Human-Computer Interaction
New Developments

Edited by
Kikuo Asai

Human-Computer Interaction, New Developments
Edited by Kikuo Asai

Republished by InTech
Janeza Trdine 9, 51000 Rijeka, Croatia

Additional hard copies can be obtained from orders@intechopen.com

Human-Computer Interaction, New Developments, Edited by Kikuo Asai
p. cm.
ISBN 978-953-7619-14-5

For EU product safety concerns:
IN TECH d.o.o., Prolaz Marije Krucifikse Kozulić 3, 51000 Rijeka, Croatia,
info@intechopen.com or visit our website at intechopen.com.

Meet the editor

Kikuo Asai
Areas of Specialty - Informatics - Multimedia Computing Research Themes - Human Computer Interaction - Haptic Interface and Applications - Virtual and Augmented Reality Education - 1998 Ph.D. in Electrical Engineering and Electronics, Nagoya University - 1993 M.E. in Electrical Engineering and Electronics, Nagoya University - 1991 B.E. in Electric and Electronic Engineering, Meijo University Career History - 2013 - Present Associate Professor, Informatics, The Open University of Japan - 2009 - 2010 Visiting Researcher, Human Interface Technology Laboratory, University of Canterbury - 2009 - 2013 Associate Professor, Center of ICT and Distance Education, The Open University of Japan - 2002 - 2013 Associate Professor, Dept. of Cyber Society & Culture, The Graduate University for Advanced Studies - 2002 - 2003 Visiting Researcher, Department of Computing Science, University of Alberta - 2000 Visiting Researcher, Electronic Visualization Laboratory, University of Illinois at Chicago - 2000 - 2009 Associate Professor, National Institute of Multimedia Education - 1996 - 2000 Research Associate, National Institute of Multimedia Education

Preface

We use computers in our daily lives, sometimes becoming so engrossed in the virtual world that we stop being conscious of the computer's presence. Computers' increasing capabilities, such as faster processing, larger capacity, and wide-band networking, make it possible for us to interact seamlessly with them. The field of human-computer interaction is the study of interaction between people (users) and computers. It is often regarded as the intersection of computer science, behavioral science, design, psychology, sociology, and several other fields. In spite of a long history of extensive research, we have not yet achieved a full understanding of the principles and mechanisms of human-computer interaction. The study of human-computer interaction is, therefore, becoming more and more important in both the physical and cognitive aspects of designing user interfaces.

A basic goal of human-computer interaction is to improve communication between users and computers by making the interfaces more accessible and responsive to the users' needs. Better design of the user interfaces of computer systems leads to the improved communication. A cognitive science viewpoint substantially contributes to the improvement of communication by clarifying cognitive elements of user interfaces and applying cognitive design principles. That is, cognitive information processing takes into account human performance, including psychological and physiological factors as well as physical factors, in interface design. Knowledge transfer through communication is a form of learning. When users manipulate computer systems, they form mental models based on the experience. This allows the users to anticipate the system's input mechanisms, yielding highly productive interactions.

When we see alteration and variety in user interfaces due to technology evolution, it may seem difficult to continue the embodiment of design principles. This book takes on the challenge of providing a forum for the dissemination and exchange of up-to-date reports on scientific trends in theoretical, generic, and applied areas of human-computer interaction. It covers topics such as universal access, engineering psychology, cognitive ergonomics, virtual and mixed reality, internationalization, design development, online communities, social computing, human modelling, and human-centered design.

The book consists of 20 chapters, each addressing a certain aspect of human-computer interaction. Each chapter gives the reader background information on a subject and proposes an original solution. This should serve as a valuable tool for professionals in this interdisciplinary field. Hopefully, readers will contribute their own discoveries and improvements, innovative ideas and concepts, as well as novel applications and business models related to the field of human-computer interaction.

Chapter 1 presents a solution for improving human-computer interaction by developing culture-sensitive applications based on common sense knowledge. It shows how meaning can be assigned to messages using common sense, thereby making user interfaces more intuitive. Chapter 2 investigates the role of head-up displays (HUDs) in computer-assisted instruction (CAI), describing the basic concept of the HUD, features of HUD-based CAI, and user performance with HUD-based CAI systems. Chapter 3 carries out structural analysis of interface and visualization metaphors, considering cognitive aspects of system engineering in order to understand how these metaphors are constructed, how they work, and how users interpret them. Chapter 4 introduces non-intrusive physiological monitoring for sensing and recognizing user emotion. It discusses methods and technologies for finding practical solutions to the affective sensing problem. Chapter 5 develops mobile design guidelines in the context of retail sales support. It focuses specifically on the research project IntExtMa, "Interactive Expert System for Made-to-measure Clothing," interpreting mostly desktop-oriented existing guidelines from a new point of view.

Chapter 6 investigates methodologies for envisioning new or improved task practices and associated technology requirements, taking into account the broader socio-technical context for human-machine interaction. Chapter 7 describes adaptive automation design as a potential solution to the problems associated with human-automation interaction by optimizing cooperation and efficiently allocating labor between an automated system and its users. Chapter 8 introduces a novel framework to assess the acceptance and usability of interaction design tools in development and design activities, discussing how work style transitions influence the tool's perception of use. Chapter 9 proposes a modelling technique that offers a novel perspective on smart spaces where sensor technology in digital and physical objects enables people to seamlessly interact with information and with their surroundings. Chapter 10 provides an overview of existing problems with mobile interaction design, particularly addressing early design stages. New approaches compiled within a user-centered design methodology for the development of a set of ubiquitous systems are proposed.

Chapter 11 compares augmented reality to standard visual warning signals in an industrial context. It explains the prospects of using this technology to warn against potentially dangerous events like machine start-ups and excessive operating speeds. Chapter 12 outlines the requirements for creating a miniature 3D controller suitable for mobile computing applications and then presents the key elements of the design of a prototype fulfilling these requirements. The miniature, low-cost device provides one-handed 6-DOF (degree of freedom) input. Chapter 13 proposes an approach to increasing the level of human-computer interaction in database access by translating queries in natural spoken language into SQL queries. This extends the concept of user database queries to something that is present in the user's natural speech. A formal query event model is presented together with a software prototype of the proposed approach. Chapter 14 describes an alternative approach to location-aware applications based on intuitive, conventional user interfaces that enable information retrieval from the physical environment. The alternative is based on design patterns of the physical space that help users get oriented in an unknown place and become more familiar with it. Chapter 15 examines the criteria for touch-screen keyboard text entry, emphasizing finger typing. A touch-screen software keyboard is designed as a customizable and adaptable touch-screen keyboard with bubble cursor-like visual feedback.

Chapter 16 introduces a practical solution for non-contact interfaces using structured-light illumination to acquire depth information about an object's surface by measuring the deformation in a projected light pattern. It realizes the direct and accurate measurement of human hands and faces. Chapter 17 investigates how midwives would use a head-mounted display to alternately observe a patient and her ultrasound scan results on the display. Chapter 18 presents adaptive algorithms for face tracking using computer vision, a fundamental technique for sensing humans using an unobtrusive layout. The real-time face tracking can be managed over long period of time, in varying illumination conditions, with complex background. Chapter 19 describes an intercultural interaction analysis tool to observe and analyze human-computer interaction behavior of users from different cultures. It can quantitatively and qualitatively identify differences of the interaction patterns based on their cultural backgrounds. Chapter 20 considers user models that detect and exploit user familiarity in natural language human-computer dialogue, so that the user models can improve the degree to which systems can adapt to human characteristics.

Editor

Kikuo Asai

National Institute of Multimedia Education

Japan

Contents

1

Improving Human-Computer Interaction by Developing Culture-sensitive Applications based on Common Sense Knowledge

Junia Coutinho Anacleto and Aparecido Fabiano Pinatti de Carvalho
Advanced Interaction Lab / Computing Department / Federal University of São Carlos
Brazil

1. Introduction

Computing is becoming ever more present in people's everyday life. Regarding this fact, researchers started to think of ways for improving Human-Computer Interaction (HCI) so that computer applications and devices provide users with a more natural interaction, considering the context which users are inserted into, as humans can do (Harper et al., 2008). Developing culture-sensitive interactive systems seems to be a possibility for reaching such goal. Bailey et al. (2001) already mentioned the importance of considering cultural issues in computer systems development. For them, culture is a system of shared meanings which forms a framework for solving problem and establishing behavior in everyday life that has to be considered in interactive system development. Since cultural knowledge is often implicit, designers often have trouble even realizing that their designs carry cultural dependencies implicitly. Moreover, it is not possible to design by hand for every combination of possible cultures, nor is it practical to exhaustively test for every possible user culture (Bailey et al., 2001). A support is necessary for making this possibility come true and information and communication technology can offer it, as it is explained further ahead.
This chapter presents the solutions of the Advanced Interaction Laboratory[1] (LIA) from the Federal University of São Carlos (UFSCar), Brazil, for developing culture-sensitive interactive systems. LIA's approach relies on using common sense knowledge for developing such kind of systems. That is because individuals communicate with each other by assigning meaning to their messages based on their prior beliefs, attitudes, and values, i.e. based on their common sense. Previous researches developed at the Lab have shown that common sense expresses cultural knowledge. So, providing this kind of knowledge for computers is a way of allowing the development of culture-sensitive computer applications (Anacleto et al., 2006a).
One idea for providing computers with common sense is to construct a machine that could learn as a child does, observing the real world. However, this approach was discarded after Minsky and Papert's experience of building an autonomous hand-eye robot, which should perform simple tasks like building copies of children's building-block structures. In this

---

[1] LIA's homepage (in Portuguese): http://lia.dc.ufscar.br

experience, they realized that numerous short programs would be necessary to give machines human abilities as cognition, perception and locomotion and that it would be very difficult to develop those programs (Minsky, 1988).
Another idea is to build a huge common sense knowledge base, store it in computers and develop procedures that can work on it. This seems to be an easier approach; nevertheless there are at least three big challenges that must be won in order to achieve it. The first challenge is to build the necessary common sense knowledge base, since it is estimated that, in order to cover the human common sense, billions of pieces of knowledge such as knowledge about the world, myths, beliefs, and so on, are necessary (Liu & Singh, 2004). Furthermore it is known that common sense is cultural and time dependent, i.e. a statement that is common sense today may not be a common sense statement in the future (Anacleto et al., 2006b). For instance, consider the statement "The Sun revolves around the Earth". Nowadays this statement is considered wrong, however, hundreds of years ago people used to believe that it was right.
One possible idea to transpose this difficulty is to build the knowledge base collaboratively by volunteers through the Web, since every ordinary people has the common sense that computers lack (Liu & Singh, 2004, Anacleto et al. 2006a). In order to make the collection process as simple as possible to the volunteers, it is kind to think of collecting the common sense statements in natural language.
Then the second big challenge arises: to represent the knowledge collected in natural language in a way that computers can make inferences over it. In order to be used by computer inference mechanisms, it is still necessary that the knowledge be represented in specifics structures such as semantic network or ontology. So, it is necessary to process the statements in natural language in order to build a suitable knowledge representation. Natural language processing is a well-known AI challenge (Vallez & Pedraza-Jimenez, 2007).
The third challenge is to generate natural language from the adopted knowledge representation, so that computer systems can naturally and effectively communicate with users. This is another well-known challenge of current AI researches (Vallez & Pedraza-Jimenez, 2007).
This chapter discusses LIA's approaches for common sense knowledge acquisition, representation and use, as well as for natural language processing, developed in the context of the Brazilian Open Mind Common Sense (OMCS-Br) project (Anacleto et al., 2008b), in order to develop applications using such approach. It shows how common sense knowledge can be used for instantiating some issues of cultural-sensitive systems in the area of HCI. For this purpose, some applications developed at LIA are presented and the use of common sense knowledge in those applications is explained. Those applications are mainly developed for the domain of education, which is extremely culture-sensitive, and one of the main technological, social and economical challenges considering globalization and the necessary digital inclusion of every ordinary person.
The chapter is organized as follows: section 2 goes over some related projects that proposes to build large scale common sense knowledge bases such as Cyc (Lenat et al., 1990), the American Open Mind Common Sense (OMCS-US) and ThoughtTreasure (Mueller, 1997); section 3 presents details on OMCS-Br architecture for acquiring, representing, making available and using common sense knowledge in computer application; section 4 suggests ways of using common sense knowledge in the development of interactive systems and

exemplifies the suggestions with computer applications developed at LIA; finally, section 5 presents some conclusions remarks and point to some future works.

2. Building Up Common Sense Knowledge Bases

Nowadays there are several projects, like Cyc, OMCS-US and ThoughtTreasure, which aim to build up large scale common sense knowledge bases. While those projects are mainly focused on Artificial Intelligence (AI) issues, OMCS-Br is more concerned about HCI. This section goes over the approach of such projects to build up large scale common sense knowledge bases, contextualizing LIA's researches.

In late 1950s, the goal of providing common sense knowledge for computers received great attention from AI researches. However, in the early 1960s that goal was abandoned by many of those researches, due especially to the difficulties they faced with for building the necessary common sense knowledge base (Minsky, 2000; Lenat, 1995).

Believing in the possibility of building up the knowledge base and making computer applications intelligent so that they could flexibly answer to users input through inferences mechanisms that would work on the common sense knowledge base, Douglas Lenat started in 1984 the Project Cyc, founding the Cycorp Inc. (Lenat et al., 1990). Nowadays, Cyc is one of the more active projects on acquiring and representing common sense knowledge computationally and on developing inferences mechanisms for common sense reasoning, as it can be verified in its scientific production[2].

At the beginning, the approach used by Cyc researchers was to construct the project knowledge base by hand. Panton et al. (2006) mention that the use of natural language understanding or machine learning techniques was considered by the project researchers, but it was concluded that, to have good results using those techniques, computers would have to have a minimum of common sense knowledge for understanding natural language and learning something from it. Therefore, it was defined a specific language for representing the knowledge, named CycL (Lenat et al., 1990), and, then, the corporation's *knowledge engineers*, trained in that language, started to codify and store pieces of knowledge in Cyc knowledge base. The knowledge was gottem from ordinary people by interviews about the several subjects that are part of people's common sense, in an effort of approximately 900 people per year (Matuszek et al., 2006).

Inspired in Cyc, Eric Mueller started the Project ThoughtTreasure in 1994, having as goal to develop a platform for making natural language processing and common sense reasoning viable to computer applications (Mueller, 1997). As in Cyc, the approach used for building ThoughtTreasure knowledge base was manual.

The existence of concepts, phrases and predicates both in English and French in ThoughtTreasure knowledge base is a differential of this project. The project also does not limit the knowledge representation to a logic language, as CycL does, but also allows knowledge representation in the format of finite automata and scripts (Mueller, 1997).

Besides the flexibility of ThoughtTreasure knowledge representation, it does not discard the need of knowing a specific structure to populate the base of the project. This issue, shared by Cyc and ThoughtTreasure projects, impedes that people who do not know the specific format that knowledge should be inserted into the knowledge base collaborate on building

[2] See Cycorp Incorporation group's publications in http://www.cyc.com/cyc/technology/pubs

it. This demands a bigger time frame for making the knowledge base rise so that robust inferences can be done over it. Cyc and ThoughtTreasure are samples of this. After more than two decades, Cyc's knowledge engineers could map only 2.2 millions of assertions (statements and rules) (Matuszek et al., 2006). ThoughtTreasure, one decade younger, has only 50,000 assertions relating its 25,000 concepts (Mueller, 2007).

Thinking about fast building a large scale common sense knowledge base, researchers from the MediaLab of the Massachusetts Institute of Technology (MIT) launched OMCS-US, taking into account that every ordinary people have the common sense knowledge that machines lack, so all of them are eligible for helping build the common sense knowledge base machines need to be intelligent (Singh, 2002). In order to involve every ordinary people, OMCS-US collects common sense statements in natural language on a website made available by its researchers, and uses natural language processing techniques to build up its semantic network, the knowledge representation adopted in the project (Liu & Singh, 2004). Therefore, volunteers need only to know how to write in a specific language - nowadays there are three OMCS projects, each one in a language: OMCS-US, in English[3], OMCS-Br, in Portuguese[4] and OMCS-MX, in Spanish[5] - and have access to the Internet in order to collaborate in building the knowledge base. In less than five years OMCS-US got a semantic network with more than 1.6 millions assertions of common sense knowledge "encompassing the spatial, physical, social, temporal and psychological aspects of everyday life" (Liu & Singh, 2004). Section 3.1 gives details on the common sense collection process used by OMCS-Br, the same used by OMCS-US.

Being aware of the importance of including ordinary people in constructing its knowledge base, Cyc also started to develop systems for populating the knowledge base from natural language statements. The first try was made by developing KRAKEN (Panton et al., 2002). The system was developed in order to allow subject-matter experts to add information to pieces of knowledge already stored in Cyc knowledge base through natural language interface. In 2003, Witbrock et al. (2003) presented a system for interactive dialog, which used a structure similar to KRAKEN for allowing amateurs in CycL to enter information in the knowledge base.

Another approach for collecting common sense knowledge is proposed by von Ahn et al. (2006). Von Ahn's team agrees that collecting common sense knowledge in natural language is a good approach. However, they criticize the absence of fun in the collection process used by Cyc and OMCS-US, blaming this absence for until nowadays no project which has proposed to construct large scale common sense knowledge bases has beaten the amount of hundreds of millions facts that are supposed to be necessary to cover the whole human common sense. Thus, they propose to use games for fast collecting common sense facts, believing that through games it is possible to collect million of facts in few weeks (von Ahn et al., 2006). Considering this premise, the group developed Verbosity, a game in which common sense facts are collected as side effect of playing the game. In the same way, OMCS-US research group developed Common Consensus (Lieberman et al., 2007), aiming to motivate volunteers to collaborate in building the project knowledge base.

Last but not least, there is another approach for acquiring common sense knowledge under

[3] OMCS-US Homepage: http://commons.media.mit.edu/en/

[4] OMCS-Br Homepage (in Portuguese): http://www.sensocomum.ufscar.br

[5] OMCS-Mx Homepage(in Spanish): http://openmind.fi-p.unam.mx

development at Cycorp, which aims to automate the collection process by using crawlers to get common sense knowledge from web pages. The developed method has six steps (Matuszek et al., 2005): *(i)* to use Cyc inference engine for selecting subjects of interest from Cyc knowledge base and composing query strings to be submitted to Google; *(ii)* to search for relevant documents on the Internet using Google's resources; *(iii)* to identify relevant statements to the subjects of interest on the retrieved documents; *(iv)* to automatically codify the statements in CycL; *(v)* to validate the new assertions using the knowledge already stored at Cyc common sense knowledge base and performing new searches on the Internet using Google; and *(vi)* to send the assertions to a knowledge engineer who decides whether they are going to be stored in the project knowledge base or not.

Although this last approach seems to be very innovative, it does not allow mapping the profile of the people from whom common sense knowledge was collected. OMCS-Br researchers defend that associating common sense knowledge to the profile of the person from whom it was collected is extremely important to make viable the use of such knowledge for HCI. This is because common sense knowledge varies from group to group of people and, therefore, the feedback that a common sense-aided application should give to users from different target groups should be different (Anacleto et al., 2006b). The variation in common sense among groups of people is what makes interesting use it for supporting the development of culture-sensitive computer application, as it is explained in section 4. That is why all OMCS-Br applications used for collecting common sense demands that users subscribe themselves and log into the system before starting interacting. In such way developers can analyze how people from different target groups talk about specific things and propose different solutions for each group.

Furthermore, the judgment performed by knowledge engineers makes possible question if the statements stored in Cyc knowledge base really represent common sense. Statements such as "Avocado is red" would not be stored in Cyc knowledge base, according to the process described by Matuszek et al. (2005), Shah et al. (2006) and Panton et al. (2006). However, if the majority of people with the same cultural background say that "Avocado is red", this should be considered as common sense for that community and should be in the knowledge base despite the knowledge engineers judge it as wrong. Because of that OMCS-Br does not judge the semantic of the statements collected in its site (Anacleto et al., 2008b).

3. The Project OMCS-Br

OMCS-Br is a project based on OMCS-US, which has been developed by LIA/UFSCar since August 2005. The project works on five work fronts: (1) common sense collection, (2) knowledge representation, (3) knowledge manipulation, (4) access and (5) use. Figure 1 illustrates the project architecture.

First of all, common sense knowledge is collected both through a website and through applications which have been developed in the context of OMCS-Br and stored in the OMCS knowledge base. After that, the knowledge is represented as semantic networks, called ConceptNets. In order to build the semantic networks, the natural language statements are exported through an **Export Module** and sent to the **Semantic Network Generator**. The generator is composed of three modules: the **Extraction, Normalization** and **Relaxation** modules. The result of these three modules is a group of binary predicates. For dealing with Portuguese natural language processing, Curupira (Martins et al., 2006), a natural language parser for Portuguese, is used. The predicates are filtered according to parameters of profile, such as gender, age and level of education, generating different ConceptNets. In order to make inferences over the ConceptNets, several inference mechanisms, which are grouped in an API (Application Programming Interface), were developed. The access to the API functions is made through a Management Server, which makes available access to instances of APIs associated with different ConceptNets. Through this access, applications can use the API inference mechanisms and can perform common sense reasoning. Details about each element of the architecture presented in Figure 1 and the OMCS-Br work fronts are presented in the following sub-sections.

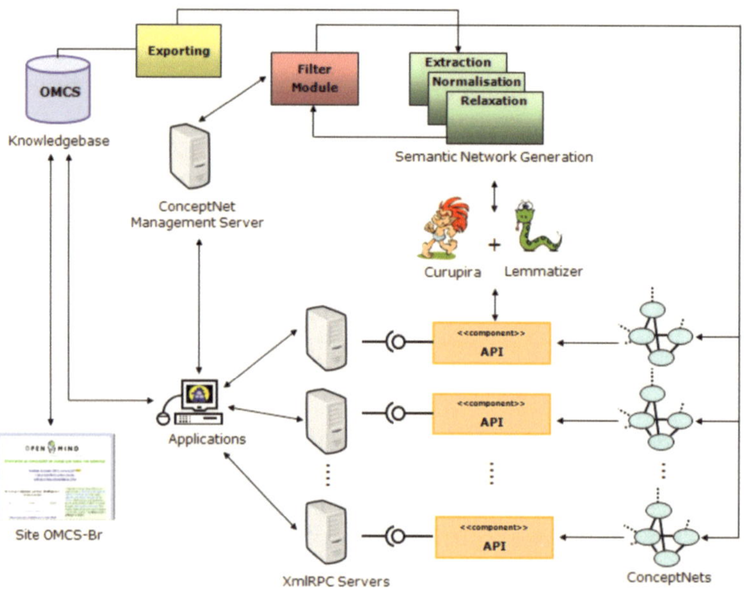

Fig. 1. OMCS-Br Project architecture

3.1. Common Sense Collection

OMCS-Br adopts template-based activities which guide users in such a way that they can contribute with different kinds of knowledge. The templates are semi-structured statements in natural language with some lacunas that should be filled out with the contributors' knowledge so that the final statement corresponds to a common sense fact. They were planned to cover those kinds of knowledge previously mentioned and to get pieces of information that will be used further to give applications the capacity of common sense reasoning. The template-based approach makes easier to manage the knowledge acquired, since the static parts are intentionally proposed to collect statements which can be mapped into first order predicates, which composes the project semantic networks. In this way, it is possible to generate extraction rules to identify the concepts present in a statement and to establish the appropriate relation-type between them. In OMCS projects, there are twenty relation-types, used to represent the different kinds of common sense knowledge, as it is presented in (Liu & Singh, 2004).

Those templates have a static and a dynamic part. The dynamic part is filled out by a feedback process that uses part of statements stored in the knowledge base of the project to compose the new template to be presented. Figure 2 exemplifies how the feedback process works. At the first moment the template "You usually find a __________ in a **chair**" of the activity Location is presented to a contributor – the templates bold part is the one filled out by the feedback system. In the example, the contributor fills out the sentence with the word "screw". Then, the sentence "You usually find a **screw** in a chair" is stored in the OMCS knowledge base. At the second moment, the template "A screw is used for _________" of the activity Uses is shown to another contributor. Note that the word "screw" entered at the first moment is used to compose the template presented at the second moment.

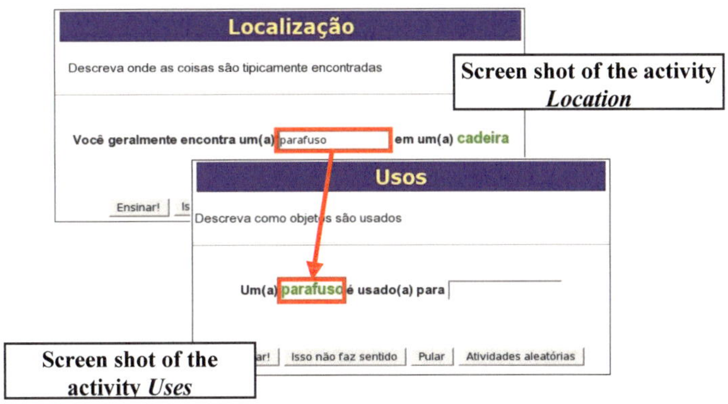

Fig. 2. Example of the OMCS-Br feedback process

The feedback process used in OMCS-Br website was planned in order to allow varied templates to be generated so that users are able to contribute on several subjects and do not get bored with always filling out the same sentence.

Still related to the feedback process, considering that the statements stored in the knowledge base will be used to compose templates that will be shown to other contributors, it is important to provide a way through what it could be selected the statements that should be used by the feedback process. Thinking in this need, it was developed in OMCS-Br an on-line review system, which can be accessed just by the ones who have administrator privileges, where the statements are selected to be or not to be used by the feedback process.

In order to perform the review, it was defined some rules to assure that common sense knowledge would not be discarded (Anacleto et al., 2008b). It is worth pointing out that during the review process the reviewer is not allowed to judge the semantic of a sentence. That is because it does not matter if a sentence seems strange in meaning or if it has already been scientifically proved as wrong. Common sense knowledge does not match scientific knowledge necessarily. Since a sentence is accepted as true by the most people who share the same cultural background, it is considered as a common sense sentence. Because of that , reviewers are not allowed to judge if a sentence is common sense statement or not. Only statements with misspelling errors are discarded, in order not to cause noisy in the semantic networks generated in the next step (Anacleto et al., 2008b).

Besides the templates about general themes such as those about "things" which people deal with in their daily life, "locations" where things are usually found and the common "uses" of things, there are also, in the Brazilian project website, templates about three specific domains: health, colors and sexual education. They are domains of interest to the researches that are under development in the research group which keeps the project (Anacleto et al., 2008b). This approach is only used in Brazil and it was adopted taking into account the necessity of making the collection of common sense knowledge related to those domains. The specific-domain templates were defined with the help of professionals of each domain. They were composed with some specifics words which instantiate the templates of general themes in the domain, in order to guide users to contribute with statements related to it. Table 1 shows the accomplishments that OMCS-Br has gotten with that approach.

domain	number of contributions	period of collection
Healthcare	6505	about 29 months
Colors	8230	about 26 months
Sexual Education	3357	about 21 months

Table 1. Contributions on specific domains in OMCS-Br

The numbers of contributions in each domain can seem to be irrelevant, however, considering the only 2 statements about AIDS found in the knowledge base before creating the theme Sexual Education, it can be noticed the importance of domain-contextualized templates in order to make faster the collection of statements related to desired domains.
Another accomplishment of the OMCS-Br is related to the variety of contributor profiles. Nowadays there are 1499 contributors registered in the project site of which 19.33% are women and 80.67% are men. The most part of contributors (72.80%) is from Brazil South-east area, followed by the South area (15.25%). Those numbers point to the tendency proved by geographic sciences, which present the South-east and South area as being the most developed areas of Brazil. Considering that, it is perfectly understandable that, being well developed areas, their inhabitants have easier access to the Internet. Table 2 and Table 3 present other characteristics of OMCS-Br contributors.

age group	percentage
Younger than 12 years	0.75 %
13 - 17	20.51 %
18 - 29	67.36 %
30 - 45	9.88 %
46 - 65	1.22 %
Older than 65 years	0.28 %

Table 2. Percentage of Contributors by Age Group

school degree	percentage
Elementary school	2.21 %
High school	18.17 %
College	65.86 %
Post-Graduation	4.52 %
Master Degree	7.04 %
Doctorate Degree	2.21 %

Table 3. Percentage of Contributors by School Degree

Another conquest of OMCS-Br is the amount of contributions. Within two years and a half of project, it has been gotten more than 174.000 statements written in natural language. This was possible thanks to the web technology and the marketing approach adopted by LIA. As the project was released in Brazil in 2005, it was realized that the knowledge base would rise up significantly just when there were an event that put the project in evidence. Figure 3 demonstrates this tendency.

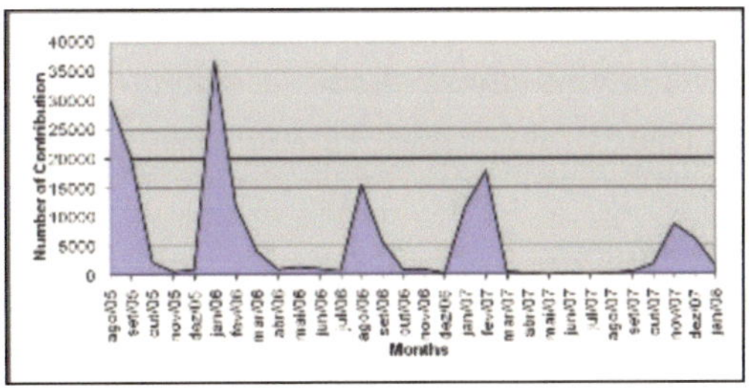

Fig. 3. OMCS-Br knowledge base tendency of growing up

It can be noticed in Figure 3 that the periods where the knowledge base grew up significantly were from August to October 2005, from January to March 2006, from August to October 2006, from January to February 2007 and from November to December 2007. This is an interesting fact, because those jumps in the knowledge base just followed some marketing appeals performed by LIA. In the first one, LIA got published some articles in newspapers of national coverage telling people about the project and asking for people contribution. After getting those articles printed, the OMCS-Br knowledge base reached the number of 50.000 statements. Three months later, the knowledge base established and passed to grow up very slowly.

Thinking of having another jump in the knowledge base size, it was released in the later January 2006 a challenge associated to the Brazilian carnival. In that challenge, it was offered little gifts as prizes to the three first collaborators that contributed with the most number of statements in the site activities. The winners received T-Shirts of the OMCS-Br Project and pens of MIT. The challenge was announced among the project contributors, who received an e-mail telling about it. The announcement was also posted in the Ueba website (www.ueba.com.br), a site of curiosities which target public is people interested in novelties. As it can be noticed, the knowledge base size had a jump as soon as the challenge was launched. The same approach was used in August 2006, January 2007 and December 2007.

Although the approach has gotten a good response from the contributors in the first three challenges, it can be noticed in Figure 3 that this approach is becoming inefficient. Thinking about keeping the knowledge base growing up, it is under development some games, following project contributors' suggestions, in order to make the collection process funnier and more pleasant.

One example is the game framework "What is it?" (Anacleto et al., 2008a), presented in section 4.3. The framework is divided in two modules: (1) the player's module, a quiz game where players must guess a secret word considering a set of common sense-based clues and (2) the game editor's module, a seven-step wizard which guides people to create game instances by using common sense knowledge. In the player's module, while the player tries to find out the secret word, the system collects common sense knowledge storing the relationship between the word suggested and the clues already seen by the player. In the game editor's module common sense knowledge is collected during the whole set up process, where the editor defines: (a) the community profile whose common sense statements should be considered; (b) the game main theme; (c) the topics, i.e. specifics subjects related to the main theme; and (d) the cards of the game. All possible combinations among the data supplied by the system and the editor's choices are stored in the knowledge base. For example, the secret word select by the editor and the synonyms (s)he are stored in the knowledge base as statements like *"secret word is also known as synonym"*. Moreover, statements relating the synonyms among them, i.e. statements like *"synonym-1 is also known as synonym-2"*,..., *"synonym-(n-1) is also known as synonym-n"*, are stored.

3.2. Knowledge Representation

As OMCS-Br adopts natural language approach to populate its knowledge base, it was decided to pre-process the contributions stored in the knowledge base so that they could be easier manipulated by inference procedures. From this pre-processing, semantic networks are generated with the knowledge represented as binary relations. These semantic networks are called ConceptNets in OMCS projects.

Currently twenty relation-types are used to build the OMCS-Br ConceptNets. Those relation-types are organized in eight classes, presented by Liu and Sing (2004). They were defined to cover all kinds of knowledge that compose the human common sense - spatial, physical, social, temporal, and psychological (Liu & Singh, 2004). Some of the relation-types, the K-Lines, were adopted from Minsk's theory about the mind. In that theory, K-Line is defined as a primary mechanism for context in memory (Minsky, 1988).

ConceptNet relations have the format:

(Relation-type "parameter-1" "parameter-2" "f=;i=" "id_numbers")

Figure 4 depicts the graphical representation of a mini ConceptNet. That semantic network was generated from a very small excerpt of the OMCS-Br knowledge base. The nodes, originally in Portuguese, was freely translated for this chapter.

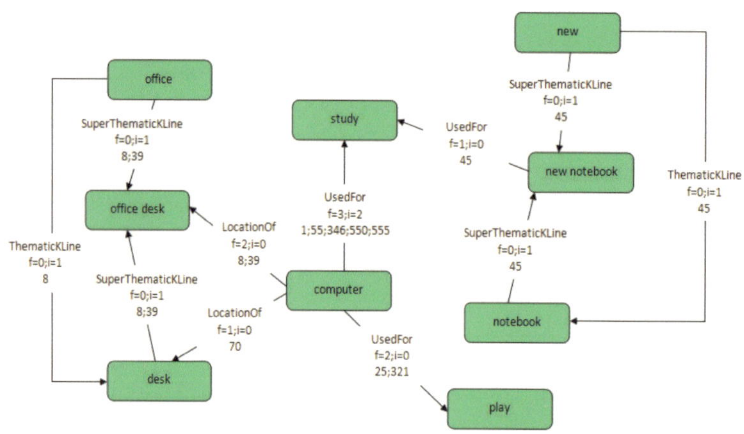

Fig. 4. Sample of ConceptNet

One example of relation that can be mapped from Figure 4 is:

(UsedFor "computer" "study" "f=3;i=2" "1;55;346;550;555")

The parameters *f* (frequency of uttered statements) and *i* (frequency of inferred statements) are part of the semantic relations. The *f* represents how many times a relation was generated directly from the statements stored in the knowledge base, through extraction rules. The *i* represents how many times a relation was generated indirectly from the statements. In this case they are submitted to the natural language parser and afterwards inference heuristics are applied on them. The generation of the *f* and *i* is explained further ahead. The *id* numbers correspond to the *id* of the natural language statements in the knowledge base which originated the relation. This allows computer programs to go back to the knowledge base and retrieve natural language statements related to a certain context of interaction.

In OMCS-Br, differently from OMCS-US, it is possible to generate several ConceptNets considering only the statements collected from a specific profile of volunteers. This feature was incorporated in the Brazilian project since it is known that common sense varies from group to group of people, inserted in different cultural context (Anacleto et al., 2006a; Carvalho et al., 2008). The profile parameters which can be used to filter the knowledge from the knowledge base and to generate different ConceptNets are: age, gender, level of education and geographical location.

Furthermore, in OMCS-Br, each non k-line relation-type has its negative version. For example, in OMCS-Br ConceptNets, it can be found both "IsA" and "NotIsA" relations, "PropertyOf" and "NotPropertyOf", and so on. The decision for the affirmative or negative relation version is made in the second phase of the ConceptNet generation process. In total there are 5 phases in the ConceptNet generation process (Carvalho, 2007): (1) **Exporting,** (2) **Extraction,** (3) **Normalization,** (4) **Relaxation** and (5) **Filtering**. Each step is presented in details in the following.

Exporting

The first step to generate an OMCS-Br ConceptNet is to export the natural language statements collected on the site and stored in the project knowledge base. This export is made by a PHP script that generates a file whose lines are seven-slot structures with the statements and information about them. The slots are separated one another through "$$". Figure 5 presents a very small excerpt of the OMCS-Br knowledge base after the export phase. Although the data in Figure 5 and in the other Figures related to the ConceptNet generation process are in Portuguese, they are explained in English in the text.

Um(a) computador é usado(a) para estudar$$M$$18_29$$mestrado$$Clementina$$SP$$1
Um(a) computador é usado(a) para jogar$$M$$13_17$$2_incompleto$$São Carlos$$SP$$25
Você geralmente encontra um(a) computador em uma mesa de escritório$$F$$18_29$$mestrado$$Campinas$$SP$$8
Pessoas usam cadernos novos quando elas começam a estudar$$M$$13_17$$2_incompleto$$São Carlos$$SP$$45

Fig. 5. Sample result of the exporting phase

As it can be seen in Figure 5, the slot 1 stores the natural language statement, the slots 2 to 6 present information about the profile of the volunteer who entered the statement in the knowledge base (gender, age group, level of education, origin city and origin state, respectively) and the last slot stores the *id* number of the sentence in the knowledge base. For example, in the first structure presented in Figure 5: *(i)* the natural language statement is "Um(a) computador é usado(a) para estudar" (in English, "A(n) computer is used for studying"); *(ii)* the profile parameters are "male" (M), "person between 18 and 29 years old" (18_29), "Master of Science" (mestrado), "Clementina City" (Clementina), "São Paulo State"

(São Paulo); and the knowledge base statement *id* number is "1". The id is very important for common sense-based applications to trace back the natural language statements related to certain interaction scenarios. This is better explained in section 3.3.

Extraction

In the extraction phase, extraction rules, i.e. regular expression patterns (Liu & Singh, 2004), are used for identifying specifics structures in the natural language statements. These regular expressions are designed according to the templates of the OMCS-Br site. Based on the templates, it is possible to identify the relation-type and the parameters of a relation. For example, considering the first statement of Figure 5, "Um(a) computador é usado(a) para estudar", through a extraction rule it is possible to identified the following structures "computador" ("computer"), "é usado(a) para" ("is used for"), "estudar" ("studying"). By these structures it is generated the relation (UsedFor "computador" "estudar"). Figure 6 shows the relations generated from the sample structures presented in Figure 5. It can be noticed in Figure 6 that the profile parameter are still in the relation structure. Those parameters are kept until the Filtering phase, where they are used to generate different ConceptNets, according to the application needs.

(UsedFor "computador" "estudar" "M" "18_29" "mestrado" "Clementina" "SP" "1")
(UsedFor "computador" "jogar" "M" "13_17" "2_incompleto" "São Carlos" "SP" "25")
(LocationOf "computador" "mesa de escritório" "F" "18_29" "mestrado" "Campinas" "SP" "8")
(MotivationOf "usam cadernos novos" "começam a estudar" "M" "13_17" "2_incompleto" "São Carlos" "SP" "265")

Fig. 6. Result of the Extraction phase for the structures in Figure 5

In this phase, it is decided which version of the relation-type should be used, the affirmative or the negative. The extraction rules decide for one of them taking into account the following heuristic: *"If there is a negative adverb before the structure which defines which relation-type should be used, then use the negative version. Use the affirmative version instead, if no negative adverb precedes the structure which defines the relation-type".*

For example, consider the following natural language statement: "Você quase nunca encontra um(a) mesa de escritório em um(a) rua" ("You hardly ever find a(n) office desk in a(n) street"). After being processed by an extraction rule, the structures "quase nunca encontra" ("hardly ever find"), "mesa de escritório" ("office desk") and "rua" ("street") are identified. In this case the verb "encontra" ("to find") expresses the semantics that leads to the relation-type "LocationOf". However, as the adverbial phrase "quase nunca" ("hardly ever") precedes the verb, the generation system decides to use the negative version of the relation-type. So, it is generated the relation (NotLocationOf "mesa de escritório" "rua").

The incorporation of negative version to the ConceptNet relation-types was an initiative of the OMCS-Br. Until 2007, the OMCS-US did not take into account this feature, and after some discussions led by the Brazilian research group, the American research group implemented the polarity parameter in their ConceptNet (Havasi et al., 2007). Nonetheless the Brazilian group decided to define new relation-types instead of implement another parameter in the ConceptNet relations, since this approach would cause a smaller impact in the inferences procedures which had been already developed.

Normalization

Since the statements collected in the site can express the same knowledge about the human aspects in several ways, such as, using synonyms, different phrase structures, and different inflectional morphology, those statements should be manipulated to increase the semantic network quality. In order not to have inflected concepts, which means the same word varying in number, tense, etc., a normalization process is performed.

The normalization process of OMCS-US makes use of Montylingua (Liu & Singh, 2004) - a natural language parser for English, that tags and strips inflectional morphology of the knowledge base statements. However, Montylingua cannot be used to parse Brazilian Portuguese statements, due to syntactic and lexical differences between those languages.

The alternative found by OMCS-Br was to adopt Curupira (Martins et al., 2003), a parser developed for Brazilian Portuguese. However Curupira does not strip the sentence inflectional morphology. Because of that, a module to normalize the statements submitted to OMCS-Br generation process was developed, using the inflectional dictionary developed by the UNITEX-PB project (UNITEX-PB, 2008), which has all inflectional forms of Brazilian Portuguese morphological classes. The "normalizer" works in 3 steps, as it is described in the following (Anacleto et al., 2008):

1. First of all, each sentence token is tagged using Curupira. Here it was necessary to develop another module which makes the bridge between the "normalizer" and the parser library, available through a *dll* (dynamic linked library) format.
2. Afterward, articles are taken off - proper names are kept in original form. Special language structures that are proper of Brazilian Portuguese are treats. For instance, the structure called *ênclise*, a case of pronominal position where the pronoun goes after the verb, is stripped from the statements and the verb is put in the infinitive form. For example, the verb "observá-la" ("observe it") is normalized to "observar" ("to observe").
3. Overall, each tagged token is normalized into its normal form found in the adopted inflectional dictionary. In this way, the statements that were separated by morphological variations, like "compraria cadernos novos" ("would buy new notebooks") and "comprou um caderno novo" ("the bought a new notebook"), are reconciled during the normalization process generating the normalized expression "comprar caderno novo" ("to buy new notebook").

For the purpose of measuring the effects of the normalization process on the semantic network, the average nodal edge-density, as well as the number of distinct nodes and of distinct relations in OMCS-Br ConceptNet, was calculated. This processing was performed using and not using the normalization process. The results of this measurement are presented in Table 4.

	non-normalized	normalized	normalized/ non-normalized
nodes	36,219	31,423	- 13.24 %
relations	61,455	57,801	- 5.95 %
average nodal edge-density	4.4643	3.3929	+ 31.57 %

Table 4. Effects of the normalization process on the Brazilian ConceptNet structure

It can be seen in the results that the number of nodes and relations were decreased after the normalization process. This confirms the tendency that the normalization process makes reconciliations between morphological variations, and thus unifies them.
Another result that can be inferred examining the connectivity of semantic network is that the nodal edge-density has increased more than 30%. This is the most relevant data of the measurement performed, since it demonstrates that the normalization process improves the connectivity of the nodes.
It is worth mentioning that the OMCS-Br research group has been facing with several difficulties regarding the use of Curupira. For instance, when an *ênclise* occurs, Curupira assigns more than a tag to the same token. The same happens with some composite words such as *"fada-madrinha"* ("fairy godmother") and *"cavalo-marinho"* (hippocampus). Moreover, some verbal phrases are tagged incorrectly. For instance, *"fazer compras"* (go shopping) is tagged as "fazer/VERB" and "compras/VERB" when it should be tagged as "fazer/VERB" and "compras/SUBST". However, some heuristics to transpose these difficulties has been developed, as it can be verified in (Carvalho, 2007).

Relaxation

Other strategy developed to improve the ConceptNet connectivity is to extract new relations from the relations uttered directly from the natural language statements. This is made applying a set of heuristic inferences over the relations generated in the Extraction phase. The heuristics applied in this phase are based on grammatical and semantic patterns, as it is explained in the following (Carvalho, 2007).
The Relaxation module receives as input a file with the relations generated in the first phase of the ConceptNet generation process normalized and tagged, as it can be notice in Figure 7.

(UsedFor "computador/SUBST" "estudar/VERB" "M" "18_29" "mestrado" "Clementina" "SP" "1")

(UsedFor "computador/SUBST" "jogar/VERB" "M" "13_17" "2_incompleto" "São Carlos" "SP" "25")

(LocationOf "computador/SUBST" "mesa/SUBST de/PREP escritório/SUBST" "F" "18_29" "mestrado" "Campinas" "SP" "8")

(MotivationOf "usar/VERB caderno/VERB novo/ADJ" "começar/VERB a/PREP estudar/VERB" "M" "13_17" "2_incompleto" "São Carlos" "SP" "265")

Fig. 7. Sample result of the Normalization phase

As an example, consider the last relation in the group. In Figure 6, that relation was like:

(MotivationOf "usam cadernos novos" "começam a estudar" "M" "13_17" "2_incompleto" "São Carlos" "SP" "265")

After the normalization process, the relation got the following representation:

(MotivationOf "usar/VERB caderno/VERB novo/ADJ" "começar/VERB a/PREP estudar/VERB" "M" "13_17" "2_incompleto" "São Carlos" "SP" "265")

As it can be noticed, the verbs "usam" ("to use") e "começam" ("to start") were put in the infinitive form and tagged as verb (VERB); the noun "cadernos" ("notebooks") was put in singular and tagged as substantive (SUBST); the adjective "novos" was put in singular, since in Portuguese adjectives have also plural form, and was tagged as adjective (ADJ); and the preposition "a" received the preposition tag (PREP). The tags are very important in this phase because they are used by the inference mechanisms as it is explained in the following.
The first step in the relaxation phase is to assign the parameters f and i to the relations. All the relations receives "f=1; i=0" at the beginning, because they are generated just once by an extraction rule and up to this point no relations were generated by inference mechanisms.
The second step is to group all equal relations, incrementing the f parameter and appending the id number. For example, consider the following two relations:

(UsedFor "computador/SUBST" "jogar/VERB" "M" "13_17" "2_incompleto" "São Carlos" "SP" "25" "f=1;i=0")

(UsedFor "computador/SUBST" "jogar/VERB" "M" "13_17" "2_incompleto" "São Carlos" "SP" "387" "f=1;i=0")

They were generated from two different natural language statements (the statements number 25 and 387). However, they are the same relation and it was collected from people with the same profile (male, between 13 and 17, high school, São Carlos, SP). Note that although the profile parameters are the same, this does not mean that the statements 25 and 387 were collected from the same person, but from people with the same profile. After this second step, the two relations are reconciled in the following relation:

(UsedFor "computador/SUBST" "jogar/VERB" "M" "13_17" "2_incompleto" "São Carlos" "SP" "25;387" "f=2;i=0")

Note that *f* received a new value (f=2) and the id numbers were groped ("25;387"). If ten people with the same profile had entered a statement which generated that relation, *f* would be "f=10" and there would be 10 id numbers in the id number slot.
The next step of the relaxation phase is to generate new "PropertyOf" relations. They are generated from "IsA" relations. All IsA relation whose first parameter is a noun or a noun phrase and the second parameter is an adjective, generates a new "PropertyOf". For example the relation:

(IsA "computador/SUBST pessoal/ADJ" "caro/ADJ" "M" "18_29" "2_completo" "São Carlos" "SP" "284" "f=1;i=0")

generates the relation:

(PropertyOf "computador/SUBST pessoal/ADJ" "caro/ADJ" "M" "18_29" "2_completo" "São Carlos" "SP" "284" "f=0;i=1")

Note that the profile parameters and the id number are kept the same as the relation used by the inference process. It is worth pointing out that for each new relation generated, it is verified whether an equal relation is already in the ConceptNet. In case affirmative the *i* parameter of the existing relation is incremented and the id number of the generated relation is appended to its id numbers. For instance, consider that when the relation previously presented is generated, there is already the following relation in ConceptNet:

(PropertyOf "computador/SUBST pessoal/ADJ" "caro/ADJ" "M" "18_29" "2_completo" "São Carlos" "SP" "45;78;171" "f=3;i=0")

Instead of registering the generated relation in ConceptNet as a new relation, the existing relation is updated to:

(PropertyOf "computador/SUBST pessoal/ADJ" "caro/ADJ" "M" "18_29" "2_completo" "São Carlos" "SP" "45;78;171;284" "f=3;i=1")

Notice that the parameter *i* is now 1 and the *id* number 284 is part of the relation id numbers. New relations "CapableOf","CapableOfReceiveingAction","ThematickKLine" and "SuperThematicKLine" are created by similar processes. For detail about the other inference mechanisms that generate such relations, see (Anacleto et al., 2008b).

Filtering

After the Relaxation phase, different ConceptNets can be generated, according to the possible combination of the profile parameter values. This generation is made on demand, as common sense based applications which use the OMCS-Br architecture need a certain ConceptNet. This is only possible in OMCS-Br, since the OMCS-US, Cyc and ThoughtTreasure do not register their volunteers' profile.

The Filtering module receives an array of arrays as input with the profile parameter values which should be considered to generate the desired ConceptNet. The first sub-array in the global array has the parameters related to the volunteers' gender; the second, to their age group; the third, to their level of education; the forth, to the city they come from; and the fifth, to the state they live. If an array in the global array is empty, it means that a specific profile parameter does not matter for the desired ConceptNet, and then it is considered all possible value for that parameter. For example, if the array *[[], [13_17, 18_29], [2_completo], [], [SP, MG]]* is provided to the Filtering module, a ConceptNet will be generated, whose relations were build from statements gotten from people of both gender, since the first sub-array is empty; who are between 13 and 17 years old and between 18 and 29 years old, whose highest level of education is high school; who come from any city located in the Brazilian *São Paulo* and *Minas Gerais states*.

The first step in the Filtering phase is to recalculate the *f* and *i* parameter values, grouping the equal relations whose profiles fit to the profile values previously provided. After that, another heuristic is applied on the relations in order to generate new "PropertyOfs". This heuristic is applied only in this step because it considers two groups of relations in the inference process and these two groups should have only relations which fit to the considered profile. Therefore, for guaranteeing this constraint, it was decided to apply this heuristic only in this stage. For details about this heuristic, see (Carvalho, 2007).

After the Filtering phase, the ConceptNet is stored in a ConceptNet Server so that it can be accessed by the ConceptNet Server Management, as it is explained in details in section 3.5.

3.3. Knowledge Manipulation

Once the semantic network is built, it is necessary to develop procedures to manipulate it, in order to make computer applications capable of common sense reasoning and, then, to use these resources for developing culture-sensitive computer applications. The procedures developed in the context of OMCS-Br are integrated in its API for being used by computer applications. Currently there are five basic functions that simulate some sorts of human reasoning ability. They are related to context, projections, analogy making, topic gisting and affective sensing (Liu & Singh, 2004). The OMCS-Br applications use mainly three of them.

The first one is the *get_context()* function, which determines the context around a certain concept or around the intersection of several concepts. For example, when someone searches for the concept "have lunch" using *get_context()*, it returns concepts like "be hungry", "eat food", "meet friend", "buy food", "take a break", and "find a restaurant". These related concepts are retrieved by performing spreading activation from the source node in the semantic network that finds related concepts by and considering the number and the intensity of connected pairs of concepts. This function is very useful for semantic query expansion and topic generation. For instance, in the "What is it?" framework (Anacleto et al., 2008a), it is important to expand an initial concept provided by the game editor in order to bring more relations about the main concept.

The second function is *display_node()*, that can be used for bringing relations about a particular concept. This function retrieves: the relation-type, the two concepts associated through it, and the id numbers of the statements in knowledge base which originated the relation. Therefore, the applications can use these results to create complete natural language statements. Basically, there are two ways of doing so: (1) the relations can be mapped in statements such as the templates used in the OMCS-Br site; for example, the relation (UsedFor "computer" "study") enable to create a statement like "A computer is used for study"; (2) the id numbers can be used to find the original statements in the knowledge base. Note that in the first case there are still difficulties to generate natural language statements grammatically correct. This is one of the AI challenges concerning natural language generation (Vallez & Pedraza-Jimenez, 2007).

Other function is *get_analogy()*, which has been developed based on the Gentner's Theory of Mapping of Structures (TME) (Gentner, 1983). From the Structure-Mapping Engine (SME) (Falkenhainer et al., 1990), an algorithm capable of generating analogies and similarities from OMCS-Br ConceptNets was developed. This algorithm uses a ConceptNet as basis domain and an ExpertNet as target domain, returning literal similarities. Details about the algorithm can be found in (Anacleto et al., 2007b). In the same way it can be found details about the other common sense inference procedures used in OMCS-Br in (Liu & Sing, 2004).

3.4. Access

The ConceptNet API is available to any computer application through XML-RPC (Remote Procedure Call) technology (XML-RPC, 2008), which allows a simple connection between a client application and a server application over the Internet. This connection is established through HTTP and all data are encoding in XML format. First of all, the application informs the ConceptNet Management Server shown in Figure 1 about the profile parameters values related to the desired ConceptNet. The server checks whether an API for that ConceptNet has been already instantiated in a specific port handled by it. If the desired ConceptNet API has been not been instantiated yet, the server asks for the Filtering module to verify whether the desired ConceptNet has been already generated in another moment so that it can instantiate an API for it. In case affirmative, the server allocates a port for the ConceptNet and makes it available also through the XML-RPC protocol. If the ConceptNet has not been generated yet, the Filtering module generates it, and then the server instantiates and makes available an API for the ConceptNet so that the application can use the API inference procedures. Since the application has been informed about the port where the ConceptNet API is available, it can connect to the port and use the API procedures.

4. Designing and Developing Culture-Sensitive Applications

As the complexity of computer applications grows, one way to make them more helpful and capable of avoiding unwise mistakes and unnecessary misunderstandings is to make use of common sense knowledge in their development (Lieberman et al., 2004). LIA has been experiencing that cultural differences registered in common sense knowledge bases can be helpful in: (a) developing systems to support decision-making by presenting common sense knowledge of a specific group to users; (b) developing systems capable of common sense reasoning, providing different feedback for people from different target group; and (c) helping designers who want to consider these differences in the interactive systems development by customizing interfaces and content according to the user's profile.
In the following, those three items are approached in details considering the domain of education and examples of cultural sensitive common sense-aided computer applications for each of them are presented.

4.1. Developing systems that show cultural issues for decision-making

There are situations in which it is interesting to know the common sense of a specific group in order to make suitable decisions. This is especially interesting in the domains of Human-Human Interaction (HHI), when two or more people from different cultural background are interacting with each other, and of Education, where it is important for educators to know how their learners talk about themes which is going to be taught, so that they can decide on how to approach those themes during the learning process. This was the first kind of common sense-aided computer application development approached by LIA's researchers.
In the following, two applications developed at LIA to illustrate how common sense knowledge can be used for this purpose are presented.

WIHT: a common sense-aided mail client for avoiding culture clashes

As the world economy becomes more and more globalized, it is common to see situations where people from two or more cultural backgrounds have to communicate with each other. Developing communication systems which show cultural differences to people who want to communicate with each other, making commentaries on the differences in the grounding that can lead to possible misunderstandings so that someone can correct him/herself before getting into an embarrassing situation, can be considered an advance in HCI that reflects on HHI. This issue has been approached by the development of an e-mail client which shows cultural difference between people from three different cultures combined two by two: Brazilian, Mexican and American (Anacleto et al., 2006a).
The application has an agent that keeps watching what the user is typing, while makes commentaries on the differences in the grounding that can lead to possible

misunderstandings. The system also uses these differences to calculate analogies for concepts that evoke the same social meaning in those cultures. This prototype is focused on the social interaction among people in the context of eating habits, but it could scale to other domains. The system interface has three sections, as can be seen in Figure 8. The first one - at the upper left - is the information for the e-mail addresses and the subject; the second one - at the upper right - is where the agent posts its commentaries about the cultural differences and the third part - the lower part - is the body of the message. The second section has four subsections: the upper one shows the analogies that the agent found and the other three show the data that are not suitable for analogy. For example, in the screen shot in figure 8, the third label for the Mexican culture - Mexicans thinks that dinner is coffee and cookies - and the second for American culture - Americans think that dinner is baked chicken - cannot make a meaningful analogy even if they differ only in one term.

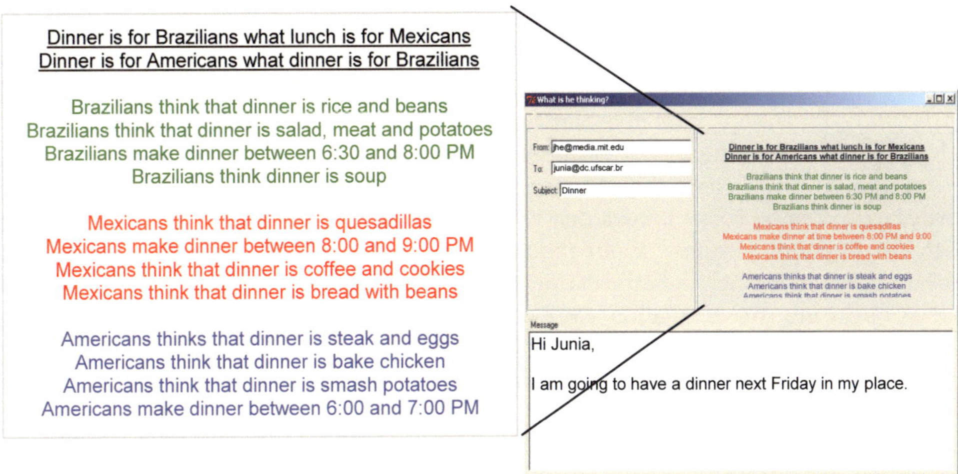

Fig. 8. WIHT screen shot (Anacleto et al., 2006a, p. 7)

In order to make the cultural analogies, the system uses three culturally specific semantic network that have knowledge about the Brazilian, Mexican and North-American culture - the ConceptNetBR, ConceptNetMX and ConceptNetUS respectively. The ConceptNetBR was built from data mined from the OMCS-Br knowledge base, originally in Portuguese. Specifically in this project, a small group of statements related to eating habits were selected and freely translated to English to be parsed by the system (Anacleto et al., 2006a).

PACO-T: a common sense-aided framework for planning learning activities

Another application developed at LIA for supporting decision making is PACO-T (Carvalho et al., 2008b), a computational tool for PACO (**P**lanning learning **A**ctivities based on **CO**mputers), a seven-step framework which aims to support educators in planning pedagogically suitable learning activities (Neris et al., 2007). PACO seven steps are: (1) define the learning activity theme, target public and general goal; (2) organize the learning activity topics; (3) choose a pedagogical/methodological reference; (4) plan the learning tasks; (5) choose computer tools to support the tasks execution; (6) edit the learning objects which are going to be used in the learning activity; and (7) test pedagogical and technological issues.

Researches developed at LIA shows that common sense knowledge can be used for educators to (Carvalho et al., 2008a) *(i)* identify topics of general interest to the target group; *(ii)* fit the learning activity content to the target group's previous knowledge; *(iii)* identify suitable vocabulary to be used in the learning activity; and *(iv)* identify knowledge from the target group's domain to which new knowledge can be anchored so that meaningful learning can be achieved (this knowledge can be used, for instance, in composing metaphors and analogies to be presented during the learning activity). Those are some pedagogical issues necessary to allow effective learning to take place, according to Learning Theories from renowned authors from the field of Pedagogy, such as Freire (2003), Freinet (1993), Ausubel (1968) and Gagné (1977).

Therefore, a case study was conducted specially to check the possibility of using common sense knowledge during the planning of learning activities by using PACO, to support teachers in answering questions brought up along the framework steps. The case study allowed a requirement elicitation, which was used for designing PACO-T. In the case study, two Nursing Professors from the Nursing Department of the Federal University of São Carlos planned a learning activity to prepare their students on how to orient caregivers in the community from which the common sense knowledge was collected. In the learning activity, the common sense knowledge was used to call the learners' attention to the way which the population talked about requirements to be a caregiver or about procedures which might be taken while home caring a sick person and to point which learners should emphasize during the orientation were presented (Carvalho et al., 2007; Carvalho et al., 2008a). Table 5 summarizes the support that common sense knowledge can give to teachers during learning activities planning using PACO, identified during the case study.

Step	Support
1	To define the learning activity theme.
	To compose the learning activity justification.
	To define the learning activity general objective.
	To define the learning activity specific objectives.
2	To decide which topics should be approached during the learning activity, so that it can fit to the students' needs.
	To decide the detail degree with which each topic should be approached.
3	To reach pedagogical issues addressed in Freire's (2003), Freinet's (1993), Ausubel's (1968) and Gagné's (1977) Learning Theories.
4	To fit the learning tasks to the pedagogical/ methodological references adopted.
	To know how the target group usually study.
5	To know with which computer tools the target group is familiar.
6	To compose the learning material.
7	-

Table 5. Support offered by common sense knowledge in each PACO's Step

In PACO-T, the target group's common sense knowledge is presented to educators, so that they can assess how people from that target group talk about topics related to the theme of the learning activity being planned and decide which topics they should approach in the learning activity, according to the needs they identify. Through common sense analysis educators can become aware about the learners' level of knowledge, avoiding approaching topics which learners already know and approaching topics which is misunderstood by that learners' profile, since common sense registers myths, believes and misunderstandings of people from whom the knowledge was collected.

The tool uses the semantic networks and the API provided by OMCS-Br to present knowledge related to the context of the learning activity planning, collected from volunteers with the profile of target group. For this purpose, teachers should define the target group's profile at the beginning of the planning so that a suitable ConceptNet can be instantiated and used during it. Figure 9 presents one of PACO-T interfaces with common sense support. The common sense support box can be noticed on the right.

Note that the items are presented in the common sense support box as links. Clicking on the link, the system performs a new search in ConceptNet, using as keyword the text of the link and updates the information in the common sense support box. This allows educators to navigate among the concepts previously presented and to analyze how people with the same profile of their target group talk about related subjects. Concerning the content in Figure 9, by analyzing it the educator can see that one of the motivations of home caring a sick person is to save money. Therefore, s(he) can consider that for her/his target group it is important to know procedures of home caring sick person which are not expensive and approach this theme during the learning activity.

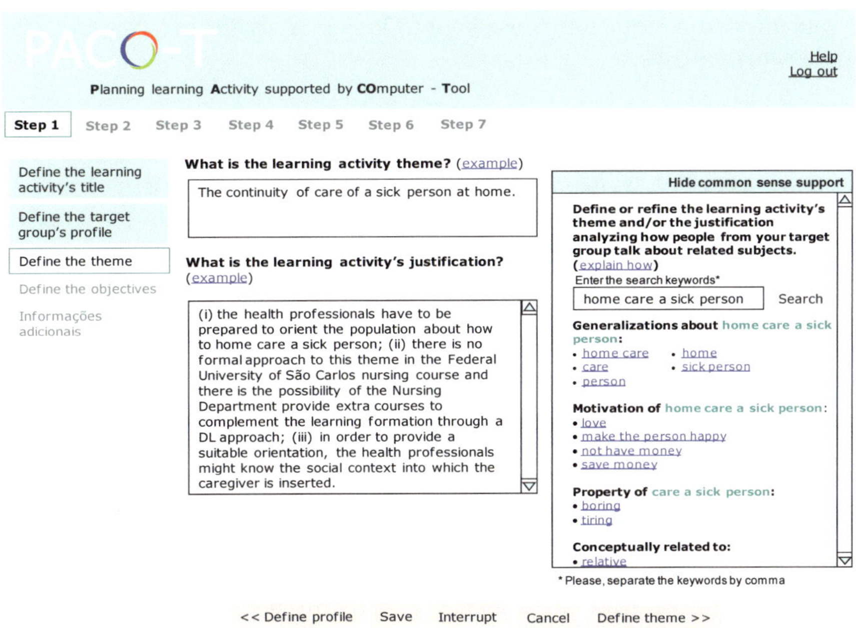

Fig. 9. PACO-T Interface – Step 1: Define the theme

Tools such as PACO-T, which can personalize the information that it is going to present to users, according to some parameters they provide, can be considered an valuable contribution to HCI, especially when the development of adjustable interfaces, which seems to be one of the main issues of HCI in a near future, is taken into account.

4.2. Developing systems which infer over cultural issues

Imagine the possibility of developing an agenda system capable of warning someone who tries to set up a meeting with an Indian in a barbecue place that this is not the best place to take an Indian, based on the information "Indians does not eat cow meat, because cows are considered holly in its culture". This is undoubtedly an advance in HCI that will allow the development of systems capable of acting flexibly to different kind of situations based on cultural information.

To support teachers contextualizing considering the educational context, the learning content they are preparing by suggesting topics of interest for the target group through inferences over a common sense knowledge base, an example to illustrate the use of common sense knowledge for the purpose of developing systems which infer over cultural issues. Moreover, when communities of people with common interests are considered like a group of learners of a certain educator in certain school year, it is possible to improve the interaction between educator and learners allowing educators to know about the learners' daily life and to prepare the content they will approach in classroom, considering the learners' cultural context. If a certain concept is explained through metaphors and analogies coming from learners' community the chances of such concept to be understood by the learners are bigger, according to pedagogical principles. Then, developing systems capable of suggesting those examples by inferring over a common sense knowledge base can be helpful. This section presents Cognitor, a computational framework for editing web-like learning content, and a Common Sense-Based On-line Assistant for Training Employees which implement those ideas.

Cognitor: a framework for editing culture-contextualized learning material

Cognitor is an authoring tool, based on the e-Learning Pattern Language Cog-Learn (Talarico Neto et al., 2008). Its main objective is to support teachers in designing and editing quality learning material to be delivered electronically to students on the Internet or on CD/DVD. It aims to facilitate the development of accessible and usable learning material, which complies with issues from Pattern and Learning Theories, giving teachers access to common sense knowledge in order to make them able to contextualize their learning materials to their learners' needs (Anacleto et al., 2007a). About using common sense knowledge in the learning process, Cognitor is being prepared to make possible the use of common sense knowledge through all the edition of the learning content, in order to instantiate the Patterns implemented in the tool, to organize the hyper document, to contextualize the content, to adjust the vocabulary used in the content and to fulfill the metadata of such learning objects.

One of the tools available in Cognitor is the implementation of the Cog-Learn Knowledge View Pattern (Talarico Neto et al., 2008), which supports the planning and the automatic generation of learning material navigational structure, by using the technique of Concept Map, proposed by Novak (Novak, 1986). For that purpose, teachers should: (i) enter into the system the Concepts which they want to approach in their learning material and organize them hierarchically; (ii) name the natural relations between concepts, i.e. the relations mapped from the hierarchy previously defined; and (iii) establish and name any other relation between concepts, which they consider important to the content understanding and exploration. See (Anacleto et al., 2007a) for more information on the process of generating a Concept Map in Cognitor, using the Knowledge View Pattern.

When the teacher chooses to use the Knowledge View pattern, Cognitor offers the common sense support to provide her/him with information about the facts that are considered common sense in the domain that s/he is thinking of. So the teacher can complete the Concept list based on that information, decreasing the time on planning the material organization. Figure 10 depicts the first step of Cog-learn Knowledge View Pattern tool, in which teachers are expected to enter into the system the concepts which they want to approach in the content.

In the example, the teacher entered the concept "Health" ("Saúde", in Portuguese), and the system suggested in the box on the right concepts such as "sick person" ("pessoa doente"), "place" ("lugar") and "drug" ("remédio"). Teachers can select one of the suggestion from common sense knowledge and click on the button "<< Include", select a concept in the list of concepts on the right and perform a search in the common sense knowledge base for related concepts through the button "Search >>", or even add another concept that is not in the common sense concepts suggestion list. By using common sense suggestion educators can contextualize the learning content they are preparing to their target group´s needs in the same way it is done in PACO-T.

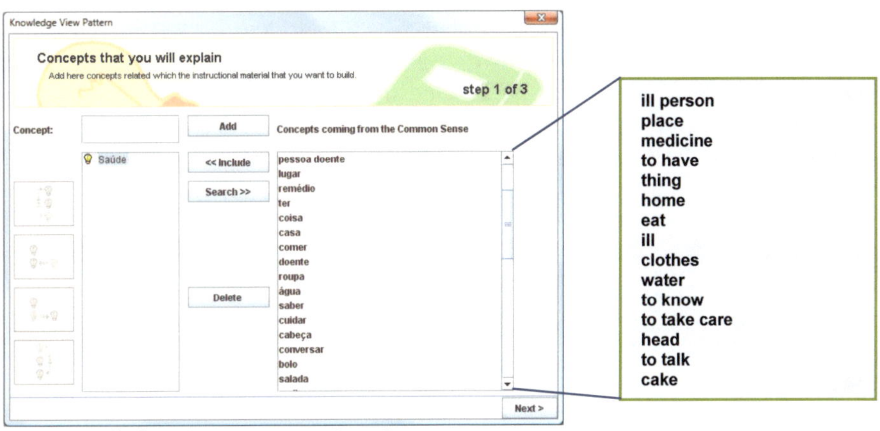

Fig. 10. Knowledge View Pattern First Step

On-line Help Assistant for Training Employees

The On-line Help Assistant is a web system to support continuing education about workplace safety issues, where the learner can ask a doubt about a certain concept in natural language and the system gives him back the formal definition and some analogies coming from common sense of that employee community to explain the concept (Anacleto et al., 2007b). In order to build the analogies, the system uses the function *get_analogy()* mentioned in section 3.3 of this chapter.

The system is basically a common sense-aided search engine. Its interface is composed for five areas, four of them presented in Figure 11:

1. **Search area**, where users should type the search query;
2. **Definition area,** where definitions for the concepts in the search query are presented;
3. **Analogy area,** where the analogies to explain the concepts are shown;

4. **Relations area,** where the relations among the concepts present in the search query and the ones in the ConceptNet are presented; and
5. **Related concept area**, where related concepts retrieved from ConceptNet are presented and users can continue their studies by exploring those concepts. For this purpose, learner can use the links offered by the assistant and browse through the concepts.

Users should type the concept they want to get explained and then click on the button "Shown information found". In order to identify the morphological variations in the query, the system uses two techniques. The first one is the expansion technique. It is useful when students use short expressions to perform the search. In this technique, the terms related to the context are retrieved by the function *get_context()* of the ConceptNet API. Then, terms that have the lemmatized expression as a substring are also retrieved. For instance, when a learner provides the expression "fogo" ("fire", in English) in the search area the system will also search for expressions like "fire alarm", "fire place", "fire door" and so on. The second technique is useful especially when large expressions are provided by the students to be searched. In this case phrasal structures, such as noun phrases, verbal phrases and adjective phrases are identified by the system and then the system performs a search for each structure identified. For example, when a student asks the system for results related to the expression "prevenir acidentes no ambiente de trabalho" (in English, "preventing accidents in the workplace"), the expression will be divided in "preventing work accidents", "work accidents", "accidents" and "accident in the workplace". This technique increases the likelihood of getting results from the search, since the terms that are searched are simpler and more likely to be found in the semantic network (Anacleto et al., 2007b).

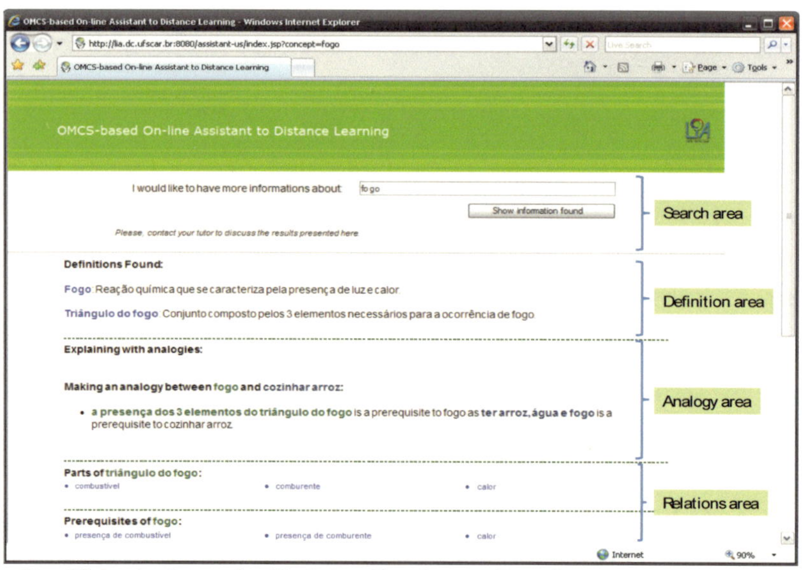

Fig. 11. On-line Help Assistant for Training Employees Interface

4.3. Designing systems considering cultural issues

Attributes as attraction, dynamism, level of expertise, confidence, intention, location, social validation and preferences have different weights in different cultures. Consequently, user

interface developers face many challenges, such as the design of the content which should be presented for users with different culture profiles. For example, which colors should be used in the design of an interface in order to make users feel comfortable or react in the desired way? Which symbols should be used so that the right message is transmitted?
Despite of the importance of these issues, developers face the almost unreachable tasks of researching culture-dependent requirements and having a contextualized development accepted due to tight budgets, limited agenda, and scarce human resources. In this context, collecting these "world views" and making them available for everyone that wants to develop culture-contextualized user interfaces, can be expensive and laborious.
Taking into account that this kind of information and that the answer for question´s such the ones stated before can be found in people's common sense. Using this kind of knowledge in the system development seem´s to be a alternative for providing cultural contextualization.
Common sense-based interface content design has been tested at LIA in an educational game called "What is it?" (Anacleto et al., 2008a), a card-based quiz game that proposes to work on curricular themes. The game framework is presented in the following.

"What is it?": a framework for designing culture-contextualized educational games

The game framework "What is it?" is a proposal to support teachers in contextualizing the content of quiz-like educational games to the students' local culture, in order to promote a more effective and significant learning. It is divided in two modules: a module for educators, called "Editor's Module" and another for learners, called "Player's Module" (Anacleto et al., 2008a). The cards designed by the educators are presented for the learners in the learner's module, which automatically considers cultural issues when the topics to be worked on are established. So, the content presented to learners is customized according the common sense knowledge shared by people with their profile, once the educator previously established the topics and statements from that learner's community to set up the game (Anacleto et al., 2008a).

Editor's Module

The game editor is a seven-step wizard which guides the teacher towards creating game instances, which fit to their pedagogical goals. It implements the principle of developing systems that shows cultural issues for decision-making, presented in section 4.1.
During the card definition, teachers receive the support of common sense knowledge. For that purpose, in the framework editor Step 1 teachers have to define the population profile which should be considered in the search for common sense statements in the knowledge base. In this way, the system guarantees that the statements which are going to be presented to the teacher were gathered from people who have the desired profile to the game instance, i.e. the statements are contextualized to the target group.
In the two next steps the teacher must define two items: (1) the game main theme that nowadays have to be related to one of the six transversal themes defined on the Brazilian curriculum (sexual education, ethics, healthcare, environment, cultural plurality, market and consumers) and (2) the topics, which are specifics subjects related to the theme chosen, to compose the game dice faces (Anacleto et al., 2008a).
The next steps consist of defining the secret words, their synonyms and the set of clues for each secret word. For each secret word defined, it is performed a search on the ConceptNet instantiated at Step1, that increasing the number of words associated with the secret work. The concepts associated with the secret word and their synonyms are presented to teachers

as natural language statements and, based on these statements, teachers can compose the card clues. For example, the relation (IsA "aids", "sexually transmitted disease"), found in the ConceptNet-Br, is presented to teachers as "Aids is a(n) sexually transmitted disease".
Then the teacher can (a) select a common sense statements as clues, adding them to the card set of clue; (b) edit a statement to make it suitable to the game purpose; or (c) just ignore the suggestions and compose others clues. It is worth pointing out that the statements edited or composed by the teachers are also stored in the OMCS-Br knowledge base as new common sense statement collected from that teacher.
It is also important to point out the fail-soft approach adopted in the framework. This means that the statements suggested to teachers can be valid or not and the teachers will decide for accepting or not the suggestion. However, the suggestion does not bring any problem to the teachers' task performance. On the contrary, it helps the teachers to finish their task faster and more efficiently.

Player's Module

Figure 12 presents an instance of "What is it?" in theme "Sexual Education". That is the interface presented to learners after teachers finish preparing the game cards. To start the game the player should click on the virtual dice, represented in Figure 12 by the letter "S", whose faces represent the topics related to the transversal theme on which the teacher intents to work. In Figure 12, the letter "S" corresponds to the topic "Sexually transmitted diseases". Other topics which can potentially compose the "Sexual Education" theme dice, according to the teachers' needs, are "anatomy and physiology", "behavior" and "contraceptives methods". The letters, which represent the topics, are presented to the player fast and randomly. When the player clicks on the dice it stops and say about which topic the secret word, which should be guessed, is.

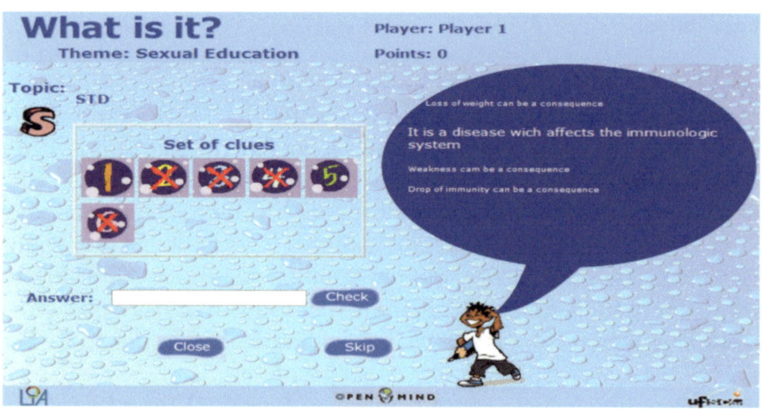

Fig. 12. Player's Module Main Interface

Each topic has a set of cards associated with, which are related to different secret words. These cards are defined by teachers in the game's editor module, using the support of a common sense knowledge base. In addition to that, it is possible to relate a list of synonyms to each secret word. These synonyms are also accepted as expected answers.

The clues play the role of supporting the player to guess which the secret word is. Each card can have a maximum of ten clues which can be selected by the learners by clicking on a number into the "Set of clues" area, which can be seen in Figure 12. After having the topic defined by the dice, a card with clues is presented to the player and, as s(he) selects a clue, it is displayed on the blue balloon. The players can select as many clues as they consider necessary before trying to guess the word.

As the players try to find out the secret word, the system collects common sense knowledge, storing the relation between the word they have suggested and clues that have been already displayed. This collection process is interesting (1) for teachers, who can identify possible misunderstanding by analyzing the answers that learners with the profile of their target group give to a specific set of clues, and, therefore, approach those misunderstandings in classroom to clarify them; and (2) for the OMCS-Br, which will get its knowledge base increased. It is important to point out that the answers provided by the learners, which do not correspond either to the secret word or to a synonym defined by the teacher, are not considered incorrect by the system.

5. Conclusion and Future Works

The advent of Web 3.0, claiming for personalization in interactive systems (Lassila & Hendler, 2007), and the need for systems capable of interacting in a more natural way in the future society flooded with computer systems and devices (Harper et al., 2008) show that great advances in HCI should be done.

This chapter presents some contributions of LIA for the future of HCI, defending that using common sense knowledge is a possibility for improving HCI, especially because people assign meaning to their messages based on their common sense and, therefore, the use of this knowledge in developing user interfaces can make them more intuitive to the end-user. Moreover, as common sense knowledge varies from group to group of people, it can be used for developing applications capable of giving different feedback for different target groups, as the applications presented along this chapter illustrate, allowing, in this way, interface personalization taking into account cultural issues.

For the purpose of using common sense knowledge in the development and design of computer systems, it is necessary to provide an architecture that allows it. This chapter presents LIA's approaches for common sense knowledge acquisition, representation and use, as well as for natural language processing, contributing with those ones who intent to get into this challenging world to get started.

Regarding the educational context adopted by LIA's researchers, the approaches presented here go towards one of the grand challenges for engineering in 21st century recent announced by the National Academy of Engineering (NAE) (http://www.nae.edu/nae/naehome.nsf): advance personalized learning (Advance Personalized Learning, 2008). Using intelligent internet systems, capable of inferring over the learning contexts which educators want to approach and presenting related themes, topics and pieces of information retrieved from is one of the possible approaches mentioned by NAE.

As future work it is proposed to perform user tests on the applications presented along this chapter, in order to check their usability and, consequently, the users' satisfaction in using such kind of application.

6. Acknowledgements

We thank FAPESP and CAPES for financial support. We also thank all volunteers who have been collaborating with the Project OMCS-Br and all LIA's researchers, who have been giving valuable contributions towards the project.

7. References

Advance Personalized Learning (2008). National Academy of Engineering: Grand Challenges for Engineering. Available in: http://www.engineeringchallenges.org/cms/8996/9127.aspx. Last access in: March 2008.

Anacleto, J. C. ; Pereira, E. N. ; Ferreira, A. M. ; Carvalho, A. F. P. De & Fabro, J. A.(2008a). Culture Sensitive Educational Games Considering Commonsense Knowledge, *Proceedings of the 10th International Conference on Enterprise Information Systems (ICEIS 2008)* , pp. 136-141 ,978-9- 898-11140-1,Barcelona, June 2008, INSTICC Press, Setúbal.

Anacleto, J. C.; Carvalho, A. F. P. de; Pereira, E. N.; Ferreira, A. M. & Carlos, A. J. F. (2008b). Machines with good sense: How can computers become capable of sensible reasoning? In: *Artificial Intelligence in Theory and Practice II*, Bramer, M. (Ed.), - , Springer, ISBN: 978-0-387-09694-0, Germany. In press.

Anacleto, J. C. ; Carlos, A. J. F. ; Carvalho, A. F. P. de & Godoi, M. S.(2007a). Using Common Sense Knowledge to Support Learning Objects Edition and Discovery for Reuse, *Proceedings of the 13th Brazilian Symposium on Multimedia and the Web (WebMedia 2007)*, pp. 290-297, ISBN: 857669150-7, Gramado, October 2007, Brazilian Computing Society, Porto Alegre.

Anacleto, J. C.; Godoi, M. S.; Carvalho, A. F. P. de & Lieberman, H. (2007b). A Common Sense-Based On-Line Assistant for Training Employees, In: Human-Computer Interaction - INTERACT 2007, Baranauskas, C.; Palanque, P.; Abascal, J. & Barbosa, S. D. J. (Eds.), pp. 243-255, Springer, ISBN: 978-3-540-74794-9, Germany.

Anacleto, J. C. ; Lieberman, H. ; Tsutsumi, M. ; Neris, V. P. A.; Carvalho, A. F. P. de; Espinosa, J. ; Zem-Mascarenhas, S. ; Godoi, M. de S. (2006a). Can common sense uncover cultural differences in computer applications?, In: *Artificial Intelligence in Theory and Practice II*, Bramer, M. (Ed.), pp. 1-10, Springer, ISBN: 978-0-387-34654-0, Germany.

Anacleto, J. C. ; Lieberman, H. ; Carvalho, A. F. P. De ; Neris, V. P. A. ; Godoi, M. S. ; Tsutsumi, M. ; Espinosa, J. ; Talarico Neto, A. & Zem-Mascarenhas, S.(2006b). Using common sense to recognize cultural differences, In: *Advances in Artificial Intelligence - IBERAMIA-SBIA 2006*, Sichman, J. S.; Coelho, H. & Rezende, S. O. (Eds.), pp. 370-379, Springer, ISBN: 978-3-540-45462-5, Germany.

Ausubel, D.P. (1968). *Educational Psychology: A Cognitive View*, Holt, Rinehart and Winston, ISBN: 0030696402, New York.

Bailey, B.P.; Gurak, L. J. & Konstan, J.A. (2001). An examination of trust production in computer-mediated exchange, *Proceedings of the 7th Human Factors and the Web Conference*, pp. 1-8, - , Madison, June 2001, - , - .

Carvalho, A. F. P. de; Anacleto, J. C. & Zem-Mascarenhas, S. (2008a). Learning Activities on Health Care Supported by Common Sense Knowledge, *Proceedings of the 23rd Annual ACM Symposium on Applied Computing (SAC 2008)*, pp. 1385-1389, ISBN: 978-1-59593-753-7, Fortaleza, March 2008, ACM Press, New York.

Carvalho, A. F. P. de; Anacleto, J. C. & Neris, V. P. A. (2008b). Supporting Teachers to Plan Culturally Contextualized Learning Activities, *Proceedings of the WCC 2008 TC3 ED – L2L Conference*, - , - , Millan, September 2008, Springer, Germany. In press.

Carvalho, A. F. P. de. (2007). Utilização de Conhecimento de Senso Comum para o Planejamento de Ações de Aprendizagem Apoiado por Computador. 2007. 241p. *Master Thesis*. PPG-CC, UFSCar. /in Portuguese/

Carvalho, A. F. P. de; Anacleto, J. C.; Zem-Mascarenhas, S. (2007). Planning Learning Activities Pedagogically Suitable by Using Common Sense Knowledge, *Proceedings of the 16th International Conference on Computing (CIC 2007)*, pp. 1-6, - , Mexico City, November 2007, - , - .

Falkenhainer, B.; Forbus, K. & Gentner, D. (1990). The structure-mapping engine: algorithm and examples, *Artificial Intelligence*, vol. 41, - , 1990, pp. 1-63, - .

Freinet, C. (1993). *Education through work: A model for child centered learning*, Edwin Mellen Press, ISBN: 0773493034, New York.

Freire, P. (2003). *Pedagogia da autonomia: saberes necessários à prática educative*, Paz e Terra, ISBN: 9788577530151, São Paulo.

Gagné, R. M. (1977). *The Conditions of Learning*, Holt, Rinehart e Winston, ISBN: 0030899656, New York.

Gentner, D. (1983). Structure-mapping: A theoretical framework for analogy, *Cognitive Science*, v. 7, n. 2, 1983, pp. 155-170, - .

Harper, R. ; Rodden, T. ; Rogers, Y. & Sellen, A. (Eds) (2008). *Being Human: Human-Computer Interaction in the year 2020*, Microsoft Research Ltda, ISBN: 978-0-9554761-1-2, England.

Havasi, C.; Speer, R. & Alonso, J. (2007). ConceptNet 3: a Flexible, Multilingual Semantic Network for Common Sense Knowledge, *Proceedings of the 2007 Recent Advances in Natural Language Processing Conference (RANLP 2007)*, - , - , Borvest, - , - .

Lenat, D. B.; Guha, R. V.; Pittman, K.; Pratt, D. & Shepherd, M. (1990). Cyc: toward programs with common sense, *Communications of the ACM*, v. 33, n. 8, p. 30-19, August 1990, ISSN: 0001-0782.

Lenat, D. B. (1995). CYC: a large-scale investment in knowledge infrastructure. *Communications of the ACM*, v. 38, n. 11, p. 33-38, November 1995, ISSN: 0001-0782.

Lieberman, H.; Smith, D. & Teeters, A. (2007). Common Consensus: A Web-based Game for Collecting Commonsense Goals. Proceedings of the 1st Workshop on Common Sense for Intelligent Interfaces (CSIUI), - , - , Honolulu, January 2007, - , USA.

Lieberman, H.; Liu, H. Singh, P. & Barry, B. (2004). Beating common sense into interactive applications, *AI Magazine*, v. 25, n. 4, p. 63-76, Winter 2004, ISSN: 0738-4602.

Liu, H.; Singh P. (2004). ConceptNet: a practical commonsense reasoning toolkit, *BT Technology Journal*, v. 22, n. 4, p. 211-226, October 2004, - .

Martins, R. T.; Hasegawa, R.; Nunes, M.G.V. (2003). Curupira: a functional parser for Brazilian Portuguese, In: *Computational Processing of the Portuguese Language*, Mamede, N.J.; Baptista, J.; Trancoso, I.; Nunes, M. G. V. (Eds.), pp. 179-183, Springer, ISBN: 978-3-540-40436-1, Germany.

Matuszek, C.; Witbrock, M.; Kahlert, R.; Cabral, J.; Schneider D. ; Shah, P. & Lenat, D. B (2005). Searching for Common Sense: Populating Cyc from the Web, Proceedings of the 20th *National Conference on Artificial Intelligence*, - , - , Pittsburgh, 2005, USA.

Minsky, M. (1988). *The Society of Mind,* Simon and Schuster, ISBN: 0671657135, New York.

Minsky, M. (2000). Commonsense-based interfaces, *Communications of the ACM,* v. 43, n. 8, pp. 66-73, August 2000, ISSN: 0001-0782.

Mueller, E. T. (1997). Natural language processing with ThoughtTreasure, Signiform, ISBN: 0966074602, New York.

Mueller, E. T. (2007). ThoughtTreasure: A natural language/commonsense platform. Available on: <http://www.signiform.com/tt/htm/overview.htm>. Access in: March 2007.

Neris, V. P. A.; Anacleto, J. C.; Zem-Mascarenhas, S. & Carvalho, A. F. P. de. (2007). PACO - A Framework for Planning Learning Activities Supported by Computers, Proceedings of the 18th Brazilian Symposium on Informatics in Education (SBIE 2007), pp. 597-606, ISBN: 9788576691570, São Paulo, November 2007, Brazilian Computing Society, Porto Alegre.

Novak, J. D. & Tyler, R. W. (1986). A Theory of Education, Cornell University Press, ISBN: 0801493781, New York.

Lassila, O. & Hendler, J. (2007). Embracing "Web 3.0", *IEEE Internet Computing,* v. 11, n. 3, pp. 90-93, May 2007, ISSN:1089-7801.

Panton, K.; Matuszek, C.; Lenat, D. B.; Schneider, D.; Witbrock, M.; Siegel, N. & Shepard, B. (2006). Common Sense Reasoning – From Cyc to Intelligent Assistant, In: *Ambient Intelligence in Everyday Life,* Cai, Y. & Abascal, J. (Eds.), pp. 1-31, Springer, ISBN: 978-3-540-37785-6, New York.

Panton, K.; Miraglia, P. & Salay, N. (2002). Knowledge Formation and Dialogue Using the KRAKEN Toolset, *Proceedings of the 14th National Conference on Innovative Applications of Artificial Intelligence*, pp. 900-905, - , Edmonton, 2002 , - , - .

Singh, P. (2002) The OpenMind Commonsense Project, *KurzweilAI.net,* - , - , January 2002, - , - . Available on: http://www.kurzweilai.net/meme/frame.html?main=/articles/art0371.html. Last access in: May 2008.

Talarico Neto, A.; Anacleto, J. C. & Neris, V. P. A. (2008). Cog-Learn: an E-Learning Pattern Language for Web-based Instructional Material Design, *eLearn Magazine,* - , - , - , - , - . To appear.

UNITEX-PB (2008). Available on: http://www.nilc.icmc.usp.br:8180/unitex-pb/index.html. Last access in: May 2008.

Vallez, M.; Pedraza-Jimenez, R. Natural Language Processing in Textual Information Retrieval and Related Topics, *Hipertext.net*, n. 5, - , 2007, - , ISSN: 1695-5498.

von Ahn, L.; Kedia, M. & Blum, M. (2006). Verbosity: a game for collecting common-sense facts, *Proceedings of the SIGCHI Conference on Human Factors in Computing Systems (CHI),* pp. 75-78, ISBN:1-59593-372-7, Montreal, April 2006, ACM Press, New York.

Witbrock, M.; Baxter, D; Curtis, J.; Schneider, D; Kahlert, R.; Miraglia, P.; Wagner, P.; Panton, K.; Matthews, G. & Vizedom, A. (2003). An Interactive Dialogue System for Knowledge Acquisition in Cyc. *Proceedings of the 18th International Joint Conference on Artificial Intelligence*, - , - , Acapulco, 2003, - , - .

XML-RPC Home Page. http://www.xmlrpc.com. Last access in: March, 2008.

2

The Role of Head-Up Display in Computer-Assisted Instruction

Kikuo Asai
National Institute of Multimedia Education
Japan

1. Introduction

The head-up display (HUD) creates a new form of presenting information by enabling a user to simultaneously view a real scene and superimposed information without large movements of the head or eye scans (Newman, 1995; Weintraub and Ensing, 1992). HUDs have been used for various applications such as flight manipulation, vehicle driving, machine maintenance, and sports, so that the users improve situational comprehension with the real-time information. Recent downsizing of the display devices will expand the HUD utilization into more new areas.

The head-mounted display (HMD) has been used as a head-mounted type of HUDs for wearable computing (Mann, 1997) that gives a user situational information by wearing a portable computer like clothes, a bag, and a wristwatch. A computer has come to interact intelligently with people based on the context of the situation with sensing and wireless communication systems.

One promising application is in computer-assisted instruction (CAI) (Feiner, et al., 1993) that supports the works such as equipment operation, product assembly, and machine maintenance. These works have witnessed the introduction of increasingly complex platforms and sophisticated procedures, and have required the instructional support. HUD-based CAI applications are characterized by real-time presentation of instructional information related to what a user is looking at. It is commonly thought that HUD-based CAI will increase productivity in instruction tasks and reduce errors by properly presenting task information based on a user's viewpoint.

However, there are not enough empirical studies that show which factors of HUDs improve user performance. A considerable amount of systematic research must be carried out in order for HUD-based CAI to fulfill its potential to use the scene augmentation to improve human-computer interaction.

We have developed a HUD-based CAI system that enables non-technical staff to operate the transportable earth station (Asai, et al., 2006). Although we observed that users of the HUD-based CAI system performed slightly better than users of conventional PCs and paper manuals, it was not clear which factors significantly affected performance in operating the system. We here conducted a laboratory experiment in which participants performed a task of reading articles and answering questions, in order to evaluate how readable the display

of the HUD is, how easy it is to search information using the system, and how it affects the work efficiency. We then discuss the characteristics of HUD-based CAI, comparing the task performance between the HUD-based CAI and conventional media.
Thus, this chapter is a study on the information processing behavior at an HUD, focusing on its role in CAI. Our aim is to introduce the basic concept and human factors of an HUD, explain the features of HUD-based CAI, and show user performance with our HUD-based CAI system.

2. HUD Technology

The HUD basically has an optical mechanism that superimposes synthetic information on a user's field of view. Although the HUD is designed to allow a user to concurrently view a real scene and superimposed information, its type depends on the application. We here categorize HUDs into three design types: head-mounted or ground-referenced, optical see-through or video see-through, and single-sided or two-sided types.

2.1 Head-mounted and Ground-referenced Types

HUDs are categorized into the head-mounted and ground-referenced types in terms of spatial relationship between the head and HUD, as shown in Fig. 1.
In the head-mounted type (Fig. 1 (a)), an HUD is mounted on the head, being attached to a helmet or a head band. It is generally called a head-mounted display (HMD). Since the HUD is fixated to the head, a user can see visual information, even though moving the head. The head-mounted type of HUD is used at the environment where users have to look around them, such as building construction, surgical operation, and sports activities. The head-mounted HUD should be light in weight, because the user has to support its weight.
In the ground-referenced type (Fig. 1 (b)), an HUD is grounded to a desktop, wall, or floor. Since the relation between the head and HUD is not fixated spatially, visual information can be viewed just in case that a user directs the head to the HUD. The ground-referenced type of HUD is used at the environment where users almost look at the same direction, such as flight manipulation and vehicle driving. The user does not need to support the weight in the ground-referenced HUD.

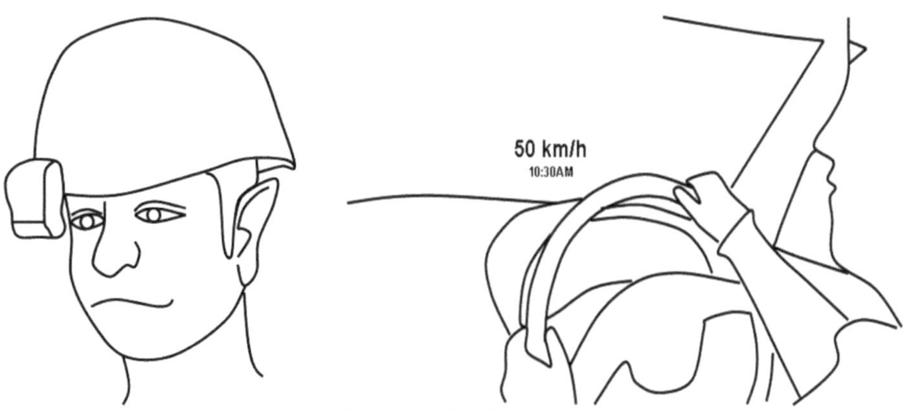

(a) Head-mounted type (b) Ground-referenced type
Fig. 1. Spatial relation between the head and HUD

2.2 Optical See-through and Video See-through Types

HUDs are categorized into the optical see-through and video see-through types in terms of optical mechanism, as shown in Fig. 2.

In the optical see-through type (Fig. 2 (a)), a user sees the real scene through a half mirror (transparent display) on which the synthetic images including graphics or text are overlaid. The optical see-through HUD has advantages of seeing the real scene without degradation of the resolution and delay of the presentation. In addition, eye accommodation and convergence responses work for the real scene. However, the responses do not work for virtual objects. That is, the real scene and the synthetic images are at different distances from the user. Therefore, the user's eyes need to alternately adjust to these distances in order to perceive information in the both contexts. Frequent gaze shifting to different depths may result in eye strain (Neveu, et al., 1998). The optical see-through HUD does not also represent occlusion correctly because the real scene goes through the half mirror at the pixel area of the front virtual objects. One more problem is of difficulty in use under a bright illumination condition such as an outdoor field because of low luminance of the display.

In the video see-through type (Fig. 2 (b)), a real scene is captured by a camera. The user sees the real scene images, in which information such as graphics or text is superimposed, at a display monitor. The video see-through HUD has the following advantages; (1) the real scene can be flexibly processed at the pixel unit, making brightness control and color correction, (2) there is no temporal deviation between the real scene and virtual objects because of their synchronous presentation in the display image, and (3) the additional information is obtained by using the captured scene, deriving depth information from parallax images and user's position from the geometric features. According to (1), the occlusion is achieved by covering the real scene with the virtual objects or culling the back pixels out of the virtual objects. While, the video see-through HUD has shortcomings due to losing rich information on the real scene. Low temporal and spatial resolution of the HUD decreases the realistic and immersive sense of the real scene. The inconsistent focus-depth information may result in high physiological load during the use. Despite (2), the video see-through HUD has presentation delay due to the image composition and rendering, which may sometimes lead to a critical accident at the environment such as a construction site.

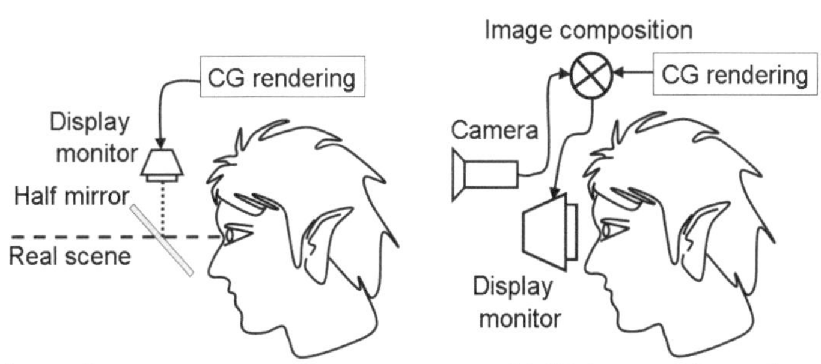

(a) Optical see-through type (b) Video see-through type

Fig. 2. Optical difference between the HUDs

2.3 Single-sided and Two-sided Types

HUDs are categorized into the single-sided and and two-sided types in terms of the field of view based on relation of the eyes and HUD, as shown in Fig. 3. Whether presenting the

synthetic images to one eye or two eyes is an important factor that dominates the range of applicable areas.
In the single-sided type of HUD (Fig. 3 (a)), the real scene is viewed by two eyes, and the synthetic images are presented to one eye using an optical see-through or video see-through display. The real scene images captured by a video camera have a time lag to be displayed at the video see-through display. A single-sided HUD is used at the environment where a user works looking at the peripheral situations or experience of the real world proceeds acquisition of the complementary information. For example, the single-sided type is usually used in a construction site due to safety reasons. When the synthetic images or the device frames interfere largely with the user's field of view, vital accidents may occur during the work.
In the two-sided type of HUD (Fig. 3 (b)), the real scene and synthetic images are viewed by two eyes using an optical see-through or video see-through display. A two-sided HUD is used at the situation where safety of the user is ensured without looking around, because the cost of visual interference would be high at the two-sided HMD, in which the overlaid information interferes with the view of the workspace. For example, the two-sided type is often used at an entertainment situation because of producing the feeling of being there.
There is a tradeoff relationship between the single-sided and two-sided types in readability of documents on the HUD and visibility of the real scene via the HUD. The single-sided HUD enables a user to easily see real objects using one eye with no occlusion, though the user has to read documents using only one eye. On the other hand, the two-sided HUD enables the user to read documents with both eyes, though the user has to view real objects through the display on which the documents are presented. The single-sided HUD is more convenient for acquiring information on real objects, and the two-sided HUD is more convenient for acquiring information on the display.
In the head-mounted type, the weight of the HUD is an important factor for user's comfort. A single-sided HUD, in general, weighs less than the two-sided HUD. Although the difference in weight is only 150 g for the HUDs, it turns out to be significant because the device is attached to the head (Asai, et al., 2005). The heavier the HUD is, the tighter the HUD has to be placed on the head without being shifted, which may result in difficulty for a long-time use.

(a) Single-sided type

(b) Two-sided type

Fig. 3. Relation between the eyes and HUD

3. Human Factors of HUDs

HUD systems have developed for improving performance of multiple tasks in aircraft landing and vehicular driving. In the aircraft landing, the HUD system supports pilots to keep operation performance in navigating through a crowded airspace. In the vehicular driving, the HUD supports drivers to keep driving performance in accessing information from multiple sources such as speed, navigation, and accidents. Although numerous information and communication tools have provided a user with a large amount of information, the user's capacity to process information does not change.

There are many researches regarding the costs and benefits of HUDs compared with head-down displays (HDDs). The benefits of HUDs are mainly characterized by visual scanning and re-accommodation. In the visual scanning, HUDs reduces the amount of eye scans and head movements required to monitor information and view the outside world (Haines, et al., 1980; Tufano, 1997). The traditional HDD causes time sharing between the tasks. For example, drivers must take their eyes off the road ahead in order to read the status at the control panel, which affects driving safety. The HUD degrades the problem because of simultaneous viewing of the monitor information and real scene. In the visual re-accommodation, HUDs reduces the adjustment time of refocusing the eyes required to monitor information and view the outside world (Larry and Elworth, 1972; Okabayashi, et al., 1989). The HDD makes the user refocus the eyes frequently for viewing the closer and far domains, which may cause fatigue. The HUD degrades the re-accommodation problem by allowing the user to read the status without shifting focus largely in case being optically focused farther.

However, use of HUDs did not always improve user performance in aviation safety studies, especially when unexpected events occurred (Fischer, et al., 1980; Weintraub, et al., 1985). The HUD users had a shorter response time than the HDD users to detect unexpected events only in conditions of low workload. The benefits of HUDs, however, were reduced or even reversed in conditions of high workload (Larish and Wickens, 1991; Wickens, et al., 1993; Fadden, et al., 2001). Measurement of the time required to mentally switch between the superimposed HUD symbology and the moving real-world scene revealed that it took longer to switch when there was differential motion between superimposed symbology in a fixed place on the HUD and movement in the real-world scene behind the symbology caused by motion of the aircraft (McCann, et al., 1993). As a result, conformal imagery (Wickens and Long, 1995) or scene-linked symbology (Foyle, et al., 1995) that moved as the real objects moved was configured on the HUD to reduce the time it takes to switch attention. The HUD can depict virtual information reconciled with physically viewable parts in the real world. This conformal imagery or scene-linked symbology is based on the same concept as spatial registration of virtual and real objects in augmented reality (AR) technology (e.g., Milgram and Kishino, 1994; Azuma, 1997).

4. HUD-based CAI

CAI has been applied to maintenance and manufacturing instructions in engineering (Dede, 1986), in which complex tasks must be performed. CAI systems have helped new users learn how to use devices by illustrating a range of functional capabilities of the device with multimedia content. However, the human-computer interfaces were inadequate for eliciting the potential of human performance, due to the limitations of the input/output devices, including inconvenience of holding a CAI system while working and mismatch of information processing between computer and human. An HUD environment may make it possible to improve human-computer interaction in CAI by allowing information to be integrated into the real scene.

4.1 Applications

Typical examples of HUD-based CAI applications are operation of equipment, assembly of products, and maintenance of machines. Many systems have been developed as applications of AR technology, including assistance and training on new systems, assembly of complex systems, and service work on plants and systems in industrial context (Friedrich, 2002; Schwald and Laval, 2003).

In the service and maintenance, the work is expected to improve efficiency by accessing databases on-line and reduce human errors by augmenting the real objects with visual information such as annotations, data maps, and virtual models (Navab, 2004). As a solution, an online guided maintenance approach was taken for reducing necessity and dependency on trained workers facing increasingly complex platforms and sophisticated maintenance procedures (Lipson, et al., 1998; Bian, et al., 2006). It has potential to create a new quality of remote maintenance by conditional instructions adjusting automatically to conditions at the maintenance site, according to input information from the machine and updated knowledge at the manufacturer. The service and maintenance of nuclear power plants also require workers to minimize the time for diagnostics (troubleshooting and repair) and comply with safety regulations for inspection of critical subsystems. The context-based statistical pre-fetching component was implemented by using document history as context information (Klinker, et al., 2001). The pre-fetching component records each document request that was made by the application, and stores the identifier of the requested document in a database. The database entries and the time dependencies are analyzed for prediction of documents suitable for the current location and work of the mobile workers.

Early work at Boeing in the assembly process indicated the advantages of HUD technology in assembling cable harnesses (Caudell and Mizell, 1992). Large and complex assemblies are composed of parts, some of which are linked together to form subassemblies. To identify the efficient assembly sequence, engineers evaluate whether the assembly operation is feasible or difficult and edit the assembly plan. An interactive evaluation tool using AR was developed to attempt various sequencing alternatives of the manufacturing design process (Sharma, et al., 1997; Raghavan, et al., 1999). On the other hand, an AR-based furniture assembly tool was introduced for assemblers to be guided step-by-step in a very intuitive and proactive way (Zauner, et al., 2003). The authoring tool was also developed offering flexible and re-configurable instructions. An AR environment allows engineers to design and plan assembly process through manipulating virtual prototypes at the real workplace, which is important to identify the drawbacks and revise the process. However, the revision of the design and planning is time-consuming in the large-scale assembly process. Hierarchical feature-based models were applied updating the related feature models in stead of the entire model. This results in computational simplicity offering a real-time environment (Pang, et al., 2006)

4.2 Effects

Compared to conventional printed manuals, HUD-based CAI using an HMD has the following advantages:

1) Hands-free presentation
An HMD presents information with a display mounted on the user's head. Therefore, although cables are attached to supply electric power and data, both hands can freely be used for a task.
2) Reduction of head and eye movements
Superimposing virtual objects onto real-world scenes enables users to view both virtual objects and real scenes with less movement of the eyes and the head. Spatial separation of the display beyond 20 deg. involves progressively larger head movements to access of visual information (Previc, 2000), and information access costs (effort required to access information) increase as spatial separation increases (Wickens, 1992).
3) Viewpoint-based interaction
Information related to the scenes detected by a camera attached to an HMD is presented to the user. Unlike printed media, there is no need for the user to search for the information required for a specific task. The user simply looks at an object, and the pertinent information is presented at the display. This triggering effect enables efficient retrieval of information with little effort by the user (Neumann and Majoros, 1998).
While many systems have been designed based on implicit assumptions that HUDs improve user performance, little direct empirical evidence concerning their effectiveness has been collected. An inspection scenario was examined in three different conditions: an optical see-through AR, a web browser, and a traditional paper-based manual (Jackson, et al., 2001). They found that the condition of the paper manual outperformed those of the others. In a car door assembly, the experimental results showed that the task performance depended on degree of difficulty on the assembly tasks (Wiedenmaier, et al., 2003). The AR condition wearing an HMD was more suitable for the difficult tasks than the paper manual condition, whereas the performance had no significant difference for the easy tasks between the two conditions.
There has been an investigation of how effectively information is accessed in annotated assembly domains. The effectiveness of spatially-registered AR instructions was compared to the other three instructions: a printed manual, CAI on an LCD monitor, and CAI on a see-through HMD, in experiments on a Duplo-block assembly (Tang, et al., 2003). The results showed that the spatially-registered AR instructions improved task performance and relieved mental workload on assembly tasks by overlaying and registering information to the workspace in a spatially meaningful way.

5. Case Study

We applied a HUD-based CAI to a support system for the operation of a transportable earth station containing many pieces of equipment used in satellite communications (Tanaka and Kondo, 1999). The transportable earth station was designed so that non-technical staff could manage the equipment in cooperation with a technician at a hub station. However, operating unfamiliar equipment was not easy for them, even though a detailed instruction manual was available. One of the basic problems staff has during the operation was to understand what part of the instruction manual related to which equipment and then figuring out the sequence of steps to carry out a procedure. Another problem was that the transmission at a session leaves little room for error in operating the equipment because mistakes of the transmission operation may give serious damage to the communication devices of the satellite.

5.1 Transportable Earth Station

A transportable earth station has been constructed as an extension of the inter-university satellite network that is used for remote lectures, academic meetings, and symposia in higher education, to exchange audio and video signals. The network now links 150 stations at universities and institutes. The transportable earth station has the same functionality as the original stations on campus but can be transported throughout Japan.

Figure 4 (a) shows a photograph of the transportable earth station. The van carries transmitting-receiving devices, video-coding machines, a GPS-based automatic satellite-acquisition system, and various instruments of measurements. The operator has to manage these pieces of equipment with the appropriate procedures and perform the adjustments and settings required for satellite communications. The uplink access test involves the operation of the transmitters and receivers shown in Figure 4 (b), and this requires some specialized expertise and error-free performance.

(a) Van

(b) Equipment

Fig. 4. Transportable earth station

5.2 HUD-based CAI System

Our HUD-based CAI system was originally designed to improve operation of the transportable earth station. Here, the outline of the prototype system assumes that the system will be used to operate the pieces of equipment in the transportable earth station, though the experiment described in the next section was done under laboratory conditions.

Figure 5 shows a schematic configuration of our prototype system. A compact camera attached to the user's head captures images from the user's viewpoint. These images are transferred to a PC through a DV format. Identification (ID) patterns registered in advance are stuck on the equipment, and each marker is detected in the video images using

ARToolkit (Kato, et al., 2000), which is a C/OpenGL-based open-source library that detects and tracks objects using square frames.

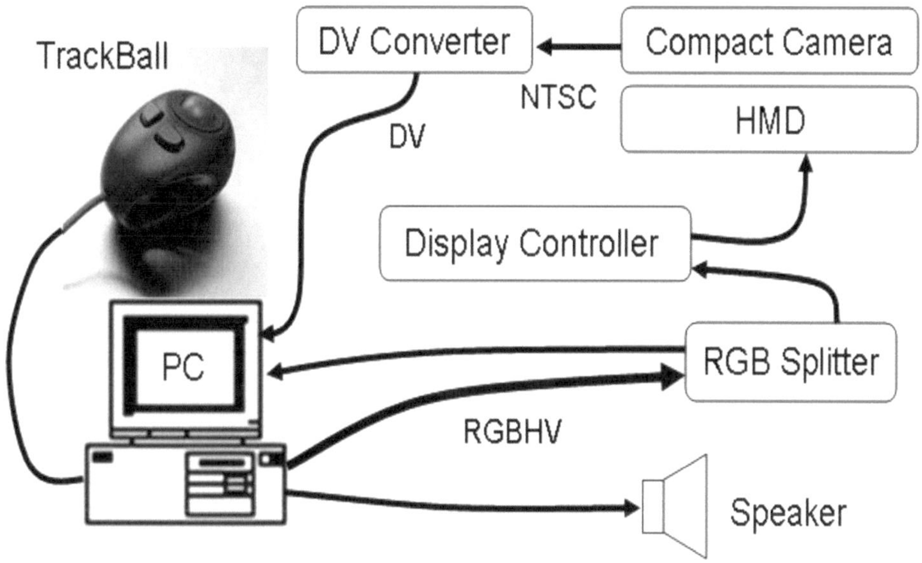

Fig. 5. System configuration

When the marker pattern is found in the registered list, ARToolkit identifies the piece of equipment and the appropriate instructions are presented to the user via an HMD. At the same time, the name of the equipment is stated audibly by a recorded voice to alert the user and make sure he or she works on the right piece of equipment. A square marker centered in or close to the center of the scene is detected, as several markers are present in the same scene. A trackball is used to control pages by, for example, scrolling pages, sticking a page, and turning pages.

5.3 Software Architecture

Figure 6 shows the software architecture of the prototype system. The software consists of two parts that have a server-client relationship: image processing and display application. The server and client exchange data using socket communications with UDP/IP. The server-client architecture enables the load to be distributed to two processors, though the prototype system was implemented on one PC.

It is common for graphical signs or simple icons to be presented with spatial registration to real objects in assembly tasks. In our case, however, using such graphical metaphors is insufficient to represent the amount of information because detailed operating instructions for the equipment should be provided based on conditions. Such documents contain too much information to be spatially registered with a single piece of equipment. Unfortunately, the resolution and field of view are currently limited in commercially available HMDs. Therefore, we displayed the manual documents with large fonts, sacrificing the spatial registration to the real equipment. The lack of spatial registration may not be a problem for us because, unlike aircraft landing simulation, there is no differential motion in the manipulation of the equipment and the background scene is stable.

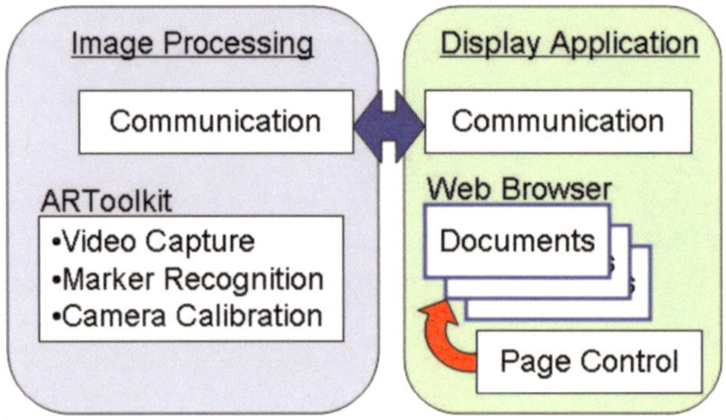

Fig. 6. Software architecture

Pages presented on the HMD are formatted in HTML, which enables a Web browser to be used to display multimedia data and makes instruction writing easier. Writing content for this kind of application, which has usually required programming skills and graphics expertise, is often costly and time consuming. Instructions must be customized to each piece of equipment and sometimes need to be revised, which may greatly increase the workload. The use of a Web browser enables fast implementation and flexible reconfiguration of the component elements in the instructions.

5.4 Implementation

The prototype system was implemented on a 2.8-GHz Pentium 4 PC with a 512-MB memory. The video frame rate of the image processing was roughly 30 frames per second. A single-sided HMD (SV-6, produced by Micro Optical) was installed as shown in Fig. 7, attaching a compact camera. The HMD has a viewing angle of roughly 20 degrees in the diagonal and the pinhole camera has a viewing angle of 43 degrees. The HMD, including the camera, weighs 80 g.

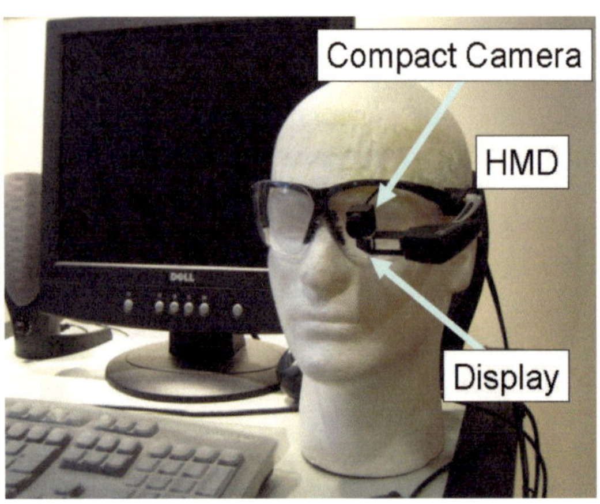

Fig. 7. HMD with a camera

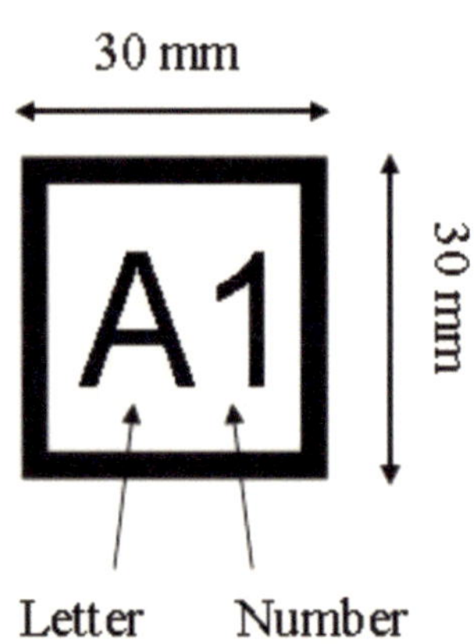

Fig. 8. Sample ID marker

Figure 8 shows a sample ID marker. When the surroundings are too dark, the camera images become less clear, degrading marker detection and recognition accuracy. Although the recognition rate depends on illumination, no recognition error has been observed at a viewing distance within 80 cm when the illumination environment is the same as that in which the marker patterns were registered.

6. Experiment

We conducted an experiment that compared the performance of participants using a HUD system, a laptop PC, and a paper manual. We hypothesized that the HUD system would make users receive the HUD profits (hands-free environments, reduction of head and eye movements, and awareness of real objects) and difficulty viewing information on an HMD. We expected that these would affect the time required to perform tasks. Figure 9 shows photos of the experiment being carried out: a) HMD system, b) laptop PC, and c) paper manual, respectively.

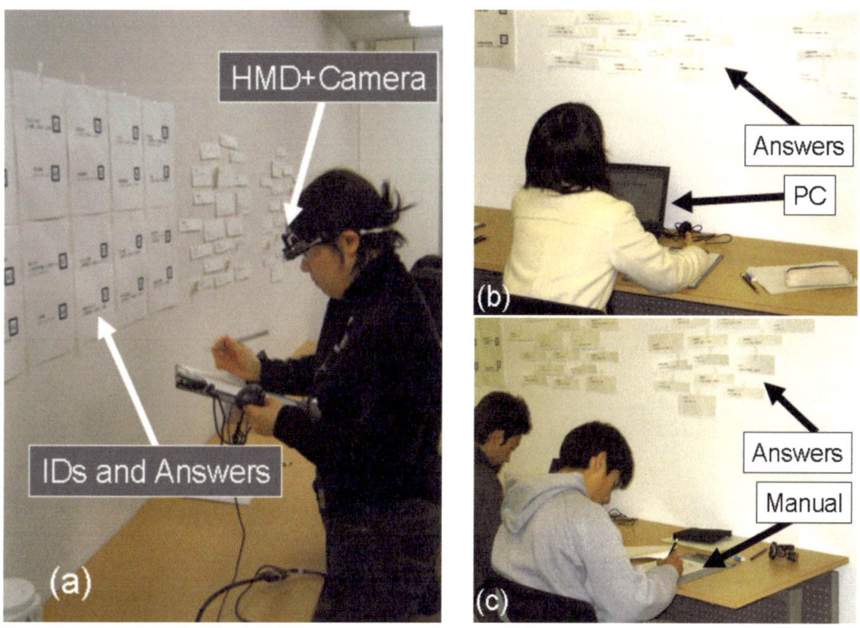

Fig. 9. Experimental tasks (a: HMD system, b: laptop PC, and c: paper manual).

6.1 Method

Thirty-five people participated in the experiment. The participants were undergraduate and graduate students who had normal vision and no previous experience of HUD-based CAI.
The task was to read articles and answer questions about the articles. The questions were multiple choices and had three possible answers each. Participants were instructed to read 20 articles with each instruction media. For each article, participants were required to write down the answer and the times when they found the answer possibilities and when they finished answering the questions. The participants were instructed to complete the task as quickly and accurately as possible.

In the experiment, slips of paper with possible answers were taped to the wall in front of the participant. In the HUD system, each possible answer slip has an ID marker, and articles and questions are presented on the HMD. In the PC and the paper manual, articles and questions are presented on the PC monitor and paper sheets, respectively.
All three media used the same format to present the articles, but there were differences among the media in how the questions and answers were presented. In the HUD system and the PC, the title and marker number were displayed in blue at the top of the page, and the headings of the article were displayed in black below the title. These headings were presented in larger fonts on the HMD (24 pt) than on the PC monitor (12 pt). When the participant centers the marker on the display, the article is identified, and the article's top page is presented on the HMD. While reading an article, a participant presses a button of the trackball to hold the page.
The time required to find and complete each article were recorded for all 20 articles. Finding time is defined as the time it took the participant to find the possible answers for a question, and completion time is defined as the time it took the participant to finish answering the question. These times were recorded by the participants themselves using a stopwatch, and participants were asked at a preference test about which media was best for performing the task. The questions are listed in Table 1.

	Question
1	The instruction medium was easy to use.
2	Practice was not necessary.
3	Looking for possible answers was easy.
4	Identifying the answer to the question was easy.
5	The task was not tiring.
6	The medium was enjoyable.

Table 1. Preference test questions

The participants were divided into three groups and each group started performing the task using one of the three different instruction media. There were three trials with each group using each medium once. For example, if a participant began with the HUD system, he or she would use the laptop PC in the second trial and the paper manual in the third trial. The preference test was conducted immediately after participants had finished all three trials.
For the HUD system to work properly, the position of the HMD and the direction of the compact camera needed to be calibrated. The calibration took approximately two minutes. The participants practiced with the HUD system, and any questions were answered at that

time. The trials started when the participants reported feeling comfortable in using the HUD system.

6.2 Results

Figure 10 shows the results of the experiment. The bars indicate average times required by participants to complete trials. The black, shaded, and unshaded bars represent times for the HUD system, the laptop PC, and the paper manual, respectively. The error bar on each bar represents the standard deviation.

Analysis of Variance (ANOVA) was carried out on the task time data. Presentation media significantly affected finding time ($F[2,32]=39.6$, $p<0.01$). Post hoc analysis for all possible pairs of presentation media showed that the trial with the HUD system was significantly shorter than those with the others. Presentation media also significantly affected work time (the time required to finish the article after the possible answers had been found) ($F[2,32]=22.4$, $p<0.01$). Post hoc analysis showed the trial with the HUD system took significantly longer than those with the other media but no significant difference between the PC system and the paper manual. Presentation media also significantly affected completion time ($F[2,32]=6.8$, $p<0.01$). Post hoc analysis showed that the trial with the PC took significantly longer than those with the other media, but there was no difference in completion time between the HUD system and the paper manual.

QuickTime™ and a
TIFF (Uncompressed) decompressor
are needed to see this picture.

Fig. 10. Experimental results (black: HUD, shaded: laptop PC, unshaded: paper manual)

Figure 11 shows the results of the preference test. Scores for questions by number, as listed in Table 1, are ranged along the horizontal axis. The bars indicate the average score reported by participants. The black, shaded, and unshaded bars represent scores for the HUD system, the laptop PC, and the paper manual, respectively. The error bar on each bar represents the standard deviation.

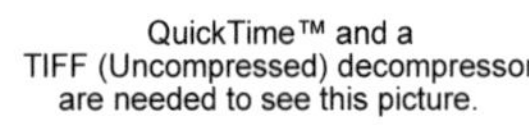

Fig. 11. Preference test results (black: HUD, shaded: laptop PC, unshaded: paper manual)

In answers to questions 1 and 2, related to ease of use and practice, the same tendency was observed: the paper manual was the most preferred instruction medium, the PC was ranked second, and the HUD system was third. In answer to question 5, which asked about how tiring the task was, participants reported that they preferred the PC and the paper manual to the HUD system, but neither of these two was clearly preferred over the other. In answers to question 4, about mental switching, all the scores were comparable. In answers to question 6, participants reported that the HUD system was the most enjoyable, the PC was next, and the paper manual was boring. In answers to question 3, the HUD system was reported to be the most helpful in searching articles, and the other media had comparable scores.

6.3 Discussion

Overall, the performance and preference test results did not show that the HUD system was clearly superior to the other media over the whole course of the task. As expected, the participants using the HUD system took less time finding the possible answers and more time reading the articles and the question on the HMD than participants using the other media. The results showed that the HUD system excelled at finding the place of the answer possibilities but seemed to spoil the excellence by careful reading of the articles and questions, which affected the task time. This suggests that the HUD-based CAI system is good at indicating which equipment the user needs to treat but not so suitable for presenting instructional information, because the HMD requires the user to see letters and characters at the limited resolution and field of view.

We also observed that the ID on the answer possibility sheet made it easy to identify the location of the answer on the wall and the article on the HMD. That is, the ID worked as a sign guiding the task procedure.

We found that there was a difference between the experimental results and those obtained in the actual operation of the transportable earth station. In the laboratory experiment, the task completion time was comparable among the three media. In the actual operation, however, people using the HUD-based CAI system performed better than those using the other two media. This was interpreted as a difference of the task or the experimental condition that worked against the HUD system or in favor of the paper manual in this experiment. It was important for the people to check if they were reading the appropriate instructions during the actual operation, because the pieces of equipment were not familiar to them. This situation could work for the HUD system.

7. Conclusion

We investigated the role of HUDs in CAI.

First, the basic concept of an HUD was introduced by briefly describing general HUD technology and its relevant applications. An HUD is basically a display medium on which information is presented, allowing a user to simultaneously view a real scene and superimposed information without large movements of the head or eye scans. The HUD has been incorporated into various applications, on which its type depends. We described HUD design types: head-mounted or ground-referenced, optical see-through or video see-through, and single-sided or two-sided types.

Second, the features of HUD-based CAI were explained by describing its applications, such as equipment operation, product assembly, and machine maintenance. These HUD-based CAI applications have witnessed the introduction of increasingly complex platforms and sophisticated procedures and are characterized by the real-time presentation of instructional information related to what the user is viewing. Common thought is that HUD-based CAI will increase the efficiency of instructions and reduce errors by properly presenting instructional information based on a user's viewpoint. We discussed the advantages of HUD-based CAI, such as a hands-free environment, reduction of head and eye movements, and awareness of real objects, compared to conventional printed manuals.

Third, a user study with our HUD-based CAI system was reported. Our system provides information using a head-mounted HUD, on which a piece of equipment is identified with identification markers, as the user looks at the piece of equipment that she tries to manipulate. User performance with the system was evaluated during a task in which participants read articles and answered questions about the articles, and this performance was compared to performance with a laptop PC and paper manual. The experimental results for the performance of the HUD-based CAI system showed less time finding pairs of questions and the possible answers and more time selecting one of the possibilities after reading the articles. This suggested that the user would receive the advantages of an HUD, but also have difficulty viewing the information because of the HUD's narrow field of view.

8. References

Asai, K., and Kobayashi, H. (2005). Computer assisted instruction using augmented reality in operating the transportable earth station - Comparison between single-sided and both-sided HMDs-, *Proc. Human Computer Interaction International,* (CD-ROM, pp. 1-8, vol. 6 - Human Factors Issues in Human-Computer Interaction)

Asai, K., Kobayashi, H., and Saito, F. (2006). Comparative effectiveness of computer-assisted instruction using a head-up display for operation of the transportable earth station, *IEEJ Transactions on Electronics, Information and Systems*, vol.126, pp. 465-473

Azuma, R. T. (1997). A survey of augmented reality, *Presence: Teleoperators and Virtual Environments*, vol. 6, pp.355-385

Bian, Z., Ishii, H., Izumi, M., Shimoda, H., Yoshikawa, H., Morishita, Y., and Kanehira, Y. (2006). Development of a tracking method for augmented reality applied to NPP maintenance work and its experimental evaluation, *Proc. ACM Symposium on Virtual Reality Software and Technology*, pp. 35-44, Limassal, Cyprus

Caudell, T. P., and Mizell, D. W. (1992). Augmented reality: an application of head-up display technology to manual manufacturing processes, *Proc. International Conference on System Sciences*, pp. 659-669

Dede, C. (1986). A review and synthesis of recent research in intelligent computer-assisted instruction, *International Journal of Man-Machine Studies*, vol. 24, pp. 329-353

Fadden, S., Ververs, P. M., and Wickens, C. D. (2001). Pathway HUDs: Are they viable? *Human Factors*, vol. 43, pp.173-193

Feiner, S., MacIntyre, B., and Seligmann, D. (1993). Knowledge-based augmented reality, *Communications of the ACM*, vol. 36, pp. 52-62

Fischer, E., Haines, R. F., and Price, T. A. (1980). Cognitive issues in head-up displays, *NASA Technical Paper 1711*, Moffett Field, CA

Foyle, D. C., McCann, R. S., and Shelden, S. G. (1995). Attentional issues with superimposed symbology: formats for scene-linked displays, *Proc. 8th International Symposium on Aviation Psychology*, pp. 98-103

Friedrich, W. (2002). ARVIKA - augmented reality for development, production, and service, *Proc. International Symposium on Mixed and Augmented Reality*, pp. 3-4

Haines, R., Fischer, E., and Price, T. (1980). Head-up transition behavior of pilots with and without head-up display in simulated low-visibility approaches, *Technical Report: NASA Ames Research Center*, Moffett Field

Jackson, P., Ealey-Sawyer, J., Stephen Jones, Lu, I.-L., and Jones, S. (2001). Testing information delivery methods using augmented reality, *Proc International Symposium on Augmented Reality*, pp.171-172

Kato, H., Billinghurst, M., Poupyrev, I., Imamoto, K., Tachibana, K. (2000). Virtual object manipulation in a table-top AR environment, *Proc. ISAR 2000*, pp. 111-119

Klinker, G., Creighton, O., Dutoit, A. H., Kobylinski, R., Vilsmeier, C. (2001). Augmented maintenance of powerplants: a prototyping case study of a mobile AR system, *International Symposium on Augmented Reality*, pp. 124-136, New York

Larish, I., and Wickens, C. D. (1991). Attention and HUDs: Flying in the dark? *Society for information Display International Symposium Digest of Technical Papers*, XXII, pp.461-464

Larry, C., and Elworth, C. L. (1972). The effects of pilot age, lighting, and head-down time on visual accommodation, Report Number D162-10378-1 TN, The Boeing Company, Seattle, WA

Lipson, H., Shpitalni, M., Kimura, F., and Goncharenko, I. (1998). Online product maintenance by web-based augmented reality, *New Tools and Workflow for Product Development*, pp. 131-143

Mann, S. (1997). Wearable computing: a first step toward personal imaging, *IEEE Computer*, vol. 30, pp. 25-32

McCann, R. S., Lynch, J. M., Foyle, D. C., and Johnston, J. C. (1993). Modeling attentional effects with head-up displays, *Proc. 37th Annual meeting of the Human Factors Society*, pp. 1345-1349

Milgram, P., and Kishino, F. (1994). A taxonomy of mixed reality visual displays, *IEICE Transactions on Information Systems*, E77-D12, pp.1321-1329

Navab, N. (2004). Projects in VR: developing killer apps for industrial augmented reality, *IEEE Computer Graphics and Applications*, vol. 24, pp. 16-20

Neumann, U., and Majoros, A. (1998). Cognitive, performance, and systems issues for augmented reality applications in manufacturing and maintenance, *Proc. IEEE VRAIS'98*, pp. 4-11

Neveu, C., Blackmon, T., and Stark, L. (1998). Evaluation of the effects of a head-mounted display on ocular accommodation, *Presence: Teleoperators and Virtual Environments*, vol. 7, pp. 278-289

Newman, R. L. (1995). *Head up displays: designing the way ahead*, Avebury Aviation

Okabayashi, S., Sakata, M., Fukano, J., Daidoji, S., Hashimoto, C., Ishikawa, T. (1989). Development of practical heads-up display for production vehicle application, paper 890559, *Society of Automotive Engineers*, pp.69-78

Pang, Y., Nee, A. Y. C., Ong, S. K., Yuan, M. L., Youcef-Toumi, K. (2006). Assembly feature design in an augmented reality environment, *Assembly Automation*, vol. 26, pp. 34-43

Previc, F. H. (2000). Neuropsychological guidelines for aircraft control stations, *IEEE Engineering in Medicine and Biology*, pp. 81-88

Raghavan, V., Molineros, J., and Sharma, R. (1999). Interactive evaluation of assembly sequence using augmented reality, *IEEE Transactions on Robotics and Automation*, vol. 15, pp.435-449

Schwald, B., and Laval, B. (2003). An augmented reality system for training and assistance to maintenance in the industrial context, *Journal of WSCG*, vol. 11, pp.425-432

Sharma, R., Molineros, J., and Raghavan, V. (1997). Interactive evaluation of assembly sequences with mixed (real and virtual) prototyping, *Proc. International Symposium on Assembly and Task planning*, pp.287-292

Tanaka, K. and Kondo, K. (1999). Configuration of inter-university satellite network "Space Collaboration System," *IEICE Transactions on Information & System*, J82-D-I, pp. 581-588

Tang, A., Owen, C., Biocca, F., and Mou, W., Comparative effectiveness of augmented reality in object assembly, *Proc CHI 2003*, pp. 73-80

Tufano, D. R. (1997). Automotive HUDs: The overlooked safety issues, *Human Factors*, vol. 39, pp. 303-311

Weintraub, D. J., Haines, R. F., and Randle, R. J. (1985). Head-up display (HUD) utility, II: Runway to HUD transitions monitoring eye focus and decision times, *Proc. Human Factors Society 29th Annual Meeting*, pp. 615-619

Weintraub, D. J., Ensing, M. (1992). *Human factors issues in head-up display design: the book of HUD* (CSERIAC State-of-the-art Report), Wright-Patterson AFB, Dayton, OH: Crew System Ergonomics Information Analysis Center

Wickens, C. D. (1992). Computational models of human performance, *Technical Report No. ARL-92-4/NASA-A3I-92-1*, University of Illinois, Aviation Research Laboratory

Wickens, C. D., and Long, J. (1995). Object- vs. space-based models of visual attention: Imprecations for the design of head-up displays, *Journal of Experimental Psychology: Applied*, vol. 1, pp. 179-194

Wickens, C. D., Martin-Emerson, R., and Larish, I. (1993). Attentional tunneling and the head-up display, *Proc. The 7th International Symposium on Aviation Psychology*, pp.865-870, OH: The Ohio State University

Wiedenmaier, S., Oehme, O., Schmidt, L., and Luczak, H. (2003). Augmented Reality (AR) for assembly processes design and experimental evaluation, *International Journal of Human-Computer Interaction*, vol. 16, no. 3, pp. 497-514

Zauner, J., Haller, M., Brandl, A. (2003). Authoring of a mixed reality assembly instructor for hierarchical structures, *Proc International Symposium on Mixed and Augmented Reality*, pp. 237-246

3

Searching and Analysis of Interface and Visualization Metaphors

Vladimir L. Averbukh, Mihkail O. Bakhterev, Aleksandr Yu. Baydalin
Institute of Mathematics and Mechanics, Inst. of Math. and Mech., Inst. of Math. and Mech.
Dmitriy Yu. Gorbashevskiy, Damir R. Ismagilov, Alexey Yu. Kazantsev
Inst. of Math. and Mech., Ural State Univercity, Inst. of Math. and Mech.
Polina V. Nebogatikova, Anna V. Popova, Pavel A. Vasev
Ural State Univercity, Ural State Univercity, Inst. of Math. and Mech.
Russia (all)

1. Introduction

This chapter is devoted to problems of interface and visualization metaphors. Really the subject-matter of metaphor is popular in modern literature on HCI and visualization. One can find hundreds interesting articles, books, technical reports and thesises on metaphors in computing. The metaphor matter is discussed regularly at workshops and seminars. The success of metaphors is apparent, all the more a well-known Desktop metaphor, which is widely used on millions and millions computers all over the world. One source of the theory of computer metaphors is classical theory of metaphor, especially the cognitive approach advanced by G. Lakoff and his colleagues. Also the sign nature of the human-computer interface and visualization allows using semiotics in the theory of computer metaphor.
Our interest in theoretical problems of a metaphor is connected with our main goal - to design specialized interactive visual systems as well as quickly. The goals of our researches are to draw up design criteria for "good" human-computer interface and "effective" visualization on the one hand and recommendations for developers of visual systems on the other hand. Our approaches are connected with our experience of design and development of specialized visualization systems including systems of scientific, informational and software visualization. The specialized systems support the decision of certain class of problems by the certain class of users (mathematicians, physicians, sociologists, etc.). Specificity of such systems frequently demands new methods of visualization and interaction that are adequate to the given task and concrete (possibly narrow) user or class of users. The practice of design and development of specialized visualization systems shows necessity of specific metaphors, and a stage of metaphor searching and designing is a part of development process. During design and development process of such systems the following aspects are distinguished:
- Computer Graphics means and means of Human-Computer Interface organization;
- Software Engineering;

- Cognitive aspects.
We consider cognitive aspects of system engineering. Cognitive aspects are the most independent from technology. There are a lot of examples, when failures with "cognitive" components of projects bring to nothing all successes and achievements in computer graphics and software engineering of projects. In connection with this we are interested in language aspects of visualization and human-computer interaction. Metaphor is considered as the source of this language, a basis of representation of visual and dialogue objects and methods of interaction with these objects. We need to search and choose "good" metaphors for specialized systems. We aim to understand how metaphors are constructed, how they work and how users interpret them. The theory of computer metaphor serves to evaluate existing visual interactive systems and to predict properties of new systems at designing stage. However in practice, there are problems both with concrete metaphor searching and with evaluation of their suitability for the given problem and user group.
Below some points of the metaphor theory are considered in connection with computer metaphors. The theory of interface and visualization metaphor is supplemented and defined more exactly. The structural analysis of concrete metaphors is carried out. Bases of the analysis are the concepts of "metaphor action" and "metaphor formula", as well as realizing the logic of metaphor choices and generations. This analysis is necessary to understand the reasons of successes of one and failures of other visualization and visual interface metaphors. In turn, it allows formulating criteria of evaluating of cognitive components of visual systems.

2. Metaphors in HCI

Above we have noted, that the theory of interface and visualization metaphor is based both on the theory of a classical metaphor on semiotics. A lot of researches are devoted to the formal description of the computer metaphor theory and to studying of interface metaphors from these positions. Now concept of metaphor is widely used for the description of concrete decisions in interactive visual systems. We have gathered near two hundreds books, articles, dissertations and technical reports on problematic of computer metaphor. Our literature sources (of course not full) can be subdivided as follows:
- general works on metaphor and semiotics;
- works on theory of interface metaphor;
- works describing the concrete systems but containing issues on metaphor theory;
- works describing the concrete systems and using the elements of metaphor theory;
- works describing the concrete systems where only the concept of metaphor is used;
- works containing the criticism of computer metaphors.

Among these works there are our researches on visualization metaphor theory as well as our specialized visualization systems where the concept of visualization metaphor using for design and development.
Studying of this literature on problems of a computer metaphor allows drawing some conclusions. One of them - the certain consensus on the computer metaphor theory takes place. First of all this consensus consists of the recognition in *cognitive* ***approach*** to metaphor theory as the base of theory of interface metaphor. (This approach is linked with names G. Lakoff and his colleagues (Lakoff & Johnson, 1980), (Lakoff, 1993)).) The cognitive approach to a metaphor considers a metaphor as the basic mental operation, as a way of cognition,

structuring and explanation of the world. The metaphor essence consists in interpretation and experience the phenomena of one sort in terms of the phenomena of other sort. Metaphorization is based on interaction structures of source and target domains. During process of metaphorization some objects of target domain are structured on an example of objects of target domain and there is a metaphorical mapping (projection) of one domain onto another. That is the metaphor can be understood as a map from source domain onto target domain, and this map is strongly structured.

Secondly, Peircean semiotics is applied to user-interface metaphor (Barr et al, 2004). (Note in this connection the researches on visual semiotics and semiotics of HCI such authors as P. Andersen, J. Goguen, M. Nadin, C. de Souza (Andersen, 2001), (Goguen, 2004.), (Nadin, 1997), (de Souza, 2005.)

Some other approaches to forming of interface metaphor theory are mentioned. Among them - M. Black's *interactive* model (see, for example, (Gardenfors 1996) and (Blackwell, 2006)) and T. Kuhn's theory of scientific metaphor (see, for example, (Harrison et al 2007), (Travers, 1996)). There is also the consideration of games as a metaphor for interface systems (Stathis & Sergot, 1996). But just Lakoff's and Peirce's approaches are prevailed in forming of interface metaphor theory. The other approaches to describing of interface metaphors are less common.

Now let's copy out the main (or may be more typical and popular) positions of existing interface metaphor theory:

1) A metaphor is a rhetoric figure, whose essence is understanding and experiencing one kind of things in terms of another (Lakoff&Johnson, 1980).

2) M. Johnson defined metaphor as a pervasive mode of understanding by which we project patterns from one domain of experience in order to structure another domain of a different kind. (Johnson,1987).

3) The two domains are commonly called the source and target domains of a metaphor and the metaphorical projection is a mapping from source to target. The target consists of the concepts the words are actually referring to (also said the original idea). The source refers to the concepts in terms of which the intended target concepts are being viewed (the borrowed idea). Conventional metaphors are represented as sets of associations, or relations, between source and target concepts. Source and target concepts usually belong to different domains, and the familiarity with the source domain is exploited to understand the target concepts. The metaphor specifies how the source concepts reflected in the surface language correspond to the various target concepts. It establishes an isomorphism between the target and source domains. Interface metaphors, in this projective view, go beyond explaining unfamiliar domains to novices. They determine how labor is distributed between a user and a system, what concepts a user has to deal with, and in what terms user and system communicate. In short, they structure application domains and organize tasks. (Kuhn W. & Frank A.U., 1991), (Catarci et al, 1996).

4) A metaphor is a device for explaining some concept or thing, *x*, by asserting its similarity to another concept or thing, *y*, in the form ***X IS Y***.

The concept being explained is often referred to as the tenor of the metaphor, while the concept doing the explaining is called the vehicle. (Barr et al., 2004)

A typical definition of metaphors might run like this:

Given two domains A and B, taking A as metaphor for B is equivalent to providing a formal mapping from the primitives defining A into the primitives defining B.

Such definition makes the metaphor question a question about representational formats, structural primitives, and the properties of formal mappings. From the standpoint of cognitive "process" these analyses reduce metaphor to primitive pattern matching operations defined over the elements and relations of structural descriptions (Carroll J. & Mack R., 1985) Structure-mapping analysis of metaphor interprets metaphor as mapping between two (graph theoretical expressed) domains, pairing the nodes of each. The relations of these two domains are constrained to be identical (Gentner, D. 1983).

User-interface metaphor is intuitively the application of this device to the user-interface. Thus, a user-interface metaphor is a device for explaining some system functionality or structure (the tenor) by asserting its similarity to another concept or thing already familiar to the user (the vehicle). The key here is that the chosen vehicle is something already familiar to the user and so the intention is to provide a base level of comfort and knowledge without necessarily understanding the underlying system (Barr et al., 2004).

5) For Peirce the sign is a genuine triadic relationship among the elements: the representamen, the object and the interpretant. The representamen refers to the material aspect of the sign and represents the object under certain aspects or "capacities". The sign only means so because the representamen can represent another thing: the object. The interpretant doesn't refer to the interpreter of the sign but it refers to a relational process occurring in the interpreter's mind, associating representamen and object (de Oliveira & Baranauskas 1998).

The interface is defined as a collection of computer-based signs, i.e., the software parts which can be seen or heard, used and interpreted by a community of users (Andersen, P. B. 1997).

The use of semiotics will help to resolve how the metaphor functions or what the metaphor really means.

A metaphor sign involves the interaction in some way of two signs, which are the tenor and the vehicle of the metaphor. The stance we take in this paper is that a metaphor may well be composed of two signs, but can plausibly be treated as a sign in itself as well. Essentially, the meaning of the metaphor intended by its author comprises the object, while the expression of the metaphor itself, usually in language, forms the representamen. An encounter with the representamen leads a reader to form an interpretant, which is what the metaphor is taken to mean by them. (Barr et al, 2004)

5) A metaphor gives the possibility to understand new and complex concepts by means of more familiar (i.e. well-known) ones. This feature has been exploited in the interfaces of several computer systems (Marcello L'Abbate & Matthias Hemmje, 1998)

6) The process of applying our experiences on things that are new to us is called "mapping". Analogy is the most obvious kind of mapping… Metaphors are mappings from source to target domains… Metaphor is the most complex kind of mapping, where the two structures - or concepts - being compared actually explains each other. (Kuhn W. & Frank A.U., 1991), (Olle Torgny 1997) A conceptual metaphor is a set of mappings from a relatively concrete domain to a more abstract domain. Through these mappings, the more abstract domain is more readily understood. (David G. Hendry, 2006). When the domains are specified algebraically, it is natural to use morphisms, which are mappings between algebras, to define metaphorical mappings . (Kuhn W. & Frank A.U., 1991)

7) Image-schemas are image-like reasoning patterns, consisting of a small number of parts and relations, made meaningful by sensori-motor experience. There is a CONTAINER

schema (things that have an inside, an outside and a boundary), a PART-WHOLE schema (something can be seen as a whole or as its constituent parts), a LINK schema (two or more things have a link between them), a SOURCE-PATH-GOAL schema (or sometimes, just a PATH, which goes from a source along a path to a destination). There is an UP-DOWN schema, a BACK-FRONT schema and so on. Schemas are gestalts - structured wholes - that structure our direct experiences. Image-schemas may in fact be the kind of structure which is preserved by interface metaphors. This assumption agrees with Lakoff's invariance hypothesis which claims that image-schemas remain invariant under metaphorical mappings (Kuhn W. & Frank A.U., 1991), (Benyon & Imaz, 1999).

8) The best known formal theory of metaphor and analogy is Gentner's structure mapping theory (Gentner, D. 1983), (Gentner, D. 1989). It describes analogies as mappings between source and target domains, each represented by semantic networks. It does not formalize the mappings themselves, however, and rests on a syntactical distinction of different kinds of relations. While Gentner's theory deals with structural aspects, it neglects the role of tasks in metaphor use. Our formalization addresses these problems by formalizing mappings as morphisms and expressing tasks and actions through algebraic operators and their effects. Describing domains algebraically rather than relationally may only be a syntactic difference; it does, however, allow for relating metaphors to task mappings .

If an image-schema is invariant in a metaphorical mapping, it must be a common part of the source and target domains. It is therefore possible to obtain the algebraic specifications of these domains by extending a common core specification which formalizes an image-schema. Such a process of adding operators to algebraic specifications is called an enrichment. Thus, a formal version of Lakoff's invariance hypothesis is:

For any metaphor, there is an algebraic specification which describes an image-schema or a combination of image-schemas and which can be enriched toward specifications of the source and target domains.

Since an algebraic specification describes a class of algebras or category, image-schemas are formalized as categories. These categories contain the algebras of the source and target domains as well as the morphisms between them . (Kuhn W. & Frank A.U., 1991).

The common perception of the word "formalization" is connected with the derivation of some formulas and equations that describe the phenomenon in analytical form. In this case, formalization is used to describe a series of steps that ensure the correctness of the development of the representation of the metaphor. Metaphor formalization in the design of semantic visualization schemes includes the following basic steps:

- *Identification of the source and target spaces of the metaphor* - the class of forms and the class of features or functions that these forms will represent;

- *Conceptual decomposition of the source and target spaces* produces the set of concepts that describe both sides of the metaphor mapping. As a rule, metaphorical mappings do not occur isolated from one another. They are sometimes organized in hierarchical structures, in which `lower' mappings in the hierarchy inherit the structures of the `higher' mappings. In other words, this means that visualization schemes, which use metaphor are expected to preserve the hierarchical structures of the data that they display. …these are the geometric characteristics of the forms from the source space, and other form attributes like colors, line thickness, shading, etc. and the set of functions and features in the target space associated with these attributes and variations;

- *Identifying the dimensions of the metaphor* along which the metaphor operates. These dimensions constitute the common semantics. ...this can be for instance key properties of the form, like symmetry and balance with respect to the center of gravity, that transfer semantics to the corresponding functional elements in the target domain;
- *Establishing semantic links, relations and transformations* between the concepts in both spaces, creating a resemblance between the forms in the source domain and the functions in the target domain. (Simoff 2001)

Formalization by itself, however, is not enough to arrive at useful theories. Concentrating on the mathematical aspects of a theory underlying an implementation can lead designers to neglect usability aspects of the resulting system and can produce undesirable effects at the user interface. Theoretical refinements sometimes burden the users with an additional load of concepts they have to master if they want to use a system effectively. Depending on the tasks and users, some concepts of a formal theory may be completely irrelevant or even unintelligible to users mappings (Werner Kuhn, 1993).

9) The structural formulation of what metaphor is allows us to define many further concepts regarding metaphor relations. [It is defined] a variety of such relations: base specificity, clarity, richness, abstractness, systematicity, validity, exhaustiveness, transparency, and scope.

"Base specificity" is defined as the extent to which the structure of the metaphor base, or source, is understood.

"Clarity" refers to the precision of the node correspondences across the mapping.

"Richness" is the density of predicates carried across the mapping.

"Abstractness" refers to the level at which the relations carried across the mapping are defined. If they are the individual predicates of the base, the mapping is less abstract than if they are relations among predicates in the base.

"Systematicity". Metaphors are "systematic" to the extent that the mapped relations are mutually constrained by membership in some structure of relations.

"Validity". Metaphors are "valid" to the extent that the base relations carry their truth values across the mapping.

"Exhaustiveness. "Base exhaustive" metaphor map each of their relations into target ("target exhaustive" metaphor are defined analogously).

"Transparency". Metaphors are "transparent" to the extent that it is obvious which relations in the base are able to be carried into the target.

"Scope" refers to the extensibility of the mapping.

(Carroll J. & Mack R., 1985)

10) The success of a metaphor depends on having a familiar domain to analogize from and on recognizing enough in the new domain so that some correspondence can be established. Structural descriptions of corresponding domains in a comparison relation provide only an abstract set of possible mappings. The actual relevance of any of these mappings to a real and usable metaphor depends fundamentally on the needs and goals of the [user]. Put another way, we need to understand the pragmatics of the [given] situation. (Carroll J. & Mack R., 1985)

11) How can we Find Metaphor Candidates? Everybody asks this question and only few researchers or designers have proposed generalizable methods to come up with useful interface metaphors. Can there be systematic approaches to generating metaphors at all? Isn't a good metaphor the result of a strike of creative thought which cannot be planned?

Clearly, much more can be done in a systematic way than what has been done in this area so far. Metaphors do not fall out of the blue sky. If they should be appropriate for a certain user community in a certain application area, they must have source domains which are meaningful to these people in their work environment. Such meaningful concepts are certain to appear in the language of prospective users, in their work regulations, documentation of existing technology, and many other manifestations of how these people think and act when they do their work. Finding metaphor candidates, therefore, means listening to users, observing their work and behavior, and reading their instructions and regulations. We have all become skeptical, with good reason, about clever ideas of interface designers for fancy metaphors, commands, and icons which are generated late at night while playing around with the latest interface design tool kit. They tend to disappear as fast as they were created. Useful metaphors are the work of design teams which have studied the work flow, tools, language and general culture of users over months or years. Seen in this way, finding metaphor candidates is a central part of task analysis. It can indeed be argued that the selection of metaphors constitutes the essence of task analysis, explaining why there is often much more synthesis than analysis involved in this process. Choosing a metaphor means deciding on the ontology of the user interface, i.e., on the concepts which users will have to master, the objects and operations they get to see, and the work distribution between them and the system. The more complex an application area is, the more time this process will take. A good example is, again, the much discussed desktop metaphor. It took years of very careful analysis and synthesis of work processes, based on detailed observations in actual office work environments, until the design of the Star interface was completed. Then, it took another couple of iterations to make it usable in practice (Kuhn W., 1995).

12) An account of the mechanisms of metaphorical understanding would tell us why one or more metaphors are useful and how they are generated and then used to support [interface]. What Makes a Metaphor Good or Bad? Once metaphor candidates have been found, an engineering design approach requires some kind of evaluation method to be able to select the best candidate among them. In practice, there often seems to be an "obvious" choice and a designer may feel compelled to use it without investigating alternatives. There are some plausible criteria to separate better from worse metaphors in a given context. Starting with qualities which make a metaphor "good" for an application, the first and decisive feature has to be its understandability. If a metaphor is not understandable to the users, it is really no metaphor at all, as its source domain should by definition be familiar. Understandability is not only a matter of the source concepts, however, but also of how these are presented to the users. A second, more subtle criterion is that a metaphor should create a useful ontology for the user's tasks. The ontology of a user interface is the collection of concepts which a user has to master in order to use the system productively. Another way to evaluate interface metaphors is by the suitability of the work distribution that they impose. If a metaphor satisfies these three criteria, it may still be "bad" for a user interface, if it has some undesirable properties. Among them are incomplete mappings from source to target domains. This means that there are either salient source concepts which the user expects to find, but are missing from the interface, or there are abstract user interface concepts not matched to appropriate parts of the source domain. The latter problem is fairly common in practice, confronting the user with a bewildering mix of metaphorical concepts and computer jargon. A second slippery slope is mixing metaphors. From our use of natural

language, we have a fairly good intuition about the possibilities and limitations of mixing metaphors. Simply applying this common sense to the evaluation of metaphor combinations in a user interface would already take care of many problems in existing interfaces. (Werner Kuhn 1995).

Also there are some important and concepts used in the theory of interface (and visualization) metaphor. Among them there are concepts of mental spaces and a mental model.

Mental spaces

Mental spaces provide a medium in which cognitive activities can take place. Cognitive models created through imaginative processes structure those spaces. We think by connecting different mental spaces. So for example, we may have a space that structures our experienced reality, another that is structuring future situations, another fictional situations and so on.

The concept of mental space refers to the partial cognitive structures that emerge when we think and talk. It is in these mental spaces that domains are defined, altered and merged. There is a source mental space, a target mental space and connectors that map elements from both spaces. However, the concepts of mental spaces and connectors apply to more general situations, involving more than two spaces (Benyon & Imaz, 1999).

A mental model

A mental model is a cognitive construct that describes a person's understanding of a particular content domain in the world. This contrasts sharply with much other work in cognitive psychology, which attempts to be domain-independent (Plantings, 1987).

There are three elements that work together in the interface. Two mental models: the user's model, the designer's model and finally the system image. One of the paramount interests next to usability testing of HCI is to improve the design of interfaces in first place. Therefore it is a proven good idea to use prescriptive mental models, so called conceptual models, throughout the design. The design goal is to reach as much as possible congruence of all the mental models (Weidmann, 2004).

The visual metaphor is seen as a transformation between abstract and visual information. In that case, the abstract information is the database schema. Therefore, the main elements of the formalisms are:

1) A data model that captures schemata,
2) A visual model that captures visualizations, and
3) A visual metaphor that is a mapping between data and visual models (Catarci et al, 1996).

Thus, the harmonious enough theory of the interface metaphor takes place, including (alongside with other elements) definitions of basic concepts, the description of metaphor formalization on base of semiotics and algebraic approaches, criterion of "good" metaphors and principles of their choice.

For the practice of applications of the interface and of visualization metaphors there is the following situation. The metaphor is considered in less strict manner, as some basic idea of bridging the gap between different areas (even if strict definitions also take place). Instead of precise metaphor evaluation criteria heuristic approaches are used. Here are rather typical examples of using the metaphor conception in papers on HCI and/or visualization:

i) The mapping from a program model (lower level of abstraction) to an image (higher level of abstraction) is defined through a metaphor, specifying the type of visualization. Most visualization techniques and tools are based on the graph metaphor (including the extensive research on graph layout algorithms). Other initiatives are the representation of programs as 3D city notations, solar systems, video games, nested boxes, 3D Space, Software World, etc. (Panas et al, 2003a), (Knight & Munro 2000). With the help of the metaphor, different views on the program representations are provided. These views are finally illustrated as one picture and can be interactively (Panas et al, 2003b).

ii) The Magic Mirror is a user interface technique that mimics a hand mirror. In addition to providing the optical effect of a real mirror, several non-physical extensions are also proposed. As a metaphor, the Magic Mirror is an intuitive and easy to learn interaction technique (Grosjean & Coquillart 1999).

iii) Our classification distinguishes between two basic structural metaphors differing in terms of the mental model being generated. First the theater metaphor, where the user has a static position and viewpoint and the world around changes. Second the locomotion metaphor, where the user has a dynamic position and will be moved through a structure.

Theater Metaphor

This metaphor resembles typical WIMP interfaces, since the user's viewpoint remains constant. In analogy to a stage portal this is symbolized through a static frame of reference. The 3Ddocument mainly stays in the center of interest. It does not necessarily have to remain in the field of view, but can also exit and reappear like a real actor. Whenever changing action spaces the "set" (i.e. 3D-widgets, displays, decorative elements...) changes, too.

Locomotion Metaphor

The user's viewpoint changes with this metaphor, made visible by a dynamic visual frame of reference (e.g. different rooms or floors). The rooms or action spaces are completely changed along with their interface elements. In some cases 3D-widgets can be shared with other action spaces. 3D-document of the application might remain in the last visited action space or can be taken to the next space. The locomotion metaphor is most suitable for applications consisting of various action spaces with simpler associated sub-tasks (Dachselt 2000).

iv) Roles of variables, which describe stereotypic usages of variables, can be exploited to facilitate teaching introductory programming. This paper describes the evaluation of visual metaphors for roles used in a role-based program animator. The evaluation is based on several criteria: properties of the images, metaphor recognition and grading, and effects on learning. The study demonstrates that as a whole the role metaphors facilitate learning. The results also identify ideas for further elaboration of the individual metaphors. Furthermore, the study suggests that the evaluation of animated metaphors may require special measures (Stutzle & Sajaniemi, 2005).

v) We interpret the rules governing an interactive system as the rules specifying a game. Under this metaphor, interactions made by the participants of an interactive system are interpreted as moves selected by the players of a game (Stathis & Sergot, 1996)

vi) We present WeatherTank, a tangible interface that looks like a vivarium or a diorama, and uses everyday weather metaphors to present information from a variety of domains, e.g., "a storm is brewing" for increasingly stormy weather, indicating upcoming hectic activities in the stock exchange market. WeatherTank represents such wellknown weather metaphors with real wind, clouds, waves, and rain, allowing users to not only see, but also feel information, taking advantage of our skills developed through our lifetimes of physical

world interaction. Metaphors-concrete images that illuminate abstract ideas - are common in user interface design. We propose to use the rich and well-understood natural phenomena of weather as metaphors to represent abstract information from other domains. Many people, irrespective of educational level, literacy, and profession, understand weather metaphors intuitively (Marti et al 2001).
Here are only the small part of hundreds works where the concept of metaphor is used. In our list we can't embrace all cases of computer metaphor using. Beyond our theme there is such interesting application of computer metaphor as system metaphor (or design metaphor) in software projects (especially in "Extreme Programming") (Khaled et al, 2004), (Stubblefield, 1998).
One can recognize that the certain discrepancy between theory and practice takes place. For example, in practice there are no distinctions between metaphors and metonymies (and even between analogies and metaphors) when using in HCI and visualization. Instead of the criteria of metaphor "goodness" designers use the insight when find and/or choose metaphors for their systems. Note, by the way, that some of positions in the interface metaphor theory are based on the general theory of analogy and some of criteria are applicable to every type of mapping but not just to metaphors much less to interface and/or visualization metaphors. On our opinion that is why some of criteria such as precision or completeness of metaphor are redundant. We need to study these metaphors as original phenomenon and to reveal their original characteristics. As in beginning of 90-th we again need to answer such questions as "what are user interface metaphors", "how can we find metaphor candidates", "what makes a metaphor good or bad", etc. (Kuhn, W., 1995). It means we need to supplement the theory of interface and visualization metaphor and to define it more exactly.
Below we'll describe our approach to the of computer metaphor theory.

3. The Theory of Computer Metaphor

In this section our approach to Computer Metaphors (mainly interface metaphors and visualization metaphors) are considered. We try to increase existing approaches and to construct new bases for criteria of metaphor choice and search.
Our main goal is to design "good" interaction visual systems and in this connection we are interested in the problems of a representation of model objects as well as recognition of visual objects and manipulations them.
As it has been noted above, the semiotics is one of the bases of both HCI theory and computer visualization theory (Andersen, 2001), (Goguen, 2004.), (Nadin, 1997). It is obvious that human-computer interface and visualization have the sign and language nature. Each interface and visualization system contains the language as its core. The language is understood as the systematical description of entities under consideration, methods of their representation, modes of changes of visual display, as well as, techniques of manipulations and interaction with them. The language is built upon some basic idea of similarities between application domain entities with visual and dialog objects, i.e., upon a *computer metaphor*. (We use the broad meaning of "metaphor" concept, not dividing it onto analogy or metonymy as it is usually used in practice of interface and visualization design.)
One can consider *mapping* a computer model of the entity under study into some visual representation based on the *mental model* of this entity in the mind of the user and/or the

developer of this visualization system. Also let us consider the conception of *model entity*, i.e., an object of the computer model to be studied, an object whose state and behavior, characteristics, attributes, and features are of interest to the researcher and, hence, are to be mapped (visualized).

The sign nature of the human-computer interface and visualization allows reveal sign systems, determining interactions, visualization and communications. (A *sign system* can be defined as a set of signs together with internal relationships among signs corresponding, in one way or another, to the relationships among denotations.) In these cases relations between object of representation (denotate) and visual sign are easily separated. Defining some context the user or the observer (interpreter) recognizes the idea caused by visualization that is the interpreting idea (interpretant). There are all relations described of *semiosis* (the process of interpreting signs or *sign process*).

The visual interface uses regularly the language based on one or other sign system. Human-computer interaction in this connection may be described precisely as sign process. Visualization also may be described as sign process similarly to human-computer interaction. Interpretation of an individual visual situation, which is outside of some context (as it has been made in some works, for example (Roberts, 2000), (Barr et al., 2004)), is problematic. It is more productive to consider interfaces and visualizations as sign systems. That is to choose a metaphor means to choose a sign system that will be used to define the dialog language of interaction and/or visualization.

Let's define a view as the abstraction of a graphic display, containing specification of visual objects, their attributes, their interpositions, possible dynamics and ways of interaction. It is possible to consider a view as standard or ad hoc techniques of visual data presentation, some kind of, visual procedures, which after realization in concrete visual environments and, after substitution of the real data is output on some graphic devices. In such "procedure" (that is the view) possible changes of images, including animation, and allowable ways of interactions with a picture can be provided. Changes of significant and meaning pictures during possible interaction with the image are here the external side of visualization. These pictures (concrete graphical displays) are a realization of an abstract concept of a view. For example, Cartesian ("precomputer") data visualization metaphor generates a function graph as the view. In turn after substitution of the data (x and y coordinates) the real curves on a plane are displayed.

The set of the given system views can be considered as a vocabulary of some visual (or visualization in case of computer visualization systems) language, whereas as grammar it is possible to consider rules of formation the concrete displays and specifying a sequence of image changes. Thus, it is realized with reasonable facility a separation of language elements. Semiotics analysis of the visual (visualization) language requires correct revealing of its spatial syntax and semantics. But it is especially important the description of true visualization languages pragmatics. The problem of pragmatics is tightly related to the fact that perception of the visual text is subjective and is dependent on cultural, psychological, and even physiological factors.

Interface metaphor is considered as the basic idea of likening between interactive objects and model objects of the application domain. Its role is to promote the best understanding of semantics of interaction, and also to determine the visual representation of dialog objects and a set of user manipulations with them.

Specificity of visualization, as independent discipline in frameworks of Computer Sciences, demands the distinction between visualization metaphors and interface metaphors. The concept of visualization metaphor is defined for generalization of metaphor using cases in all domains of Computer Visualization.

Visualization metaphor is considered as a map establishing the correspondence between concepts and objects of the application domain under modeling and a system of some similarities and analogies. This map generates a set of views and a set of methods for communication with visual objects. We consider the metaphoricalness of any visualization. *(In our opinion there are no "metaphorless" visualizations of computer models and program entities* (Averbukh 2001)
Thus, one can define a computer metaphor as a mapping from concepts and objects of the application domain under modeling to a system of similarities and analogies generating a set of views and a set of techniques for interaction with and manipulation by visual objects.

In terms of semiotics the metaphor is something dynamic, in contrast to a stable sign. We can describe a metaphor as the act or the process of a designation of one concept by means of a sign, traditionally connected to other concept.
Another function of a metaphor is to determine the context for a correct interpretation of language elements, and to reveal the sense of *visual texts*. Thus, interface and visualization metaphors provide understanding represented entities of the application domain, and also metaphors help to create new entities based on the internal metaphor logic.
The conception of metaphor dominating at the moment is based on representing phenomena that are new or rather untypical for the user by means of phenomena familiar from everyday life; the latter phenomena must possess the same main properties as the phenomena they explain (Tscheligi & Musil 1994). Thereby constraints of metaphor habitualness and completeness are brought forth (Richards et al, 1994). Certainly, the appeal to ordinary human experience and interest activization while using habitual analogies facilitates understanding and learning of basic moments of the source phenomenon or process. But practice of the use of visual interface metaphors gives examples of habitual and full metaphors in which designer has achieved scrupulous conformity between entities of source and target domains and excellent recognition of almost all metaphorical objects. However, these metaphors may appear practically useless because of their bulkiness or occurrences additional and undesirable analogies connected to ordinary things. On the other hand there is a set of examples obviously incomplete, but fruitful metaphors.
So when does the metaphor work well? Examples show, that not only in that case when familiar concepts and images are used. Here it is possible the occurrence of additional, "parasitic" senses. Users may connect these senses with real concepts and images harmful to interpretation. Requirement of completeness of mapping from source domain onto target domain also may not always be suitable. Metaphors are successful, when their usages reduce the complete abstractiveness of computer modeling, including the abstractiveness of user interface with the system. Interpretation of visualization and the interactive manipulations constructed on the basis of the given metaphor, reconstructs (or creates anew) for users some mental structures in which the picture of the phenomena is represented. As a matter of fact a metaphor designs for the user some world frequently by means of objects, concepts or operations, not existing in a reality, creating as though "magic" opportunities for the user. Logics of new reality on the one hand reflect user ideas about the interface and objects of the modeled domain, and on the other - should coincide

(or to be close) with logic of development of processes and changes of objects in source domain, including logics of user activity.

We propose the approach to the understanding of metaphor as a main principle of mapping an application domain to visual universe. The understanding of metaphors as mapping from source to target domains is incomplete at least in case of interface and visualization metaphors. We offer more complex mechanism, which underlies functioning of metaphors. Our approach differs from traditional ones that in its frameworks the metaphor generates some independent metaphor domain at the expense of correspondence that puts to objects of target domain some objects from the source domain. And more exactly, structures and/or characteristics of objects from target domain are put in the correspondence structures and characteristics of objects from source domain. Cite an example of a classical metaphor LIFE IS A JOURNEY, where LIFE is target domain, and JOURNEY is source domain. Some structures of JOURNEY (beginning, ascent, descent, end, etc.) are considered in the given metaphor as a basis for the description of life structure. Similarly in other classical metaphor RICHARD - THE LION some lion qualities (for example, courage, but not tail, fangs, and claws) are transferred on a human being, who now becomes in frameworks of the metaphor domain.

An action of visualization metaphor consists of extractions of structures from target domain on the base of certain structures from source domain and transfers them in metaphor domain, which in this case has a visual nature. (Metaphorically speaking, it is possible to compare the action of a metaphor with the action of messenger RNA in molecular biology.) The visualization metaphor is mapping (more exactly operator) to certain visualization world, where unshaped objects get its visual presentations.

(There are the similar approaches to metaphor understanding, see for example (Old & Priss, 2001) or (Turner & Fauconnier, 1995). Note also that our approach is based on initial understanding of metaphorical processes. Compare with Lakoff's point of view: "*A metaphor consists of the projection of one schema (the source domain of the metaphor) onto another schema (the target domain of the metaphor). What is projected is the cognitive topology of the source domain, that is the slots in the source domain as well as their relation with each other.*" (Lakoff & Johnson 1980), (Lakoff, 1993).

As we noted above computer metaphors promote the best understanding of interaction and/or visualization semantics, as well as provide visual representation of the appropriate objects and determine the user's manipulations set. A metaphor, considered as a basis of the sign system, underlies in a basis of a dialog visualization language in its turn. User formulates the problem with the help of this language and achieves its solving from the computer. The metaphor helps to describe abstraction, structures understanding of new applied area, but also assigns dialog [visual] language objects.

The use of metaphors should increase expressiveness of objects under investigation. To achieve it objects of target domain (with a set of structures, properties) are selected. As this takes place not all objects are chosen (and even not all their characteristic or structure elements), but only that, which are under interest most of all. Analogues for these objects (by way of structures, qualitative properties) are searched in source domain. Further the following operation takes place. Object of target domain together with object from source domain are located in *metaphorical domain*, or more exact in doing so the metaphorical domain is generated. In this domain the investigated object now starts to function. (It is possible to consider, that it is already a new object of a new domain.) The *metaphorical domain* gets autonomy from domains generated it. Many properties of its objects only mediately are connected (if at all are connected) to properties of source domain objects. There is a new logic of development metaphorical domain. So, for example, the use of the scientific metaphor of an electromagnetic field its intensity is studied. But it is obviously absent on a field of wheat. In that specific case of visualization metaphors mapping to some world of visualization, where imageless objects obtain their visual representations, takes place.

There are the questions - what are nature and structure of metaphorical domain; how its generation is produced? The natural answer to them is connected to understanding of that the consideration of a metaphor as a sign or as a pair of signs is not fruitful. First of all the metaphor generates some sign system, that is integral sign set, in which existing internal relations between signs somehow map relations between designates. Our metaphorical domain as a matter of fact is a sign system.

The understanding of *a metaphor as a sign system* gives us a basis for evaluations of metaphors offered in concrete cases. If the used affinity (comparison or a set of comparisons) matches the *systemness* requirements, then we may speak about existence of a useful metaphor. If not, if condition changes of source domain objects are connected with changes of target domain objects poorly, then such comparisons usage can't help us to understand an investigated situation better. (See the approach to semiotic model of interface metaphor in. (Barr et al., 2004).)

In case of a metaphor the generation of a sign system is possible to consider as the adaptation of two metaphor operators, the basic:

"Let A is similar to B"

and the additional operator:

"The following attributes /elements/characteristics of A are selected for assimilation to the following attributes /elements/characteristics of B"

Where ***A*** is a source domain, and ***B*** is a target domain.

The analysis of the use of visual interaction systems reveals that the metaphor has a "focus" making the greatest impact on the user of the visual language generated by this metaphor. Sometimes, the metaphor focus is founded upon dissimilarity between metaphoric and model entities. In other cases, the metaphor affects the user by placing an object of the metaphor to a semantic context unusual to this object. Note possibilities of presence several foci in metaphors and absences focus in the concrete metaphor. Also note that focus of the metaphor is always perceived subjectively and can be missed by some particular user.

The computer metaphor can be specified as a set consisting of the following parts:

- imagery of the metaphor;
- operations directed by metaphor both animation operations and user's manipulations (in degenerated case the observation may be considered as these operations);
- the set of similarities between model and metaphoric entities or elements of semantic discrepancy;
- the focus of the metaphor responsible for the greatest part of the impact the metaphor makes on the user.

Now when our extended approach to metaphor meaning was described, in the next section we'll consider our approach to metaphor generation.

4. Metaphors Generation

In this section the scheme of metaphors generation is considered. Note that this scheme is suitable both for computer, and for literary and rhetorical metaphors. It is necessary to determine relation between metaphor and target system of meanings, for which metaphor was formed. This relation might be expressed in the terms of "meanmarks".

Let's start with an example of a well-known metaphor "RICHARD - the LION". In this case notion "RICHARD" is the object of methaphorization. Some his qualities, in particular, bravery, nobleness, force, etc. are well known. There is some image of Richard [king] in our mind, along with insights about bravery, nobleness, force etc. Connections between Richard's image and these notions take place, so one can write down:

Richard - brave;

Richard - noble;

Richard - strong.

Note, that Richard is only simple name, which may be turned off the real world, and actually, is really free label (as, for example, "true" in classical logic). In the same time the label "brave" means an opportunity to attach the other labels or labels to a subject, or (may be) vice versa their obligatory absence. That's mean, that "brave" is the true conceptual label having the tree of implications, and as well as the tree of preconditions. If to say from the theory aspect side, one can consider it as the target domain of a metaphor. The goal here is to define a relation between the metaphor and the target system of meanings, for which the metaphor was formed. This relation might be expressed in the terms of "meanmarks". To define what meanmark is, let us consider the word "brave". The meaning of that word may be established through ***if-then*** (implication) relation of it to other words. The implication is important because it is a base for reasoning, and metaphors assist the process of reasoning. For the word "brave" one may define outgoing implications. For instance, if ***A*** is "brave" then ***A*** is "not timid". This relation is denoted with →, in the following form as *"brave" → "not timid"*. Besides outgoing arrows every word has incoming ones. So the following object emerges. ***{I}*** → "brave" → ***{O}***, where ***{I}*** is set of words implying "brave" and ***{O}*** is set of those which are implied by "brave" itself. Now the graph of such implications can be considered, and it is assumed here that the topology of graph's paths passing through node defines mean of that node. Meanmark is simple the label for node in such oriented graph. The graph may not be the graph of implication relations of words; it may depict any such relation.

We use a symbol arrow (→) to describe concepts sequence in this case. This symbol, against formal logic, designates what concepts entail the following concepts, which may be attached to the object under consideration. For example:

Richard → brave, strong; king;

or

there are red and dark blue and green → there is motley.

Concept under metaphorization is considered here as a way of meanmarks ascription to various entities, as interrelation of this meanmarks set. It's revealed - what meanmarks with what are connected in our cogitative metaphorization concepts model. Also it's detected following levels of arrows (the second, the third, the fourth etc.) that stand up for each of meanmarks in the given conceptual system. It turns out the graph consisting of meanmarks. This graph may be covered on a graph consisting of meanmarks from source domain of metaphor. It is obvious, that the sets of meanmarks in these graphs are differing, but their general structures are similar. Both metaphorical system of meanings and target system have such graphs which show how meanings are connected within them. According to that representation the correspondence between meanings at target system and meanings at metaphor can be established through homomorphism from target system meanmarks graph onto meanmarks graph of metaphor.

If we want to illustrate the target system "King Richard is brave", firstly we must define meanmarks graph of that system. It is simple enough: "Richard → king, brave". But the meanmarks "king" and "brave" mean nothing without their language contexts: incoming and outgoing implications in the system of meanings of English. It is very difficult to find meanmarks in some graphs which will have the same topology of implications as "king": and "brave" in that system. So the required metaphor should include both these meanmarks. We are looking now for "somebody" → king, brave. And, of course "somebody" is "Lion".

So the following object appears in the general case:

{I} → M → {O},

where ***M*** - considered concept; ***{I}*** - set of concepts, implying ***M***; and ***{O}*** - set of concepts, generated by ***M***.

When methaphorization proceed, the graph of meanmarks for a source domain is determined. Searching of a metaphor - is searching of the structure of interrelations which are similar to structure of interrelations in the target domain. On covering (*not exact, not one to one*) it may become, that it will be necessary to remove some bottom levels. But the additional level absent in target domain may appear. Exactly this second meanmark system with its interrelations is our metaphor to the object considered originally. It may be much more interrelations between concepts in the metaphorical system than in the source. Note that some interrelations may correspond to those arrows which are present also in the first set, but just wasn't noticed up before the metaphor construction. And here they can be seen obviously. In a considered example the required structure is "LION", with traditionally implied bravery, nobleness, force. (Here we should notice that all these properties basically differ from similar, inherent to Richard).

The suggested model may also help to describe how metaphor allows establishing new properties of target system. One can consider implication dependence graphs not only for words, but also for other similar dependences in the same way.

Let's assume that we have certain time sequence of values ***{X}***. That is ***{X}*** is a set of elements with one linear discrete coordinate and some value. Problem of presentation of this sequence is raised. For example, let's transform these values into music notes with certain melody. It is possible because notes may be interpreted as values, and duration of music notes is always discrete. Then:

Melody → time sequence of notes → a set of elements with one linear discrete coordinate and a certain value.

Recognition ***{X}*** through a similar metaphor may lead to interesting conclusions. The sequence of notes has the special property - notes may compose (or not) beautiful melodies. And if our way of formal transformation values ***{X}*** to notes may generate melody, that, probably, ***{X}*** has interesting properties, which may be found out by means of a metaphor. (One can consider sonification as a special form of visualization see, for example, (Reed et al, 1995), (Osawa, 1998). There are examples of cognitive visualization with music in (Zenkin1991)..)

The process of metaphor generation (metaphorization) first of all includes (may be implicit) analysis of target domain of the future metaphor. The hierarchical structure of object interrelations of target domain and their properties is revealed on a basis of the metaphor objects and its properties. At the following stage a source domain and its main object are searched. Criteria of a choice are criteria of metaphor quality.

Firstly, the main object of a source domain should have the properties, similar (closed) to properties of metaphorization object. The structure of these object interrelations and its properties should be *similar* to structure of interrelations of object under metaphorization and its properties, at least on the first level of a structural tree. Secondly, a *source domain* should be **visualized**. *That's mean that the nature of the source domain should be like, that its objects have dimension, extent, length, form, color or other visual characteristics.* (For example - a metaphor of the railway for the functional description of operational systems.)

The person distinguishes any general logic in a picture, breaking it on the set (perhaps enclosed) of fragments, abstracting from minor elements. One can consider the structures of user's internal mental model. In these structures (so called "representative cognitive structures") images of external world phenomena and inward habit are presented (Chuprikova, 2003). Thus, there is the set of structures including cognitive structures, structures of entities under analysis and structures of visual objects and images. It is necessary to support conformity between these three types of visualization structures.

"Visualizeness" (in a broad sense) of source domain provides the interpretation. A process of interpretation is exactly the generation of representative cognitive structures on base of visual images. This process is inverse or more exactly dual to visualizations. Similarly to visualization principles the interpretation principles should exist. So, the metaphor's quality is connected with an opportunity of easy interpretation of the [visual] language, which is generated by this metaphor. Also the visualizeness requirement is connected with the known for a long time criterion of "good" metaphorization - habitualness, recognition of source domain objects. (The concept of habitualness and recognition in the specialized systems of the human-computer interface should be connected mostly not with everyday realities, but with potential user activity in that sphere for which the interactive system is created).

The analysis of a source domain is carried out at the next stage of methaphorization process. On the basis of the interrelations analysis and dependences in the context of a source domain, as well as on the basis of analogies with them, both the methaphorization the analysis of the object and its properties is carried out. Objects dependences in the context of target domain are revealed. It is necessary for a source domain to have the deeper structure of interrelations than target domain in order to search for new dependences in the target domain. It's one of the factors of a "successful" metaphor. (See also the examples of metaphors in (Barbosa & de Souza 2000).) It's clear, that the metaphor's success is connected first of all with interrelations concepts structure of a source domain and with a possibility to obtain on its base the new understanding of dependences in the target domain that was of interest to us initially.

The duality of interpretation and visualization processes (or any other form of representation) is shown here through a metaphor. Sign process in visual interactive systems (or more exact part of this process connected with the interface interpretation) is supported through metaphor action. Metaphor action and, in particular, the user reaction to properties and dependences carried out at objects of metaphorization are connected with imposing of rich structures of interrelations concepts of a source domain on a target domain.

5. Metaphor Analysis

Some different interface and visualization metaphors are analyzed in this section. These metaphors include popular "Desktop" metaphor, "room" metaphor, and also metaphors used in highly specialized scientific and information visualization systems. We paid attention on genesis of metaphors, opportunities of data presentation and manipulation using concrete metaphors, potential properties of metaphorical objects, and also potential opportunities of user interpretation of these objects and manipulations with them. The purpose of analysis is to reveal structures of successful metaphors and to build a basis for comparison and evaluation of metaphors. Such concepts as "metaphor action" and "metaphor formula" are considered to construct the basis of analysis (Averbukh et al, 2007).

5.1 Metaphor Action and Metaphor Formula

Let's define the concept "metaphor action". This characteristic is constructed by answers to the following questions:

"How can this metaphor assist to represent the information? "

"How can this metaphor assist to interact with data or to manipulate them? "

"What properties of metaphorical objects (that is visual and/or dialogue objects generated by the metaphor) take place?"

"What actions or ideas are arisen from the process of the user interaction (including observations of pictures) with metaphorical objects?"

It is possible to construct a "formula" of metaphor actions. **The metaphor "formula" includes simplified descriptions of source and target domains, an idea of likening using in the metaphor and results of metaphor actions.**

We begin our analysis with the most popular "Desktop" metaphor. (Note, that one of the first works on the interface metaphor formalization was dedicated to this metaphor and was published as 1991 (Kuhn W. & Frank A.U. 1991))

In the case of desktop metaphor the formula may be written as follows:

Source domain: Desk with folders containing documents (documents are structured, but folders may be disordered);

Target domain: Office automation system;

Idea of likening: "Folders with papers" = "structure of the data, a set of files";

"Opening of a folder " = "demonstration of file structures and/or files";

"Processing of documents" = "execution of functions, by means commands of the visual language".

Result: The direct access to data structures by means manipulations of icons placed on the screen; calls of some [user] predetermined functions by means a visual dialog language.

Microsoft Windows uses the extended version of this metaphor.

Addition of source domain:

A desk is combined with control panel where starting buttons are placed.

Besides the "*magic*" idea is added: All actions within the framework of system are made by means of ***double click*** on icons.

Result: icons that can represent as data structures as programs calls.

There is also one more idea - opening of new windows when program executions are begun. One can speak about carrying out of "metaphorical" interface space, constructed on the basis of desktop realities. But not all entities of real desktops (the source domain of the metaphor), which are richer and poorer than metaphorical objects in the same time, were equally useful in new metaphorical space. Often icons moving on the screen are needed only for its grouping and for concrete user work convenience. Images of folders do not play a main role in users' actions with operational system and frequently they are not placed on "desktop". But the major value (not having analogues in initial area) double "click" using for program starts has obtained. Usually double "click" results in new window opening, and, in Internet-browsers case windows are opened almost in literal sense. In result we have logical commands system of visual (iconic) language, based on basic double icon "click" operation.

The desktop metaphor became a basis of comfortable and clear users interface. Doubtless, the metaphor's success connected not only with natural icon figurativeness, clear users, but also with logicality and systemness of the visual dialog language.

5.2 Metaphor Properties

One can consider "room" metaphor as development of "desktop" metaphor. Really at first realizations of this three-dimensional metaphor for office automation systems were simple extensions of desktop successes. Then the room metaphor got its independent value and was actively used in human-computer interface systems and the software visualization (Greenberg & Roseman, 1998). The other three-dimensional metaphor - a "landscape" metaphor is also actively used in systems of software visualization and information visualization (Balzer et al, 2004), (Charters et al, 2002).

In case of "room" metaphor we can't write the full metaphor formula because there are no a common application area, successful and convincing examples of its usage, and, that is there is no a unity of target domain. However we shall result the review of ***properties*** of room metaphor. Realizations of this metaphor are characterized often by a combination of three-dimensional space of the room with bidimensionality of objects, placed on its "walls", a "ceiling" or a "floor". Such combination on the one hand preserves principles of structural correspondence between model entities and visual objects, on the other - provides successful spatial placement of images. (See for example (Reed et al, 1995) and (Bajdalin & Ismagilov 2006).)

Let's carry out the analysis of a room metaphor from two positions: the room metaphor itself and how it is possible to represent the information with its help.

The room metaphor possesses the following properties:

1. Ability to contain any objects inside itself.

The room not only represents separate object, but also is the container for others ones.

2. Restriction of a perception context. Objects inside a room are considered in a separation from "external worlds".

3. Closeness. There are no any additional elements to use Room metaphor (excepting possible inner objects).

4. Inclusion in structure. It is possible "to build buildings of rooms", that is to consider set of rooms. Therefore the room may be an element of construction of some complex construction.

5. Naturalness of a metaphor. The room is natural metaphor, with presence of corresponding objects in the real world. Functionality and characteristics of real objects are transferred in the virtual world with only minor extended understanding.
(See also analysis of "room" metaphor properties in (Dieberger, 1994).)
The "landscape" metaphor and "city" metaphor (which may be considered as the variant of landscape) are well-known in information and software visualization. This spatial metaphor can show for example structures of program projects as a map of some district. Components of the software are represented as the geographical conventions having an exact spatial site in geographical space. Such map may serve as fine means for development of projects, and also as means for visualization of program executions. (See (Balzer et al, 2004) for the full survey of landscape metaphor using in Software Engineering.) Our analysis shows following metaphor properties:
1. An unlimited context.
In case of landscape metaphor user's context is not limited by any special means. As result, an user needs in additional efforts to identify an object among set of others.
2. Naturalness of a metaphor.
Naturalness of a metaphor reduces efforts on interpretation of the resulting image. With reference to a landscape metaphor one can mention additionally to naturalness of spatial orientation, also naturalness of navigation. That is why the landscape metaphor is a good choice for using in virtual reality systems.
3. "Nesting" of landscapes, the organization of internal structure
The landscape metaphor structures the data, "putting" them in larger components.
4. Clues
The landscape metaphor may use for representing of large volumes homogeneous in visual sense data. In this case it is necessary clue elements which are "starting points" for user interpretation of complex data. For example these clues may use in debuggers to represent erroneous or other "especial" elements.
Let's note also, that the more is the volume of data the more expedient is using of the "landscape" metaphor. Thus, the landscape metaphor is good for using in debuggers and performance analysis systems.
These properties of metaphors are taken into consideration when real systems are designed for constructing ***views*** with rich methods of information representation, in particular, by means of objects accommodation inside volumes, changes of space characteristics and/or objects, etc. Landscape metaphor is used actively in visualization environments with virtual reality applying.
Below we'll show how this analysis turns out to be useful in development of specialized visual systems on the basis of new computer metaphors.

5.3 Metaphors in Specialized Visualization Systems

In the majority of the specialized visualization systems the representations of abstract per se mathematical, program, or information objects takes place. There are cases, when existing visualization methods are not applicable. Therefore search of source metaphorical domains for them is rather serious problem. So, it is necessary to search for visualization metaphor and to build a view set on its basis, including additional, assisting interpretations visual objects, and also the techniques for manipulation of these objects. There is our experience of search of new metaphors for scientific, information and software visualization systems.

5.3.1 Germ Metaphor

Let's consider the following example of abstract metaphor which is used in visualization of one type of 4-dimensional datasets. These datasets are the result of High Performance Computer modeling of some chemical processes. It is obvious that there is no natural way to represent multidimensional sets. Another problem was that typical dataset is relatively large - about 1 million 4D points. After long research, the following metaphor was found useful. It was known that original dataset have one structural aspect, which allows making projection of 4D data onto 2D surface using first two coordinates of point and cutting out two last. For each point on this 2D surface, we can construct corresponding "germ" - another 2D surface formed by coordinates wiped during projection. Let us explain it. Original dataset contains *{(x,y,u,v)}* values. We remove *(u,v)* coordinates and thus get another dataset: *{(x,y)}*. Each *(x,y)* pair of this new dataset has a corresponding set of *(u,v)* values. This *{(u,v)}* set is called "germ" of particular *(x,y)* point. The *{(x,y)}* set is called "projection".

- First, user can choose any point on projection and visually see its germ.
- Secondly, germ's properties such as width, height, radius, element's count are useful. We show these properties on a projection by color. User chooses which property he wants to visualize and sees colored projection immediately. This allows him to see the whole picture of data distribution.

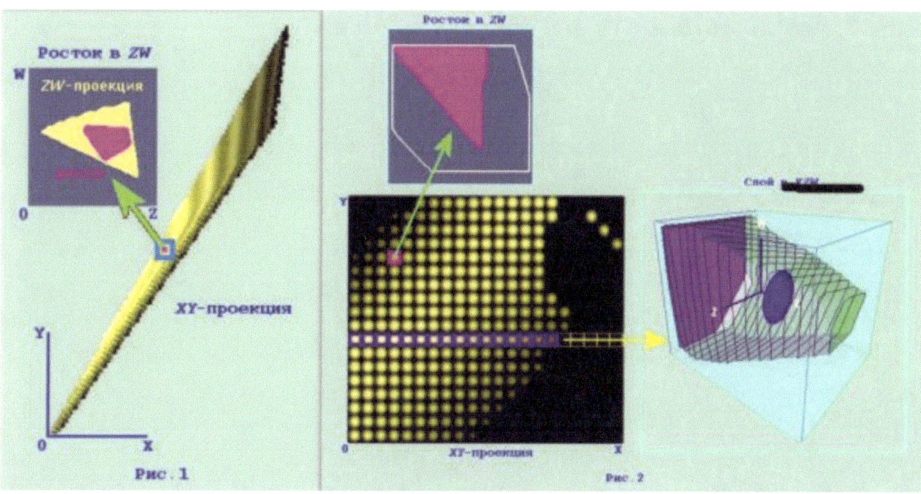

Fig. 1. The Germ in visualization of 4D set

This simple scheme of interaction allowed user to navigate inside original 4D dataset and to perceive data after each computational experiment.

One important feature of this example is that germ object has no analogies nor in application area nor in mathematical model. In spite of its abstract nature the "germ" metaphor became actually usable in practice.

Note in the metaphor analysis the abstractness of applied area models, and the abstractness of the figurativeness used in the visualization. Interpretation is made not by recognition of known images and processes, but via possibility to examine image changes in connected

view areas (projection and germ) during interoperation with the system. This connection is made by user manipulation with projection when he selects current point and sees its corresponding germ.
The construction of visualization model was based on knowledge of mathematical structure of original dataset. This allowed to escape rendering difficulties - we never render 4d object as is. Metaphor's idea was created specifically for this datasets structure and nature. Implementation of this idea has allowed to achieve new results in chemical research being made (Vasev & Pervalov, 2001). (See Figure 1).

5.3.2 Molecula Metaphor

Call graphs are used in Software Visualization for performance tuning of parallel and distributed computing. They allow to observer which program functions used most part of processor time. Three-dimensional visualization techniques may improve the quality of graph structure perception. Suggested idea is to search analogies with natural objects. Let's place in nodes-functions (which is usually represented like spheres) an electrostatic charge (Averbuh et al, 2004).

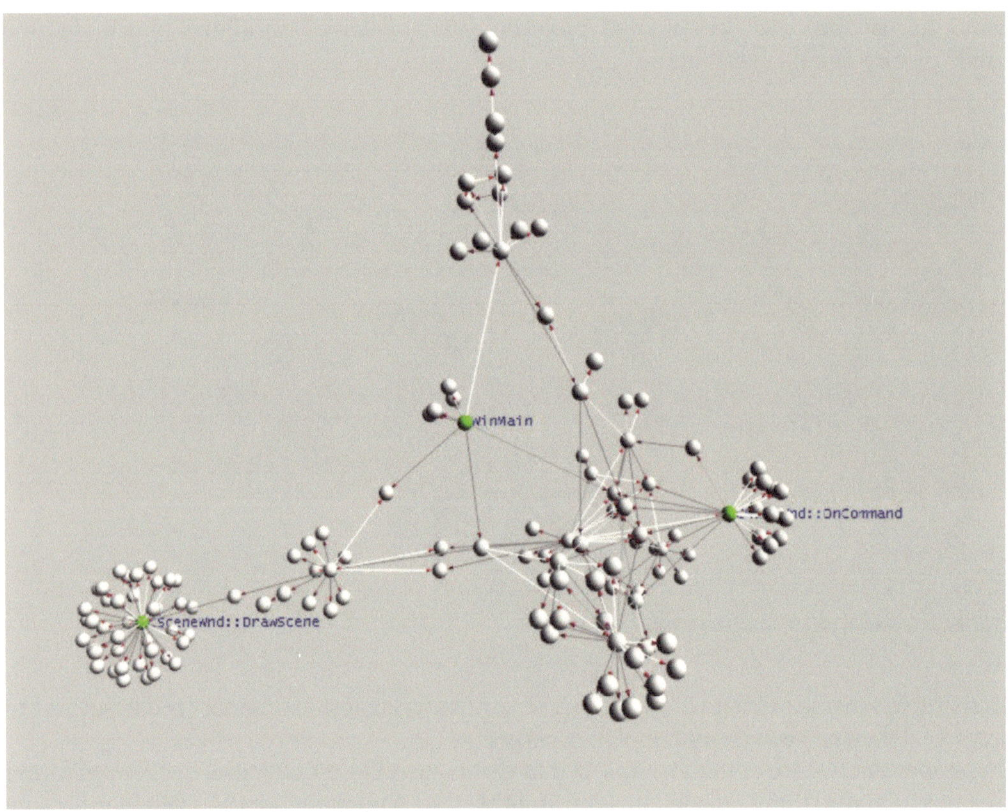

Fig. 2. Call graph of "Callgraph drawing" program

Connections between nodes are replaced by elastic interaction. Let's name the metaphor "a molecule metaphor" because at the given approach the visualization similar to the structure of benzol molecules. Thus there are two types of interactions: springy between bound nodes and electrostatic between all other nodes-"atoms"'. Electrostatic interaction may reflect temporary features of the calling functions, then springy - a number of calls. Consideration of the "molecule" energy allows us to construct the effective drawing algorithm for about thousand of objects. The displays meet the symmetry criteria. Animation (molecule rotation) allows exploring graph structure better. Color may be used for accentuation of interesting features of visualized graphs. The molecule metaphor is constructed on analogies to natural objects. The graph structure is looked over easily and is distinctly perceived and interpreted by the person, not demanding special intellectual efforts. At the subsequent analysis and algorithm modification it was found out that the molecule metaphor may be used successfully at visualization of large databases, and in general at representation large systems structures (See Figure 2). Thus, the effect of metaphor "reverse motion" took place in this case when properties of the metaphor are investigated, and then the target domain (and new application) for this metaphor may be found. Such approaches to metaphor construction based on "physical" conceptions are popular in Software Visualization and Graph visualization systems (Osawa, 1998), (Malloy & Power, 2005). Note also the similarity of visualization in (Malloy & Power, 2005) and (Averbuh et al, 2004).

5.3.3 Magic Lancet Metaphor

The search of effective interface led to the metaphor of human in medical information system - "a human figure in a glass cube" (Averbuh et al, 2005). In this case three-dimensional model of a human body is displayed and there are an opportunity to make visible or invisible those or other systems of an organism, for example skin integument, skeleton, nervous and blood systems, etc. Information inquiry may represent as "*semantic immersing*" to the human organism. For example circulatory system, the digestive apparatus or some other organs connected in the context of any disease, may be shown. Something like a set of semantic filters or the special virtual ("magic") glasses, allowing to see and to isolate, for example, the ill organ with the adjoining struck tissue, turns out. Figurativeness of this metaphor is natural has three-dimensional representation. Figurativeness of this metaphor is natural has three-dimensional reflection. Due to a semantic filtration, the user obtains additional opportunities at data output that considerably reduces manipulations amount necessary for information inquiry. However without the "manipulator", that is some device, allowing operating in this metaphor context, realization of systems on its base is pretty difficult. As an additional manipulator's metaphor the idea of "magic lancet" is offered. "Lancet" allows "to cut" this or that organism area for the profound exploring. During any human organism object "cutting", all physical changes are visualized, as if we did it in a reality. On the other hand, one "cut" is not enough sometimes. Semantic immersing allows to come nearer to object as far as it will be necessary, passing through some systems of an organism, making it invisible and visible again. This property helps us to obtain more exact medical data visualization. In case of a combination the "magic lancet" metaphor with three-dimensional model of human body, we may obtain the virtual model of operations. On basis of these metaphors the prototype system of information visualization for the medical purposes is realized now (See Figures 3). Systems based on this metaphor may be used for example for surgery learning.

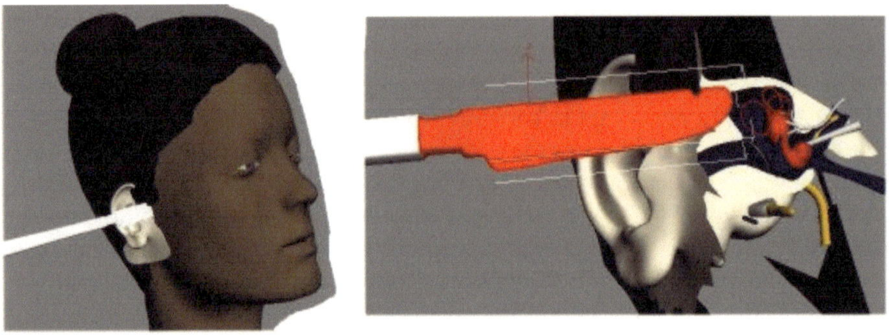

Fig. 3. Screenshots of "Magic Lancet" System

5.3.4 Using of Local Metaphors

In a number of interactive systems several interface metaphors are used at once. It can be metaphors for various widgets, or even metaphors of separate operations. Sometimes a set of additional metaphors is created for a basic metaphor enhancement. It was made in works (Kocjan, 2007) and (Trushenkova, 2007), where new interface solutions within a concept of a desktop metaphor were found for office automation tasks. Another example is in (Dieberger, 1994), where it is possible to build a lot of additional metaphors (a post, a bulletin board, etc.) within a city metaphor.

Sometimes such combination of metaphors is successful and sometimes it becomes a heap of obscure images and manipulations. There exist theoretical works on a subject of the mixed metaphors (Lee. & Barnden 1999). However they are not intended for practical application in the process of designing interactive systems.

It seems that presence of hierarchy of metaphors is a condition of success in such cases. Interface metaphors should generate a language of user-application interactions and should not conflict with each other.

Let's consider the following hierarchy:

- A global metaphor conveys the basic idea of application design (e.g. the world as an office);
- A basic metaphor of an application, such as a desktop metaphor, a landscape or a city metaphor;
- A local metaphor describes a specialization of an application (e.g. a card file metaphor);
- A metaphor for widgets and separate operations, for example, a metaphor of scissors in (Kocjan, 2007) and dashboard metaphor in RDM +(see below).

Further one can find two examples of the interface metaphors hierarchy. The first program is an office automation system and the second one is a mobile application for remote computer management.

Office Automation System for Municipality Clerks

An office automation system which is intended for registration of citizens and a housing stock of a municipality is taken up. The basic functionality consists of effective storing and processing information and report forming.

A well-known desktop metaphor was chosen as a basic metaphor of the interface. It is widespread in office automation applications as clerks (users of the system) work with documents at their desks. Some significant properties of the desktop metaphor have been specified earlier.

As a local interface metaphor the card file metaphor was chosen. The following are the most important properties of this metaphor which have affected our choice.
Property 1. A card file metaphor is a natural metaphor. It means that there is an object of the real world which is well-known to users.
Property 2. The concept of a card file implies precise data structuring.
Clerks have to obtain callers and work with the application simultaneously. It is a very important feature to note. Users, who work with people, should be stress-resistant, disciplined, and attentive both to people and to their work. A majority of users are middle age women. They are poorly familiar with operation on a computer, but they have a great paperwork experience. Thus it is very important, that they perceived a new working procedure, as something familiar, similar to in what they were engaged earlier.
Working with people and operation on a computer increase probability of mistakes, therefore data should be well-defined. Data structuring also plays an important role at forming of a mental model of the application of a user and gives positive psychological effect.
Now it is clear, that both properties of the card file metaphor are very important for the application (from the standpoint of information on functionality of the program and its users).
It's worth to mention that the metaphor was adapted for the application. The adapted metaphor changes the way of object handling. For example, searching and ordering of documents are replaced with "magic" (automatic) operations (for example, immediate returning of a card to the place after its process ending or appearing all family members at once in active cards "list"). This is an example of a metaphor action.
Let's consider another example of hierarchy of interface metaphors.

RDM+ (Remote Desktop for Mobiles)
RDM+ is an application for a remote computer management from Apple iPhone. It allows to edit documents, to get access to network resources, to surf web and many other things. It is also possible to carry out simple administrative tasks.
Besides direct manipulation with Windows' objects (icons, menus and so forth) the application allows to send shortcuts to operating system and to accelerate user's work.
A user can keep data about several computers that he or she usually connects to.
It is important to note that the interface of the program was created for a touchscreen mobile device. iPhone's screen is rather small (in comparison with a computer screen), therefore a compact representation of an information is required. And as we speak about a mobile device fast access to all functions of the application is required (especially for users on the go).
As the basic metaphor of the application a dashboard metaphor was chosen. A dashboard is a visual display of the most important information needed to achieve one or more objectives, consolidated and arranged on a single screen so the information can be monitored at a glance. (Few, 2005)

Fig. 4. A dashboard metaphor on iPhone's homescreen

Fig. 5. A dashboard metaphor on the home page of RDM+

Compactness of information representation and fast access to any information are the main properties of the dashboard metaphor.
iPhone's homescreen also uses the dashboard metaphor and to some extent this experience made for the choice of the basic metaphor.
As a local metaphor an address book metaphor was taken. The address book metaphor helps to organize a list of remote computers and its handling.
iPhone users are familiar with a telephone directory. An address book of RDM+ works on the same principle as the telephone directory. Addition, editing and deletion of computers form an address book. The choice of a concrete computer from the list starts operation of "call" to the remote computer and connection to it.
Simplicity and habitualness of the operations connected with the local metaphor of address book provide fast performance. And successful experience of other programs suggests that the use of an address book in mobile applications is effective both in the view of understanding by users, and in the view of compactness.
In this case speed of work with the application is provided with both interface metaphors and their interrelation.

5.4 New Metaphors

Yet one can't achieve the important goal of metaphor generation, that is to automate a choice of the metaphor source domain. The creation of new metaphors realizes, as a rule, by insight. We suggest examples of new invented metaphors, such as "basket" interface metaphor and "manga + anime" metaphor for information visualization.
Now the interface based on hierarchy is most popular. Realizations of the hierarchy are used such structures as a tree. However this approach is not always convenient for "end" users. One can consider other principle, the metaphors of gathering interface operations in a "shopping basket". Let a set of possible operations, depicted by icons, takes place. Users may collect them in a basket to form the interface that is essential for their work. That is an user visits "interface self-service store" and gathering of the "goods" (i.e. icons representing operations) in a "shopping basket", and then she/he assembles new interface operations using this collection.(See the similar idea in (Stuckenschmidt, 2004), where there is using a "shopping basket" to collect search results.)
"Manga + anime" metaphor is offered for information visualization systems. Manga is Japanese comics, based on well-defined visual language. This language is well and unequivocally interpreted by readers. Anime is a type of the Japanese animation films. The visual language of anime also is well understood by skilled spectators. All over the world there are a lot of fans of manga and anime. Our idea consists in using comics (manga) metaphor for the description of processes. A sequence of windows may be output on a screen the. In turn a film may be shown in each window, for example, to describe details of a process. The metaphor can be used also to design animated tutorials and user's guides.
"Magic" is often considered in design and development of the interface for "end user programming" systems and for social computing. A "magic" idea is an idea of "miraculous, impossible in a real life things, actions, situations and events. Magic ideas are interesting and useful to create interface and visualization metaphors and new techniques for dealing in virtual environments. The conception of "magic" metaphors is rather popular in the literature on HCI (for example (Poupyrev, 2001), (Kuhn, W.1995), (Rohrer, 1995), (Kim Halskov Madsen, 2000), (Grosjean & Coquillart 1999).

Even the superficial analysis shows, that in some cases the magic expands opportunities of real objects and characters, and in some cases the phenomena, essentially distinguished from habitual are described. In connection with search of metaphors both cases are interesting. Note also, that the magic ideas from literary fairy tales (fantasy stories) are the most useful for our purposes.
Examples of the metaphors generated on the basis of literary fairy tales, can be considered. Among them there are "speaking portrait" and "speaking map", that is the intellectual agents with spontaneous activity. Such agents can be used as means for the organization "end user" interface. Prototypes of specialized interactive systems based on these metaphors are under construction now.
'Magical approach does not try to incorporate properties of the physical world into the virtual environment, but rather extends them by inventing "magical" interfaces. All of these techniques are based on certain "magical" metaphors and are very easy to understand if one knows the metaphor. Many metaphors are available that can be used and they do not needed to be learned if the user already knows about them. Thus the resulting interface can be very easy to learn and used right away (Poupyrev, 2001). The virtual reality may call for the diverse magic metaphors, as it (a virtual reality) as a matter of fact also is "not fantastic" magic. Some sorts of fantastic stories may be bases of scenarios for actions and manipulations in virtual environments.

6. Discussion and Conclusion

To sum up our studies, let's consider some propositions of this chapter.
The sign nature of HCI and visualization allows applying the semiotics analysis to them. The basic idea of similarities between application domain entities with visual objects is required when visual language is designed. It is possible to speak about some idea of metaphoric representation. A metaphor is a framework of visual language which provides both depicting by an author of the visual text (that is a designer of the interactive [visualization] system) and user interpretation of the visual text.
The main approaches to Computer Metaphor Theory are based on the cognitive approach to metaphors linked with G. Lakoff and his coauthors. In frameworks of these approaches the analysis of a metaphor goes back to analysis of "Lakoff's" structures. Metaphor formalization in this case describes steps of metaphor designing.
As a rule the concept of a visualization metaphor is not separated from the concept of human-computer interface metaphor. Metaphor is considered as an usage everyday and well-known (often technical) realities. The concept of visual interface metaphor is based on presentation of new or unusual for user phenomena by means of other phenomena that are known to him from everyday life. These phenomena should have the same basic properties, as the phenomena which they explain. Thereby constraints of metaphor habitualness and completeness are brought forth. Advantages of such approach are the appeal to ordinary human experience and activation of user interest that relieves understanding and assimilation of the processes under modeling. But there are some limitations of this approach among them - potential loss of details and some specific notions, in cases when there are no analogues to them in the given domain; necessity of comparison of concepts from different domains during training; potential additional and undesirable analogies connected with everyday metaphors.

Our approach to computer metaphor in some aspect does not comply not only traditional for philology understanding of a metaphor, as ornaments of speech and increase its informativeness due to bright comparisons, but also understanding of metaphors as an application of everyday experience for abstract conceptions as it is usual in theory and practice of HCI. Interface and visualization metaphors may be considered as a special case of scientific metaphor used for generation of new or additional senses for understanding of the new facts and the phenomena.

Interface and visualization metaphors are not completely identical to the metaphors investigated in other disciplines. Practical use of metaphors frequently does not submit to the criteria chosen at the previous stage of development of discipline. On our opinion to form the qualitative and constructive theory of interface and visualization metaphors it is necessary to update and to supplement the existing theory. Then practice applications of metaphor can base on stronger basis.

The criticism of HCI metaphors, as a rule, is caused by an unsuccessful choice of a source domain or sometimes a misunderstanding takes place, as the criticism is concerned to other aspects of using analogies and metaphors in Computer Sciences.

The conception of "metaphor action" is important for the theory of computer metaphor. This conception has formed a basis for the analysis actions of concrete interface and visualization metaphors. Techniques of data representation generated by means the given metaphor, property of metaphorical objects and results of their interpretations by users are the subject of the analysis. Also the conception of metaphor "formula" is offered. The "formula" includes simplified descriptions of source and target domains, an idea of likening using in the metaphor and results of metaphor actions and additionally some "magic" (not existing in the reality, but useful) possibilities of the interface. The purpose of analysis is to reveal metaphor structures, to understand principles of their functioning, to obtain a basis for comparison and evaluation of metaphors.

A metaphor generates some "metaphorical" domain constructed on basis of realities of source and target domains. Just in this domain the metaphorical objects exist, act and interact and just its logic determines their behavior and relations. Another function of the metaphor is to specify a context for better interpretation of elements of the given interaction and visualization language. The computer metaphor helps to understand entities of the application domain that are being modeled, as well as to create new entities based on the internal logic of the metaphor. The components of the metaphor are the imagery (and/or a set of dialog objects) it generates and actions it dictates for updating visual images and manipulating visual objects.

On our opinion one can formalize the suggested concepts, including concepts of the "metaphor action" and "metaphor formula" within the framework of the theory computer metaphor for example on Natural Deduction logics (Pelletier, 2000). The formula of already existing metaphor and the description of the structure of its source domain may help to find objects corresponding to the target domain which satisfies qualitative criteria. One can choose a metaphor, as well as construct on its base a correct set of views for a visual interactive system. Criteria of a choice may be considered as criteria of metaphor quality. The analysis of metaphor properties shows applicability for our goals the conceptions of image-schemas and representative cognitive structures.

Criteria of correctness choice (or designing) of views are necessary. In particular, construction of views can be based on a rule that *the constructed structure of the visual image should not contradict to the structure of the initial entity.* Interpretation of the visual object representation should not result in relations that are absent in the initial entity originally. For example representation of the modelling entity with a bidimentional structure as 3D object may lead to wrong interpretation. Though the increase of an image dimension is often useful for better interposition of represented objects in a scene. While a reduction of dimension, as well as a reduction of all structures is not a mistake provided that the user (interpreter) is informed about it. The criteria of metaphor and view quality can be considered in more general context of cognitive principles of visualization design. (See (Tversky et al, 2007), (Tversky et al, 2002) and also Lakoff's ideas of image schemata (Kuhn W. & Frank A.U. 1991)

The analysis and formulas of known metaphors set the general rules of their genesis and functioning. These rules will help to estimate and compare already known metaphors, as well as to search and/or to generate new ones. What are criteria of success for visualization and interface metaphors?

Ability to generate sign systems can be considered as an attribute of quality of metaphors. Classical requirements such, as habitualness, completeness, and smaller abstractness of a source domain in comparison with a target domain should be supplemented and formulated anew.

Let's write out a set of versatile requirements to a choice of metaphors.

First of all one can specify the requirement of entirety and systemness of interface and/or visualization. This requirement is connected with the sign nature and visualization and human-computer interactions as a whole. HCI and visualization should describe as sign systems, instead of separate sign situations. Generation of sign system of an interactive environment occurs due to a choice of corresponding metaphor. The problem of the designer is the description of the whole visual language, instead of its separate dialogue elements. Some unrelated to each other metaphors describing details and components of a dialogue, cannot become a basis of such language.

It is necessary to conform to the main metaphors used in system, and also to global metaphors. It is known, that the metaphors basing on jargons and, especially, on the slangy verbs are not good.

The successful HCI and visualization are constructed on base of "good" metaphors, and they should be supported on the already existing user model of phenomena and/or processes (representative cognitive structures).

It is necessary *to depict entities under visualization, but not to describe them.*

Magic fairy tales and fantasy stories are one of sources for metaphor searching.

Now let's do assumption about the sign nature of computer modeling. One can hold that a process of computer modeling is a process of generation of sign systems. Really, in some model one can easily isolate objects of the modeled phenomenon or processes as a set of denotates, that makes possible to consider model objects as signs. True, this consideration is not necessary for the purposes of the modeling; however it allows doing the further derivation of a theory. Next one can consider the hierarchy of computer models such as physical, mathematical, algorithmic, programming. There is the cycle of computer modeling including these stages and providing possibilities of returns on each cycle stages. The level of abstraction increases naturally at each modeling hierarchy level. It is possible to consider a metaphor (and, in particular, a visualization metaphor) as scientific model, and as the stage of computer modeling. The goal of the visualization in modeling process is to provide interpretation and the analysis of data, and also to support all stages of the computer modeling cycle. A visualization metaphor, and more precisely the visualization generated by metaphor is the last sign system in hierarchy of models. After the whole series of abstraction, which are inherent in modeling process, it is necessary to provide a specificity inherent visual images (that is really perceived by eyesight). Generally visualization should reduce (and not increase) the general abstractness level of all modeling hierarchy. We suggest considering the idea of "disabstract operations" (reducing of abstractness) by means of visualization. In terms of semiotics it is possible to consider "disdesignation" by means visualization. That is the removal of levels of designation (and abstractness) takes place during visualization. These several levels of designation are linked with series of sign systems, inherent to given hierarchy of models. The "disdesignation" is the most explicit when direct visualization of source object of modeling takes place. Visualization should support direct connection between a picture, which in this case is an iconic sign (in Ch. Peirce's sense), and designated objects. It is possible to consider the purpose of visualization as the removal at least one abstraction layer for needs of better (more adequate) interpretation of modeling results, instead of occurrence of additional layers. Also there are successful examples of visualization that support the modeling process without increasing or reducing of abstractness levels. A quality evaluation of a visualization metaphor may be considered in connection with the account of abstractness levels assigned on the number of layers (levels of hierarchy), laid between the examined model and the first entity under modeling (for example, a partial differential equation system and a fluid flow modeled by these equations). Then one can estimate how many layers of model abstractness the visualization have lowered to evaluate quality of a visualization metaphor. (Note that a graph of functions lowers an abstractness level on several layers all at once.) One can evaluate metaphor quality through its opportunity to lower an abstractness level of models. (However one can estimate only metaphors, rather then visualization systems themselves since in concrete systems there are a lot of external circumstances connected with realization.) Success and failures of visualization systems may be explained with the help of these evaluations. One can consider a set of requirements to a choice of metaphors and views.

The metaphor has to generate integral and systematic interface and/or visualization systems. As we mentioned above, it means an undesirability of the interface based on several fine metaphors describing details and components of dialog. This requirement means also necessity to conform as to others already existing computer metaphors, and to general ideas of global metaphors. Reduction of interpretation complexity is considered as a condition of "good" metaphor. Therefore direct interpretation of images is required, but decoding and interpretation of complex [visual] texts is considered as a source of failures.

A set of the criteria, imposed on initial and target domains in a process of metaphor generation includes:

- similarity of object properties in source and target domains,
- ability to visual presentation for object in the source domain,
- habitualness (recognition) of objects in the source domain,
- rich set of interrelations between objects in the source domain.

In the interactive visual systems a metaphor is realized as a system of *views*. Just this system of views defines the visual language of the system. Also one can write out criteria of generation for views based on metaphors. These criteria include such well-known requirements, as truthfulness, laconicalness, expressiveness, clearness. It is necessary to add in this list the interdependency between views and good manipulation abilities for their dialog elements.

Researching metaphors, views and their structures allows to analyse and evaluate existing design decisions and to project interactive visual systems with necessary properties. This is the main goal of Computer Metaphor theory. On our opinion both semiotics and metaphor theory are only the tools for analysis of computer metaphors, but not the main object of research on Computer Metaphor domain.

Thus, we know how metaphors are structured and how they are generated. We are able to find new metaphors and to evaluate their properties and opportunities. We have an experience in design and developing of specialized interactive visual systems which are based on these metaphors. Now we design specialized visualization systems based on virtual reality environments. One of our future research directions is connected with problems of metaphors for virtual reality environments. On the one hand we need in metaphors to write scenarios for user's activities in virtual reality. On the other hand we need in interface metaphors for new (real and virtual) devices to manipulate virtual reality objects. We have to take into consideration that users of specialized visualization systems are first of all the "problem solvers", and these problems may be connected with very abstract mathematical problems. The question is: what metaphors may help users to navigate and manipulate in virtual reality environments especially dealing with abstract computing models.

7. References

Andersen, P. B. (1997) *A Theory of Computer Semiotics*. Updated ed. of 1990. Cambridge University Press, New York, 1997.

Andersen P.B. (2001) What semiotics can and cannot do for HCI. *Knowledge-Based Systems*, Volume 14, Number 8, 1 December 2001 , pp. 419-424, Elsevier

Averbukh V.L.(2001) Visualization Metaphors. *Programming and Computer Software*. Vol. 27, No. 5, 2001 pp. 227-237.

Averbukh V., Bakhterev, M., Baydalin, A., Ismagilov, D., Trushenkova, P. (2007). Interface and Visualization Metaphors. J. Jacko (Ed.): Human-Computer Interaction, Part II, HCII 2007, Lecture Notes on Computer Sciences 4551, Springer-Verlag Berlin Heidelberg, Germany, 13-22.

Averbukh V.L., Baydalin A.U., Ismagilov D.R., Kazantsev A.U., Timoshpolskiy S.P. (2004) Utilizing 3D Visualization Methophors. *Proccedings of THE 14th International Conference on Computer Graphics & Vision GRAPHICON'2004*, pp. 295-298. Moscow Russia. September 6 - September 10, 2004, MSU, Moskow, Russia (In Russian.)

Averbuh V.L., Baydalin A.J., Kazantsev A.J.,Ryabinina L.B. (2005) Metaphors and complex views for Information Visualization systems. *Proceedings of Conference "Problems on Pure and Applied Mathematics"*. Pp. 314-315. Ekaterinburg, IMM UrB of the Russian Academy of Science, 2005. (In Russian.).

Bajdalin A., Ismagilov D. (2006) Structure Representation in Software Visualization Systems. *The 16th International Conference on Computer Graphics and Applications GraphicCon'2006*, pp. 271-274 Novosibirsk, Akademgorodok, Russia, July 1-5, 2006. (in Russian.)

Balzer M., Noack A., Deussen O., Lewerentz C. (2004) Software Landscapes:Visualizing the Structure of Large Software Systems in Joint EUROGRAPHICS - IEEE TCVG Symposium on Visualization, pp. 261-266.

Barbosa S.D.J., de Souza C.S. (2000) Extending software through metaphors and metonymies. *Proceedings of the 5th international conference on Intelligent user interfaces.* pp. 13-20. New Orleans, Louisiana, United States, January 09-12, 2000.

Barr P. Noble J., Biddle R. (2004) *A Semiotic Model of User-Interface Metaphor. Virtual, Distributed and Flexible Organisations Studies in Organisational Semiotics*, Springer, ISBN 978-1-4020-2161-9 2004. 189-215, Netherlands

Benyon D., Imaz M. Metaphors and Models: Conceptual Foundations of Representations in interactive Systems Development. *Human-Computer Interaction*, Volume 14, Issue 1 & 2 March 1999 , pp. 159 - 189

Blackwell A.(2006) The Reification of Metaphor as a Design *ACM Transactions on Computer-Human Interaction (TOCHI)* Volume 13, Issue 4 (December 2006) Pp.: 490–530.

Harrison, S., Tatar, D. and Sengers, P. (2007) The three paradigms of HCI. Presented at the Alt.Chi. *Session at the SIGCHI Conference on Human Factors in Computing Systems* San Jose, California, USA, April 28 - May 03, 2007 CHI '07.

Carroll J., Mack R. (1985) Metaphor, computing systems, and active learning. *International Journal of Man-Machine Studies*, Volume 22 , Issue 1 (January 1985), Ellis Horwood series in artificial intelligence pp.: 39 - 57.

Catarci T., Costabile M.F., Matera M. (1996) Which Metaphor for Which Database? *Proceedings of the HCI'95 conference on People and computers*, pp: 151 - 165, Huddersfield, United Kingdom 1996.

Charters S., Knight C., Thomas N. & Munro M. (2002) Visualisation for Informed Decision Making; From Code to Component. *Proceedings of the Workshop on Software Engineering Decision Support, 14th International Conference on Software Engineering and Knowledge Engineering*, Ischia, Italy, July 15-19 2002. pp. 765-772

Chuprikova N.I. (2003) *Mental Development and Learning (toward Motivation of System-Structural Approach).* RAO Publishing House. Moscow-Voronezh. 2003. (in Russian)

Dachselt R. (2000) Action Spaces - A Metaphorical Concept to Support Navigation and Interaction in 3D User Interfaces. *Proceedings of 'Usability Centred Design and Evaluation of Virtual 3D Environments'*, Paderborn (Deutschland), ISBN 3-8265-8252-7, April 2000.

Dieberger A. (1994) Navigation in Textual Virtual Environments using a City Metaphor PhD thesis. Submitted at the Vienna University of Technology Faculty of Technology and Sciences November, 1994.

Few S. (2005) Dashboard design: Taking a metaphor too far. In *DM Review Magazine*, March 2005.

Hendry D. G. (2006) Sketching with Conceptual Metaphors to Explain Computational Processes In *Proceedings of IEEE Symposium on Visual Languages/Human-Centric Computing 2006*, September 4-7, 2006, Brighton, UK (pp. 95-102). IEEE Computer Society Press.

Gardenfors P. (1996) Mental Representation, Conceptual Spaces and Metaphors, Synthese, Volume 106, Number 1 / 1996, 21-47

Gentner, D. (1983) Structure-Mapping: A Theoretical Framework for Analogy. *Cognitive Science* Vol 7 : 155-170.

Gentner, D. (1989) *The mechanisms of analogical learning.* In *Similarity and Analogical Reasoning.* Edited by S. Vosniadou and A. Ortony. 199-241. Cambridge, UK: Cambridge University Press.

Johnson, M.(1987) *The Body in the Mind.* Chicago: The University of Chicago Press. 1987

Goguen J. A. (2004) Compassion and Value-Centered Design in *Virtual, Distributed and Flexible Organisations Studies in Organisational Semiotics,* Springer Netherlands, ISBN 978-1-4020-2161-9 2004. 3-14.

Greenberg S. and Roseman M. (1998) *Using a Room Metaphor to Ease Transitions in Groupware* / Research report 98/611/02, Department of Computer Science, University of Calgary, Calgary, Alberta, Canada, January

Grosjean J., Coquillart S. (1999) The Magic Mirror: A Metaphor for Assisting the Exploration of Virtual Worlds. In *Spring Conference on Computer Graphics*, pp 125—129

Khaled R., Barr P., Noble J., Biddle R. (OrgSem 2004) *System Metaphor in "Extreme Programming"': A Semiotic Approach.* Presented at OrgSem 2004, Portugal

Kocjan, J. (2007) Vidi Windows - A Step towards the Plurality on the Desktop. *Electronic Proceedings of HCII 2007,* Beijing, 2007.

Knight C., Munro M. (2000) Virtual but Visible Software Information Visualization. *Proceedings of IEEE International Conference* on Volume , Issue , 2000 Pp.:198 - 205

Kuhn W. (1993) Metaphors Create Theories For Users. Lecture Notes in Computer Science, Volume 716, 1993 Springer Berlin / Heidelberg 1993, pp. 366-376

Kuhn, W. (1995): 7±2 Questions and Answers about Metaphors for GIS User Interfaces. *Cognitive Aspects of Human-Computer Interaction for Geographic Information Systems.* (Nyerges, T.L., et al., eds.), Series D: Behavioural and Social Sciences, Vol. 83, Dordrecht, The Netherlands, Kluwer Academic Publishers, pp. 113-122.

Kuhn W., Frank A.U.(1991) A Formalization of Metaphors and Image-Schemas in User Interfaces In Cognitive and Linguistic Aspects of Geographic Space. Edited by D. M. Mark and A. U. Frank. *NATO ASI Series.* Dordrecht, The Netherlands: Kluwer Academic Press. 419-434.

Marcello L'Abbate, Matthias Hemmje VIRGILIO (1998)- The Metaphor Definition Tool. Technical Report: rep-ipsi-1998-15 Sankt Augustin: GMD Forschungszentrum Informationstechnik, 1998.

Lakoff, G. (1993). The contemporary theory of metaphor. *Metaphor and Thought.* (2nd ed., pp. 202-251). Cambridge: Cambridge University Press.

Lakoff G., Johnson M. (1980). *Metaphors we live by.* Chicago: University of Chicago Press.

Lee, M.G. & Barnden, J.A. (1999): Mixing metaphors.*In Procs. Symposium on Metaphor, Artificial Intelligence, and Cognition (at AISB'99 Convention, Edinburgh, April 1999),* pp.11-16.

Madsen K. H. (2000) Magic by Metaphors in Designing Augmented Reality Environments *Proceedings of DARE 2000 on Designing augmented reality environments Elsinore, Denmark* , pp.: 167 - 169.

Malloy B.A., Power J.F. (2005) Using a Molecular Metaphor to Facilate Comrehension of 3D Object Diagrams in *IEEE Symposium on Visual Languages and Human-Centric Computing,* Dallas, Texas, USA, September 20-24, 2005, pp.233-240.

Marti S., Seetharam D, Hiroshi Ishii (2001) WeatherTank: A Tangible Interface using

Weather Metaphors December 2001, 2 pp., *technical report media.mit*

Nadin M. (1997) Signs and Systems. Signs and Systems. A Semiotic Introduction to Systems Design, chapter Visible Signs - The Language of Multimedia. University Press, Cambridge, 1997.

Old L. J., Priss U. (2001) Metaphor and Information Flow Proceedings, *Twelfth Midwest Artificial Intelligence and Cognitive Science Conference* (MAICS'2001), Ohio, April 2001, pp. 99-104.

Oliveira O. L. de , M. Cecilia Calani Baranauskas (1998) Interface Understood as Communicating Entities - a Semiotic perspective. Instituto de Computacao da UNICAMP, Relatorio Tecnico IC-98-42

Osawa N. (1998) An Enhanced 3-D Animation Tool for Performance Tuning of Parallel Programs Based on Dynamic Models SPDP 98 Welches Or. USA. pp. 72-80.

Panas Th., Berrigan R., Grundy J. (2003a) A 3D Metaphor for Software Production Visualization *Seventh International Conference on Information Visualization (IV'03)*, pp 314-319.

Panas Th, Lowe W., Assmann U., (2003b) Towards the Unified Visualization Architecture for Reverse Engineering, International *Conference on Software Engineering* Research and Practice - SERP 03, 2003

Pelletier F.J. (2000) A History of Natural Deduction and Elementary Logic Textbooks J. Woods, B. Brown (eds.) Logical Consequence: Rival Approaches and New Studies, Vol. 1. (Oxford: Hermes Science Pubs). pp. 105—138.

Plantings E. (1987) Mental Models and Metaphor Theoretical Issues In Natural Language *Proceedings of the 1987 workshop on Theoretical issues in natural language processing.* Las Cruces, New Mexico, pp.: 185 - 193.

Poupyrev I. (2001) 3D interaction strategies and metaphors http://people.cs.vt.edu/~bowman/3dui.org/course_notes/siggraph2001/metaphors.pdf

Reed D., Scullin W., Tavera L., Shields K., Elford Ch. (1995) Virtual Reality and Parallel Systems Performance Analysis. In *IEEE Computer*, V.28, N 11, (November 1995), pp. 57-67.

Richards S., Barker P., Banerji A., Lamont C., Manji K. (1994) The Use of metaphors in iconic interface design. Intelligent Tutoring Media 1994. Volume 5. Number 2, pp. 73-80.

Roberts J.C. (2000) Display Models - ways to classify visual representations // International Journal of Computer Integrated Design and Construction. V. 2, N 4 (December 2000), pp. 241-250.

Rohrer T (1995 Feelings Stuck in a GUI web: metaphors, image-schemas, and designing the human computer interface, or Metaphors we compute by: bringing magic into interface design. 1995.

Simoff S.J. (2001) Towards the development of environments for designing visualisation support for visual data mining. Proceedings International Workshop on Visual Data Mining, 2001, pp. 93-106.

de Souza C. (2005)The semiotic engineering of human-computer interaction MIT Press, 2005, ISBN-10: 0-262-04220-7, ISBN-13: 978-0-262-04220-8

Stathis K., Sergot M.(1996) Games as a Metaphor for Interactive Systems. *Proceedings of HCI on People and Computers.* XI Springer-Verlag, London, UK , 1996, pp.19 - 33.

Stubblefield W. A. (1998) Patterns of Change in Design Metaphor. A Case Study Conference on Human Factors in Computing Systems. *Proceedings of the SIGCHI conference on Human factors in computing systems.* Los Angeles, California, United States pp.: 73 – 80. 1998

Heiner Stuckenschmidt, Frank van Harmelen, Anita de Waard, Tony Scerri, Ravinder Bhogal, Jan van Buel, and Ian Crowlesmith, Christiaan Fluit, Arjohn Kampman, Jeen Broekstra, Erik van Mulligen (2004) Exploring Large Document Repositories with RDF Technology: *The DOPE Project in IEEE INTELLIGENT SYSTEMS May/June 2004* (Vol. 19, No. 3) pp. 34-40.

Stutzle T., Sajaniemi J. (2005) An Empirical Evaluation of Visual Metaphors in the Animation of Roles of Variables. *Informing Science Journal* Volume 8, 2005, pp.87-100.

Torgny O.(1997) Metaphor - a Working Concept in Proceedings of EAD conference Contextual Design - Design in Contexts, Stockholm, April 1997.

Travers M. D. (1996) Programming with Agents: New metaphors for thinking about computation Submitted to the Program in Media Arts and Sciences, School of Architecture and Planning in partial fulfillment of the requirements for the degree of Doctor of Philosophy at the Massachusetts Institute of Technology, June 1996 http://xenia.media.mit.edu/~mt/thesis/mt-thesis.html

Trushenkova, P. (2007). Local Application Metaphor: How to Create and Use. In *Electronic Proceedings of HCII 2007*, Beijing, 2007.

Tscheligi M., Musil S (1994) An Information Manipulation Environment for Monitoring Parallel Programs. Proceedings of the Workshop on Advanced Visual Interfaces, AVI 1994: Bari, Italy. AVI'94, June 1--4, 1994, Bari, Italy. ACM, 1994. P. 246-248.

Turner M., Fauconnier G. (1995) *Conceptual Integration and Formal Expression Metaphor & Symbolic Activity*, 1995, v10 (n3):183-204

Tversky B., Agrawala M., Heiser J., Lee P., Hanrahan P., Phan D., Stolte Ch., Daniel M.--P. (2007) Cognitive Design Principles for Automated Generation of Visualizations. In *Applied Spatial Cognition; From Research to Cognitive Technology.*Mahwah, N.J. Lawrence Erlbaum Associates, 2007. pp. 53-74.

Tversky B., Morrisony J.B., Betrancourt M. (2002) Animation - can it facilitate. In *Int. J. Human-Computer Studies*, (2002), 57, pp. 247-262.

Weidmann K.-H. (2004) Metaphors, Conceptual Models and Evolutionary Epistemology. *8th ERCIM Workshop "User Interface for All" Workshop Adjunct Proceedings*

Vasev P.A., Pervalov D.S. (2001) One method of visualization of four-dimension sets. *Proceedings of conference "Supercomputing technologies in physical and chemical researches"*, Chernogolovka, Russia, 2001, pp. 32-36. (in Russian.

Zenkin A.A. (1991) *Cognitive Computer Graphics* Moskow, Russia, Nauka. 1991 (in Russian).

4

Non-intrusive Physiological Monitoring for Affective Sensing of Computer Users

Armando Barreto
Florida International University
USA

1. Introduction

The last two decades have, undoubtedly, brought about an amazing revolution in the relationship between computers and their users. This relationship has evolved from an initial state in which the full "burden" of the communication was placed on the shoulders of the user, when early computer models had to be programmed one instruction at a time, toggling individuals switches (which restricted computer usage to very few, highly trained individuals), to the current status, in which, thanks to highly intuitive graphic user interfaces (GUIs), even young children can have some meaningful interaction with the personal computers that are now present at many homes.

Further, it is now possible for users to employ alternative means, such as their speech, or even the direction of their eye gaze, to interact with computers. In cases such as these, it is clear that now the computer has taken over a larger portion of the interaction "burden", as ancillary programs (speech recognition, eye image processing, speech synthesis) will be running in the computer system to match the actions (speaking, shifting the point of gaze on the screen, listening) that the user naturally and almost effortlessly performs during the interaction.

One may think that computers are fast approaching a level of development in which they may recognize our speech, perceive our gaze shifts and speak to us just as well as another human could, to the point of being able to substitute, under certain scenarios, a human counterpart in a dialog. However, it is very likely that, in spite of the efficiency of the recognition of our speech and the fidelity and cadence of the synthesized voice, we would soon realize we are interacting with a machine, as the subtle modulation and adjustments that occur in human-human interaction due to phenomena such as empathy and sympathy would be found missing, substituted instead by mechanistic and often inflexible templates that have been pre-designed for short interaction segments, which disregard what the affective state of the user might be or how it might be changing. In summary, the goal of a human-computer interaction that should be inherently natural and social, following the basics of human-human interaction, as proposed by Reeves & Nass [Reeves & Nass, 1996], has not yet been reached.

2. Affective Computing and its Requirements

In response to the challenge outlined above, a whole new sub-discipline of Human-Computer Interaction has emerged, under the name of Affective Computing. One of its pioneers, Rosalind Picard, describes Affective Computing as 'Computing which relates to, arises from, or deliberately influences emotions' [Picard, 1997]. In analyzing the specific capabilities that a computer would require to fulfil Picard's description, Hudlicka [Hudlicka, 2003] proposed that the following are the key processes involved:

1. Affect Sensing and Recognition
2. User Affect Modelling / Machine Affect Modelling
3. Machine Affect Expression

The interaction of these key processes involved in an Affective Computing implementation is shown in Figure 1.

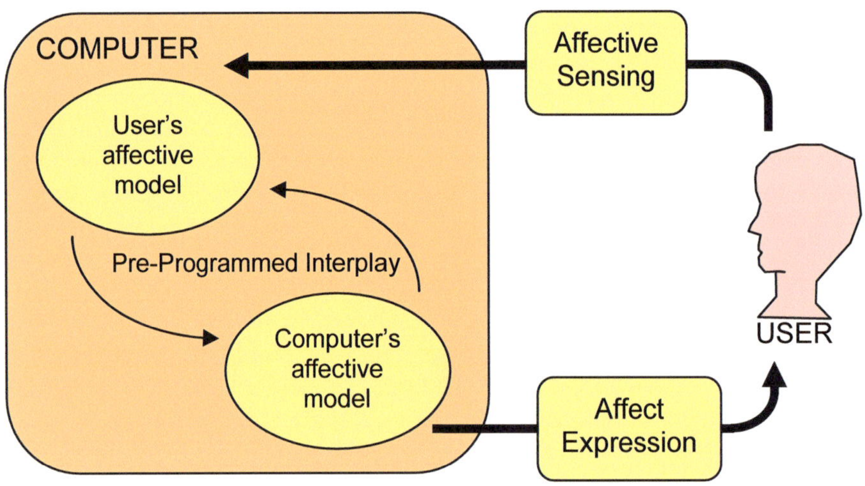

Fig. 1. Simplified diagram showing the interaction between the key processes in affective computing identified in [Hudlicka, 2003].

The interrelation between these basic building blocks for an affective computing system may be understood as follows: Just like humans are capable to "respond" to the affective state of another human by, for example, expressing empathy, an affective machine (affective computer) would first need to assess the affective state of its user, through affective sensing and recognition, in order to determine an appropriate reaction, based on an affective model of the user and its own affective model. The interplay between these models in the machine, for a given affective state identified in the user, and considerations derived from the functional purpose of the specific computing system, will determine what the reaction of the affective machine should be. Then, it is possible that the affective reaction of the machine may need to go beyond the modification of the state of its own (machine) affective model, and it may require that a resulting expression of affect be generated and directed to the user. For example, an affective avatar may be developed to provide support to the user during computer-based tutoring activities. If this affective system were to detect sadness in the user (perhaps caused by being notified of a low score in a quiz), it would update the user's affective model and, if programmed to be supportive, it may also alter its internal affective model to a state of "sadness". Further, the affective machine may then express its empathy with the user by, perhaps, adopting a "sad" facial expression and changing to a soft and slow synthesized speech pattern.

3. Affective Sensing

It is clear, from the previous simplified description and example, that the initial task of affective sensing, i.e., the ability of a computer to remain aware of its user's affective states and transitions, is essential to the practical implementation of the complete affective computing paradigm. In fact, Picard has identified "Sensing and recognizing emotion" as one the key challenges that must be conquered to bring the full promise of affective computing concepts to fruition [Picard, 2003]. However, it is just as clear that the implementation of a real-time, robust mechanism for the assessment of affective states and transitions in a computer user, as considered within a realistic interaction environment, remains an elusive goal.

The difficulty implicit in resolving the challenge of machine-based affective sensing may prompt researchers to actually question the feasibility of such task. Nonetheless, the very observation that has prompted researchers to pursue machine-based recognition of emotions provides evidence of the existence of clues that signal the emergence of affective states in humans, and the transitions between them. That is, we want to endow computers with affective sensing abilities because we wish they did what humans do when we interact with each other. Thus, the fact that humans are capable (according to their individual levels of perception) to "read" affective clues from people that engage them in interaction, indicates that such objective clues exist and that they are readable by an entity that is external to the subject being observed. Therefore, the actual challenge is to select the most appropriate set of clues to watch for, and then to develop systems with enough sensitivity and specificity to detect (and interpret) the occurrence of those clues, with a moderate level of "false detections".

It should also be noted that the goal of providing computers with an awareness of the affective states of their users for the purpose of enhancing the interaction between the user and the computer implies, indirectly, that the means utilized to achieve that assessment should not, simultaneously, be detrimental to the quality of the interaction. Specifically, this consideration limits the monitoring mechanisms that a realistic affective sensing system may involve to achieve its objective, restricting them to those that would not be considered hindrances for an ordinary computer user.

3.1 Affective Sensing Approaches based on Audio, Video or Text

Perhaps due to the preference of avoiding extraordinary devices or components that could be considered to hinder the ordinary activities of the computer user in an abnormal manner, some research groups have placed a strong emphasis on attempting the assessment of user affective states using streams of data that are (more or less) commonly available to many contemporary computing systems. In this sense, it could be considered that many personal computers these days are equipped with a camera that captures video of the face of the user and it can also be considered that a microphone could be continuously recording the speech of the user. Certainly, since much of our interaction with computers is still through text typed on a keyboard, this could also be considered a pre-existing stream of information from the user that could, potentially, be used to attempt the assessment of user affective status.

Zeng et al. [Zeng et al., 2007], provide an interesting survey of relevant systems that use video (typically of the user's face) or audio, or both, to attempt the assessment of the user's affective state. Most vision-driven approaches are based on the known changes that occur in the geometrical features (shapes of eye, mouth, etc.) [Chang et al., 2006] or appearance features (wrinkles, bulges, etc.) [Guo and Dyer, 2005] of the faces of the subjects, according to different affective states. The approaches based on speech monitoring search for affective clues in the explicit components of speech, i.e., in its linguistic aspects and also in the implicit (or paralinguistic) aspects. In this area, the work of Cowie et al. is significant, as it associated acoustic elements to prototypical emotions [Cowie et al., 2001]. Further, some groups have recently begun to explore the coordinated exploitation of audio-visual clues for affective sensing [Fragopanagos & Taylor, 2005].

Liu et al. argue that the utilization of text typed by the user is particularly important, since "the bulk of computer user interfaces today are textually based" [Liu et al., 2003]. They also provide a basic taxonomy for most common textual affect sensing approaches, consisting of four groups. The first group is "Keyword Spotting", in which the presence of words considered affective indicators is detected [Elliot, 1992]. The second group is formed by approaches based on "Lexical Affinity", where more than just obvious affect words are assigned a probabilistic "affinity" for a particular emotion [Valitutti et al., 2004]. The third category is for approaches based on "Statistical Natural Language Processing", in which a machine learning algorithm is trained using a large corpus of affectively annotated texts [Goertzel et al., 2000]. The final category is reserved for highly customized or "Hand-Crafted Models", such as Dyer's "Daydreamer" project [Dyer, 1987].

3.2 Affective Sensing Approaches based on Data Collected Directly From the User

In contrast with the audio, video and text approaches outlined above, other research groups have considered that the changes in the subject's facial expression, or in the words the user speaks or types, are all external manifestations of much deeper changes that the user undergoes as he or she modifies his/her affective state. These research groups have set out to identify the intrinsic physiological modifications that are directly associated with the affective states and transitions that occur in human beings, and have proposed methods for sensing those physiological changes in ways that are non-invasive and non-intrusive for a computer user. The following sections of this chapter explain the rationale for this school of thought, present some of the most relevant implementations of physiological monitoring systems for affective sensing in computer users and preview some of the most innovative approaches in this area of work.

4. Rationale for Physiological Monitoring Towards Affective Sensing

In trying to devise mechanisms that would enable a computer to gain awareness of the affective state of its user through monitoring of his/her physiological signals, one could also ask: How does a human become aware of the emotional state of another? How does one change when affected by an emotional stimulus? Most of us can attest to some clear, involuntary and unmaskable changes in our bodies as reactions to strong emotional stimuli: our hearts may change their pace during climatic moments in a sports event we witness; our hands may turn cold and sweaty when we are scared; we may feel "a rush of blood to the head", when we get into a strong argument. These are not imaginary changes, but instead reflect the perception of an actual reconfiguration of our organism that takes place as a reaction to the psychological stimuli listed.

Just like we are capable of identifying an affective shift in another human being by sensing his/her physiological reconfiguration (e.g., seeing the redness in the face of an angry colleague, feeling the wetness and cold of a fearful person's hand) computers could, potentially, measure these physical quantities from their users and utilize those measurements to assess their affective states. This approach to affective sensing follows the lead of studies on the "detection of deception" (lie detectors), in that it attempts to capitalize on the physiological reconfiguration associated with transitions between affective states. The reconfiguration experimented by a human subject as a reaction to psychological stimuli is controlled by the Autonomic Nervous System (ANS), which innervates many organs and structures all over the body. It is known that the ANS has the ability to promote a state of restoration in the organism, or, if necessary, cause it to leave such a state, favouring physiologic modifications that are useful in responding to the external demands. These changes in physiological variables as a response to manipulations of the psychological or behavioural conditions of the subject are the object of study of Psychophysiology [Hugdhal, 1995] .

The Autonomic Nervous System coordinates the cardiovascular, respiratory, digestive, urinary and reproductive functions according to the interaction between a human being and his/her environment, without instructions or interference from the conscious mind [Martini et al., 2001]. According to its structure and functionality, the ANS is studied as composed of two divisions: The Sympathetic Division and the Parasympathetic Division. The Parasympathetic Division stimulates visceral activity and promotes a state of "rest and repose" in the organism, conserving energy and fostering sedentary "housekeeping" activities, such as digestion [Martini et al., 2001]. In contrast, the Sympathetic Division prepares the body for heightened levels of somatic activity that may be necessary to implement a reaction to stimuli that disrupt the "rest and repose" of the organism. When fully activated, this division produces a "flight or fight" response, which readies the body for a crisis that may require sudden, intense physical activity. An increase in sympathetic activity generally stimulates tissue metabolism, increases alertness, and, from a global point of view, helps the body transform into a new status, which will be better able to cope with a state of crisis. Parts of that re-design or transformation may become apparent to the subject and may be associated with measurable changes in physiological variables. The alternated increases in sympathetic and parasympathetic activation result in a dynamic equilibrium achieved by the ANS, and produce physiological changes that can be monitored through corresponding variables, providing, in principle, a way to assess the affective shifts and states experienced by the subject.

However, the physiological changes caused by sympathetic or parasympathetic activations are not well-focused, and do not impact just a few organs at a time. Instead, parasympathetic and sympathetic activations have effects that tend to be distributed over numerous organs or subsystems, appearing with a subtle character in each of them. So, for example, sympathetic activation (in general terms) promotes the secretion of adrenaline and noradrenaline, inhibits bladder contraction, promotes the conversion of glycogen to glucose, inhibits peristalsis and secretion, dilates the bronchi in the lungs, accelerates the heartbeat, inhibits the flow of saliva, dilates the pupils of the eyes and reduces the peripheral resistance of the circulatory system. In contrast, parasympathetic activation (in general terms) stimulates the release of bile, contracts the bladder, stimulates peristalsis and secretion, constricts the bronchi in the lungs, slows the heartbeat and stimulates the flow of saliva.

The distributed effects of the sympathetic-parasympathetic tug-of-war set up an interesting paradox for the assessment of affective states: There are (potentially) many points where the effects of ANS changes might be observed, yet none of those variables displays strong effects that could unequivocally reveal an affective state or transition. In some instances this ambiguity is further compounded by the fact that the observable physiological variables may be changed by ANS reactions to non-affective stimuli. That is, for example, the case of the pupil diameter, which is known to respond strongly to the amount of light impinging on the retina, through the Pupillary Light Reflex (PLR).

5. Selection of physiological signals that can be monitored non-intrusively

In spite of the fact that the effects of sympathetic and parasympathetic activation, as physiological expressions of affective states and transitions, surface in numerous locations around the body, only a subset of those changes can be monitored by currently available means in ways that can still be considered "non-intrusive" in the context of human-computer interaction. According to this consideration, the following physiological signals, which are likely to be influenced by the ANS, are nonetheless impractical for affective sensing in the context of ordinary computer use:

Electrocardiogram (ECG) - The activity of the heart, directly reflected by the ECG is clearly affected by ANS changes. However, measurement of the ECG would require the application of electrodes to the chest of the computer user, which is an unrealistic assumption, even if the signals could then be transmitted wirelessly, to avoid having the user tethered to the computer.

Electroencephalogram (EEG) - The electrical signals produced by the activity of the brain may be influenced by ANS changes. Similar to the case of ECG, the measurement of the EEG would require the application of multiple electrodes to the scalp of the computer user, which is an impractical pre-condition for most computer users.

Pneumograph - The breathing pattern of a subject is likely to reveal ANS shifts. However, the collection of breathing data would ordinarily require the placement of a respiration transducer (pneumograph) fitted tightly around the chest of the computer user and the transmission (wired or wireless) of the signals to the computer, which is not practical by today's computer usage standards.

From the above remarks, it is clear that the collection of data from a computer user in ways that will not interfere strongly with the activities that are needed to operate the computer is an important limitation in the selection of physiological signals for affective sensing. An interesting alternative that emerged in the 1990's is the collection of physiological signals that can be retrieved by sensors that touch the skin of the user, particularly the skin of the hand. In 1999 Ark, Dryer and Lu [Ark et al., 1999] noticed that

"One obvious place to put the sensors is on the mouse. Through observing normal computer usage (creating and editing documents and surfing the web), people spend approximately 1/3 of their total computer time touching their input device. Because of the incredible amount of time spent touching an input device, we will explore the possibility of detecting emotion through touch"

Although the title of the paper in which these researchers included the above key reflection is "The Emotion Mouse" [Ark et al., 1999], it must be noted that the experiment described in the paper did not actually use a mouse-like device with the sensors. Instead they asked their subjects to hold two contact sensors (galvanic skin resistance and temperature) in their left hands while using a (normal) mouse with their right hands: "Participants were asked to sit in front of the computer and hold the temperature and GSR sensors in their left hand, hold the mouse with their right hand and wore the chest sensor". Through the means described in the previous excerpt, these researchers measured the heart rate (from a chest sensor), the temperature (from a contact sensor), the galvanic skin resistance (from a contact sensor) and assessed the General Somatic Activity (from the movement of the mouse), while the subjects attempted to emulate Ekman's six basic emotions: anger, fear, sadness, disgust, joy and surprise [Ekman and Rosenberg, 1997].

At about the same point in time, it was proposed that the variations observed in the "Blood Volume Pulse" (BVP) signal, which can be recorded from the subject's finger using an infrared photoplethysmograph (PPG), may also be appropriate to evaluate the ANS function [Nitzan et al., 1998]. More recently, it has been confirmed that the BVP signal from a photoplethysmograph may provide basic information about the heart rate and its variability [Giardano et al., 2002] in a non-intrusive form. In a sense, the BVP signal may offer additional information about the ANS function, as it is also affected by the peripheral cardiovascular resistance changes associated with increased sympathetic or parasympathetic activation.

Therefore, three contact-based physiological measurements seem to be viable candidates for the assessment of affective states in computer users, since their corresponding sensors may be incorporated in a customized mouse-type device: The galvanic skin response (GSR), the blood volume pulse (BVP) and the skin temperature (ST).

Additionally, as "webcams" become more and more common in computer systems, it is feasible that, in a near future, the analysis of a fourth physiological signal: the pupil diameter (PD) could be also used for the purpose of affective sensing.

The next section provides additional information about these four physiologic variables and their expected behavior under sympathetic activation. Typically, increased parasympathetic activation would have the opposite effect in each of the variables.

6. Effects of ANS changes in GSR, BVP, ST and PD signals

When a subject experiences stress and nervous tension, associated with increased sympathetic activation, the palms of his/her hands become moist. Increased activity in the sympathetic nervous system will cause increased hydration in the sweat ducts and on the surface of the skin. The resulting drop in skin resistance (increase in conductance) is recorded as a change in electrodermal activity (EDA), also called galvanic skin response, or galvanic skin resistance (GSR). So, in everyday language, electrodermal responses can indicate 'emotional sweating' [Hansen et al., 2003]. The GSR is measured by passing a small current through a pair of electrodes placed on the surface of the skin and measuring the conductivity level. In spite of its simplicity, GSR measurement is considered one of the most sensitive physiological indicators of psychological phenomena. GSR is also one of the signals used in the polygraph or 'lie detector' test. Figure 2 shows a typical increase in the GSR signal, known as a "Skin Conductance Response"

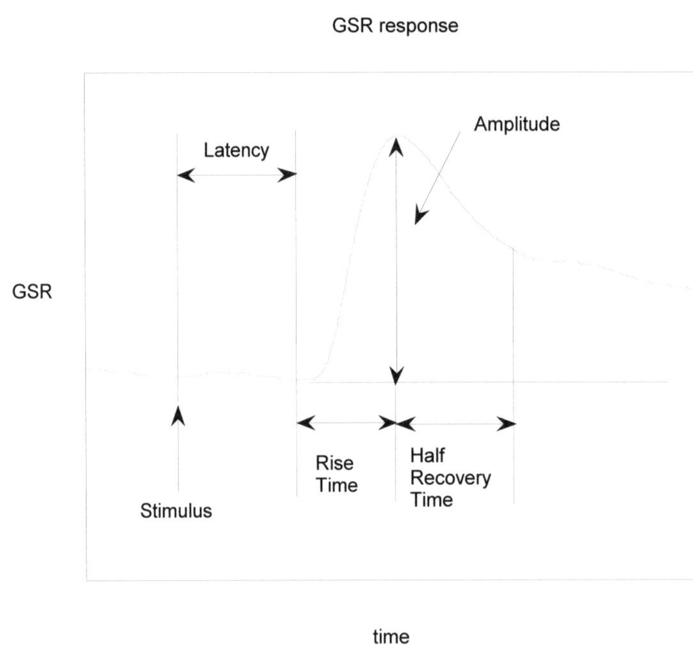

Fig. 2. Example of recorded GSR signal, showing a single Skin Conductance Response (SCR)

The measurements of blood volume pulse (BVP) may be obtained using the technique called photoplethysmography (PPG), to measure the blood volume in skin capillary beds, in the finger. PPG is a non-invasive monitoring technique that relies on the light absorption characteristics of blood, so it does not require costly equipment or specialized personnel. Traditionally, the Blood Volume Pulse has been used to determine the heart rate only. However, if measured precisely enough, it can be used to extract estimates of the heart-rate variability, which is another indicator of user affective state to be considered for human-computer interaction [Dishman et al., 2000; Picard & Klein, 2002]. Figure 3 shows a short segment (3 cardiac cycles) of a BVP signal recorded with a finger photoplethysmograph.

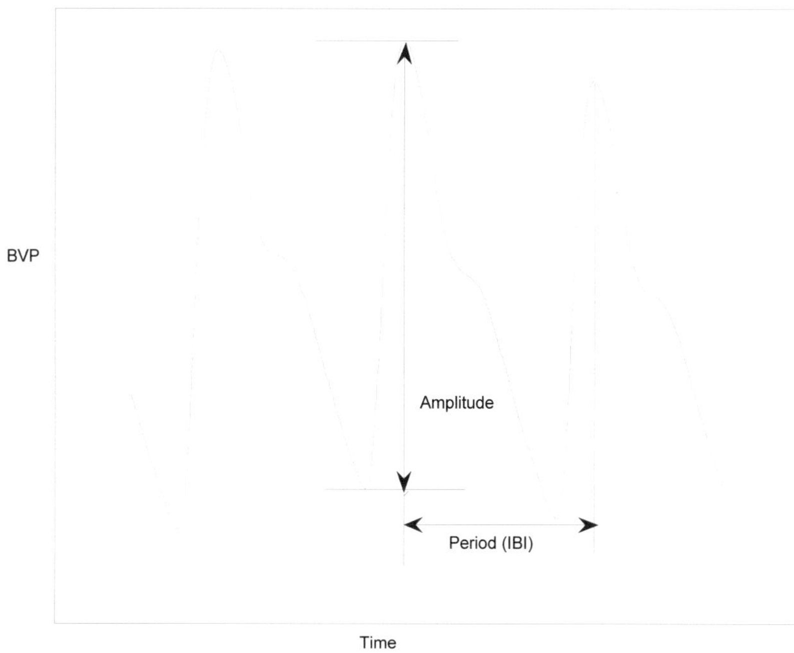

Fig. 3. Example of recorded BVP signal, showing three cardiac cycles (beats)

Changes of acral skin blood flow are also a commonly used indicator for sympathetic reflex response to various stimuli. In response to stimuli that produce sympathetic activation, the blood volume in the finger vessels is expected to decrease due to the vasoconstriction in the hairless areas of the hand but not in the hairy skin of the hand [Krogstad et al., 1995]. If this assumption is true, the finger temperature should transiently decrease according to this effect. A thermistor can be put in contact with the subject's finger to sense the temperature changes. Figure 4 shows an example of the temperature variations that may be observed as a manifestation of affective changes in a subject.

The diameter of the pupil is determined by the relative contraction of two opposing sets of muscles within the iris, the sphincter and dilator pupillae, and is influenced primarily by the amount of light and accommodation reflexes [Beatty & Lucero-Wagoner, 2000]. The pupil of the human eye can constrict and dilate such that its diameter can range from 1.5 mm to more than 9 mm. The pupil dilations and constrictions are governed by the Autonomic Nervous System (ANS) in humans. Several researchers have established that pupil diameter increases due to many factors. Anticipation of solving difficult problems, or even thinking of performing muscular exertion will cause slight increases in pupil size. Hess [Hess 1975] indicated that other kinds of anticipation may also produce considerable pupil dilation. Previous studies have also suggested that pupil size variation is related to cognitive information processing. This, in turn, relates to emotional states (such as frustration or stress) since the cognitive factors play an important role in emotions [Grings & Dawson, 1978]. Partala and Surakka have found that using auditory emotional stimulation, the pupil size variation can be seen as an indication of affective processing [Partala & Surakka, 2003]. There are several techniques available to quantify pupil size variations [Grings & Dawson, 1978]. Currently, automatic instruments, such as infrared eye-tracking systems, can be used to record the eye information including pupil diameter and point of gaze. It is foreseeable that, in the near future, the resolution and quality of "webcams" and personal communication cameras may evolve to a point in which they will be able to assess the pupil diameter of a computer user in a continuous fashion.

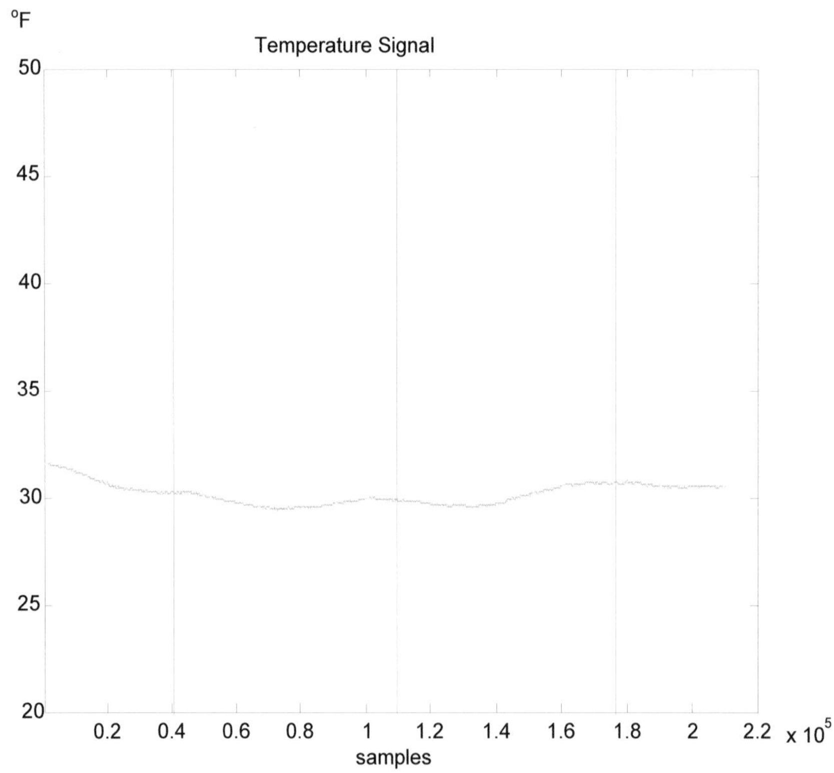

Fig. 4. Example of recorded skin temperature signal. Each vertical line indicates application of a stress stimulus. Total duration of segment shown is approximately 9.72 min (sampling rate was 360 Hz)

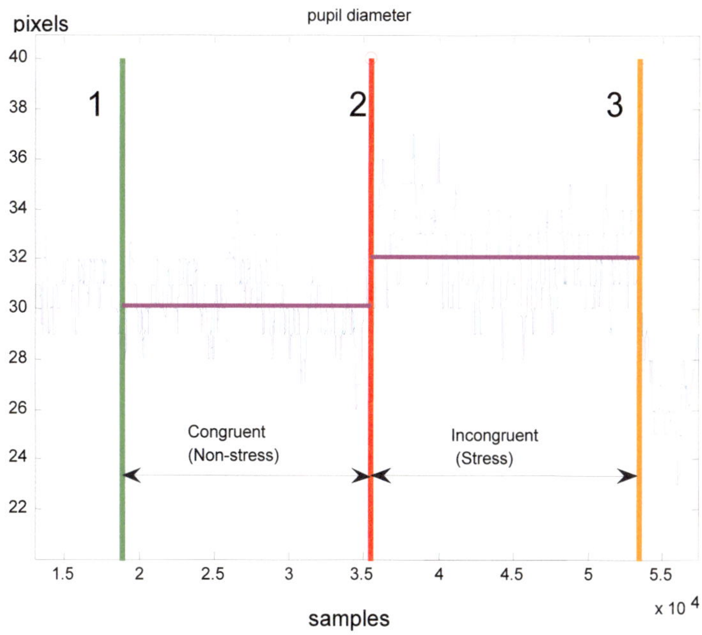

Fig. 5. Example of recorded pupil diameter signal (in camera pixels). A stress stimulus is applied in between vertical lines "2" and "3". Total duration of segment shown is approximately 2.08 min (sampling rate was 360 Hz)

7. Affective Sensing Systems Based on Physiological Monitoring

Several research groups have attempted the development of emotion recognition systems based on the analysis of physiological signals. The Affective Computing group of Dr. Rosalind Picard at the Media Laboratory of The Massachusetts Institute of Technology (MIT) has explored different approaches for affective sensing, which include the monitoring of physiological signals, since the mid-1990's [Picard, 1997; Picard et al., 2001; Picard & Klein, 2002].

One of the early efforts of this group, with respect to the monitoring of physiological signals for affective sensing, was reported in the paper by Healey and Pickard [Healey & Picard, 1998]. In this effort, four physiological variables were collected from a single subject over an extensive period of time (32 days). In every session the subject would be asked to "experience and intentionally express eight affective states" when directed by a prompting system. The eight emotion states used were: no-emotion, anger, hate, grief, (platonic) love, romantic love, joy and reverence. The physiological signals monitored were the electromyogram (EMG) from the masseter muscle; the blood volume pulse measured with a finger photoplethysmograph; the skin conductance measured between the index and middle fingers of the left hand and the respiration pattern measured with a Hall-effect sensor strapped around the diaphragm. In this preliminary effort, Healey and Pickard derived eleven features from these physiological variables and attempted the discrimination of the 8 emotions from the features using a Fisher linear discriminant projection. With this initial approach, the authors were not able to separate (classify) individual emotions, but were able to distinguish six groups of three emotions each with correct classification levels ranging between 75% and 82%.

In 2001, Picard, Vyzas and Healey [Picard et al., 2001] published new results from more advanced analysis on the same type of data (also long-term recordings, from a single subject, of the same four physiological measurements, obtained while the subject expressed the same eight emotions). In this new report the researchers used an additional signal labeled "heart rate signal, H", said to be "derived from the blood volume pressure signal, B, by a nonlinear transformation performed automatically by the ProComp sensing system." The analysis involved the calculation of six features from each one of the five physiological signals (four measured directly and "H"): Mean of the raw signal; standard deviation of the raw signal; mean absolute value of the first differences of the raw signal; mean absolute value of the first differences of the normalized signal; mean absolute value of the second differences of the raw signal; and mean absolute value of the second differences of the normalized signal. In addition to these 30 features, these researchers also derived 10 "physiology-dependent" features (f1 - f10), for a total of 40 features. The classification approaches included the Sequential Floating Forward Search (SFFS) and Fisher Projection (FP), as well as a combination of both (SFFS-FP), which proved to be the most successful, achieving an overall classification accuracy of 81.25%, which consisted of only 30 misses in a test set of 20 instances of each of the 8 emotions (160 test instances in total).

In 2004 Kim and colleagues [Kim et al., 2004] reported the development of an emotion recognition system based on short-term monitoring of physiological signals from multiple (5) subjects. This system monitored four physiological signals: The electrocardiogram (ECG), measured between two electrodes ("from both upper arms"), the blood volume pulse obtained through a finger photoplethysmograph (PPG), the skin temperature measured from the ring finger of the left hand and the galvanic skin resistance, also known as electrodermal activity (EDA), measured between the index and middle fingers of the right hand. Although two different cardiovascular sensors were used, the ECG and PPG signals were used to study the same aspects: heart rate and heart rate variability (HRV). In this work, only a limited number of features were extracted form the original signals. The ECG signal was used to determine the basic heart rate by R-peak detection. The resulting "spike train" was transformed into a time series labeled by the authors "HRV time series". They studied the mean and standard deviation of the HRV time series, as well as its spectral composition in the low frequency (LF) band (0.03 Hz - 0.15 Hz) and high frequency (HF) band (0.15 Hz - 0.4 Hz). From the EDA signal, this group identified the occurrence of characteristic features called "Skin Conductance Responses" (SCRs) and used the frequency of their occurrence (in 50-second signal segments), the mean value of SCR amplitudes, their duration and the DC level of the EDA signal as features. Only two features were extracted from the skin temperature signal segments: its maximum and mean values. These features were then analyzed with a Support Vector Machine classifier, and this group reported a correct classification ratio of 78.4% in identifying instances of "sadness", "anger" and "stress", and 61.8% in identifying instances of "sadness", "anger", "stress" and "surprise".

In 2003, Barreto and Zhai [Barreto & Zhai, 2003] reported on the development of an instrumentation setup for the monitoring of four physiological signals towards the determination of the assessment of affective states in computer users. The four signals chosen for non-invasive and non-intrusive monitoring of subjects while they performed a specific computer task were: The galvanic skin resistance measured between two fingers of the left hand; the blood volume pulse measured through a finger photoplethysmograph worn by the subjects in the ring finger of their left hands, the skin temperature measured with a integrated circuit temperature sensor attached to the thumb of the left hand of the users and the pupil diameter, obtained as a secondary measurement from a desk-mounted infrared eye gaze tracking system. This setup was capable of recording the GSR, BVP and ST signals, as well as additional time marker channels at 360 samples/second, for each signal. The pupil diameter was obtained as numerical values (expressed in pixels of the eye image captured by the eye gaze tracking system), every 1/60 of a second. These researchers used the monitoring setup to observe variations of BVP, GSR, ST and DP when the subject was presented with alternating neutral and stressing stimulation delivered as sequences of "congruent" and "incongruent" Stroop test trials. In a Strop test trial the subject is presented with a word naming a color, written with a color font, and he /she is asked to identify verbally (or, in the case of a computerized version of the test, click on the screen button corresponding to) the font color [Stroop, 1935]. In a "congruent" trial the word presented spells the name of the color font used. In contrast, in an "incongruent" trial the color spelled by the word is different from the font color used, which elicits a mild level of mental stress in the subject [Renaud & Blondin, 1997]. Zhai and colleagues verified that the increased sympathetic activation during "incongruent" Stroop segments produced characteristic modifications on the four signals monitored. They derived a total of 11 features from the physiological signals monitored and used those features to attempt the differentiation of non-stress (Stroop congruent) and stress (Stroop incongruent) segments , by means of three different classifiers: A Naïve Bayes classifier; a Decision Tree classifier, and a Support Vector Machine classifier [Zhai et al., 2005; Zhai & Barreto, 2006]. These researchers found that the Support Vector Machine classifier performed best for the classification task, achieving a correct classification percentage of 90.10% [Barreto et al., 2007a].

8. Future Research Direction

An additional finding of Zhai and colleagues was that if the pupil diameter signal was removed from the ensemble of physiological signals monitored in their experiments, the performance of the classifiers, even the Support Vector Machine, would decrease significantly (to 58.85%), while the classification performance would remain essentially unaltered if, for example, the skin temperature signal were to be removed from consideration [Barreto et al., 2007a]. This observation has prompted further study of the potential of the pupil diameter signal, specifically, to determine the affective states or transitions of a computer user. Barreto et al. [Barreto et al., 2007b] were able to verify that the populations of PD values measured before and after a transition from a non-stress (congruent Stroop) experimental segment to a stress (incongruent Stroop) experimental segment were statistically different. Furthermore, these researchers also compared the Receiver Operator Characteristic (ROC) curves of individual features derived from the (mean) PD signal, the ST (mean slope) signal, the mean value of the BVP signal and the mean period from the BVP signal, considered as single-variable detectors, and found that the detector derived from the PD signal exhibited clearly superior characteristics (the area under the ROC curve was 0.96, versus 0.65 for the second-best detector) [Barreto et al., 2007c]. The indications of potential use of the pupil diameter measurement as a strong contributor to the identification of affective states and shifts in computer users is exciting because this signal is not currently considered in many instrumental setups developed for affective sensing purposes. As such, it may very well represent an additional source of information that could be very useful in future studies of affective sensing. It should be noted, however, that all the studies described above which measured the variations of pupil diameter were performed in controlled environments, in which the ambient illumination and the light intensity emanating from the computer display were kept reasonably constant, by design, to minimize the unwanted influence of the pupillary light reflex (PLR) on the measured pupil diameter values. The practical application of the pupil diameter measurement for affective sensing purposes depends on the emergence of signal processing techniques that would be capable to differentiate pupil diameter changes caused by PLR from those derived from affective responses in the subject. The definition of such signal processing techniques is currently an open research topic.

9. Conclusion

It is clear, from the considerations briefly outlined in this chapter, that the definition of robust, non-intrusive methods for affective sensing in human-computer interactions is still an open challenge, which must be conquered as an essential pre-requisite to the fulfillment of the promise of Affective Computing concepts and their widespread application in everyday computing. While the goal of robust affective sensing may seem distant, it is also evident that a tremendous amount of progress has been made in the past two decades in many of the aspects that will necessarily be involved in a viable solution. Our understanding of affective states and their correlates to physiological changes has evolved, the sensing mechanisms used to monitor physiological variables have improved, the signal and image processing techniques used to analyze the physiological signals from the computer user continue to be enhanced, and the computing power that can be utilized to implement them (potentially in real-time) increases continuously. Additionally, research groups are now contemplating the use of multi-modal collaborative approaches in which the strengths of physiological monitoring can be combined with other sources of information about the user's affect available to the computer, such as face expression recognition and textual assessment of affect. When all of this is brought into consideration, it is foreseeable that practical solutions to the affective sensing problem might be found in a near future.

10. References

Ark, W.; Dryer, D. and Lu, D. (1999). The Emotion Mouse. *Proceedings of the 8th International Conference on Human-Computer Interaction*. Vol. I, Ergonomics and User Interfaces, pp. 818-823.

Barreto, A., & Zhai, J.(2003) Physiologic Instrumentation for Real-time Monitoring of Affective State of Computer Users, *WSEAS Transactions on Circuits and Systems*, Vol. 3, Issue 3., pp. 496-501.

Barreto, A.; Zhai, J. & Adjouadi M. (2007a) Non-intrusive Physiological Monitoring for Automated Stress Detection in Human-Computer Interaction, *Lecture Notes in Computer Science* Vol. 4796, pp. 29–38, Springer-Verlag.

Barreto, A.; Zhai, J, Rishe, N. & Gao, Y. (2007b) Measurement of Pupil Diameter Variations as a Physiological Indicator of the Affective State in a Computer User, *Biomedical Sciences Instrumentation*, Vol. 43, pp. 146-151.

Barreto, A.; Zhai, J., Rishe, N. & Gao, Y. (2007c), Significance of Pupil Diameter Measurements for the Assessment of Affective State in Computer Users, in Advances and Innovations in *Systems, Computing Sciences and Software Engineering*, K. Elleithy, ed., Springer, (ISBN: 978-1-4020-6263-6). Dordrecht, The Netherlands, pp. 59 - 64.

Beatty, J. & Lucero-Wagoner, B. (2000) The Pupillary System. In: *Handbook of Psychophysiology*. J.T. Cacioppo, L.G. Tassinary, and G.G. Berntson, editors. pp. 142-162. Cambridge University Press

Chang, Y.; Hu, C.; Feris, R. & Turk, M. (2006), Manifold Based Analyis of Facial Expression, *J. Image and Vision Computing*, Vol. 24, No. 6, pp. 605-614.

Cowie, R.; Douglas-Cowie, E.; Tsapatsoulis, N.; Votsis, G.; Kollias, S,; Fellenz, W. & Taylor, J. (2001). Emotion recognition in human-computer interaction. *IEEE Signal Processing Magazine* 18(1): 32-80.

Dishman, R.K.; Nakamura, Y.; Garcia, M.E.; Thompson, R.W.; Dunn, A.L. & Blair, S.N. (2000) Heart rate variability, trait anxiety, and perceived stress among physically fit men and women. *International Journal of Psychophysiology* 37:121-133

Dyer, M. (1987). Emotions and their computations: Three Computer Models. *Cognition and Emotion* 1(3): 323-347.

Ekman, P. & Rosenberg, E. (1997) *What the Face Reveals: Basic and Applied Studies of Spontaneous Expression using the Facial Action Coding System (FACS)*, New York: Oxford University Press.

Elliott, C. (1992). *The affective reasoner: a process model of emotions in a multi-agent system*, Doctoral Dissertation, Northwestern University.

Fragopanagos, N. and Taylor, J. (2005). Emotion recognition in human-computer interaction. Neural Networks 18(4): 389-405.

Giardano, N.; Lehrer, P & Edelberg, R. (2002) Comparison of finger plethysmograph to ECG in the measurement of heart rate variability, *Psychophysiology*, v.39, pp. 246–253.

Goertzel, B.; Silverman, K.; Hartley, C.; Bugaj, S. & Ross, M. (2000). The Baby Webmind Project. *Proceedings of the AISB'00 Symposium*, The Society for the Study of Artificial Intelligence and the Simulation of Behaviour.

Grings, W.W. & Dawson, M.E. (1978) *Emotions and Bodily Responses A psychophysiological Approach*. Academic Press.

Guo, G. & Dyer, C. (2005). Learning from examples in the small sample case -- face expression recognition. *IEEE Transactions on Systems, Man and Cybernetics - Part B* 35(3): 477--488.

Hansen, A.L.; Johnsen, B.H.& Thayer, J.F. (2003) Vagal influence on working memory and attention. *International Journal of Psychophysiology* 48:263-274

Healey, J. & Picard, R. (1998) Digital processing of affective signals. *Proceedings of the 1998 IEEE International Conf. on Acoustics, Speech and Signal Processing*, pp. 3749-3752.

Hess, E. H., (1975), *The Tell-Tale Eye: How your eyes reveal hidden thoughts and emotions*, Van Nostrand Reinhold Co.

Hudlicka, E. (2003). To feel or not to feel: the role of affect in human-computer interaction. *International Journal of Human-Computer Studies* 59(1-2): 1-32.

Hugdahl, K.(1995) *Psychophysiology: The Mind-Body Perspective,* Harvard University Press, Cambridge, MA.

Kim, K.H.; Bang, S.W. & Kim, S.R. (2004) Emotion Recognition System using Short-term Monitoring of Physiological Signals. *Medical & Biological Engineering & Computing* 42:419-427

Krogstad, A.L.; Elam, M.; Karlsson, T. & Wallin, B.G. (1995) Arteriovenous anastomoses and the thermoregulatory shift between cutaneous vasoconstrictor and vasodilator reflexes. *J. Auton. Nerv. Syst.* 53:215-222

Liu, H.; Lieberman, H. & Selker, T. (2003) A model of textual affect sensing using real-world knowledge. *Proceedings of the 8th international conference on intelligent user interfaces.* Miami, Florida, USA, ACM, pp. 125-132.

Martini, F.H.; Ober W.C.; Garrison C.W.; Welch, K.; & Hutchings, R. T.(2001) *Fundamentals of Anatomy & Physiology,* 5th Edition, Prentice-Hall, Upper Saddle River, NJ.

Nitzan, M.; Babchenko, A.; Khanokh, B. & Landau, D. (1998) The variability of the photoplethysmographic signal - a potential method for the evaluation of the autonomic nervous system, *Physiological Measurement,* Volume 19, pp. 93 - 102.

Partala, T. & Surakka, V. (2003) Pupil size variation as an indication of affective processing. *International Journal of Human-Computer Studies* 59:185-198

Picard, R. (1997). *Affective computing,* MIT Press.

Picard, R.; Vyzas , E. & Healey, J. (2001) Toward Machine Emotional Intelligence: Analysis of Affective Physiological State. *IEEE Transactions on Pattern Analysis and Machine Intelligence* 23(10): 1175-1191.

Picard, R. & Klein, J. (2002) Computers that recognize and respond to user emotion: theoretical and practical implications. *Interacting with Computers* 14:141-169

Picard, R. (2003) Affective computing: challenges. *Int. J. Hum.-Comput. Stud.* 59, pp. 55-64.

Reeves, B. & Nass, C. (1996) *The Media Equation.* Cambridge Univ. Press

Renaud, P.& Blondin, J.-P. (1997) The stress of Stroop performance: physiological and emotional responses to color-word interference, task pacing, and pacing speed. *International Journal of Psychophysiology* 27:87-97

Stroop, J.R. (1935) Studies of the interference in serial verbal reactions. *Journal of Experimental Psychology* 18:643-662.

Valitutti, A,; Strapparava, C. & Stock, O. (2004) Developing Affective Lexical Resources. PsychNology *Journal* 2(1): 61-83.

Zeng, Z.; Pantic, M; Roisman, G. & Huang, T. (2007). A survey of affect recognition methods: audio, visual and spontaneous expressions. *Proceedings of the 9th international conference on Multimodal interfaces.* Nagoya, Aichi, Japan, ACM, pp. 126-133.

Zhai J., & Barreto A. (2006) Stress Detection in Computer Users Through Noninvasive Monitoring of Physiological Signals, *Biomedical Science Instrumentation,* vol. 42, pp. 495-500.

Zhai, J., Barreto, A., Chin, C., & Li, C. (2005) User Stress Detection in Human-Computer Interactions, *Biomedical Sciences Instrumentation,* Vol. 41, pp. 277-282.

5

Mobile Design Guidelines in the Context of Retail Sales Support

Rainer Blum, Karim Khakzar & Werner Winzerling
Fulda University of Applied Sciences
Germany

1. Introduction

Mobile technology is an inherent part of today's private and professional life in the developed nations, with mobile telephony at the forefront. Optimization of business processes with mobile technology presents a topic of interest for enterprises for several years focusing primarily on the sales force and logistics (Wichmann & Stiehler, 2004).
Though still rare in practice, by supporting the duties of the retail sales staff in their daily personal sales activities, mobile technology is assumed to generate added value in the retail context for customers, sales staff and shop owners as well. Individual innovative companies still test these techniques, for example the METRO Group with its "Future Store Initiative". But, also in a broader context and independently of today's enormous diffusion of mobile technology, mobile design still remains an area of active research.
In this regard, employing mobile devices for the retail sales support at the point of sale was a subject in the research project IntExMa, "Interactive Expert System for Made-to-measure Clothing" at Fulda University of Applied Sciences. In doing so, usability was regarded as a fundamental quality criteria.
Many standards, guidelines and scientific papers document the existing usability knowledge in the field of HCI. While this expertise has predominantly evolved in the desktop computer domain over a period of several decades, interface design for mobile services is still regarded to be "in its infancy" (USE-ME.GOV, 2004). Yet, only a few scientific and hardly any generally accepted guides for mobile interface design exist. These are naturally not based on such a broad basis of experiences than in the desktop domain.
Gong & Tarasewich propose a range of usability guidelines for the mobile devices domain (Gong & Tarasewich, 2004). They start from Shneidermans & Plaisants eight "Golden Rules", implicitly termed desktop-oriented, and base them on their own and other research findings. Many other studies concentrate exclusively on the optimized display of web pages on handheld devices, e.g. (Kärkkäinen & Laarni, 2002). The two major companies offering operating systems for handhelds, Palm Source and Microsoft, have each published their own more or less product specific guidelines (see below).

1.1 Objectives and Significance

Facing the heap of well-established desktop-descending guidelines, standards and recommendations, like e.g. the outstanding ISO 9241, one objective of this work is to answer

the question if these resources are also relevant and applicable for the mobile context. In addition, existing mobile guidelines are also taken into account.
Putting it all together, a compilation of design principles is proposed, each rationally explained and detailed with a range of exemplary, more concrete rules and clarifying examples. Thus, we aim to contribute to the state-of-the-art by interpreting existing, mostly desktop-oriented guidelines under a new point of view. In doing so, the lack in the mobile interface design domain shall be attenuated.
All recommendations are specifically shaped for the context of use at hand: support of personnel selling activities at the point of sale with handheld technology in the hands of the sales persons.

1.2 The IntExMa Sales Support System

The basic concept of the IntExMa system is to effectively support in-store, "real world" sales processes with e-commerce technology ("virtual shopping"), thus generating added value for customers, sales staff and shop owners. Made-to-measure shirts constitute the particular sales context to which the system is adapted. According to the customers' body measures, a 3D figure is automatically generated and dressed in the desired shirt applying a highly realistic physical simulation. Customers are able to use a subset of the system's interactive features via a simple custom-made knob and buttons interface.
Via a PDA, the salesperson has mobile access to the entire functionality of the system: electronic product catalogue with capacious ordering functions, customer data, and 3D scene interaction. This includes interaction with the stationary display showing the "virtual try-on" via the PDA. Within this scope we investigated to what extent mobile devices can support the duties and responsibilities of the retail sales staff in their daily personal selling activities.

2. Method

Several distinct steps were taken in order to gather the necessary theoretical basis to be able to compile the desired specific collection of design guidelines. They were chosen following ISO 13407 (ISO 13407, 1999).
First, the specific characteristics of handheld computing and the PDA device class were analyzed and compared with the desktop computing domain. Thereby, the manifold possibilities concerning interaction techniques and forms became apparent but also the limitations to be considered were diagnosed. Then, a detailed context of use analysis was conducted and accordant requirements were formulated.
Apart from that, some of the most important and accepted usability standards, guidelines and scientific papers were analyzed in order to assess which insights are also valid for the mobile domain and can be transferred into the present context.
Taking these results as a theoretical basis, finally, the desired compilation of design principles, concrete rules and clarifying examples was developed.
This project specific standard was applied for the development of mobile applications for the aforementioned IntExMa system. Usability evaluation of these implementations will imply also the indispensable evaluation of the developed guidelines.

3. Context of Use and Requirements

The context of use analyses was conducted in-depth following ISO 13407 (ISO 13407, 1999). Some major points are reproduced in the following.
Sales support as a central activity is characterized by a broad spectrum of tasks aiming to enhance sales. This study focuses on the domains of the retail business not dominated by self-service but where consultation-intensive products are sold and the customers are served by well-trained personnel. This personal selling is primarily characterized by a direct communication between customer and sales person.

3.1 User Characteristics, Tasks, Environment

Sales process support in the retail business is characterized by a high heterogeneity concerning users' respectively salespersons' characteristics - gender, age, education, experiences, knowledge, etc.
Skills and knowledge about the business processes and methods to be supported can be estimated as comprehensive. Furthermore, experiences with PDA usage are expected to be very low, but to substantially rise with the usage period. Previous knowledge concerning interaction techniques and modes may exist but can't be assumed for all users. Using a portable touch screen of this size is certainly novel for most of them. A short, e.g. one-day training on the application is expected.
Tasks groups to be supported by the mobile application are informing and giving advice, utilizing and administering customer data, processing payments, providing service and sales preparation and follow-up. The present context of use is characterized by a "hierarchy of tasks" like described by Gorlenko & Merrick (Gorlenko & Merrick, 2003): During interaction, the tasks external to the device are in the centre of interest while system-internal tasks, e.g. entering a search keyword, accrue additionally. Also, the social environment only provides minimum freedom for interaction with the mobile device, as mostly the customer is in the focus of the attention of the personnel.

3.2 Resulting Requirements

Following the results of the context of use analysis, an important requirement is to design the system for users with diverse experiences, skills and knowledge concerning information technology and to cater for novices as well as for "power users". In order to reduce the acceptance threshold users must be enabled to acquire basic functionality by themselves.
Seamless integration into the existing environment supports the flexible functionality changeover of sales persons during work.
The customer must be taken into account as "indirect user" constantly present during service and with needs taking the centre stage of personnel selling. Therefore, the demand of resources, e.g. of attention or time, of the application should be as small as possible. One-hand or, even better, hands-free operation of the device is desirable in order to keep interacting with real objects as much as possible.
The users should - only to a small extent - have to „make place" for the device operation. Their imposed mental workload should be kept low, while simultaneously staying informed about the current process status, despite frequent interruptions.
Also, the sales person should have the possibility to present output information visually to the customer, e.g. if the "spoken word" is not sufficient due to product complexity or lack of the completed product (e.g. mass customization).

The mobile interactive system must provide required information on the spot and in the desired level of detail with flexible search and meaningful comparison options. In addition, a methodical and controlled proceeding of the sales person must be supported and ensured. Where possible, interaction with physical objects, e.g. via product bar codes, as "information bearers" should be possible, in order to avoid unnecessary searching in electronic resources and to further enhance integration with the real environment.

4. Existing Guidelines

A selection of the most important representatives of desktop-related standards and guidelines was analyzed concerning their relevance and their transferability for the handheld/PDA domain.

The most well-known user interface design standard is probably ISO 9241 (ISO 9241, 1993-2002). Parts 2, 10 and 11 can be fully applied. In part 12 only the addressed window technique is subject to severe limitations on the handheld platform. User guidance in part 13 is absolutely relevant, with reservations concerning the extent and design of online help due to limited display space. Part 14 has relevance, though only small-sized menu dialogues make sense on PDAs. Command dialogues in part 15 are hardly relevant, unless it comes to speech control. Many recommendations for the direct manipulation concept in part 16 are applicable though the graphical representation and the manipulation features of objects and their states should be much less comprehensive than on the desktop. Furthermore, direct manipulation beyond basic interaction (e.g. dragging objects) demands to much concentration from the user to be reasonably applied in the mobile context (Kristoffersen & Ljungberg, 1999). Part 17 is again mostly of high relevance for the handheld domain. Some of the recommendations imply a cursor. Though existent for form fields and text documents, mouse pointers are not standard. They may be activated in certain operating systems or simulated by applications.

ISO 14915 (ISO 14915, 2002-2003) is basically relevant for handheld design, due to similarity to ISO 9241 though it must be considered that the multimedia capabilities of these devices do not approximate those of multimedia desktop computers.

The analyzed "Ten Usability Heuristics" by Nielsen (Nielson, 1994) and eight „Golden Rules" by Shneiderman & Plaisant (Shneiderman & Plaisant, 2004) are valid for handheld design, as they are independent of specific technologies and device form factors. They must be individually interpreted in order to apply them practically in a specific context of use.

The basic principles for user interface design and many of the more concrete guidelines and rules presented in the "desktop-descending" IBM Common User Access (CUA) Guidelines, refer to (IBM Corporation) for a condensed presentation, in the Microsoft Official Guidelines for User Interface Developers and Designers (Microsoft Corp, 1999) and in the Apple Human Interface Guidelines (Apple Computer, Inc., 2005) are applicable for the present setting.

The Windows Mobile Guidelines (Microsoft Corp., 2005) and the Palm OS User Interface Guidelines (PalmSource, Inc., 2003) are the only available more comprehensive mobile guidelines. Here, Microsoft does not provide basic design principles but some more general guidelines which are converted into very practical Windows Mobile specific recommendations. The Palm starts with basic principles, moves on to concrete design guidelines and ends with detailed technical layout guidelines. Main focus from the point of view of functionality is the Personal Information Manager (PIM) domain, e.g. administrating contact details, dates, tasks, notes or even documents. So, practical applicability is ensured in both cases. Both compilations contain relevant information also for the context of use at hand.

5. Specific Design Guidelines Compilation

Based on the insights and recommendations in the previous chapters, seventeen design guidelines are presented in the following.
Every principle consists of a short title, followed by a more detailed wording as a complete sentence in the first paragraph. As interpreting and applying these principles first requires to fully understand their logical foundation, the second paragraph contains accordant explanations. Then, for lack of space, one exemplary of several rules is listed, that focus specific design questions. The reproduction of concrete design examples and the listing of references to existing standards and guidelines is abandoned here. In the full research report (Blum, 2006) this serves the underpinning of the scientific significance of each principle and its corresponding rules as well as pointer to further resources.

5.1 Choose "Low-absorbing" Interaction Techniques

Design the system in such way, that its use occupies the user's manual resources and sensory functions (vision, hearing, perception in general) as little as possible.
Interaction with an application draws upon the sense of the user and requires manual activity: The system's output has to be perceived visually, acoustically, potentially also tactilely, processed in the brain and subsequently converted into motor reactions. Resources tied up in this process are at the same time required for the primary tasks of the sales person in the sales process support. Due to the importance of non-verbal communication for the personnel selling, the visual senses are highly significant.
An exemplary rule is to make the operation of the system possible without the usually obligatory pen and, even better, with only one hand.

5.2 Design on the Basis of the Real Tasks

When designing the user interface, refer primarily to the requirements of the tasks to be completed in the real environment and the requirements of the context of use.
Thereby, the components of the user interface shall "take a back seat" in the perception of the user. An additional charge of the sales person with system-internal tasks during the customer dialogue should be preferably avoided. Also, frustration by reason of inability to tackle tasks adequately is counteracted.
To choose terminology, symbols and metaphors according to the real tasks and, as such, to build on existing knowledge of the user, is one concrete rule.

5.3 Design for Short, Frequently Interrupted Tasks

Map tasks in such a way that the separate steps may be processed in a flexible order and action sequences may be interrupted and resumed later.
The hardly to plan course of a customer dialogue demands for a variable but thorough completion of the separate work tasks (task sequence) and a spontaneous and flexible response to the remarks and requests of the customer. The interactive system needs to show

the same degree of flexibility while ensuring a well-structured advancement and an exhaustive task processing.
One exemplary corresponding rule is to provide the processing status of a task "at a glance", concretely by presenting all necessary information in one screen form and indicating data fields that are already treated.

5.4 Strive for Consistency

Question all user interface components whether they can be designed consistent to the experience of the sales personnel, other employed applications and among each other.
Consistency enables the users to apply existing knowledge and to quickly build a mental model of the application's functional concept. They come across familiar objects and training period can be reduced. Thereby, the user interface should furthermore be operated intuitively and without surplus mental load and additional concentration effort. Consistent positioning of controls enables the salesperson to operate the application "blindly" (without concentrating on the display).
An exemplary rule is to rarely make exceptions but in situations that justify their use - and to design them coherently.

5.5 Cater for Easy and Intuitive Interaction

Give interactive elements a design as simple as possible and make sure, that the user intuitively detects how to interact with them.
Controls, whose operation is apparent should result in a faster learnability and a lower mental workload for the user. If, in addition, the interaction techniques are straightforward, the application should demand less attention from the user.
Exemplary rule: For text fields, make clear which kind of input is expected.

5.6 Offer Instantaneous, Informative Feedback

Provide a feedback for every interaction, that, with its "magnitude", reflects appropriately the significance and frequency of occurrence of the particular action and that considers the context of use.
Prompt reaction to the user's interaction supports a sense of controllability. On the one hand, users are informed, that their input was recognized, on the other hand the "new" system state is communicated. Panic, that may occur due to too long response times when pressure to perform is high, can be avoided. A suitable degree of clarity and demand of attention must be ascertained.
A rule is to acknowledge every interaction with a prompt feedback.

5.7 Provide Simple and Unambiguous Navigation

Design navigation instruments in such a way, that the user can answer the questions "Where am I, how did I get here?", "What can I do here?", "Where can I go next?" at all times.
Due to frequent interruptions, the salespersons must be enabled to recognize at a glance at which position in the task sequence they are currently. Also, it must be transparent how

they got there (or what the previous steps were) and which options to proceed are offered, i.e. which elements are available for follow-up interaction.
For example, an option for navigating backward and, if applicable, forward in a list of lastly visited dialogue pages should be provided.

5.8 Cater for Effective, Usable Content

Prepare content (product data, customer data etc.) and structure the design in such a way, that an effective handling by the salespersons is ensured and that, at the same time, their limited attention is considered.
Parts of the information taken from the PDA is passed on to the customer, partly it is needed for processing the more formal steps of the sales process. Preparation and reproduction of information must be oriented along this process and has to consider that the salespersons have to pay the bigger part of their attention to the customer.
One corresponding rule is to make it possible to output content otherwise than via the PDA display (e.g. graphically as product comparison chart), in order to communicate it to the customer not only verbally.

5.9 Design Well-defined Dialogues

Structure tasks in small action groups with obvious start and end; inform the user explicitly about their successful completion.
In a working environment characterized by lots of disruption and distraction, the explicit confirmation about a successfully completed (even small) working process creates a feeling of release and satisfaction by the user. The user can tick off one item on his mental task list and focus on the remaining steps.
An exemplary rule is to structure tasks such that they can be "displayed" on a single screen page.

5.10 Reduce Functionality to its Minimum

Reduce the variety of the application's functions to the minimum mainly required by the salesperson during the customer dialogue conducted mobile.
The fewer functions need to be accommodated in the application, the higher are the chances to achieve a good usability. This can lead to a clearer structure and the possibility to dimension control elements more generously. These facts should in turn reduce the practical training for the salesperson, as well as the cognitive load and the demand for concentration. Too many details can obfuscate the structure, complicate the conceptual model on the user's part and produce confusion - especially if the users cannot pay most of their attention to the application.
One corresponding rule is to not try to port a desktop application - in the sense of transforming it with only minimal adjustments.

5.11 Consider Different User Characteristics

Try to cover a wide spectrum of user characteristics by providing alternative possibilities of interaction.

Even in a small shop you will find different kinds of characteristics amongst the salespersons, e.g. regarding perception-related abilities, motor coordination skills and cognitive capacity or education, knowledge, abilities and experiences. These differences can be considered with a thoroughly designed device.
Exemplary rule: Alternative interaction paths and short cuts should be offered.

5.12 Ensure Easy and Permanent Access to Important Options

The availability of important and frequently used options should vary only little and access to these options should be eased explicitly.
Learnability decreases and cognitive load increases if certain command options are available in some, but not in all situations. Such variations can cause discontent and concern, and potentially complicate the user's mental model of the application.
An exemplary rule is to avoid operation modes, particularly as their marking requires additional status messages.

5.13 Minimize the Quantity of Required Interaction and Input

Demand as little interaction from the user as possible and take advantage of already available information.
A low quantity of required elementary interactions, which in addition require only little concentration, should keep the salesperson's stress low. The intensive usage of data that is already available in the system and respectively in the shop, reduces the necessity to reproduce information from memory.
For example, meaningful standard values should always be provided, that constitute a basis for further processing.

5.14 Prevent Errors

Analyze which errors can occur. Indicate which error situations can arise or better, eliminate those from the very beginning.
The present context of use with frequent disruptions of the work process is susceptible to operator errors. The salespersons should have the impression that the handling of the PDA is "foolproof" and that they can hardly make a mistake if at all. This feeling should reduce their mental stress.
A corresponding rule is to explicitly indicate unsaved data in order to avoid accidental discarding.

5.15 Offer Straightforward Error Recovery

Indicate errors to users and support them during the recovery process.
The possibility to easily recover from errors is a precondition for a self-confident operation of an application by the user. This leads to less mental workload for the salesperson as well as a lower demand of attention during a potentially error-prone stress situation. Being able to cancel a previous action in case of an unexpected reaction of the application can avoid frustration.
Rule: Cancelling of actions should be offered with different granularities, from elementary interaction steps (e.g. not releasing a pressed button) to complete task sequences.

5.16 Offer Concise, Context-sensitive Help

Offer an online help corresponding clearly and briefly to the current dialogue context.
The leading principle should be that the system is usable without documentation. Nevertheless, the users should be able to recall help, which refers to the current dialogue situation. This enables them to self-help even during the customer dialogue. Comprehensive help should be offered via the manual or separate learning software.
To specify concrete actions in the help information is a corresponding rule.

5.17 Design Easily Perceivable, Readable, Rich in contrast and Aesthetic Dialogues

During the design process, aspire after clearness, simplicity, visual attractiveness and a harmonic overall picture.
On the one hand, the goal is to facilitate the perception and handling of the available information by the salesperson. Variable environmental characteristics (e.g. changing lighting conditions) should not have a negative influence. On the other hand, the visual design should appeal to the users and animate them to use the device.
Example rule: Icons should be simple and rich in contrast and have clear contours.

6. Conclusions

The aim of this chapter was to contribute to the development of guidelines for mobile (handheld respectively PDA) design, a domain not yet sufficiently covered especially when it comes to business process support. A rather complete set of principles and exemplary rules is presented, based on analysis, interpretation and amendment of established guidelines for desktop user interfaces and some of the rare mobile design guides.
The question if desktop-descending guidelines, standards and recommendations are also relevant and applicable for the mobile context could be answered positively for a range of well-established representatives. It is important to notice, that the presented guidelines compilation is adapted to the specific context of use at hand: handheld support for the sales person at the point of sale being involved in personnel selling. Though this setting restricts some of the variable factors to be considered, its heterogeneity is still so high, that applying these guidelines requires a thorough consideration of the specific situation. Therefore, this work should be generally useful to practitioners and HCI researchers.
It proved to be challenging to find a balance between complete coverage of all relevant aspects and treatment of each in sufficient level of detail. Starting from basic principles, explaining their rationale, providing several exemplary, more concrete rules and giving concrete examples is the proposed way to ensure practical applicability but to also allow to assess and integrate new developments.
Evaluation by application and analysis in concrete implementations and the consideration of further related quality aspects, e.g. accessibility or joy of use, are options for next steps.

7. Acknowledgments

This research was financially supported by the German Federal Ministry of Education and Research within the framework of the program "Angewandte Forschung an Fachhochschulen im Verbund mit der Wirtschaft" (FH[3]).

8. References

Apple Computer, Inc. (2005). *Apple Human Interface Guidelines*, http://developer.apple.com/documentation/UserExperience/Conceptual/AppleHIGuidelines/OSXHIGuidelines.pdf, Last retrieved 16/05/08

Blum, R. (2006). *Gestaltungsempfehlungen für PDA-Benutzungsschnittstellen am Beispiel der Verkaufsunterstützung im Einzelhandel*, Master Thesis, Fulda University of Applied Sciences

Gong, J. & Tarasewich, P. (2004): Guidelines for Handheld Mobile Device Interface Design, *Proceedings of the 2004 Decision Sciences Institute (DSI) Annual Meeting*, pp. 3751-3756, ISBN 0966711807, Boston, Nov. 2004, Decision Sciences Institute, Atlanta

Gorlenko, L. & Merrick, R. (2003). No wires attached: Usability challenges in the connected mobile world, In: *IBM Systems Journal*, Vol. 42, No. 4, pp. 639-651

IBM Corporation: *Design Principles*, Last retrieved 16/05/08 https://www.306.ibm.com/software/ucd/designconcepts/designbasics.html

ISO 13407 (1999). *Human-centred design processes for interactive systems*

ISO 14915 (2002-2003). *Software ergonomics for multimedia user interfaces*, Parts 1-3.

ISO 9241 (1993-2002). *Ergonomic requirements for office work with visual display terminals (VDTs)*, Parts 2, 10 to 17

Kärkkäinen, L. & Laarni, J. (2002): Designing for Small Display Screens, *Proceedings of the second Nordic conference on Human-computer interaction*, pp. 227-230, Aarhus, Oct. 2002, ACM Press

Kristoffersen, S. & Ljungberg, F. (1999): „Making Place" to Make IT Work: Empirical Explorations of HCI for Mobile CSCW, *Proceedings of the International ACM SIGGROUP Conference on Supporting Group Work*, pp. 276-285, ISBN 0897910651, Phoenix, Nov. 1999, ACM Press

Microsoft Corp. (1999). *Official Guidelines for User Interface Developers and Designers*, Microsoft Press, ISBN 0735605664, Redmond

Microsoft Corp. (2005). *Design Guidelines, Windows Mobile Version 5.0 SDK*, Last retrieved 16/05/08 http://msdn.microsoft.com/en-us/library/ms879586.aspx

Nielson, J. (1994). Heuristic evaluation, In: *Usability Inspection Methods*, Nielson, J. & Mack, R.L. (Eds.), pp. 25-62, John Wiley & Sons, ISBN 0471018775, New York

PalmSource, Inc. (2003). *Palm OS User Interface Guidelines*, http://www.accessdevnet.com/docs/uiguidelines.pdf, Last retrieved 16/05/08

Shneiderman, B. & Plaisant, C. (2004). *Designing the User Interface - Strategies for Effective Human-Computer Interaction*, 4th ed., Addison Wesley, ISBN 0201694970, Amsterdam

USE-ME.GOV (2004). *Review of State of the Art in User Interface Design for Mobile Applications*, Deliverable D4.1

Wichmann, T. & Stiehler, A. (2004). *Prozesse optimieren mit Mobile Solutions*, Berlecon Research GmbH, Berlin

6

Envisioning Improved Work Practices and Associated Technology Requirements in the Context of the Broader Socio-technical System

Joan Cahill
School of Psychology, Trinity College Dublin
Ireland

1. Introduction

Work practice and technology innovation presents a number of challenges for Human Computer Interaction (HCI) designers. Chief among them is the question of devising suitable HCI methods, for future process and task envisionment and related technology design. Methods must facilitate work practice re-engineering/envisionment and the development of user friendly work tools. Despite the future oriented nature of this activity, and its associated outputs, research must be predicated on a clear model of existing processes, task practices and tools usage.

HCI research in both commercial and technology research settings, is undertaken in the context of the broader software development process. As such, HCI methods must deliver clear user requirements for use by Software Developers. Nonetheless, HCI resources may be limited, or the research subject to time constraints - impacting on the scope of HCI research. As such, a valid research design which delivers on the core research brief, while taking into account project constraints, is required.

HCI design methodologies are used at different points in the software development lifecycle to design new technologies or re-design existing technologies, in the context of both open and closed systems. Typically, open systems involve the performance of a series of work processes requiring both individual and/or group task activities. Usually, these activities require operator interaction with a range of technical (e.g. IT systems) and human agents. Further, such interactions are subject to external influences. In contrast, closed systems are characterized by one to one user interaction with simple software packages in office or home computing settings. These interactions are unaffected by external influences.

This chapter focuses on the use of HCI methods in the context of open systems (or socio-technical systems). Specifically, it investigates methodologies for the envisionment of new or improved task practices and associated technology requirements, taking into account the broader socio-technical context for human machine interaction. First, an overview of the methodological implications of a range of conceptual frameworks, relevant to an understanding of human interaction with computer systems in socio-technical settings is provided. Following this, a summary of the software development process and the different requirements distinguished in this process, is presented. An introduction to Human Factors and HCI is then provided. Proposed HCI methodological requirements are then specified. Following this, specific HCI and work analysis methodologies are reviewed, as part of identifying an overall integrated HCI design approach. This is followed by an examination of certain practical challenges facing HCI practioners. In so doing, the author will consider the application of best practices in a real world setting, where HCI research is subject to commercial, technical and organisational constraints.

The HCI methodology outlined in this chapter may be of interest to HCI researchers or practitioners tasked with process and technology envisionment, and/or investigating the links between HCI theory and methods. The specific HCI research methodology proposed and related discussion of practical issues is also relevant to HCI researchers working with limited resources in both commercial software development and/or technology research settings. Further, the specific user requirements gathering methods examined, may be of interest to Software Developers and/or Business Analysts.

2. Conceptual Frameworks and Methodological Implications

2.1 Background

It is well established in the HCI literature that technology systems either fail, or do not perform as well as they might do, because they are not optimised from a user task perspective (Norman, 1988, 1993 and Preece, 2002). Perhaps this seems an obvious point. However, defining the nature of the task, and envisioning new or improved work practices and associated tool requirements, is not a straightforward activity. The question 'what is the task' must be explored on a number of levels. This links to certain theoretical models concerning the relationship between process, task and technology design, and specifically, the relationship between operator task performance and tools and information flow design. Importantly, an investigation of these models suggests certain methodological requirements for HCI design.

2.2 Introduction to Socio-technical Systems

In order to understand the methodological requirements for technology design in socio-technical settings, we must first understand the nature of socio-technical systems and how they perform. A 'socio-technical system' is defined as any instantiation of socio and technical elements engaged in goal directed behaviour. In place of a formal definition, engineering psychologists have proposed a range of characteristics to describe these systems. Characteristics include: large problem spaces, social, heterogeneous perspectives, distributed, dynamic, potentially high hazards, many coupled subsystems, automated, uncertain data, mediated interaction via computers and disturbances (Perrow, 1984, Vicente, 1999).

2.3 Basic Concepts Socio-technical Systems

The definition of a number of basic concepts in socio-technical systems helps illuminate certain aspects of the HCI design problem, which should be considered by HCI professionals. Before discussing socio-technical systems theories, a brief explanation of a number of basic socio-technical concepts is provided.

The operational goal refers to the purpose of the operation or the state of affairs to be achieved (e.g. safe and on time flight). This is associated with a series of operational states necessary to the achievement of the goal and a specific 'end state' which marks the successful accomplishment of the operational goal. The operational process defines the logic or structure of work, so that the operational objective is achieved. This includes the distribution of work or task activities between different human and technical agents and the overall timeline for this (e.g. sequencing of tasks). An operational process can be divided into a number of sub processes. Typically, this includes a planning process and the active operation. The active operation requires certain prior work to be accomplished (e.g. all technical and human resources in place). This work is undertaken in the planning phase. In the active operation, the planned work is executed. The operational process can be conceptualized in relation to a series of process gates (or critical points in the operational process). At each process gate, work must be accomplished by different operational agents, so that the process can move forward. Overall, the collective accomplishment of work at each of these process gates, results in the achievement of the operational goal. The process state refers to the status of the process at any point in time, in relation to the achievement of specific operator tasks. A process dependency refers to a relationship between two different parts of a process or two sub-processes. For example, the relationship between the planning sub process and the active operations sub process. Process dependencies also include dependencies between two related but different processes. In terms of a flight operation, this could be the relationship between the active flight operation, and the line maintenance process. Underlying these process dependencies are specific task dependencies. The operational plan describes how the operational goal will be achieved from an organisational perspective. This includes a definition of what human and technical resources will be used at different points in the operation. It also includes any regulatory requirements to be adhered to. Certain background organisational processes are required to ensure that the operational objective is achieved in a safe, efficient and legal manner. This includes the management of a range of organisational functions such as procedures design, documentation management, training, human resources, safety management and risk management.

The realisation of the operational goal requires the accomplishment of work or tasks by different members of the operational team. In socio-technical systems, work is realized by a number of operational agents or resources. This includes human and technical resources. Human resources refer to the people in the system. Technical resources denotes both the tools used by operator to perform their tasks (e.g. procedures, paper tools, IT systems), and all relevant technology (e.g. machines or systems) required to achieve the operational objective. In socio-technical systems, the work environment is distributed in space. As such, both human and technical resources can be situated in similar or remote locations.

Individual units of work are described in terms of tasks. As defined by Kirwan and Ainsworth, a task is 'a set pattern of operations, which alone, or together with other tasks, may be used to achieve the goal' (1992). Task performance is the enactment of the relevant operational task in time and space. The literature distinguishes between the performance of technical and non technical tasks. Technical tasks refer to specific physical tasks undertaken in order to achieve the operational goal. Typically these tasks are described in company standard operating procedures documentation. Non technical tasks denote the cognitive and social aspects tasks that underlie technical task performance. This includes situation assessment, decision making, task management, communication and co-ordination. Often these are not defined in company documentation. Further, it should be noted that task practice does not necessarily follow the task descriptions provided in company SOP. As such, SOP task descriptions should not be read as definitive.

Depending on the work requirements, operators may perform individual tasks in a sequence, or a number of tasks may be performed in parallel. Typically, tasks are analysed in terms of a hierarchy (e.g. task, sub-task and actions). Depending on the complexity of the task, the task might be grouped into a number of smaller steps or sub-tasks. A sub-task reflects a grouping of related actions, which form an overall step in a task. An action refers to the smallest unit of activity. Actions are associated with human roles, machines/tools and technologies. In relation to human performance, this includes technical activity (e.g. selecting a control on an information display or panel) and non technical activity. Non technical activity includes a range of cognitive (e.g. attending to information on a display, decision making) and social functions (e.g. communicating or co-ordinating with other operators in relation to work activities).

Task dependencies refers to relationships between tasks (both technical and non technical tasks) performed by individual operators or by a group of operators (collaborating on the same task, or producing outputs relevant to each others tasks) at different points in time, throughout the process. Two types of task dependencies can be distinguished. This includes prior or sequential dependencies and parallel dependencies. Prior dependencies refer to task activities and associated task outputs performed by the same or other operators, which are inputs to next phase of work. Critically, there are two aspects to this. Firstly, task performance must be considered in terms of task completion. The task needs to be completed, so that the process can continue. In the example of a flight operation, the Captain must obtain technical signoff of aircraft, before proceeding to close the doors and commencing aircraft push-back. Certain tasks can span a number of process gates or not. However, at a certain point in the operational timeline, tasks become mandatory from a process stability perspective. Also, the quality of task performance must be considered. Tasks may be performed, but the quality of task performance may be weak. For example, poor briefing or situation awareness at one point in flight can have a knock on effect on task performance at a later point in flight. Parallel dependencies concern work undertaken in parallel by other agents, which is an input to the operator's task.

In socio-technical systems, human actors are assigned a role. This corresponds to a set of functions or tasks that they are required to perform in relation to the achievement of the operational goal. Certain actors may have the same overall role, but perform different tasks based on their rank or seniority. Further, in team work situations, a number of actors may collaborate in the performance of the same task or different tasks, either in sequence or in parallel. These actors might have similar roles and ranks, or similar roles and different ranks, or different roles. Consequently, for each task we must distinguish the (1) active role (directly involved in the task) and the (2) supporting roles (contributes or provides inputs but is not directly responsible for the task). The supporting role might include actors with a similar role to the active role, or with different roles. Importantly, the supporting role may or may not be involved in the performance of other tasks at the same time. As such, we must consider how the actions of other agents relate to primary role actions.

Task performance often requires the use of different types of tools. A number of definitions of tools are provided. Overall, a tool can be defined as a thing (concrete or abstract) that supports task performance - either directly indirectly. From a workplace perspective, the term 'tool' refers to a range of entities - both real and abstract - which are used to perform tasks or to assist in the performance of tasks. This includes paper based information resources (e.g. paper based descriptions of a task or procedure, checklists etc), machines (e.g. mechanical machines, simple computer systems and complex computer systems) and human based information resources (e.g. memory, mental models, expertise, cognitive methodologies and so forth). In this respect, workplace tools can be physical (e.g. paper tools or IT systems) or non physical (e.g. best practice methods or expertise). Critically, workplace tools allow operators to perform tasks that are difficult or impossible given certain physical and/or cognitive limitations. For example, tools can provide a mechanical means to undertake certain physically complex or dangerous tasks. Further, tools enhance our ability to complete difficult cognitive tasks (e.g. processing large amounts of information). In this way tools shape task performance and in particular, extend our cognitive abilities (Norman, 1988, 1993). Certain types of tools are referred to as 'information resources'. An information resource is a tool that provides information relevant to the performance of a task. Information resources include physical resources (e.g. paper tools and IT systems) and human resources (e.g. other operators in the system who provide information to the operator or the operators own memory or expertise). IT systems can provide different levels of information. This ranges from raw data relevant to the performance of a task, to specific decision instruction - depending on the level of automation provided. Depending on the task and tool design, one or more physical tools and/or information resources are used by operators in the performance of task functions. In complex systems (e.g. such as aviation and process control), operators interact with a range of part-task tools, to complete a task. In this instance, the range of part task tools form a system of tools which taken collectively support task performance. From a task performance perspective, integration between different systems or tools is critical (Wickens, 2000).

2.4 Socio-technical Systems Theories & Methodological Implications

What is the nature of socio-technical system performance? How do the elements of a socio-technical system relate? Further, what are the implications of socio-technical system performance theories in terms of HCI research design? A number of theories have been advanced in relation to the overall elements of a socio-technical system. Collectively, these theories build on the basic conception of a socio-technical system as containing three overall elements. This includes the social system, the technical system and the environment. This follows from the socio-technical models of Pasmore (1988) and Trist (1981). Further, it links to frameworks associated with Activity Theory (Leontev, 1974). Overall, socio technical theories emphasize the inter-related nature of the social and technical aspects of a work process. Central to these theories, is the contention that there is a relationship between individual task performance and the design of the overall operational and organisational system (McDonald, 2004, 2006). Specific theories highlight the importance of certain social aspects of organisational performance. This includes the role and organisation of people (e.g. linking to the design of processes and procedures) and the specific social interactions that underlie task performance (e.g. communication and co-ordination). Further, theories point to the gap between formal processes and actual operator task practices. The implication of these theories is that design methodologies should allow for an understanding of the socio-technical context for task performance. Specifically, proposed technology concepts should be embedded in a broader system model. In particular, future technology envisionment must take into account the relationship between task and process. This includes both operational and organisational processes.

2.5 HCI & Information Behaviour Frameworks & Methodological Implications

A range of theoretical frameworks have been proposed to describe human interaction with computer systems, in the context of socio-technical systems. This includes HCI theories and information flow theories. Critically, these theories can be interpreted as suggesting certain methodological requirements for HCI practioners.

HCI theories such as Distributed Cognition (Hutchins, 1992, 1995, Hollan et al, 2000) and Group Supported Co-operative Work (Bannon, 1991), point to the role of tools and information in shaping operator task performance. Further, such theories emphasize the sense in which operator task performance often involves collaboration with other human and technical agents. The implication of these theories is that proposed methodologies should allow the researcher to understand how tools and information shape task performance. Further, methodologies might facilitate the identification of information flow requirements linked to the task performance of all relevant team agents - both human and technical.

In relation to task performance, HCI theories refer to the task problem to be solved or the task objective. Critically, the tools that operators use provide a means to solve the task problem. In this respect, HCI theorists (Norman, Carroll and Bannon) argue the specific design of a tool influences both the nature of the task and how it is performed (e.g. task workflow and level of complexity). Specifically, Norman (1993) uses the term 'cognitive artefacts' to describe those tools that given their design (e.g. task representational qualities), simplify the nature of the task.

As observed by Carroll (2000, 2001), the introduction of new tools can change the overall nature of the task. Further, it can change the nature of the operational process (Mc Donald, 2004). Carroll's (2000, 2001) concept of the task artefact lifecycle is relevant here. New technology requirements cannot be premised on existing task practices and associated problems alone. Carroll argues that we must envisage improved task practices (or future use scenarios) and consider how technology might support this. That is, we must consider how technology might be used to transform the task. In identifying future technology requirements, the researcher must balance two task pictures. This includes the existing task performance picture and the potential new task performance picture, facilitated by the introduction of new or improved technologies.

The literature highlights the necessity of developing tools from the perspective of the full task and not in isolation. As noted by Wickens (2000), individual displays supporting part task functionality cannot be designed in a vacuum. Rather, the wider tools picture must be evaluated. Here HCI designers must consider issues related to design consistency and information integration across the range of tools used by different operators. This is no easy task, but nonetheless requires consideration.

Information behaviour theories (Wilson, 1999) illuminate a range of operator information management processes in socio-technical contexts. This includes processes related to information gathering, information interpretation, information classification and prioritisation, information communication and information use. From a methodological perspective, this suggests that HCI methodologies should allow the research to model human information behaviour and associated information management strategies, so the proposed new technologies are predicated on an appropriate task and information picture, prioritise key user information and facilitate information sharing with all relevant human and technical agents involved in the task activity. Further, it is well documented that the format in which information is presented to the user, impacts on the perception, interpretation and use of this information. Here, we need to consider the HCI aspects of information access and presentation. As such, methods should allow the researcher to properly assess such issues so that user friendly design solutions are advanced.

3. Introduction to Human Factors & Human Computer Interaction

3.1 Human Factors

The Human factors discipline arose in relation to understanding the human role in socio-technical systems. The International Ergonomics Association (IEA) defines Ergonomics (or Human Factors) as

'The scientific discipline concerned with the understanding of interactions among humans and other elements of a system, and the profession that applies theory, principles, data and methods to design in order to optimize human well-being and overall system performance' (2000).

The IEA distinguish three domains of specialization within the discipline of ergonomics: Physical ergonomics is concerned with human anatomical, anthropometric, physiological and biomechanical characteristics as they relate to physical activity. Cognitive ergonomics is concerned with mental processes, such as perception, memory, reasoning, and motor response, as they affect interactions among humans and other elements of a system. Organizational ergonomics is concerned with the optimization of socio-technical systems, including their organizational structures, policies and processes.

3.2 Human Computer Interaction

Human computer interaction is a multi-disciplinary subject focused on the design of human friendly technology. Different definitions of HCI have been provided. In certain definitions, HCI is regarded as a subset of Human Factors concentrating on the design and evaluation of technologies, while in others it described in similar terms as Human Factors. This is also complicated by the fact that the term HCI is often used interchangeably with 'Engineering Psychology', 'Cognitive Ergonomics' and 'Human Factors'. In this analysis, HCI can be considered as a sub-set of theory and methodologies within HF, concerned with the design and evaluation of technology for use in the context of both open and closed systems. In terms of the three strands of Human Factors defined above, it can be broadly classified as Cognitive Ergonomics.

According to HCI theorists and practioners, to design human friendly technology which fits the work context, we must adopt a 'user centered design' methodology/process. The HCI literature defines a range of methods for this. Collectively, these methods emphasize: (1) the necessity of involving users in design process, (2) the degree to which design is an iterative process (e.g. designs are prototyped and evaluated and the modified and evaluated again), and (3) the extent to which evaluation provides an empirical basis in which to evaluate/justify designs.

4. Software Development Process

HCI methodologies are adopted in the context of developing software/technologies following project goals and timelines. This process is referred to as the software development process. This process follows a number of high level stages including, (1) specifying user requirements, (2) specifying functional requirements, (3) application development, (4) testing, (5) trials and (6) full implementation. Critically, a range of HCI techniques are used for different purposes (e.g. specifying requirements, designing prototypes, evaluating prototypes etc) at various points in this process.

The software development process involves the specification of a number of different types of requirements. This includes user requirements, system/functional requirements, user interface design requirements and usability requirements. User requirements refer to what the system needs to do from the user's perspective (taking into account that there might be a range of different users). System requirements refer to what the system actually does (e.g. list of functions that the system performs and analysis of each function). User interface design requirements refer to what the user interface will look and feel like, and how users will interact with different system functions. Finally usability requirements refer to the acceptable level of user performance and satisfaction with the system. It is important to note that both user requirements and user interface design requirements can be defined at different levels. Depending on the level of specification (e.g. requirements stated in the form of general guidelines or visual prototypes) more or less design instruction is provided to Interface Designers and Software Developers. Evidently, both user requirements and user interface design requirements must be specified at a sufficiently concrete level so that (1) Software Developers can document the functional specification (e.g. functional requirements) linking to application development and (2) Graphic and Interaction Designers can produce the full interaction and visual design model. According to participatory design advocates, one of the weaknesses of formal HCI methods, is that typical outputs (e.g. lists of users and tasks, task analysis diagrams, task scenarios and so forth), fail to provide sufficient design guidance. This is discussed in more detail, later in this chapter.

5. HCI Design Methodological Challenges

So what should HCI design methodologies achieve? How should the range of HCI methodologies serve HCI design practioners in terms of envisioning new or improved work practices, and associated technologies in socio-technical system settings?

It is argued that HCI design methods should fulfil the following objectives:

1. The development of an appropriate task model
2. Evaluation of existing tools & information resources
3. Envisionment of new tool requirements & associated task practices
4. Understanding broader organisational and technological implications of proposed tool concepts
5. Specification and evaluation of proposed user interface for new or improved tool concepts
6. Facilitation of communication of user requirements and design concepts to Software Developers & Graphic Designers

5.1 The Development of an Appropriate Task Model

Firstly, HCI design methods should allow for the development of an appropriate task model. This involves a consideration of both existing task practice and future task practice. In relation to the former, methodologies should assist the following:

1. Modelling actual task practice, taking into account different operational and environmental contexts (e.g. ecological validity)
2. Modelling operator task activity and information flow (including collaborative work activity)
3. Modelling the relationship between task and process (e.g. design of both operational process and background organizational processes).
4. Modelling the both technical and non technical aspects of task performance
5. Modelling information flow requirements (e.g. information in an out and how this is facilitated by the use of tools and information resources (both human and technical)

In terms of future task practice, methods should allow the researcher to identify how task practice might be improved given new technology possibilities.

5.2 Evaluation of Existing Tools and Information Resources

Design methods should also allow the researcher to assess the use of existing tools and information resources. For example, task problems associated with existing technology design constraints might be ameliorated by rethinking the current design.

5.3 Envisionment of New Tool Requirements & Associated Task Processes

Proposed HCI design methods should allow for the identification of new tool requirements and associated operational processes based on the task model and evaluation of existing tools. Critically, the resulting tools should represent an improvement on the existing situation. This may involve the envisionment of new operational processes along with new task practices. As such, the design methods should allow for both process and task envisionment. Further, to mitigate problems in relation to the task artefact lifecycle (Carroll, 2000, 2001), such methods might allow the researcher to evaluate the future use situation and associated tool concepts. Importantly, new designs should not inherit the weaknesses of earlier designs, no introduce any new HCI problems.

5.4 Specification and Evaluation of Tool Concepts

Further, design methods should facilitate the prototyping of new tool concepts, thereby bridging the gap between requirements specification and design. Also methods should allow for the evaluation of tool concepts, to ensure that they are optimised in terms of user tasks and conceptual models. Further methods should allow researchers to assess whether human performance and environmental constraints are factored into the proposed HCI design solution.

5.5 Understanding Broader Organisational & Technological Implications of Proposed Tool Concepts & Associated Feasibility Issues

Also, methods should facilitate the assessment of whether or not the proposed technology requirements are achievable. First the researcher must consider feasibility in terms of existing organisational structures and roles, resource capacity and redesign requirements. To this end, methods should facilitate the identification of the task/performance requirements embedded in the proposed technology design, and whether this requires changes to existing work practices and/or resource allocations. There may be organisational barriers to changing existing work practices. For example, new tool concepts may require communication or sharing of information between different roles or departments. Certain departments may not want to share information. Further, there may be data protection issues linked to Union agreements or regulatory rules, which prohibit data sharing. In addition, new tool functionality (e.g. the provision of task support information customised to an operation) may require additional work effort/human resources. Does the organisation have the capacity for this? Can new functions be incorporated in existing roles, or are new employees required? What are the training implications?

The design of technology for use by individual groups of operators in socio-technical contexts often links to the design of technologies used by other roles in the organisation. In particular, the provision of information to specific end users, related to collaborative work activities necessitates information sharing across the different human and technical agents involved in the work activity. As such, methodologies should assist researchers in identifying the relevant information integration requirements inherent in the proposed technology concepts. Further, proposed methods should permit the identification of any additional technology requirements linked to the task performance of other operational roles, which may or may not be supported by existing tools.

5.6 Facilitate Communication of User Requirements and Design Concepts to Software Developers & Graphic Designers

Lastly, it is critical that the analysis and design outputs of the HCI design methodologies adopted, can be utilized by Software Developers, in terms of specifying the functional requirements of the system. Moreover, the outputs need to be instructive in terms of specifying the user interface design requirements for the proposed system, which is managed by the Graphic Design team.

6. Overview of HCI Methods

Do HCI methodologies facilitate the above objectives? Or, are other methods required? The literature distinguishes two high level sets of methods, namely formal and informal HCI methods. In general, formal methods are characterized as being closer to scientific methods. Alternatively, informal methods are strongly linked to design activities and considered to have a more qualitative focus

6.1 Formal HCI Methods

Formal methods in HCI allow for user involvement at specific points in the software development lifecycle (Nielsen, 1993, Constantine et al, 1999, Mayhew, 1999).

First, a task analysis is conducted, to understand how the operator interacts with the existing system and to identify the user requirements for an improved or new system. According to Kirwan and Ainsworth (1992), a task analysis *'is a method of describing what an operator is required to do, in terms of actions or cognitive processes, to achieve a system goal'*. Usually, this occurs at the beginning of a project and takes the form of structured or semi-

structured interviews focused on understanding and evaluating current work practices and supporting technology (Hackos et al, 1998). This follows ethnographic research methods, advanced in the Social Science field (e.g. Interviews and Observation).
A number of analysis and design steps are then completed by HCI professionals without the participation of end users. These techniques aim to represent the cognition, practice or logic of the task. In addition, they aim to identify user requirements. Typical analysis methods include content analysis, hierarchical task analysis and task workflow analysis.
Design concepts are then modelled with the help of Graphic Designers. This involves mapping user tasks and workflows to a set of interface screens with a defined information structure and presentation logic. Initially, HCI designers might map a high level storyboard. Following this, a more detailed storyboard is modelled. Detailed storyboards include rough sketches of screen layouts and designs that correspond to the use sequence outlined for a detailed level of a task performance by a system. This process is supported by a wealth of advisory information relating to user interface design. This includes International Organisation for Standardisation (ISO) user interface design approaches and standards (ISO, 1995, 1997), and usability design principles/heuristics (Nielsen, 1993, Preece et al, 2002).
Following this, prototypes are modelled. Developing prototypes is a central part of user centred design. A prototype is an experimental or incomplete design. This links to the distinction between specification and implementation. A prototype belongs to specification/design phase, as opposed to the implementation phase. Different kinds of prototyping are appropriate for different stages of design. Once the prototypes are completed, user workflows and interface features/behaviours are evaluated. In HCI design, evaluation is part of the design process. Evaluation is part of the design process. Feedback is obtained about the usability of designs via inspection, testing or enquiry. This is an iterative process. Evaluation occurs at different points in the development process. The goals of evaluation are multiple and varied. Evaluation can be used to investigate what users want, if user requirements are being met and what problems users have. Further, it can be used to test out design ideas/concepts quickly and to assess the usability of a UI and improve the quality of the UI. Two main evaluation methods are used. This includes (1) user testing and (2) heuristic evaluation. User testing involves the assessment of a user interface (UI) by observing representative users performing representative tasks using the UI (Rubin, 1994). This is used to identify any aspects of a design that cause users difficulty, confusion, or misunderstandings. These may lead to errors, delays, or in extreme cases inability to complete the tasks for which the UI is designed. User testing also provides insight into user preferences. In addition, a heuristic evaluation may be conducted. In a Heuristic Evaluation, the UI is examined against a set of agreed usability /user experience principles (the heuristics). This is undertaken by a team of experienced usability professionals (the evaluators). As such, the evaluation does not involve end users. The evaluator or team of evaluators step into the shoes of the prospective end user - taking into account their profile, mental models of the task, typical learning styles and task requirements. Following iterative prototyping and evaluation, high fidelity prototypes are developed by software developers.

6.2 Informal HCI Methods

Formal HCI methods have been the subject of much debate in the HCI literature. Specific challenges have come from the fields of Ethnography and Participatory Design.

Ethnographers argue that classical HCI methods do not take work practice seriously; failing to address the social aspects of work (Hutchins 1995, Vicente 1999). In particular, they argue that user interviews cannot provide actual insight into real work practices. Participatory design theorists have questioned the separation between design and evaluation in formal methods (Bødker and Buur, 2002). Specifically, they have challenged the instructiveness of traditional user and task analysis outputs for design guidance. Also, they argue that user testing provides insufficient information concerning user problems. Further, PD theorists have questioned the usefulness of these methods for the design of both socio-technical systems and ubiquitous technology (Bodker and Buur, 2002).

The field of participatory design originated in Scandinavia in the early 1970s, in response to union mandates that workers should be involved in the design of new workplace technology. This heralded the introduction of new HCI methodologies, many of which were pioneered in the Utopia Project (Bødker, 1985). Central to PD theory is the idea that usability engineers design 'with' end users, as opposed to 'for' them. Accordingly, users are active participants in the design process, and the traditional HCI design team (e.g. Usability Engineers and Graphic Designers) is broadened to include end users (workers and worker organizations), stakeholders and domain experts. Crucially, PD theory stresses the relationship between design and evaluation. PD theorists argue that to design effective work tools, design teams must first experience and evaluate future technology and practices (Bannon, 1991, Muller 2003). As such, PD techniques (such as, the co-creation and evaluation of prototypes and scenario role playing), allow design teams to envision and evaluate future workplace practices and related technologies, without the constraints of current practice. Overall PD techniques have been adapted from Ethnography. This includes concept generation, envisionment exercises, story collecting and story telling (through text, photography and drama), games of analysis and design and the co-creation of descriptive and functional prototypes.

The PD contention that users must be active participants in the design process, (and related argument that Usability Engineers should be receptive to user's own ideas and explanatory frameworks) reflects certain underlying phenomenological conceptions of knowledge. Participants are not objects but partners or 'experts' whose ideas are sought. Thus, it is inappropriate for human factors researchers to formulate design models in advance of collaboration with end users. In this respect, PD theorists argue that there are four dimensions along which participation could be measured. This includes: (1) the directness of interaction with the designers, (2) the length of involvement in the design process, (3) the scope of participation in the overall system being designed and (4) the degree of control over design decisions.

Critical to PD methodology is the envisionment of future work situations. According to PD theorists, users need to have the experience of being in the future use situation, or an approximation of it, in order to be able to comment on the advantages and disadvantages of the proposed system. As argued by Bannon, some form of mock-up or prototype needs to be built in order to let users know what the future use situation might be (1991). This allows users to experience how emerging designs may affect work practice.

Carroll proposes a scenario based design approach (2000, 2001). This links to the development of persona's and task scenarios, used in formal HCI approaches. This approach distinguishes the development of existing task scenarios (describing current practice), and future task scenarios (or future use scenarios). According to Carroll, future use scenarios are narrative descriptions of a future task state. This relates to the participatory design techniques of imagining future work processes and supporting technology (described above). Further, it relates to Carroll's concept of the task artefact lifecycle. For Carroll, the task artefact cycle is the background pattern in technology development (2000, 2001). Possible courses of design and development must be envisioned and evaluated in terms of their impacts on human activity (before they are pursued). If - If Designers model technology in terms of the existing task practice (e.g. model what is), the technology will be one step behind (Carroll, 2000, 2001).

Further, the application of participant observation methods developed in the Social Science field, have also been proposed. The purpose here is to obtain a picture of real world task practices and associated environmental constraints. This is based on the idea that participant feedback in interviews (used in formal methods) may not provide a true or accurate picture of the actual work reality. These methods have been supported by Hutchins. According to Hutchins, it is through Ethnography that we gain knowledge about how a distributed system actually works (1995).

7. Overview of Methods Used in Organisational Ergonomics Fields

HCI methods are influenced and/or have much in common with specific work analysis methods used in the organisational ergonomics domain. This includes Process Mapping and Cognitive Work Analysis.

7.1 Process Mapping

The objective of process mapping is to model the current process and identify process re-design requirements for the purpose of improving safety, or productivity. This relates to business process modelling (e.g. modelling 'as is' and 'future processes'), with the objective of improving efficiency and quality. Process mapping involves the production of a diagrammatic representation of the overall process, and associated sub-processes. Specifically it represents the sequential and parallel task activities of both human and technical agents, which collectively result in the achievement of the operational goal. This approach originates in the research of Gilbreth and Gilbreth (1921). Underlying this visual map is an analysis of the process as a functional system (e.g. transformation of inputs into outputs, process dependencies), as a social system (e.g. team performance requirements, co-ordination and communication mechanisms) and as an information system (e.g. transformation of information across different technical and human resources). Typically process mapping is conducted in a workshop format involving all relevant stakeholders involved in the operational process. First, the researcher reviews the high level process and then drills down to chart the related task activities of different roles. As part of this, there is usually some form of trouble-shooting related to identifying existing process problems and redesign solutions.

7.2 Cognitive Work Analysis

Vicente argues that in dynamic work settings, there are many factors outside the individual affecting their interactions with computer systems and these factors must be considered in the design of such systems (1999). In this regard, Vicente contends that to understand work demands both cognitive and environmental constraints must be considered. Vicente methodology is based on Rasmussen's argument that the work environment determines to a large extent the operator constraints and the ability of the operator to choose his/her own strategy. In Vicente's view, environmental constraints come first (Vicente, 1999). To this end, Vicente (1999) proposes a cognitive work analysis (CWA) methodology to analyse work. This includes both task and work domain analysis. CWA consists of five concepts and corresponding analysis. This includes, (1) an analysis of the boundaries and restrictions of the work domain, (2) an analysis of the information processing parts of the task, (3) an analysis of the process and associated task performance, (4) an analysis of social organisational and co-ordination and (5), an analysis of worker competencies. This methodology has been applied to diverse work situations involving varying degrees of process control/automation.

8. Analysis

Operator work in socio-technical contexts can be quite complex. Often it involves the performance of collaborative activities with a range of human and technical agents. As such, task activity and human computer interaction in open systems is more demanding than in closed systems. It is argued that (1) the modelling of task activity and (2) the envisionment, design and evaluation of improved task support tools in socio-technical contexts, necessitates the application of a range of design methods, above and beyond what is outlined in the HCI literature (e.g. both formal and informal HCI methods). Taking into account the methodological requirements outlined earlier, it is suggested that HCI researchers adopt a mix of methodologies associated with two of the three Human Factors fields, namely Cognitive Ergonomics and Organisational Ergonomics. Specifically, an integration of formal HCI methods, informal HCI methods and both process mapping and cognitive work analysis methods is proposed. Typically, HCI practioners working in socio-technical settings use a range of both formal and informal HCI methods. Further, certain work analysis techniques such as Cognitive Work Analysis have been applied by HCI practioners. Other methods such as process mapping methods have not been used.

Existing HCI methods do not support an analysis of the relationship between task, process and technology requirements. Specifically, to design 'operational' technologies, HCI researchers must understand how existing and future technologies relate to the design of the existing process and/or future process. The introduction of new technologies has implications for broader task practice (e.g. task practice of other agents) and the design of the operational process. As such, we cannot just think of technology from the perspective of the task performance of one role, or in isolation from the broader process design. To this end, in analysing task performance, we must distinguish two perspectives on task activity – (1) the specific user perspective and (2) the broader system perspective (e.g. takes into account the broader operational and organisational aspects of task performance). Insofar as both perspectives relate, this is not a real distinction. However, this distinction is useful from an analytic perspective. The individual perspective focuses on task performance in terms of unique roles. Here we consider the overall task picture, how tasks relate, actual task workflows (e.g. difference between SOP and actual practice), task information requirements, use of tools and environmental constraints. Critically, this perspective prioritises the task requirements of the individual operator. The system perspective investigates task performance on two other levels – the operational level and the organisational level. The operational level takes into account collaboration with other roles and associated task information inputs and outputs. As such, it reflects a process perspective on task activity - factoring team collaboration requirements into task models. This links to the computer supported cooperative work frameworks proposed by Bannon (1991) and others. The organisational level examines task performance in terms of those processes in the organisation that support task performance. For example, training, safety management and procedures design. Process mapping workshops can be used to model the existing operational process and envisage future processes and associated re-design requirements. Also, interviews and observations can be used to map relevant work processes.

Formal HCI design methods do not support the envisionment of future work practices and associated technology requirements. To this end, informal HCI methods are required. It is argued that participatory design methods facilitate technology envisionment and provide concrete design instruction. Collaborative prototyping of proposed tool concepts with end users allows both the researcher and participants to envision future use scenarios and associated technology requirements. Further, these techniques enable practioners to elicit feedback relating to the usability of future technology concepts - thereby circumventing the task artefact lifecycle. Crucially, the application of these methods results in the advancement of meaningful requirements. User requirements and associated interface concepts are translated into actual user interface features and behaviours. Prototypes can be used as a basis for exploring, evaluating and communicating design ideas. Indeed, it is difficult for participants to fully envisage and evaluate design ideas, without such prototypes. Essentially, techniques allow both users and designers to experiment with different visual/interactive affordances (e.g. menu structures, icons, presentation of form fields) until a design consensus is reached. Further, certain visual and interaction issues require 'hands-on' problem solving. In this way, research does not stop short of concrete solutions. However, as a stand-alone methodology, participatory research methods are insufficient. To design tools that improve upon current practice, we must start from current practice. To interpret and weight participant opinions related to specific design solutions, the researcher must be familiar with the existing problem space. As such, naturalistic research methods (e.g. interviews and observations) are a necessary precursor to PD methods.

Both HCI methods and organisational analysis methods do not facilitate the identification of the broader organisational and technological implications of new tool concepts. It is suggested that process workshop methods are adapted to this purpose. The specific methodology for this is outlined in subsequent sections.

9. Proposed Methodological Approach & Case Study Examples

The proposed integrated HCI design methodology can be grouped into a series of design steps at different points in the user centred design process. The specific steps proposed relate to HCI research only. Some of these steps are required, while others are optional. Further, certain steps depend on the project context. It is recommended that practioners adopt this methodology for their own purpose, taking into account relevant project considerations. Other work, relevant to the performance requirements of the wider software development team is alluded to in terms of dependencies with HCI work, but not described in terms of actual steps. This includes the production of the graphic design, the specification of functional requirements, software development, software testing, software and hardware integration and testing, trial implementation of proposed systems and full implementation of proposed systems.

Step	Description	Required, Context Dependent Or Optional	Methods	Output
1	Literature Review	Optional	Review literature available – comparative tools, known problems	Report
2	Identifying the process context underlying operator task performance	Required	Process mapping workshops (existing process) Follow up observation of work practice, or interviews with different stakeholders	Process map of existing process Process analysis templates Role/task descriptions
3	Modelling existing task practice and tool usage	Required	Observation of work practice Interviews with different operational roles User testing User and task analysis	User/task matrices Task scenarios Procedural workflow diagrams User testing report
4	Specification of preliminary user requirements	Depends on project context	Advancement of future use scenarios and associated technology brief Analysis and documentation of requirements	Future use scenarios Preliminary user requirements specification Prototypes (optional)
Management review and decisions				
5	Envisioning new work practices and associated user requirements for new or improved technologies	Required	Process workshops (future process) Technology envisionment exercises Role play Collaborative prototyping	Future / To be process map Future use scenarios High level tool concepts High level paper or MS Visio prototypes
6	Prototyping and evaluating of proposed tool concepts	Required	Mix of individual and collaborative prototyping User testing	Prototypes (MS Visio Prototypes)
7	Dry run implementation of proposed tool concepts to assess organisational and technological implications	Required	Review of proposed scenarios and prototypes, as part of an implementation workshop	Prototypes Implementation Report

Management review and decisions				
Step	**Description**	**Required, Context Dependent Or Optional**	**Methods**	**Output**
8	Further prototyping and evaluation	Depends on previous - scope of changes	Further prototyping and evaluation (if required)	Prototypes
9	Overall Research Analysis, Further Prototyping & Specification of User Requirements and User Interface Design	Required	Analysis and weighting of all feedback Further prototyping Specification of user requirements	User requirement specification User interface design specification Prototypes Updated process map
10	Handover to Software Developers & Graphic Designers	Required	In person review session - review proposed tool prototypes and relevant documentation	User requirement specification Prototypes
Production of graphic design				
Definition of functional specification				
Initial software development				
Handover of graphic design to software developers				
Further software development				
11	Review Software Prototypes	Required	In person review session (ongoing)	Updated software prototypes
12	Evaluation of High Fidelity Prototypes	Optional	User testing Heuristic Evaluation	Updated software prototypes
13	Tool Certification (ongoing once tool concepts defined)	Depends on project context	Review of regulatory guidance Evaluation with authorities	Certification report
Software testing				
Integration with other software systems and hardware				
Integration Testing				
Trial implementation of new systems in organisation				
Full implementation of new systems in organisation				
14	Ongoing feedback and improvements (after go live)	Optional	Observation of work practice using new tools Interviews with different operational roles Surveys	Implementation report

Table 1. Summary of Proposed HCI Methodology & Associated Steps, Methods and Outputs

Such method triangulation has been used in two different studies conducted by the author. Each of these studies has involved the application of some or most of the design steps outlined above. It should be noted that one of these studies is complete while the other is ongoing. Before presenting the proposed the design steps for the integrated HCI design

methodology, I will first provide a high level background to these studies. Design steps will then be discussed in the context of the HCI methodologies used in these projects.
The first study involved the re-design of an electronic flight bag application as part of a commercial software project (Cahill and McDonald, 2006). HCI resources for this project were limited, thus limiting the scope and depth of HCI research.
The second study concerns the development of improved Flight Crew task support tools, linking to the advancement of improved processes and technologies supporting airline performance management, safety/risk management and continuous improvement activities (Cahill and McDonald, 2006, Cahill et al, 2007, Cahill and Losa, 2007). This project started in 2005 and is due to be completed in 2009. A core requirement for the research was to map the existing process and envision future work processes. As such, process mapping was built into the overall HCI research design.

9.1 Step 1: Literature Review

Before embarking on HCI research, it is necessary to familiarize oneself with the proposed research domain. As such, the first step involves conducting a literature review, specifically investigating what is reported in relation to existing process and task descriptions, existing technologies and future technology concepts. Project sponsors may have certain preconceptions about future technology objectives and requirements. In this respect, the researcher should assess the feasibility of the initial technology development proposal. It is important that a neutral perspective on any of the concepts reported (e.g. both the literature and company requirements) is adopted, so as to avoid prejudicing the research.
In relation to the second study, the literature review highlighted a number of task performance concepts linked to certain theoretical models of Flight Crew task performance (e.g. situation assessment, information management and task management) and related training concepts (e.g. crew resource management and threat and error management), requiring validation in field research. Interestingly, the initial evaluation of these concepts proved critical in terms of the directing future field research, and generating tool requirements (Cahill and Losa, 2007).

9.2 Step 2: Identify the Process Context

The second step involves identifying the process context underlying task performance. The objective is to map the existing operational process, and in particular, to identify the relationship between the task performances of the operator under study, with the task performance of other operational agents involved in the work process and associated information inputs and outputs. This necessitates conducting process mapping workshops with all relevant stakeholders. Depending on time constraints, workshop information can be substantiated by follow up observations of the work activities or de-brief interviews with different operators.
In the case of the second study, the high level process and associated sub-processes were first mapped. Following this, detailed aspects of each sub process were mapped. This included the process gates, process states, the specific tasks and collaboration required by different agents to achieve the process state and relevant dependencies (both at a task and process level). In terms of tools, process mapping can be undertaken using a marker and whiteboard, or using specific process mapping software. In this instance an 'off the shelf' process mapping product was used. Given the notational and visual display logic inherent

in this tool, not all of the information captured was amenable to representation in a visual display. This information was recorded and linked to the visual map display. Specifically, the process map was supplanted with process analysis templates defining process pre-requisites, operator roles, task dependencies and relationships and so forth. Further, role task descriptions and associated performance requirements were documented.

9.3 Step 3: Modeling Existing Task Practice & Tool Usage

The next step involves modelling actual task practice, taking into account the wider socio-technical process. Ideally, this follows from process mapping activities. As such, the researcher is driving down on the high level process picture to understand in more detail the task activity of the operator for whom the future technology is intended. As part of this, specific task workflows, the use of existing tools and information resources, and overall collaboration and information flow with the different human and technical agents involved in task activity should be analysed. If formal process mapping has not been undertaken, the researcher should endeavour to establish the relationship between task and process and associated dependencies, as part of the task analysis methodology.

Typically, the first point of analysis is company documentation such as standard operating procedures. Usually this documentation does not refer to the social or cognitive aspects of a work process, and the performance requirements of other agents, which link to operator task activity. In relation to modelling existing task practices, it is critical that this reflects what operators actually do as opposed to normative descriptions of task practice (e.g. airline SOP). As noted in the literature, there is often a gap between operator descriptions of work activity (relayed in user interviews), and actual task practice. This necessitates the application of a range of naturalistic research method such as user interviews and observations of work practice. Interviews may be conducted with the primary users. It is useful to create interview templates which guide the researcher through a series of questions, linking task and process and eliciting information about tools and information flow. Further, questions should be asked in relation to the cognitive and social aspects of task performance. Specifically, information management behaviour and communication and co-ordination tasks should be addressed. This links to Vicente's Cognitive Work Analysis approach (1999). In the second study, two phases of interviews were undertaken. The first set of interviews focussed on modelling task workflows and task relationships. The second set of interviews investigated issues related to tools usage, information management behaviour and associated strategies and workflows and techniques related to certain non technical tasks (e.g. situation assessment and joint decision making).

To lend ecological validity to work descriptions, interview data should be co-related with data gathered during observations of actual work practice. Critically, observation of task practice must include both the operators under study (e.g. for whom the proposed new technology is designed for) and any other operators with whom they collaborate. Information gathered can be co-related with interview feedback and analysis templates updated. Further, additional interviews may be conducted to clarify research findings.

In relation to understand the tools and information picture, the researcher might engage in a walk-through of existing tools with research participants. This will help the researcher to understand the strengths and weaknesses of existing technologies and future tool requirements. Alternatively, user testing of existing tools might be undertaken. User testing of existing tools was conducted in the first study. In the second study, a walk-through of existing tools was performed.

The output of this research can include the following: user/task matrices, existing task scenarios, task analysis templates, procedural workflow diagrams and diagrams of the workspace.

9.4 Step 4: Specification of Preliminary User Requirements

In commercial situations, a preliminary specification of proposed tool objectives and functions and associated user requirements, may be required. Typical reasons include the necessity to report to management, or to furnish Software Developers with draft high level requirements, so that software development activities can be initiated. This is often required in situations where the HCI budget and/or timeline is limited, and HCI research and software development must be undertaken in parallel.

The fourth step therefore involves conducting an overall analysis of the aggregated findings of all preceding research, to envision preliminary future use scenarios, tool objectives and functions and high level user requirements. It should be noted that this step is conducted without the involvement of end users. This can result in a range of outputs - depending on the specific analysis undertaken. This includes future task scenarios and a preliminary user requirements specification. Further, it is possible to produce a draft high level prototype based on this first phase of research. Both future use scenarios and prototypes can be used to help direct envisionment exercises and collaborative prototyping activities at a later point. It should be noted that both future use scenarios and associated prototypes are advanced to illustrate the research findings. These are by no means final. Much can change following subsequent envisionment and collaborative prototyping research with end users. In the case of both study one and two, such an approach was undertaken.

9.5 Step 5: Envisioning Future Work Practices and Associated User Requirements for New or Improved Technologies

The fifth step involves the envisionment of future work practices and the associated requirements for new or improved technologies. The objective is to identify the future work process and associated task scenarios for all relevant agents, and following from this, to scope the requirements for new or improved task support tools. This entails the application of one or a number of the following techniques - future use process workshops, future use scenarios definition and role play, and collaborative prototyping with end users. Typically the application of these methods requires a mix of individual and group participatory sessions.

Future process mapping can be undertaken following the mapping of the existing process or in a separate workshop session. Process mapping of the existing process will have identified a range of process barriers and facilitators. Barriers might include human factors problems (e.g. communication and co-ordination with other human agents) or HCI problems with existing technology (e.g. information not provided, complex or unintuitive interaction or visual design). Problems identified can be recorded on post-it notes and pinned to the walls, for the purpose of group review and joint problem solving. During the workshop participants review all issues, prioritise key problems and engage in joint problem solving. This problem solving is directing at identifying an improved process, new task workflows and associated technology tool requirements. Both short and long terms re-design recommendations can be identified.

A number of future use scenario based design approaches can be undertaken. Prior to the session, the researcher may have documented a future use scenario based on earlier research (e.g. process and task analysis). In the session, participants are invited to review the scenario, for the purpose of generating a discussion around future use situations and associated tool requirements. As part of this, both participants and researchers can engage in role play activities, to further clarify the future use scenario and technology implications. Alternatively, the researcher might invite participants to identify their own future use scenario. As before, participants role play specific task activities, detailing what information they would expect to obtain, how they would obtain this information, and how they would use this information. In so doing, the researcher can commence collaborative modelling of high level prototypes with participants. This entails evaluating and further scoping prototypes produced in the earlier analysis (if produced). Conversely, participants are invited to draw out their concepts on paper, with the assistance of the researcher.

Finally, collaborative prototyping techniques can be used (Muller, 1991). Again, depending on the nature of the preceding analysis, this may involve joint envisionment of high level prototypes, or the review and scoping of preliminary prototypes created by the researcher. A series of prototyping sessions is conducted. This starts with the production of paper prototypes. As the research progresses, the researcher can model prototypes using a prototyping tool such as Microsoft Visio. Following this, the researcher updates the prototypes based on an analysis of aggregated findings. Prototypes can be advanced by means of either individual or group session. However, it is important to validate prototypes in group sessions at the end, to ensure an overall design consensus is obtained.

Depending on the approach taken, the outputs of this analysis include the following: future or 'to be' process maps, future use scenarios, high level tool concepts and high level paper or MS Vision prototypes.

In the first study, a range of participatory techniques were used to problem solve usability issues which arose in prior user testing and ethnographic research, and to provide a concrete interaction design model for the proposed new EFB tool (Cahill and Mc Donald, 2006). Specific PD activities involved a combination of requirements' envisionment and the co-creation and evaluation of prototypes. First, a task was described and users were requested to outline the workflow and information requirements (including workarounds and bottlenecks and so forth). For example, participants were asked "If you noticed a new defect on landing, what would you do? What usually happens?" Participants were also encouraged to verbalize workflows, and sketch task-flows, using pencil and paper. As part of this, participants were invited to consider group/collaborative work requirements. Further, participants were shown task workflow drawings (specific user and task analysis outputs) and asked to edit them, where appropriate. This led participants to scrutinize both their own conceptions of workflows, and that of others. This is close to Carroll's (2000) investigation of task scenarios via claims analysis. This resulted in a clear task picture (e.g. task hierarchies, sequences and relationships).

In the second study, the research design involved an integration of technology envisionment and collaborative prototyping approaches, outlined by Muller (1991) and Bodker (1985), with the future use scenario based design approach proposed by Carroll (2000, 20001). Four phases of research were undertaken. First, all prior research was analyzed. This resulted in the production of high level 'future use scenarios' and associated tool concepts. Following this, initial high level prototypes were advanced for the emerging tool concepts. These indicated the high level workflows and information flow for these applications. The third phase involved the co-evaluation and development of low fidelity prototypes using an off the shelf prototyping tool - namely Microsoft Visio. This required iterative modelling of tool concepts with twelve participants over four days. The overall user interaction design model for each of the prototypes was first reviewed (e.g. navigation and information classification and structure) and feedback elicited. Following this, the high level screens for each of the application concepts were reviewed. Prototype screens were used as a talking point from which to establish more detailed requirements concerning task workflows, information requirements and information structure and presentation. The final phase involved further prototyping and modification of tool concepts following the analysis of all prior research.

9.6 Step 6: Prototyping & Evaluation of Tool Concepts

The sixth step involves further scoping and evaluation of the initial system prototypes advanced in last phase of research, with end users. The objective here is to bridge the gap between high level tool concepts and associated user requirements, and the specification of user interface functions and behaviours. To this end, prototypes are co-developed with end users following the collaborative prototyping techniques outlined earlier. This can involve a mix of collaborative prototyping sessions with individual end users, and/or group sessions. This is an iterative activity and involves a number of prototyping sessions and updates. Following each series of sessions, the research will engage in additional prototyping based on a review of aggregated findings. As part of this, the researcher must consider relevant design guidelines. In the case of the first study, the researcher followed regulatory guidance in relation to EFB human factors. Further, additional written documentation may be provided to outline proposed user workflows and provide an explanation of any user interface objects. For example, the full contents of drop down menus/combo boxes should be specified. Further, user testing of prototypes can also be undertaken. The output of this activity is usually low or mid fidelity tool prototypes.

In the first study, three phases of prototyping and evaluation were undertaken involving four participants per phase. Participants included Flight Crew, Maintenance Engineers, Training Personnel and Domain Experts. Individual sessions were conducted with all participants. Informal group sessions were conducted with project stakeholders/ management, after each PD phase to relay project progress and elicit feedback on specific design decisions. Further, as participatory design work progressed, design feedback was relayed to software developers. After phase two, a provisional model (EFB visual/interaction prototype) was provided to the software development team. Specific task interactions were translated into formal use cases and UML models, by development teams. Later, user interface design and HCI rules (series of behaviours for different widgets and screen elements) were drafted. Both the design model and HCI rules were updated, as research progressed. This often necessitated software edits. This wasn't ideal from a software development perspective (e.g. time and costs rewriting code), but was unavoidable given project requirements (e.g. software development and HCI research to progress in parallel with on-going HCI feedback and updates).

The first phase involved the collaborative design and evaluation, of basic paper prototypes drawing from Muller's PICTIVE technique (1991, 1993). In Muller's technique, users actively participate in the design of the user interface. Typically, users mock up a design (either individually or collectively) using basic materials (e.g. pencil, markers and paper), with the assistance of Designers and/or Developers. The mock up/prototype is modified repeatedly (users evaluate the mock up and problem solve changes) for a specific time period. Often, the session is videoed to record the specific design iterations and the rationale behind proposed changes. Underlying this technique is the idea that users must experience the proposed technology solution (e.g. either by prototyping the solution or interacting with the solution), to properly critique the emerging work practice and supporting technology solution. In this context, individual participants were invited to draw concepts for specific screens/workflows. Videotaping was not used. Some participants had difficulties visualizing basic screen structures. In these instances, drawings were produced collaboratively. After a number of participant sessions, generic drawings emerged (e.g. integration of results across a number of sessions). In later sessions, participants were asked to compare their drawings with the evolving concept. Again, this encouraged participants to explore complementary workflow concepts and related visualizations. Following on from this some Visio prototypes for specific task scenarios were developed based on the emerging EFB concept. A second phase involved detailed evaluation of these prototypes. First, participants were asked to appraise a simulation of certain interaction concepts explored in Phase One. After this, participants evaluated specific screens/workflows. All participants evaluated the same prototype. Where problems arose, 'on the fly' design changes were made to clarify solutions. Individual problems and recommendations were recorded for each evaluation, and analyzed. A further Visio prototype was designed, based on the findings of prior co-evaluations. The final phase, involved further collaborative evaluations of the Visio prototype. Individual evaluations were conducted and problems and solutions recorded. The output of this phase was a tentative model for the redesigned EFB solution.

In the second study, a series of individual and group participatory prototyping sessions were conducted with end users. Feedback was provided to Software Developers at different points during this activity. First, a series of collaborative prototyping and evaluation sessions were conducted over a two day period. On the first day, collaborative prototyping and evaluation of tool prototypes with conducted with twelve participants. The sessions focussed on evaluating and extending the initial prototypes which emerged in the earlier envisionment activities. Following the analysis of feedback from all sessions, the prototypes were updated. On the second day, the revised prototypes were reviewed with One Pilot. Further, additional user interface screens were scoped. This was followed by a presentation of proposed concepts to a broader airline group. Feedback from this presentation was factored into further prototyping activities by the researcher. Further prototyping and evaluation of proposed tool concepts was then undertaken with one Pilot, over the course of two additional individual sessions. As part of this, the researcher reviewed issues relating to the broader operational and organizational processes underlying the proposed tool concept. This included scoping of existing company tools and links to other tools advanced in the project. This was followed by further prototyping on the part of the researcher.

9.7 Step 7: Implementation & Evaluation of Proposed Tool Concepts in Organization

The preceding research will have generated new work practice concepts and associated user requirements for new or improved tools. The introduction of new work processes may not be possible. Further, the development costs in relation to the introduction of certain tool functions for primary end users, or the extension of existing tools used by other operational agents to support the work of these primary end users (e.g. supporting information sharing), may be too high. Trade offs may be required. The seventh step therefore involves reviewing and evaluating proposed work practice scenarios and associated tool concepts with different organisational stakeholders, to assess the overall feasibility of proposed tool concepts from an organisational, technical level and commercial perspective. The objective is to assess the feasibility of the proposed technology concepts, and obtain a consensus as to what functions to retain and what to omit. In this regard, technology development might be split over a number of phases. As such, both short term and long term technology development priorities are agreed.

Typically this takes the form of a group workshop with all relevant stakeholders. First the researcher presents the proposed new work practice task scenarios taking into account the task requirement of all relevant roles. Following this, the proposed user interaction with specific new or improved technology tools is described. This can be accompanied by a review of the proposed HCI model for the new or improved system, specific user interface workflows for important tasks and any relevant background documentation. As part of this, the researcher elicits feedback from the group in relation to the proposed work practices for the different agents involved in the work process, and related tool concepts. Problems can be identified and solutions suggested. There may be different views as to the suitability of the new work practices and tool concepts. Feedback may reflect the biases of different roles. In addition, the prototypes may raise certain complex technical issues. This may require a more detailed review. Moreover, proposed organisational changes may be perceived as controversial by certain personnel. As such, a number of workshop sessions may be required. Further, it may be useful to pursue certain discussions on an individual basis. In such cases, the researcher can handover proposed user scenarios, tool prototypes and supporting documentation to the relevant project contact or advocate in the organisation. This person can elicit further feedback from relevant partiers. This feedback can be relayed to the researcher at a later point. Alternatively, the researcher can follow up with specific individuals. This step was undertaken as described above, in relation to the second project only.

9.8 Step 8: Analysis of Feedback & Further Prototyping

The eight step involves the analysis of implementation workshop feedback and further prototyping. Further, the researcher may engage in further review and evaluation of prototypes with end users, if so required. This can become an unending activity. Knowing when to stop is important! The review and evaluation of prototypes typically ends once the researcher is satisfied that the proposed solution meets the agreed requirements and that relevant problems have been surmounted. However, there may not be time (e.g. budget/resources) for exhaustive prototyping and evaluation, and the scope of this evaluation may be curtailed.

9.9 Step 9: Overall Research Analysis, Further Prototyping & Specification of User Requirements & User Interface Design

Step nine entails the analysis of all prior research, for the purposes of specifying the user requirements and user interface design features of the proposed new tool. This necessitates ensuring that all prototypes and associated documentation is in order, to facilitate the communication and handover of requirements. Prototypes should be updated to ensure that all revisions have been modelled. Further, specific user interface screens should be reviewed to check that all required user instructions are provided, that agreed terminology is used on all menu items and interface objects (e.g. checkboxes), and that the contents of drop down menus are complete. The user requirements document should be clearly linked to the prototype so that it is clear to Software Developers, how specific user requirements are executed in terms of the proposed HCI design model. Further, the 'to be' process map and future task descriptions which underlie the proposed technology concept might be updated.

9.10 Step 10: Handover of Requirements to Software Developers & Graphic Designers

Step ten involves the communication and handover of user requirements and the associated user interface design specification to both Software Developers and Graphic Designers. It is the task of the Software Developer to translate user requirements into functional requirements. Similarly, it is the task of Graphic Designers to translate the HCI and information design model into a full visual design - taking into account issues highlighted in relation to information priority and use and presentation of graphics including icons. Usually both user and design requirements are reviewed in person with relevant team members. Prior to this, HCI professionals may have provided advance feedback to the team, and so they may have a broad understanding of the proposed tool requirements. It is recommended that HCI professional involve other team members in the research as early in the process as is possible, to facilitate this handover.

9.11 Step 11: Review & Evaluation of Software Prototypes & Graphic Design

Step eleven involves the review and evaluation of software prototypes (with embedded graphic design), as these activities progress. Prototypes can be reviewed either with team members and/or with end users. In relation to the former, this typically takes the form of a walk-through and evaluation of prototypes with team members. It is important that the software prototypes cohere with the agreed HCI design specification. There may be problems which need to be resolved with the broader team. For example, the implementation of workflows as specified in the URD and associated prototypes may require more software development effort than planned. Alternative solutions may need to be agreed with the team. Further, a number of graphic design options may be suggested. As such, HCI professional may be required to assist Graphic Designers in terms of the selection of specific design options. Usually, the evaluation of prototypes with end users involves some form of user testing.

9.12 Step 12: Evaluation of High Fidelity Prototypes

Once the software prototypes are fully developed, HCI researchers can engage in additional user testing of the system.

9.13 Step 13: System Certification

Step thirteen involves the certification of the system. This is not applicable to all systems. If required, this follows established procedures detailed by the relevant authorities. Usually this process is conducted in parallel to many of the earlier HCI activities.

9.14 Step 14: Ongoing Feedback & Improvements, Post Go Live

The final step - also an optional step - involves the evaluation of the live system once it has been implemented in the organisation. A range of methods such as surveys, interviews and observations can be used. The output of this activity is an assessment of the systems usability and a specification of the re-design requirements for future development activities (if these are being undertaken). Usually any minor problems identified are corrected in the short term.

10. Practical Issues to Consider

In relation to the selection and application of specific methodologies, a number of practical issues must be considered. As mentioned previously, one of the key challenges facing HCI designers is identifying suitable HCI design methods. That is, identifying methods that facilitate work practice re-engineering/envisionment and the related development of user friendly work tools. This question is intensified if research is conducted as part of a commercial software project. Here, HCI activities are subject to constraints. Both research budgets and project time may be limited (product time to market is critical). This may necessitate concurrent HCI and software development activities. Also, HCI practitioners and management teams may have different views regarding research rigour and product quality. Management may want problems solved swiftly and not understand the iterative nature of HCI work and/or specific method limitations. In this environment, HCI practitioners must select methods which provide concrete design instruction/feedback so that products are developed both on time and within budget. HCI practioners working in research laboratories may face similar problems. The research plan may priortise software development activities and a limited budget may be dedicated to HCI research. Again, researchers may need to be opportunistic in terms of the choice and specific application of HCI methods, to ensure that the core brief is delivered on.

Certain of the HCI methodologies outlined above present more or less challenges in terms of time constraints linked to data capture and analysis. Firstly, process mapping activities are quite time consuming. The development of a robust process map requires considerable effort in terms of gathering data (e.g. conducting process workshops, interviews and observations of a range of stakeholders) and analysis and visualization of data (e.g. development of the process map). In most cases, it is not possible to develop a detailed process map for all processes. As such, it is recommended, that the researcher maps all the key processes and the key tasks of operational agents, at a high level. If time allows, the researcher might then explore those processes which are most critical to the technology development agenda, in more detail. The envisionment of future processes is best undertaken through collaborative future process envisionment workshops involving all key stakeholders.

Similarly, the scope of task analysis requires careful consideration. Before embarking on a task analysis, the researcher should review his/her specific objective and the required outputs. Is a detailed task model required? Or, is the advancement of task scenarios for critical tasks sufficient? It is imperative that task analysis activities focus on the primary user roles and key tasks. However, in the case of collaborative tasks, team task requirements must be considered. To obtain a true picture of team task activity and associated constraints, specific workflows must be modelled from the perspective of all agents involved in the

activity. Depending on time and budget, it may not be possible to interview or observe all agents. As such, research must focus on those tasks where collaboration/co-ordination activity is most complex and requires re-design.
To develop a system model of task activities and associated processes - requires conducting research across different organisational processes and functions. In short, this necessitates recruiting a wide range of participants. Releasing personnel from the operation for user interviews or workshops can be costly. Companies are often most disposed towards methods that are least taxing on operations (e.g. preference for observations or short group workshops). Further, participants may be more or less willing to discuss their work and associated problems. Certain participants may be more 'highly involved' in the operation and motivated to improve both processes and technologies. Others may be resistant to change. It is important that the participant panel reflects a range of operational and organisational functions, such that future process and technology envisionment addresses a range of perspectives and the proposed solution is amenable to all.

11. Conclusions

Crucially, the introduction of new technologies follows from the envisionment of new or improved work processes and related task workflows. Proposed technology concepts must be derived in conjunction with end users. Further, the advancement of new or improved work technologies must be predicated on operational requirements and fit the organisational environment. Technology innovation should support operational and organisational goals, as opposed to been driven by new or innovative technical advances. Crucially, the development of new workplace technology affords the opportunity to rethink existing practices and tool support from a process redesign/improvement perspective.
Traditional HCI design methods are unsatisfactory in terms of task and technology envisionment in socio-technical contexts. A number of alternatives such as the application of participatory techniques (e.g. role play, envisionment exercises and collaborative prototyping) and scenario based design approaches have been proposed. Although useful, such methods do not take into account the broader process context and associated information flow which underlies operator task performance. To this end, a blended HCI methodological approach involving the integration of a range of methods is suggested. Drawing from two HCI studies in the Aerospace industry, a new blended HCI design methodology – involving the integration of a range of methodologies associated with two of the three Human Factors fields is advanced. This integrates both formal and informal HCI methods associated with Cognitive Ergonomics, with process mapping methods used in the Organisational Ergonomics domain. Collectively, the application of the above methods ensures that future work practices and technology solutions are properly embedded in the operational and organisational context.

It is argued that HCI designers cannot develop systems/technology without investigating broader work design issues (e.g. operational and organisational aspects of task performance). As such, there is a link between methodologies used both in the Cognitive Ergonomics and Organisational Ergonomics fields. To identify specific operator technology requirements, we must first develop a real world model of the overall operational and organisational system in which the operator works. Such an approach is not typically used in the HCI field. Typically, HCI methods study user task workflows and technology/tool interactions in isolation from the broader operational and organisational processes and related information flow.

This chapter has reviewed a number of design steps in an overall user centred design process. It is suggested that HCI researchers follow this research design, albeit taking into account project constraints. To understand the relationship between task and process, some kind of process mapping is necessary. The advancement of a high level process map is better than none. This will help scope the direction of follow on task analysis - specifically in terms of the selection of tasks that are most complex in terms of process and/or task dependencies. The analysis of system information flow is also critical. The design of future task practices and tool design might be considered from an information flow perspective. As such, HCI activities might focus on identifying what information is relevant to the performance of a task or group of tasks, at a particular point in operational process/timeline, taking into account role of context. To this end, proposed tool concepts can be evaluated in terms of delivering on specific information requirements at certain points in operation, in an appropriate way (e.g. presentation and timing). Further, the application of a range of participatory methods (e.g. technology envisionment, role play, participative prototyping) is also necessary, both in terms of the envisionment and evaluation of future work practice and associated technologies, and the specification of user interface design features. Proposed design solutions must be both realistic from an organisational and technical perspective. As such, proposed work practice and technology concepts should be reviewed with relevant personnel to assess what is feasible. Although modelling the specific aspects of technology integration or broader organisational processes is not the remit of HCI designers, it is important that HCI Designers are mindful of these issues, and that the proposed design solution is advanced following appropriate discussion and negotiation in relation to this. Importantly, these issues need to be reviewed as early as is possible in the user centred design process, so that unnecessary time is not spent on concepts that are not possible for a variety of technical or organisational reasons. The early evaluation of proposed concepts in the form of implementation workshops with relevant stakeholders is useful here.

Evidently, task models and associated design solutions require justification. How can we be sure that the task picture and proposed tool concept is both valid and reliable? If the requirements for developing a valid task picture - as detailed earlier -are addressed, then this provides some degree of certainty. Critically, the application of process mapping techniques ensures that technology development is predicated on operational concepts and requirements. Further, the use of observational methods helps ensure high ecological validity. Moreover, the use of collaborative prototyping and evaluation techniques entails that end user constraints and requirements are factored into the design solution. This follows from the participatory design mantra of designing with end users and not just for end users. Also, this mitigates the task artefact lifecycle, as outlined by Carroll (2002). In addition, the use of implementation workshops ensures that proposed technology concepts are evaluated from a broader organisational and technology level. Lastly, recruiting a suitable panel of participants - representing the range of operational and organisational processes under consideration, is also important.

12. References

Bødker, S. & Burr, J. (2002). The Design Collaboratorium - A Place for Usability Design, *ACM Transactions on Computer Human Interaction*, Vol. 9, No 2, June 2002, pp 152 - 169.

Bødker, S., Ehn, P., Romberger, S., & Sjögren, D. (Eds.). (1985). *The UTOPIA Project: An alternative in text and images (Graffiti 7)*. Swedish Center for Working Life, the Royal Institute of Technology, Stockholm, Sweden and the University of Aarhus, Denmark.

Bannon, L., (1991). 'From Human Factors to Human Actors: The Role of Psychology and Human Computer Interaction Studies in System Design'. In Greenbaum, J., & Kyng, M. (Eds), *Design at Work: Cooperative Design of Computer Systems*. Hillsdale, NJ: Lawrence Erlbaum Associates, pp 25-45.

Cahill, J and McDonald, N. (2006). 'Human computer interaction methods for electronic flight bag envisionment and design', *Cognition, Technology and Work*, 2006, VOL 8; NUMBER 2, pages 113-123 Springer London

Cahill, J and McDonald, N. (2006). 'HILAS Flight Operations Research: A New Framework for System Performance Monitoring ', *Proceedings of the International Conference on Human-Computer Interaction in Aeronautics (HCI-Aero 2006)*. 20-22 September. Seattle, WA

Cahill J , Mc Donald N., Ulfvengren P, Young F., Ramos Y., Losa G (2007). HILAS Flight Operations Research: Development of Risk/Safety Management, Process Improvement and Task Support Tools. In D. Harris (Ed.): *Engin. Psychol. and Cog. Ergonomics, HCII 2007*, LNAI 4562, pp. 648–657, 2007. Springer-Verlag Berlin Heidelberg

Cahill, J and Losa G. (2007). 'Flight Crew Task Performance and the Design of Cockpit Task Support Tools', Proceedings of the European Conference on Cognitive Ergonomics 2007 (ECCE 2007), 28-31 August, Covent Garden, London, UK.

Carroll, J. (2000). *Making Use*. Cambridge, MA: MIT Press.

Carroll, J. (2001) *Human Computer Interaction in the New Millennium*, New York: ACM Press.

Constantine, L. L., & Lockwood, L. A. D. (1999). *Software for Use: A Practical Guide to the Models and Methods of Usage Centred Design*. MA: Addison-Wesley.

Engestrom, Y. & Middleton, D. (1998). *Cognition and Communication at Work*, Cambridge: Cambridge University Press.

Gilbreth, F. and Gilbreth, L. (1921) Time and Motion Study As Fundamental Factors in Planning and Control, New Jersey, The Mountainside Press

Hackos, J. A., & Redish, J. C. (1998). User and Task Analysis for Interface Design. New York: Wiley Computer Publishing, John Wiley & Sons Inc.

Kirwan, B. and Ainsworth, L.K. (1992). *A Guide to Task Analysis*, London: Taylor & Francis Ltd.

Hollan, J., Hutchins, E. & Kirsh, D. (2000). Distributed cognition: toward a new foundation for human-computer interaction research. *ACM Transactions on Computer-Human Interaction*, 7, 174-196.

Hutchins, E. and T. Klausen (1992): Distributed Cognition in an Airline Cockpit. In D. Middleton and Y. Engeström (eds.), *Communication and Cognition at Work*, Beverly Hills, CA: Sage Books.

Hutchins E (1995). *Cognition in the wild*. MIT Press, Cambridge, MA.

ISO/DIS 9241-11 (1995). Draft International Standard. Ergonomic requirements for office work with visual display terminals (VDTs). Part 11: Guidance on Usability, International Organisation for standardisation, Genève, Switzerland.

ISO/DIS 13407 (1997). International Standard -Human-centred design processes for interactive systems, International Organisation for Standardisation, Genève, Switzerland.

Leontev, A. N. (1974). The problem of activity in psychology. *Soviet Psychology*, 13(2), 4-33.

Mayhew, D. (1999). *The Usability Engineering Lifecycle: A practitioner's handbook for user interface design*, San Francisco, CA: Morgan Kauffman.

McDonald, N. (2004) 'Managing the human role in system safety' in *Human and Organisational Issues In The Digital Enterprise* (eds. Fallon E. & Karwowski, W), Galway: National University of Ireland. (P. 23)

McDonald, N. (2006). Organisational resilience and industrial risk. In E.Hollnagel, D.D. Woods & N. Leveson (Eds.), *Resilience engineering. Concepts and precepts*. Aldershot: Ashgate.

Muller, M. (2003). Participatory Design: The Third Space in HCI. In Jacko, J., & Sears, A. (Eds). *The Human Computer Interaction Handbook: Evolving Technologies and Emerging Applications*. Mahwah, NJ: Lawrence Erlbaum Associates, pp 1051 - 1069.

Muller M., & Kuhn S. (1993). Special issue on Participatory Design. *Communications of the ACM*, 36 (4).

Muller M. (1991). PICTIVE - An exploration in participatory design. In *Proceedings of the SIGCHI conference on Human factors in computing systems: Reaching through technology. New Orleans, 1991, pp* 225-231.

Nielsen, J. (1993). *Usability Engineering*. San Francisco, CA: Morgan Kaufmann

Norman, D. O. (1988). *The Design of Everyday Things*, New York: Basic Books.

Norman, D. O. (1993). *Things That Make Us Smart: Defending Human Attributes in the Age of the Machine*, Cambridge MA: Perseus Books.

Pasmore, W (1988), Designing Effective Organizations, John Wiley & Sons, New York, NY

Perrow, Charles (1984) *Normal Accidents: Living with High-Risk Technologies*, New York: Basic Books.

Preece, J., Rogers Y., & Sharp H., (2002) *Interaction Design: Beyond Human Computer Interaction*, New York: John Wiley & Sons.

Rubin, J (1994). *Handbook of Usability Testing: How to Plan, Design and Conduct Effective Test*, New York: John Wiley & Sons.

Trist, E. 1981. The evolution of socio-technical systems. Occasional paper No. 2. Ontario Quality of Working Life Centre. Toronto, Canada.

Vicente, K. J. (1999). *Cognitive Work Analysis: Toward safe, productive and healthy computer based work*. Mahwah, NJ: Lawrence Erlbaum Associates.

Wickens, C. D., & Hollands, J. G. (2000) *Engineering Psychology and Human Performance*: Third Edition, New Jersey: Prentice Hall.

Wilson, T, D. (1999) 'Models on Information Behaviour Research'. *Journal of Documentation*, Vol. 55, No. 3, June

7

The Adaptive Automation Design

Caterina Calefato
University of Turin, Department of Computer Science
Roberto Montanari, Francesco Tesauri
University of Modena and Reggio Emilia, Department of Science and Methods of Engineering
Italy

1. Introduction

During last years Adaptive Automation (AA) has received considerable attention in the academic community, in labs, in technology companies, because of the large use of automation in several domains (e.g. aviation; manufacturing; medicine; road, rail, and maritime transportation). AA is a potential solution to the problems associated with human-automation interaction, regardless of the complexity of the application domain.

The adaptive automation concept was firstly proposed about 30 years ago (Rouse, 1976), but technology has provided the empirical evidence of its effectiveness in more recent times. Several studies have shown that adaptive systems can regulate operator workload and enhance performance while preserving the benefits of automation (Hilburn et al., 1997; Kaber & Endsley, 2004; Moray et al., 2000; Prinzel et al., 2003). Still, inappropriate design of adaptive systems may even bring to a worse performance than full manual systems (Parasuraman et al., 1999). Therefore, methods and skills for designing adaptive automation systems should be fully mastered, before taking the implementation step.

Before analyzing the concept and impact of adaptation features, the meaning and definition of automation should be defined, in order to stress how human characteristics and limitations influence the use (or misuse) of automation

Andy Clark (2003) successfully tried to summarize the technological relationship between human and automated system: "humans have always been adept at dovetailing our minds and skills to the shape of our current tools and aids. But when those tools and aids start dovetailing back - when our technologies actively, automatically, and continually tailor themselves to us just as we do to them - then the line between tool and human becomes flimsy indeed".

Several researchers tried to define what adaptive automation is, using different and complementary concepts. In order to achieve a complete, if it is possible, definition of adaptive automation, it is needed to analyse the definition and the implication of automation itself.

AA aims at optimizing the cooperation and at efficiently allocating labor between an automated system and its human users (Kay, 2006) and it can be considered as an alternative method used to implement automation in a system, whose purpose is to bridge the gaps of traditional automation.

AA refers to systems in which either the user or the system can modify the level of automation by shifting the control of specific functions, whenever specific conditions are met. In an adaptive automated system, changes in the state of automation, operational modalities and the number of active systems can be initiated by either the human operator or the system (Hancock & Chignell, 1987; Rouse, 1976; Scerbo, 1996). In this way adaptive automation enables the level or modes of automation to be tied more closely to operator's needs at any given moment (Scerbo, 1996).

2. From automation to adaptive automation

Automation refers to "systems or methods in which many of the processes of production are automatically performed or controlled by autonomous machines or electronic devices" (Billings, 1997). Automation may be conceived as a tool, or resource, that allows the user to perform some task that would be difficult or impossible to do without the help of machines (ibidem). Therefore, automation can be conceived as the process of substituting some device or machine for a human activity (Parsons, 1985).

Besides the conceptual definitions, a starting point for the understanding of what automation is, is the theoretical work of Sheridan about the Levels of Automation (LoA) (Parasuraman et al., 2000). LoA represent the 10-point scale which describe step by step the automation continuum of levels1. This approach takes into account the control assignment of the system between the human and the machine, focusing on the participation and the autonomy that humans and machines may have in each task to be performed. In the Sheridan model the human machine interaction is particularly stressed; the purpose is to find the best level that fits human needs, in order to maximise the system performance and to optimize its use2. Billings (1991) instead focuses his attention on automation at work: how automation may correctly perform some activities or parts of them, how automation may interact with humans or support them in their tasks. Billing (ibidem) defines LoA in functional terms: a level of automation corresponds to the set of function that an operator can autonomously control in a standard situation united to system ability at providing answer and solutions, at acting properly according to the proposed solution, and to check the results of its actions.

Tightly coupled with Billings definition are Rouse's observations (1988): the adaptive automation provides variable levels of support to human control activities in complex systems, according to the situation. Moreover, the situation is defined by the task features and by the psychophysical status of human operator. As a consequence, the human machine interaction should depend on what has to be automated, and on how and when this should

---

[1] This model (Parasuraman et al., 2000) is made of ten levels: 1) the computer offers no assistance: human must take all decisions and actions; 2) the computer offers a complete set of decision/action alternatives, or 3) narrows the selection down to a few, or 4) suggests one alternative, 5) executes that suggestion if the human approves, or 6) allows the human a restricted time to veto before automatic execution, or 7) executes automatically, then necessarily informs the human, and 8) informs the human only if asked, or 9) informs the human only if it, the computer, decides to 10) the computer decides everything, acts autonomously, ignoring the human.

occur. Through empirical studies Rouse (1977) showed the advantages of implementing AA; specifically, AA allows a dynamic roles and tasks definition that is consistent for the operators and inserts into the system the capability to maintain adequate the human mental workload operating with the system.
The importance of the operator's psychophysical status is a crucial aspect examined by Parasuraman et al. (1992): the AA is the best combination between human and system abilities. This combination, or more properly integration, is leaded by a main decision criterion: the operator mental workload. In fact the first adaptive automation systems were implemented in associate systems based on models of operator behavior and workload (Scerbo, 1996). Particularly, the adaptive automation research has primarily focused on evaluation of performance and workload effects of dynamic allocations of control of early sensory and information acquisition functions as part of human-machine system operations (Kaber et al., 2002). There are several studies reviewing empirical researches about AA (Parasuraman, 1993), (Hilburn et al., 1993), (Scallen et al., 1995), (Parasuraman et al., 1996), (Kaber, 1997), (Kaber & Riley, 1999) that focused on the performance effects of Dynamic Function Allocation (DFA) in complex systems, specifically monitoring and psychomotor functions. These studies brought into evidence that AA significantly improves monitoring and tracking task performance in multiple task scenarios, as compared to static automation and strictly manual control conditions.
A further development for AA systems is the Neuroergonomics approach, which uses psychophysiological measures to trigger changes in the state of automation. Studies have shown that this approach can facilitate operator performance (Scerbo, 1996). Less work has been conducted to establish the impact of AA on cognitive function performance (e.g., decision-making) or to make comparisons of human-machine system performance when AA is applied to various information processing functions (Kaber et al., 2002).
AA carries all the established levels of automation: Scerbo (1996) specifies that the AA can start different types of automation, in relation with the context (system and operator). An integration to this conclusion is provided by Kaber and Riley (1999), which defined adaptive automation as a programming or a pre-definition of the control assignment between human and system, in order to improve the human performance. Human performance is in fact a crucial aspect of the functioning of complex system. As a consequence, the human operator should be involved in the control task, in order to avoid the out-of-the-loop performance. As stated by Norman (1989), without appropriate feedback people are indeed out-of-the-loop; they may not know if their requests have been received, if the actions are being performed properly, or if problems are occurring. Sharing the functions control is not only a matter of quantitative task to accomplish, but it involves the responsibility of the whole operation execution.
The dynamic function allocation (DFA) is a peculiar aspect of AA (Kaber et al, 2001). It basically consists of assigning the authority on specific functions to either the human operator or the automated system, depending on the overall context (i.e. operator's state and outer conditions) and on a defined set of criteria. DFA should therefore be designed by taking into account both the human and the system status, and considering the means for allowing context recognition.
Focusing on the participation and the autonomy that humans and machines may have in each task to be performed there is some debate. Some researches face the crucial issue of the authority that each part should have in controlling the system. Historically, humans played

the role of the supervisory control i.e. the machine decides about the actions and the humans evaluate these decisions; depending on this assessment, control on the actions is either regained by human operators or provided (Sheridan, 1992). In this effort a crucial role is played by the human skills and abilities and by the systems natural limits (Parasuraman et al., 2000).

There is a clear difference between the AA approach and the Level of Automation (Kaber & Endsley, ibidem). By contrast with the traditional view of automation that is shortly a fixed and highly regulated process designed to eliminate human interaction, AA is designed to expect and anticipate changes under active control of a developer while maintaining precise control of all background variables not currently of interest (Kay, 2006). AA is based on the dynamic allocation of the control of the whole task or of some parts, crossing along time manual and automated phases. The Levels of automation instead allow only a static function assignment, because the task level of automation is established in the design phase (Kaber & Endsley, ibidem). AA allows users to experiment with variables seen as key parameters in a system while preventing undesired secondary effects that could unexpectedly arise from variations in parameters not under study, which in manual systems might not be precisely controlled. Through adaptive automation, developers gain flexible control of parameters under study and confidence as well as automatic control of the rest of their systems (Kay, 2006). In this way, adaptive automation can be considered as a design philosophy with a heavy impact on the technological development. Rather than focusing on repetition of the same events, adaptive automation focuses on flexible process design and rapid process development. AA allows process development facilities to move beyond limited "automated instrument" development into a more fully integrated "automated process," in which individual instruments become part of a universal, fully-automated cycle (Kay, 2006).

3. Adaptation and the problem of authority: from the delegation metaphor to the horse-rider paradigm.

An accurate automation design includes an high level of flexibility, in order to allow the system to perform different operational modes, according to the task or to the environment. The flexibility level determines the type of system: adaptive automation systems can be described as either adaptable or adaptive. In adaptable systems, changes among presentation modes or in the allocation of functions are initiated by the user. By contrast, in adaptive systems both the user and the system can initiate changes in the state of the system (Scerbo, 1996). The distinction between adaptable and adaptive technology can also be described with respect to authority and autonomy. "As the level of automation increases, systems take on more authority and autonomy. At the lower levels of automation, systems may offer suggestions to the user. The user can either veto or accept the suggestions and then implement the action. At moderate levels, the system may have the autonomy to carry out the suggested actions once accepted by the user. At higher levels, the system may decide on a course of action, implement the decision, and merely inform the user (...). In adaptive systems, on the other hand, authority over invocation is shared. Both the operator and the system can initiate changes in state of the automation".

There is some debate over who should have control over system changes: the debate arises about the final authority on the control process: some researchers believe that humans should have the highest authority over the system, because s/he has the final responsibility of the whole system behaviour. This position is supported by the conviction that humans are more reliable and efficient in the resources and safety management when they encompass the control over the automation change of state (Billings & Woods, 1994; Malin & Schreckenghost, 1992). To ensure the safety of the system is the issues about. However, it may be that strict operator authority over changes among automation modes is always justified. There may be times when the operator will be not the best judge of when automation is needed. Scerbo (1996) argues that in some hazardous situations where the operator is vulnerable, it would be extremely important for the system to have authority to invoke automation, because, for example, operating environments change with time, and it may not be easy for humans to make correct decision in a changed environment, especially when available time or information is limited (Inagaky, 2003) or when operators are too busy to make changes in automation (Wiener, 1989). The authority shared between humans and machines becomes a question of decision during design.

It is important to notice that human and automation roles are structured as complementary: one of the main approach to human interaction with a complex system is "delegation", that is patterned on the kinds of interactions that a supervisor can have with an intelligent trained subordinate. Human task delegation within a team is in fact an example of adaptable system, "since the human supervisor can choose which tasks to hand to a subordinate, can choose what and how much to tell the subordinate about how (or how not) to perform the subtask s/he is assigned, can choose how much or how little attention to devote to monitoring, approving, reviewing and correcting task performance, etc." (Miller et al., 2005).

Despite this such a system shows also adaptive elements in its behaviour. Delegating a task to a subordinate (in this case the automation), the subordinate may have at least a partial authority to determine how to perform those task. Moreover a good subordinate may have opportunities to take initiative in order to suggest tasks that need to be done or to propose information that may be useful (Miller et al., 2005). Note that the main difference between task delegation as performed by a supervisor and task allocation performed by a system designer has been that the supervisor had much more flexibility in what when and how to delegate and better awareness of the task performance conditions. The system designer, instead, has to fix a relationship at design time for static use in all context (Miller & Parasuraman, 2007). To vary the quantity of control and authority is an important issue, because in the case of emergency it may be needed to rapidly transfer the control, without distraction from the outcome problem.

The control and authority variation is also a communication matter (Norman, 2008). A way the machine can communicate its objectives and strategy is to present them to the human in an explicit manner. Miller proposes the playbook metaphor, that propose a model of shared knowledge, used to communicate. The Playbook model allows humans to interact with the subordinate automated systems almost as with human subordinates, originating a type of adaptive automation.

Despite of all the efforts to create a human-machine communication, there are no real communication capabilities built into systems. As Norman (2007) states: "Closer analysis shows this to be a misnomer: there is no communication, none of the back-and-forth discussion that characterizes true dialogue. Instead, we have two monologues. We issue commands to the machine, and it, in turn, command us. Two monologues do not make a dialogue". The collaboration and communication failure by a even more powerful technology becomes a very crucial point. Collaboration requires synchronisation and trust, achievable only through experience and understanding (Norman, 2007).

The need of sharing trust and knowledge between humans and machines leads to the so called H-Metaphor, that studies and tryes to reproduce the relationship between a horse and its rider. The "horse-rider paradigm" is introduced at first time in 1990 by Connell and Viola, then it was developed by Flemish et al (2003), that named it "H-metaphor" and faced also by Norman (2007). The "Horse-Rider paradigm" explains the relation between human and automation like the relation that a rider establishes with his/her horse: the human receives information about the actual system status through an osmotic exchange with it. Human intention and actions become the parameters the system uses to offer him the correct solution or answer to the faced context. In this way it is possible to improve the human performance that represents the crucial hearth of the interaction in complex systems. Besides the operator is maintained in loop during the system control, in order to avoid or reduce the out-of-the-loop performance.

2. Implementation of Adaptive Automation principles

The main purposes of adaptive automation are to prevent errors and to reduce the out-of-the-loop performance, preserving the adequate level of situation awareness and of mental workload (Kaber Riley, Endsley 2001).

These approaches redefine the assignment of functions to people and automation in terms of a more integrated team approach. Hence, the task control has to be shared between the human and the system, according to the situation. The adaptive automation tries to dynamically determine in real time when a task has to be performed manually or by the machine [Endsley 1996] (see figure 1).

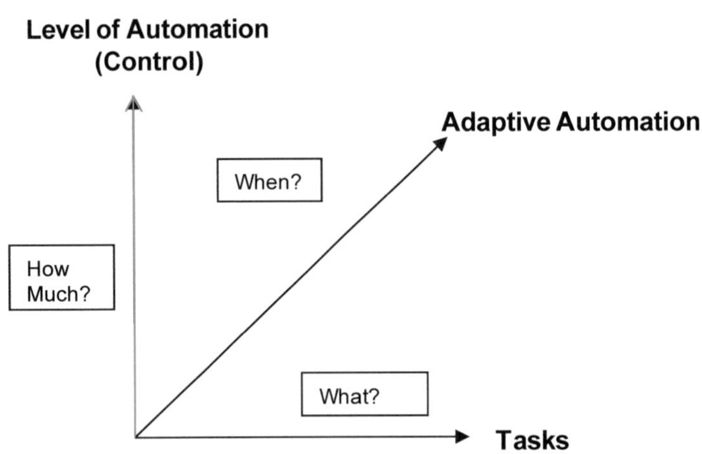

Fig. 1. *Automation Design Consideration* (Endsley 1996).

Along the axes of figure 1 are shown two orthogonal and complementary approaches: one approach (Level of Automation - Control) tries to find to optimisation in the assignment of control between the human and automated system by keeping both involved in system operation. The other (Adaptive Automation, AA, or Dynamic Function Allocation, DFA) illustrates how the control must pass back and forth between the human and the automation over time, and seeks to find ways of using this to increase human performance [Endsley 1996]. Although the adaptive automation is very promising, some problems are still unsolved, i.e. to identify the task features that determines the optimal level for the AA implementation. It has to be carefully taken into account the effects on the cognitive and physically activities, specifying the best AA implementation for each activity. Besides, the human machine interfaces have to be studied in order to support correctly the AA [Kaber, Riley, Endsley 2001]. Another difficult issues is about when AA should be invokes. It is needed to work in order to address questions of periodic insertion of automation into manual task. "Research is also needed to explore the interaction between adaptive automation and level of control - how much automation needs to be employed may be a function of when it is employed" [Endsley 1996]. It should be determined also how to implement AA, that is another controversial matter. Many systems allow operators to invoke automation, but in critical sistuaations, the human my be 1) so overloades as to make this an extra encumber, 2) incapacitaded or unable to do so, 3) unaware that the situation calls for automated assistance, or 4) a poor decision maker. Otherwise leaving the system with the authority to turn itselef on and off may be even more problematic, as this forces the operator to passive accept the system decision [Endsley 1996]. The final authority may be traded flexibly and dynamically between humans and automation, because there can be the cases in which automation should have the final authority for ensuring the safety of the system [Inagaky 2001].

2.1 Human centred automation

The studies about adaptive automation share their field of interest with the researches about the human centred automation, that is a design practice that takes into account the human factors [Parasuraman, Sheridan 2000]. As Sheridan (1997) states, the human-centered automation has many
alternative meanings ranging from: "allocate to the human the tasks best suited to the human, allocate to the automation the tasks best suited to it," through "achieve the best combination of human and automatic control, where 'best' is defined by explicit system objectives." The meanings he presented span from a function-oriented perspective to a mission-oriented view. As we have explained, automated systems, have negative consequences on the human situation awareness, expecially in the understanding and projection of future states and favourites the out-of-the-loop performance. The human-centred automation will is to correct this aberrant effects typical of the technology centered automation, facilitating the human system cooperation in the control and managing of complex systems [Kaber, Endsley 2004].
The design of complex systems supporting the operator situation awareness is the bridge between human centred automation theory and adaptive automation techniques [Kaber, Riley, Endsley 2001]. Since the human centred automation claims an acceptable workload and a good situation awareness, then the adaptive automation is the vehicle for the reaching of these purposes. Hence the AA can be defined as a kind of human centred automation. On

this hand there are empirical evidence on positive effects of AA on SA and workload [Kaber 1997], on the other hand there is not a unique theory that give designer a general guideline suitable for each application field, such as aviation, automotive, rails, tele-robotics and manufacturing.
The human centred automation refers both to the system output and to the human input. Automation may involve different phase of the whole decision and action processing, that involves four main steps, and copes with the Sheridan ten-point scale of level of automation [Parasuraman, Sheridan 2000].

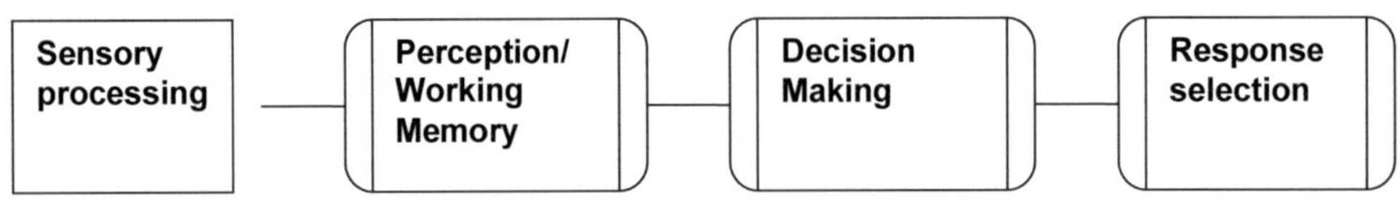

Fig. 1. Stages of Human Information Processing

This four-stage model is certainly a relevant simplification of the many components of human information processing as deeply explained cognitive psychologists [Broadbend 1958].
The sensory-processing phase refers to the acquisition and registration of multiple sources of information. In this stage the positioning and orienting of sensory receptors, sensory processing,
initial pre-processing of data prior to full perception, and selective attention are included. The perception/working memory phase considers conscious perception, and manipulation of processed and retrieved information in working memory [Baddadely 1996]. The decision phase involves the decision reaching based on such cognitive processing. The final action phase refers to the implementation of a response or action according with the decision choice [Parasuraman, Sheridan 2000]. Adaptive automation can be applied to the output functions of a system (automation of decision and action selection) and also to the input functions (sensory processing and perception) that precede decision making and action [Parasuraman, Sheridan 2000].

2.2 Design adaptive automation

In order to develop an adaptive system, some theoretical instruments guiding designers are available. In this paper task analysis and function allocation methods will be presented. These methods are applied during the preliminary study phase. Task analysis and function allocation both aim at matching the human abilities with the system ones, in order to automate the tasks best suited to machines and to maintain as manual the functions best suited to human (Harrison, Johnson, Wright, 2001). The task analysis is namely a graphic representation (as flow chart) of tasks and sub tasks that the operators may accomplish with the system. Once the basilar functions have been founded, they will be allocated, in order to consider the consequences of the match of functions with roles and scenarios. As Harrison, Johnson, Wright [2001] defined, a function is an activity that the man-machine system is required to be capable of performing in order to achieve some result in the domain under

consideration. From this point of view it is possible to state that Work systems perform functions or units of work. Roles, instead, are more difficult to define. They make sense to consider it as an activity that can be performed either by human or machine (Harrison, Johnson, Wright, 2001).
The York Method (developed at the Department of Computer Science, University of York) provides theoretical instruments to define functions, rules and scenarios, and then represents them by some specific grids. The aim is to decide which functions are suitable to which rules, considering different scenarios [Calefato, Montanari, Tango 2007]. "A function may be separable from all roles, and technically feasible and cost effective to automate, in which case the function may be totally automated. Alternatively it is possible that the function maps entirely to one of the roles, and is infeasible to automate, in which case the function is totally performed within that role. In most cases however functions fit into neither category. In this situation the function is to be partially automated" (Harrison, Johnson, Wright, 2001). Functions and roles have to be set into one or more scenarios.
The scenario development process involves several steps [Calefato, Montanari, Tango 2007] : 1) identification of goals and objectives; 2) scenario definition, including specifications and development of needed model elements and performance measures; 3) preparation of specific component models; 4) program specific performance measures; 5) scenario programming; 6) testing, upgrading and validating of the system on the chosen scenarios. In taking into account the driving scenario, it has to be measured the driver's competences in tasks critical to performance and safety.
These concept can be clarified by an example belonging to the automotive domain. We can hypnotize to have to design a preventive safety system. In order to design the application, the driving scenario and its corresponding manoeuvres have been broken down into functions and sub-functions in order to outline which functions have to be performed manually, automatically or both. Secondly, system and driver's roles have been combined with functions in order to outline which functions suite best to which roles, considering the given scenarios. The scenarios have been selected in order to measure the driver workload and situation awareness. Consequentially the selected scenario shows the whole behaviour of the system, along the seven LoA implemented [Calefato, Montanari, Tango 2007].

3. Side effects of automation

Despite of the wide advantages of automation such as the increased capacity and productivity, reduction of small errors, manual workload and mental fatigue, the relief from routine
operations, and decrease of performance variation due to individual differences, there are several drawbacks that must be taken into account. Since automation brings same changes in the task execution (i.e. setup and initialization), in the cognitive demands (i.e. requirements for increased situational awareness), in the people roles related to the system (i.e. relegating people to supervisory controllers). Beside a decrease of job satisfaction automation lead to a lowered vigilance and an increased mental workload, fault-intolerant systems, silent failures, false alarms. This framework is strictly connected with other

negative effects due to the human interaction with the system: over-reliance, complacency, over trust and mistrust, manual deskilling [Prinzel 2003].
Nowadays the adaptive automation is claimed as the solution for the problems inducted by the automation. In this paper we aim to show how the adaptive automation may be successfully used in the design of automotive user interfaces that control automatic or partially adaptive systems, named ADAS (Advanced Driver Assistance Systems).

4. Automotive applications: preventive safety systems

One of the most important application field of the adaptive automation design principles is the automotive domain, where the preventive safety approach is applied in the designing of the driving task, turning the automation in a safety tool. The ergonomic studies about the driving safety are a wide and well-known field (Campbell et al. 1998; Mariani, Bagnara, Montanari 2001; Bekiaris et al. 2003; Green 2003). Particularly, the systems that foresee the integration of automation elements into the driving task (i.e. the ACC, adaptive cruise control) are studied by the information ergonomics, that deals with the improvement of signalling and command devices whose efficient information is often crucial. It is specifically the case of in-vehicle information systems (IVIS), that nowadays include also the nomadic devices, like pocket pc and mobile phones; of the new integrated dashboards, that show the driver, apart from traditionally information (such as speedometer, odometer, rev counter, etc.), other information about the trip (instantaneous consumption, fuel autonomy, covered distance, direction to follow, etc.); of innovative commands like haptic devices or vocal commands.
These systems are based on several technologies: sensing technologies for environment perception, in-vehicle digital maps and positioning technologies, wireless communication technologies

One of the current research area in automotive is aimed at improving driving safety with regards to the development of so-called preventive warning systems, also called ADAS (i.e. Advanced Driver Assistance Systems). These are systems able to detect an incoming dangerous in advanced, allowing a time to perform a repairing manoeuvre. ADAS (Advanced Driver Assistance Systems), thanks to their sensors, are able at monitoring the external environment and if a critical situation is detected, and at alerting the driver about a possible danger (Berghout et al. 2003), supporting him/her in several driving tasks. The driver needs to be supported with scenario and task information especially when some dangerous events can occur all-around the vehicle, because preventive information can improve the road-safety, such as in the case of the collision avoidance system and of blind spot systems. Other situations that can be supported by ADAS are low visibility (night vision systems) or correct driving behaviour handling (lane keeping or lane warning).
The solution offered by AA can be applied not only to the automatic functions but also to the user interface that manage them. There may be interesting solutions of dynamic adaptation of interface to the external context and to the user psychophysical condition. An contemporary research field is about the introduction of dynamic displays into adaptive system interfaces. Dynamic displays allow *ad hoc* configurations of informative needs and of interaction styles. For instance, dynamic in-vehicle displays can provide specific interface features on the basis of the time of the day, like what happens with the night modality of

navigator displays, which invert their colours. Flexible display configurations that satisfy driver's information needs are able at improving the situation awareness and the driving performance (Calefato, articolo di HCI).
It comes into evidence the importance of the design of in-vehicle interfaces to carefully evaluate which kind of information to take into account. From the human side the choose is among visual, auditory, and haptic information. From the automation side the choose is among psychophysical information: i.e. workload, situation awareness, distraction, ecc.
From the human factors point of view (Green 2003), driving is considered as a complex cognitive task that can be summarized by four main sub-processes: perception, analysis, decision and action. To be performed, each phase presumes the achievement of the previous one.
ADAS, both the prototype and the devices already available on the market, alert the driver by visual, acoustic and tactile alarms that a critical situation has been detected, but they also modify the driver behaviour: the driver is earlier warned about dangers, but as it happens with automation, the same warnings may interfere with the driving task (Wickens 1984; 1989), augmenting the driver's mental workload, often already high (De Waard 1996) and favouring the failure of the whole human-machine system.
The European Project PREVENT (www.prevent-ip.org) has been dedicated to developing of preventive safety applications and technologies, able to help drivers to avoid or mitigate an accident through the use of in-vehicle systems which sense the environment and the importance of a possible danger, taking also into account the driver's state. Preventive safety makes use of information, communications and positioning technologies to provide solutions for improving road safety. Generally speaking, the PREVENT technologies should progressively act, according to the significance and timing of the threat. The preventive applications have to early inform the driver, warn him or her if no repairing manoeuvre has been undertaken, and finally actively assist or intervene in order to avoid an accident or mitigate its consequences. The main applications taken into consideration by these researches are:

- maintaining a safe speed
- keeping a safe distance
- driveing within the lane
- avoiding overtaking in critical situations
- safely passing intersections
- avoiding crashes with vulnerable road users
- reduce the severity of an accident if it still occurs

Apart from ADAS, other new in-vehicle technologies are being introduced on the market: they are the In-Vehicle Information Systems (IVIS), that are often connected with a wide range of nomadic devices (i.e. mobile phones, personal digital assistants and other portable computing devices). The use of these technologies can be a benefit for the road safety enhancement. On one hand IVIS and nomadic device provide in-vehicle access to new information services, on the other hand they may induce dangerous levels of workload and distraction. The general objective of another relevant EU project named AIDE is to generate the knowledge and develop methodologies and human-machine interface technologies required for safe and efficient integration of ADAS, IVIS and nomad devices into the driving environment (www. aide-eu.org). More in details AIDE aim is to develop innovative technologies able to maximise the efficiency and the safety benefits of preventive safety system and minimize the side effects of IVIS, and finally to reduce the level of workload and distraction induced by the even more complex cockpit.

5. Conclusions

After considering the positive effects of adaptive automation implementation, this chapter focuses on two partly overlapping phenomena: on the one hand, the role of trust in automation is considered, particularly as to the effects of overtrust and mistrust in automation's reliability; on the other hand, long-term lack of exercise on specific operation may lead users to skill deterioration. As a future work, it will be interesting and challenging to explore the conjunction of adaptive automation issues and neuroergonomics, multiple and intelligent user interfaces, distributed cognition.

6. References

Baddeley A. D. (1986), *Working Memory*, Oxford University Press, 978-0198521167, USA

Billings, C. E. (1991) Human-centered aircraft automation: A concept and guidelines (NASA Tech. Memo. No.103885), Moffet Field, CA: NASA Ames Research Center

Billings, C. E. (1997). *Aviation Automation: The Search for a Human-Centered Approach,* Lawrence Erlbaum Associates, 978-0805821260, USA

Billings, C.E., & Woods, D.D. (1994). Concerns about adaptive automation in aviation systems. In M. Mouloua & R. Parasuraman (Eds.), *Human performance in automated systems: current research and trends* (pp. 264-269). Hillsdale, NJ: Erlbaum.

Broadbent, D. E. (1958) *Perception and Communication*, Pergamon Press, ISBN not available, U.K

Clark, A. (2003), *Natural-Born Cyborgs: Minds, Technologies and the Future of Human Intelligence*, ISBN not available, Oxford University Press, USA

Flemisch F., Adams C., Conway S., Goodrich K., Palmer M., and Schutte P., (2003). The H-Metaphor as Guideline for Vehicle Automation and Interaction, (NASA/TM—2003-212672). Hampton, VA: NASA Langley Research Center.

Hancock, P.A., & Chignell, M.H. (1987). Adaptive control in human-machine systems. In P.A. Hancock (Ed.), *Human factors psychology* (pp. 305-345). North Holland: Elsevier Science Publishers

Hilburn, B., Molloy, R., Wong, D., & Parasuraman, R. (1993). Operator versus computer control of adaptive automation. In R. S. Jensen & D. Neumeister (eds.), *Proceedings of the 7th International Symposium on Aviation Psychology* (pp. 161-166). Columbus, OH: Department of Aviation, The Ohio State University

Hilburn, B., Jorna, P., Byrne, E., & Parasuraman, R. (1997). The effect of adaptive air traffic control (ATC) decision aiding on controller mental workload. In M. Mouloua & J. Koonce (Eds.), *Human automation interaction*, 84–91. Mahwah, NJ: Erlbaum.

Inagaky, T., (2003), Automation and the cost of authority. *International Journal of Industrial Ergonomics*, Vol. 31, 169-174.

Kaber D. B. (1997). The Effect of Level of Automation and Adaptive Automation on Performance in Dynamic' Control Environments' (Tech. Work. Doc.: ANRCP-NG-ITWD-97-01). Amarillo, TX: Amarillo National Resource Center for Plutonium.

Kaber, D. B. and Riley, J. (1999). Adaptive automation of a dynamic control task based on secondary task workload measurement. *International Journal of Cognitive Ergonomics*, Vol. 3, No. 3, 169-187.

Kaber, D. B., Riley, J. M., Tan, K., Endsley, M. R, (2001), On the Design of Adaptive Automation for Complex Systems, *International Journal of Cognitive Ergonomics*, Vol. 5(1), Lawrence Erlbaum Associates, Inc.

Kaber, D. B., & Endsley, M. (2004). The effects of level of automation and adaptive automation on human performance, situation awareness and workload in a dynamic control task. *Theoretical Issues in Ergonomics Science*, Vol. 5, 113–153.

Kaber, D., Prinzel III, L., Wright, M., Clamann, M., (2002), Workload-Matched Adaptive Automation. Support of Air Traffic Controller Information Processing Stages, ...

Kay M., (2006), Adaptive automation accelerates process development, *Bioprocess international* 4(4):70-78.

Malin, J. T., & Schreckenghost, D.L. (1992). Making intelligent systems team players: Overview for designers. NASA Technical Memorandum 104751, Johnson Space Center, Houston, TX.

J. & Chapman, M. (2005) The Playbook™ Approach to Adaptive Automation *Proceedings of Human Factors and Ergonomics Society Annual Meeting, Aerospace Systems*, pp. 15-19, ISBN, Orlando (USA).

Miller, C.; Funk, H.; Wu, P.; Goldman, R.; Meisner, et Wu, P. (2005). Implications of adaptive vs. adaptable uis on decision making : Why "automated adaptiveness" is not always the right answer. *In Proceedings of the 1st International Conference on Augmented Cognition*, Las Vegas, NV.

Miller, Parasurman, Designing for flexible interaction between humans and automation: delegation interfaces for supervisory control

Moray, N., Inagaki, T., & Itoh, M. (2000). Situation adaptive automation, trust and self-confidence in fault management of time-critical tasks. *Journal of Experimental Psychology: Applied*, Vol. 6, 44–58.

Norman, D. (1989) The problem of automation: Inappropriate feedback and interaction not overautomation (ICS Report 8904). La Jolla, CA: Institute for Cognitive Science, U. C. San Diego.

Norman, D. (2007) *Design of future things*, Basic Books, 978-0465002276, USA

Parasuraman, R., Bahri, T., Deaton, J., Morrison, J., & Barnes, M., 1992, Theory and design of adaptive automation in aviation systems (Progress Rep. No. NAWCADWAR-92033-60) Warmister, PA: Naval Air Warfare Center, Aircraft Division, Factors, 30.

Parasuraman, R., Mouloua, M., Molloy, R., & Hilburn, B. (1993). Adaptive function allocation reduces performance costs of static automation. In R. S. Jensen & D. Neumeister (eds.), Proceedings of the 7th International Symposium on Aviation Psychology

Parasuraman, R., Mouloua, M., & Molloy, R. (1996). Effects of adaptive task allocation on monitoring of automated systems. *Human Factors*, Vol. 38 (4), 665-679.

Parasuraman, R., Mouloua, M., & Hilburn, B. (1999). Adaptive aiding and adaptive task allocation enhance human-machine interaction. In M. W. Scerbo & M. Mouloua (Eds.), *Automation technology and human performance: Current research and trends* (pp. 119–123). Mahwah, NJ: Erlbaum.

Parasuraman Raja, Sheridan Thomas B., Wickens, C. (2000.) A Model for Types and Levels of Human Interaction with Automation, Fellow, in *Transactions on systems, man, and cybernetics – Part A: Systems and humans*, vol. 30, no. 3, May 2000, IEEE

Parsons, H.M. (1985). Automation and the individual: Comprehensive and comparative views. *Human Factors*, Vol. 27, 99-112.

Prinzel, Lawrence J., 2003, Team-Centerede perspective for Adaptive Automation Design, Langley Research Center, Hampton, Virginia, available from NASA Center for Areospace Information (CASI).

Prinzel, L., Freeman, F., Scerbo, M., Mikulka, P., & Pope, A. (2003). Effects of a psychophysiological system for adaptive automation on performance, workload and event-related potential P300 component. *Human Factors*, Vol. 45, 601–614.

Rouse, W.B. (1976). Adaptive allocation of decision making responsibility between supervisor and computer. In T.B. Sheridan & G. Johannsen (Eds.), *Monitoring behavior and supervisory control*, 295-306. New York: Plenum Press.

Rouse, W. B., 1988, Adaptive aiding for human/computer control, in *Human Factors*, Vol. 30, 431-438.

Scallen, S., Hancock, P. A., & Duley, J. A. (1995). Pilot performance and preference for short cycles of automation in adaptive function allocation. *Applied Ergonomics*, Vol. 26, 397-403.

Scerbo, M.W., (1996). Theoretical perspectives on adaptive automation. In R. Parasuraman & M. Mouloua (Eds.), *Automation and human performance: Theory and applications*, 37-63. Mahwah, NJ: Erlbaum

Sheridan, T. B. (1997). Supervisory control. In G. Salvendy (ed.), *Handbook of human factors* (pp. 1295-1327). New York: John Wiley & Sons.

Wiener, E.L. (1989). Human factors of advanced technology ('glass cockpit') transport aircraft. Technical report 117528. Moffett Field, CA: NASA Ames Research Center.

8

How Workstyle Transitions Influence the Tools' Perceptions of Use

Pedro Campos
University of Madeira
Portugal

1. Introduction

Software engineers need better interaction design tools: tools that will help them create higher quality user interfaces. Looking back at the evolution of interaction design and software development tools, what we see is a relentless march of ever heavier, more complex and less usable systems, systems that prevent the designers from focusing on their real important tasks: building usable and useful products.

There is increasing evidence from research claiming that real-world designers and modellers prefer to use general-purpose, unrestrained, tools instead of formal, rigid tools (Jarzabek and Huang, 1998; Wu et al., 2003), something that our previous research also showed (Campos and Nunes, 2007). However, the industries' tool vendors "who sell us the software tools that make disciplined design possible" do not use the tools themselves (Constantine, 2001). Companies often force designers to adopt certain tools or tool suites as a consequence of management intentions to instil standards and best practices. The designer has been framed into a vicious plot of imposed tools and methods: tools are not widely adopted and used.

In this paper, we propose a novel framework to assess the acceptance and usability of interaction design tools. Instead of leveraging on usability engineering work, we use a popular technology acceptance model from the Management Information systems (MIS) field and combine that model with usability evaluation techniques to study how interaction designers actually work.

Throughout this paper, we use the concept of work style (Campos and Nunes, 2005b) as a compact way to describe the user's way of working (working alone or collaboratively, thinking at problem level or at solution level, using a sound semantic or simply being creative).

Although some research has been dedicated to studying why modelling tools are not used (Ilvari, 1996), leading to some frameworks that can measure the tool usability in a cost-effective way (Seffah and Kline, 2002); our approach is distinctive because it combines work style quantitative data that can be easily obtained with logging tools (tools that measure the user's actions running unobtrusively in background) with qualitative data that predicts a given tool level of acceptance. By quantitative, we mean data that we can easily measure in numbers, like e.g. the number of times the user switches from a high-level view of the User

Inter-face (UI) into lower-level, detailed views of the UI. By qualitative, we mean data collected from subjects, which express their subjective feelings regarding any aspect of using a system, like e.g. the extent to which users found the system easy to use. The HCI field has surprisingly little research on evaluation methods that try to combine and make use of both quantitative and qualitative data. Combining them can contribute to obtaining a "bigger picture" of a system's level of usability and usefulness.

This paper is organized as follows: in Section 2, we describe some studies and frameworks about usability and evaluation methods with a particular focus on development or design activities. Section 3 describes the foundations of our proposed framework. Section 4 presents field study's results and discussion. Finally, section 5 concludes and discusses some implications of our findings to tool developers and designers.

2. Studying and Supporting the Designer's Behavior

Our research goal is to better understand the usability and acceptance factors of interaction design tools. We follow a two-phase approach: (i) study everyday interaction design tasks and (ii) exploit the information obtained in the design of new tools.

We devised an approach that aimed for an empirically sound framework that could be used to inform as well as to validate the design of new tools. This research objective is not new, but the question is very timely: the argument that the practitioner's behaviour must be studied in order to make better tools has been used recently by Seffah and Kline (2002); Ko and Myers (2005). There has also been a growing body of research aimed at building models for e.g. the design of interactive systems within their physical environments. Graham et al. (2000) describe a Dimension Space "intended to help designers understand both the physical and virtual entities from which their systems are built, and the tradeoffs involved in both the design of the entities themselves and of the combination of these entities in a physical space".

This need for better studying and supporting the interaction designer's work is even more evident in the case of model-based tools (Paternò, 2005; Navarre et al., 2001; Vanderdonckt and Berquin, 1999), which are our main research focus. In model-based tools it is common to provide the designer with a set of tools suited for each aspect of the development. For instance Sinnig et al. (2004) describe a set of tools for task modelling, dialog modelling and for designing the presentation and layout models. The problem with this approach is that it is difficult to go back and forth from one model to another: even if tools provide full traceability between models, there is a cognitive load in the designer's mind that gets higher as the number of transitions between different models increases.

Paternò (2005) has recently described how tools can support the development of task models, particularly for multimodal UI development, and has also analyzed a series of new challenges for model-based tools. Paternò also acknowledges that models can be represented with different levels of formality, which we also ad-dress in our proposed work style model.

Thevenin and Coutaz (1999) have also argued for "plastic" UI's, interfaces that must run on heterogeneous devices, where the contexts of use vary and may even change at runtime, according to the user's preferences and needs. This line of thought clearly supports our argument that more effort is needed for designing tools that are capable of transparently adapt to the interaction designer's work styles.

2.1 The Technology Acceptance Model

Complex work activities increase the difficulty of predicting the level of acceptance of novel technology and how it will be used in practice. An important and open research question is how to translate usability evaluation results into concrete design decisions (Morris and Dillon, 1997; Wright et al. 2000).

The Technology Acceptance Model (TAM) developed by Davis and colleagues (Davis, 1989) is a widely used theoretical model in the Management Information Systems (MIS) field. Basically, it attempts to predict and explain computer-usage behaviour, offering both researchers and practitioners a direct, pragmatic instrument to measure a technology degree of acceptance. Morris and Dillon (1997) pointed out that TAM offers HCI professionals a "theoretically grounded approach to the study of software acceptability that can be directly coupled to usability evaluations".

In TAM, depicted in Figure 1, there are five primary constructs: Perceived Usefulness (PU), the extent to which the user expects the system to improve his/her job performance within an organizational setting; Perceived Ease Of Use (PEOU), the degree to which the user believes the system's use will be free of effort; Attitude toward Using (A), the user's desire to use or favourableness feelings towards using the system; Behavioural Intentions to Use (BI), which measures the strength of a user's intention to use the system in the future; and the Actual Use, i.e. the amount of usage per time unit.

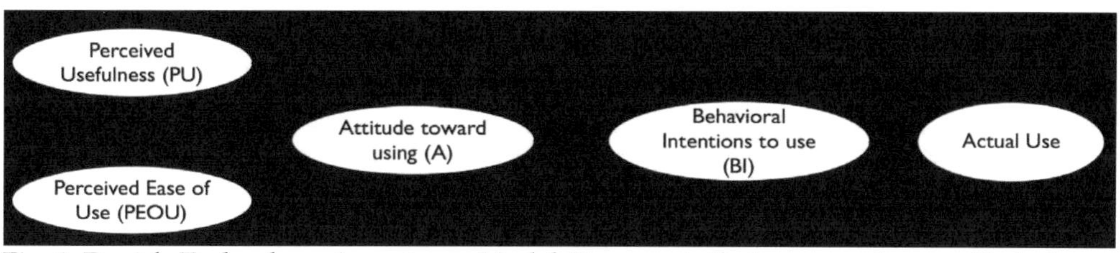

Fig. 1. Davis's Technology Acceptance Model. It suggests that a person is more likely to actually use a technology if he believes that it will be both useful and usable.

As depicted in Figure 1, the actual use of a system is a direct function of the behavioural intentions to use it. These are in turn influenced by perceived usefulness and attitude toward using. Perceived ease of use and perceived usefulness are both crucial to determine the attitude toward using the system.

TAM has been effectively used (Taylor and Todd, 1995; Mathieson, 1991) to predict system's acceptability, but it cannot be used to explain specific design flaws (Morris and Dillon, 1997). However, it presents the important advantage of being a reliable and cost effective way to evaluate systems at any life cycle time. The value of TAM stems from several aspects: it has a solid background on psychological theory, it is easy to apply and understand; it links to usability evaluations (Davis, 1993); and finally it has been replicated in different contexts and tools (Adams et al., 1992; Taylor and Todd, 1995; Morris and Dillon, 1997).

3. Styles for Work Styles: a Study Framework

Interactive Systems Design methodologies, such as Wisdom (Nunes and Cunha, 2001) and Usage-Centred Design (Constantine and Lockwood, 1999), often describe users in context by using the concept of actors. UsageCD (Constantine and Lockwood, 1999), for example, separates the actors of a system from the roles they play during the system's usage. Indeed, users adopt several roles during the usage of a system, just like film actors do, but they also switch roles during the process. Although interaction design methods are well conceived to develop systems supporting the roles of usage, few systems provide support for flowing from different contexts/needs of usage. In our research, we found that interaction designers often engage into different work styles, a term coined by Wu and Graham (2004), who studied the activities and collaboration is-sues of software designers.

We define a work style as an informally defined set of values in n-dimensions. These dimensions describe the most important aspects of the way users work in order to achieve their tasks. A work style transition (or change) is a change in one or more values of a work style. A region (or plane) in a work style model is a set of work styles. Systems supporting work style regions are systems that can adapt to and support transitions in the users' styles of work. Figure 2 illustrates an example of a work style transition in the life of an interaction de-signer: on the left hand-side, a team of developers works together using post-it notes for task clustering in a spatially useful style. After this, the team splits and each designer is assigned a set of tasks and builds a concrete mock-up of the interface using an interface builder. Each designer transitioned from a low-detail, collaborative, low-tech work style to a high-detail, high-tech, individual work style.

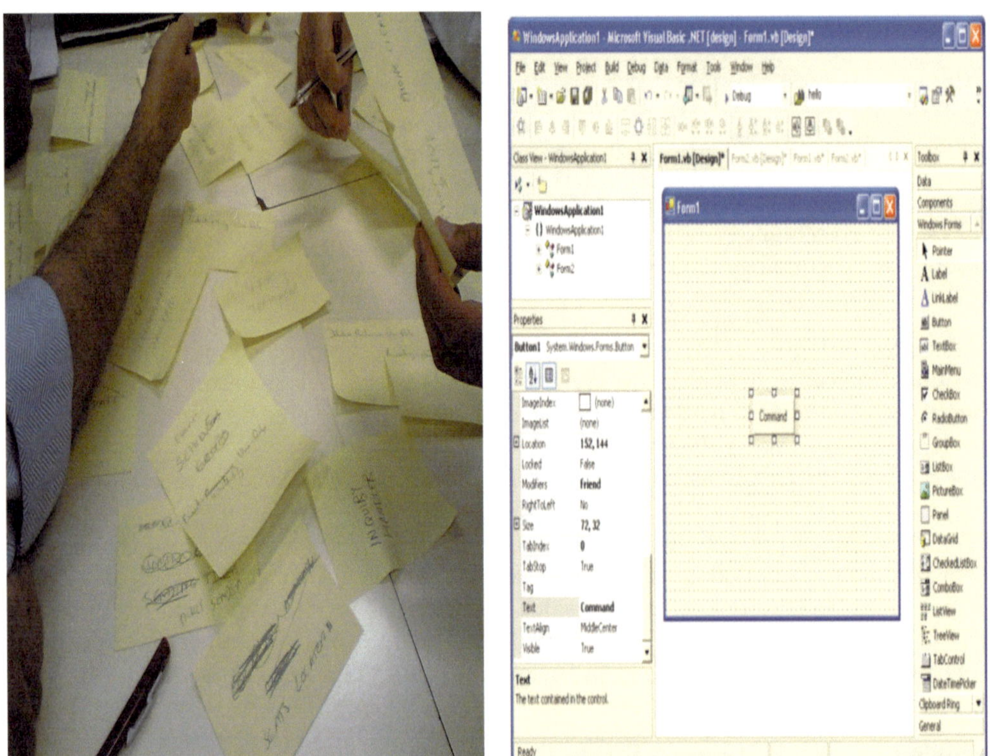

Fig. 2. Davis's Technology Acceptance Model. It suggests that a person is more likely to actually use a technology if he believes that it will be both useful and usable.

This is not the only example of a work style transition. "Moving from collaboratively modelling using a whiteboard into a digital version (using e.g. a UML tool)", "Moving from high-level descriptions of the user interface (e.g. sitemaps, navigation maps, etc.) to detailed screens of the user interface (concrete widgets, but-tons, etc.)", "Moving from sketching informal ideas/concepts (using e.g. blackboards or sheets of paper) into formal models (e.g. UML digital models), and back.", "Moving from non-functional prototypes toward fully-functional prototypes" and "Moving from business rules, use cases and problem space concepts into final solution design, and back" are concrete examples from a day in the life of an interaction designer.

3.1 Supporting the Work Style Model for User-Centered Design

In order to aid the characterization of different work styles as well as transitions in those work styles, we developed a novel model called the Work Style model for UCD (Campos and Nunes, 2005a). The model consists of eight continuous axes. These axes are grouped under three main categories:

- Notation style-related dimensions (Perspective, Formality and Detail),
- Tool usage style-related dimensions (Traceability, Functionality and Stability) and
- Collaboration style-related dimensions (Asynchrony and Distribution).

Each of these dimensions is described in more detail in (Campos and Nunes, 2005a), and for each dimension there is a set of questions that can act as guidelines, thus aiding the process of work style classification.

Perspective plots whether one is working at problem (business) level or at solution (design) level. Formality plots whether the designer is being informal (ambiguous, sketchy, creative) or formal (rigorous, semantically-sound). Detail refers to the level of abstraction being employed: at one extreme Traceability depicts whether one is interested in maintaining (or not) traceability between design models. Functionality describes the amount of working components in the prototype(s) being designed: a paper-based prototype has no functionality at all, whereas an interface designed in ubiquitous graphical interface builders shows a reasonable degree of functionality. Stability plots the rate of change and modification in the designs. And finally, collaboration-style dimensions plot Asynchrony (editing designs at same time or different times) and Distribution (working at the same place or remotely).

One of the main advantages brought by the work style model for UCD comes from the fact that, for the first time, there is a fundamental approach that can justify what kind of tool should be used, as well as when and how. For this purpose, we need to know which style is needed at what stage and what transition afterwards. Therefore, according to the development path (e.g., top down, bottom up, or middle out), different transitions might be explored. The model is also useful for driving the development of new design tools. We will de-scribe some aspects of the TaskSketch tool (Campos, 2005; Constantine and Campos, 2005) that were directly designed to support work style transitions.

The TaskSketch tool was developed both as a research proof-of-concept instrument used to test and validate our ideas, as well as an instructive tool, which has proven effective in supporting the teaching of UCD concepts at the undergraduate and graduate levels. Figure 3 shows a partial screenshot from the tool, illustrating briefly all the views and models that are currently supported.

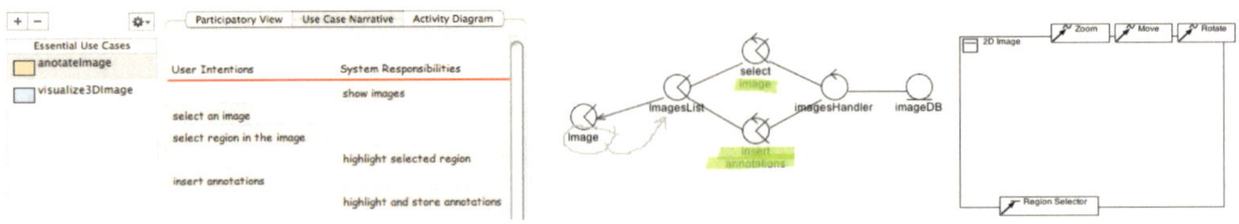

Fig. 3. TaskSketch briefly illustrated (From left to right): Use Case View, Task Flow View, Conceptual Architecture View and Canonical Abstract Prototype View.

As an example of how tools can be designed by direct inspiration of the work style model, consider the following example from the TaskSketch tool. How can we support the perspective dimension? Instead of merely supplying the users with a set of constructs and views for use case modelling, TaskSketch provides drag-and-drop mechanisms for extracting an initial conceptual architecture for an interactive system.

As another example of work style support, the tool allows editing of task flows at three different - but synchronized - views: the participatory view, which is a typical result of a participatory session with end users (obtained by manipulation of sticky notes); the use case narrative proposed by Constantine that can also be printed in index cards for stacking and ordering by the different stakeholders; and the activity diagram which could include additional details relevant to developers but that are not depicted in the other views.

3.2 A Framework for Studying the Designer's Tools and Work Styles

We argue that professional practitioners of interaction design engage into different work styles throughout their daily activities. We performed a survey distributed to professional interaction designers associations and mailing list, and collected 370 usable responses (Campos and Nunes, 2007). This study had two main goals:

- Assess the practical aspects of the work style model: in particular whether asking questions about work-styles would be understandable and would lead to interesting findings;
- Find interesting patterns of tools' use and/or work style transitions among industrial designers.

Among other issues, we were interested in finding out which work style transitions did the practitioners considered more frequent and more difficult, in their everyday work practices. By frequent, we mean, "how many times [the respondent] engages and transitions in those work styles", and by difficult we mean, "how difficult [the respondent] finds to perform that transition". We confronted respondents with several concrete scenarios of work style transitions and asked them to rate frequency and cost by selecting a value from a 7-point Likert scale, labelled from 1-low, to 4-moderate and 7-high.

Results showed that the most frequent and the most difficult transition was "Moving from business rules, use cases and problem space concepts into final solution design, and back". This is a perspective work style transition, and the average rating was 4.6 on the 7-point Likert scale for the frequency and 4.5 for the difficulty.

Combining the Technology Adoption Model, the Work style Model for UCD and our survey's results, we designed an experimental framework aimed at studying the interaction designer's tools and work styles. Figure 4 summarizes the constructs in our framework, as well as the hypotheses we tested.

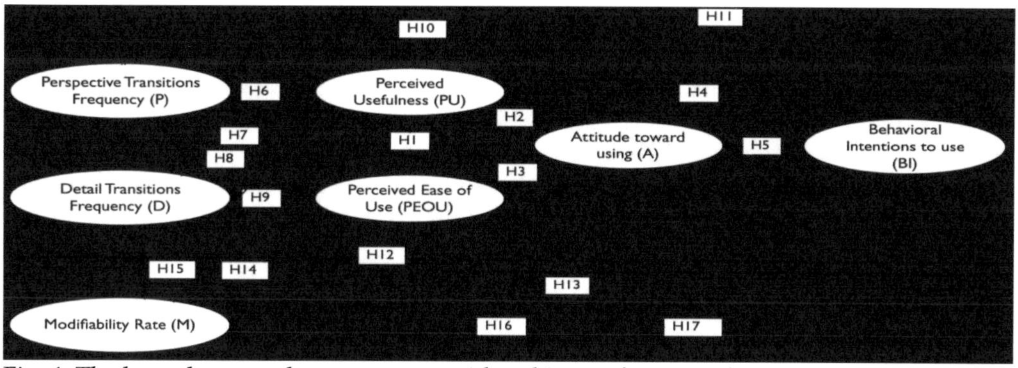

Fig. 4. The hypotheses and constructs considered in our framework.

As illustrated in Figure 4, we wanted to test the following variables:
Perception-related variables operationalize the constructs of this framework. Four perception-based variables are measured, just like in the TAM:
- Perceived Usefulness (PU) is defined as the degree to which the user believes that using the tool will enhance his or her performance in designing interactive systems;
- Perceived Ease Of Use (PEOU) is defined as the degree to which the user believes that using the design tool will be free from effort;
- Attitude toward using (A) measures the feelings of favourableness toward using the tool;
- Behavioural intention to use (BI) measures the strength of a designer towards using the tool in the near future.
Work style-related variables measure some aspects that come from our Work style model and from the transitions considered most difficult and frequent by professional interaction designers (according to our survey):
- Perspective Transitions Frequency (P) is defined as the rate (per minute) of transitions from different perspective views, i.e. the frequency of transitioning from problem space concepts (use cases, task flows) to solution space (architecture, abstract prototype) and back;
- Detail Transitions Frequency (D) is defined as the rate (per minute) of "drill-down" or "roll-up" between model elements, i.e. switching from high-detail views of an element to low-detail or the opposite;
- Modification Frequency (M) is the rate (per minute) of change made to any element of the artefact(s) being designed. This might include changing names, colour, size, values or any other property of elements.

As shown in Figure 4, our framework extends the technology adoption model (TAM). We augmented it by including work style quantitative data that can be automatically obtained from the usage of a given design tool. Both the perspective and detail transitions frequency can be obtained by logging mechanisms. The same happens to the modifiability frequency measurement. We extended TaskSketch in order to produce detailed statistics regarding the following quantitative variables:
- Perspective Transitions Frequency, the number of times (per minute) that a designer switches from a view to another (e.g. use cases view to abstract prototype view); in TaskSketch this is measured by counting the number of times the user switches his focus from one view to another;

- Detail Transitions Frequency, the number of times (per minute) that a designer switches from high (low) detail view of the user interface to low (high) detail view; in TaskSketch this is measured by counting the number of times the user switches from the Architectural view (which can be used to define navigation maps of the user interface) to the Abstract Prototype view and back;
- Modification Frequency, the number of times (per minute) that a designer performs changes to any given model element (e.g. changing the text/title of a use case, changing the layout of a prototype, etc.).

We chose to include only these transitions in our framework and experimental study because of two main reasons: first, according to our survey's results, these are the transitions rated with the highest combination of frequency/cost perceptions (between practitioners). This means they are among the most important ones. And secondly, because they are also the simplest transitions to measure. Functionality and Traceability are also easy to measure quantitatively but are more difficult to implement in a tool. For instance, a tool that supports Functionality transitions should allow designers to create fully-functional prototypes, partially-functional or non-functional at all. Collaboration-style transitions are easier to measure in intrusive ways, e.g. by videotaping users and/or running "think-aloud" protocols.

Since we were measuring the rate of modifications to modelling artefacts, we also gathered data regarding the percentage of time users were engaged in creation activities (e.g. adding a new use case, drawing a new element, etc.), modification activities (e.g. changing the text/title of a use case, changing the layout of a prototype, etc.) and searching activities (e.g. looking for a particular element using the search facilities).

4. Test Results and Analysis

Since there is currently no other tool for Usage-Centred Design, we didn't evaluate TaskSketch against a control method. We could compare it with, e.g. ArgoUML or MS Visio, but they would have to be adapted to ensure they supported the same notations equally. We examined the usage of TaskSketch in a field study that used subjects enrolled in an undergraduate 3rd year Human-Computer Interaction course at the University of Madeira in a similar procedure as (Ko and Myers, 2005; Abrahão et al., 2005). In this section, we describe in detail the experiment's procedure, variables, results and discussion.

4.1 Procedure and Variables

Our sample size was 15 students. Subject's average age was 22.71 (SD = 2.78). Five participants were female. In order not to bias the experiment, subjects' participation was entirely optional, and the experimenter was not an instructor in the course. The experiment took place in a single laboratory equipped with 15 eMacs, and to avoid ceiling effects, we gave no time limit for the execution of the task. The third year HCI students had already experience in using modelling tools, and their perceptions of use map very closely to what a professional designer might think or believe, because their objective is very much alike.

We asked participants to design a Use Case, Task Flow, Conceptual Architecture and an Abstract Prototype for an interface to a weather system for travellers, as Landay and Myers (2001) did. This problem is described in Usability Engineering (Nielsen, 1993) and provides a solid benchmark, since possible design errors are well-documented (Nielsen, 1993). It is also small-enough for a study session and large-enough to ensure sufficient coverage of design situations.

After finishing the tasks, subjects were asked to answer a post-experiment survey. The survey included 14 questions, based on the variables of the theoretical model. The items used were formulated through a 7-point Likert scale, where the order of items' presentation was randomized and half the questions negated to avoid monotonous responses and prevent systemic bias in a process very similar to current research techniques such as the ones conducted by Abrahão et al. (2005), Morris and Dillon (1997).

We measured quantitative and qualitative variables. The questionnaire we developed uses scales for each qualitative variable in the theoretical model presented earlier. The whole set of constructs in this experiment and how they were built and measured are shown in Table 1.

PEOU-Perceived Ease of Use	1. Learning to use TaskSketch would be easy to me. 2. It's easy to create models using TaskSketch. 3. It would be easy for me to become skillful at using TaskSketch. 4. I would find TaskSketch easy to use.
PU-Perceived Usefulness	5. Using TaskSketch would improve my performance in designing UI's 6. Using TaskSketch would enhance my effectiveness in designing UI's. 7. Using TaskSketch would improve my productivity in designing UI's. 8. I would find TaskSketch useful in the University.
A-Attitude toward Using	9. Using TaskSketch is a (good/bad) idea. 10. Using TaskSketch is a (wise/foolish) idea. 11. I (like/dislike) the idea of using TaskSketch. 12. Using TaskSketch would be (pleasant/unpleasant).
BI-Behavioral Intentions to Use	13. I intend to use TaskSketch during the remainder of the semester. 14. I intend to use TaskSketch frequently this semester.
P-Perspective Transitions' Frequency	Number of times the user switches from a view to another (per minute), e.g. switching from use cases (problem perspective) view to abstract prototype (solution perspective).
D-Detail Transitions' Frequency	Number of times the user switches from a high (low) detail view to a low (high) detail view (per minute), e.g. switching from navigation map (low detail) to abstract prototype (high detail).
M-Modifiability Rate	Number of times per minute that the user edits or changes any property of any model element, e.g. changing the layout of a prototype, changing a use case description, changing the title of a task.

Table 1. Constructs and how they were built.

4.2 Validity and Reliability of the Model's Constructs

In order to evaluate the validity of the constructs in our model, we performed an inter-item correlation analysis. We assumed that all items associated with a particular construct had equal weights and measured the convergent and discriminant validity proposed by Campbell and Fiske (1959), which was used in several re-search reports in the SE field with similar sample sizes (Abrahão et al., 2005).

Convergent validity (CV) assesses if measures of constructs that theoretically should be related to each other are, in fact, observed to be related to each other. It is measured by the average correlation between the indicator and the other indicators that are used to measure the same construct.

Discriminant validity (DV) assesses if measures of constructs that theoretically should not be related to each other are in fact observed to not be related to each other.

The important thing to recognize is that these concepts work together: if one can demonstrate that there is evidence for both convergent and discriminant validity, then by definition, one can demonstrate that there is evidence for construct validity.

	CV	DV	VALID?
PEOU1	0.691	0,503	YES
PEOU2	0.821	0,443	YES
PEOU3	0.698	0,424	YES
PEOU4	0.772	0,457	YES
PU5	0.687	0,440	YES
PU6	0.725	0,529	YES
PU7	0.791	0,478	YES
PU8	0.745	0,491	YES
A9	0.794	0,430	YES
A10	0.795	0,439	YES
A11	0.792	0,644	YES
A12	0.689	0,498	YES
BI13	0.859	0,419	YES
BI14	0.859	0,496	YES

Table 2. Correlation between survey items (construct validity analysis).

Table 2 shows the correlation results (single inter-tem correlation values for every item in the survey was omitted for brevity). For every question in the survey, the convergent validity is always higher than the discriminant validity (by a factor of almost 2). This demonstrates the validity for the constructs. From the data, we conclude that the survey is a valid instrument for the intended study.

We also performed a reliability analysis on the items of our survey. The reliability of an instrument de-scribes the consistency (or repeatability) the instrument gives in measuring the same phenomenon over time or by different people. To ensure reliability of the scales, we calculated Cronbach's alpha for each variable. Cronbach's alpha is the most common form of reliability coefficient. By convention, behavioural studies are considered reliable if the alpha's value is greater than .60 (Nunally, 1978).

Construct	Cronbach's Alpha
Perceived Usefulness	0.902
Perceived Ease of Use	0.898
Attitude toward using	0.899
Behavioral intentions to use	0.937

Table 3. Reliability analysis.

The results that sustain the reliability of the constructs for qualitative evaluation in our survey are shown in Table 3. We have obtained high values for the four variables (all alpha values are around 0.9), meaning that the items on the survey are reliable and valid measures of the underlying constructs of the proposed theoretical model. In practice, this means there is a great chance of obtaining very similar measures for each construct over time or by different subjects.

4.2 Results and Discussion

The descriptive statistics results from the participants' perceptions of use, as well as their attitude and intention to use are shown in Table 4.

Descriptive Statistics	PU	PEOU	A	BI
Number of observations	15	15	15	15
Minimum	3.75	2.50	3.50	1.00
Maximum	7.00	7.00	7.00	7.00
Mean	5.8667	5.2667	5.6167	4.2000
Standard deviation	1.0892	1.4744	1.2206	1.8400

Table 4. Descriptive statistics for PU, PEOU, A and BI.

These results (all averages are well above the 3.5 neutral value in our scale) mean we empirically corroborate that participants find TaskSketch both useful and usable, show a positive attitude towards this tool, and they intend to use TaskSketch in a near future. The ideal method to measure this would be using a control condition, i.e. comparing the data from a group of subjects using another tool against the data from the group using TaskSketch. However, this would be unfair since there is currently no other tool (to our knowledge) specifically aimed at Usage-centred Design.

From our log analysis tool, we also extracted the mean frequency of usage time subjects spent on each view. The pie chart in Figure 5 shows the distribution of this time. We can see that work at the abstract proto-type has the largest usage time, followed by use cases, architecture and finally task flows. We also measured the time spent creating new model elements (mean=28%), modifying model elements (mean=79%) and searching (mean=1%). All these results corroborate our expectations and are according to what we expected. Also, these results contribute to increasing empirical data on how tools are actually used, and they also assured us of the correct functioning of our logging tool. They carry with them important implications to the de-sign of interaction design tools: use cases and abstract prototype views exhibited the largest time share of usage, which means more attention should be devoted to the UI supporting these views. In the same manner, if users spend most of the time (79% according to the logging tool's measurements) modifying model elements, then it is clear that this activity is the most frequent, and therefore its performance should be carefully supported by the design tool at stake.

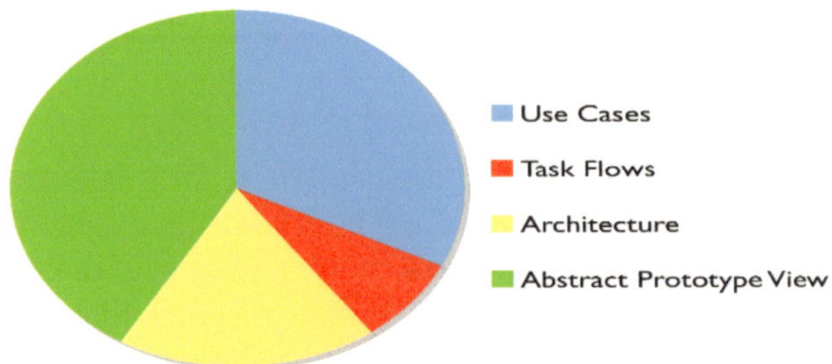

Fig. 5. Frequency distribution of the several views used by subjects (recorded through automatic logging tools).

After combining the work style transitions data, obtained by the logging tools and TAM, and the data obtained from the follow-up questionnaire, we performed regression analysis in order to test the hypothesis in our model. Table 5 shows the details of our simple linear regression analysis we performed. The grey-background rows are the hypothesis taken directly from the TAM model. All the other hypotheses are introduced by us, having in mind the proposed model (depicted previously in Figure 4).

Hyp.	Relationship	β	Std. error of β	t	p	R^2	Result
H1	PEOU→PU	0.44	0.164	2.71	0.018	0.362	Supported
H2	PU→A	0.96	0.158	6.13	0.000	0.743	Strongly supported
H3	PEOU→A	0.43	0.196	2.19	0.047	0.270	Supported
H4	PU→BI	0.89	0.397	2.26	0.042	0.282	Supported
H5	A→BI	0.81	0.352	2.32	0.037	0.293	Supported
H6	P→PU	-0.61	0.695	-0.89	0.397	0.202	Not supported
H7	P→PEOU	-2.45	0.530	-4.63	0.001	0.805	Strongly supported
H8	D→PU	-2.16	1.655	-1.31	0.219	0.147	Not supported
H9	D→PEOU	-7.34	1.499	-4.90	0.001	0.706	Strongly supported
H10	P→A	-0.24	0.788	-0.30	0.765	0.243	Not supported
H11	P→BI	-2.65	0.694	-3.82	0.004	0.735	Strongly supported
H12	D→A	-1.83	2.003	-0.91	0.381	0.077	Not supported
H13	D→BI	-8.07	1.768	-4.56	0.001	0.676	Strongly supported
H14	M→PEOU	-0.95	0.333	-2.86	0.019	0.477	Strongly supported
H15	M→PU	-0.46	0.317	-1.45	0.179	0.191	Not supported
H16	M→A	-0.92	0.234	-3.93	0.003	0.633	Strongly supported
H17	M→BI	-0.96	0.380	-2.53	0.032	0.415	Supported

Table 5. Regression results.

Table 5 shows, for in-detail analysis purposes, several commonly used regression results variables, which we will briefly describe as follows:
- β is the regression coefficient (the amount of change in y per unit change in x); in other words, it is the slope of the line, which describes the relationship between the independent and dependent variables;
- the standard error of β is the estimated standard deviation of error in estimating y from x;
- t is the statistic for determining whether the relationship is statistically significant;
- p is the statistical significance of the test;
- R2 tells us the percentage of the variation in y (the dependent variable) that is explained by the scores on x (the independent variable).

We considered a relationship was strongly supported when the level of significance p would be < 0.01 and R2 greater than 0.4, since in current research results are much more tolerant. Morris and Dillon (1997), for ex-ample consider relationships firmly supported even with R2 values lower than 0.2.

Figure 6 and Figure 7 depict the results visually and we can conclude that the tool's perceptions of use influence both the attitude toward using the tool as well as the behavioural intentions to use it. Also, we observed a strong influence of the work style-related constructs in the tool's perceived ease of use as well as in the behavioural intentions to use the tool. The actual use of the tool (following a time period, after the first contact with the tool) was not evaluated in this study.

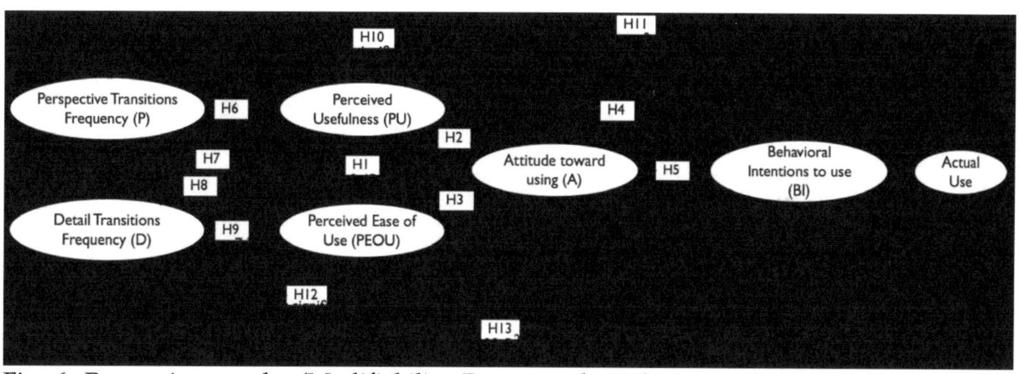

Fig. 6. Regression results (Modifiability Rate not shown). For each hypothesis tested we present the regression coefficient (b), R-square and the level of significance of the relationship.

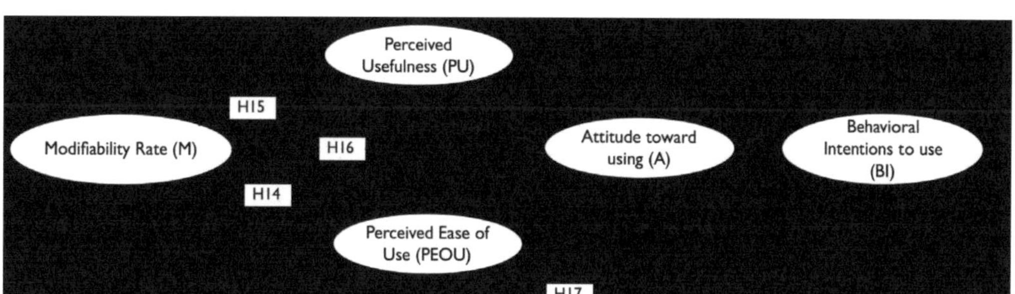

Fig. 7. Regression results for Modifiability Rate.

The final revised theoretical model is presented in Figure 8, where we use the stroke width of the hypotheses' arrows to depict the strength of the statistical significant relationships between constructs of our framework.

The results presented here firmly support all the hypotheses derived from TAM. As we expected, the TAM model's relationships were verified to be statistically significant. Some of the relationships were not found to be significant. Regarding the work style constructs, these were not found to significantly influence the perceived usefulness of the tool. However, they do play an important role when it comes to perceived ease of use and intentions to using a tool. Detail and Perspective transitions strongly influence Perceived Ease of Use and Behavioural Intentions to use. Modifiability rate influences not so strongly Perceived Ease of Use and (more significantly) the Attitude toward using, as well as Behavioural Intentions to use. In other words, work style transitions can influence the tool's perceptions of use.

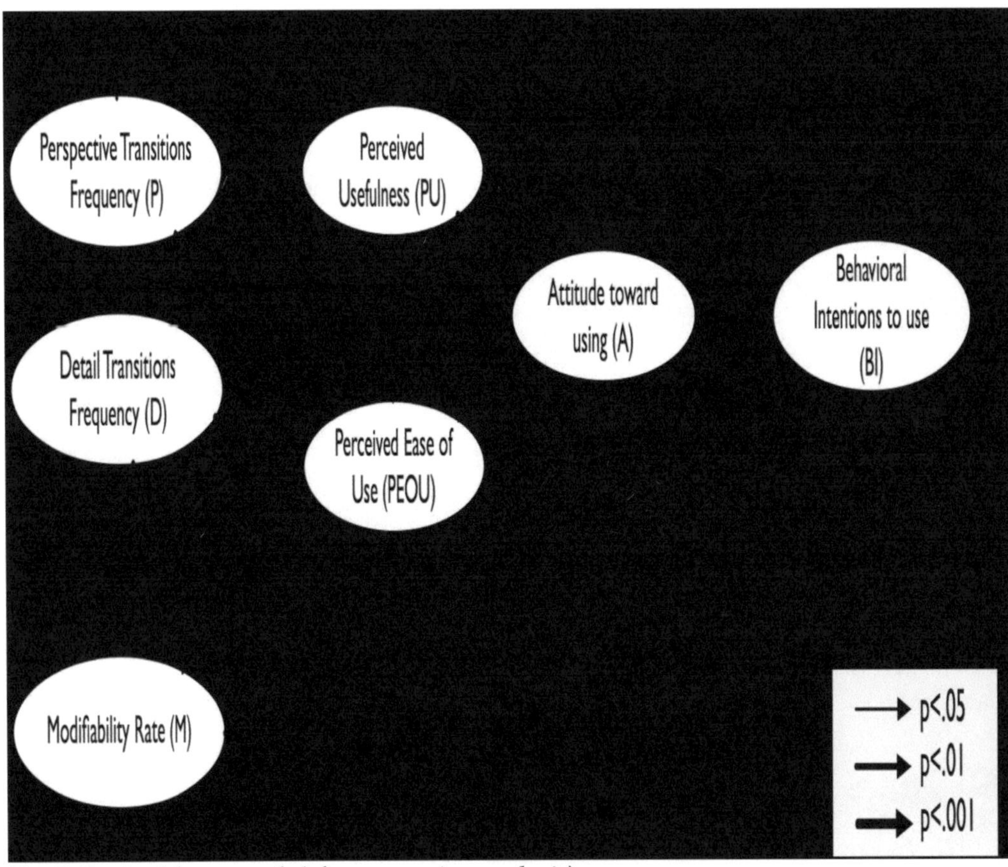

Fig. 8. Revised framework (after regression analysis).

5. Conclusions

In this paper, we have captured the interaction design styles into an empirically-based framework that can be cost-effectively used to study existing design tools as well as to inspire the development of new design tools like TaskSketch. We don't claim that our framework completely addresses all the issues related to the current interaction design tools, but we do find our framework a useful discussion and evaluation instrument.

Here we also presented the TaskSketch tool, specifically designed in order to support work styles and work style transitions. In particular perspective-style transitions, which we previously showed to be regarded as one of the most frequent and difficult work style transitions, among professionals (Campos and Nunes, 2007). The results of TaskSketch's evaluation empirically corroborate that subjects found the tool useful and usable, and they also showed a positive attitude towards using it.

We have augmented the Technology Acceptance Model with quantitative work style data from users, which was easy to obtain in a transparent way thanks to automatic logging tools.

We know that user perceptions influence software use. We currently know that work style transitions can influence the user perceptions for the case of interaction design tools. Therefore, if we better support work style transitions we might be able to build better design tools, tools capable of achieving higher adoption levels than current ones. Our results suggest that work style transitions do have an influence on the tools' perception of usability and usefulness as well as behavioural intentions to use it.

One limitation of our study is related to how well do the results generalize. This is partly due to our small sample size and partly because the population is not sufficiently close to real world designers. However, HCI students are tomorrows' users of the design tools and their perceptions of use map very closely to what a professional designer might think or believe, because their objective is exactly the same. Also, since we are dealing with perceptions of use and attitudes toward future use, no previous significant experience is required.

This study carries with it important implications regarding the design of new interaction design tools. Some are based on our own development and evaluation experiences, some are based on the model itself, and some are based on the survey and experiment's concrete results.

Based on our experience and subjects written and oral comments on the tools (both in this study and in a previous one), we believe one of the major areas of weakness of tools is related to the expressive power of tools and the comparison and exploration of alternative designs that a tool can foster. Most of the times it is so much easier to grab a sheet of paper and explain (or explore) a design idea without using a digital tool.

Aesthetics are also important. Most of the positive remarks for our tool are related to how well the models created look either in screen or in print. Work style support clearly implicates stylish user interfaces for the sup-porting tools, an issue that's being more and more debated (Norman, 2004).

If perspective and detail transitions are viewed by professional interaction designers as the most difficult (perspective) and frequent (detail) kind of transitions, and if our results show that these transitions' frequency has negative impacts on the tools' perceptions and intentions of use, then tool designers should find innovative ways to ease those transitions.

The same happens with modifiability: the results suggest that the more modifications, the lower the positive feelings regarding the tool. Since we have showed that almost 80% of the time is spent modifying artefacts, effort should be targeted at easing this activity.

If more research is targeted at studying the interaction designer's behaviour and work styles, and if we start designing tools that actually implement these ideas, then the future of interaction design tools is bright be-cause they will be fit into the work practices and usage intentions of designers.

Acknowledgements. The authors wish to thank to Prof. Jean Vanderdonckt for the suggestions on applications of the UCD Work style Model as well as to the participants of the empirical study.

6. References

Abrahão, S., Poels, G. & Pastor, O. A Functional Size Measuremes, D. A., Nelson, R. R. & Todd, P. A., 1992. Perceived Usefulness, Ease of Use, and Usage of In-formation Technology: A Replication. *MIS Quarterly*, 16:(2), 227–247.

Caetano, A., Goulart, N., Fonseca, M. & Jorge, J., 2002. JavaSketchIt: Issues in Sketching the Look of User Interfaces. In Proceedings of the 2002 AAAI Spring Symposium - Sketch Understanding, 9–14, Palo Alto, USA, 2002.

Campbell, D. T. & Fiske, D. W., 1959. Convergent and Discriminant Validation by the Multitrait-Multimethod Matrix. *Psychological Bulletin*, 56, 81–105.

Campos, P., 2005. User-Centered CASE Tools for User-Centered Information Systems. In CAiSE 2005, 12th Conference on Advanced Information Systems Engineering, Doctoral Consortium, 13-14 June 2005, Porto, Portugal.

Campos, P. & Nunes, N. J., 2005. Galactic Dimensions: A Unifying Workstyle Model for User-Centered Design. In Lecture Notes in Computer Science, Volume 3585, pp. 158–169.

Campos, P. & Nunes, N. J., 2007. Practitioner Tools and Workstyles for User-Interface Design. *IEEE Software*, vol. 24, no.1, pp. 73-80, Jan/Feb, 2007.

Constantine, L. & Campos, P., 2005. CanonSketch and TaskSketch: Innovative Modeling Tools for Us-age-Centered Software Design. In Conference on Object Oriented Programming Systems Languages and Applications (OOPSLA'05), Companion to the 20th annual ACM SIGPLAN conference on Object-oriented programming, systems, languages, and applications, San Diego, CA, 162–163.

Constantine, L. & Lockwood, L., 1999. *Software for Use. A Practical Guide to the Models and Methods of Usage-Centered Design*. Addison-Wesley, Reading, MA.

Constantine, L., 2001. Back to the Future. *Communications of the ACM*, 44:(3), 126–129.

Davis, F. D., 1989. Perceived Usefulness, Perceived Ease of Use and User Acceptance of Information Technology. *MIS Quarterly* 13:(3).

Davis, F. D., 1993. User Acceptance of Information Technology: System Characteristics, User Perceptions and Behavioral Impacts. *International Journal on Man-Machine Studies*, Vol. 38, pp. 475-487.

Graham, T. C., Watts, L. A., Calvary, G., Coutaz, J., Dubois, E., & Nigay, L. 2000. A dimension space for the design of interactive systems within their physical environments. In Proceedings of the Conference on Designing interactive Systems: Processes, Practices, Methods, and Techniques (New York City, New York, United States, August 17 - 19, 2000). D. Boyarski and W. A. Kellogg, Eds. DIS '00. ACM Press, New York, NY, 406–416.

Green, T. R. G. & Petre, M., 1996. Usability analysis of visual programming environments: a 'cognitive dimensions' framework. *Journal of Visual Languages and Computing*, 7, 131–174.

Ilvari, J., 1996. Why are CASE Tools Not Used? *Communications of the ACM*, 39:94–103.
Jarzabek, S. & Huang, R., 1998. The Case for User-Centered CASE Tools. *Communications of the ACM*, 41:(8), 93–99.
Ko, A. J. & Myers, B. A., 2005. A Framework and Methodology for Studying the Causes of Software Errors in Programming Systems. *Journal of Visual Languages and Computing*, 16:(1-2), 41-84.
Landay, J. & Myers, B. 2001. Sketching Interfaces: Toward More Human Interface Design. *IEEE Computer* 34(3), 56–64.
Mathieson, K., 1991. Predicting User Intention: Comparing the Technology Acceptance Model with the Theory of Planned Behavior. *Information Systems Research*, 2:(3), 173–191.
Morris, M. G. & Dillon, A., 1997. How User Perceptions Influence Software Use. *IEEE Software*, 14:(4), 58–55.
Navarre, D., Palanque, P., Bastide, R. & Sy, O., 2001. A Model-Based Tool for Interactive Prototyping of Highly Interactive Applications, p. 0136, 12th IEEE International Workshop on Rapid System Prototyping (RSP'01).
Nielsen, J., 1993. *Usability Engineering*. Morgan Kaufman, San Francisco, CA.
Norman, D., 2004. *Emotional Design – Why we love (or hate) everyday things*. Basic Books, NY.
Nunnaly, J., 1978. *Psychometric Theory*, 2nd ed., New York, NY, McGraw-Hill.
Nunes, N. J. & Cunha, J. F., 2001. WISDOM: Whitewater Interactive System Development with Object Models. In Mark van Harmelen (Editor), Object-oriented User Interface Design, Addison-Wesley, Object Technology Series.
Paternò, F., 2005. Model-based tools for pervasive usability. *Interacting with Computers* 17, 291–315.
Rescher, N., 1973. *The Primacy of Practice*. Oxford, Basil Blackwell, 1973.
Seffah, A. & Kline, R., 2002. Empirical Studies on Software Developers' Experiences. In WESS'02: Eighth IEEE Workshop on Empirical Studies of Software Maintenance. October 2nd, 2002. Montreal, Canada.
Seffah & Metzker, E., 2004. The Obstacles and Myths of Usability and Software Engineering. *Communications of the ACM*, 47:(12), 71–76.
Sinnig, D., Gaffar, A., Seffah, A. & Forbrig, P., 2004. Patterns, Tools and Models for Interaction Design. In IUI/CADUI 2004 Workshop on Making model-based practical: usable and open methods and tools. January 13, 2004. Madeira, Portugal.
Suchman, L., 1995. Representations of Work. *Communications of the ACM*, 38:(9), 33–68.
Taylor, S. & Todd, T., 1995. Understanding Information Technology Usage: a Test of Competing Models. *Information Systems Research*, 6:(2), 144–176.
Thevenin, D. & Coutaz, J., 1999. Plasticity of User Interfaces: Framework and Research Agenda. In Proceedings of INTERACT'99. Edinburgh: IOS Press 1999.
Vanderdonckt, J. & Berquin, P. 1999. Towards a Very Large Model-Based Approach for User Interface Development. In Proceedings of the 1999 User interfaces To Data intensive Systems (September 05-06, 1999). UIDIS. IEEE Computer Society, Washington, DC.
Wright, P., Dearden, A. & Fields, R., 2000. Function Allocation: A perspective from studies of work practice. *International Journal of Human Computer Studies*, 52:(2), 335–356.
Wu, J., Graham, T. C. N. & Smith, P. W., 2003. A Study of Collaboration in Software Design. In International Symposium on Empirical Software Engineering (ISESE'03), p. 304.

Wu, J., Graham, T. C. N., 2005. The Software Design Board: A Tool Supporting Workstyle Transitions. In Collaborative Software Design, Lecture Notes in Computer Science, Volume 3425, Jun 2005, pp. 363–382.

9

Modeling Human-Computer Interaction in Smart Spaces: Existing and Emerging Techniques

Yngve Dahl
Telenor Research and Innovation
Norway

1. Introduction

The main focus of human-computer interaction (HCI) research during the 1980s and much of the 1990s was on desktop computers applied in office settings. Developments within mobile and wireless communication technology, however, have contributed to make computer interaction beyond fixed and predictive desktop settings a reality. This has opened up for new interactive possibilities in and across various use situations. These trends can be seen as a partial implementation of Mark Weiser's ubiquitous computing (UbiComp) paradigm as envisioned almost two decades ago in his seminal article "The Computer for the 21st Century" (Weiser, 1991).

The ubiquitous computing paradigm implies that our interaction with computers becomes more physical in nature. Weiser predicted that we would have continuous interaction with multiple interconnected computers and sensors embedded in rooms, furniture, clothes, utilities, and other items we use on a daily basis. This way, people, places, and physical objects in the world would become potential elements of computer interaction, analogue to virtual widgets (e.g., buttons, hyperlinks, mouse cursors) of graphical user interfaces. Environments, in which digital and physical artifacts are used with sensor technology to implement seamless interaction with technology and surroundings, are often referred to as *smart spaces* (or sometimes context-aware, intelligent, or ambient spaces).

Although we see the rise of smart spaces, the tools designers have at their disposal for modeling computer systems that are part of such environments have not developed accordingly. Conventional modeling formalisms such as UML are essentially intended for communicating software designs, describing the structure of systems and the interactions between software objects. Using UML use case and sequence diagrams, it is difficult to represent physical aspects that are central for human-computer interaction in smart spaces. The same problem also applies to formal HCI methods like task analysis. These shortcomings have motivated designers to employ more informal modeling techniques, such as storyboards and sketches. Arguably, these techniques are more suited for describing how smart spaces present themselves to users. The informality of these modeling techniques, however, can make it more difficult to recognize similarities between different designs, and to re-use former solutions on new problems. One also risks introducing unambiguousness in the generated models.

Drawing on the above, ubiquitous computing and emergence of smart spaces arguably raise the need for methods that extends conventional modeling techniques with capabilities for describing *formal physical models* of computer systems. Motivated by this, we have investigated a technique for describing human-computer interaction in smart spaces through a set of formal notational building blocks and related semantics. The building blocks represent physical and virtual interactive elements that, taken together, form smart spaces. Currently, the formalism supports modeling of location-aware and token-based interactive systems. Both types of systems have received considerable attention in ubiquitous computing research, e.g., (Cheverst et al., 2000; Holmquist et al., 1999). This makes the proposed formalism highly applicable for modeling large number of systems that can implement smart spaces.
In the current work we aim to investigate features that characterize some of the existing techniques available for modeling computer systems and interaction in smart spaces, and discuss the added value the proposed formalism can bring to this collection.
To demonstrate the applicability of the proposed formalism we will address various services proposed and explored in relevant research literature, and show how these services can be represented by means of formalized physical models.

2. Background and motivation

To understand the modeling issues that the emergence of smart spaces raise, there is a need to give a more elaborate account of how interaction in such environments distinguishes itself from conventional desktop interaction.

2.1 Ubiquitous Computing vs. Desktop Computing

Weiser's 1991 vision of ubiquitous computing predicted how our interaction with computer technology would change in years to come. Weiser saw it as a fundamental use criterion that technology allows itself to fade into the background of the users' attention. He suggested that by integrating computers and sensors into our everyday physical environments, and by imbuing computer systems and applications with context-aware capabilities (i.e., enabling them to automatically sense and respond to their physical and social use context) computers would effectively become "invisible" in use. This stands in contrast to interaction with conventional desktop-based systems, which to a much larger extent is a foreground activity.
Dourish (2001) uses the concept of *embodiment* to distinguish how interaction with UbiComp systems is separate from interaction with traditional desktop systems. *Embodied interaction,* as argued by Dourish, unfolds real-time and real-space "as part of the world in which we are situated". This draws attention to both the physical and the social aspects of the use situations.
The ubiquitous computing paradigm, also known as *third paradigm computing,* is distinguished from previous interaction paradigms in terms of the underlying interaction model, points of interaction, the number of devices we use, and types and appearances of computer devices we interact with. Table 1 gives a conceptual overview of how these aspects have changed over various HCI paradigms.

Interaction paradigm	Period	Interactive devices	User-device relation	Interaction Model	Point of interaction
Mainframe computing	mid 1960s - ca. 1980	Mainframes	N users - 1 computer	Centralized	Corporations and larger institutions (universities, hospitals, etc.)
Personal computing	ca. 1980 - mid 1990s	PCs	1 user - 1 computer	Distributed	The desktop in the home or in the office.
Ubiquitous computing ("third wave")	mid 1990s - present	Interconnected laptops, tablet PCs, PDAs, mobile phones and "gadgets".	N users - N computers	Distributed and interconnected	"Anywhere, Anytime"

Table 1. Conceptual view of the three paradigms that have shaped human-computer interaction.

In contrast to what the situation was almost two decades ago, when Weiser expressed his vision, many of the technical components required for building smart spaces are now available. Developments in hardware and in wireless and mobile ICT have motivated research on the smart spaces in various use settings. In particular, this includes settings in which many activities are mobile by nature, e.g., hospitals (Bardram, 2004), construction (Sherry et al., 2004), and the domestic arena (Kosekela et al., 2004; Howard et al., 2006).

2.2 The Physical Reality of Human-Computer Interaction

Over the years, desktop-based interaction has become highly standardized in terms of input and output devices. The typical I/O devices for a PC include a computer mouse, a keyboard, and a screen. This standardization can be seen as a result of the relatively stable and predictable physical and social use conditions for which desktop-based systems are made - a single user sitting in front of a computer screen with required interaction devices ready at hand.

Because of the assumptions designers of software intended for desktop computers can take about the physical and social use conditions, removing these aspects from computer system models are in many ways rational simplifications - they have no significant impact on the system being described. In models constructed by means of de facto languages such as UML we find a high degree of device abstraction hiding details about how user input and output is provided. In the ontology of object-oriented modeling, the user and other system components are in many ways considered conceptually equivalent. For example, in UML use case and sequence diagrams all interactions between the actors of a system (e.g., users, hardware, and software components) are represented notational symbols.

With the emergence of smart spaces, however, the traditional distinction between software systems and the physical world they are situated in is blurred. Conceptually, smart spaces provide computer systems with a physical interface mediating between users and computer technology. This interface is analogous to (and often supplementary to) screen-based interfaces. This highlights the need for modeling principles allowing designers to represent the physical reality of human-computer ienteraction. Within ubiquitous computing and mobile human-computer interaction this has motivated the use of alternative modeling techniques such as storyboards and sketching, which are more suited for representing physical aspects of interaction (Van der Lelie, 2006; Davidoff et al., 2007).

3. Dimensions in Applicable Modeling Techniques

Modeling is a fundamental part of all scientific activity. It refers to the process of creating conceptual representations of more complex phenomena. A central aim of scientific modeling is to reduce the complexity of phenomena by focusing only on a limited set of relevant aspects, and to represent these at a specific level of abstraction.
The complexity of computer-based systems has long since made modeling techniques essential tools in the design process. Different computer-related research disciplines have developed various kinds of modeling techniques tailored to fulfill particular needs, and to improve the expressiveness required to describe relevant concepts. Hence, modeling techniques from two distinct disciplines (e.g., interaction design and software engineering) can produce very different representations of the same phenomenon.
The current section aims to give a more precise idea of where the modeling technique proposed in the current work positions itself in the landscape of existing modeling techniques from computer-related research disciplines.–For the purpose of comparing different approaches we will distinguish three dimensions in representations generated with computer-related modeling techniques—*perspective*, *formality*, and *granularity*.

3.1 Perspective

The perspective of a model corresponds to the viewpoint from which a given representation is represented. For the current purpose we will make a conceptual distinction between models that exclusively represent the software system as such, and models that draws attention to the external real-world context in which computer systems are used. We will refer to the first category of models as *system models*, while the second category of models is referred to as *physical models*. Computer modeling formalisms (e.g., UML) have mainly focused on generating system models. In interaction and scenario-based design, sketches and storyboards (picture scenarios) have frequently been employed to represent how computer systems work for people in a context. As apposed to UML representations, the resulting representations are often physical models.
Fig. 1 illustrates a system model (UML use-case diagram) and physical model (storyboard) of a hypothetical location-aware system in a clinical setting. The system automatically presents a patient's electronic record on a mobile device carried by a clinician, as he enters the virtual "presence" zone surrounding the respective patient's bed.

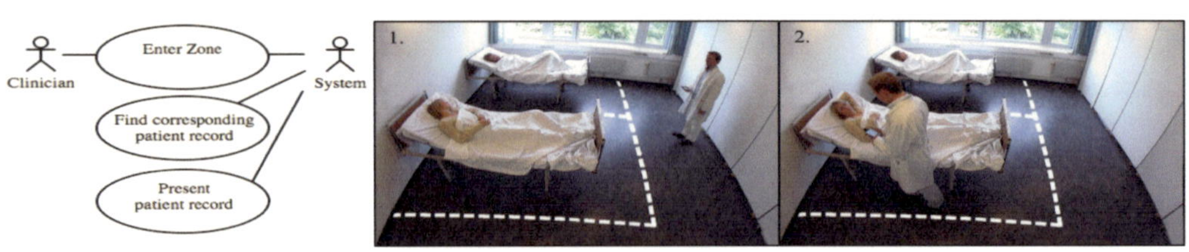

Fig. 1. (*Left*) System model. (*Right*) Physical model.

3.2 Formality of representations

Most conventional computer modeling techniques involve the use of a standardized modeling language. These approaches have been developed to describe computer systems in a consistent way, thereby creating a basis for common understanding among computer professionals. Formal representations can also help professionals recognize similarities between different designs, and thereby support reuse of former solution on new design problems. Automatic code generation and validation of models are some of the additional benefits associated with formal approaches.

Other modeling techniques generate representations that are informal and often more specific with regard to use situations and devices involved. Freehand sketching and storyboarding, informal system charts, and use cases are examples of informal modeling techniques. While formal models are domain specific and require professional experience to comprehend, informal representations, such as those noted above, can potentially act as a common language for a broader group of stakeholders involved in a design process.

Fig. 2 illustrates a formal UML sequence diagram and an informal system chart diagram of the location-aware medical information system represented in Fig 1. The use-case diagram and the storyboard shown in Fig. 1 is another example of a formal model and an informal model, respectively.

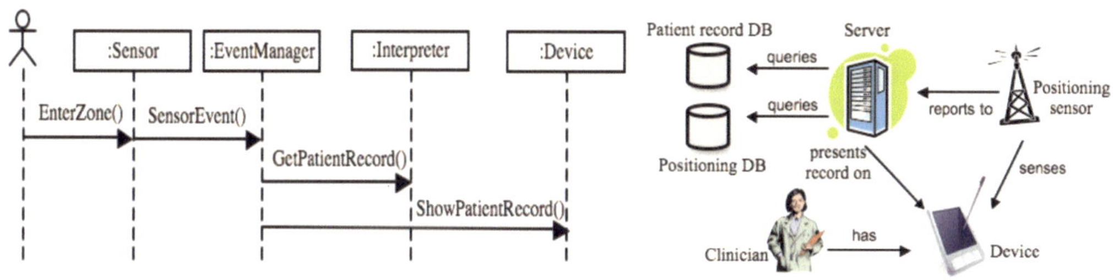

Fig. 2. (*Left*) Formal model (UML sequence diagram). (*Right*) Informal model (informal system diagram)

3.3 Granularity

Granularity refers to the level of detail that a model provides on a phenomenon being described. Both system models and physical models can be described at various levels of granularity. This, however, manifests itself differently. System models aiming to give a generic overview of a software system (e.g. Fig. 2) typically present only key system operations of a system, while sub-operations are hidden from view.

Sketches and storyboards showing physical models can be rendered rough or incomplete to hide details about certain aspects of the phenomenon or behavior being described. As we will show later, increasing or decreasing the number of picture frames included in a storyboard sequence can also adjust the granularity of the representation.

3.4 Defining the problem area

The conceptual differences between common modeling techniques applied in software engineering and interaction design are given in Table 2. Each technique can be classified in a 2×2 matrix along the dimensions: *informal representations* versus *formal representations* and *system models* versus *physical models*. The resulting matrix also helps to illustrate the gap in available modeling techniques the current work is attempting to bridge—a technique that supports the construction of formal physical models.

	Informal representation	Formal representation
System models	- Use cases - Informal system diagrams	- UML use case and sequence diagrams - HCI task analysis
Physical models	- Storyboards (picture scenarios) - Sketches - Videos	**- Formalized physical models**

Table 2. Categorization of modeling techniques.

4. Design Elements and Semantics

Having established that designers of smart spaces could benefit from formal models that put focus on the physical reality of human-computer interaction, we now turn the attention toward how this can be realized with respect to location-aware and token-based interactive systems.

4.1 Design Elements

To formalize the interaction with location-aware and token-based systems, we have developed a set of building blocks representing the following key components: *users, virtual zones, tokens* and *computer devices*. In smart spaces these are core design elements that can act as links to digital information objects such as web pages, messages, GUI states, communication sessions, etc.

Tokens, as conceptualized in ubiquitous computing, are tangible objects that can contain references to digital information (Holmquist et al., 1999). To access this information a user must take a deliberate action (i.e., scan the token). A post-it note with a barcode identifying a particular web page (also known as *WebStickers* (Ljungstrand et al., 2000)) is an example of a token.

Virtual zones refer to the detection area of a sensor capable of responding to the presence of a user or his physical position. Bluetooth, WLAN positioning, and face recognition, are examples of technologies that have been used to implement location-awareness in indoor environments. Location-based interaction, as apposed to token-based interaction, is typically consequential rather than intentional.

Computer devices can mediate system responses triggered by physical interactions, e.g., present an associated web page when a user enters a virtual zone or scans a token.

Users interact with other design elements contained within the smart space through physical presence, proximity, or touch.

Virtual zones, tokens, and *computer devices* can be either portable or fixed to a physical position (Fig. 3).

In addition to the core design elements described above, we have defined two supplementary elements. The *remote communication* component is used to denote network communication over physical distances (i.e., from remote locations). *Token containers* are physical objects that can hold one or more mobile tokens. A refrigerator with barcode stickers acting as bookmarks to electronic recipes is an example of a fixed token container.

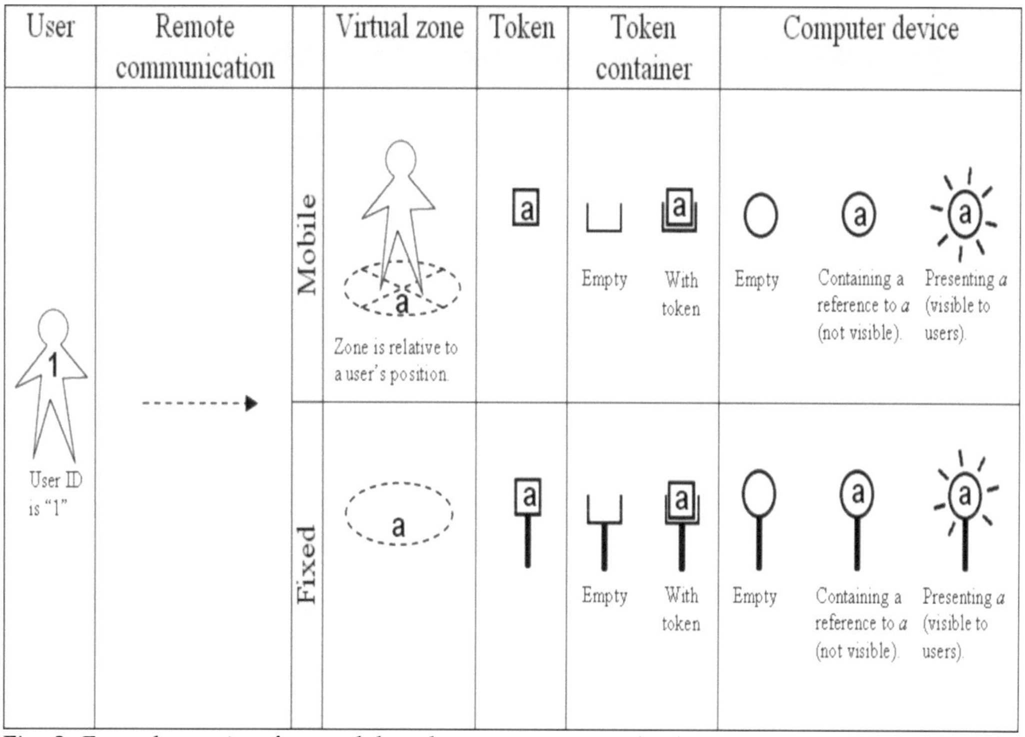

Fig. 3. Formal notation for modeling location-aware and token-based interactive systems. "a" represents an information object.

4.2 Semantics

The semantic relationship between the design elements can be summarized:

- Computer devices, tokens, virtual zones, and users can contain information objects.
- Information objects can be transferred between interaction elements based on proximity or presence (virtual zones), touch (tokens an users), or via remote communication channels.
- Users can carry mobile tokens, mobile token containers, and mobile computer devices, and have mobile virtual zones (that follow a user as he moves around).
- Tokens can be placed in token containers.
- Users can enter and leave virtual zones.
- Virtual zones can sense users and mobile computer devices that users carry with them.
- Mobile computer devices can sense tokens and other computer devices.
- Fixed computer devices can sense mobile tokens, and mobile computer devices.

The general semantic relationship between the core design elements and information objects is illustrated in Fig. 4. Fig. 5 shows the semantic relationship between the various design elements.

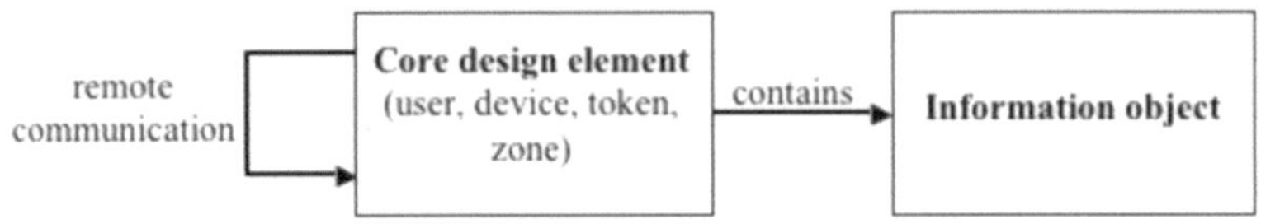

Fig. 4. Semantic relationship between design elements and information objects.

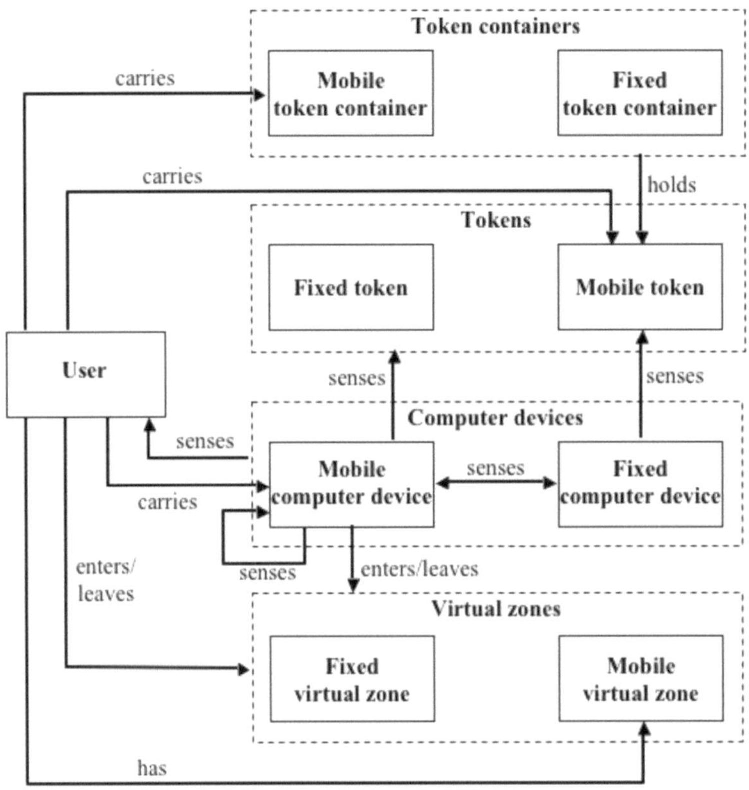

Fig. 5. Semantic relationship between design elements.

5. Applying the Formalism

To demonstrate the added value of formal and structured physical models of smart spaces, we will address some functionalities proposed and explored in earlier research on ubiquitous computing. First we will focus on basic interactions with location-aware and token-based systems. Next, we will demonstrate how *session mobility*, i.e., seamless transfer of media content from one interaction device to another, can be represented using the proposed formalism. Lastly, we will present some examples of how the technique can help represent interpersonal information exchange mediated through digitally augmented places or physical objects.

5.1 Basic Interactions

Given the building blocks described above, the basic interaction with location-aware and token-based systems can be described through simple transitions in the state-space of the system and the physical environment. Figs. 6-11 show the underlying interaction design patterns for presence, proximity, and touch-based interaction in smart spaces.

In Fig. 6, an information object associated with a virtual zone is automatically presented on the user' mobile device as he or she enters that zone. Fig. 7 shows a similar variant, where a fixed device replaces the mobile device used in the previous solution. In the location-based solution shown in Fig. 8, the virtual zone is anchored to the user. It remains fixed to the user as he or she moves about, and it can respond to physically proximate computer devices.

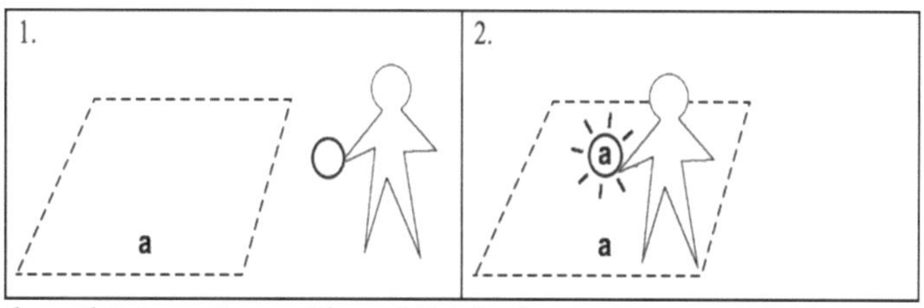

Fig. 6. Location-based interaction with mobile device.

QuickTime™ and a
TIFF (Uncor)ressed) decompressor
are needed to see this picture.

Fig. 7. Location-based interaction with fixed device.

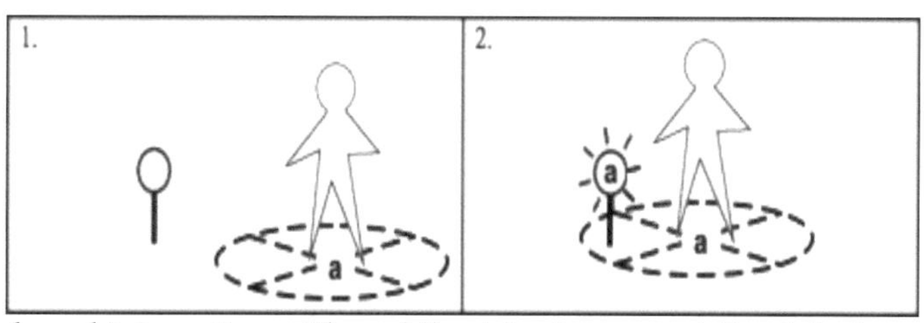

Fig. 8. Location-based interaction with mobile virtual zone and fixed device.

Figs. 9-11 show some basic token and touch-based interactions. In Fig. 9, a user carrying a mobile device accesses the information object associated with a fixed token as he scans the token. In Fig. 10 the roles of token and the device are switched vis-à-vis Fig. 9. Alternatively, in smart spaces the user can also act as a token or physical link to an information object. This is illustrated in Fig. 11.

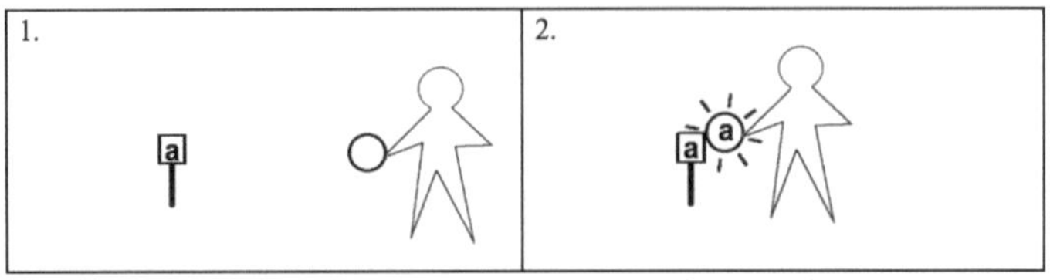

Fig. 9. Token-based interaction with mobile device and fixed token

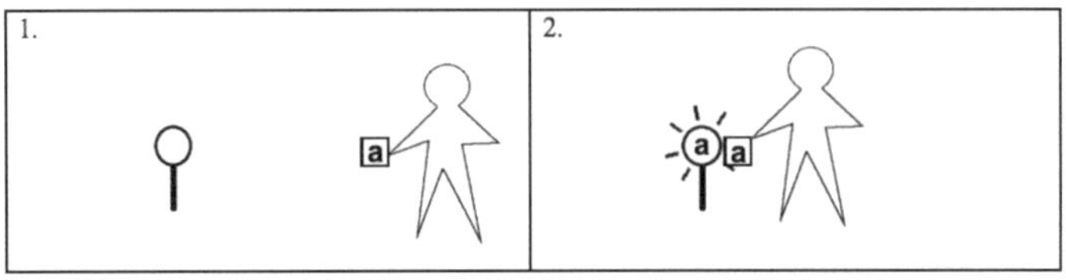

Fig. 10. Token-based interaction with fixed device and mobile token.

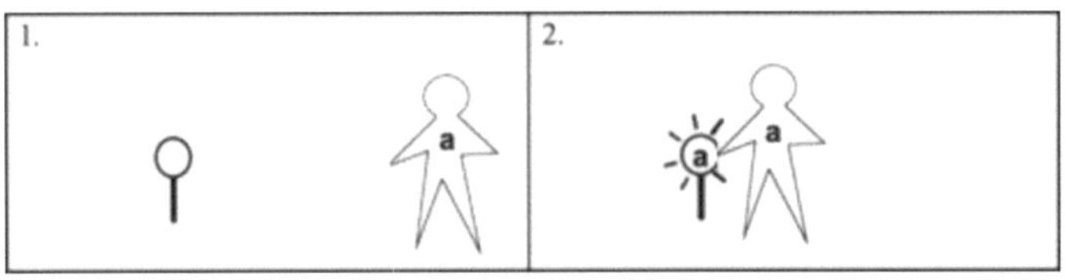

Fig. 11. Touch-based interaction. The user acts as a token or physical link to a specific information object.

The design patterns shown in the current subsection form the basis of many of the services that implement smart spaces. In the following two sections we will explore two such services in greater detail.

5.2 Session Mobility

Session mobility is commonly understood as seamless transfer of media of an ongoing communication session from one device to another (Østhus et al., 2005). A simple example of how session mobility can be modeled as a location-based service using the described notation is shown in Fig. 12. Here, the user enters a virtual zone with an associated information object. This causes the information object to be presented on the device contained within that zone. As the user moves from one zone to an adjacent zone the presented information object (session) is relocated to a compatible device.

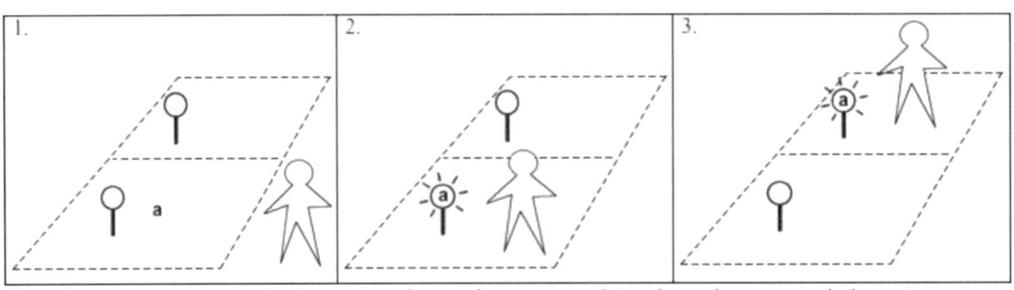

Fig. 12. Presentation and relocation of an information object based on a user's location.

Fig. 13 shows session mobility modeled as a token-based service. Here the user relocates an ongoing session by first associating it with a mobile token, and then carrying the token along and transferring the contained information object (session) to a compatible device at a different location.

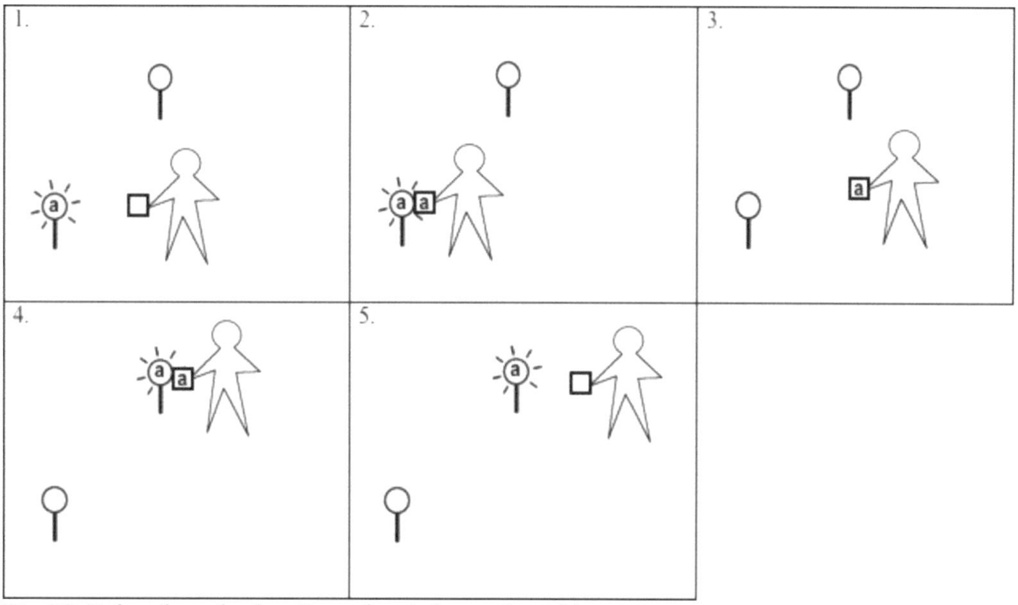

Fig. 13. Token-based relocation of an information object.

A slightly different variant is shown in Fig 14. Here, removing a token from a container associated with one device, and replacing it in a container linked to another device, relocates an ongoing session.

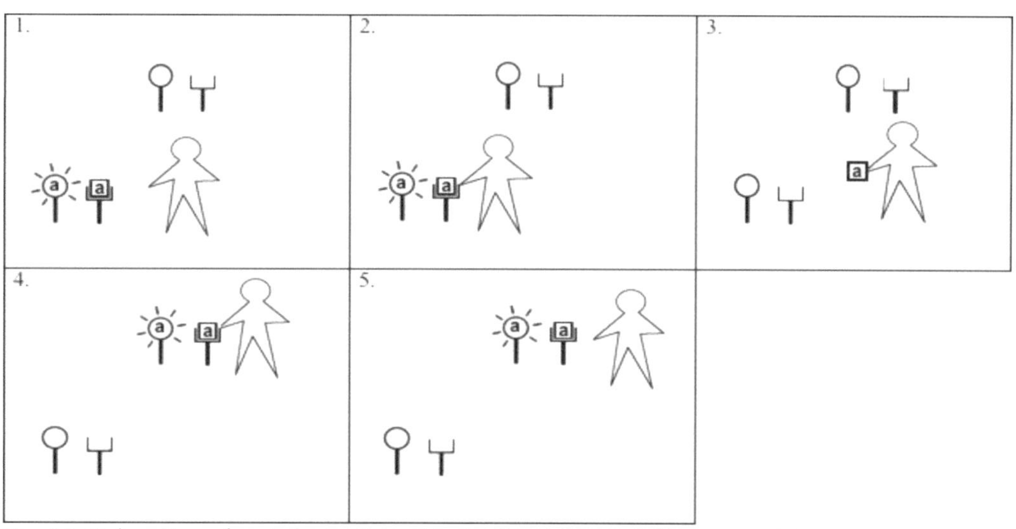

Fig. 14. Relocation of an information object using tokens and token containers.

Another solution would be to let the user take the role as token as shown in Fig. 15.

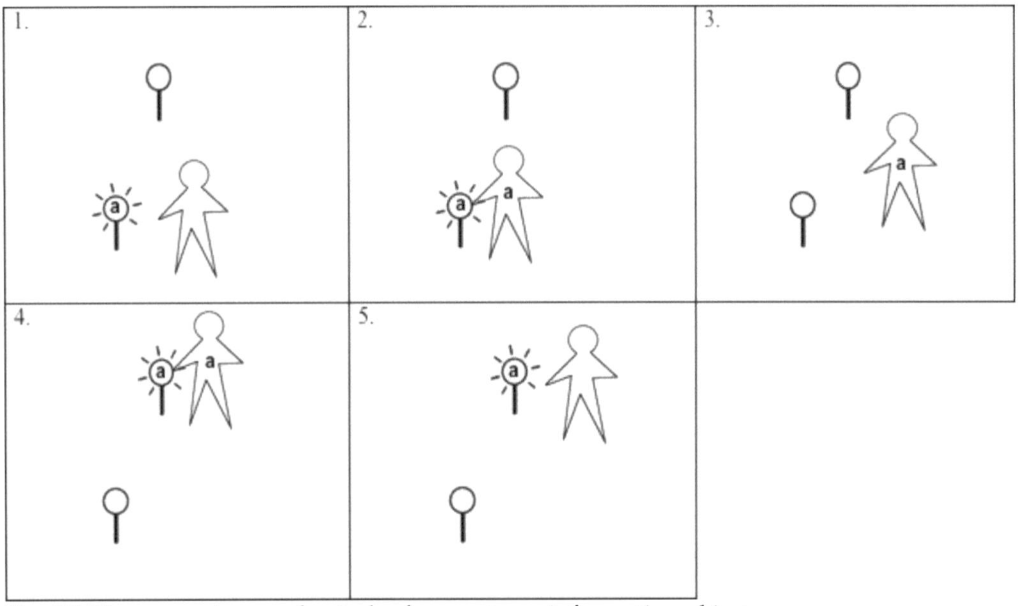

Fig. 15. The user acts as a physical reference to an information object.

5.3 Interpersonal Communication

While much of the research on smart spaces has focused on single-user scenarios, smart spaces and contained physical and digital resources can also be shared among people inhabiting these spaces. Figs. 16-20 show how different variants of information exchange between people can be modeled using the proposed design elements.

Fig. 16 and Fig. 17 show two examples of how synchronous information exchange can be modeled. In the first example, the mobile virtual zones associated with each user act as extensions of the users' bodily spaces. The mobile devices that a user is carrying can respond to the presence of another user (i.e., his extended bodily space).

In the latter example, the mobile devices must touch or be in immediate proximity of another device in order to hand over an information object.

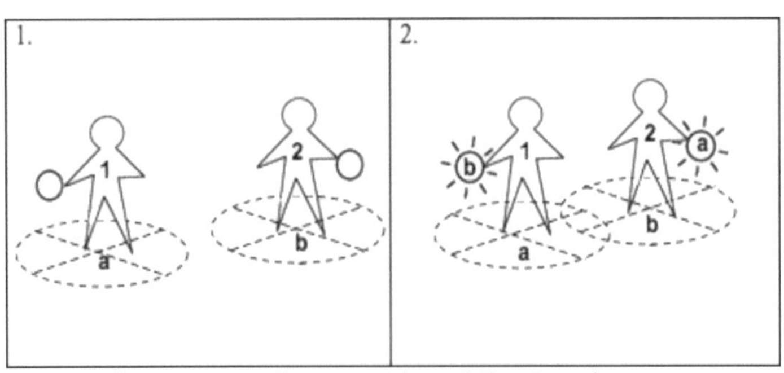

Fig. 16. Synchronous information exchange with mobile virtual zones.

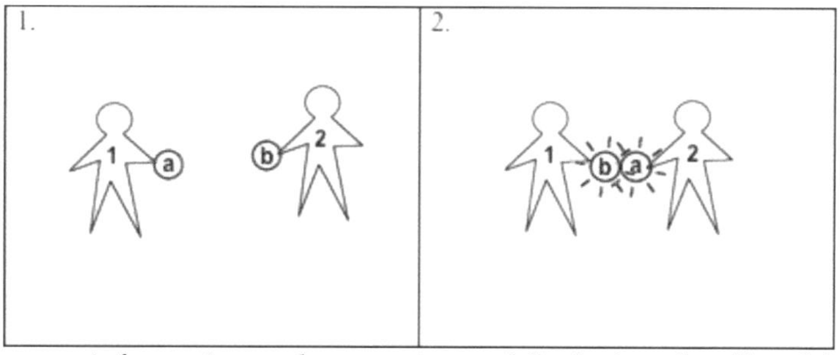

Fig. 17. Synchronous information exchange using mobile devices that "handshake".

Figs. 18-20 illustrate methods for asynchronous information exchanges. The representation shown in Fig. 18 is a conceptual model of the token-based CybStickers system (Rahlff, 2005). It allows users to communicate via tokens that can be physically distributed, and then be linked with digital information from a remote location. Other users can access the information object by scanning the respective token.

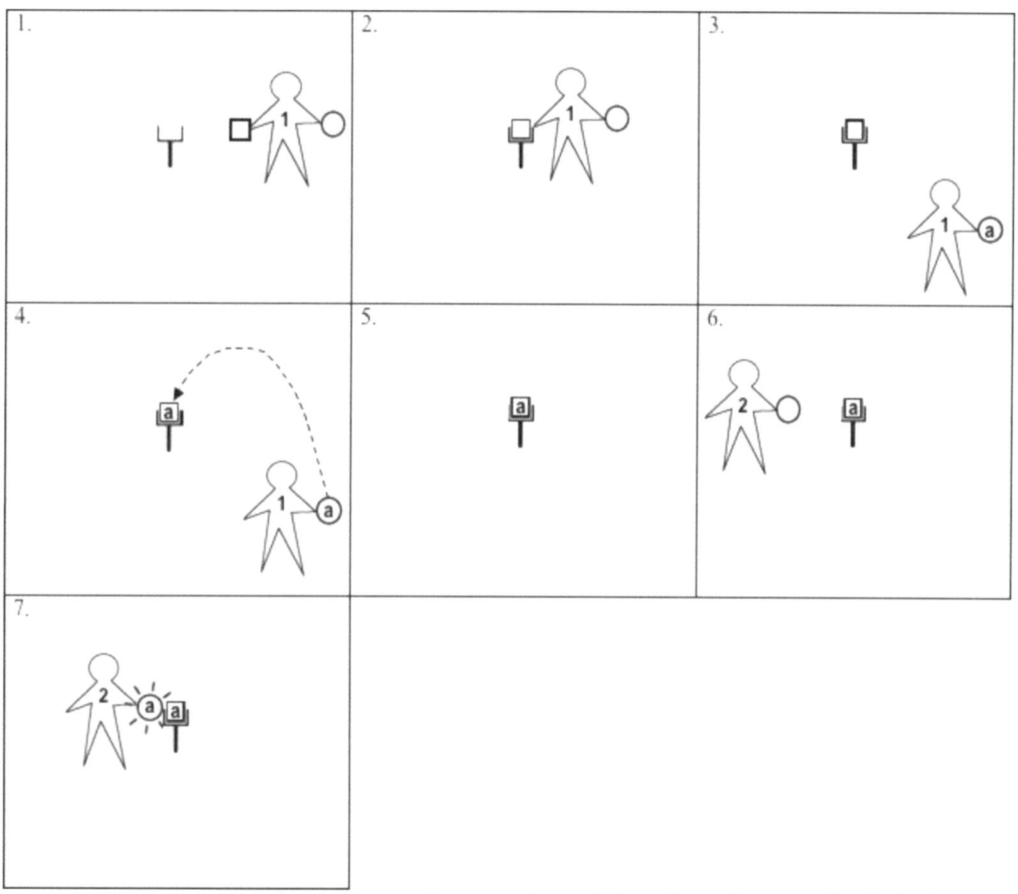

Fig. 18. Token-based information exchange via mobile token that can be linked to an information object from a remote location.

A location-based alternative implementing the same principle is shown in Fig. 19. In this setup a user can link an information object to a remotely located virtual zone. Potential recipient can then access the information object as they enter that zone. The location-based reminder service described by Sohn et al. (2005) is an implementation of this model.
Fig. 20 shows another instance of token-based information exchange. Here, a user distributes a set of tokens (e.g., RFID tags) with reference to two distinct information objects (*a* and *b*). The tokens are initially held in a mobile container (e.g., a book or folder). After the tokens have been distributed the can be accessed by other users at the respective locations.

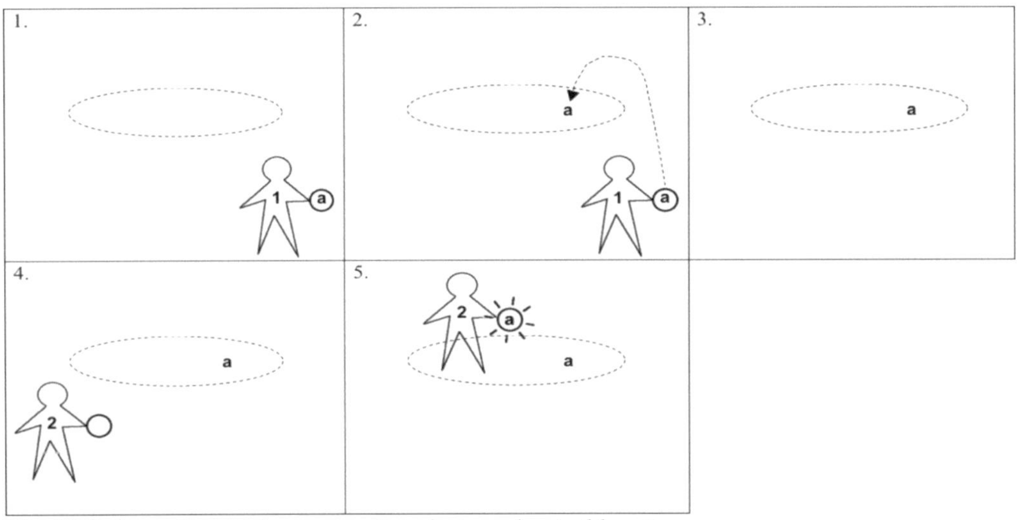

Fig. 19. Information exchange mediated via a physical location.

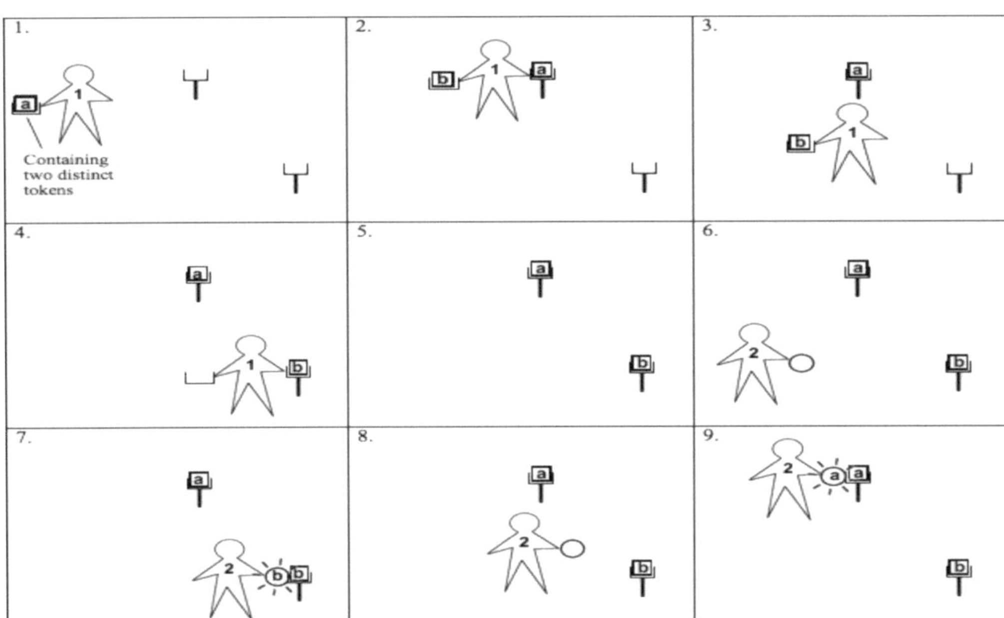

Fig. 20. Instance of token-based information exchange.

6. Discussion

In this section we will briefly discuss how the presented modeling technique can contribute to inform design of ubiquitous computing and smart spaces. We will also point out some limitations.

6.1 Main Contributions

De facto computer system modeling formalisms tend to remove physical features of the system that is modeled. This makes it difficult to use such approaches to guide thinking about design of smart spaces, in which digital services and real-world user actions and events merge.

How users can provide computer input, properties of the devices and tools, and collocation between elements of interaction are not easily communicated through system models. This highlights need for physical models.

In this essay, we have argued that one way to accommodate physical design aspects of smart spaces is to think visually. The proposed method has adopted features from narrative modeling techniques such as storyboarding. By describing interaction in smart spaces sequentially through snapshots or frames it offers a simple way for designers to "zoom" in or out on an interaction sequence by adding or removing frames. As illustrated in previous section this makes it possible to represent both high-level interaction patterns, as well as more specific use scenarios.

By introducing a set of formal design elements the proposed modeling technique allows designers to create structured representations. This can help draw attention to the different roles design elements can play in interaction in smart spaces. Essentially, the design elements reflect the basic physical capabilities (mobility, immobility, portability) of the real-world entities they represent. The semantic relationship between the design elements reflects the most common methods of physical interaction (proximity, presence, and touch) supported by UbiComp technology. The examples provided in the previous section highlights that while the actual system operations (i.e. the functional specification) are likely to be constant, the composition of design elements that form the physical interface of smart spaces is highly flexible.

Being able to describe such compositions in a structured way can make it easier for designers to recognize similarities and distinction between different interaction design solutions, and re-use or adjust previous models to new design problems.

Results from a preliminary focus group evaluation (Dahl, 2007) also suggested that one of the key benefits of the formalism is that the generated models promote reflection and discussion among designers concerning how design solutions present themselves to users.

6.2 Limitations

As with any modeling technique from computer-related disciplines there are also certain limitation associated with the approach we have presented and discussed.

Firstly, it is limited to representing location-aware and token-based systems only. Alternative interaction techniques for smart spaces, however, include pointing and gesturing (Levin-Sagi et al., 2007), speech-based (Potamitis et al., 2003), and gaze-based interaction (Bonino et al., 2006). Formalizing these interaction techniques will require custom designed notations and semantics.

Secondly, the proposed building blocks are rough. Details concerning interaction elements and usage are hidden from the constructed models. For example, computer device may support different interaction styles such as stylus and touch-based interaction. Most token-based systems require that users hold or maneuver tokens in specific way in order to successfully scan them. For example, an ATM requires that credit cards are inserted the correct way into the ATM card slot. For some token-based system the different ways a token is manipulated can have different semantic meaning (Shaer et al., 2004). Modeling such details require richer representations for which informal sketches or icons may be more appropriate.

Thirdly, because the modeling technique focuses on generating physical models the underlying software methods that implement location and token-based abstracted away.

As the limitations above suggest, the proposed modeling technique is a supplement rather that a substitution to other modeling formalisms.

7. Conclusion and Future Work

The merging of the physical and the digital is a hallmark for smart spaces. In the current work we have argued that this raises the need for modeling techniques that can help direct thinking about physical aspect of human-computer interaction. Inspired by visual modeling techniques, such as storyboards and sketching, and the structure characterizing conventional system models, the proposed formalism offers a novel perspective on smart spaces.

Through this essay we have shown that it can be an effective visual "thinking" tool for exploring the interaction design opportunities that smart spaces can offer.

To form a more comprehensive understanding of its practical applicability, the modeling technique needs to be evaluated more extensively with designers and as part of a design process.

8. Acknowledgements

This work has been conducted in the context of the ISIS project (Infrastructure for Integrated Services), which is financed by Norwegian Research Council (NFR # 180122).

9. References

Bardram, J. (2004). Applications of context-aware computing in hospital work: Examples and design principles, *Proceedings of the 2004 ACM symposium on Applied computing*, pp. 1574-1579, ISBN: 1-58113-812-1, Nicosia, Cyprus, ACM Press

Bonino, D.; Castellina, E., Corno, F. & Garbo, A. (2006). Control Application for Smart House through Gaze interaction," *Proceedings of the 2nd COGAIN Annual Conference on Communication by Gaze Interaction*, Turin, Italy, September 2006

Cheverst, K.; Davies, N., Mitchell, K. & Friday, A. (2000). Experiences of developing and deploying a context-aware tourist guide: The GUIDE project, *Proceedings of the 6th annual international conference on mobile computing and networking*, pp. 20-31, Boston, MA, ACM Press, New York, NY, USA

Dahl, Y. (2007). Toward a Visual Formalism for Modeling Location and Token-Based interaction in Context-Aware Environments. *Proceedings of the 2nd IASTED International Conference on Human-Computer Interaction*, pp. 183-192, ACTA Press

Davidoff, S; Lee, M. K., Dey, A. K. & Zimmerman, J. (2007) Rapidly Exploring Application Design Through Speed Dating. *Proceedings of the 9th International Conference on Ubiquitous Computing*, pp. 429-446, Innsbruck, Austria, September 2007

Dourish, P. (2001). Seeking a foundation for context-aware computing, *Human-Computer Interaction*, Vol. 16, No. 2-4, (February 2001) pp. 229-241, ISSN: 0737-0024.

Holmquist, L.E.; Redström, J. & Ljungstrand, P. (1999). Token-Based Access to Digital Information. *Proceedings of the 1st International Symposium on Handheld and Ubiquitous Computing (HUC'99)*, pp. 234-245, ISBN: 3-540-66550-1, Karlsruhe, Germany, Springer-Verlag, London, UK

Howard, S.; Kjeldskov, J. & Skov, M.B. (2007). Pervasive computing in the domestic space. *Personal and Ubiquitous Computing*, Vol. 11, No. 5, pp. 329-333, ISSN: 1617-4909.

Koskela, T. & Väänänen-Vainio-Mattila, K. (2004). Evolution towards smart home environments: Empirical evaluation of three user interfaces. *Personal and Ubiquitous Computing*, Vol. 8, No. 3-4, (July 2004) pp. 234-240, ISSN: 1617-4909

Ljungstrand, P.; Redström, J. & Holmquist, L.E. (2000), WebStickers: Using physical tokens to access, manage and share bookmarks to the Web, *Proceedings of DARE 2000 on Designing augmented reality environments*, pp. 23-31, Elsinore, Denmark, 2000

Levin-Sagi, M.; Pasher, E., Carlsson, V., Klug, T., Ziegert, T. & Zinnen, A. (2007) A Comprehensive Human Factors Analysis of Wearable Computers Supporting a Hospital Ward Round. *Proceedings of the 4th International Forum on Applied Wearable Computing (IFAWC)*, Tel Aviv, Israel, March 2007

Østhus, E.C.; Osland, P.-O. & Kristiansen, L. (2005). ENME: An ENriched MEdia Application Utilizing Context for Session Mobility; Technical and Human Issues, Springer LNCS, 316-325, ISBN: 978-3-540-30803-4, Springer-Verlag

Petrelli, D.; Not, E. & Zancanaro, M. (1999) Getting Engaged and Getting Tired: What is in a Museum Experience. *Proceedings of the Workshop on Attitude, Personality, and Emotions in User-Adapted Interaction*, UM'99, Banff, Canada.

Potamitis I.; Georgila, K., Fakotakis, N. & Kokkinakis, G (2003). An Integrated System for Smart-Home Control of Appliances Based on Remote Speech Interaction. *Proceedings of the 8th European Conference on Speech Communication and Technology (EUROSPEECH)*, pp. 2197-2200, Geneva, Switzerland, September 2003.

Rahlff, O.-W. (2005). CybStickers - Simple Shared Ubiquitous Annotations for All, *UbiPhysics workshop at UbiComp 2005*, Tokyo, Japan, September 2005.

Shaer, O.; Leland, N., Calvillo-Gamez, E. H. & Jacob, R. J. (2004). The TAC paradigm: specifying tangible user interfaces. *Personal and Ubiquitous Computing*. Vol. 8, No. 5, pp. 359-369, ISSN: 1617-4909

Sohn, T.; Li, K.A., Lee, G., Smith, I., Scott, J. & Griswold, W.G. (2005) Place-Its: A Study of Location-Based Reminders on Mobile Phones, *Proceedings of the 5th International Conference on Ubiquitous Computing (UbiComp 2005)*, pp. 232-250, Tokyo, Japan

Van der Lelie, C. (2006). The value of storyboards in the product design process, *Personal and Ubiquitous Computing*, Vol. 10, No. 2, pp. 159-162. ISSN: 1617-4909

Weiser, M. (1991). The Computer for the 21st Century. *Scientific American*, Vol. 265, No. 3, (September 1991) pp. 66-75.

10

Mobile Interaction Design: Techniques for Early Stage In-Situ Design

Marco de Sá, Luís Carriço & Carlos Duarte
LaSIGE and Faculty of Sciences, University of Lisbon
Portugal

1. Introduction

The recent globalization of mobile technology and its overwhelming presence on everyday life through various societal groups and activities has raised its importance to unprecedented levels. Mobile devices' diverse shapes, small size and distinctive characteristics impel their use in diverse and ubiquitous scenarios, cementing their presence within our work, social and entertainment activities. Accordingly, as they assume a greater meaning and a wider role of functionalities, a corresponding amount of new usage paradigms is also emerging. Consequentially, designers are increasingly faced with new design challenges, needing to cope with added difficulties of creating solutions for multiple contexts, users, purposes and new ubiquitous usage behaviours. Simultaneously, they need to cope with and leverage the small size factor and the peculiar or mixed interaction modalities (e.g., touch screen in concert with keyboard or voice) that define the trends of emerging mobile devices.

Contrastingly, design problems for mobile devices, and corresponding solutions, have only recently begun to be partially and superficially addressed. Difficulties and challenges are spread through various stages of design. Three phases are particularly interesting: (1) requirements and data gathering on mobile contexts; (2) prototyping for small devices and (3) evaluation on real-world settings. Currently used approaches and existing methodologies still lack specific techniques to support design on such demanding conditions, hindering the design process and resulting in poor software regarding usability. Even recent approaches generally rely on simulations, lab experiences or derive directly from non-mobile techniques, colliding with studies that have clearly demonstrated the need to take the design process out of the lab when it comes to mobile devices.

This book chapter focuses on these problems and discusses recent advances on mobile interaction design, reviewing existing attempts to overcome the added challenges brought by mobility, pervasiveness and mobile devices' characteristics. As its main contribution, it identifies key concerns and issues brought by mobility, also presenting ways to complement current efforts and proposing new approaches that aim at overcoming existing challenges and problems. It introduces findings and work developed thus far, offering improvements and solutions that tackle out-of-the-lab design procedures and support in-situ participatory design and evaluation. These approaches are compiled within a User Centred Design (UCD) methodology that emphasizes initial stages of design and identifies techniques and guidelines for (1) early stage data gathering and scenario generation for design; (2) low-fidelity prototyping techniques particularly suited to mobile devices which also propel an easier transition to (3) evaluation on real-world contexts and settings. Case studies where these techniques have been applied are presented, detailing the used procedures and tools, achieved results and eliciting the implications and benefits that emerged from the application of such techniques. As a conclusion, suggestions and guidelines on how to apply similar endeavours on different domains are presented, also defining further research goals and directions within mobile interaction design.

2. Motivation and Related Work

The somewhat recent appearance of ubiquitous and pervasive computing, supported by an ever growing diversity of mobile technology, has introduced a set of additional challenges into the design process of interactive application for mobile devices (Blom et al., 2005). While attempting to overcome such difficulties, designers often choose to port to mobile devices, existing applications available for larger platforms, adjusting the necessary details (Nakajima, 2006). However, such approach generally leads to cumbersome and unusable applications that even if containing brilliant content, quickly become obsolete and avoided by users (Brewster, 2002; Lee, 2003).

A major factor for designers to adopt such strategies is the absence of specific methodologies for mobile, handheld and ubiquitous devices (Hagen, 2005; Raptis, 2005). Although some guidelines, available in current user-centred design (UCD) methodologies, might apply to this specific design process, the unique features and constraints that ubiquity, pervasiveness and the devices' physical characteristics introduce require new, or at least deeply refined, approaches.

Three design stages are particularly sensitive and present a wider set of difficulties (Sá & Carriço, 2006a):

- (1) Gathering requirements in mobile scenarios, where the constant use of the mobile device or application is done in changing contexts, introduces details that are hardly detectable with the use of traditional methods. One can imagine, for instance, that if all contexts are known, traditional methods can acceptably assess the influence of each context in specific scenarios. However, the implications of changing from one context to another and how this might influence the user and his/her requirements towards the applications fail to be understood.
- (2) On the sketching process and construction of low-fidelity prototypes, several problems that retract from the process are also evident. Low-fidelity prototypes are, as currently used, poorly suited to the peculiarities of mobile devices and their usage scenarios (Sá & Carriço, 2006a). These ill-suited prototyping methods also have implications on the later stages of evaluation.
- (3) In fact, when it comes to the evaluation of mobile applications, given the absence of specific methods and guidelines, this stage is frequently discarded (Kjeldskov & Graham, 2003). Overall, the difficulties inherent to the design process of applications for such devices urge for different approaches and extensions to current user-centred design processes.

Aligned with these preoccupations, mobile interaction design has been recently addressed on various emerging researches (Hagen et al., 2005; Jones & Marsden, 2006; Kjeldskov and Stage, 2003; Weiss, 2002). Generally, these approaches try to adjust existing and traditional techniques to mobile settings or, in some cases, introduce new methods that cope with ubiquity and the small size factor that commonly characterizes mobile devices. Nevertheless, serious deficiencies are pointed in the available literature affecting the advance of mobile interaction design (Hagen et al, 2005; Kjeldskov & Graham, 2003; Lee, 2003; Sá & Carriço, 2006a; Marcus & Chen, 2002). As a consequence, it is common practice to overlook determinant design stages such as prototyping and evaluation (Kjeldskov & Stage, 2003; Nielsen et al., 2006), which impacts directly on the quality of available applications (Lee, 2003). Alternatively, simulation and role playing are recurrently used as quick patches (Barnard et al., 2005; Svanaes & Seland, 2004). However, these also fall short while trying to grasp realistic usage requirements (Nielsen et al., 2006).

The main motivation behind this work, builds upon the aforementioned lack of relevant guidance within mobile interaction design and on the difficulties that emerged during the design of several projects for mobile devices (Beyer & Holtzblatt, 1998; Mayhew, 1999). Overall, problems affect design teams throughout the entire process, requiring constant adjustments to each stage particularly hindering, as mentioned, the analysis and requirements gathering, prototyping and evaluation phases. Each of the following sections stresses, in deeper detail, the particular issues that affect the aforementioned design stages addressing the state-of-the-art and existing approaches to each task and design stage.

2.1 Data Gathering

Data gathering is the essential bootstrap to the design process of most interactive applications. This stage's goal is to provide designers with relevant data on how users work or act within their usual working settings and how a technological solution can improve that process. Several techniques can be used to achieve this purpose. The most common are questionnaires, interviews, contextual inquiry and user observation.

User questionnaires are, as the name points, questionnaires that are delivered to large groups of users trying to gather opinions and data based directly on the users' input and perspective on existing issues. The remaining techniques aim at gathering richer information and data by including designers directly on the process and by introducing interaction between designers and future users, allowing the former to make use of their expertise and experience while gathering information from users.

Interviews are used to obtain personal opinions from representative users from a target audience, gathering information on needs, wishes and preferences. Interviews are generally preceded by the construction of a script and questionnaire that is presented and responded orally. Although interviews can provide richer data and information when compared to questionnaires, mainly because designers can adjust, on-the-fly, their questions as the interview goes along, as well as to witness users' reactions to specific questions and details, they are generally applied to a much smaller population. Given the time and resources that they require, it is difficult to interview as many target users as those that can be reached through questionnaires (e.g., on-line questionnaire or street survey). Furthermore, interviews can be biased and influenced by the interviewer's input (Read et al., 2004). However, a major advantage is that they can be used with a varied type of population (e.g., children, elderly, visually impaired, etc) (Consolvo et al., 2004). Still, they are very focused on user input and might provide little information regarding paramount details (e.g., location, settings, and cooperation) that result from activities that users accomplish even without noticing. To overcome some of these problems designers often conduct interviews in context while observing some of the user's activities. This type of dynamic and on-the-spot interview is called contextual inquiry. With contextual inquiry the interview is conducted on the location where users work, with the usual settings, focusing activities that are taking place during that interview. It usually includes conversation and interaction

between the designer that conducts the interview and the user that is accomplishing the activities.
Since it occurs at the location where work is usually accomplished, it provides extra detail on the work context and existing problems. It merges some of the advantages of interviewing with some of the advantages of user observation. It has also been successfully used on critical scenarios. Coble et al. used the contextual inquiry method to assess requirements on a clinical setting, overcoming previous experiences that provided poor information on physicians' needs and consequently ended with poorly designed solutions and attempts (Coble et al., 1997).
However, taking into consideration ubiquitous applications, where tasks can be accomplished on multiple settings and extend through various contexts, contextual inquiry becomes extremely difficult, if not impossible to apply. Conducting contextual inquiry on a ubiquitous activity would necessary imply that the interviewer would have to follow the user around interrupting him whenever necessary in order to ask questions. Moreover, user's behaviour is usually affected by designer's questions and interruptions, thus providing a less realistic notion of how activities are accomplished, users' reactions and if, how and why behaviour changes occur. To avoid this type of problem, a simpler method is direct user observation. The user observation technique comprehends direct observation of a user accomplishing specific activities on realistic settings without any interference by the designer that is observing. Its main advantages reside on the richness of the gathered data and the unbiased perspective of the work flow. However, in order to correctly observe users while accomplishing specific task some cautions have to be taken. For instance, in Mazzone et al. (2004), the authors conducted a preliminary ethnographic study in order to understand the best locations and settings and where and how to observe the users. Nevertheless, similarly to contextual inquiry, user observation has limitations when ubiquity and mobility are involved. To properly observe a user while using a mobile device, the designer would have to follow the user everywhere while accomplishing a specific task. Moreover, the designer would have to be extremely close to the user in order to view the user's interaction with the device possibly hindering the process which also poses restrictions to the user's behaviour, especially during private tasks.
Throughout various experiences, on mobile design, the application of these techniques, suggested by the used UCD methodologies, posed problems and proved to be inadequate to some of the settings and activities that were being addressed. On pervasive and mobile activities as those that were targeted on the projects at hands (e.g., thought registration and activity scheduling during user's daily lives, Cognitive Behavioural Therapy, homework), these data gathering techniques failed to provide sufficient detail and reliable data for designers to use (Sá & Carriço, 2006). Globally, these difficulties pointed the need for adjusted and more flexible means and techniques do gather data and analyse requirements on mobile and ubiquitous settings, especially for pervasive activities.

2.2 Prototyping

Prototypes can be either low-fidelity prototypes, focused on this chapter, used in early stages of design, or highly usable prototypes, close to the final application. During the design process of a certain software program, prototypes allow designers to test their ideas and concepts with final users before the final product is completed (Beyer & Holtzblatt, 1998; Hanington, 2006; Mayhew, 1999). Low-fidelity (low-fi) prototypes are non-functional

User Interfaces (UIs) sketched on paper cards or post-its, put together with glue, pins and cut out with scissors (Beyer & Holtzblatt, 1998; Holtzblatt et al., 2005; Robert A. Virzi, 1996), that are used to simulate an actual system, while evaluating its features and detecting its flaws during early design stages. Prototypes are an essential tool for UCD and many other methodologies.

In (Frishberg, 2006a) the importance of low-fidelity prototypes to drive design and evaluate ideas with low-cost is addressed. The author stresses the need to provide users with objects that reflect ideas, illustrating assumptions and concepts on a physical and tangible manner. Accordingly, the use of prototypes facilitates user interaction with design concepts and challenges users to provide input and generate ideas. However, advantages for designers are also paramount. As detailed in (Rosenberg, 2006), low-fidelity prototypes provide a way for designers to assess user satisfaction at very early stages. They also provide a common reference point for all the design team members, improve the completeness of the product's functional specification and substantially reduce the total development cost of the product. Accordingly, this type of easy to use and highly configurable prototypes is particularly interesting for early design stages since they can be quickly built using inexpensive material (Chandler et al., 2002; Connelly et al., 2005; Kangas & Kinnunen, 2005).

Summarizing, low-fidelity prototypes, present an important tool for designers to test their designs and solutions during early design phases (Beyer & Holtzblatt, 1998; Black & Hawkes, 2006; Mayhew, 1999; Robert A. Virzi, 1996; Svanaes & Seland, 2004; Weiss, 2002). They enable developers with a quick and inexpensive way to evaluate and assess some design ideas without programming and implementing real and functional solutions. In fact, in some cases, their efficiency is almost as high as software prototypes. Several studies (Kangas & Kinnunen, 2005; Robert A. Virzi, 1996) have demonstrated that paper prototypes can be efficiently used to prevent posterior design errors and unusable applications.

However, even if they are to be viewed as a mere designing tool, many times these are perceived by users as a very resembling solution to the final application. In (Holmquist, 2005), the author points designers' attention to avoid misleading users while creating prototypes. Often, designers create very appealing prototypes which please users but are too expensive or impossible to actually implement generally leading to failure or disappointment. On a more user concerned level, this can also affect the usability of the resulting applications whereas during evaluation no major usability issues are detected while on a final version they are present in a very obtrusive way. This is particularly true for mobile devices. For instance, using a Letter sized paper to draw a UI, and using post-its as menus might be an acceptable way to prototype a desktop application. However, when it comes to mobile applications, specific attention must be taken to details which compromise their usage on real settings. In fact, here, paper prototyping may pose a considerable problem and mislead users. For instance, using a post it with a few key buttons to simulate the use of a PDA with a GPS card might seem a great idea to test a future application. However, using the real device on one's hand throughout the day may be a demanding task, requiring a much different UI or might be unsuitable for certain users (e.g., elderly) or scenarios (e.g., hiking). Testing an application with an artificial keyboard might work if the size of the letters is large, but using a real device keyboard might be quite different, suggesting the need to use alternative solutions. These details may pass without notice if one does not create suitable prototypes and perform tests on real life scenarios. It is true that low-fidelity prototypes need to be quick to build and easy to use (Beyer & Holtzblatt, 1998;

Robert A. Virzi, 1996) but the trade-off between the effort in building them and the misleading results that they might provide needs to be carefully analysed. To be as profitable and useful as acclaimed, low-fidelity prototypes for mobile devices require special attention. In general, when ill-implemented they might even produce the opposite effect than that expected (Hanington, 2006; Holmquist, 2005) since users and sometimes designers, tend to visualize mobile prototypes, even low-fidelity ones, as extremely resembling to final solutions. If care is not taken, this misleading conduct can affect the evaluation process, the use of the prototype itself, and the final result.

Also, and of great importance, is the fact that with mobile prototypes, external characteristics to the sketches may influence the validity of the prototype. Details such as weight, interaction modalities, size or shape may influence the way in which the sketch is perceived. Furthermore, simpler restraints such as the screen resolution or area might imply that common prototyping techniques need to be adapted to such details. Traditionally, mobile prototypes are regarded as just another case of prototyping. Clearly, due to the aforementioned characteristics, special attention must be taken when prototyping for mobile devices, suggesting the need for new approaches regarding this practice. Currently, low-fidelity prototyping for mobile devices is generally done in a classic way, creating sketches on paper cards and using post-its as buttons or menus. The few examples available in literature apply common techniques with no particular emphasis on the specific characteristics of the devices and their interaction. Recently, research directed to this stage of design, applied to mobile devices (Hanington, 2006; Holmquist, 2005; Weiss, 2005) including some of the experiences that originated this work (Sá & Carriço, 2006) has addressed these issues. Given mobile devices' portability and adequateness to intensive usage and their physical characteristics and peculiar interaction modalities, the distinction between the device and the UI, although rarely addressed and implemented, seems to be crucial to take into account while creating mobile low-fidelity prototypes.

In (Hanington, 2006) this topic is discussed and some experiences described. The author explains how paper and physical prototyping are essential to provide users with notions such as screen real estate, input mechanisms, and weight and so on. Moreover, the authors suggest that integrating the device prototype with the sketching process inspires inventive and creative products. The research experiences that were conducted included the construction of physical prototypes using materials such as foam, slides and other found materials. Sketches were drawn on paper and used in concert with the physical prototypes. Positive results demonstrated that merging both concepts and actually creating physical prototypes enhanced the evaluation and testing processes.

Other research experiences that focus on how prototypes should be built and what should be their characteristics consider the utilization of various fidelities of prototypes, including more or less details depending on what is being evaluated. In (McCurdy et al., 2006) the authors point the differences between prototype fidelities and present an example of a mixed-fidelity prototype. Accordingly, they suggest five different dimensions that can be adjusted according to the evaluation that needs to be conducted. The first is the visual refinement which can vary from hand drawn sketches to pixel-accurate mockups. The second dimension refers to the breadth of functionality which defines what the user can actually do with the prototype, ranging from no functionality where no action can be done with the prototype, to highly functional prototypes where most of the final functionalities are available. Closely related is the third dimension, depth of functionality, which pertains to how accurate the simulation and level of functionality of each feature is. Finally, the richness of interactivity and the richness of the data model which refer to how close the interaction with the prototype is to the final product and to how representative the actual domain data employed in the prototype is. Overall, these dimensions allow designers to categorize their prototypes depending on the type of UI or device they want to evaluate or design for. As previously mentioned, given mobile device's characteristics, dimensions such as the level of visual refinement and richness of functionality, especially on low-fi prototypes, are paramount.

Globally, it is clear that prototyping is an extremely positive endeavour that allows designers to propel design, include users on the design process and evaluate concepts and ideas on early stages of design. However, as some research already points, with mobile devices particular care must be taken while generating effective prototypes. Current literature, although stating some evidences of evolution and suggesting some new approaches, does not provide practical guidelines on how to develop or use low-fi prototypes for mobile devices. Existing examples, although well intentioned, offer suggestions that do not comply with the evaluation that is required on mobile usability, showing inability to cope with the specific characteristics that mobile devices and their usage requires. Other examples found in the literature follow different approaches, pointing directions which generally require expensive material and can not be easily used on early stages (Sá & Carriço, 2008).

On the experiences that motivated this work, as projects evolved to the prototyping stage, the type of procedures that were, as abovementioned, proposed by the literature introduced a set of problems on the usage of the prototypes that were created. Components and their size generally confounded users and resulted in unrealistic, misunderstood and quickly rejected prototypes. Since screen measurements (e.g., fonts, scroll-bars) were sometimes disregarded and prototypes quickly hand drawn, the information that each card started to include was excessive and impossible to include on actual devices. User participation was problematic since users' requests, suggestions and their own sketches were unattainable given the dimensions and features of the targeted devices. Moreover, together with the design fidelity details (e.g., size, components), more realistic tools than post-its or cards, as exemplified in (Beyer & Holtzblatt, 1998; Jones & Marsden, 2006; Mayhew, 1999; Weiss, 2002) were needed. These materials also mislead users regarding weight, size or the interaction with the devices. The cards often deteriorate during outside evaluation sessions and simulations, especially each time users try to put a paper PDA prototype in his/her pocket, while mimicking their common behaviour on common daily life situations.

Globally, both literature and some of the problems and results from the mentioned experiences stressed the need for particular care and new prototyping methods for mobile devices, addressing issues such as shape, format, fidelity levels, adequateness to evaluation and so on.

2.3 Usability Evaluation

Usability evaluation out of the lab, especially during early design stages, which has been proved to be critical on various design projects (Sá et al, 2007; Reis et Al, 2008), is not yet a common procedure (Kjeldskov & Graham, 2003). Although some researches have addressed this subject, stressing its importance and effective results (Duh et al., 2006; Jones & Marsden, 2006; Kjeldskov & Graham, 2003; Nielsen et al., 2006), most rely on simulations and role

playing and generally take place within controlled scenarios (Barnard et al., 2005; Kjeldskov & Stage, 2003; Svanaes & Seland, 2004). Accordingly, used methodologies provide no insight on how to conduct any type of multiple context/setting evaluation.
For instance, the use of the Wizard of Oz technique (Kelley, 1984) with mobile prototypes can be extremely demanding. Following a user while he/she tests a prototype on every imagined scenario might even be impossible to achieve. The procedure itself generally causes ethical and social problems and provides erroneous results. To support this type of activity, some approaches have been experimented and technological systems (Carter et al., 2007; Froelich et al., 2007; Reich et al., 2007) are being developed to support the remote evaluation of mobile applications on real-settings. However, they generally require working software prototypes and applications or use expensive material that is not commonly accessible.
Although, from a generic perspective, traditional techniques have been successfully used on a variety of tests for different systems and applications, the particular requirements that mobile devices introduce, mainly due to their use on a multitude of contexts, requires further effort and adjustments to these methods (Hagen et al., 2005; Kjeldskov & Stage, 2003; Nielsen et al., 2006; Scholtz & Consolvo, 2004). Recent research experiences suggest that given their intensive and pervasive use, mobile devices and correspondent applications should be evaluated on multiple and realistic settings. Contrarily to fixed and desktop hardware, when using mobile devices, users are constantly faced with distractions and obstacles and often accomplish several tasks at the same time. Accordingly, recent studies have been addressing this topic. Duh et al. conducted a series of tests that aimed at determining the differences between usability tests conducted within laboratories or field tests with mobile devices (Duh et al., 2006). Similar tests took place in the laboratory and on the field. In the laboratory test, digital cameras were used to capture the mobile device's interface and the user's facial expressions. On the field test a camera assistant captured only the facial expression of the user while walking around a specific setting. Results revealed field observation and tests enabled the detection of many more usability problems. Furthermore, most of the problems that were detected on the field tests were categorized as critical.
Nielsen at al. conducted a similar experience (Nielsen et al., 2006). Their results also demonstrate that field tests provide more valid results and identify significantly more usability problems. Moreover, task completion times almost duplicated on field tests and on real usage settings, suggesting that laboratory tests might provide erroneous results.
In Barnard et al. the authors show, through a series of tests how context affects human performance in mobile computing systems (Barnard et al., 2007). In this study, users were requested to perform some activities on different scenarios. The experiences focused lighting and movement (e.g., if the user is standing or walking) conditions. Results show that the user's surroundings can greatly influence his/her behaviour. Accordingly, the authors suggest that context and the environment should take a primordial role while designing and evaluating mobile applications and new methods to achieve so are necessary. Even so, the reported experiences were conducted within controlled and simulated environments. Despite the evident advantages of field evaluation tests, there are still few reports of successful experiences and even fewer suggestions and guidelines on how to address such type of evaluation. Kjeldskov & Graham presented a study that clearly demonstrates that designers tend to engineer systems using applied approaches rather than designing and

evaluating them (Kjeldskov & Graham, 2003). Furthermore, even when these are evaluated, evaluation sessions are generally conducted on laboratories. In addition, the authors conclude that contextual evaluation and phenomena observation on real settings is not widely used, presenting an increasingly required research track on the field of HCI. Curiously, one of these authors conducted a survey on new emerging techniques to evaluate mobile systems on laboratories. Here, the authors justify this approach, opposing to field and contextual evaluation, due to three difficulties that are generally felt while trying to do so. The first pertains to the scenarios and settings in which tests should be done. It is difficult to select specific situations that represent a set of contexts to evaluate. Summarizing, key settings are hard to identify.

The difficulty to apply existing evaluation techniques on mobile settings is the second reason whilst the third is caused by the complicated data collection. On field evaluations it is demanding to cope with the physical surroundings and environment that might affect the set-up. This is noticeable both on the designers that gather the data and on the users which accomplish tasks. On the other hand the authors defend that in laboratory settings these difficulties can be reduced. Although user mobility can be difficult to recreate, according to the authors, it is preferable to lose realism towards a better quality of collected data. Accordingly, they propose two frameworks for mobile evaluation in laboratories. The first focuses on the user's physical movements while using the mobile system and on the attention needed to navigate through the software. These two dimensions allow designers to arrange tests according to different configurations simulating various levels of movement and attention. For instance, if there is constant moving the authors suggest the use of a treadmill with varying speed to simulate real situations. As a consequence, conscious attention is required from the user. The second framework aims to evaluate divided attention, frequently distracting the user in order to simulate the use of a mobile system in a real world setting.

To evaluate both frameworks, experiences were conducted to assess their validity comparing them to real world evaluations. The frameworks were compared to an experience where users moved through a pedestrian street while using the mobile system. Overall, conclusions state that there are no significant differences between the use of the frameworks or real setting evaluations. In fact, the situation where most usability problems were identified was while the user was seating at a table.

However, these experiences reduced real settings and contextual influence to physical movement and degree of attention, introducing limitations on the evaluation. Using these techniques, it is extremely difficult to assess how users react to different social environments and the impact of public or privacy issues on the usability of the mobile system. Pering (Pering, 2006) conducted a study, which clearly concluded that users' behaviour changes according to the privacy settings of his/her location and working context and that these changes must be incorporated into applications and usability studies. This kind of issue is further noticeable when using location-enhanced technology that allows social communication.

Consolvo et al. state that it is crucial to understand why, when and what users want to share with each other and how this influences their social behaviour as well as the use of technology (Consolvo et al., 2005). Therefore, it is paramount to undertake evaluation studies with realistic settings (Duh et al., 2006; Nielsen et al., 2006), where more than physical characteristics of the environment are emulated. Following these findings, recent studies have addressed the need to evaluate mobile systems on actual scenarios and emerging techniques that aim to support these procedures (Duh et al., 2006; Hagen et al., 2005).

Hagen et al. categorized currently used techniques as mediated data collection, simulations and enactments and combinations. On the first, both users and the used technology collect usage data on natural settings. On the second, simulations of real settings are used whilst on the third, combinations of several techniques are utilised. These three categories comprise a set of different techniques which can rely on the use of specific data collecting hardware or on participants collecting data themselves. In fact, this last approach seems to be gaining momentum (Consolvo & Walker, 2003; Froehlich et al., 2006).

The Experience Sampling Method (ESM) is a technique inherited from the field of psychology, which relies on questionnaires to gather usage information on natural settings. Participants of evaluation sessions, using mobile devices, are prompted with questionnaires, providing usability data that can be later analysed and statistically evaluated. Furthermore, since designers are not present during questionnaire filling-in, bias associated to observation is reduced. However, despite the positive results, this technique has some problems as well. It depends greatly on the participants' availability to respond to the questionnaires and to the content of each questionnaire. While user observation provides factual data and facilitates the detection of unexpected usability problems, questionnaires generally point and lead users at problem detection on specific directions. Nevertheless, the technique has proved to be useful. However, the practical advice on how to apply it is limited and suggestions on how to use it with complementary techniques, providing more trustful results is required.

Finally, some evaluation procedures that take advantage of specific hardware are also being experimented (Isomursi et al., 2004; Lukander, 2004; Thompson et al., 2004). In (Isomursi et al., 2004) the authors present an experience where users were filmed and followed while using a mobile device. However, given their presence and the public environment, the user experience was affected. Another alternative experimented on this work relied on users to capture images from other users while utilizing the applications. Moreover, since most of the photographs provided little information when analysed individually, some users also provided annotations of the events in which the photos were taken. However, once again users' annotations did not provide detailed information about usability issues.

Consequentially, the authors suggest a new approach called the "experience clip". The method is based on the usage of a camera phone and a PDA. The PDA contains the application that is being evaluated whereas the camera phone is used to capture clips that seem relevant to users. The experience demonstrated that the technique is able to provide rich data about user emotions and feelings. However, users have to be well motivated and have to be clearly instructed on what they are supposed to capture. Furthermore, the utilization of two devices generally requires the participation of more than one user. Similarly to what was discovered with the first experience that motivated the study, it is likely that the second presence and experience per se might change and influence the evaluation results. Nevertheless, the method provides better results than simulating real-life scenarios within laboratory settings. However, most of these require working software prototypes or expensive equipment.

Overall, on early stages of design, low-fidelity prototypes are scarcely used for mobile devices. Even so, there are some examples that proved to be successful (Svanaes & Seland,

2004). However, even these were tested in controlled scenarios with role playing within the laboratory (Duh et al., 2006; Kjeldskov & Graham, 2003; Svanaes & Seland, 2004). Furthermore, as previously demonstrated, it is important to conduct evaluations studies on actual settings since these highlight specific problems that might pass undetected on laboratory evaluations (Bodker & Buur, 2002; Nielsen et al., 2006). Despite some existing techniques, currently used evaluation approaches are still ill suited to mobile scenarios and contexts of use. The existing literature, although providing some pointers and advice on how to conduct evaluation for mobile devices, generally does so for laboratory settings, contrasting with results that show the benefits and an imminent need for in-situ evaluation.

3. A Design Methodology for Mobile Devices

In order to overcome the stated difficulties, this chapter proposes a design methodology that focuses the new challenges introduced within design stages by mobility and the specific characteristics of mobile interaction. The methodology follows a user centred design approach and suggests the use of alternative techniques on all the initial design stages. As the experiences and examples that are provided here confirmed, the use of the methodology propelled the experimentation of new methods and tools that cope with the user centred design of mobile user interfaces, promoting in-situ design and evaluation and resulting in diverse solutions for various problems. The following sections detail how and which techniques can be used and some findings that emerged along the experiences that are presented.

3.1 Pervasive Data Gathering

For designers to understand currently faced problems and define more suited solutions, they must work together with future users and understand their needs so that created alternatives are innovative and usable.

As mentioned before, existing techniques provide designers with some directions to gather this information and analyze it. However, these techniques focus mainly on a specific setting and scenario. Even if they are repeated for every imagined scenario and setting, none of these methods provides means to relate the gathered requirements when settings are changed. Furthermore, the requirements and their causes are commonly lost during these transitions. This problem is generally non existent on fixed solutions since scenarios are usually immutable or usage restrictions, and their influence on the user's behaviour, are constant.

With mobile technology the case is hardly the same. Due to its pervasive and ubiquitous nature, the context, settings and usage scenarios are constantly changing, such as the requirements and needs that these imply. Therefore, it is crucial to understand the changes between settings and scenarios, which is possibly attainable with current methodologies, but it is also paramount to understand why and how these changes occurred. To achieve such results, the experiments that follow show how alternative techniques were used in order to gather information on pervasive activities on the field.

3.1.1 Example 1

On this experience, to tackle the aforementioned problems, alternative methods to evaluate and assess requirements on mobile settings were used. The envisioned application that was being designed aimed at supporting ubiquitous cognitive behavioural therapy, allowing patients to register their thoughts, emotions and problems throughout their daily lives on handheld devices (Sá & Carriço, 2007). The tool also included relaxation procedures and tutorials accompanied by pro-active aids and hints that had to be displayed whenever the user showed (through his/her answers to short questions) signs of stress. Particular care was directed to understand how usage and user's behaviours were affected by the surrounding environment, emphasizing not only the changes but also their causes and effects. Firstly, a high level conceptual framework was established, pointing specific directions and highlighting crucial concerns that had to be taken into consideration (e.g., user position, activity and goal, environment settings - lighting or noise conditions, cooperation with others, social context).

Fig. 1. User completing a task in-situ while seated at a coffee with some friends.

This framework was used to define and select some scenarios which included a set of details, derived from the framework, which needed to be taken into account while designing the envisioned applications, each including various contexts. The main goal was to assess the influence of personal, social, cultural, and cooperation issues on each context without disregarding dimensions that relate directly to the user and his/her behaviour. Accordingly, scenarios varied through multiple instances containing different user positions while working (e.g., walking, standing, seating, etc); different social/cultural events and distractions (e.g., conversation, school, work, meetings, on the bus), with special focus on those that could increase users' stress levels. This also permitted the understanding of user's reactions to transitions and subtle changes within contexts providing information on how the applications should adjust and correspond to these behaviours.

To gather data in situations where users could not be observed or followed a specific type of questionnaires was distributed by users to be filled in-situ. Users were requested to complete the questionnaires while accomplishing their activities using their traditional means and procedures and to provide information on how, at that moment and on that location, a technological solution could be helpful. Moreover, these suggestions and answers had to be followed by a short description of the location and context in which the user responded to that questionnaire. Here, once again, details that were relevant were already included in the questionnaire through multiple-choice questions. This allowed designers to focus the details that mattered but still contextualising what users should provide.

The use of specific and contextual questionnaires and their completion in-situ provided insight on contextual details and information about the user's location even without the presence of the designer. Moreover, by requesting that information while the user was working or during a certain activity, the information about problems and suggestions of new features and solutions was much easier to recollect. Here, instead of using generic questionnaires, that could be filled through the internet or on any given time, this technique gathered answers and data in-situ, relying on users to characterise the environment in which they were, requesting information that designers needed but also stressing the details that seemed important to the user at that point.

3.1.2 Example 2

On the second example, the goal was to design a digital white cane for visual impaired users. Besides replacing the traditional cane, the digital one should include features that allowed users to get information of their context while moving around different locations. On this particular experience, the data gathering stage also followed different methods and procedures. Once again, a short amount of scenarios was established. Since these included most of the dimensions and concerns that were targeted by the framework used on the first experience, they covered a wide range of situations and variations. Locations included busy subway stations, corridors full of obstacles, supermarkets and open locations in order to assess users' needs and the way they used the traditional cane.

To gather data, the experience sampling method (Consolvo, 2007) and diary studies were used (Sohn et al., 2008). As previously explained, these methods rely on the users to gather data, requiring them to annotate and register situations where they feel that a solution could be used by describing their experience, the problems that they faced and, if possible, suggesting features and requesting functionalities that could aid them, much alike probing techniques (Hulkko et al., 2004).

To support this process without adding an extra burden to the visually impaired users, these registries were recorded on digital devices that users carried along with them (e.g., audio recorder, cell-phone with recording capabilities, PDA). This allowed users to record and register specific events, also providing a description of the settings and background of the experience in-situ, without the need to write or interrupt their current activity to do so. Moreover, since the recorders were continuously gathering data and the user's voice/thoughts, users were asked to keep providing information while walking. Overall, besides the requested information about the situation, the settings and encountered difficulties, this allowed designers to gather some information regarding transition between settings and on how users' behaviour and feelings changed while transiting from context to context.

3.1.3 Resulting Guidelines

Overall, these two experiences showed that the data gathering process within mobile settings and during the design of mobile applications/tools is also achievable, with better results then when traditional techniques are used by using simple yet effective methods. Moreover, the used techniques relied on inexpensive material (e.g., paper and pencil) or even on material that was owned by the users (e.g., cell-phone to record audio). Since a large part of the data that was gathered did not require the designer's presence and direct observation, the entire procedure required less effort and posed fewer problems to users' privacy also providing less biased results. Also, it allowed data to be gathered by a larger number of users throughout the various iterations of each experience. Globally, from these two experiences, the following guidelines can be presented:

- The definition and selection of scenarios that address details that can affect the usability of the solution and the user's behaviour should be done and is paramount to the subsequent data gathering process.
- To gather data whenever direct observation is unachievable and when mobility and multiple settings are involved, contextual questionnaires can be provided to users. These should include questions that take into account the user's location, the environmental conditions, social context, etc.
- When completed in-situ, contextual questionnaires can provide information about the surrounding environment and facilitate recollection about problems and issues that emerge while performing specific activities.
- The experience sampling method, commonly applied to the evaluation of mobile applications, can also be used successfully to the initial data gathering stages.
- When necessary, data can be gathered with the aid of digital equipment (e.g., voice recorders, cell-phones) providing a less intrusive method. Moreover, since it is easier to talk than write, users generally provide richer data and more details. This approach also allows users to continue recording data while on-the-move, providing information even during transitions between contexts and settings.

3.2 Early Stage Prototyping

As already discussed, common low-fidelity prototyping techniques can result in misleading and erroneous results when used in mobile contexts to support the design of mobile applications. Accordingly, this section describes two of the experiences that took place during the design of several mobile systems and the lessons that emerged from that process. The prototypes that were used, how they were built and their advantages are shown, followed by a summary of the guidelines that can be applied on other projects and solutions.

3.2.1 Example 1

The main goal for the tool that was being conceived and designed during this experience was to allow students to use a mobile application to achieve a set of activities ubiquitously. The three main activities that needed to be included were the support for on-class test completion and annotation, homework completion and on-the-move analysis of content and registration of data. The initial stages followed the updated data gathering techniques that were addressed on the previous section. Once that data was analysed and design ideas started to be developed, the prototyping stage took place. While prototyping the application, and in order to provide users with a realistic experience and overview of the various design ideas, overcoming the problems mentioned in the related work, a frame was created using a light wooden material with about the same weight and size of a Palm Tungsten T3 (Figure 2).

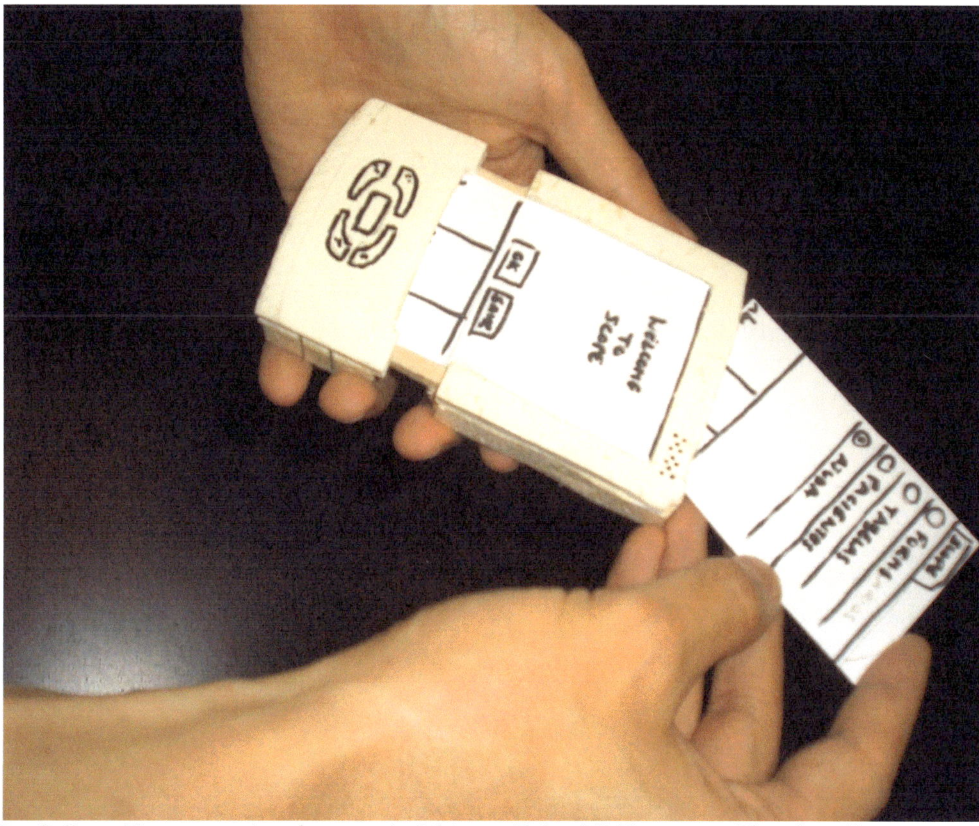

Fig. 2. Low-Fi prototyping frame mimicking a Palm T3 Tungsten. The slot allows users to easily exchange cards/sketches).

The frame had a small opening on the top, which allowed the sketched cards (screens) to be switched very easily. It took about forty minutes to build. Even so, it allowed users to have an accurate notion on the device and interaction techniques that they would use. By providing an actual solid artefact/prototype instead of only a set of cards, users were able to have a tangible experience, grasping details that would not have been visible with a traditional approach. Furthermore, it was quickly noticeable that this procedure and the resulting frame allowed the detection, and consequent correction, of a set of UI problems that would not have been found using just cards. For instance, buttons on the bottom of the screen had to be moved to the top for easier access and so that they would not move or

disappear if the screen was extended (screen extension is a T3 feature). Also, buttons and lists that extended to, or were placed near, the borders of the screen were difficult to read and interact with.
This rigid frame and the realistic prototyping techniques also provided additional benefits. Using it, users were able to test the applications while walking from one place to another, switching screens at will. This showed that the size of some components that were used when the user was walking, which was a common situation in some tasks (e.g., taking notes or checking the agenda while walking on the schools corridors), needed to be larger because of the lower accuracy in this position. Overall, the use of the rigid frame allowed users to have a realistic idea of the design concept which, consequentially, provided designers with much richer information regarding their satisfaction towards the solution that was being developed.

3.2.2 Example 2

The second prototyping experience took place during the design of the digital white cane mentioned in the previous data gathering section. In this project, in order to show final users the design concept and to support in-situ evaluation, a low-fidelity prototype of the digital cane was built. The primary goal was to allow users to interact with it and to offer a hands-on experience that could provide user feedback regarding the envisioned tool as well as the software and functionalities that would be included on it. The prototype was created using paper, glue, a lighter's wheel to strike the spark (i.e., *ferrocerium*) and a strap. To support the audio warnings that were issued to the user a Bluetooth headset was also created.

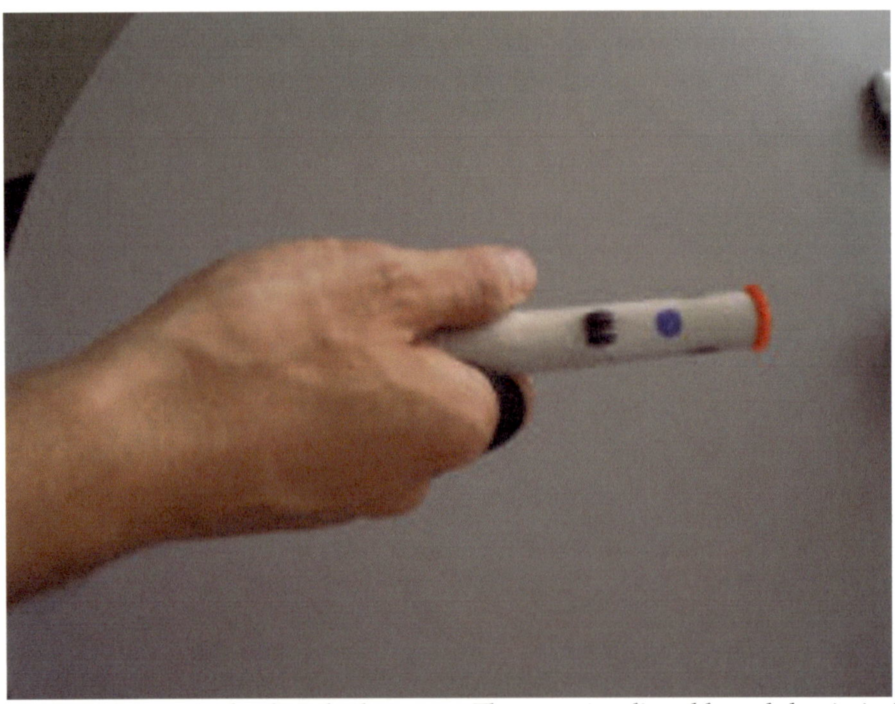

Fig. 3. Low-fi prototype of a digital white cane. The strap is adjustable and the tip includes an infra-red sensor that detects distance and reads bar-codes. The wheel on the centre allows users to select different options and to control the cane.

The low-fi cane was then handed to several users that tried to re-enact their usual behaviour while walking within a furnished room and a corridor. Moreover, to test the prototype on realistic settings, users tried to use it on the same scenarios that were used for the data gathering stages. Accordingly, the prototype was used on a busy subway station, on a supermarket and several other locations.

The combined use of the rigid prototype and the realistic scenarios allowed designers and users to detect several problems that needed to be solved. The size of the cane was adjusted in order to easily fit in users' pockets. This was noticed while entering the subway, where users needed to secure themselves on the subway by grabbing the poles in order to maintain balance and needed to quickly store the cane. Moreover, it was noticed that using the cane on busy settings, where bumps occurred occasionally, the cane's strap needed to be adjustable so it would not fall. Moreover, new functionalities also emerged from these experiences on the field. For instance, when the prototype was used within a supermarket, one of the users suggested that besides being used as a proximity sensor, the cane should also use the infra-red sensor to read code-bars, providing information directly to the user's headset. Another innovation that emerged from this experience was the haptic feedback that was added to the cane. While walking within noisy locations or when talking with friends, users did not want to be disturbed by auditory warnings through the Bluetooth headset. Accordingly, the cane was updated in order to vibrate whenever a warning or new information was available.

3.2.3 Resulting Guidelines

The results from these projects and experiences suggested that these techniques can be used in various domains and situations. Accordingly, the following guidelines emerged:

- Common techniques and material do not apply directly for most mobile devices/applications.
- A careful distinction between the device prototypes and the application/UI prototype has to be made.
- The device prototype should be created using rigid materials in order to be used in real-life settings and it should have approximately the same dimensions of an actual device.
- When applicable, a slot where cards can be easily and quickly inserted and removed needs to be available. When this option is unavailable, alternatives that facilitate screen substitution should be provided.
- Sketches must be drawn with the same size of the device's screen using similar components and fonts to those available for a real device.
- The interaction type of the actual device should also be emulated (e.g. stylus/pen, joystick/small coloured drawing pin or a thumb tack).
- Using low-fidelity prototypes that resemble closely actual devices allows designers to test their design concepts with larger amounts of users still keeping the design costs low (e.g., handing 10 wooden prototypes to users, instead of real devices). Moreover, using this type of prototype brings the possibility for users to take the prototypes home and interact with them away

from designers without the need to use their own devices (if they have any) or to purchase extra hardware.

- Although these hints might imply more effort from the designer, they are compensated with more accurate results.

3.3 Mobile Evaluation

Complementing the aforementioned procedures to create low-fidelity prototypes, the corresponding evaluation procedures must also be updated in order to take advantage of them. Particularly, it is essential to emphasize the importance of context and location while evaluating mobile applications. In fact, as already discussed, prototypes of various fidelities are usually tested on controlled settings and fictitious scenarios retracting from the evaluations sessions and preventing the detection of some usage errors.

3.3.1 Example 1

During the early evaluation of various applications, including the previously mentioned digital white cane, the context and settings of use proved to be of extreme importance. With the developed prototypes, users were able to carry the design concept with them to simulated and real situations. These findings led to the experimentation of similar evaluation sessions but using different prototypes. Accordingly, this procedure was also applied to the design of a GPS application that was being developed targeting mobile devices. The application was directed to users that needed to carry a mobile device along with them during their daily lives (e.g., traditional use of the GPS) with particular focus to highly physical activities (e.g., jogging, cycling, driving).

To test the GPS application users carried the sketches with simulated applications from one place to another, using them and exchanging them as needed during their activities. Besides evidencing some design problems that could occur, the ubiquitous evaluation sessions promoted participatory design, allowing users to engage actively on the process. In fact, most of the innovations appeared when testing the prototypes on real situations and scenarios. Since the frameworks were handed to users and they were free to use the prototypes whenever desired, most of the users involved in the process stated that whenever awkward design choices were found or whenever they thought there was a better solution, it was easier to immediately draw and annotate their idea. Here, the rigid frame that was used was also helpful, allowing users to easily write or draw on the cards or even create new ones without compromising the overall feeling of the prototype and experience.

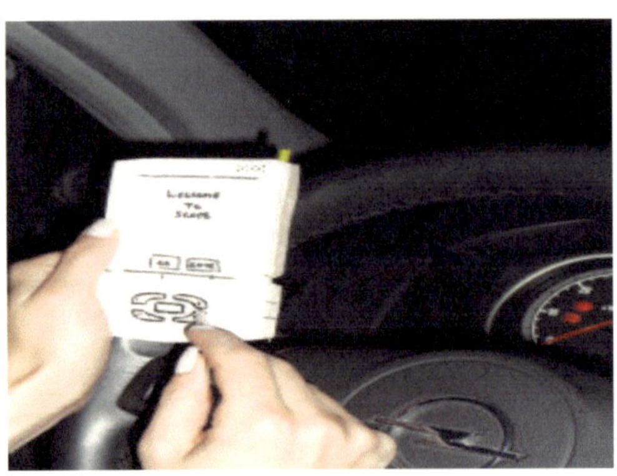

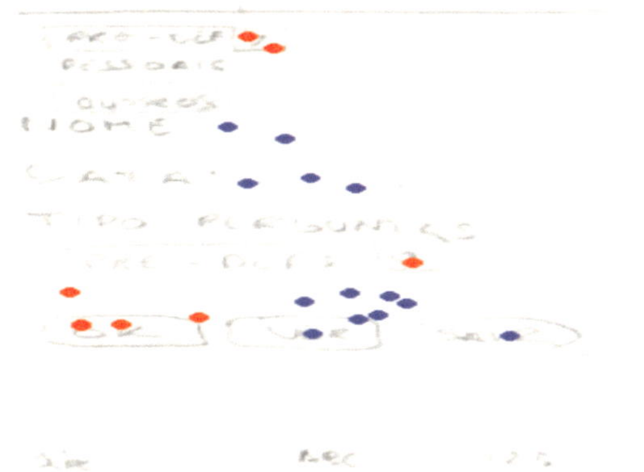

Fig. 4. Left: Low-fidelity prototype of a GPS application being used in-situ, while the user was in her car. Right: Sketch after an in-situ evaluation session.

To gather information regarding user activities while using the prototypes in-situ and to avoid following users around, users were also requested to use different colours for different tasks that they tried to accomplish while using the prototype (coloured pens were used in replacement of the usual stylus and/or fingers). The same procedure was suggested for different contexts and locations. By using specific colours for specific tasks or contexts, designers were able to detect problems that occurred in each of those contexts or activities. For instance, users were asked to use the red and blue colours for activities that were accomplished while walking. The sketches that were later returned to designers and that were marked with red paint clearly showed that users had lower accuracy towards buttons and that these needed to be enlarged (figure 4 on the right). Furthermore, users were asked to organise or "card-sort" the sketches when in specific contexts. This also allowed designers to notice that the same activities should have different sequences for different contexts, suggesting the need for a wider set of customization options on the application's user interface.

3.3.2 Example 2

On the second experience, to complement the evaluation information that was captured by the low-fidelity prototypes used according to the procedures that were introduced, a mobile video kit was used. The aim was to gather reliable information without requiring a large amount of evaluators following each user around while filming. The inexpensive video kit was comprised by a webcam that the user carried on his/her shoulder (figure 5). This camera weighed about ¼ pounds and was connected to a light (3 pounds) laptop computer that was kept in a backpack that the user also carried (figure 5). Overall, according to the users, the entire set of equipment was not very intrusive and required little effort to carry. The main concern regarding this kit was the embarrassment that it could cause while using it. The laptop had battery for 6 hours and could capture the same amount of video. The camera pointed at the average height to which users' held their device while using it. This position was established after several tries with different users on various positions/postures. It also followed the user's movement, providing information regarding the direction to which the user was moving and the objects that were in his/her way (figure 5).

After the initial experiences, users were questioned about the procedure. The general opinion was that the kit was less intrusive than being followed by designer/evaluator during the day. Moreover, as most of the users stated, they were aware and uncomfortable with the kit on the initial minutes but got used to it very quickly and almost didn't notice it on the final stages of the evaluation sessions.

Fig. 5. Mobile video evaluation kit. The camera attached to the user's shoulder captures video footage of his interaction with the device/application.

In addition to the kit, and in order to gather unbiased qualitative data, collected when using the application while all the problems and flaws are easy to recollect, user satisfaction questionnaires were provided to the users once again. However, taking advantage of the video and audio capturing capabilities of the kit, users could express their opinions orally and even during interaction with the prototypes/devices (e.g., think-aloud). Moreover, since the context and environment in which the user was navigating was automatically captured by the kit, it was no longer necessary to request the user to provide this information.
The use of the kit allowed designers to detect other interaction details that were unnoticed when using only the previous techniques. For instance, the user's behaviour when interacting or cooperating with other users or even different postures and behaviours towards obstacles and paraphernalia that was used in concert with the prototypes were easily analysed by the designers and taken into account into the following prototypes. These positive results also propelled the use of the video kit even in later stages of evaluation with actual devices and software prototypes (figure 5).

3.3.3 Resulting Guidelines

From the experiences that were conducted while evaluating several prototypes, even during later design stages, the following guidelines were encountered:

- Using rigid materials on the prototypes allows users to carry them, keep them in their pockets, take them home and participate on the sketches' design directly on the device, conducting evaluation on relevant locations.
- Context of use is essential for effective usability testing and, similarly to the initial data gathering stages, evaluation should be done in several possible scenarios that are sufficiently detailed to range a wide scope of settings and use contexts.
- The use of adequate material allows users to participate on the sketching process during contextual sessions, further promoting innovation and adequate ideas that cope with the contextual requirements.
- Tasks should be defined previously (e.g. using scripts), but the possibility of creating new features and test them on the spot should be provided.
- Colour schemes can be used to trace users' activities during and after the evaluation sessions. Moreover, if tasks/locations/screen arrangements are matched with specific colours or notations, evaluators can trace the users' behaviours without direct observation.
- Questionnaires can also be given to users together with the low-fidelity prototypes, so that they can complete them during out of the lab sessions. Here, the rigid prototyping frames also facilitate questionnaire filling. Moreover, using similar colour schemes to those previously mentioned, questionnaires can be filled with different colours according to specific locations or situations (e.g., around other users, at home, walking), eliciting problems that pertain to those using contexts.
- Mobile video capturing kits can be quickly arranged without using expensive material. Yet, these provide rich data and do not require designers to follow users constantly.
- The use of video and audio equipment also support a multi-media experience sampling method, relieving users from questionnaire answering and thought registering tasks. With the media hardware, users can simply think aloud about the current experience or video footage capturing the interaction and the surroundings can be used.

4. Discussion and Further Research Directions

So far, the work presented in this chapter has allowed the detection of several shortcomings on existing design methodologies when applied to the design of mobile applications and corresponding user interfaces. These findings, and the "on-the-fly" solutions that were used to cope with them, motivated the development of a methodology with techniques that apply specifically to mobile devices and ubiquitous applications. Globally, these problems led to the belief it was necessary to introduce solid guidelines on the various stages of design focusing on the mobility factor and on the users' varying context.

On the data gathering processes, the updated techniques provided means for designers to gather contextual information by requiring users to complete questionnaires in-situ. Moreover, the use of audio recording when using the ESM method permitted a pervasive data gathering process, allowing designers to understand users' behaviour while transiting between scenarios/settings. While not as rich or complete as user observation and contextual inquiry, these techniques are especially adequate to the initial stages of design because of their low-cost, ease of use and range. Moreover, they are particularly adequate to mobile scenarios since user observation on-the-move is difficult to achieve and inherently impossible to accomplish in every imaginable scenario/context. Also, it is noteworthy that these techniques do not aim at replacing traditional ones but aim at complementing them.

Regarding the prototyping stage, as the results showed, the used techniques gave users a much more detailed idea of the designers' vision and facilitated their in-situ evaluation. In general, although at times these procedures might require added effort to apply, they enhance the evaluation process and the detection of errors in very early stages. In fact, these techniques highlighted the close relationship between the prototyping and the evaluation stage since procedures often merge and have a direct impact and influence between these two design stages.

For the evaluation stage, the experiences that were undertaken clearly demonstrated that in-situ trials and evaluation stages can be successfully achieved even without the use of expensive material. By using adequate prototyping techniques and evaluation methods, designers can easily test their design concepts and ideas on realistic settings. Moreover, some of these techniques (especially the use of the video kit) can also be used on the initial data gathering stages.

Finally, it is noteworthy to mention that the initial setup and definition of scenarios, each containing several aspects and dimensions that are paramount to mobile activities, which can be contextualized to particular projects, is highly beneficial and influences the effectiveness of the entire design process.

As a result from the advances and concepts that emerged from these experiences, a prototyping framework for mobile devices, which takes advantage of these guidelines, is being developed. Overall, the tool aims at supporting prototyping and evaluation of applications with the peculiarity of creating the prototypes on actual devices. Some of its contributions are (1) the support for prototypes with various fidelities; (2) an automatic mechanism to gather contextual data; (3) the inclusion of ESM and probing techniques; (4) the support of on-the-spot participatory design and (5) the use of pre-established design guidelines. Accordingly, the tool will support design through the in-situ generation and evaluation of prototypes, using actual devices, even at very early design stages.

5. Conclusions

Current design approaches, although providing extensive detail on various stages of the design process, fail to support most of the related activities and tasks when mobility of the system is paramount. Existing techniques, particularly for initial stages of development and evaluation, are rarely applied, especially taking into account the volatile settings in which the applications are likely to be used. Furthermore, these techniques aren't always applicable and, when ill-used, hinder the overall process.

In this chapter, the problems that emerged while using common user centred design methodologies on the development of a set of ubiquitous systems were described. Throughout these experiences, mobility, pervasiveness and ubiquity required the adoption of new techniques and the adjustment of existing ones in order to cope with the challenges

that derived from the constant change of context and multitude of settings that could be envisioned for each specific system.
Overall, these techniques and resulting findings allowed the gathering of data on relevant locations and settings on a pervasive manner. Moreover, they propelled the detection of user interface problems on both low-fidelity and high-fidelity prototypes during the various evaluations sessions that were conducted. The use of methods that connect the various stages and that were conceived in order to facilitate the transition and evolution from stage to stage enhanced the overall process, resulting in sounder solutions and usable products and application. In comparison with existing techniques, which were used on initial stages of these processes, the new techniques provided insight to problems which would not have been detected otherwise.
This chapter provided an overview on existing problems with mobile interaction design, particularly addressing the early design stages, and proposed techniques and solutions that can be applied to projects in various domains. As a validation and as a medium to clearly show how to apply each technique, several experiences were presented and discussed highlighting the methods that had positive outcomes and the procedures that were used.

6. Acknowledgements

This work was supported by LaSIGE and FCT, through project JoinTS, through the Multiannual Funding Programme and scholarship SFRH/BD/28165/2006.

7. References

Barnard, et al. Capturing the effects of context on human performance in mobile computing systems. Personal and Ubiquitous Computing, Vol. 11, No.46, pp.81-96, 2005.

Black, J.T. & Hawkes, L.W. (2006). A prototype interface for collaborative mobile learning. In IWCMC'06, 1277–1282, ACM Press, Vancouver, British Columbia, Canada.

Beyer, H., Holtzblatt, K., 1998. Contextual Design: Customer Centered Approach to Systems Design, Academic Press, San Francisco, CA, USA.

Bodker, S. & Buur, J. (2002). The design collaboratorium - a place for usability design. Transactions on Computer Human-Interaction, 9, 152–169.

Brewster, S. (2002). Overcoming the lack of screen space on mobile computers. Personal and Ubiquitous Computing, Vol. 6, No. 3, 188–205.

Carter, S., et al. Momento: Support for Situated Ubicomp Experimentation. CHI'07, pp. 125-134, ACM.

Coble, J.M., Karat, J. & Kahn, M.G. (1997). Maintaining a focus on user requirements throughout the development of clinical workstation software. In Proceedings of the SIGCHI conference on Human factors in computing systems CHI '97.

Chandler, C.D., Lo, G. & Sinha, A.K. (2002). Multimodal theater: Extending low fidelity paper prototyping to multimodal applications. In CHI2002 Extended Abstracts, CHI 2002, ACM, Minneapolis, Minnesota,USA.

Connelly, K.H., Rogers, Y., Siek, K.A., Jones, J., Kraus, M.A., Perkins, S.M., Trevino, L.L. & Welch, J.L. (2005). Designing a pda interface for dialysis patients to monitor diet in their everyday life. In Proceedings of the 11th Human Computer Interaction International Conference, HCII05, Las Vegas, USA.

Consolvo, S. and M. Walker, Using the Experience Sampling Method to Evaluate Ubicomp Applications. IEEE Pervasive Computing, 2003. 2(2): p. 24-31.

Consolvo, S., Roessler, P., Shelton, B., LaMarca, A. & Schilit, B. (2004). Technology for care networks for elders. IEEE Pervasive Computing,3, 22–29.

Consolvo, S., Smith, I.E., Mathews, T., LaMarca, A., Tabert, J. & Powledge, P. (2005). Location disclosure to social relations: Why, when and what people want to share. In CHI 2005 , 81–90, ACM, Portland, Oregon, USA.

Duh, H.B.-L., G.C.B. Tan, and V.H.-h. Chen. Usability Evaluation for Mobile Device: A Comparison of Laboratory and Field Tests. in Mobile HCI'06. 2006., Finland, ACM.

Frishberg, L. (2006). Presumptive design, or cutting the looking-glass cake. Interactions, 8, 18–20.

Froehlich, J., Chen, M., Smith, I. & Potter, F. (2006). Voting with your feet: An investigative study of the relationship between place visit behaviour and preference. In UbiComp 2006 , Orange County, California, USA.

Froehlich, J., et al. MyExperience: A System for In Situ Tracing and Capturing of User Feedback on Mobile Phones. MobiSys'07, pp. 57-70, ACM.

Hagen, P., et al. Emerging Research Methods for Understanding Mobile Technology Use. Proc. of OZCHI 2005, Camberra, Australia, 2005.

Hanington, B.M. (2006). Interface in form: Paper and product prototyping For feedback and fun. Interactions, 8, 28–30.

Holmquist, L.E. (2005). Generating ideas or cargo cult designs? Interactions, 7, 48–54.

Holtzblatt, K., Wendell, J.B. & Wood, S. (2005). Rapid Contextual Design: A How-To Guide to Key Techniques for User-Centered Design. Morgan Kaufmann, San Francisco, CA, USA.

Hulkko, S., et al. Mobile Probes. NordiCHI'04. ACM.

Isomursi, M., Kuutti, K. & Vainamo, S. (2004). Experience clip: Method for user participation and evaluation of mobile concepts. In Proceedings of Participatory Design Conference 2004, ACM, Toronto, Canada.

Jan, Blom et al. Contextual and Cultural Challenges for User Mobility Research, Communications of the ACM, Vol 48, No.7, 37-41, 2005.

Jones, M. and G. Marsden, Mobile Interaction Design. 2006, West Sussex, England: John Wiley & Sons Ltd.

Kangas, E. & Kinnunen, T. (2005). Applying user-centered design to mobile application development. Communications of the ACM, 48, 55–59.

Kelley, J. (1984) An iterative design methodology for user-friendly natural language office information applications. Trans. Office Information Systems, 2.

Kjeldskov, J. and C. Graham, A Review of Mobile HCI Research Methods. Mobile HCI'03. Vol. 2795/2003. 2003: Springer Berlin / Heidelberg. 317-335.

Kjeldskov, J. and J. Stage, New Techniques for Usability Evaluation of Mobile Systems. International Journal of Human Computer Studies, Elsevier, 2003.

Lee, Young E. Interface Design for Mobile Commerce. Communications of the ACM,Vo.46, No.12, 2003, 49-52.

Lukander, K. (2004). Measuring gaze point on handheld mobile devices. In Extended Abstracts of CHI2004, ACM, Vienna, Austria.
Marcus, A., Chen, E., Designing the PDA of the Future. Interactions, 9:1, pp.32-44, ACM, 2002.
Mayhew, D.J. (1999). The Usability Engineering Lifecycle. Morgan Kaufmann, San Francisco, CA, USA.
Mazzone, E., Horton, M. & Read, J. (2004). Requirements for a multimedia museum environment. In Proceedings of the third Nordic conference on Human computer interaction NordiCHI '04 .
Nakajima, T., How to Reuse Existing Interactive Applications in Ubiquitous Computing Environments? SAC'06, Dijon, France, pp 1127-1133.
Nielsen, C.M., et al. It's Worth the Hassle! The Added Value of Evaluating the Usability of Mobile Systems in the Field. NordiCHI'06. ACM.
Pering, T. (2006). Evaluating the privacy of using mobile devices to interact in public places. In Permid 2006, Workshop at Pervasive 2006 , Dublin, Ireland.
Raptis, D., N. Tselios, and N. Avouris. Context-based Design of Mobile Applications for Museums: A Survey of Existing Practices. in MobileHCI'05. ACM.
Reich P., et al, The LiLiPUT Prototype. CHI'07 (extended abstracts),pp.1833-1838,ACM.
Tiago Reis, Marco Sá, Luís Carriço. Designing Mobile Multimodal Artefacts. Proceedings of ICEIS 2008, the 10th International Conference on Enterprise Information Systems, Barcelona, Spain, INSTICC, June 2008.
Robert A. Virzi, D.K., Jeffrey L. Sokolov (1996). Usability problem identification using both low- and high-fidelity prototypes. In Proceedings of CHI 1996, ACM, Vancouver, Canada.
Rosenberg, D. (2006). Revisiting tangible speculation: 20 years of ui prototyping. Interactions, 8, 31–32.
Sá, M., Carriço, L., Low-Fi Prototyping for Mobile Devices. In Proceedings of CHI'06 (extended abstracts), Montréal, Canada, pp. 694-699, ACM.
Sá, M., Carriço, L., Handheld Devices for cooperative Educational Activities. In Proc. of SAC'06, Dijon, France, pp. 1145-1149, ACM Press, April, 2006
Sá, M. Carriço, L., Antunes P., Ubiquitous Psychotherapy. IEEE Pervasive Computing, vol. 6, nº 1, pp. 20-27, IEEE Press, 2007.
Sá, M. Carriço, L., Lessons from Early Stages Design of Mobile Applications. Proceeding of MobileHCI'08, 10th International ACM Conference on Human Computer Interaction with Mobile Devices and Services, Amsterdam, Netherlands, 2008.
Scholtz, J. & Consolvo, S. (2004). Toward a framework for evaluating ubiquitous computing applications. IEEE Pervasive Computing, 2, 82–86.
Svanaes, D. and G. Seland. Putting the users center stage: role playing and low-fi prototyping enable end users to design mobile systems. in CHI'04, Vienna, Austria ACM.
Sohn, T., Li, K. A., Griswold, W. G., and Hollan, J. D. 2008. A diary study of mobile information needs. In Proceeding of the Twenty-Sixth Annual SIGCHI Conference on Human Factors in Computing Systems (Florence, Italy, April 05 - 10, 2008). CHI '08. ACM.
Thompson, K.E., Rozanski, E.P. & Haake, A.R. (2004). Here, there, anywhere: Remote usability testing that works. In Proceedings of SIGITE'04,

ACM, Salt Lake City, Utah, USA.
Weiss,S.(2002).Handheld Usability.Wiley & Sons, England.

11

Application prospects of the augmented reality technology for improving safety of machine operators

Marek Dzwiarek, Anna Łuczak
Central Institute for Labour Protection-National Research Institute
Poland

1. Introduction

Basing on the results of industrial accident analysis (Dzwiarek, 2004) one can arrive at the conclusion that every year accidents happen because a warning signal is either not heard or not heeded (Haas & Casali 1995). Therefore, one of the important measures to prevent undesired events consists in informing a machine operator about the appearance of hazardous situation quickly and effectively enough. Standard ISO 12100-2:2003 recommends employing warning signals as an additional means for risk reduction, especially in the cases when other safety measures are not effective enough. This additional means plays an especially important role in the courses of machine regulating, maintaining and repair since in those cases the protective devices are usually disconnected and a direct access to dangerous zones is required. One can deal with such a situation also when maintaining an assembly line, where the operator should work during the line standstill and has to leave the dangerous zone before the line moves on. The warning signals are of crucial importance also in the cases when it is impossible for the operator starting a machine for control all the access zones. In such a case there arises the necessity for signaling the intention of starting a machine in the way ensuring that all the persons present nearby will be warned against the danger early enough.

Therefore, the warning signals are employed for emergency event alert e.g., in case of unexpected machine start or sudden increase in a tool speed. Those signals can be used for warning the operator before the dangerous situation could have activated the safety devices. Those signals should:

(a) be generated before a dangerous event occurs,
(b) be unambiguous,
(c) be clearly distinguishable from other signals generated within the workplace.

Nowadays, visual and acoustic warning signals are most common. However, their main disadvantage consists in the fact that they may be received by many people instead of a person in danger alone. That may distract many people causing disturbances in other workstations. Additionally, visual signals can be seen only when displayed within the visual area of the person in danger. The operator usually focuses the attention and sight on the operations he/she is carrying out, therefore often neglects those signals.

The Augmented Reality (AR) devices satisfy all the requirements imposed on warning signals and suffer from no drawbacks mentioned above, therefore, the development in technology will bring about broadening of the scope of their applications covering also the field of safety at work.
The main aim of the paper consist in on presenting and discussing of the methodology of proving (by means of the perception assessment) that the warning signals generated using the AR approach reveals the same effectiveness as standard visual signals coming from an industrial signaling device that is of common use in machinery (Dzwiarek at al., 2007).

2. Case studies of emergency signs applied to machinery

In order to analyze thoroughly a possible applicability of the AR warning signals to machine operation several factories were visited for case studies. Six workstations were analyzed, and four of them indicated the applicability of the AR signals.

2.1 Automated production line

Each automated production line comprises several work centers. In each center the products are processed automatically. On the considered case production cycle takes about 10 minutes.
After a cycle has been completed the operator should enter a work centre and remove waste material. Then after leaving the work centre he/she should start the next cycle of automatic processing. Usually, the line is operated by two operators. Each work centre is supplied with a device signaling dangerous situations and warning the operator against entering the work centre area after the signal of processing cycle start has been generated. The signal can be seen only outside the centre area. A person working inside the work centre area has no possibilities of catching the signal that actually caused an accident during the line operation. The accident could have been prevented if the operator was warned about the danger early enough; e.g., using the AR signal.

2.2 The workstation of automated press forming in the „SETUP" mode

Two workers make a replacement of extrusion dies in an automatic press line. The extrusion dies are stored in piles next to the line. One of the workers makes a chosen extrusion die ready to be lifted by an overhead traveling crane, while at the same time the other worker is lifting the extrusion die that has been prepared before. An accident happened during the operations since the worker standing behind the pile extrusion dies did not notice the approaching overhead traveling crane that crashed the pile of extrusion dies. The only way of prevention such accidents consists in warning a worker against the approaching traveling crane. The warning signal applied in the case had failed since it was generated to forbid the outsider to approach the crane operation zone while the workers replacing the extrusion dies were inside the zone during work. The AR signal could be an effective in the case since it would be received by the person in danger.

2.3 Workstation of fork lift truck operation

The operator of fork lift truck provides workstations with materials. While driving from a store there are many places of possible impacts to both pedestrian and other equipment. According to the rules followed in the whole factory the fork lift trucks have the right of way. All the employee know the rule and should follow it. Despite the fact the accidents happen at the cross-roads, mainly due to missing the approaching fork lift truck by a distracted person. If the safety glasses, the workers wear, were supplied with the AR signal systems warning against the approaching trucks, at least some of the accidents could have been avoided.

2.4 Workstation of car roof assembly

The workstation is operated by two workers (Fig.1.). They should put on manually the car body sides and start an automatic car roof assembly. After the tasks have been executed the assembly line travels a little - the car body is shifted to the next workstation, allowing space for another car body.

Fig. 1. Workstation of car roof assembly.

During the assembly line travel as well as when the car roof is put on the body both the operators should be outside the zone marked on the floor with a yellow line. The zone is controlled by a laser scanner that stops the assembly line when anybody is present within the area. The time allowed for the task is 1 min. 43 s. During their work the operators wear the safety glasses.

In the course of normal operation no warning signals appear. The dangerous situations, about which the operators should be warned, consist in the events when due to a failure or fault, the production line starts its travel or the automatic car roof assembler starts its work at the instant when the operators are within the marked area. Such situations are extremely rare, however, do happen and for that reason the standard warning signal device was mounted (see Fig. 1). The signal, however, is not effective enough and supplying the safety glasses worn by the workers with the AR systems would considerably improve the protection.

The Hierarchical Task Analysis (HTA) has been conducted using the workstation considered above. The warning signal is generated when the automatic machine starts unexpectedly at the instant when the workers are executing their tasks. The event is completely independent of the operators' activities (and therefore, needs additional warning) and might occur at an arbitrary instant during any operation. One cannot, therefore, distinguish any particular operation that would be associated with the risk.

3. The Augmented Reality in a workplace

Some information about the attempts made at application of the augmented reality approach to workplace in industry has been available from the literature for the last few years. To the best of our knowledge, however, those attempts consisted in employing the AR systems for improving the efficiency of inspection and maintenance as well as for training purposes.
A general analysis of the AR systems serviceability when applied to inspection and maintenance was carried out (Kyung et al., 2002), as well as the possibilities of the AR system application to trainings for maintenance technicians were examined (Bound et al. 1999). A way of AR system application to periodic inspection of machinery was presented (Chung et al. 1999; Weidenhausen et al., 2003). Same authors (Anastassova et al., 2005) presented primary results of currently conducted investigations into AR system application to improving the work efficiency in automotive maintenance and the possibility of AR system application to manufacturing system design was discussed (Dangelmaier et al., 2005). A large scale application of the AR technology has allowed for solving many important problems in the field of car service. Car mechanics in many garages in the USA are provided with portable AR systems supplied with semi-permeable glasses that are connected with a central computer managing the expert software packages, supporting that way proper conducting of particular repair/service operations. The garage owners have estimated that the application of AR systems allows for shortening the repair time by 1/3.
All the aforementioned applications were characterised by the following features:
(a) AR images were directly associated with the executed task;
(b) AR images were displayed continuously and should have been situated in the vicinity of the devices the operator kept his sight on;
(c) Operator's attention was concentrated on the images he expected to appear.
Therefore, the investigations were planned basing within the HTA approach and, where possible, conducted on the real workstations.

3.1 Requirements for the AR warning signals

As far as we know, there is lack of information available in the literature about the investigations into application of the AR systems to generation of visual warning signals used in machinery operation for warning operators. The results of analysis presented in chapter 2 have proved that the AR systems can be applied in the cases where standard warning systems are not effective enough; especially in the cases of: warning about the machine start, when the operator's sight of dangerous zones is limited, warnings in transportation operations – e. g. in the case of overhead cranes and warning signals in semi-automatic manufacturing systems.
Some basic features have been specified to distinguish between the warning and information signals, respectively:

(a) usually, warning signals are hardly ever connected with the current operations;
(b) warning signals appear only occasionally in unusual situations and are displayed far enough from the device the operator keeps his/her sight on;
(c) warning signals appear unexpectedly, when the operator's attention is focused on other operations.
Due to the aforementioned features of warning signals, as well as the fact that there is a broad variety of workplaces they can be used it is impossible to determine using the HTA approach the operations typical for all users of the warning signals. It is possible, however, to determine special categories of psycho-motoric and cognitive skills as well as other abilities the workers should have that are necessary for safe and efficient operation in workplaces equipped with machinery. After analyzing the characteristics of respective occupational groups and workstations equipped with machinery it was stated that main abilities necessary for efficient machine operation consisted in reaction time and attention (Luczak, 2001).

4. Some AR system designs suggested for warning signal generation

The considerations presented in the previous chapter have proved that the AR systems occur to be extremely effective within a broad scope of their applications. Up till now, the AR systems were employed for providing additional information useful for the operator. Comparative analysis results have proved that work efficiency in the case of AR signal support is much higher as compared to the standard warning methods, improving the efficiency indicators; like number of mistakes and reaction time (Chunga et al., 2002). However, special characteristics of the warning signals require special AR systems for signal generation.
Special equipment has been designed and constructed at the Wrasaw University of technology in co-operation with the Central Institute for Labour Protection - National Research Institute (CIOP-PIB). The background information was collected basing on the analysis of available systems and taking into consideration the following assumptions (Dzwiarek et al., 2003; Dzwiarek et al., 2004; Dzwiarek et al., 2006):
(a) it should be a system of the see-through type. In such systems in case of no warning signal the real workstation is being observed. While in the systems, which provide additional signals emitted by a camera, the surrounding area is being displayed on a monitor screen. However the at present stage of technology development those systems should not be used for industrial applications due to their inaccuracy and low reliability (Hagele et al., 2002).
(b) the glasses on which the AR signal is generated should be as comfortable as possible.
(c) in case of no warning signal the glasses should limit the sight area in the slightest possible way and involve the minimal number of disturbances, distortions and fading of the image displayed.
Additionally, since the systems are to be used in machine operation, the requirements specified in standards EN 981:1996 and IEC 61310-1:1995 should be satisfied as well, because recommendations on visual warning signal features are specified in the standards. The designed glasses are shown in Fig.2.

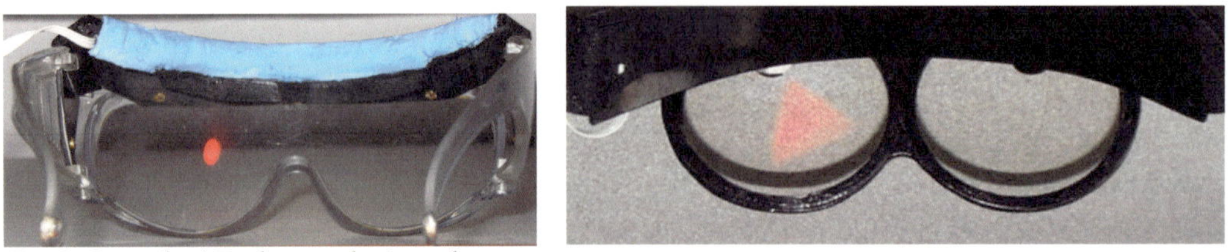

Fig.2. Sample AR glasses designed

Moreover, to introduce alphanumerical signs into the images displayed, the LITEYE-500 (see Fig. 3) glasses available on the marked were used

Fig.3. "Stop" signal displayed on the external side of LITEYE-500 eyepiece

5. Methods

The AR systems can be applied to generation of visual warning signals provided that perception of such signals is effective enough in the considered case. The main aim of the research consists in examination of the AR signal perception in the context of applicability of AR approach to warning signal generation in case of hazard in workplaces equipped with machinery. To this end we have decided to verify experimentally the following hypotheses:
Hypothesis 1
There is a substantial difference in perception of warning signals generated using the AR and standard (ST) approaches, respectively, in view of both objective and subjective indicators assessment.
Hypothesis 2
The perception of visual warning signals generated using the AR approach varies in view of the assessment of objective indicators - for different types of the AR signals.

5.1 Most common methods for examination of warning signal perception

Basing on the available literature one can conclude that a typical method for examination of perception of industrial warning signals consists in application of the „criterion task set" (CTS) (Shingledecker, 1984) while version 2.1 i.e., „probability monitoring task", is most common in the case of machine operation. In the course of experiment throughout the tracking task (Burt et al., 1995), a warning against the hazard of system failure was displayed at 30 s intervals and the circular target changed into a square. If the square target then went out of the joystick control and started to drift outside the specified rectangular boundaries, the tracking system had failed. The subjects were required to press the push-button in order to resume tracking. The reaction time was recorded from the instant when the tracking system failed until the push-button response moment. A similar experiment was described by others (Cohn, 1996), where due to accommodation accompanying warning signals: (a) the icon jumped from side to side, (b) the curved arrow moved circularly, (c) wavy lines marched across from left to right. In the course of the experiment aiming at the perception assessment of visual and acoustic warning signals generated in both the synchronous and asynchronous ways (Chan & Chan, 2006) the subjects sat in front of a computer screen wearing stereophonic headphones, through which acoustic signals were emitted. The visual signals had a form of red circles of 20 mm in diameter displayed on the computer screen at a distance of 80 mm to the left or right of a green circle of the same diameter. The subjects were required to keep their sight on the green circle and respond to the visual or acoustic signals appearing in the left or right hand side through pressing of one of the two buttons. The response time was measured. The response correctness was registered as well. In al the aforementioned experiments the perception indicator of warning signals consisted in the response time and possibly in the number of mistakes made in the course of task execution.

5.2 Experiment

Due to the features of warning signals concluded in chapter 3.1, as well as the fact that there is a broad variety of workplaces they can be used it is impossible to determine using the HTA approach the operations typical for all receivers of the warning signals. It is possible, however, to determine special categories of psycho-motoric and cognitive skills as well as other abilities the workers should have that are necessary for safe and efficient operations in workplaces equipped with machinery.

Therefore, when planning the experiment it was decided that the task should be simulated in view of engaging the specified mental processes and abilities, shared by the broadest possible group of workers instead of taking the performed operations into consideration. After analyzing characteristics of different professions and trades, also in the cases when the work is done in an assembly room (Widerszal-Bazyl, 1998; Łuczak, 2001) and the characteristics of respective occupational groups and workstations equipped with machinery it was stated that main abilities necessary for effective machine operation consisted in reaction time and attention. It was then planned that, the task executed by the operator during the experiment would involve those abilities. The requirement is satisfied by the „criterion task set" (CTS), in its „dual task" form (Shingledecker, 1984), on the basis of which the experiment was planned. The task executed during the experiment by the tested subjects consisted in putting the element of one colour into the hole of the same colour made in a palette, e.g. blue-to-blue, green-to-green, etc. After all holes in the palette had been filled a tested subject put it aside in the place of console situated within two strips. Then he took the next palette and repeated the whole cycle of putting elements into the proper holes. Each session lasted for 20 minutes. During the whole session time a robot standing in the vicinity was simulating the movements made usually when measuring the element size. The aforementioned sequences were repeated consecutively until the session ended. In the course of experimental task execution visual warning signals were generated using either a standard industrial signalling device or augmented reality glasses. The tested subject had to press a push-button as soon as a signal was generated. The warning signals were randomly generated during the test session. Each warning signal lasted for 10 seconds and if during

that time the push-button was pressed the signal was cut off and the reaction time was registered. In case the push-button was not pressed within 10 seconds the signal omission was registered. Each tested subject took part in 3 testing sessions. In one session two variants of the experiment were performed, each of 20 minutes in duration. In the first variant standard warning signals were generated, while in the second variant the AR signals were applied having one of six forms given below (AR1 - AR6). Between both the experimental sessions at least 20-minute-break was made so that the effect of fatigue could be eliminated.
Following the recommendations of EN 981:1996 i EN 61310-1:1995 and accepting the conclusions drawn by other researchers (Cohn, 1996; Gros et al., 2005) the following types of warning signals were employed during the experiment:
1. Standard warning signal; i.e., appearance of a red light signal (ST),
2. AR warning signal in the form of red circle displayed on the eyepiece (AR1),
3. AR warning signal in the form of flashing circle displayed on the eyepiece (AR2), of 4 Hz flashing frequency,
4. AR warning signal having the form of word „ STOP” displayed in red on the LITEYE-500 eyepiece (AR3).
5. AR warning signal in the form of yellow circle displayed on the eyepiece (AR4),
6. AR warning signal in the form of red flashing circle displayed on the eyepiece (AR5), of 8 Hz flashing frequency,
7. AR warning signal in the form of red triangle displayed on the eyepiece (AR6).
The experiment was performed in two cycles. The first one comprised the following sessions:
(a) Session E I - standard warning signal + AR1 warning signal (ST + AR1)
(b) SessionE II - standard warning signal + AR2 warning signal (ST + AR2)
(c) Session E III - standard warning signal + AR3 warning signal (ST + AR3)
While the second cycle of experiments was performed in the following three sessions:
(a) Session E 4 - standard warning signal + AR4 warning signal (ST + AR4)
(b) Session E 5 - standard warning signal + AR5 warning signal (ST + AR5)
(c) Session E 6 - standard warning signal + AR6 warning signal (ST + AR6)
That means that each subject during one session underwent the two types of experiments;, i.e. executing the task with the standard warning signal then executing the same task with one of the AR type signals.
All signals were generated against the same background. During the experiment the artificial lighting was employed with the colour rendering index of 82, which is typical for workstations. Within the task execution zone the luminance was measured continuously, and its change ranged from 440Lx to 550 Lx. Standard EN 12464-1:2004 recommends the lighting of luminance higher than 300 Lx at the inside work, while the investigations conducted at workstations (Pawlak & Wolska, 2004; Pawlak & Wolska, 2005; Pawlak & Wolska, 2006) have proved that actually at workstations the luminance changing within 350Lx - 600Lx.

5.3 Subjects

Subject were 21 to 25 years old, with a mean age of 23 years. Each subject having normal sight, with no needs for glasses and no sight defects (e.g. daltonism). Twenty three male volunteers constituted the paid subject population for the 1-sth cycle of experiment and 30 for the 2-nd cycle. Different groups of subjects underwent each cycle. The group of 53 people underwent tests, therefore during 159 experimental sessions the number of 318 different experiments (in view of warning signal combinations) were performed.

5.4 Results

To assess properly the perception of AR warning signals and standard warning signals both objective and subjective indicators were used. The following objective indicators were assumed: reaction time, number of signal omissions, number of mistakes made when putting elements into the holes. A subjective indicator has a form of questionnaire including four questions about the assessment of tested subject's reaction time to stimuli of both kinds and about preferences between the kinds of signal.

The results obtained were then analysed in view of the hypotheses that had been put forward before. The reaction times measured were subject to statistical analysis on the assumption of normal distribution. The results obtained from each experimental cycle were analysed independently of the other ones. Basic statistics were determined for each set of results:

(a) mean value T^i_m

(b) mean standard deviation σ^i

(c) maximal and minimal values (T^i_{max} and T^i_{min})

where "i" stands for the i-th subject.

The analysis results justified the hypotheses put forward. During the first experimental cycle the AR signal having the form of red circle was really better receivable as compared to the standard one, in view of both the reaction time and working speed. However, in view of the reaction time, the AR signal having the form of word "STOP" occurred to be visibly more hardly perceptible as compared to the standard one. During the second experimental cycle the AR signal having the form of yellow circle occurred to be significantly better in view if the working speed and visibly worse in view of the reaction as compared to the standard one. Additionally, during the same experiment the AR signal having the form of red circle flashing at 8 Hz frequency occurred to be visibly better as compared to the standard one since the scatter of the reaction times measured was narrower.

Substantial differences appeared in signal perception between the standard and AR warning signals also in view of subjective assessment of the perception quality. The comparative analysis of subjects' preferences have proved that the AR signals were received as the better ones in the case when they had the form of red circle, flashing or not, despite the flashing frequency. While during the task execution the red inscription STOP was considered to be more disturbing than the standard warning signal. The AR warning signal having the form of yellow circle was also considered as more disturbing, being however much easier to notice as compared to the ST one. In view of visibility the standard signal was consider to be better than the AR signal having the form of red triangle, that signal however, was considered to be noticeable much sooner than the standard one.

It can be concluded that in view almost every considered indicators, both objective and subjective ones, the AR signal occurred to be better as compared to the standard one. One of the reasons behind obtaining such a result consists in the fact that the AR signal, being displayed on the eyepiece, is always visible by the working person, while visibility of the standard warning signal changes, depending on the position the working person assumes or occupies.

It occurred, however, that the standard warning signal was more effective than the AR one having the form of red inscription STOP. The reaction time to the stimuli was really shorter. As far as we know, the results can be explained basing on the theory of perception, within which the two levels of perception are distinguished; i.e., sensomotor and semantic-operational (Tomaszewski, 1975). One can assume that perception of the standard warning signal take place on the sensomotor level (figurative perception), allowing for distinguishing geometrical objects (e.g. points, lines, solids). While perception of the inscription STOP takes place on the semantic-operational level (physical perception), and is not restrained to physical properties of singular objects (things, persons, events) but allows also for perception of their representations (models, diagrams, words).
Moreover, it can be assumed that following the whole perception process, i.e. impression phase (sensor registration), organisation phase (emotional assessment), recognition and metaphoric assessment; may in that case take much more time as compared to the red light generated by a signalling device, mainly due to the third phase (recognition) time (Kosslyn&Rosenberg, 2006).
At this stage of the perception process the semantic assessment of stimuli is carried out, allowing for its categorisation. Due to the set size effect the higher the number of stimuli to be compared the longer the perception process (Maruszewski, 2001) . In our case the inscription STOP is a more complicated stimuli than the red light.
The inscription STOP was considered as a more disturbing one, as well that subjective assessment may result from the fact that the inscription covers a larger part of the sight area than the red circle signal. Moreover, it was found that in experimental cycle 1 in view of the reaction time the red circle signal displayed on the eyepiece occurred to be the best one, while the inscription STOP - the worst signal. During experimental cycle 2, however, in view of the working speed the yellow circle signal displayed on the eyepiece occurred to be the worst one.
It can be concluded that the AR signal having the form of red circle was most advantageous: the reaction time to that stimuli was shortest and the working speed observed was most suitable. Additionally, it resulted from the subjective assessment that the red circle was considered to be best visible, most easy to catch and would be used most often at the actual workstations. When comparing between the signals differing in colour; i.e. red and yellow circles, more advantageous have occurred the red one. It seems that the reasons behind such assessment result from the social significance system, where the red colour usually means - "danger". The aforementioned system was detected e.g., in the course of investigations into perception of words and colours connected with danger, where it occurred that about 75% of subjects had considered the red colour to have meant "danger" (Baun&Silver, 1995; Borade et al., 2008). It was very important in view of the research completing also to find out what the subjects felt about different warning signals. Most of the subject population considered the AR signals as more "user-friendly" than the standard one. At the same time, however, almost everyone emphasized that the ergonomics of glasses was of crucial importance. Improving ergonomic properties of the glasses could make them more useful.

6. Conclusions

The considerations presented in Chapter 2, as well as the analysis results of the accidents that happened in machine operation (Dźwiarek, 2004) have proved that the appropriate use of warning signals is always the issue of crucial importance. The results obtained from the experiment conducted indicate that the warning signals generated using the augmented reality technology may occur much more efficient as compared to the standard warning signals. On the other hand thanks to the technological development signals of that type will soon be more easily available. Successful applications of the AR systems to solve other, not safety-related problems; like,

- supporting of service and assembly tasks in industry;
- training and supporting of diagnostics in medicine;
- "virtual guides" in museums;
- computer games;

also indicate the possibility of broadening the scope of AR system applications to improve the safety at work. Especially in the cases when standard warning devices occur to be ineffective and insufficient. Major drawback the standard warning systems suffer from consists in the fact that they are fixed, and therefore after the operator has moved they could be situated outside his/her visual area. The warning devices of that type can also be hidden from view by machinery elements or other equipment.

The AR signals are considered as the active visual ones. It is due to the fact that by means of changes in contrast, brightness, colour, shape size or location of a symbol they provide the information about any change in the state of machinery. If the information relates to risk changes they are warning signals.

To make the perception of visual warning signal easier the signal should be situated in the way ensuring that they will be seen from each place they should be. Active safety-related signals should be positioned so that they are visible to operators from working positions, and to exposed persons, and should have as wide a viewing angle as needed for safe detection. The examples shown in Chapter 2 have proved that when dealing with the standard visual warning systems it might be difficult. The idea of AR signal ensures that those requirements are satisfied since the signal will always remain within the operator's visual area. Moreover, it is very important that the AR signal is received only by a person in danger instead of involving any disturbances in the work of other people.

All safety-related signals should be designed in the way ensuring that their meaning is always clear, obvious, exact and unambiguous to the expected user. The safety-related information should be provided using means adapted accordingly to the perception capabilities of operators or other people in danger. The effective warning signals should be properly designed. The investigations conducted have proved that the type of applied signals is here of crucial importance. It is obvious that in warning signal design only "see-through" systems should be considered. In such systems in case of no warning signal the workstation is being observed. In the systems where additional signals are displayed the workstation is being observed on a monitor screen. That type of design is neither precise nor reliable enough to be applied in industry. Even most advanced systems can not reconstruct the real images in the way precise enough and supply the reality with virtual images.

The symbols as simple as possible should be used as warning signals. The results we have obtained have proved that most effective are circles, the reception of which does not require further semantic-operational analysis. Each additional sign considerably extends the perception time, which might reduce their effectiveness. One should consider also the risk of „sensory overwork" due to the information overload, which might cause that the operator misses the warning signals. A proper colour of sign is also important. Actually, our

experiment has excluded the use of colours other then red, ehich agrees with the results obtained by other researches as well as with commonly accepted rules and standards on the warning signals. However, it is recommended to support the signal perception by means of flashing signals. From the experiment it was found that the signals flashing at 4-8 Hz were best received. Lower flashing frequency may cause reaction delays since the time between flashes is comparable with the operator's reaction time. Higher flashing frequencies are perceived as a continuous signal.
When designing the AR devices for industrial applications one should concentrate efforts on their ergonomics, which could be clearly seen from the subjects' remarks. It is recommended that the personal protective equipment used at the workstation be adapted accordingly for AR applications. If it is impossible, new designs should be as close to those being in use as possible, taking into consideration the conformity assessment with the relevant regulations on working equipment.
It can be concluded, therefore, that the AR devices can be successfully applied to warning against any dangerous event; like machine start, too high speed, etc; as the devices supporting standard warning signals. That concerns especially the cases when the operator should look in many different directions.

7. Acknowledgments

This paper has been prepared on the basis of the results of a task carried out within the scope of the second stage of the National Programme "Adaptation of Working Conditions in Poland to European Union Standards", partly supported - within the scope of research - in 2005 -2007 by the Ministry of Science and Higher Education. The Central Institute for Labour Protection - National Research Institute was the main co-ordinator of the Programme.

8. References

Anastassova, M., Burkhardt, J.M., Mégard, C., Ehanno, P. (2005). Results from a user-centred critical incidents study for guiding future implementation of augmented reality in automotive maintenance. *International Journal of Industrial Ergonomics,* Vol. 35 No. 1, pp. 67-77

Borade A., Bandos S., Gandhewar V (2008). Hazards perception from safety words and colors: an Indian perspective. *International Journal of Occupational Safety and Health,* (w druku).

Bound, A.C., Haniff, D.J., Baber, & Steiner, S.J. (1999). Virtual reality and augmented reality as a training tool for assembly tasks. *Proceedeings of 1999 IEEE International Conference on Information Visualization,* pp. 32-36, USA, 1999, Los Alamitos.

Braun C. C., Silver N. C. (1995) Interaction of signal word and colour on warning labels: differences in perceived hazard and behavioural compliance. *Ergonomics,* Vol. 38, No. 11, pp. 2207-2220.

Burt J. L., Bartolome D. S., Burdette D. W., Comstock J. R. (1995). A psychological evaluation of the perceived urgency of auditory warning signals. *Ergonomics,* Vol. 38, No. 11, pp. 2327-2340.

Chan A.H.S, Chan K.W.L. (2006) Synchronous and asynchronous presentations of auditory and visual signals: Implications for control console design. *Applied Ergonomics*, Vol. 37 p. 131-140.

Chung, K.H., Shewchuk, J.P., Williges, R.C. (1999). An application of augmented reality to thickness inspection. *Human Factors And Ergonomics In Manufacturing*, Vol. 9, No. 4, pp. 331-342.

Chung K. H., Shewchuk J. P., Williges R. C., (2002) An analysis Framework for Applying Virtual Enviroment Technology to Manufacturing Tasks. *Human Factors and Ergonomics in Manufacturing*, Vol. 12, No. 4, pp. 335-348.

Cohn T. E. (1996) Engineered Visibility Warning Signals: Tests of Time to React, Detectability, Identifiability and Salience. *IDEA Program Transportation Research Board*, National Research Council, May 1, 1996

Dangelmaier, W., Fischer, M., Gausemeier, J., Grafe, M., Matysczok, C., Mueck, B., (2005). Virtual and augmented reality support for discrete manufacturing system simulation. *Computers in Industry*. Vol. 56, No. 4, pp. 371-383.

Dzwiarek M., Holejko K., Nowak, R. (2003) Augmented Reality - a new kind of hazardous situation indicator. *Proceedings of International Conference Safety of Industrial Automated Systems*, pp. 3-41 ÷ 3-45, France, October 2003, IRNS, Nancy.

Dzwiarek, M., (2004). An analysis of Accident Caused by Improper Functioning of Machine Control Systems. *International Journal of Occupational Safety and Ergonomics*, Vol. 10 No. 2, pp. 129-136.

Dzwiarek, M., Holejko, K., Nowak, R., Czarnecki, T., (2004). A system for signalling of emergency situation based on the augmented reality concept. In: *Human & Organisational Issues in the Digital Enterprise*. Enda F. Fallon (Ed.), pp. 479-488 The Department of Industrial Engineering, National University of Irlend, ISBN 0-9538974-1-9, Galowey, Irland.

Dzwiarek, M., Czarnecki, T., Holejko, K., Nowak, R. (2006). Application of augmented reality to the industrial systems for signalisation of emergency situations. In: *Photonics Applications in Astronomy, Communications, Industry, and High-Energy Physics Experiments IV*. Ryszard S. Romaniuk (Ed.), pp. 1147-1156, The International Society for Optical Engeenering.

Dzwiarek, M., Łuczak, A., Strawiński, T. (2007). Badania percepcji wizualnych sygnałów ostrzegawczych generowanych metodą rzeczywistości wzbogaconej celem ich optymalizacji. Raport końcowy. (Inwetigation of of perception of visual warning signals generated using an augmented reality system for their optimalisation purpuses. Final report.) *Publications of Cental Institute for Labour Protection - National Research Institute (in Polish).*

EN 981:1996 Safety of machinery - System of auditory and visual danger and information signals. *European Committee for Standardisation.*

Gros B. L., Greenhouse D. S., Cohn T. E. (2005) Visual warning signals optimized for human perception: What the eye sees fastest. *Applied Bionics and Biomechanics*, Vol. 2, No. 1, pp. 45-52.

Haas E, C, Casali J., G. (1995), Perceived urgency of response time to multi-tone and frequency-modular warning signals in broadband noise. *Ergonomics*, Vol. 38, No 11, pp. 2313-2326.

Hagele M., Helms E., Schaaf W., (2002) Robot assistants at manual workplaces: effective co-operationand safety aspects. *Proceedings of the 33rd International Symposium of Robotics*. October 2002.

IEC 61310:1995 Safety of machinery - Indication, marking and actuation - Part 1: Requirements for visual, auditory and tactile signals. *International Electrotechnical Committee.*

ISO 12100-2:2003. Safety of machinery. Basic concepts, general principles for design - Part 2: Technical principles. *International Standard Organization.*

Kosslyn S.M., Rosenberg R.S., (2006) Psychologia. Mózg. Człowiek. Wydawnictwo Znak, Kraków (in polish).

Kyung H. Chung, John P. Shewchuk, Robert C. Willinges. (2002). An analysis Framework for Applying Virtual Environment Technology to Manufacturing Tasks. *Human Factors and Ergonomics in Manufacturing,* Vol. 12, No. 4, pp. 335-348.

Luczak A., (2001) Wymagania psychologiczne w doborze osób do zawodów trudnych i niebezpiecznych. ISBN 83-87354-61-9 (in polish).

Maruszewski T., (2001) Psychologia poznania. Sposoby rozumienia siebie i świata. *GWP,* Warszawa (In polish).

Pawlak A., Wolska A. (2004) Ocena występowania olśnienia na stanowiskach montażu opraw rastrowych. CIOP-PIB (in polish).

Pawlak A., Wolska A. (2005) Ekspertyza warunków pracy na 6 wybranych stanowiskach pracy w ABB, Łódź. CIOP-PIB (in polish).

Pawlak A., Wolska A. (2006) Ocena warunków oświetleniowych na stanowisku kontroli jakości w POLAR S.A. we Wrocławiu. CIOP-PIB (in polish).

Shingledecker, C. A. (1984) „A task battery for applied human performance assessment research". *Technical Report AFAMRL-TR-84-071,* Air Force Aerospace Medical Research Laboratory, Wright - Patterson Air Force Base USA.

Tomaszewski T. (1976) Procesy spostrzegania. IN: *Psychologia.* T. Tomaszewski (Ed.), pp. 226-246, PWN, Warszawa (in polish).

Weidenhausen, J., Knoepfle, C., Stricker, D. (2003) Lessons learned on the way to industrial augmented reality applications, a retrospective on ARVIKA. *Computers & Graphics,* Vol. 27 No. 6, pp. 887-891.

Widerszal-Bazyl, M. (1998) Przewodnik po zawodach. MPiPS, ISBN 83-86313-75-7, Warszawa (in polish).

Wogalter, MS., Mayhorn, CB. (2005). Providing cognitive support with technology-based warning systems. *Ergonomics,* Vol. 48, No 5, pp. 522 - 533.

12

Miniaturized Human 3D Motion Input

Kynan Eng
Institute of Neuroinformatics
University of Zurich and ETH Zurich
Switzerland

1. Introduction

Imagine that you are sitting on a train, standing in a queue or walking down the street. You are, like a majority of people in the world, carrying one or more mobile computing devices. It could be a mobile telephone, a portable media player, a personal digital assistant (PDA) or a portable gaming console (e.g. Nintendo DS, Sony Playstation Portable). Your particular device has 3D graphics capabilities, and you have some application - perhaps a game, a navigation tool or a computer-aided design (CAD) model - that needs 3D input. How do you provide 3D input to your device as intuitively and quickly as possible, preferably using only one hand? And how can you provide the input while standing and without needing to use a stable surface such as a table or wall?

An increasing number of hand-held computers, portable gaming devices and mobile telephones are sufficiently powerful to run 3D applications. There is thus a need for miniature one-handed input devices that combine small size, many input degrees of freedom (DOF) and acceptable usability compromises. Users of 3D applications need to manipulate virtual objects in up to six degrees of rotational and translation freedom (DOF). A wide range of devices for providing the required input is already available on desktop computer and gaming console platforms. However, due to technological and human physiological constraints none of them can be easily scaled down to a form that could conceivably be part of a truly portable device. Here I detail the requirements for a useable portable "walk-around" 3D input device, reviews currently available 3D input technologies and describe a candidate design fulfilling the requirements.

2. 3D Input Technologies

2.1 Existing Technologies

How many input degrees of freedom are necessary to control a 3D software application? The answer depends on the application. The most common families of 3D applications, and the currently most popular ways of controlling them, are:

- Driving simulations: 3DOF total - left hand 1DOF (steering wheel), right hand or feet 2DOF (keyboard/pedals: accelerate, brake)

- Flight simulators (fixed-wing): 4DOF total - right hand 3DOF (joystick: nose up/down, bank left/right, rudder), left hand 1DOF (throttle: thrust).
- First-person games ("ego shooters") or virtual world free navigation: 4DOF total - right hand 3DOF (mouse: look left-right, look up-down), left hand 2DOF (keyboard: torso left/right, torso forwards/backwards). Many games include extra special movements such as leaning, crawling and jumping which are controlled using the same DOFs with an extra key or button press.
- CAD models: 6DOF total - left hand 6DOF (SpaceBall/SpaceNavigator: translate X, Y, Z and rotate X, Y, Z)

Examples of the most popular devices implementing these control methods are listed and described in Table 1. Note that in controller jargon, a "digital" input is one which uses on/off buttons or switches, and an "analog" input is one that allows graded input on an axis with multiple-bit digital output resolution. The terms "aDOF" and "dDOF" are used to refer to analog and digital degrees of freedom.

	**Sony Dualshock3 (formerly Sixaxis)** Left hand: 4-way digital direction pad (2 dDOF) plus a 2-way analog joystick (2 aDOF). Right hand: 2-way analog joystick (2 aDOF). Other: the entire controller can be translated and rotated in three translational plus three rotational degrees of freedom (6 aDOF).
	**Sony Playstation Portable** Controller very similar in operation to the Dualshock3. Left hand: as for Dualshock3, except the 2 aDOF analog joystick is replaced by a flat analog input point (similar to the Trackpoint found on some laptops).
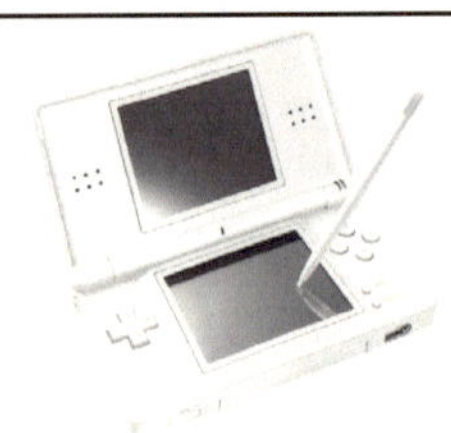	**Nintendo DS** Left hand: 2 dDOF digital direction pad. Right hand: two touch screens for a nominal extra 2 x 2 aDOF. However, the vast majority of Nintendo DS applications use the touch screens for selection of on-screen objects rather than 3D navigation.
 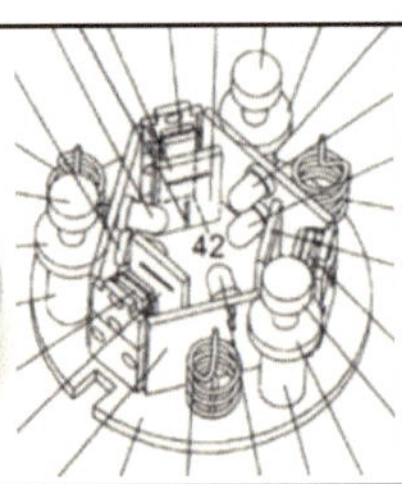	**3Dconnexion SpaceNavigator** Left hand: 6 aDOF translation and rotation (Gombert 2004), achieved by pushing, pulling and rotating the black cap (left) small distances. Inside the cap is an arrangement of six light-emitting diodes and corresponding optical detectors (right) which detect motions of the cap relative to the base on which the electronics are mounted.

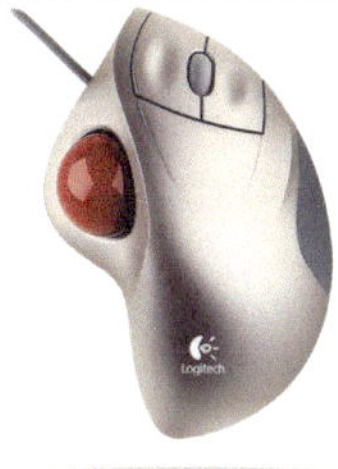	**Logitech TrackMan Wheel** Right hand: analog trackball (2 aDOF) incorporating a textured ball with an internal vision sensor (Bidiville et al. 1994), operated using the thumb which leaves the index finger free to operate the scroll wheel (1 dDOF).
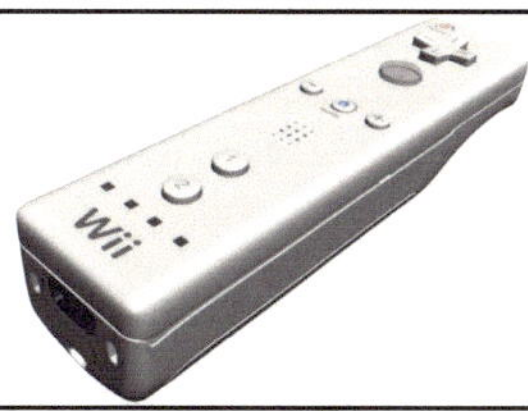	**Nintendo Wiimote** Left/right hand: thumb-operated 4-way digital direction pad (2 dDOF) with 3-axis accelerometers (3 aDOF) and a imager-based point tracker (2 aDOF) which senses analog movement relative to a "sensor bar" normally placed above the television.
	**Thrustmaster Hotas Cougar** A typical high-end joystick. Right-hand: X-Y analog joystick motion (2 aDOF) with axial twist (1 aDOF), plus a thumb-operated digital 4-way direction pad on the joystick handle (2 dDOF). Left hand: analog thrust lever (1 aDOF).
	**Microsoft Wireless Laser Mouse 8000** Left/right hand: mouse movement (2 aDOF) and a 2-way digital scroll wheel (2 dDOF), usually used for horizontal and vertical window scrolling.
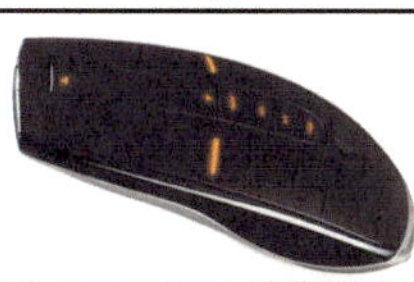	**Logitech MX Air Mouse** Left/right hand: designed to be used either on a flat surface or in the air using accelerometers (2 aDOF in each case) and has a capacitive scroll pad on its top surface (1 aDOF).
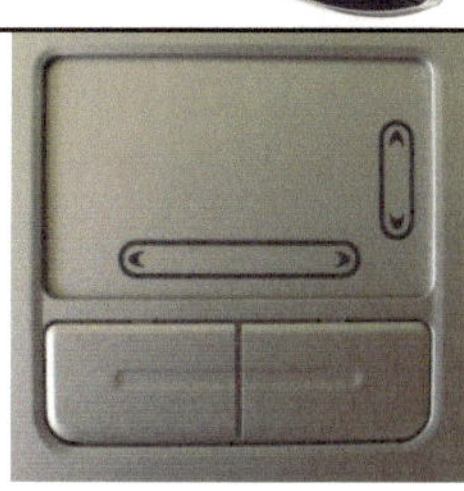	**Touch pad with integrated scroll bars** Made mainly by Synaptics and ALPS. Left/right hand: 2 aDOF with single-finger pointing. Recent versions such as the one illustrated here contain in-built scroll bars to allow 4 aDOF pointing (Bisset and Kasser 1998), although controlling all DOFs simultaneously using one hand is virtually impossible. Another variant differentiates between two-finger and one-finger gestures to alternate between pointing and scrolling operations.
	**Thrustmaster RGT Force Feedback Pro Clutch Edition Racing Wheel** Left hand: steering wheel (1 aDOF). Right hand: gear lever (1 dDOF). Feet: three foot-operated pedals (3 aDOF).

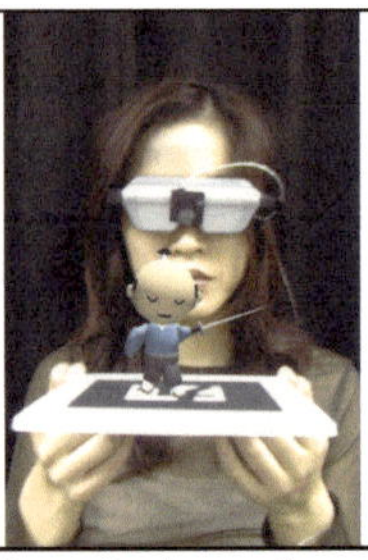	**ARToolkit** An open-source software library (ARToolworks 2007) which provides 6 aDOF camera tracking of specially designed markers. Has been used to produce a 6 aDOF mouse (Woods et al. 2003). ARToolkit and its related projects (ARToolkit+, ARTag) are examples of a class of "outside-in" trackers which use an imaging device to track special markers attached to an object to be manipulated.

Table 1. Description of currently available 3D controllers.

2.2 Requirements

An ideal miniature walk-around 3D input device would:

- provide for input in up to six independent analog DOF (3 translation plus 3 rotation).
- be operable using only one hand, with the other hand free to support the device and provide command input.
- work reliably even when the user and device are moving in unknown directions, either on foot or standing on a bus.
- be small enough to be mounted on a mobile computing device such as a mobile telephone or ultra-mobile PC.
- not require any extra devices to be worn or carried around, apart from the mobile computing device itself (optional).
- provide reasonable accuracy.
- be insensitive to everyday interference from light, sound and magnetic fields.
- be cheap and easy to manufacture.

Table 2 shows how the input devices described in the previous section match up against each other when miniaturized in terms of usability, manufacturability and implementation cost. The above-listed requirements act as strong constraints on the range of feasible input devices. In fact, there is currently no available device that satisfies all of the requirements. Most of the listed input devices support only 2-4 DOF in one-handed operation, while more degrees of freedom are very difficult to achieve. Since the user is not attached to a fixed reference frame such as a table or wall, the computing device itself must act as the reference frame for measuring movements. In unstable environments where the user can be moving around, free-floating inertial input devices such as the Sony Dualshock3, the Logitech MX Air Mouse, the ARToolkit tracker and the Nintendo Wii-mote accelerometers are unsuitable. The Wii-mote imaging sensor is also unsuitable since it uses an imaging sensor which would prone to interference from stray light and bright reflections.
The device which comes the closest to meeting all of the requirements is the 6 DOF SpaceNavigator from 3Dconnexion. It provides one-handed control which can be attached to any computing device by using an arrangement of springs and optical sensors inside the device's hand grip. However, the required volume of the custom sensor inside the hand grip currently limits its minimum size to about 4 cm diameter, making it currently unsuitable for ultra-mobile applications. It may be possible to reduce the size of the sensor further, but miniaturizing the multiple discrete parts in the sensor which include light-

emitting diodes, several springs and metal stop elements (Gombert 2004) could affect manufacturability and therefore cost. What would be ideal is a that works as well as the SpaceNavigator, but uses fewer discrete parts and can be easily miniaturized.

Existing Controller	**Miniaturized for 1-handed walk-around**	
Native DOFs	**1-handed walk-around usability**	**Manufacturability Cost**
Sony Dualshock3 4 analog: 2 joysticks 2 digital: direction pad 6 analog: accel. + gyroscope	Good for 2DOF only Moderate for 2+2DOF Poor for 6DOF (no reference point for whole-body motion)	Good Low
Sony PSP 2 analog: trackpoint 2 digital: direction pad	Good for 2DOF Moderate for 2+2DOF	Good Low
Nintendo DS 2 digital: direction pad 4 analog: 2 touchscreens	Good for 2DOF only	Good Low
3Dconnexion SpaceNavigator 6 analog: custom optical-spring sensor	Good for 6DOF	Poor: sensor must fit inside cap Medium
Logitech TrackMan Wheel 2 analog: trackball 1 digital: scroll wheel	Good for 2+1DOF	Good Low
Nintendo Wii-mote 2 analog: screen pointer 2 digital: direction pad 3 analog: accelerometers	Good for 2DOF Poor for 2+2DOF: no fixed reference point available for screen pointer	Good Low
Thrustmaster Hotas Cougar 4 analog: joystick with stick rotate, throttle 2 digital: direction pad	Good for 3DOF Moderate for 3+2DOF: move joystick with hand while thumb/finger controls direction pad	Moderate Low
Microsoft Wireless Laser Mouse 8000 2 analog: mouse 2 digital: 2D scroll wheel	Poor: must keep mouse on large flat stable surface	Good Low
Logitech MX Air Mouse 2 analog: mouse surface or accelerometers in air 1 analog: scroll pad	Moderate for 3DOF: no fixed reference point for air operation	Good Medium
Touch pad with scroll bars 4 analog: touch pad, scroll bars	Moderate: can only actuate 2-3 DOF at a time with one hand	Good Low
ARToolkit 6 analog: camera tracking of marker patch pose	Poor: highly sensitive to ambient lighting conditions, requires extra object to be carried around, CPU intensive	Good Low

Existing Controller Native DOFs	Miniaturized for 1-handed walk-around	
	1-handed walk-around usability	Manufacturability Cost
Thrustmaster RGT Wheel 4 analog: wheel, brake, clutch, accelerator 1 digital: gear shift	Good for 1DOF Poor for >1DOF - must use feet or other hand	Good Low

Table 2. Assessment of potential of current 3D controllers for miniaturization for one-handed "walk around" operation.

3. A Miniature 3D Input Device

3.1 Design

This section describes the design of a prototype of a 3D controller for providing one-handed 6 DOF input with miniature size and low cost. An overview of the device is shown in Fig. 1. In terms of operation it is similar to the SpaceNavigator, providing a single grip, designed to be held between the thumb and index finger, which can be translated and rotated in 6 DOF. Movements of the finger grip are detected by an imager placed underneath, and the grip is permitted to move and rotate by a system of planar springs.

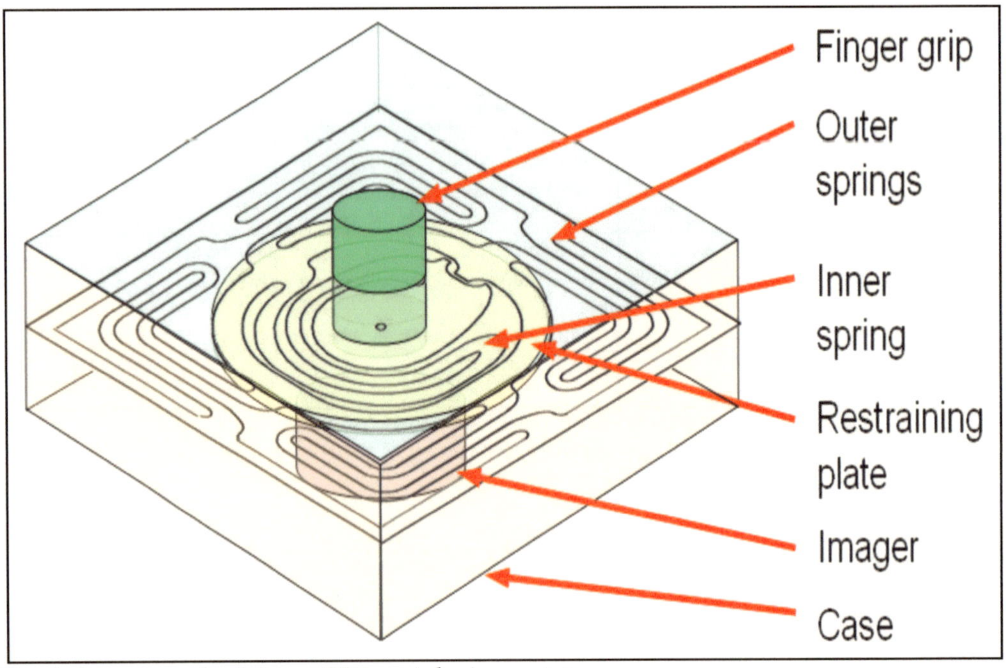

Fig. 1. Overview of miniature 3D input device prototype.

The detail of the planar spring mechanism is shown in Fig. 2. Translational and rotational movements of the finger grip move the inner frame relative to the outer frame, via the outer linear springs. With this arrangement it is relatively straightforward to design the outer springs in the L-shape shown so that the forces required to translate the finger grip and rotate it about the in-plane axes are approximately equal. However, the arrangement always results in the rotational stiffness of the spring about the perpendicular axis being much higher, impairing usability. To reduce the stiffness about the perpendicular rotational axis, the inner torsional spring is used. Its effect is limited to rotation about the perpendicular axis by the two restraining plates attached to the inner frame, completely enclosing the torsional spring. A circular hole in the center of the upper restraining plate allows the close-fitting grip shaft to protrude, which is fixed to the finger grip. A similar circular hole in the center of the lower restraining plate makes visible the underside of the grip mount, to which the grip shaft is attached.

To prevent excessive rotational displacement, the grip mount has two stopping tabs located on it. These tabs match a similar stopping tab on the inside of the inner frame, to limit the maximum rotational displacement approximately 8.2°. The outer springs self-contact to limit in-plane translation to 1.5 mm in each horizontal direction, and vertical displacements of the restraining plates are limited to 2 mm by external parts of the frame and case holding the controller. By comparison, the laptop version of the SpaceNavigator limits translational motion to approximately 1.0 mm in each direction and rotation to 8.8°.

Fig. 3 shows an assembled prototype of the planar spring made from laser-cut 2mm thick Plexiglas. The black rubber finger grip is 18 mm in diameter and 12 mm high. The total functional area used by the planar spring is 50 mm square. The internals of a USB webcam (Logitech QuickCam, 320x240 pixels) are mounted inside the case, and the USB power is connected to two red light-emitting diodes aligned to illuminate the underside of the grip mount (Fig. 4).

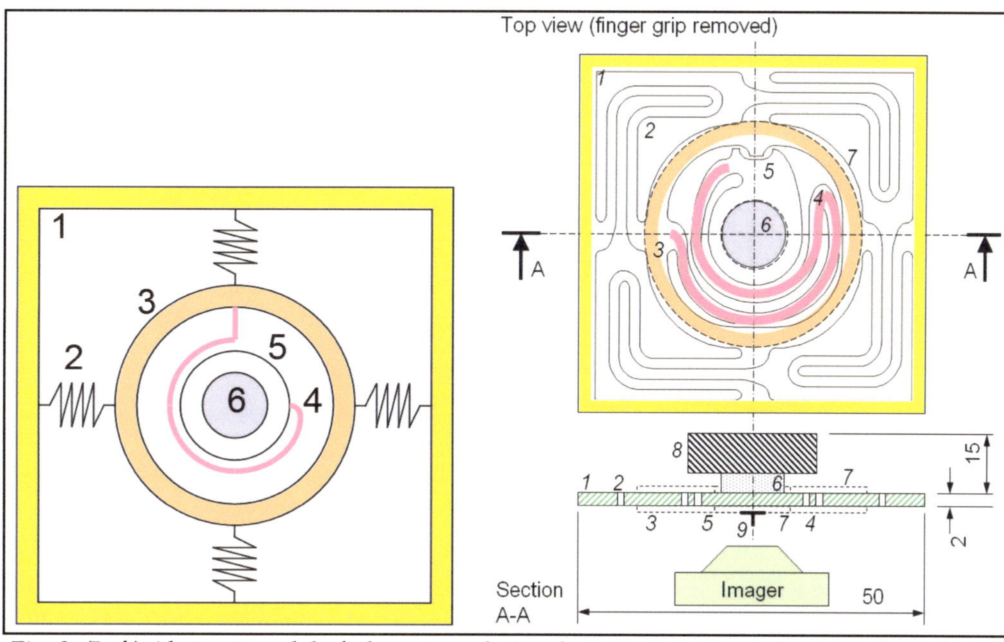

Fig. 2. (Left) Abstract model of planar translational-torsion spring mechanism. (Right) Realised design of spring mechanism. 1: outer frame (yellow); 2: outer springs; 3: inner frame (apricot); 4: inner torsion spring (pink); 5: grip mount; 6: grip shaft (light blue); 7: restraining plates; 8: finger grip; 9: index points. Adapted from (Eng 2007).

Fig. 3. (Left) Prototype spring mechanism with controller knob on top. The torsional spring can be seen inside the cavity formed by the two restraining plates.

Fig. 4. (Left) Internal view of the controller, showing the webcam lens and illumination provided by two light-emitting diodes. (Right) The assembled controller.

The purpose of the webcam is to track the movements of the grip mount and therefore the user's movements applied to the finger grip. The camera tracks the movements of specially arranged white index points on a black background attached to the grip mount (Fig. 5). By considering the relative movements of the index points compared to the rest position using simple heuristics, 6 DOF simultaneous movements can be decoded using a 3D index point arrangement. If the central point is in the same plane as the other points, the number of

DOFs that can be decoded reduces to four. In the prototype the 4 DOF version of the index point pattern was used, laser printed on normal paper. Each point was 0.5 mm in diameter and aligned at the corners of a square of side length 2.0 mm. The fifth point was of the same size and set in the center of the square.

Ideally, the index points should be positioned at the exact center of rotation of the controller finger grip to avoid applied rotations about the in-plane axes causing simultaneous offset translation of the index points. These offset translations can be ambiguous and hard to decode, since they are indistinguishable from "real" translations applied to the controller. The design presented here has the index points just below the plane of the springs, which is slightly too low to be fully correct. A future improved version would feature a recess in the center of the grip shaft so that index point rotations occur about the natural center of rotation of the mechanism.

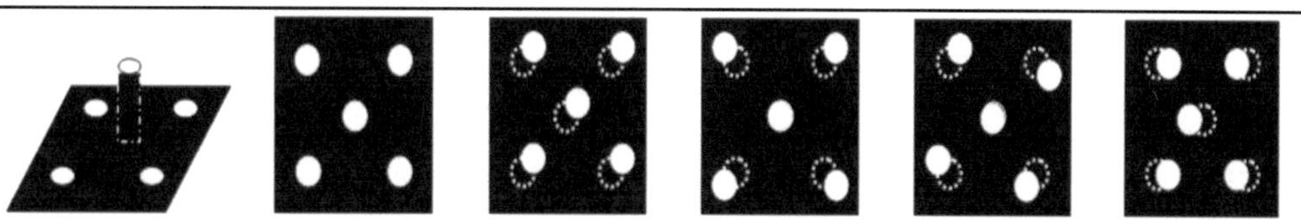

Fig. 5. Schematic of methods for deducing 3D motion from 2D motion of index points (not to scale). Dotted circles indicate original positions of index points. Adapted from (Eng 2007).

One of the biggest usability problems with all user input devices is zero-position drift. This phenomenon occurs when some hysteretic deformation or movement of the device results in the measurement of the device in the home (unloaded) position being non-zero. Applying a movement threshold often does not solve the problem on its own, as the zero position can drift above the threshold over an extended time period. It is also undesirable to use very high thresholds since it reduces the output resolution and increases the forces needed to move the device. One solution, as applied to the miniature 3D controller described here, is to have an adaptive zero level. When the current device reading is below threshold, the zero position is continually adapted slowly towards the current sub-threshold reading. The adaptation stops during above-threshold readings when force is applied to the device, and only starts again once the device has been released. Depending on the controller the adaptation process can be applied at a number of processing steps; in this case it was applied at the image processing level detecting the movements of the index points.

3.2 Testing

The mechanical response of the planar spring was measured as 2.2 N/mm (horizontal plane dX, dY), 1.0 N/mm (out of the plane dZ) and 0.016 N/degree = 1.8 Nm/degree (rotation about Z-axis at the finger grip contact point). These figures were roughly comparable with values measured from the laptop version of the SpaceNavigator (2.0 N/mm for dX/dY translation, 2.4 N/mm for dZ translation , 0.08 N/degree = 3.6 Nm/degree for rotation about the Z axis).

Even using the standard low-cost optics of the webcam it was possible to focus the lens reliably on the pattern of index points, corresponding to a spatial resolution of approximately 0.05 mm. This spatial resolution corresponded to approximately 4-5 bits of translation resolution and 3-4 bits of rotational resolution for the controller.

The controller proved to work well enough for users to position and orient a virtual cube (Fig. 6) in 4 DOF with a little practice. Because the springs were made of plastic and were thus highly damped, no measurable unwanted mechanical oscillations occurred when the user let go of the device. The tolerances involved in production of the hand-made prototype created significant zero-position hysteresis but the adaptation algorithm to eliminate zero-position noise worked as designed. The CPU load on a desktop PC (Pentium 4 2.8 GHz) was approximately 20% including the graphics display.

No reliable method was found for producing the 3D version of the index points required to support full 6 DOF motion. Producing such small index points in 3D would require development of specialized molding or machining processes, together with methods for very precisely applying high-contrast black and white paint, neither of which were available during development of the prototype.

Fig. 6. Prototype miniature 3D motion controller in use manipulating a virtual cube. From (Eng 2007).

4. Outlook

This chapter has outlined the requirements for creating a miniature 3D controller that is suitable for mobile computing applications, and presented the key elements of the design of a device fulfilling these requirements. Its key feature is a novel mechanism that provides for full 6 DOF motion using only one moving part, combined with standard image processing. While its feasibility has been demonstrated, several improvements are required to achieve a truly usable mobile controller. The two key necessary improvements include:

- Redesign the imaging device packaging and optics to reduce the depth of the controller within the case from >40 mm to <15 mm, so that it can fit inside a typical mobile computing device.
- Find methods for producing the out-of-plane calibration point, probably using machining or plastic molding, so that full 6 DOF output can be supported instead of the current 4 DOF.

More straightforward improvements include further optimization of the spring design, increasing the stiffness of the casing to reduce zero-position hysteresis, and a switch to higher resolution imagers. Using a 1.3 megapixel imager would improve sensitivity by approximately 2 bits, at the cost of increasing image processing requirements. It would thus be desirable to create an embedded version of the vision processing algorithm to create a stand-alone, platform-independent device with minimal power consumption. Direct usability comparisons comparing the presented device with existing devices are also needed.

5. Acknowledgments

Thanks to Rodney Douglas and Wolfgang Henggeler for their advice and encouragement during the development of the device, and to Adrian Whatley for his corrections to the manuscript.

6. References

ARToolworks. (2007). ARTookit, from http://www.hitl.washington.edu/artoolkit/.

Bidiville, M., Arreguit, J., van Schaik, F. A., Steenis, B., Droz-Dit-Busset, F., Buczek, H. and Bussien, A. (1994). *Cursor pointing device utilizing a photodetector array with target ball having randomly distributed speckles*. United States Patent and Trademarks Office. United States of America.

Bisset, S. J. and Kasser, B. (1998). *Touch Pad with Scroll Bar, Command Bar*. WO 98/37506. WIPO, Logitech, Inc.

Eng, K. (2007). *A Miniature, One-Handed 3D Motion Controller*. LNCS4662 Part 1: Interact 2007, Rio de Janeiro, Brasil.

Gombert, B. (2004). *Arrangement for the detection for relative movements or relative position of two objects*. US6804012. USA, 3DConnexion GmbH, Seefeld (DE).

Woods, E., Mason, P. and Billinghurst, M. (2003). *MagicMouse: an Inexpensive 6-Degree-of-Freedom Mouse*. Proceedings of the 1st international conference on Computer graphics and interactive techniques in Australasia and South East Asia, Melbourne, AU, ACM Press.

13

Modeling Query Events in Spoken Natural Language for Human-Database Interaction

Omar U. Florez and SeungJin Lim
Computer Science Department
Utah Sate University
Logan, UT 84322-4205, USA

1. Introduction

The database-related technologies have been extensively developed over the past decades and are used widely in modern society. In response to the increasing demands upon high performing database interaction, many efforts have been made to improve database system performance. For example, indexing technologies enable us to efficiently retrieve information from very large databases [1]. However, the user interfaces to database systems essentially remain unchanged: SQL is the *de facto* standard language used either directly or indirectly through an API layer. It is, however, interesting to note that the most common mode of human interface is the communication through a natural language, which motivates us to use a natural language as a human-database interface [2]. Let us compare SQL and natural language in a database query.

- While a query in natural language expresses the mental representation of the goal by the user, an SQL expression describes the structure of the data stored in the database [3].
- While SQL is a declarative language to describe a fixed set of actions to manipulate data in a relational database, the set of actions supported by the verbs in a natural language [4] is large and can be extended.
- Nevertheless, the primary user intention of data manipulation is the same both in SQL and natural language.

Clearly, there is an important gap to be filled between the cognitive model of the user interaction with databases by humans in natural language and the structured model in SQL. This gap represents the different layers of the abstraction of the user interaction carried out by the user and by the database system over the data. In this work, we attempt to bridge the gap between spoken natural language and SQL to enable the user to interact with the database through a voice interface. This goal is achieved by recognizing a *query event*, whose structural complexity is moderate, presented in a spoken natural language phrase, and then translating it to an SQL query. The presence of a query event in a spoken language expression is detected in our approach by recognizing linguistic patterns in which a verb triggers a query action followed by a set of words which specify the action. In other words, our approach works as a linguistic *adapter* which converts the structure of the spoken language expression to that of SQL at three different abstraction layers: lexical, syntactic, and semantic. The structure to be identified and the corresponding actions involved in these three layers are summarized in Table 1. They will be discussed in depth in later sections.

Abstraction layer	**Spoken natural language**	**Actions to bridge natural language and SQL**	**SQL**
Lexical	Voice signal from the user	Detection of phonemes from the voice signal and word formation from the phonemes	Words
Syntactic	Parts of speech of words by the proposed grammar	Syntactic analysis of parts of speech	Keywords and literals by the SQL grammar
Semantic	Queries in natural language	Representation of queries as events in a word stream	No meta data or events are considered. Syntactically valid actions are to be executed.

Table 1: The characteristics of the three linguistic abstraction layers in spoken natural language and SQL.

There are a wide range of interesting applications that can benefit from the proposed spoken language-based database interaction, ranging from an alternative user interface to perform database queries to voice-enabled retrieval of medical images in surgery. To this end, our contribution to the study of human-computer interaction is threefold. First, we formalize the detection of the presence of database queries in the user speech by modeling them as special events over time, called *query events*. Second, we provide a mechanism to translate a query event in a spoken natural language to an SQL query. Finally, we developed an application prototype, called Voice2SQL, to demonstrate the proposed user-database interaction approach in an application.

2. Previous Work

The work to enhance the interaction between humans and database systems has evolved over time. The approaches that are found in the literature can be classified into two by the way in which the interaction is carried on: textual and visual. While the use interaction in textual query systems (TQS) consists of typing SQL sentences using a keyboard, in visual query systems (VQS) the human interaction is assisted by the visual representation of the database schema by means of a graph which includes classes, associations and attributes [5, 6]. In VQS, the user formulates the query by means of a direct manipulation of the graph. The output of the query is also visualized as a graph of instances and constants. One advantage of this approach is that users with limited technical skills still can access the database without too much effort. In recent years, Rontu *et al.* provided an interactive VQS on general databases and Aversano *et al.* suggested in [7] an alternative visual approach that employs an iconic query system in the interaction with databases in which each icon is a semantic representation of attributes, relationships and data structures. In contrast to other VQSs, this iconic query system provides a high level language that expresses queries as a group of different icons. Moreover, the output of a query is also an icon which can be reused in further operations. Catarsi and Santucci made a comparison between TQS and VQS in [8] and concluded that visual query languages are easier to understand than traditional SQL expressions. While all the previous works have been proved to be effective for human interaction with databases and are getting momentum in recent years, a query system exploiting spoken natural language is rare in the literature. In fact, a spoken query system (SQS) may have unique advantages as summarized as follows:

- The use of VQS and TQS may be restricted in some scenarios. For example, visually impaired people or people with Parkinson's disease may have hard time to use a mouse or a keyboard in such a way these devices are primarily designed. The voice can be an alternative interaction method to databases and will allow us to set aside visual representations and pointer devices [9]. Thus, an SQS may provide a general purpose interface which only relies on the user's voice captured through a microphone.
- From the ergonomics point of view, the use of concurrent and similar input methods increases the user's mental load and produces interference during the interaction with computers [10]. Hence, the degree of interference in the interaction can be reduced when we use an alternative interaction method like a spoken interface. As an example, a surgeon might need to retrieve medical images of the patient while he is operating. However, the use of traditional methods to retrieve images (e.g. pointer devices or keyboards) may distract the surgeon's attention which is focused on his hands and sight. A voice-enabled interface seems to be a suitable alternative interface in this context.
- The formulation of queries in natural language is generally more intuitive for users than the use of text-based queries. Li *et al.* showed in [2] that a natural language query interface leads to the creation of queries with a better quality than a keywordbased approach. The quality in queries was measured in this study in terms of average precision and recall of different queries.

3. A Linguistic Approach from Human Voice Queries to SQL

The Merriam-Webster dictionary defines a language as "a formal system of signs and symbols including rules for the formation and transformation of admissible expressions" [11]. This definition stresses the presence of a well-defined set of symbols and rules in a language. Both natural language and SQL can be thought of as two languages with different layers of abstraction of the underlying user intention; natural language being a higher abstraction than SQL. Since natural language is used in everybody's daily life, it would be an appealing alternative interface for interaction with computers to most users as long as it can be understood by computers. However, the potential ambiguity in the meaning of a natural language expression remains to be resolved. In fact, the translation of sentences from natural language to SQL is still far from a satisfactory solution.

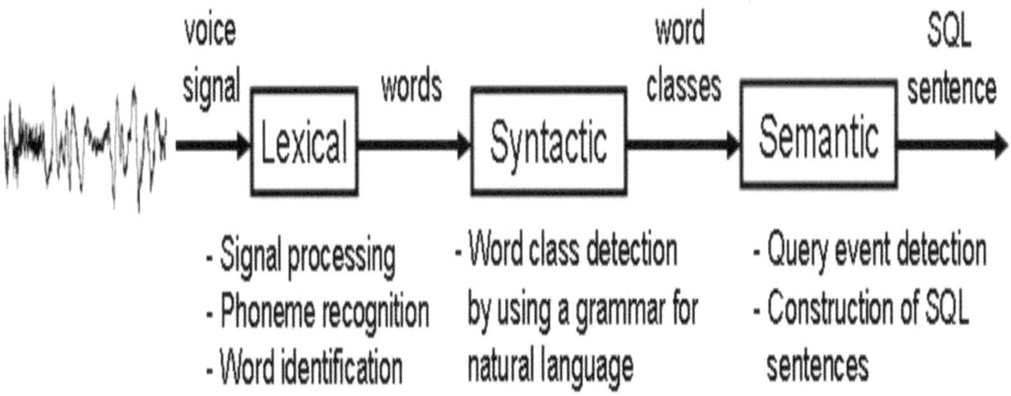

Fig. 1. Flow of data through the three processing components involved in the translation of queries in spoken natural language to SQL queries.

Our approach to the translation of query phrases from a spoken natural language to SQL is mainly to detect *query events* (which are discussed later) by three processing components, *lexical, syntactic* and *semantic,* as depicted in Figure 1, and then translate them as an SQL expression. The lexical component models common low-layer symbols in both languages to generate words. The syntactic component exploits the arrangement in the words to distinguish the associated word classes, e.g., adjective, verb, determiner, subject, preposition, and adverb, by employing a context-free grammar for natural language. Once the class of each word is identified, the semantic component checks for valid query events and builds SQL sentences.

Example 1. Consider the next sentence in Spanish[1] as an example of a query pronounced by the user.

Recuperar el nombre, el curso y la nota de los alumnos que tengan un profesor el cual les enseña un curso.

which is translated in English as follows:

Retrieve the name, the course and the grade of the students that have a lecturer which teach them a course.

We will use this sentence as an aid in presenting the proposed approach in this chapter. !

3.1 Lexical Component

The lexical component of our approach represents the lowest level of abstraction of the input voice signal captured via a microphone. While the words pronounced by the user are the basic units of information in spoken natural language, SQL employs a set of keywords and user-defined literals to express a query expression. Our goal here is to recognize words expressed in the input voice signal. To this end, we apply a typical signal processing technique that involves splitting the input signal into small segments by considering significant pauses in the signal as delimiter, digitizing each signal segment into discrete values, applying a machine learning algorithm to the discrete values to detect phonemes from them, and recognizing valid dictionary words. We believe that the detection of silent periods in the voice signal and subsequently phonemes, such as /r/, /e/, /c/, /u/, /p/, /e/, /r/, /a/, and /r/ in *recuperar* (*retrieve* in English) leads us to the recognition of the words pronounced by the user. Since phonemes have a short duration, we analyze each signal segment by using short-time slicing windows of time length w with the goal of finding phonemes inside. The window length $|w|$ is an external parameter and should be long enough to contain phonemes. In the literature this value is commonly set to a value between 15 to 25 milliseconds [12, 13], and set to 20 milliseconds in our approach. Since some phonemes may not be detected if they appear in the two consecutive time windows $w1$ and $w2$, we let the third time window $w3$ overlap $w1$ and $w2$ half way in order to capture the eventual presence of those phonemes. From each window slice, we extract the most representative features as a vector for further processing. This procedure, denoted as *segmentation* in the literature [14], is repeated for the entire voice signal as it arrives through the microphone.

Among the number of descriptors to extract features from a voice signal within a fixed length time window, such as Linear Predictive Coding [15], Perceptual Linear Predictive [16] and RASTA [17], Mel-Frequency Cepstrum Coefficients (MFCC) are widely used because they have shown to be a robust and accurate approximation method [18]. In practice, a feature vector of 12MFCC coefficients is enough to characterize any voice segment. In other words, the entire spoken query can be divided into segments and each segment is characterized by a feature vector of 12 coefficients. Clustering of these vectors helps us identify the phonemes contained in the input signal. Among the several existing clustering methods, we chose the Kohonen's Self-Organizing Map (SOM) which is trained with a set of feature vectors, each of which is labeled with a phoneme. The detection of phonemes in the user speech is then reduced to obtain the neuron with the most similar feature vector on the SOM. The shape and members of the clusters on the SOM map changes over time while the SOM learns different phonemes through successive iterations. After training the SOM, we perform a calibration step where a set of feature vectors with well-distinguished labels are compared against the map. An example of the resulting map after training and calibration is depicted in Figure 2. (The signal processing details and program parameters used in our lexical procedure are fully explained in [19].)

Example 2. Consider the input spoken query in Example 1 again. The SOM training after calibration recognizes phonemes from the corresponding voice signal. Examples of the detected phonemes include: /r/, /e/, /c/, /u/, /p/, /e/, /r/, /a/, and /r/ for "recuperar" (*retrieve*), /l/, /a/ for "la" (*the*) and /n/, /o/, /m/, /b/, /r/, and /e/ for "nombre" (*name*).

Once phonemes are recognized from each signal segment, the detection of words becomes our final task at this layer. It seems reasonable to think that a sequence of phonemes forms a word, but some words may not be correctly formed since the presence of noise in the feature extraction process may lead to the recognition of false positive or false negative phonemes. Since we are interested in obtaining dictionaryvalid words only, we approximate each word, formed by a sequence of phonemes, to the most similar word in a dictionary by using the *edit distance* as similarity function.

3.2 Syntactic Component

We have obtained a sequence of valid words from the previous lexical component. In the syntactic component, we employ a lightweight grammar to discover the syntactical

Fig. 2: Illustration of the SOM after the training and calibration process. Note that some neurons have learned certain phonemes. For example, the phonemes 'ñ', 'y' and 'z' are treated differently from others in Spanish due to their unique pronounciation. These phonemes are located, individually or together, in clusters isolated from other phonemes.

class of each word such as noun, verb, determiner, and adjective from the given word sequence.

There are different types of grammars that define a language such as context-free, context-sensitive, deterministic, and non-deterministic. Although all natural languages can be easily represented by context-sensitive grammars which enable simpler production rules than other types of grammar, the problem of detecting if a language is generated by a context-sensitive grammar is *PSPACE-complete* [20], making it impractical to program such a language. In contrast to context-sensitive grammars, context-free and deterministic grammars (Type-2 in the Chomsky hierarchy) are feasible in programming without generating ambiguous languages and can be recognized in linear time by a finite state machine. Thus, we propose a context-free, deterministic grammar to process the word sequence. The proposed grammar is shown in Figure 3 by means of the Backus-Naur Form notation. The production rules in the grammar identify the syntactical class of each word.

Example 3. By applying the proposed grammar to the words found in the user query sentence, we obtain the class of each word as follows: *recuperar (retrieve:verb), el (the:determiner), nombre (name:noun), el (the:determiner), curso (course:noun), y (and:copulative-conjunction), la (the:article), nota (grade:noun), de (of:preposition), los (the:determiner), estudiantes (students:noun), que (that:preposition), tienen (have:verb), un (a:determiner), profesor (lecturer:noun), el (the:determiner), cual (which:preposition), les (them:determiner), enseña (teach:verb), un (a:determiner), curso (course:noun).* !

3.3 Semantic Component

In our work, user queries given in the voice stream data are recognized as especial query events from the sequence of (word:class) pairs generated by the syntactic component. For this purpose, we propose an event model as follows:

Definition 1 (user query event) A user query is an event that consists of five event attributes

<What, Where, Who, When, Why>

such that

1. *What* denotes the target action specified in the given query such as to retrieve, insert, delete, or update information,
2. *Where* denotes the set of data sources implied in the query,
3. *Who* denotes the set of attributes that are presented in the query,
4. *When* denotes the temporal aspect of the query (optional), and
5. *Why* denotes a description of the query (optional). !

The role of the *what, where* and *who* event attributes are self-explanatory in the definition. The distance between user queries with respect to time, i.e., the *when* event attribute, seems irrelevant in our context since we are focusing on detecting a single

```
MESSAGE -$ verb DIRECTOBJECT
DIRECTOBJECT -$ determiner DETERMINER1
DETERMINER1 -$ determiner DETERMINER2
DETERMINER1 -$ adverb ADVERB1
DETERMINER1 -$ adjective ADJECTIVE1
DETERMINER1 -$ noun NAME1
DETERMINER2 -$ noun NAME1
ADVERB1 -$ adjective ADJECTIVE1
ADJECTIVE1 -$ noun NAME1
ADJECTIVE1 -$ preposition INDIRECTOBJECT
NAME1 -$ . END
NAME1 -$ adjective ADJECTIVE1
NAME1 -$ adverb ADVERB1
NAME1 -$ and ENDLISTOFNAMES
NAME1 -$ adjective ADJECTIVE1
NAME1 -$ preposition INDIRECTOBJECT
NAME1 -$ comparative COMPARATIVE1
NAME1 -$ relative-pronoun CONJUNCTION1
NAME1 -$ copulative-conjunction CONJUNCTION2
NAME1 -$ relative-conjunction NAME2
NAME1 -$ determiner DETERMINER1
ENDLISTOFNAMES -$ determiner determiner1
COMPARATIVE1 -$ to NAME1
COMPARATIVE1 -$ than NAME1
CONJUNCTION2 -$ verb DIRECTOBJECT
CONJUNCTION2 -$ relative-conjunction NAME2
CONJUNCTION2 -$ relative-pronoun CONJUNCTION1
INDIRECTOBJECT -$ the THE1
INDIRECTOBJECT -$ noun NAME1
THE1 -$ table TABLE
TABLE -$ noun NAME1
NAME2 -$ noun CONJUNCTION1
CONJUNCTION1 -$ bool BOOL1
CONJUNCTION1 -$ auxiliary-verb AUXILIARYVERB
CONJUNCTION1 -$ verb VERB1
BOOL1 -$ verb VERB1
AUXILIARYVERB -$ verb VERB1
VERB1 -$ determiner DETERMINER1
VERB1 -$ adjective ADJECTIVE1
VERB1 -$ noun NAME1
```

Fig. 3. The grammar used to detect the role of each word

query event from a voice input. Note also that the *why* event attribute should be defined ideally as an unambiguous description of the user query to be useful. One way is through adopting a canonical definition of an event as many authors have considered canonical representations of natural language [21, 22] with the goal of reducing the ambiguity in meaning. Canonical representations often require a semantic analysis which identifies the roles of entities and the relationships between the entities, and an analysis of the domain where these entities are defined. Although each user query can be described in a canonical form, the detailed description of each query and their corresponding semantic analysis are currently beyond the scope of our work. Thus, we model a user query event with three obligatory attributes: *what, where* and *who* leaving the other two attributes *why* and *when* optional. Finally, the meaning of a missing or unknown attribute is *any* by default in our work.

Event Detection Intuitively, a user query event is an action that responds to a user goal (**what**) performed on a set of attributes (**who**) that belong to certain database entities (where) at a particular time (**when**) with intuitive description of the query (**why**). The degree of equivalence among different query events is measured by the user's intention expressed in these event attributes. Hence, a query event recognition consists of the recognition of these event attributes in the (word:class) stream generated at the syntactic layer, i.e., (w_1, c_1), (w_2, c_2), . . ., (w_n, c_n) where w_i is a word and c_i is the syntactic class of w_i. The query event model serves as a template for a user query in this process. We present the essence of our event attribute detection approach below without presenting the complete list of linguistic rules used in our work.

- Detection of *what*: The detection of a *what* attribute is accomplished by finding the verbs that are likely used to express a query action, such as *retrieve, enumerate, show, calculate, list, select*, etc. We maintain a controlled set of such words in our approach.

- Detection of *who*: The *who* attribute is detected by finding the following patterns:

• *<verb>* [*<determiner>*]* *<noun>* *<preposition>*
• *<verb>* [*<determiner>*]* *<noun>* *<comparative>*
• *<verb>* [*<determiner>*]* *<ad jective>* *<noun>*

where !*verb*" is the one used to detect a *what* attribute above. If the (word:class) stream matches any of the patterns above, the *noun* word in the stream is likely the *who* event attribute.

- Detection of *where*: The word '*table*' is a strong indication for a data source in the user query. In such a case, nouns following the word '*table*' are taken as dana source names. Otherwise, those nouns which occur after the *who* nouns in a close proximity are considered as the data sources.

We demonstrate the query event detection process in the following example.

Example 4. Consider the following (word:class) stream to illustrate the detection of the *who* event attribute from it.

(Retrieve:verb), (the:determiner), (name:noun) (of:preposition) (the:determiner), (students:noun) (which:preposition), (take:verb), (the:determiner), (course:noun), (of:preposition), (cs203:noun), (with:preposition), (age:noun), (greater than:comparative), (twenty:noun), (and:copulative-conjunction), (that:preposition), (have:verb), (the:determiner), (best:adjective), (grades:noun).

From the (word:class) stream, the following *who* attributes are detected accordingly:

1. The pattern !*noun*" !*preposition*" !*noun*" in conjunction with "course of cs203" yields the expression course = 'cs203' as the preposition 'of' is translated to '='.

2. The pattern !*noun*" !*comparative*" !*noun*" found in "age greater than 21" yields the expression: age > 'twenty'. Additional comparatives *greater than*, *less than*, *equal to*, and *different from* are interpreted as >, <, =, and ! respectively.

3. The pattern !*ad jective*" !*noun*" matches "best grades" in the word stream. In our work, this pattern yields an SQL expression invoking the user-defined function MAX(grades). However, since the meaning of an adjective frequently depends on the context, it is difficult to translate it to an SQL expression without consulting with the context. In our present work, we assume that the context is given.

User Query Specification The underlying structure of query events detected can be represented in XML. Queries expressed in XML format have the advantage of being independent of the language (whether natural or SQL language) and allow us to share query events and subsequently the embedded data in the events across different information systems. In XML, we can define the structure of query events by the following Document Type Definition (DTD):

```
<!ELEMENT QUERIES (QUERY)*>
<!ELEMENT QUERY (WHAT)>
<!ELEMENT WHAT (TEXT, WHERE+, WHEN?, WHY?)>
<!ELEMENT WHERE (TEXT, WHO+)>
<!ELEMENT WHO (TEXT)>
<!ELEMENT WHEN (TEXT)>
<!ELEMENT WHY (TEXT)>
<!ELEMENT TEXT (#PCDATA)>
```

We now show an example of how a query in natural language can be rewritten as a query event using the XML DTD presented above.

Example 5. Consider the following user query again presented in Example 1:

Retrieve the name, the course, and the grade of the students that have a lecturer which teach them a course.

The event associated to this query in expressed in XML as follows.

```
<?xml version="1.0"?>
<QUERIES>
  <QUERY>
    <WHAT><TEXT>Retrieve</TEXT>
      <WHERE><TEXT>Students</TEXT>
        <WHO><TEXT>Name</TEXT>
        <WHO><TEXT>Course</TEXT>
        <WHO><TEXT>Grade</TEXT>
      </WHERE>
      <WHERE><TEXT>Lecturer</TEXT>
        <WHO><TEXT>Name</TEXT>
        <WHO><TEXT>Course</TEXT>
      </WHERE>
      <WHY><TEXT>if is(y, lecturer(y)) and is(x, student(x))
```

```
            then SELECT(<name, course, grade> in x
            such that teach(y, x))</TEXT>
        </WHY>
    </WHAT>
  </QUERY>
</QUERIES>
```

in which the *why* attribute is manually made up for a demonstration purpose.

Note that the query event DTD implies hierarchical relationships among the event attributes: the *what* attribute is the highest container which contains *where* attributes which, in turn, contain *who* attributes. The *when* and *why* attributes are optional.

As we add instances of attributes to the *what* container, the query becomes more specific. This idea is captured in Figure 4. In the figure, we make the general query goal, *retrieve*, more specific by adding two *where* attributes with values *students* and *lecturer*. The same query becomes even more specific by adding *name*, *course* and *grade* as *who* attributes. An addition of *when* and *why* will further increase the level of specificity of the query.

Moreover, if two events *e*1 and *e*2 have the same hierarchy structure, we can perform an *algebraic operation* over them to produce a new event which is likely of a different level of specificity. For example, *e*1 % *e*2 may yield the union or intersection of the two events depending on the definition of %. Figure 5 illustrates the union of the two following query operations:

- *Retrieve the id, name, and course values from the students table.*
- *Retrieve the id, course, grade and lecturer values from the students table.*

4. Prototype

We developed a software prototype, called Voice2SQL as shown in Figure 6, to demonstrate the proposed query event identification approach and tested it with a number of queries spoken in Spanish.

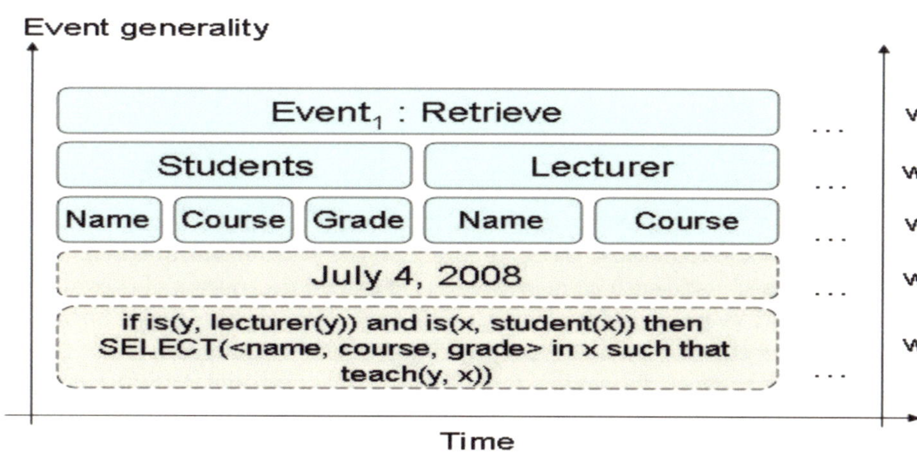

Fig. 4. The hierarchy implied among the event attributes in our event model. As more attributes are added to the general *what* attribute, the query becomes more specific.

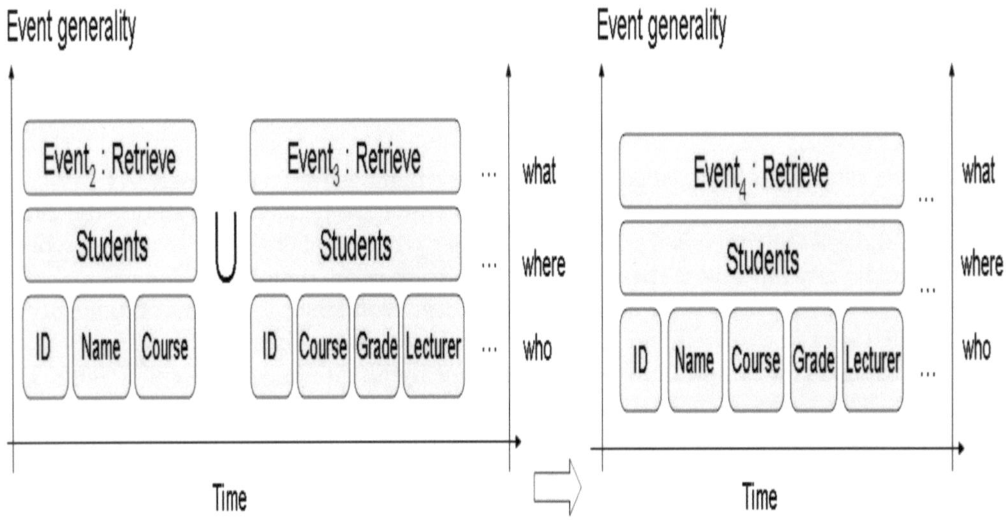

Fig. 5. Union of two query events in the proposed event model (*e*4 = *e*2 & *e*3). In this case, each event represents a query operation in the database and the result of the union of *e*2 and *e*3 is *e*4.

The upper part of Voice2SQL in Figure 6 shows the pseudo-SQL expression obtained from the natural language query in Spanish: "Calcular el nombre y la nota de los alumnos de el curso de redes cuya ciudad sea igual a Arequipa de la tabla registros" which is equivalent to "Recover the name and the grade of the students of the course of network whose city is Arequipa from the table records" in English. From the user query, Voice2SQL generates the SQL expression shown in the lower part: "CALCULAR nombre, nota WHERE curso = redes AND ciudad = arequipa AND son(alumnos) FROM registros" which is equivalent to "SELECT name, grade WHERE course = 'networking' AND city = 'arequipa' AND are(students) FROM records" in English. Additional examples of Spanish user queries that have been translated successfully by Voice2SQL are also provided in Table 2 in English.

5. Conclusion

We have presented in this chapter an approach to translate queries in spoken natural language to queries in SQL to increase the level of human-computer interaction in database access. Our focus in developing such an approach was to extend the concept of user queries as the presence of query events in the user speech. A formal query event model is presented together with a software prototype of the proposed approach. The proposed event model finds a correspondence between queries in a spoken natural language and the SQL language by studying the common linguistic components that are present in both languages. The proposed approach was moderately evaluated by developing a software prototype. A rigid, large scale evaluation is necessary to validate the benefit of the proposed event model and query event identification.

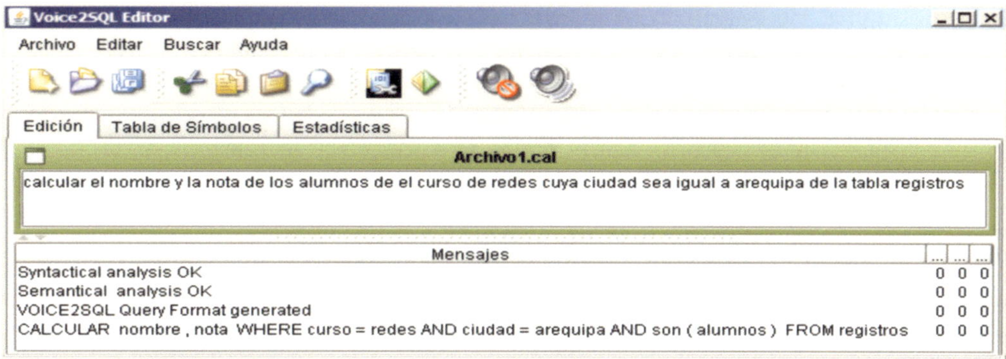

Fig. 6. Voice2SQL GUI. The upper part shows the input user query and the lower part shows the pseudo-SQL expression produced by Voice2SQL.

Spoken user query	SQL generated by Voice2SQL
Calculate the average mark in the students of the course of AI	SELECT AVG(Mark) FROM students WHERE course = 'AI';
Select the students of fifth cycle that are not registered in the course of AI	SELECT * FROM students WHERE course <> 'AI' AND cycle = 5;
Enumerate the approved students in the course of AI	SELECT * FROM students WHERE course = 'AI' AND approved(students);
Select the students of fifth cycle that are not registered in the course of AI	SELECT * FROM students WHERE course <> 'AI' AND cycle = 5;

Table 2: Query examples processed by Voice2SQL.

6. References

T. Kahveci and A. K. Singh, "Efficient index structures for string databases," in *Proceedings of the 27th International Conference on Very Large Data Bases*, San Francisco, CA, USA, 2001, pp. 351–360.

Y. Li, H. Yang, and H. V. Jagadish, "NaLIX: A generic natural language search environment for XML data," *ACM Transactions on Database Systems*, vol. 32, no. 4, p. 30, 2007.

A. Witkowski, S. Bellamkonda, T. Bozkaya, N. Folkert, A. Gupta, J. Haydu, L. Sheng, and S. Subramanian, "Advanced SQL modeling in RDBMS," *ACM Transactions on Database Systems*, vol. 30, no. 1, pp. 83–121, 2005.

P. Merlo and S. Stevenson, "Automatic verb classification based on statistical distributions of argument structure," *Computational Linguistics*, vol. 27, no. 3, pp. 373–408, 2001.

S. Polyviou, G. Samaras, and P. Evripidou, "A relationally complete visual query language for heterogeneous data sources and pervasive querying," in *Proceedings of the 21st International Conference on Data Engineering*, April 2005, pp. 471–482.

R. Harrathi and S. Calabretto, "A query graph for visual querying structured documents," in *Proceedings of the 2nd International Conference on Digital Information Management.*, vol. 1, 2007, pp. 116–120.

L. Aversano, G. Canfora, A. D. Lucia, and S. Stefanucci, "Understanding SQL through iconic interfaces," in *Proceedings of the 26th International Computer Software and Applications Conference on Prolonging Software Life*, Washington, DC, USA, 2002, pp. 703–710.

T. Catarci and G. Santucci, "Diagrammatic vs textual query languages: a comparative experiment," in *Proceedings of the 3rd IFIP Working Conference on Visual Database Systems 3 (VDB-3)*, London, UK, UK, 1995, pp. 69–83.

S. Harada, J. O.Wobbrock, and J. A. Landay, "Voicedraw: a hands-free voice-driven drawing application for people with motor impairments," in *Proceedings of the 9th international ACM SIGACCESS Conference on Computers and Accessibility*, New York, NY, USA, 2007, pp. 27–34.

C. D. Wickens and J. G. Hollands, *Engineering Psychology and Human Performance (3rd Edition)*. Prentice Hall, September 1999.

"Merriam-Webster dictionary," http://www.merriam-webster.com, 2008.

R. C. F. Tucker, M. Hickey, and N. Haddock, "Speech-as-data technologies for personal information devices," *Personal and Ubiquitous Computing*, vol. 7, no. 1, pp. 22–29, 2003.

H. Xie, P. Andreae, M. Zhang, and P. Warren, "Learning models for English speech recognition," in *Proceedings of the 27th Australasian Conference on Computer Science*. Darlinghurst, Australia, Australia: Australian Computer Society, Inc., 2004, pp. 323–329.

D. Ponceleon and S. Srinivasan, "Structure and content-based segmentation of speech transcripts," in *Proceedings of the 24th Annual International ACM SIGIR Conference on Research and Development in Information Retrieval*. New York, NY, USA: ACM, 2001, pp. 404–405.

G. Antoniol, V. F. Rollo, and G. Venturi, "Linear predictive coding and Cepstrum coefficients for mining time variant information from software repositories," *ACM SIGSOFT Software Engineering Notes*, vol. 30, no. 4, pp. 1–5, 2005.

E. H. C. Choi, "On compensating the Mel-frequency Cepstral coefficients for noisy speech recognition," in *Proceedings of the 29th Australasian Computer Science Conference*, Darlinghurst, Australia, Australia, 2006, pp. 49–54.

H. Hermansky and N. Morgan, "RASTA processing of speech," *IEEE Transactions on Speech and Acoustics*, vol. 2, pp. 587–589, October 1994.

T. Ganchev, N. Fakotakis, and G. Kokkinakis, "Comparative evaluation of various MFCC implementations on the speaker verification task," in *Proceedings of the International Conference Speech and Computer*, vol. 1, 2005, pp. 191–194.

O. U. Florez and S. Lim, "A spoken natural language-based interface for querying SQL databases," *International Journal of Information Technology and Intelligent Computing (to appear)*, 2008.

J. Zhu, "Towards scalable flow and context sensitive pointer analysis," in *Proceedings of the 42nd Annual Conference on Design Automation*. New York, NY, USA: ACM, 2005, pp. 831–836.

S. Wintner, "Formal language theory for natural language processing," in *Proceedings of the ACL-02 Workshop on Effective Tools and Methodologies for Teaching Natural Language Processing and Computational Linguistics*. Morristown, NJ, USA: Association for Computational Linguistics, 2002, pp. 71–76.

S. Nirenburg and V. Raskin, "Ontological semantics, formal ontology, and ambiguity," in *Proceedings of the International Conference on Formal Ontology in Information Systems*. New York, NY, USA: ACM, 2001, pp. 151–161.

14

HCI Design Patterns for Mobile Applications Applied to Cultural Environments

R. Tesoriero, J. A. Gallud, M. D. Lozano & V. M. R. Penichet
University of Castilla-La Mancha
Albacete, Spain

1. Introduction

Nowadays, mobile activities such as entertainment, commerce (m-commerce) or learning (m-learning) are being increasingly adopted by people. A new activity being explored in mobile computing is the support of Augmented and Immersive Reality (A&IR) features on public physical spaces (shops, libraries, museums, etc). The adoption of these new technologies is due to the physical space constraints to display information and the information media support restriction to text and images, because synchronous media, as audio and video, are difficult to play in public spaces (people must be "synchronized" at the beginning of the reproduction to be meaningful). This situation is very common in museums and art expositions. Each art piece has lots of information associated to it, but only a small part of this information is available to visitors.

People in charge of museums and libraries started using electronic technology more than 20 years ago. It began with electronic libraries and was intensified with the introduction of Web technologies offering new opportunities to open up the walls of the museum to the world (Schweibenz, 1999) (Dolgos, 1999) (Falk & Dierking, 1992) (Jackson, 1998) (McKenzie, 1998). Some authors (Léger, 2004) (Georgiev et al., 2004) (Elliot & Phillips, 2004) (Gary & Simon, 2002) suggest that m-commerce and m-learning are the "next step" of Web applications. This tendency will be soon reflected on museum electronic guides. Following the emerging notation, we refer to this kind of applications as m-space applications (mobile applications for physical spaces).

The application of mobile technologies to museums and exhibition environments has been an area of special research interest in the last years. There are numerous approaches and applications that employ location awareness techniques to retrieve information from art pieces and exhibition rooms (Bristow et al., 2002) (Ciavarella & Paternò, 2004) (Gallud et al., 2005). Although some of these approaches seem to be suitable for small museums, it may result expensive in large deployments.

In this sense, we propose an alternative approach to location-aware applications based on an intuitive classic user interface that allows visitors to retrieve information from the physical environment. This alternative is based on HCI design patterns because they seem to be the appropriate tool to solve recurrent problems in this area. This proposal can be used together

with different cultural space solutions or location awareness techniques. A particular solution is employed to evaluate the catalogue of interaction design patterns proposed.
Thus, this chapter starts presenting related work in museums guides and design patterns. Sections 3, 4, 5, 6 and 7 expose a catalogue of HCI design patterns organized in categories. Later, in section 8, we describe how patterns are applied in a real scenario and an evaluation of the improvements based on design patterns is presented. Finally, we expose the conclusions and future work.

2. Related Work

This section exposes the origins of the application of design patterns to the computer science discipline. Then we present a set of HCI design patterns catalogues that are related to our work. Next, we define a mobile design patterns catalogue. Finally we present our conclusions about previous works.
In the late seventies Christopher Alexander (Alexander et al., 1977) studied how people interacted with physical spaces and found a new method of architecture and scheduling. Alexander exposes that life is about patterns of events and the architecture that supports these patterns help us to feel better.
Alexander said that "A pattern language is really nothing more than a precise way of describing someone's experience of building".
Alexander kept these observations using a format, known as "design pattern". Thus, a design pattern summarizes the context of a problem and its solution. It should be concrete enough to be used as a rule of thumb with good results, and yet sufficiently abstract to be applied to countless situations. So a "pattern language" is a group of "design patterns".
However, the concept of pattern languages was firstly adopted by the programming community in computer science. The most important contribution in this field is the book "Design Patterns: Abstraction and Reuse in Object-Oriented Designs" (Gamma, E. et al, 1995). The book describes solutions to common software design problems defining four essential elements that feature design patterns.
The **name** of the pattern identifies it and is used to describe a design problem, the solutions and the consequences in a word or two. Giving names to patterns increases vocabulary and allows us to get a higher level of abstraction. The **problem** describes when the pattern should be applied explaining the problem and the context it solves. The **solution** describes the elements that are part of the design, the responsibilities and collaborations. It does not describe a concrete solution; it is like a template that can be applied in different situations. The **consequences** are the result of applying the pattern to solve a problem. They expose the advantages and disadvantages of the solution proposed. They also include the impact on flexibility, extensibility and portability of the system.
This work groups patterns on categories according to the problem they solve. It defines three categories: creational patterns, structural patterns and behavioural patterns. Each pattern belongs to only one category.
Communities related to HCI adopted Alexander ideas too. One of the first attempts to define design pattern collections applied on HCI was the book "Common ground: A Pattern Language for Human-Computer Interface Design" (Tidwell, 1999).

These general purpose patterns were loosely coupled. It means that each pattern may belong to more than one category. To organize them they were grouped into primary patterns and sublanguages.

There are primary patterns related to content and actions. There are also patterns related to the deployment of content and actions, and patterns that describe the basic form of content and actions, how available actions are shown to the user, how the space and user attention are used, how the content is organized in working surfaces, how the user is able to navigate, what are the actions the user is able to carry out, how the user is able to modify the interface, how to achieve a clean and attractive interface and how the interface is able to support user tasks.

An evolution of this seminal work was published in a new book entitled "Designing Interfaces: Patterns for effective Interaction Design" (Tidwell, 2005). This publication presents patterns in a general way, organized in "pattern languages".

She grouped patterns according to the function they perform on the interface, as follows: organizing the content, getting around, organizing the page, commands and actions, showing complex data, getting input from users, builders and editors and making it look good.

Other collections and languages followed, for instance, Martijn van Welie's work "Interaction Design Patterns" (van Welie & Trætteberg, 2000). In this case patterns were organized according to interface types (Web Design Patterns, GUI Design Patterns and Mobile UI Design Patterns). Within these categories, these patterns are grouped by the functionality they provide. These patterns are close related to the usability concepts: visibility, affordance, natural mapping, constraints, conceptual models, feedback, security and flexibility.

In (van Walie et al., 1999) there are some usability conditions that are related to learnability, memory, performance, error rate, satisfaction and task completeness. According to these indicators, to describe a design pattern the following elements are used: the problem that is related to categories defined by (Norman, 1988), the usability principle that was also defined by (Norman, 1988), visibility, affordance, constraints, models, feedback, security, flexibility, context, solution, rationality, performance, learnability, memory, satisfaction, completeness rate, errors and samples.

Another interesting book related to patterns in HCI (Borchers, 2001) and recently a complete collection of patterns oriented to Web site applications by the same author.

Design patterns were also applied to mobile applications. For instance, in (Roth, 2002) Roth defined classes of patterns (as pattern languages or categories) related to mobile interaction. He groups patterns in the following classes: security, authentication, streaming, mobile service, mobile code, mobile data and user interface. Within the UserInterfaces class, he grouped patterns related to UI interaction patterns of mobile applications.

Design patterns are the natural choice to represent a generic solution in the design of user interfaces related to mobile applications for cultural spaces because: (a) The domain model of the problem we want to solve is closely related to architectural problems, the origin of design patterns, (b) They have been successfully applied in computer science for years and they have proved to be a good solution to common problems and (c) Design patterns are also applied in two fields that are closely related to the one we tackle, the HCI and mobile computing field.

Based on these facts and the need to solve the problem of designing an intuitive and natural interface that allows users to retrieve information from the environment though a mobile device, it is logical to think about defining design patterns for mobile devices to browse information related to physical objects in physical spaces.
In the next section we present our proposal of HCI mobile design patterns.

3. HCI Mobile Design Patterns for m-space applications

Before introducing design patterns, we will introduce the concept of m-space applications. These applications are a subset of mobile applications that are designed to browse information related to physical spaces (buildings, floors, rooms, halls, etc.) and the objects that these spaces contain.
Examples of this kind of applications are the museum tour guides. These guides show information about the art pieces the museum exhibits.
In this section we present the characteristics of design patterns for m-space applications.
Patterns emerge from the experience of solving problems in real scenarios. We have based the construction of this pattern catalogue on usability evaluations (Tesoriero, 2007) performed in a real m-space system, the Cutlery Museum of Albacete or MCA (Gallud, 2005).
Analyzing the usability evaluations, we detected some problems related to HCI using a PDA running in the MCA system. To solve these problems we designed a brand new user interface.
From this interface design, we extracted a set of HCI design patterns that were defined to solve related to the design of m-space applications. These patters were introduced in (Tesoriero et al., 2007c).
Mobile devices do not have the processing power neither the screen resolution of desktop computers, so the information to be presented to the user should be carefully organized.
Some advantages of implementing m-space systems are:

- **The improvement of information availability in physical spaces**: Information that is not available in a physical form (a text panel or a photo) may be so virtually.
- **The provision of physical context to the information**: The information is easily assimilated if there is a physical representation that is associated to it.
- **Information update**: Information is easily updated in a virtual form. For instance, it is cheaper and quicker to change the information stored in a database than the information displayed in a text panel.

Examples of public spaces that can take advantage of this type of applications are museums, libraries, shops etc.
When building these applications, there are some aspects that should be carefully designed to keep the application simple, intuitive and easy to use. Based on our experience we have summarized the findings and the lessons learned in the following list:

- It is vital to reflect the user position and orientation into the interface to keep the virtual/physical synchronization between the real and virtual location of the user.
- Mobile devices should be manipulated with the least possible effort because users usually are manipulating other objects while using the device.

- People should be able to use their own mobile devices as a guide in physical spaces. Additional information about users may be used to guide them across buildings and rooms.
- Accessibility is a key issue to tackle because mobile devices may become a powerful tool that may help disabled people to interact with the environment.

Once we have talked about the aspects covered by this pattern catalogue, we will describe how these patterns are documented.

We have based the design patterns description on the one given by Roth (Roth, 2002) that is indeed based on Gamma's description.

The elements were used to describe these patterns were:

- **Name**: The name of the pattern should indicate the problem and proposed solution in one or two words.
- **Synopsis**: It is a brief description of the pattern.
- **Context**: Describes the problem to be solved.
- **Solution**: Describes the proposed solution.
- **Consequences**: Describes the advantages and disadvantages of applying this pattern.
- **Schematic Description**: Most patterns described in this catalogue have a generic graphical representation that is represented in this section.
- **Related Patterns**: This section is used to relate patterns of this or other catalogues. We have included relationships to W3C Common Sense Suggestions for Developing Multimodal User Interfaces principles (W3C, 2006), Tidwell's sublanguages (Tidwell, J., 1999)(Tidwell, J., 2005) and Van Welie's patterns[1] (Van Welie, M. & Trætteberg, H., 2000).

We have kept Gamma terminology using the term Category to describe groups of patterns. And we have also found more useful the classification of patterns where each pattern belongs to just one category.

Each category represents a set of related problems. In this sense, we defined four categories as follows:

- **Location**: The set of patterns to keep people situated within the physical space.
- **Layout**: Patterns proposed in this category expose different interface organizations to cope with mobile device screen resolution restrictions.
- **Routing**: These patterns guide users through a physical space.
- **Accessibility**: These patterns help disabled people to explore physical spaces.

The detailed explanation of each design pattern category will be described in sections 4, 5, 6 and 7.

4. Location Patterns

Public spaces, as museums and art exhibitions, are usually visited by people that have not been there before. So, usually they get a feeling of insecurity when visiting these places because they are going through an unfamiliar place.

---

[1] http://www.welie.com

This feeling should be minimized in order to improve user experience into these spaces. To cope with this feeling, mechanisms that improve people knowledge of the place should be provided.

There are many alternatives to achieve these improvements and the most common are web pages, maps and panels. Web pages are good alternative to those people that plan their visit, but it is not practical to those that perform ad-hoc visits. Maps seem to be a good alternative for small spaces that do not have much information to show because they are small and easy to manipulate, but on large spaces and lots of information to expose, this alternative is not the best because of map dimensions. Finally, panels seem to be a good alternative because they are able to expose information about a specific space, and all the information is kept in context with the space it belongs to, but this information may not be available to all visitors because of space restrictions.

However, an application containing information about physical space can be deployed into visitors' mobile device to help them to know the place **while** they are visiting the space. Besides, as this information is displayed individually, a personalized view of the information may be provided to visitors.

To display information according to physical spaces, we have to use a metaphor that relates different levels of spaces (i.e. buildings, floors, rooms, etc.) each other. This relationship seems to be the "contains" relationship because buildings are composed by floors, floors are composed by rooms and halls, furniture is placed in rooms and halls, and each piece of furniture contains objects.

Thus, most of these patterns are based on this relationship to help users get oriented into an unknown space and get more familiar with it. They are used to make visitors aware of orientation and position within a physical space. They also tend to synchronize real space with virtual space creating a virtual representation into mobile device screen that could be easily matched to the real scenario.

4.1 Breadcrumbs

Synopsis: A marquee is used to identify a space into large sets of buildings or floors.

Context: M-space applications present information about a space or object into the mobile device screen. This information should be in context with the space that contains it to keep the user situated into the place.

Large spaces are difficult to explore because there are lots of places to see and most of them have a similar appearance. Consequently, visitors usually get lost.

Solution: This problem could be solved applying a simple concept that is present in our daily life, the address. When we have to locate a house, we usually identify it by its address (street, number, state, country and so on). So, the same idea is applied to physical spaces. For instance, buildings have names, floors have numbers, rooms or halls also have names or numbers, and showcases or concrete objects have a way to be identified too.

A simple implementation of this concept may be achieved by adding a small address bar on the top or bottom of the screen. This bar shows the path of names of the space levels that are required to get to the place is being represented on screen.

An address bar may be composed by the names, in text form, of spaces separated by a symbol that represents the relationship between neighbour spaces.

Besides, the low resolution of mobile device screens leads to a landscape based design to avoid using several rows to expose addresses.

Consequences: The first advantage of applying this pattern is the achievement of visitor location awareness in a simple and direct way. Spaces can be reviewed easily, because the user is able to uniquely name them. Besides, it is useful to perceive how far a user is from a place because any visitor can be aware of distances just by relating two addresses (i.e. two rooms are near if they are in the same floor). It also provides an easy way to identify places or objects to visitors when they are communicating experiences. Finally, as consequence of the last fact, when visitors have to reach a known place, the path name may be used as an implicit guide to reach the destination.
On the other hand, there are some disadvantages of this approach. For instance, it has a direct impact on the screen because it takes some space from screen, particularly when long addresses are needed. Thus, depending on screen resolution, it is probable that space names do not fit in one line.
An alternative to solve this problem is the addition of a second line, but we will be wasting space on information that is probably not used at all times (address information is useful but it should not be the centre of attention of users). Another alternative is based on displaying the lower level space names only, because they are more relevant to visitors; but we are not displaying the whole space context. And, close related to the last alternative is the possibility of including key controls to show this information (right-left, up-down), but buttons are really important resources, and they should not be used unless they were unused. Finally, we can propose a marquee based alternative where text is moving through bar. However, this alternative should not take too much attention of the user.

Schematic Description:

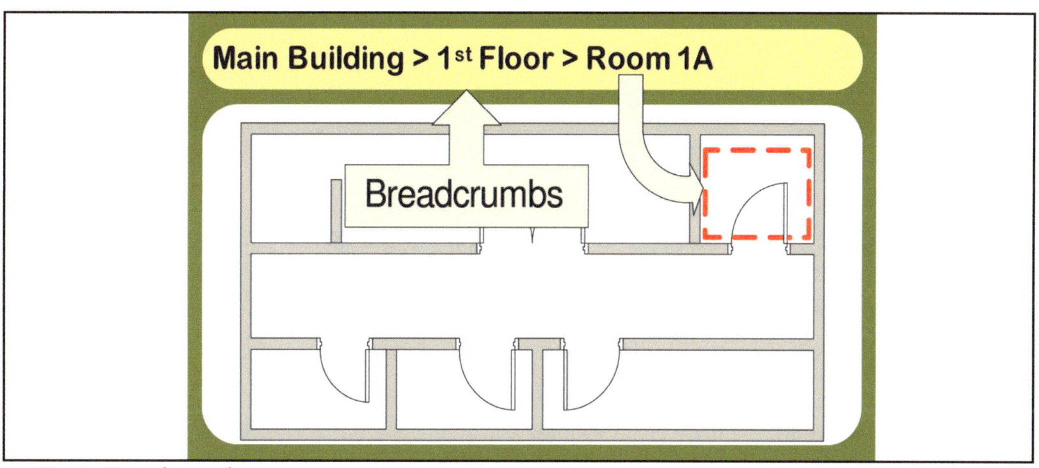

Fig. 1. Breadcrumbs

Related Patterns
Patterns in this catalogue: This pattern is related to Landscape because it provides

Breadcrumbs with a wider space to display path names. A graphical alternative to Breadcrumbs is Multi-Layer Map.
W3C Common Sense Suggestions for Developing Multimodal User Interfaces: This pattern focuses on two principles. The first one is the ability to communicate clearly, concisely, and consistently with users because the information is shown to the user in the same way through all spaces and synchronizes virtual and physical space in some way. The second principle is related to make user comfortable because: it always presents the current status of the system to the user, it also eases stress in the users' short-term memory, and it helps users to know where they are.
Tidwell's sublanguages: It is related to Go Back One Step, Go Back to a Safe Place and Navigable Spaces. Breadcrumbs pattern is used to navigate backwards, one step or any.
Van Welie's patterns: Breadcrumbs is related to its homonymous in Welie Web design patterns group because it is essentially the same idea applied to a physical space.

4.2 Multi-Layer Map

Synopsis: A set of small icons, photos or schemas are used to identify user location into the space.

Context: Some m-space applications are centred on space location (i.e. guide or map applications). It means that the information these applications provide is basically the location of something instead of information about something. When large spaces are composed by spaces that are similar in appearance, the user can easily get lost. Even more, if spaces are not identified. And these applications should avoid this situation. Besides, sometimes users do not know exactly what they are looking for and they just start browsing to find something interesting for them. So, to improve user location awareness a rich space representation is needed.

Solution: A solution to this problem may be based on showing a stack of sketches, images or icons that that represent each level of space hierarchy. This stack displays the path to the lower level space being showed on screen in a graphical way. Generally, it is enough to represent space levels in 2D. However, space representations may be expressed in 3D.

Consequences: The consequence of using this pattern is the possibility to locate objects or spaces in unnamed or unidentified locations, due to the expression richness of the representation. Another good consequence of applying this pattern is the provision to users with "virtual" and graphical distance perception because, if representation is scaled to real dimensions, the user perceives the distance between two points. This pattern can easily be adapted to portable device screen layout design because it can be placed horizontally, on the top or the bottom of screen; or vertically, on the left or on right of screen. Besides, if there is enough screen space and spaces have names assigned, a label indentifying them can be added accordingly to avoid user deducing it. It also provides users with the ability to perceive space neighbourhood. It is a very interesting tool for those that do not know exactly what they are looking for. The main disadvantage of this approach is the amount of screen space this representation takes from screen. It is only advisable if the location is the centre of the application, otherwise Breadcrumbs solution is preferable.

Schematic Description:

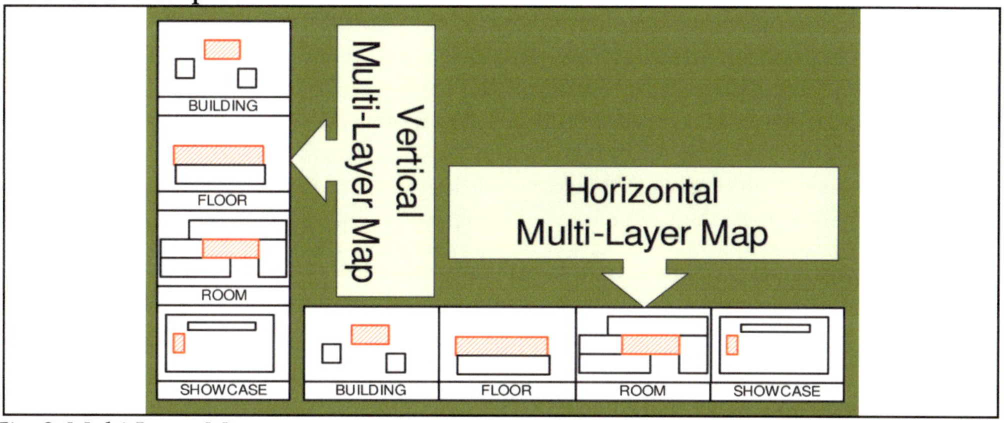

Fig. 2. Multi-Layer Map

Related Patterns

Patterns in this catalogue: It is close related to Breadcrumbs pattern because it performs the same functionality, but graphically. If *routes* pattern is applied, the next space to be visited can be easily shown.

W3C Common Sense Suggestions for Developing Multimodal User Interfaces: This pattern focuses on communicate clearly, concisely, and consistently with users because information is shown to the user in the same way through all spaces. It also synchronizes virtual and physical space in some way. It also makes user comfortable because it always present the current status of the system to users, it also eases stress in the users' short-term memory and it helps users to know where they are.

Tidwell's sublanguages: As this pattern is close related to Breadcrumbs, it is related to Go Back One Step, Go Back to a Safe Place and Navigable Spaces; and it provides a flexible way of navigating across spaces, because you are not showing a path, but nodes on the tree hierarchy.

Van Welie's patterns: This pattern is related to Breadcrumbs in Welie Web design pattern group because it is essentially the same idea applied to a physical space.

4.3 Door at Back (aka Exit)

Synopsis: A sign is drawn into a space representation is used to point the way used by the visitor to enter the space.

Context: There are two types of problems this pattern addresses. The first one is related to large spaces, where people spend lots of time exploring this area. As consequence, they get lost because they get focused on the content of this space instead of the location they are in. The second problem lays on space transitions. A space transition occurs when people pass through one space into another. If transitions occur between spaces that have similar appearance, the user may get confused and probably lost.

Solution: To represent spaces, maps are used. So due to screen resolution restrictions, spaces are represented in many screens that contain information about a portion of a map describing a space unit (a room, a floor, a building, etc) where users can select subspaces to browse information in them. The solution is based on a simple question that is asked when we get lost in any place: "How did we get in?" To answer this question, we can use the virtual map provided by the virtual device. It can easily provide us with a mark that points the entrance to the space. This mark should match to a physical sign to get the real point into the map at any time. The mark works as an automatic bookmark, when visitors enter to any space, the entrance is automatically bookmarked to go back any time they need it. It is also important to notice that when we come into a space it is preferable to have the entrance mark at the bottom of the map, so when users enters any space the map is automatically oriented according to users' location.

Consequences: The application of this pattern provides users with the ability to get oriented when a space transition occurs. They can match virtual and real scenarios at first sight as soon as they enter the space. Another advantage of applying this pattern is the support for user memory to remember a familiar point. The entrance point of any space is always a milestone providing short stops in the visit that are long enough to avoid keeping user attention more that the necessary, and short enough to avoid users to go a long way back in the visit. However, to implement this pattern, an icon to mark the entrance in the map should be provided. Therefore, the marks in the map may obscure it, even more in low resolution screens; they also may cover other interesting points in the map, and make the map more difficult to read.

Schematic Description:

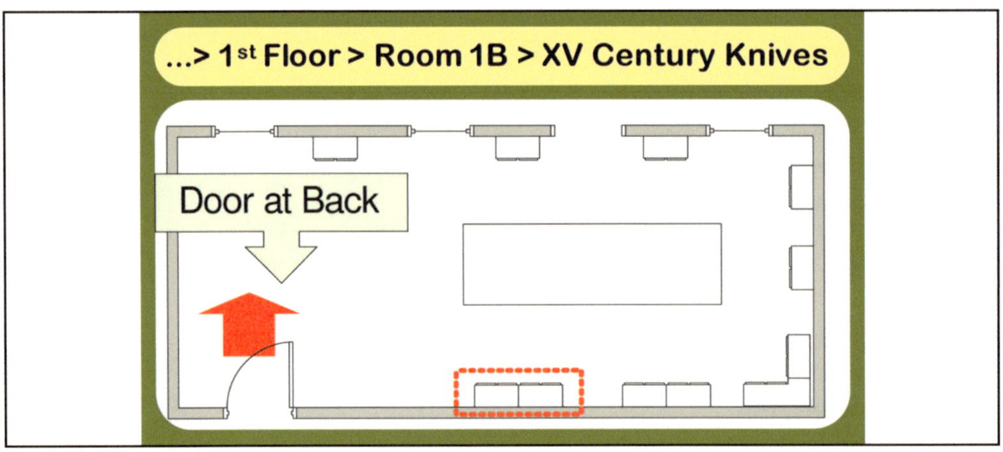

Fig. 3. Door at Back

Related Patterns

This catalogue patterns: This pattern can be used jointly with Breadcrumbs to help users to get oriented in a natural and intuitive way. Besides, it can be combined with layout patterns, such as Vertical-Horizontal layout to adapt screen layout to map shape and Layout Transitions to make users aware of layout changes. Finally, there is a close relationship between this pattern and Signs because they relate real and virtual spaces explicitly.

W3C Common Sense Suggestions for Developing Multimodal User Interfaces: There are three principles that are close related to this pattern. The first one focuses on Satisfying Real-world constraints, as physical and environmental suggestions, due to real space orientation is treated in this pattern. The second one is about communicating clearly, concisely, and consistently with users because a representative icon is placed in the screen to represent user entrance direction (i.e. an arrow). Finally, the third one makes users comfortable by easing users' short term memory because the icon helps users to get "back to the basics" when users enters a room.

Tidwell's sublanguages: The following sublanguages are related to this pattern definition: Go Back One step and Go Back to a Safe Place are related because the arrow is used as a way to go to a safe place and get the user oriented. It is also related to Bookmark because the entrance is automatically bookmarked as a safe place. And, at last, Remembered State because it signals the moment the user entered into the room.

Van Welie's patterns: This pattern can be related to Feedback because user gets oriented based on a previous known position and visibility to solve the user guidance problem. Besides, it improves the Learnability and Memorability aspects of the usability.

4.4 Signs

Synopsis: A real sign matches a virtual representation to the map to identify subspaces.

Context: On large spaces, as rooms or halls visitor may get lost because their attention is focused on the contents of the space. After a while, because of the lack of knowledge of the space, users get lost. Another problem arises when users are looking for something in large spaces filled with lots of objects. To find it they should be able to identify some subspaces within the space in order to locate the desired object. Finally, a common situation that usually affects visitors is getting lost in spaces that present a homogeneous appearance.

Solution: The solution to the proposed problem is based on the point of reference or neighbourhood idea. It means that we identify some places based on the relationship on a remarkable or known place; for instance, the house next to the bank, the statue in middle of the park, and so on. Mobile devices provides maps to identify spaces, so to identify subspaces (i.e. stops) within the space a set of signs is placed in different locations of a room or hall. These signs are also indentified in the map by iconic representations. Real signs may be labels, pictures or some remarkable object in the room or hall. Virtual icons representing these objects or signs should be representative of them, to ease the real to virtual matching to users.

Consequences: Users become aware of their own orientation/position virtually and physically just by looking both (the real and the virtual in the map) signs.

This pattern tends to reduce the gap time that users need to get oriented after spending a long time inside a space because the user can easily identify physical objects or location with a map representation in the mobile device screen, achieving A natural and intuitive user orientation. Users are guided across spaces by signals that do not need translation because they are represented in the same way into the map. Besides, if remarkable objects are used as signals, they are identified in the map easily, too. Visitors may use these signs to communicate object locations each other precisely because signals identify subspaces. A disadvantage of applying this pattern is the possibility to obscure the map with icons and remarkable objects representations. Another disadvantage is the possibility of polluting the physical environment visually with signs. However a solution to this problem is the use of remarkable objects instead of signs.

Schematic Description:

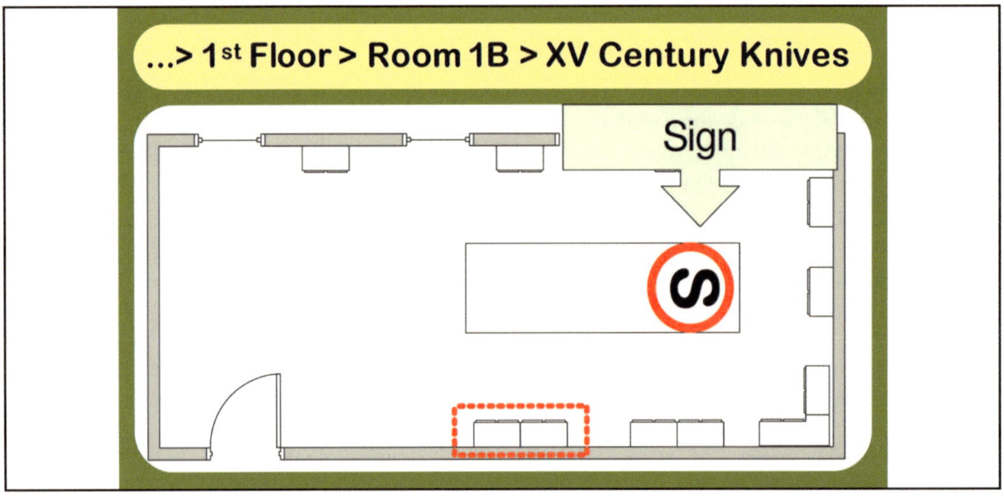

Fig. 4. Signs

Related Patterns

This catalogue patterns: This pattern is close related to Door at Back. The main difference lies on the space application level because Door at back is targeted to solve space transition awareness, and this pattern intent is to cope with long stays in the same space. As a location pattern, it is related to Breadcrumbs and Multi-Layer Map too. All these patterns can be combined providing users with powerful orientation tools.

W3C Common Sense Suggestions for Developing Multimodal User Interfaces: This pattern focuses on communicating clearly, concisely, and consistently with users because it synchronizes multiple modalities appropriately, the real and virtual one. It also makes users comfortable by advertising and suggesting using signs like landmarks, helping them to know where they are.

Tidwell's sublanguages: This pattern is related to Bookmark because it can be seen as a fixed bookmark in the space.

Van Welie's patterns: The only pattern related to this one is Like in Real World because it associates a real life object to a virtual one.

5. Layout HCI Design Patterns

Mobile devices have several resource restrictions compared to desktop computers. One of the low resolution of screen. As consequence, screen organization should be carefully designed. These patterns deal with this problem because they propose solutions to this common situation that usually arises when m-space applications are designed. They exploit screen dimensions according to the data that will be presented to users. Most solutions in this category are based on a dynamic layout adaptation of the UI components of the screen according to the data they should render. Screen layouts are usually based on two types of information, primary information and secondary information. Primary information is related to the goal of the screen, for instance showing information about an art piece or an object of user interest. On the other hand, secondary information is about information that is useful to the user, but it should not take user attention unless the user is really interested on it. An example of this type of information is awareness information. In order to optimize screen size and resolution, information type should be taken into account to modify screen layout and get the best results.

5.1 Landscape

Synopsis: It applies a landscape based interface design to implement m-space applications

Context: M-Space applications should provide users with information that is not usually available on traditional spaces, for instance, photo galleries, audio and video. Photos are usually wider than higher and videos are usually displayed in panoramic screens. However PDA applications are usually designed to run in portrait position. Besides, people that are visiting public spaces usually carry baggage and they have only one hand free to operate any device. Using a mobile device such as a PDA in portrait orientation requires the user to use both hands to use the keyboard.

Solution: The solution of these problems is the landscape design of mobile device user interfaces.

Consequences: The use of mobile devices in landscape position will provide users with the capability of take advantage of low screen resolution while seeing photos or watching videos. Besides, using PDA in landscape position allows users to hold the device and access cursor controls using one hand only. However, controls and application orientation must be synchronized for right and left handed people. Thus, up and down, and left and right buttons should be swapped to get desired behaviour. Finally, cursor keys are the best way to manipulate portable devices on one hand only and the use of mobile devices in landscape position allows it.

Schematic Description:

Fig. 5. Landscape

Related Patterns
This catalogue patterns: This pattern is closely related to Vertical - Horizontal Layout because the data to be displayed should be optimized to be shown on landscape format. It is also close related to Right-Left Handed Users, because cursor keys should be used by the most skilled hand of the user.
W3C Common Sense Suggestions for Developing Multimodal User Interfaces principles: This pattern focuses on Satisfy Real-World Constraints because most of media information is prepared to be presented on landscape format, so the best way to fit this information is by using this format on screen. Besides, it communicates clearly, concisely and consistently with the user by making the focus consistent across information media by using PDA in landscape position.

5.2 Vertical-Horizontal Layout

Synopsis: This pattern adapts screen layout according to importance of information level to optimize the screen size.

Context: Information to be displayed on portable device screens should be carefully presented to the user because screen resolution is low and screen dimensions are reduced. In this kind of systems, we can define two types of information to be displayed. The primary information fulfils the screen objective. On the other hand, secondary information provides additional information to perform other operations. Primary information shape and size varies; for instance there are photos that should be displayed in portrait or landscape position, videos are usually displayed in landscape position and text is preferably to be displayed in portrait position. So, how should we design the interface to cope with a multimodal interface?

Solution: To solve this problem, we captured the solution proposed by most of video players. When no video is being played, controls are the focus of the application. However, when a video is being played by the player, controls are hidden or they are placed at the bottom of the screen to avoid interference with user attention. In this case, when no video is being played, the primary information is represented by the player controls. On the other hand, when a video is being played, the primary information is represented by the video and secondary information is represented by player controls. The solution is based on laying out the interface according to the shape and size of the primary information. And to optimize screen visualization for main information, screen layout is changed to fit main information the best way as possible. Secondary information is displayed "around" main information where space is available.

Consequences: Primary data information is optimized to fit screen and secondary information is displayed on available space. So, the interface displays the primary information the best way possible. However, secondary information is not sacrificed in pro of primary information space; instead it is placed on where it does not injuries primary information. A disadvantage that presents this approach is the possibility of the user to get confused when layout transformation is applied to interface. For instance, suppose that we are watching a photo in landscape position and we have breadcrumbs on the top, then we want to see a photo in landscape position, and title bar on the right. As consequence, the user may get disoriented with the interface, because same actions are in different places of the screen.

Schematic Description:

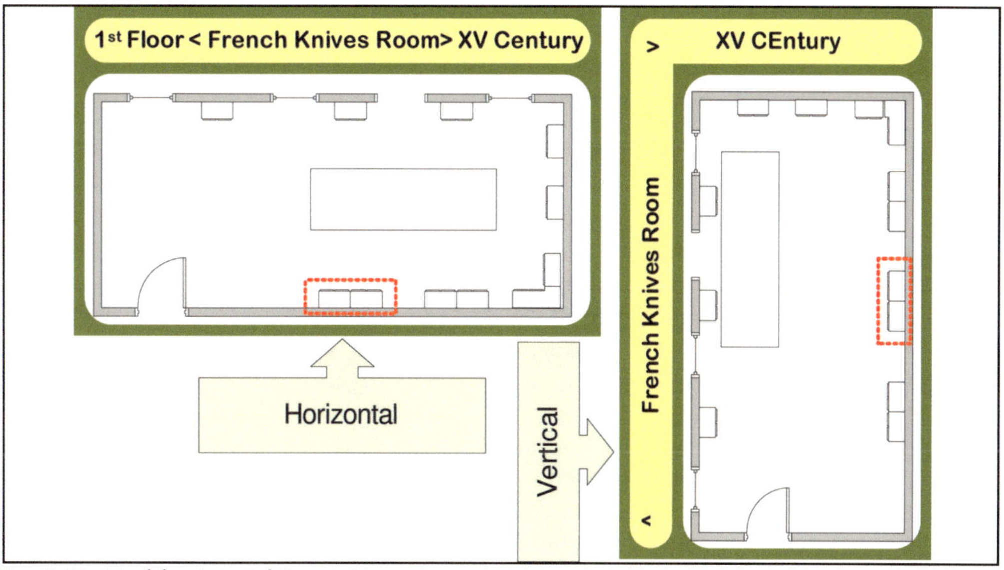

Fig. 6. Vertical-horizontal Layout

Related Patterns

This catalogue patterns: Because this pattern belongs to Layout category, it is close related to Landscape and Layout Transition. Landscape can be applied when video or photos in landscape position are displayed, and portrait when text is being displayed. To address the problem of transitions between different layouts, the Layout Transition can be applied.

W3C Common Sense Suggestions for Developing Multimodal User Interfaces: This pattern satisfies the ability to communicate clearly, concisely, and consistently with users by switching presentation modes when information is not easily presented in current mode. This pattern performs this operation based on primary information requirements. It also suggests keeping the interface as simple as possible because information layout is changed, keeping information to be displayed intact. Besides, this pattern makes users comfortable by reducing learning gap of a new user interface because information to be displayed is the same, only layout is changed.

Tidwell's sublanguages:_A sublanguage related to this pattern is Disabled Irrelevant things. Although secondary items are not disabled, they are not treated in the same level of relevance as primary information. Good Defaults sublanguage is also related to this pattern because information default layout changes according to primary information to be displayed.

5.3 Layout Transition

Synopsis: It gives feedback about layout transition to users.

Context: It is a good practice to keep information in the same screen zone to avoid users look for this information every time they need it. However, mobile devices have screen restrictions, so it is important to optimize screen space usage. One of the mechanisms to achieve this goal is the arrangement of data display components according to information to be displayed. However it causes user disorientation.

Solution: The solution is based on two ideas. The first one states that people learn how to operate something based on previous experience. That is to say, if they know how to read temperature from a car dashboard, it does not matter if is on top of speedometer or if it is at the bottom. The second one is based on the fact that people learn quicker when is able to see how a process is performed. As information is usually organized in panels, the layout usually affects these panels and the solution to the problem stated before is based on presenting users a smooth animation of affected panels, providing feedback about the new layout and information distribution of the application. There are many ways to achieve this commitment, for instance, panels may be stretched and enlarged until they get the desired shape. Another way to achieve this goal is using arrows that show the user what is going to happen with the interface.

Consequences: The first consequence of applying this pattern is the achievement of user confidence about what is going to happen with the application. It is really important to note that these transitions also save user learnability time because interface is not changing, it is being transformed. Interface is showing how information is arranged instead of letting users notice the change. However, it introduces a delay into HCI interactions. It is really worthy for beginners, but it may be a little annoying when when expert users are interacting with the application. It is recommendable to allow users enable and disable this application feature.

Schematic Description:

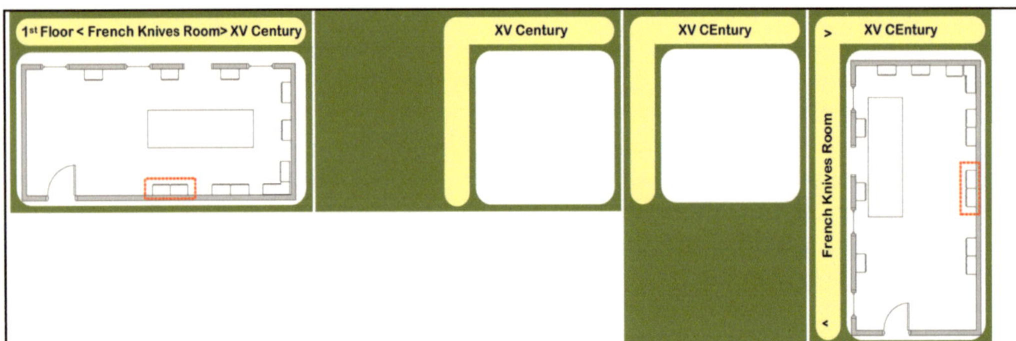

Fig. 7. Layout Transition

Related Patterns

This catalogue patterns: This pattern is very close related to Vertical - Horizontal Layout pattern because it proposes arranging UI components according to importance of information level.

W3C Common Sense Suggestions for Developing Multimodal User Interfaces: It accomplishes the advertising suggestion principle because it encourages the use of animations and sound to show transitions while organizing interfaces, stating that the use of these resources to get users' attention.
Tidwell's sublanguages: This pattern is mainly related to the Progress Indicator because screen layout transformation is a process that is being exposed to the user.

6. Routing HCI Design Patterns

M-space applications are designed to allow users to browse information related to the physical environment they are exploring. The browsing process is based on a metaphor that enables users to match objects and physical spaces to their virtual representation. In this case, we have to match this representation into a mobile device. Mobile devices have screen resolution and processing power restrictions that should be taken into account when virtual representations are used. Navigation across spaces should be natural and intuitive because if they find out that the use of the device is more complicated than performing the same tasks by themselves, the application will be futile. To carry out this goal we present this category of design patterns that groups patterns related to space navigation. These patterns provide, among other important features, user awareness about virtual space navigation controls and location. They also provide different ways of navigation and guidance help for users according to their preferences.

6.1 Free Will Navigation (aka left-right & up-down)

Synopsis: It provides users with access to any virtual space at any level using cursor keys only.

Context: M-Space application objective is to browse and retrieve information about objects and spaces. A key task to carry out this objective is the provision of a versatile, intuitive and natural navigation interface. There are some issues that should be taken into account when designing navigation interfaces for m-space applications. For instance, the importance level of information that the navigation system has assigned is defined as the most important of secondary information. So, it should take enough space to be easily identified by users, but not too much to obscure the main content of the screen. Besides, navigation controls should be natural and intuitive to keep learnability gap to the minimum because it may become useless if users find out that it is easiest to browse information without using the application. Another important issue to take into account is the fact that public spaces are usually accessed by people that are carrying baggage. As a consequence, they have only one hand free at a time to use any electronic device. So, it is necessary to introduce a way to navigate through the m-space application using one hand only.

Solution: The solution is based on the interface presented in most of electronic devices. These devices have shortcuts to most used functions of the device. For instance, MP3 players provide controls to most common operations (play, stop, pause, volume control, etc) directly on the keyboard. However, it does not mean that these are the only operations available, but they are the easiest to access.
Thus, the proposed solution is based on using cursor buttons, available in any mobile device, as navigation controls. Interface is based on a map that shows a virtual space, for

instance a room containing furniture. And, three actions are available; the first one is the selection of any furniture piece of the room; the second one enables users to go into selected furniture to see the objects it contains; and finally, the third one enables users to get out of the room, and get into the floor map to be able to select another room.
Therefore, the same situation is analogous in almost any space level; for instance, you can see a floor map to select rooms or exit to the building to select another floor. Users can also see the building map to select floors, or they can see an object, and select an audio or video associated to such object. Once application interface is defined, key assignments should be performed. For a landscape layout, adapted to right handed people, we propose to use **up** and **down** keys to select an element into the map. In the room example exposed before, we will use these cursor keys to select a furniture piece into the room. The **right** cursor key will be assigned to go into selected space. In the room example it will display a screen to browse the objects contained into the selected furniture piece of the room. And finally the **left** cursor key is used to get out of the map and go into the previous space level. In the room space, this key shows the floor the current room belongs to, so the user is able to go another room. It is recommendable to **label** the arrows representing cursor buttons on screen to provide user feedback about actions.

Consequences: The first consequence is the possibility for users to control the space navigation naturally and intuitively with one hand only using cursor keys. An important issue to note is the possibility to make the proposed combination of keys a standard; making it the "natural key combination" for m-space applications. This fact will drastically reduce the learnability time. Unfortunately, because of the lack of actual standards, labels may obscure map.

Schematic Description:

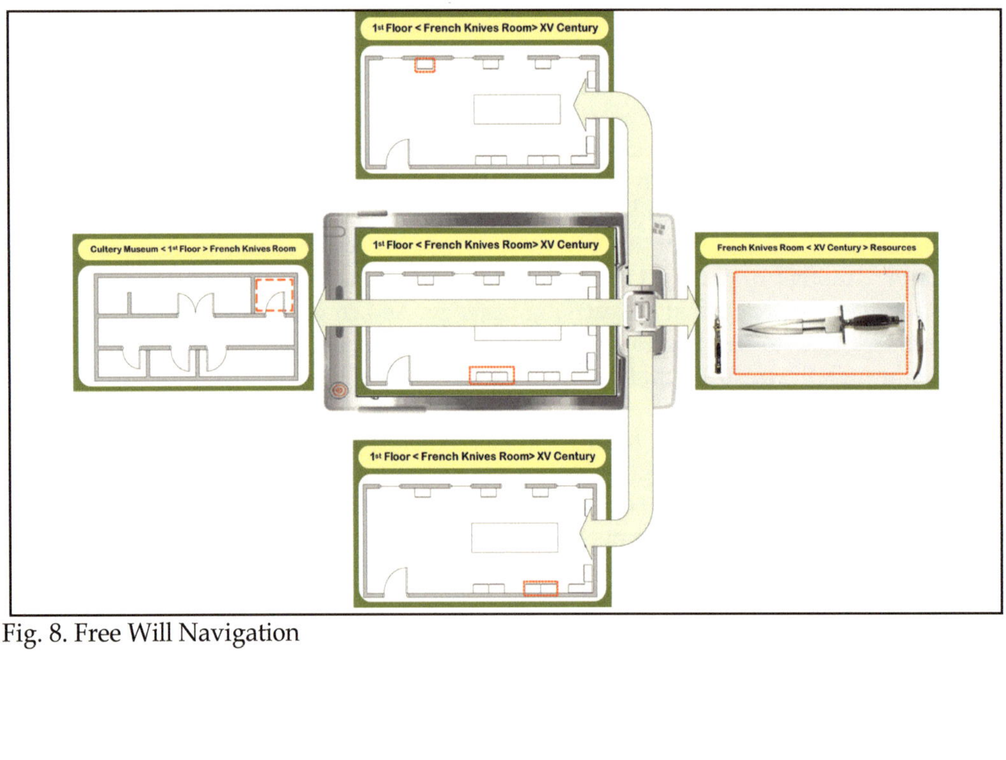

Fig. 8. Free Will Navigation

Related Patterns

This pattern catalogue: Main relationship is established to Landscape Layout pattern because portable devices (such as PDAs) can be used with one hand only, if they are in landscape position. The device should be used with the most skilled hand of the user so it is also related to Right-Left handed users design pattern..

W3C Common Sense Suggestions for Developing Multimodal User Interfaces: This pattern satisfies real-world constraints by assigning cursor keys to most common operations on this kind of applications. It also applies physical suggestions by using one hand only instead of both hands. This pattern also communicates clearly, concisely, and consistently with users by using the same keys through the whole navigation system regarding of space level, keeping interface simple.

Tidwell's sublanguages: This pattern is related to: Optional Detail On Demand because user access the information according to space level, Short description because information about navigation is displayed on screen, and Convenient environment Actions because people usually goes one level up and down only.

Van Welie's patterns: The problems this pattern affords are related to: Visibility because user guidance and navigation can be used to guide users across buildings, Affordance because it uses the space metaphor, and Feedback because operations are labeled. In relation to usability issues, this pattern try to cope with Learnability and Memoability.

6.2 Routes

Synopsis: Routes pattern provides users with predefined routes that guide them according to their interest.

Context: Large spaces are difficult to explore, because they may contain huge amounts of information that is not manageable by visitors. So, information is usually divided according to subjects. This division is not exclusive and cannot be grouped into separate spaces. There are many examples about this situation in museums, for instance, we can group art pieces according the year they were created, or we can group them by author. Sometimes visitors do not have enough time to explore the whole physical space, so they decide to explore the part of the space they are more interested. For instance, a user can decide to see XIV Century Swords instead of all swords.

Solution: The solution is based on the provided in large museums, where visitors can choose a route to follow. This route is related to a specific subject and it guides visitors through the museum where most important art pieces, related to this subject, are exposed. To extend this solution to a mobile device based applications, a bi-panel view is employed. First panel is the **Map panel**. It shows actual space map and navigation control is provided by the application of Free Will Navigation pattern. This map shows the stop points defined by the selected route. Selection keys moves to the next and previous points of visit instead of next and previous object or space within the map. To select the route, you have to swap panels and the **Route selection panel**. To do it, a mobile device key is assigned (usually it is the home key). To disable routes, a special route called Free is used.

Consequences:

First advantage of using Routes pattern is the possibility for users to focus their visit on part of the information provided by the m-space application. Consequently, it optimizes the visit times and provides an easy way to look for specific objects or spaces in a close range search. Another advantage of applying this pattern is the simplification of device control because only two controls (keys) are needed to navigate across a defined route the **previous** and **next**.

Schematic Description:

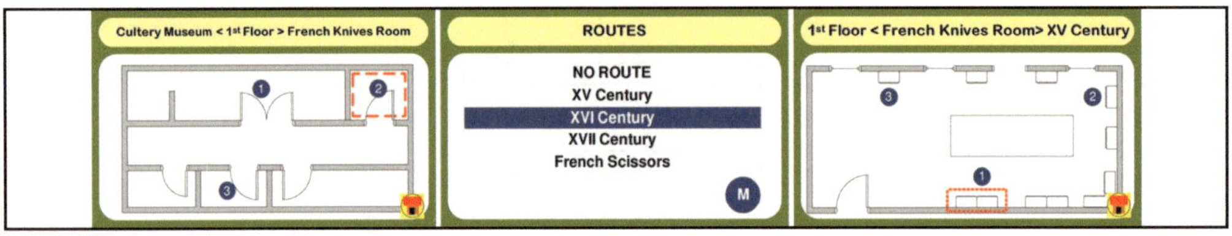

Fig. 9. Routes

The key is used to switch between views.

Related Patterns

This catalogue patterns: This pattern is close related to Free Will Navigation because when the No Route route is selected, Free Will Navigation is applied.

W3C Common Sense Suggestions for Developing Multimodal User Interfaces: This pattern satisfies real world constraints by suggesting an easy way to perform a task because it allows users to look for a group of related objects. It also communicates clearly, concisely and consistently with users keeping user interface simple because the map is used as a part of routing interface. Finally, it makes user comfortable by improving Human-memory constraints.

Tidwell's sublanguages: We found out this pattern is related to Clear entry points because routes list panel represents a list of entry points of a physical space; Bookmarks because each route can be seen as a list of ordered bookmarks; Convenient Environment Actions because action feedback is shown on screen; Navigable spaces because cursor keys are used to move across stop points; Step by step Instructions because Route navigation can be seen as a sequence of actions; Map of navigable spaces because Routes could be seen as "filtered maps"; Go Back One Step because it allows navigating across spaces; and finally, the Control panel sublanguage is applied on Routes panel too.

7. Accessibility

Public spaces should be available to everybody. An m-space application goal is providing users with a tool to browse and retrieve information from physical spaces. This tool should be available to all people, so accessibility issues are a must of any m-space application. Besides, these applications may provide disabled people with a powerful tool that easies their life because information that could be difficult to reach, due to architectonic barriers, may be available through this type of applications. So, a category that groups patterns dealing with the improvement of m-space application accessibility is defined.

7.1 Space Audio Perception

Synopsis: A voice notifies the user the space he or she has selected or entered.

Context: Blind people cannot see selection or environments from screen.

Solution: We base our solution on voice based interfaces by adding voice awareness to m-space applications when any action occurs.

Consequences: Blind people can enjoy the application and get profit of it.

Related Patterns: It can be used with Free Will Navigation pattern to provide blind users access to application. This mechanism jointly with voice oriented content will provide accessibility to the whole content of the space.

7.2 Right–Left Handed Users

Synopsis: This pattern adapts Landscape based interfaces of m-space applications to be used by right-left handed people.

Context: Usually people do not have the same skills on both hands. So, if an application can be used with one hand only, it is logical that the hand used to perform operations be the skilled one.

Solution: The solution lays on two issues. The first one is mirroring screen horizontally to get the screen view accordingly and the second one is the swapping of cursor keys behavior. **Up** swaps to **down** and **left** swaps to **right**.

Consequences: The most important consequence is the fact that accessibility is improved, and the system can be used by people more efficiently.

Schematic Description:

Fig. 10. Left-Handed users

Related Patterns

This pattern catalogue: This pattern is close related to FreeWillNavigation because it allows left handed people to use device keys with most skilled hand. It is also very close related to Landscape, because it allows users to use mobile device with one hand only.

W3C Common Sense Suggestions for Developing Multimodal User Interfaces: This pattern satisfies real-world constraints because it allows users to use the device in the easiest way to perform a task. Besides it communicates clearly, concisely, and consistently with users because it makes commands consistent. And with organizational suggestions keeps interface simple, too.
Tidwell's sublanguages: We found this pattern is related to convenient environment actions because actions are adjusted to user's perspective. It also improves flexibility by providing explicit control to the user. Finally, this pattern improves learnability and memorability too.

7.3 Zoom

Synopsis: The aim of this pattern is the provision of controls to change font size easily when users are reading documents.

Context: Elder people usually have problems to read documents from portable devices.

Solution: When a text is being shown, it is wrapped and cursor keys to left and right are used to increase - decrease font size. Up and down buttons are used to scroll text.

Consequences: Accessibility is improved, and the system can be used by people more efficiently.

Schematic Description:

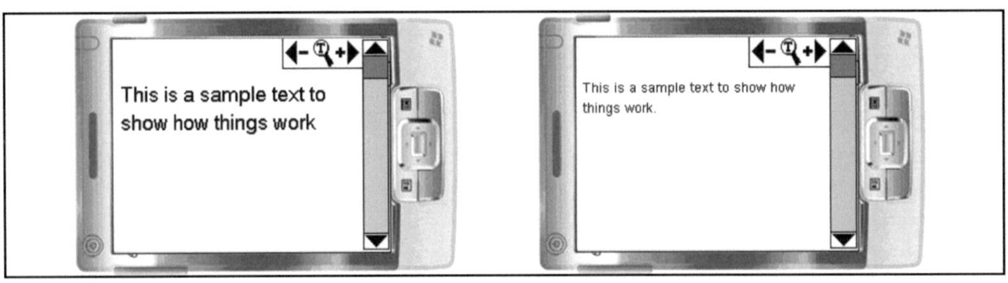

Fig. 11. Zoom

8. Applying HCI Design Patterns in an m-space application

In this section we present the evaluation performed to guarantee the validity of these patterns regarding usability issues. To achieve this goal, we have developed a prototype employing the design patterns described in previous sections based on a real m-space application. The former application is completely available to visitors, who can rent a pocket computer (PDA) to explore the museum pieces and spaces, in the Cutlery Museum of Albacete (MCA) in Spain (Gallud et al, 2005). The application of these patterns is exposed in detail in (Tesoriero et al., 2007b).To compare usability issues, a usability evaluation was performed on the original system (Tesoriero, et al., 2007) and then we performed the same evaluation to the prototype. We briefly explain the functionality and interface design of the original system. Then, we describe how design patterns have been applied to build the new prototype. And finally, we compare the evaluation results standing out some final remarks.

8.1 MCA Original System

This section describes the main features regarding the UI of the original MCA m-space application. The diagram depicted in Fig. 12 shows the application UI transitions to explain how people interact with the application. In this diagram, each box represents a screen; arrows represent a transition from one screen to another. Actions that perform a screen transition are identified by a label above the arrow line. An arrow without label expresses an implicit transition (more than one, expresses selection). Once the application navigation has been defined, we will explain the application screens and its main functionality. The system provides four ways of guiding visitors through the space:

The first one is **Recommended Routes** mode. This mode was designed to guide users interested in specific subjects through concrete routes. Samples of these routes are: knives of XVII century or French scissors. To provide this service, a list of recommended routes is displayed to the user. Once a route is selected, the first piece's location is shown on the screen. Users can see the information of the selected piece, by pressing *Ver Pieza* (see Fig. 13a); or can select the next piece according to a defined order, by clicking on *siguiente*; or can go to the previous piece by clicking on *anterior* (see Fig. 13a).

The second one is the **Guided Tour** mode. It was designed as a general purpose route to guide inexperienced visitors through the *whole* building. Functionality and behaviour is identical to a selected route on "Recommended Routes".

The **Access to finder** is used to look for pieces or showcases in the museum. This search can be performed on two ways. The first one is by using piece characteristics (Fig. 13b). The second one is by entering the code of a piece or a showcase (Fig. 13c). Once the search process is concluded, the piece or the list of pieces is shown to the user. If a list of pieces is the result of the searching process, then, users may select pieces to display their information, as shown in Fig. 13g.

The **Unguided Tour** allows users to navigate across the application to get information about pieces and showcases. The information is displayed on levels and three levels were defined: exhibitions, rooms, showcases and pieces. The user interfaces for each level are depicted in Fig. 13 (d), (e), (f) and (g) respectively.

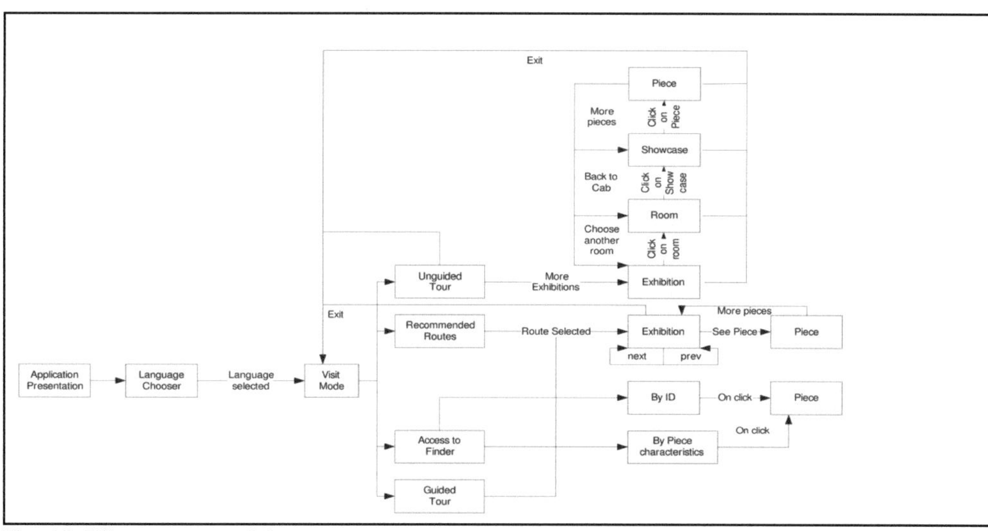

Fig. 12. UI screen transitions.

Fig. 13. UI screen transitions.

8.2 MCA Pattern based Prototype

As the previous version of the system interface, the new one is organized in levels. The first and upper level represents the whole museum (see Fig. 14a). A museum can be composed by several buildings. A building may be composed by several floors (Fig. 14b). A floor may be composed by several rooms (Fig. 14c) and a room may contain some furniture pieces as cabinets or showcases (Fig. 14d). A furniture piece contains objects or art pieces, as depicted in Fig. 14e. Finally, the lower level is defined by piece information, as shown in Fig. 14f.

To navigate across spaces we applied Free Will Navigation.

As Free Will Navigation allows users to control the application using cursor keys only, the application can be controlled by blind people; so if we combine this pattern with Space Audio Perception pattern by adding sounds on space transitions the application can be used by blind people. Free Will Navigation can be combined with Landscape pattern too. So, PDA can be used with one hand only.

Although Free Will Navigation solves many problems, it adds a new accessibility problem. Left-handed and right-handed people should use the application. To cope with this situation we apply Right-Left handed users, design pattern. This pattern proposes control keys switching and screen mirroring to solve this problem.

To improve user orientation and localization, we applied Signs and Door at back design patterns.

A space transition happens when a user moves virtually and physically from one space to another; for instance form a room to another. As room shapes may vary, the Vertical-Horizontal Layout pattern is applied. As consequence we applied Layout Transition pattern, too. When text documents are reached, Zoom pattern proposes to use left and right cursor keys to change font size (bigger and smaller, respectively) and up and down cursors to scroll text.

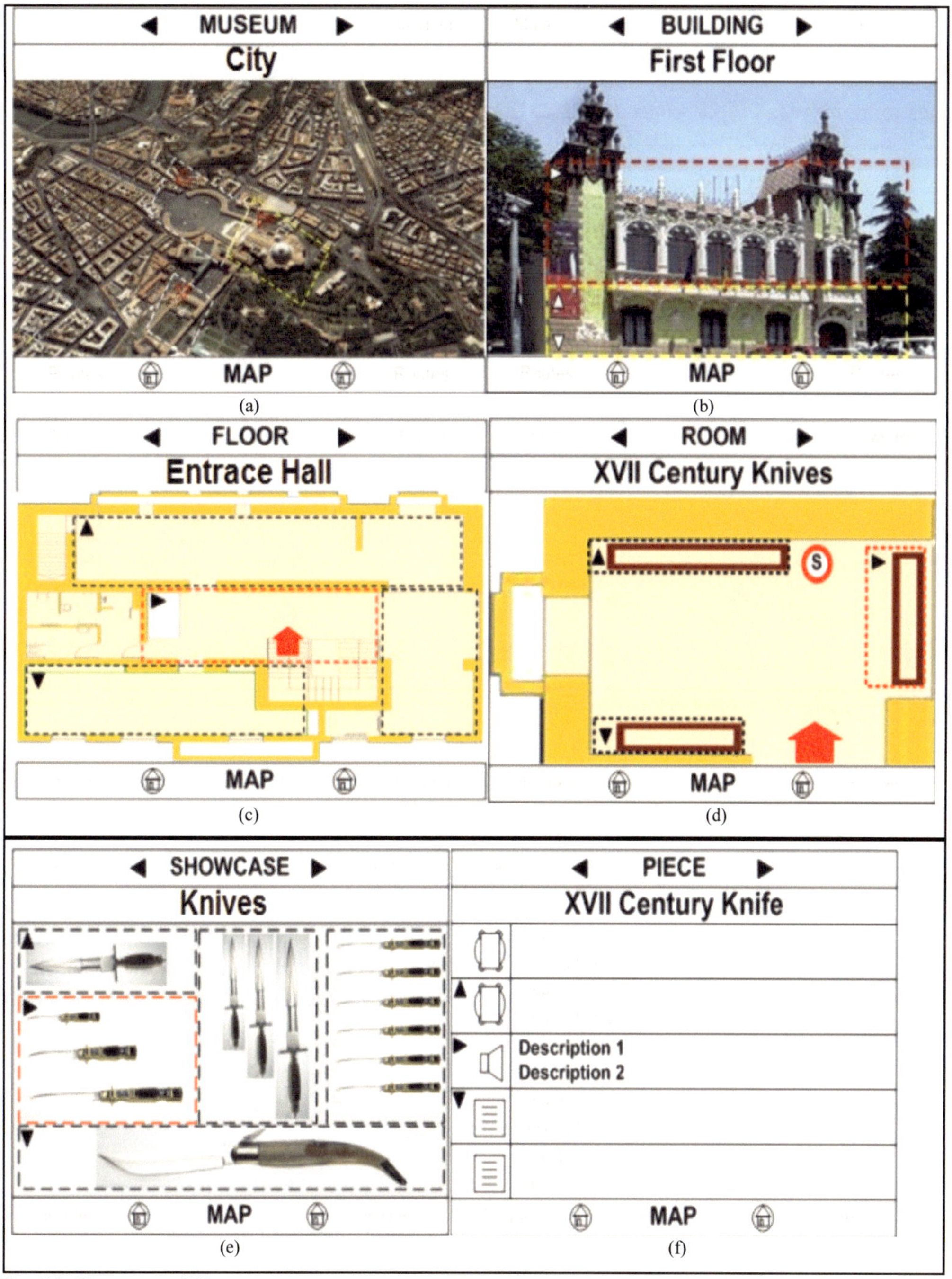

Fig. 14. Prototype UI.

8.3 The Evaluation

In this section we describe the satisfaction evaluation of the PDA client in both systems. The evaluations were based on a satisfaction questionnaire (Table. 1) that was prepared according to the CIF (Common Industry Format for Usability Reports) standard defined by the ISO/IEC DTR 9126-4.

People were queried about the system and were asked to express their feelings about MCA application. To get general impression about user satisfaction of MCA application a questionnaire was prepared according to the standard. Details and results of the study were published on (Tesoriero et al., 2007).

Nº	Question	Level of Satisfaction					
		1	2	3	4	5	6
1	Do you like application design?						
2	Do you like application appearance?						
3	Do you feel graphics have good quality?						
4	Is it easy to learn this application?						
5	Did you get a good feeling about using the application?						
6	Was it difficult to choose the language?						
7	Is it easy to choose a room?						
8	Is it easy to get a showcase?						
9	Is it easy to find a piece?						
10	What do you think about usability?						

Table 1. Satisfaction questionnaire

The questionnaire is composed by ten multiple choice questions. Each question has six possible answers according to the users' level of satisfaction. The least satisfying answer scores 1 while the most satisfying scores 6. The experiment embraced three aspects of the application covered by this questionnaire. The first aspect is about graphic design and visual impact and it is covered by questions 1, 2 and 3. The second aspect is about application general usability and it is covered by questions 4, 5 and 10. Finally, the third one is about application concrete functionality (i.e. finding a showcase) and it is covered by questions 6, 7, 8 and 9. To measure users' experience satisfaction for a Question q the following formula is applied:

$$Sq = \sum_{l=1}^{L} \frac{l}{L} \cdot \frac{x_l}{N} \tag{1}$$

Where (Sq) is the satisfaction level of question q, (L) is the amount of possible answers (in this case 6), (x_l) is the amount of people that answered l in question q and (N) is the amount of people that filled the questionnaire.

The result of applying formula (1) is a value between 1/6 and 1, the greater the better. Although the satisfaction evaluation embraces three aspects due to the fact we have developed a prototype using design patterns we will focus on the last two aspects of the application general usability and concrete functionality because appearance details were left to a later stage of development. System evaluation results are exposed in Fig. 15.

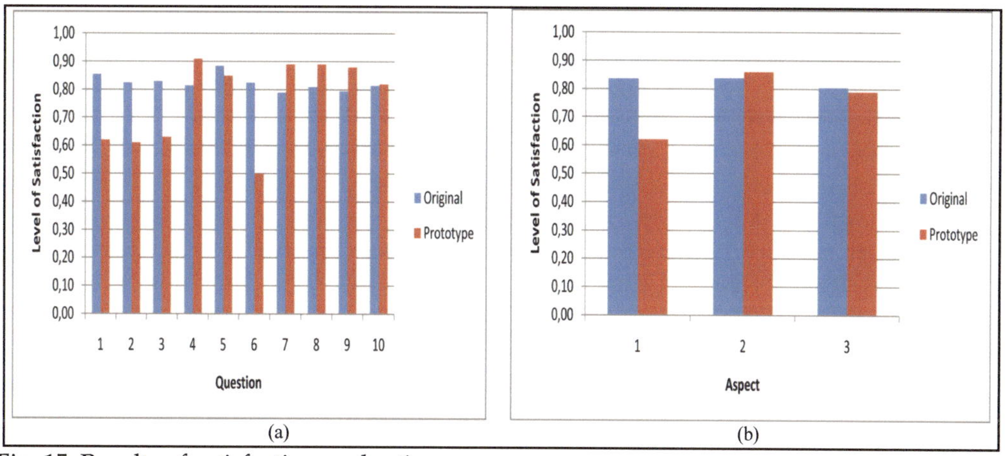

Fig. 15. Results of satisfaction evaluation

Comparing results we found that application design, graphic quality, application appearance and language selection are below of the mean. The main reason of UI appearance targeted a low score is the fact that it is just a preliminary prototype and we did not care about graphical design at this stage because the application supports skins and it should be customized according the specific situation, we focused our efforts on usability issues leaving details for later. Language selection was finding, because we thought that people only think about changing language in the beginning only, but experience demonstrated that it is not true.

Other issues are above 82% of satisfaction and it is remarkable because it is a good mark in general, taking into account that the scale starts at 17.67% and 83.33% represent a level of satisfaction of 5 point on 6. If we see Fig. 15b where we based our analysis on three aspects defined before: graphic design and visual impact, general usability, concrete functionality, we found that first aspect was discussed on previous analysis, so we will center the discussion on aspect 2 and 3. On Aspect 2, we can deduce that people are not aware or underestimate general usability issues because scoring in question 10 (usability in general) is 82.14% and it is the lower value of usability questions, because the other two questions averages 87.5 %. We think that the poor performance on Aspect 1 affected this item, although indirectly. As we discussed before, on Aspect 3 language selection had affected the result on 9.72 % and concrete functionality would have scored almost 89%.

9. Conclusions and Future Work

As new types of applications emerge, technology advances and a new set of applications (m-space applications) arises. These applications have characteristics and constraints related to

the physical space that define them. Some problems associated to these issues should be coped. To solve these problems, we have proposed an HCI design pattern language. These patterns have been grouped in categories that solve related problems providing a useful way to identify them. As we can see from the evaluation results we can deduce that usability is improved applying these patterns. We want to remark also that the catalogue could be extended with new patterns covering new needs, making it as open and flexible as possible.
Our work in progress is currently focused on patterns evaluation. Usability evaluation tests are being designed to measure usability before and after the application of these patterns. We are also thinking about performing these tests inside and outside an HCI Lab and compare these measurements.
From our perspective, we think that m-space applications are not mature enough and more research is needed to achieve natural interaction and better user experience. So we propose some future wok on this field to improve HCI on this environment. In order to improve interaction on m-space applications, sensors could be also used to suppress manual navigation with cursor keys. To provide this functionality, there are many technologies currently available (RFID, Barcodes, IRDA, etc) that could be used to provide location aware applications (Tesoriero et al, 2008).

8. References

Alexander, C.; Ishikawa, S.; Silverstein, M.; Jacobson, M.; Fiksdahl-King, I. & Shlomo A. (1977). *A Pattern Language: Towns, Buildings, Construction*. New York: Oxford University.

Barber, C.; Bristow, H.; Cheng, S.; Hedley, A.; Kuriyama, Y.; Lien, M.; Pollard, J. & Sorrell, P. (2001). Augmenting Museums and Art Galleries, *Proceedings of Human-Computer Interaction INTERACT '01. The International Federation for Information Processing*, pp. 439-447, ISBN: 978-1-58603-188-6, Tokyo, Japan, July 2007, IOSPress, Amsterdam, The Netherlands.

Bristow, H. W.; Baber, C.; Cross, J.; Woolley, S. & Jones, M. (2002). Minimal Interaction for Mobile Tourism Computers. *The Workshop "Mobile Tourism Support" at MobileHCI 2002.* http://www.eee.bham.ac.uk/pcg/docs/Mobiletourismv4.1.pdf.

Ciavarella, C. & Paternò, F. (2004). The design of a handheld, location-aware guide for indoor environments. *Personal and Ubiquitous Computing*, Vol 8, No 2, April 2004, 82-91, Springer Verlag, London, England. ISSN: 1617-4909.

Borchers J. (2001). *A Pattern Approach to Interaction Design,* John Wiley & Sons, May, 2001. ISBN 0471498289

Dolgos, C. (1996). *Visiting the Virtual Museum: The World Wide Web and its Impact on Museum Education*. Thesis (M.S. Ed.). Bank Street College of Education, New York.

Elliot, G. & Phillips, N. (2004). *Mobile Commerce and Wireless Computing Systems*. Pearson Education, ISBN 0201752409. New York.

Falk, J. H. & Dierking, L. D. (1992). *The Museum Experience*. Whalesback Books. Washington.

Gallud, J. A.; Penichet, V. M. R.; Argandoña, L.; González, P. & García J. A. (2005). Digital Museums: a multi-technological approach. *Proceedings of HCI-International Conference 2005*. ISBN 0-8058-5807-5, Las Vegas (USA), 2005, Lawrence Erlbaum Associates

Gamma E.; Helm R.; Johnson R. & Vlissides J. (1995). *Design Patterns: Abstraction and Reuse in Object-Oriented Designs*, Addison-Wesley Professional, ISBN 0201633612.

Gary, S. & Simon, S. Y.. Shim (2002). A Service Management Framework for M-Commerce Applications. *Mobile Networks and Applications*, Vol 7, 2002, 199–212. ISSN: 1383-469X.

Georgiev T.; Georgieva E. & Smrikarov A. (2004). M-Learning - a New Stage of E-Learning. *Proceedings of International Conference on Computer Systems and Technologies (CompSys-Tech'04)*.

Jackson, R.; Bazley, M.; Patten, D. & King, M. (1998). Using the Web to Change the Relation Between a Museum and its Users. *Proceedings of the Second International Conference Museums and the Web*. Ed. David Bearman and Jennifer Trant: Museums and the Web 1998: Selected Papers published on CD-ROM, Toronto, Canada, April, 1998. Pittsburgh, PA: Archives & Museum Informatics.

Léger, P. M.; Cassivi L. & Fosso Wamba S. (2004). Determinants of the Adoption of Customer-Oriented Mobile Commerce Initiatives, International Association of Management of Technology. *Proceedings of IAMOT, Virtual Organizations and Partnerships / E-Commerce Track*, Washington D.C.

McKenzie, J. (1998). Building Virtual Museums. From Now On. *The Educational Technology Journal*. URL = http://www.fromnowon.org/museum/museum.html. Last visited 09/14/1998.

Norman, D. A. (1988). *The design of everyday things*, Basic Books. ISBN 0-262-64037-6

Roth, J. (2002). Patterns of Mobile Interaction. *JournalPersonal and Ubiquitous Computing*, Vol 6, No 4, September, 2002, 282-289, ISSN 1617-4909.

Schweibenz W. (1999). The Learning Museum: How Museums use information Technology to present value added Collection Information for Lifelong Learning. *Proceedings of the 7th International BOBCATSSS Symposium Learning Society – Learning Organisation – Lifelong Learning*, Bratislava, Slovak Republic, January, 1999, Sandra Beheim, Stephan Cradock, Eva Dächert, Sonja Pfurr.

Tesoriero, R.; Lozano, M. D.; Gallud, J. A. & Penichet, V. M. R. (2007). Evaluating the Users' Experience of a PDA-Based Software Applied in Art Museums. *Proceedings of 3rd International Conference on Web Information Systems and Technologies (WebIST07)*, pp. 351-358, ISBN 9789728865788, Barcelona, Spain, March, 2007, INSTICC Press.

Tesoriero, R.; Montero, F.; Lozano, M. D. & Gallud, J. A. (2007b): HCI Design Patterns for PDA Running Space Structured Applications. *Proceedings of 12th International Conference on Human-Computer Interaction (HCII 2007)*, pp. 1206-1215, ISBN 978-3-540-73104-7. Vol 4550, Beijing, China, July, 2007. Springer LNCS, Berlin, Heidelberg, Germany (2007)

Tesoriero, R.; Lozano, M. D.; Gallud, J. A.; Montero, F. (2007c): Applying HCI Design Patterns to PDA Applications on Art Museums. *Proceedings of 3rd International Conference on Web Information Systems and Technologies (WebIST07)*, pp. 490-496, ISBN 9789728865771, Barcelona, Spain, March, 2007, INSTICC Press.

Tesoriero, R.; Gallud, J. A.; Lozano, M. D. & Penichet, V. M .R. (2008): A Location-Aware System Using RFID and Mobile Devices for Art Museums. *Proceedings of The Fourth International Conference on Autonomic and Autonomous Systems (IARIA-ICAS 2008)*, ISBN 0-7695-3093-1, Gosier, Guadeloupe, March, 2008, IEEE Computer Society Press.

Tidwell, J., (1999). *Common Ground: A Pattern Language for Human-Computer Interface Design.* URL http://www.mit.edu/~jtidwell/common_ground_onefile.html.

Tidwell, J. (2005). *Designing Interfaces: Patterns for Effective Interaction Design*, O'Reilly, ISBN 0596008031

van Welie, M. & Trætteberg, H. (2000). Interaction Patterns in User Interfaces, *Proceedings 7th Pattern Languages of Programs Conference (PLoP 2000)*, Allerton Park, Monticello, Illinois, USA.

van Welie, M.; van der Veer, G. C. & Eliëns, A. (1999). Breaking down Usability. *Proceedings of Interact '99*, Edinburgh, Scotland

W3C Working Group. Common Sense Suggestions for Developing Multimodal User Interfaces 2006. URL http://www.w3.org/TR/mmi-suggestions/.

15

Touchscreen Software Keyboard for Finger Typing

Kentaro Go[1] and Yuki Endo[2]
[1]*Interdisciplinary Graduate School of Medicine and Engineering, University of Yamanashi*
[2]*Yamanashi R&D Center, HAL Laboratory, Inc.*
Japan

1. Introduction

Touchscreen interfaces have attracted attention in recent years because their flexibility, functionality, and usability for design have become better known. They have been used in public-use terminals such as automated teller machines, ticket machines, and information kiosks. Recently, they are used for small, mobile device interfaces such as Apple's iPhone and iPod touch (Apple Inc., 2006). Furthermore, they are employed as large tabletop interfaces such as Microsoft Surface (Microsoft Corp., 2007) and MERL DiamondTouch (Dietz & Leigh, 2001).

For touchscreen interfaces, touchscreen keyboards are a fundamental function because text entry is a primary and frequently used task in several applications. Physical screen size affects the touchscreen keyboard design. A keyboard might include a different type of keyboard, display fewer keys on a small screen, or enable selection of an appropriate typing device such as a finger or stylus. Fundamentally, the touchscreen keyboard is created by software. It therefore has flexibility in visual presentation and software-based technique.

In this chapter, we specifically examine touchscreen software keyboards for finger typing. We first examine criteria for analyzing and discussing touchscreen keyboards. Then the chapter presents a description of our ongoing efforts at designing a Customizable and Adaptable Touchscreen Keyboard with bubble cursor-like visual feedback (CATKey). We are particularly interested in addressing the needs of a wide range of user classes by improving its perceived usability without decreasing the text entry rate. Many touchscreen systems are targeted at the public-use market. For that reason, users' skills and experiences are expected to vary widely. Users would refuse to use a touchscreen keyboard if the text entry method were to provide low perceived usability.

2. Touchscreen Keyboard for Finger Typing

A touchscreen keyboard is a virtual keyboard: it displays a keyboard image on a computer display and is operated mainly with a finger or stylus. It is intended to be used in place of a physical keyboard. The keyboard image is created and controlled by software and displayed on a screen. Therefore, the touchscreen keyboard is categorizable as a soft keyboard (software keyboard) or onscreen keyboard. Although several alternative approaches for onscreen-based methods have been used for text entry such as handwriting recognition-based approaches and alphabetic gesture-based approaches (e.g., Graffiti, Unistrokes), we specifically examine display of a keyboard image onscreen and typing with a finger or stylus because of the user's familiarity with physical keyboards. Figure 1 shows our criteria for classifying touchscreen keyboards for text entry. Listing the criteria, we specifically examine important factors related to text entry with touchscreen keyboards.

Screen size
- Small (Mobile and smart phones, Personal Digital Assistant, Handheld computer)
- Medium (Standard PC, Tablet PC)
- Large (Tabletop, Wall-sized display, projector)

Touchscreen keyboard types
- Soft keyboard
- Gesture-based keyboard (menu-based)

Number of keys
- Alphabetical (selection keyboard)
- Numerical (10-key numeric keypad)

Typing device
- Finger typing
- Stylus typing
- Hybrid use (Finger + Stylus)

Technique
- Prediction of input word
- Customization of keyboard layouts
- Adaptation
- Visual appearance (size, shape, color, visual feedback, etc.)

Fig. 1. Criteria for classifying touchscreen keyboards for text entry

2.1 Screen Size

The touchscreen device size and the touchscreen's effective area affect the touchscreen keyboard design. The device sizes are categorizable into three groups: small, medium, and large. Small touchscreen devices include mobile and smart phones, Personal Digital Assistants (PDAs), and handheld computers. Their effective touchscreen area is small; hence onscreen objects become small. Therefore, users are assumed to use a stylus for manipulating them. The finger use of small touchscreen devices has become more popular in the research community since Apple's iPhone and iPod touch were released.

Medium-size touchscreen devices include standard PCs and tablet PCs.

Finally, large touchscreen devices contain table-top displays, wall-sized displays and projectors. Recently, researchers started to examine text entry specifically for tabletop displays (Hinrichs et al., 2007). They analyzed properties of tabletop displays and summarized existing text entry methods for tabletop use.

2.2 Touchscreen Keyboard Types

Touchscreen keyboards of two types have been investigated: soft keyboards and gesture-based keyboards. Soft keyboards can have various keyboard layouts. The QWERTY layout is the standard for soft keyboards, but an alphabetical layout is used as a selection keyboard in some cases. These two layouts are suitable for walk-up-and-use scenarios (Hinrichs et al., 2007). For example, with a public terminal, people might come to use it briefly then leave. Consequently, we cannot assume their prior knowledge and experience of sophisticated tools and methods. Users can transfer their knowledge related to alphabetical order if we use a selection keyboard with alphabetical order for a touchscreen keyboard on a public terminal. Users can transfer their skills and experience gained using common hardware keyboards if we were to use QWERTY layouts for touchscreen keyboards (MacKenzie et al., 1995). Notwithstanding, previous studies have shown that the text entry rate for a touchscreen keyboard is considerably lower than that for a hardware QWERTY keyboard, even for expert typists (Shneiderman, 1991; Sears et al., 1993).

Although public terminals usually use these layouts for touchscreen keyboards, private devices might implement any keyboard layout. Because the primary emphasis of text entry is its performance, several efforts have been conducted to find a keyboard layout with higher performance for text entry: the Dvorak layout, the Metropolis layout (Zhai, Hunter & Smith, 2000), and so forth.

On the other hand, with a gesture-based keyboard, the user inputs a gesture, drawing a line without lifting up the finger or stylus. Gesture-based approaches might display specialized menus (Venolia & Neiberg, 1994; Guimbretiere & Winograd, 2000), provide a dedicated input area (Perlin, 1998; Mankoff & Abowd, 1998), or a dedicated soft keyboard for gesture input (Zhai & Kristensson, 2003). Finally, Masui (1998) provides combined usage of a soft keyboard and a gesture-based keyboard.

2.3 Number of Keys

Onscreen keyboards present several advantages over physical keyboards. The main advantage is their flexibility to keyboard design. For example, keyboard layouts, even the number of keys, can be modified easily and tested for actual use. Two typical cases for the number of keys include alphabetical (full-size) keyboards such as the 101 keyboard for standard PCs and the numerical 10-key pad for mobile phones.

MacKenzie and Tanaka-Ishii (2007b) described the number of keys for text entry from the concept of a *key-ambiguity continuum*. In their concept, if each symbol is assigned to a dedicated key, it has no ambiguity. If some symbols are assigned to a key, such as a key with upper and lower case letters, it creates ambiguity. The ambiguity increases if we assign more symbols to a key. A typical example is a 10-key pad with the assignment of English letters: three or four letters are assigned to each key. In general, the fewer keys we provide, the greater the ambiguity, given set of letters.

A technique to resolve the ambiguity must be used when we design a keyboard with ambiguity. Two approaches exist: multi-tap method and prediction-based method. Using the multi-tap method, the user presses a key one or more times to specify a desired letter from a cyclic sequence of letters. The multi-tap method is a standard for numeric 10-key pad text entry. Using a prediction-based method, the user presses a series of keys; then, the system creates a list of possible words from the combinations of assigned letters to the keys using a dictionary. A typical example of this method is T9 (Tegic Communications).

2.4 Typing Device

Although a soft keyboard might be used with a mouse or other pointing device, a touchscreen keyboard is typed in mainly with a finger or stylus. For large keys or buttons on screen, finger typing is a reasonable approach. Sears et al. (1993) investigated the effect of touchscreen keyboard size on text entry speed. Results showed that expert typists achieve 32.5 wpm using the largest keyboard (24.6 cm wide) out of four levels of keyboard size condition. The narrower the keyboard, the fewer words typed per minute. Nevertheless, expert typists achieved 21.1 wpm using the smallest keyboard: 6.8 cm wide.

For small screen devices such as mobile and smart phones, PDAs, and handheld computers, stylus typing is used. However, in some daily situations, people feel that taking out a stylus is cumbersome, especially in brief use. Vogel & Baudisch (2007) proposed a technique for operating stylus-based interfaces with touch: a hybrid approach. It displays an offset call-out when the finger occludes small dense targets; the user operates the offset cursor in the call-out area to select a target. Tsurumi et al. (2008) applied this concept for a touchscreen keyboard to implement a hybrid approach.

2.5 Technique

As noted already, the touchscreen keyboards are created and displayed onscreen with software. For that reason, they have flexibility of design and functionality as opposed to hardware keyboards. A gesture-based keyboard described in Section 2.2 is a typical approach for software-based dynamic control. A menu can be created and displayed easily on a touchscreen. It is easy to record a sequence of typed characters, predicting subsequent characters based on a dictionary, and showing a menu of candidate words.

A customization function can be realized easily when we design a touchscreen keyboard. For example, its appearance--the size, shape, color, font, and borderline--can be set. Visual feedback when the user types can be modified if we design the software as it is. In addition, the keyboard layout itself can be modified to fit the size and shape of the keyboard to the user's hands. The concept of adaptation is realized if we frequently customize the keyboard layout. Himberg et al. (2003) proposed online personalization of the keyboard layout.

3. CATKey: Customizable and Adaptable Touchscreen Keyboard using Bubble Cursor-Like Visual Feedback

3.1 Motivation

Text entry tasks undertaken using touchscreen keyboards are cumbersome because (1) the user cannot touch, feel, or distinguish the positions of the keys displayed on the screen; and (2) it is difficult to feel the visual and tactile feedback from the keys, especially with conventional touchscreen devices, even though tactile displays have developed rapidly (Benali-Khoudja et al., 2004). However, as described in the previous section, touchscreen keyboards present practical advantages because (1) they can be designed as customizable

and adaptable keyboards; and (2) they can be designed to display the visual feedback of they keys and on the keys.
Our approach to designing touchscreen keyboards is to address the weak points using customizable and adaptable functions and effective visual feedback to improve their perceived usability. We designate the method as Customizable and Adaptable Touchscreen Keyboard with Bubble Cursor-Like Visual Feedback: CATKey (Go & Endo, 2007).

3.2 Customizable Key Layout

Figure 2 portrays the concept of Voronoi key area of our keyboard design. Figure 2(a) depicts a typical QWERTY layout keyboard, consisting of rectangular keys. Figure 2(b) is the initial key layout of our CATKey. Each key has a maximum area; consequently, the overall key area forms a Voronoi diagram (Aurenhammer, 1991). Himberg et al. (2003) employ this approach for an onscreen numeric 10-key pad. In the keyboard, each key consists of a set of points.

$$V_i = \{ x \mid d(x, c_i) < d(x, c_j), \text{ for all } j \neq i \} \quad (1)$$

In that equation, x is the coordinate of a point, d is the Euclidean distance, and c signifies the coordinate of the key centroid.

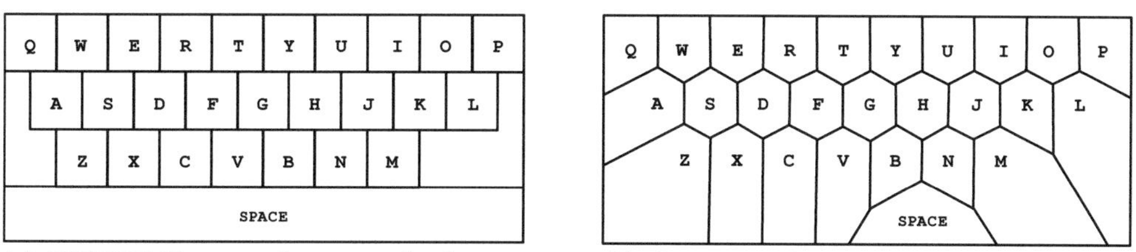

(a) QWERTY layout of rectangular keys

(b) QWERTY layout of keys with Voronoi area

Fig. 2. The Voronoi key area concept

Figure 3 presents a key layout customized by a user in the customization mode of CATKey. In this mode, the user adjusts each key by touching and manipulating it directly so that the user feels that the layout is easy to use. The customized key area also forms a Voronoi diagram.

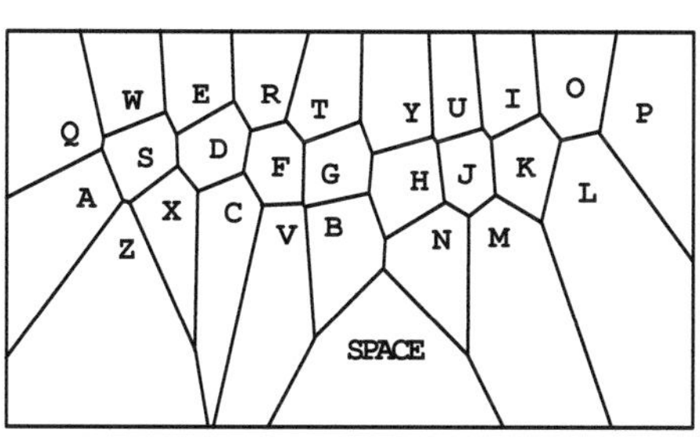

Fig. 3. A key layout customized by a user

3.3 Adaptable Keys

We designed an adaptable function similar to that presented by Himberg et al. (2003). In the adaptive mode of CATKey, the key centroid is moved to the centroid of recorded keystroke points in each key (Fig. 4). The keystroke coordinates are recorded for the period of the pre-specified number of keystrokes.

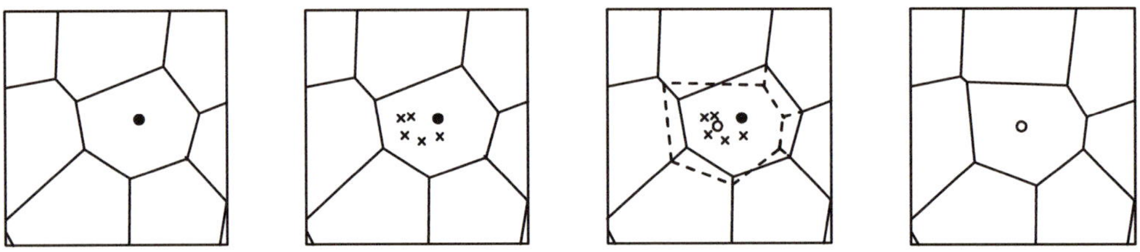

(a) Original key area (b) User's typing points (X-mark) (c) Recalculated centroid of the typing points (d) Adjusted key area

Fig. 4. The key adaptation mechanism of CATKey: Black point, the original centroid. X-mark: keystroke points; White circle, the centroid of the keystroke points and the weighted original centroid; Dotted line, recalculated key area.

3.4 Visual Feedback

Figure 5 depicts the design of visual feedback in CATKey. Figure 5(a) portrays an actual view of CATKey. We assigned a round key area to communicate the touched location to the user. The yellow f and j keys show home positions of the index fingers. The presence of the line and color of keys can be modified using the parameter-setting dialogue.

Figure 5(b) shows the bubble cursor-like visual feedback (Grossman & Balakrishnan, 2005). The bubble-shaped cursor in red adjusts dynamically to the closest key and provides the sensation of an offset cursor (Sears & Shneiderman, 1991). Figure 6 presents the concept of bubble cursor-like visual feedback used in CATKey. Figure 6(a) shows the Voronoi area of a key that has a colored circle with the centroid as its middle. It redraws the circle in a different color as visual feedback when the user touches inside the color circle (Fig. 6(b)). When the user touches outside the color circle, it redraws the circle in a different color, draws a circle with its keystroke point as its middle, and merges them (Fig. 6(c)). The radius of the second circle is the distance from user's keystroke point to the color circle.

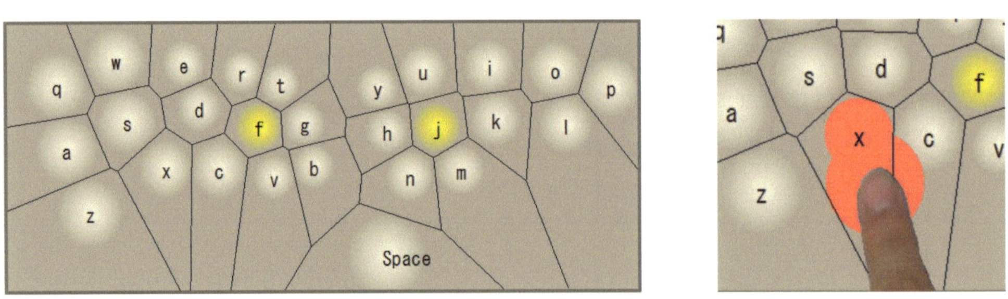

(a) Overview of CATKey with lines and color circles (b) Bubble cursor-like visual feedback

Fig. 5. Design of visual feedback in CATKey

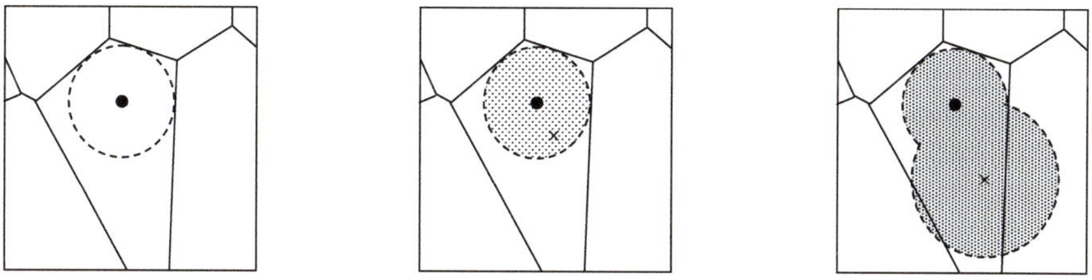

(a) Color circle (b) User's keystroke point is in the color circle (c) User's keystroke point is outside the color circle

Fig. 6. Concept of bubble cursor-like visual feedback: Black point, the centroid of the key; Dotted line, the inscribed circle of the key; X-mark, keystroke point.

4. Evaluation of CATKey

We evaluated the usability of CATKey based on ISO 9241-4 (1998). We measured the text entry speed and error rate using a hardware QWERTY keyboard, a software QWERTY keyboard, and CATKey, and assessed its comfort; finally, we conducted a debriefing interview.

Ten college students (two women and eight men) participated in the evaluation. Each uses a hardware QWERTY keyboard regularly, but seldom uses a touchscreen keyboard for daily activities.

A CAD Center NEXTRAX 15 touchscreen computer was used for evaluation. It has a 15-inch TFT monitor with 1024 × 768-pixel resolution. Also, CATKey was implemented using C# (Visual Studio.Net 2003; Microsoft Corp.). Figure 7 shows a user typing with NEXTRAX 15, which has a 20-deg mounting angle. For hardware keyboards, standard QWERTY keyboards (Dell Computer Corp.) were used. The sentences were chosen randomly from among pangrams such as "a quick brown fox jumps over the lazy dog," "how quickly daft jumping zebras vex," and "pack my box with five dozen liquor jugs."

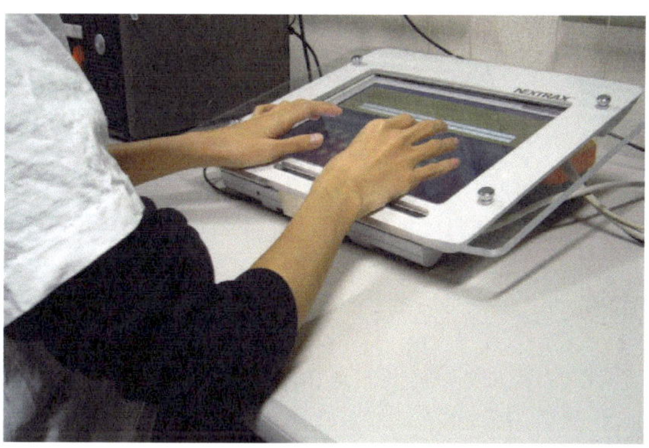

Fig. 7. Experimental setting (NEXTRAX 15).

Each experimental session included 10 sentences for the typing task. Each participant performed two practice sessions, then completed four sessions for measurement. The presentation order of keyboard types was counterbalanced.

Results indicate that the respective mean entry speeds of the hardware QWERTY keyboard, software QWERTY keyboard, and CATKey were 33.5, 23.8, and 22.8 wpm. A significant difference was found among the keyboards ($F(2, 18) = 7.5$, $p<0.05$); but no significant difference was found between the levels of the software QWERTY keyboard and CATKey. Similarly, the respective mean error rates of the hardware QWERTY keyboard, software QWERTY keyboard, and CATKey were 3.4, 5.9, and 6.8%. A significant difference was found among the keyboards ($F(2, 18) = 6.3$ ($p<0.05$)); but no significant difference was found between the levels of software QWERTY keyboard and CATKey. Furthermore, no significant difference was found from the assessment of comfort between the software QWERTY keyboard and CATKey.

5. Conclusion

In this chapter, we examined the criteria of touchscreen keyboard text entry. We specifically emphasized the use of a touchscreen keyboard use for finger typing. We analyzed it from five aspects: screen size, touchscreen keyboard types, number of keys, typing device, and technique.

Additionally, we described the CATKey design: it is a customizable and adaptable touchscreen keyboard with the bubble cursor-like visual feedback. Our criteria suggest that CATKey is better used for medium or larger touchscreen devices. Incorporating a soft keyboard approach, it has alphabetical keys. It specifically examines finger typing, but is useful for a stylus also. Although it has no prediction function, its keyboard layout can be customized. It has an adaptation function. Finally, its visual appearance has a bubble cursor-like visual feedback.

Early results of evaluation show that the mean text entry speed and mean input error rate of CATKey are not significantly different from those of a standard software QWERTY keyboard. This result might indicate limitations of our design: users need a compelling reason to replace their text entry device from a static standard QWERTY keyboard from a performance viewpoint. Notwithstanding, during the debriefing interview, the participants expressed their preference for the design and usability of CATKey.

6. References

Apple, Inc. (2007). iPhone and iPod touch, http://www.apple.com/ (Last accessed: May 19, 2008)

Aurenhammer, F. (1991). Voronoi diagrams--a survey of a fundamental geometric data structure, *ACM Computing Surveys*, Vol. 23, No. 3, pp. 345-405.

Benali-Khoudja, M.; Hafez, M.; Alexandre, J.M. & Kheddar, A. (2004). Tactile Interfaces: A State-of-the-art Survey, *Proceedings of 35th International Symposium on Robotics*, pp. 721-726, Paris, France, March 2004.

Dietz, P. H. & Leigh, D. L. (2001). DiamondTouch: A Multi-User Touch Technology, *Proceedings of the ACM Symposium on User Interface Software and Technology (UIST 2001)*, pp. 219-226.

Go, K. & Endo, Y. (2007). CATKey: Customizable and Adaptable Touchscreen Keyboard with Bubble Cursor-like Visual Feedback, *C. Baranauskas et al. (Eds.): INTERACT 2007, LNCS 4662*, Part I, pp. 493-496.

Grossman, T. & Balakrishnan, R. (2005). The Bubble Cursor: Enhancing target acquisition by dynamic resizing of the cursor's activation area, *Proceedings of the SIGCHI Conference on Human Factors in Computing Systems 2005*, pp. 281-290.

Guimbretiere, F. & Winograd, T. (2000). FlowMenu: Combining command, text, and data entry, *Proceedings of the ACM Symposium on User Interface Software and Technology (UIST 2000)*, pp. 213-216

Himberg, J.; Hakkila, J.; Kangas, P. & Mantyjarvi, J. (2003). On-line personalization of a touch screen based keyboard, *Proceedings of the 8th International Conference on Intelligent User Interfaces (UIST 03)*, pp. 77-84.

Hinrichs, U.; Hancock, M.; Collins, C. & Carpendale, S. (2007). Examination of Text-Entry Methods for Tabletop Displays, *Proceedings of the Second Annual IEEE International Workshop on Horizontal Interactive Human-Computer Systems (TABLETOP 2007)*, Oct 2007, pp. 105-112.

ISO9241-4 (1998). *Ergonomic requirements for office work with visual display terminals (VDTs), Part 4: Keyboard requirements.*

Isokoski, P. (2004). Performance of menu-augmented soft keyboards, *Proceedings of the 2004 Conference on Human Factors in Computing Systems (CHI 2004)*, Vienna, Austria, April 2004, pp. 423-430.

MacKenzie, I. S. & Tanaka-Ishii, K. (2007a). *Text Entry Systems: Mobility, Accessibility, Usability*, Morgan Kaufmann.

MacKenzie, I. S. & Tanaka-Ishii, K. (2007b). Text entry using a small number of buttons, in *Text Entry Systems: Mobility, Accessibility, Usability*, Morgan Kaufmann, pp. 105-121.

MacKenzie, I. S. & Zhang, S. X. (1999) The design and evaluation of a high-performance soft keyboard, *Proceedings of the SIGCHI Conference on Human Factors in Computing Systems: the CHI is the limit*, May 1999, Pittsburgh, Pennsylvania, United States, pp. 25-31.

MacKenzie, I. S.; Zhang, S. X. & Soukoreff, R. W. (1995). Text entry using soft keyboards. *Behaviour and Information Technology*, Vol. 18, pp. 235-244.

Mankoff, J. & Abowd, G. D. (1998). Cirrin: A word-level unistroke keyboard for pen input, *Proceedings of the ACM Symposium on User Interface Software and Technology (UIST98)*, pp. 213-214.

Masui, T. (1998). Integrating pen operations for composition by example, *Proceedings of the ACM Symposium on User Interface Software and Technology (UIST98)*, pp. 211-212.

Microsoft Corporation (2007) Microsoft Surface, http://www.microsoft.com/surface/ (Last accessed: May 19, 2008)

Perlin. K. (1998). Quikwriting: Continuous stylus-based text entry, *Proceedings of the ACM Symposium on User Interface Software and Technology (UIST98)*, pp. 215-216.

Shneiderman, B. (1991) Touch Screens Now Offer Compelling Uses, *IEEE Software*, March, pp. 93-94.

Sears, A.; Revis, D.; Swatski, J.; Crittenden, R. & Shneiderman, B. (1993). Investigating touchscreen typing: The effect of keyboard size on typing speed. *Behaviour and Information Technology*, Vol. 12, No. 1, pp. 17-22.

Sears, A. & Shneiderman, B. (1991). High-precision touchscreens: design strategies and comparisons with a mouse. *International Journal of Man-Machine Studies*, Vol. 34, No. 4, pp. 593-613.

T9, Tegic Communications, http://www.t9.com (Last accessed: May 19, 2008).

Tsurumi, L.; Watanabe, R.; Matsuura, Y. & Go, K. (2008) Dynamic assignment of symbols to keys for soft keyboard, *The 70th Annual IPSJ Convention (4)*, 5ZC-6, pp. 177-178 (in Japanese).

Venolia, D. & Neiberg, F. (1994). T-Cube: A fast, self-disclosing pen-based alphabet, *Proceedings of the SIGCHI Conference on Human Factors in Computing Systems (CHI 94)*, pp. 265-270.

Vogel, D. & Baudisch, P. (2007). Shift: A Technique for Operating Pen-Based Interfaces Using Touch. *Proceedings of the SIGCHI Conference on Human Factors in Computing Systems (CHI 2007)*, pp. 657-666.

Zhai, S.; Hunter, M. & Smith, B.A. (2000). The Metropolis Keyboard: An Exploration of Quantitative Techniques for Virtual Keyboard Design, *Proceedings of the 5th International Conference on Intelligent User Interfaces (UIST 00)*, pp. 119-128.

Zhai, S.; Hunter, M. & Smith, B.A. (2002). Performance Optimization of Virtual Keyboards, *Human-Computer Interaction*, Vol. 17, Nos. 2–3, pp. 229-269.

Zhai, S. & Kristensson, P-O. (2003). Shorthand Writing on Stylus Keyboard, *Proceedings of the SIGCHI Conference on Human Factors in Computing Systems (CHI 2003)*, pp. 97-104.

16

Structured Light Illumination Methods for continuous motion hand and face-computer interaction

Charles J. Casey, Laurence G. Hassebrook and Daniel L. Lau
University of Kentucky
Department of Electrical and Computer Engineering
Lexington, Kentucky
USA

1. Introduction

Traditionally, human-computer interaction (HCI) has been facilitated by the use of physical input devices. However, as the use of computers becomes more widespread and applications become increasingly diverse, the need for new methods of control becomes more pressing. Advances in computational power and image capture technology have allowed the development of video-based interaction. Existing systems have proven themselves useful for situations in which physical manipulation of a computer input device is impossible or impractical, and can restore a level of computer accessibility to the disabled (Betke et al., 2002). The next logical step is to further develop the abilities of video-based interaction. In this chapter, we consider the introduction of third dimensional data into the video-based control paradigm. The inclusion of depth information can allow enhanced feature detection ability and greatly increase the range of options for interactivity. Three-dimensional control information can be collected in various ways such as stereo-vision and time-of-flight ranging. Our group specializes in Structured Light Illumination of objects in motion and believe that its advantages are simplicity, reduced cost, and accuracy. So we consider only the method of data acquisition via structured light illumination. Implementation of such a system requires only a single camera and illumination source in conjunction with a single processing computer, and can easily be constructed from readily available commodity parts. In following sections, we will explain the concept of 3D HCI using structured light, show examples of facial expression capture and demonstrate an example of a "3D virtual computer mouse" using only a human hand.

2. Structured Light Illumination

Structured light illumination (SLI) allows one to measure the depth information of a surface by measuring the deformation in a projected light pattern (Schmaltz, 1932). A simple example would be a pattern of stripes projected onto a sphere. When viewed obliquely, the light stripes on the sphere appear curved as shown in Fig. 1. For a given arrangement of the projector and camera, the variation in a pattern can be characterized extremely accurately, such that a precise model of the surface can be reconstructed. Most modern implementations of SLI systems make use of digital projectors to illuminate the subject and a digital camera to capture an image of the illuminated subject, though in certain cases static projection devices (slide projectors, for example) may be used.

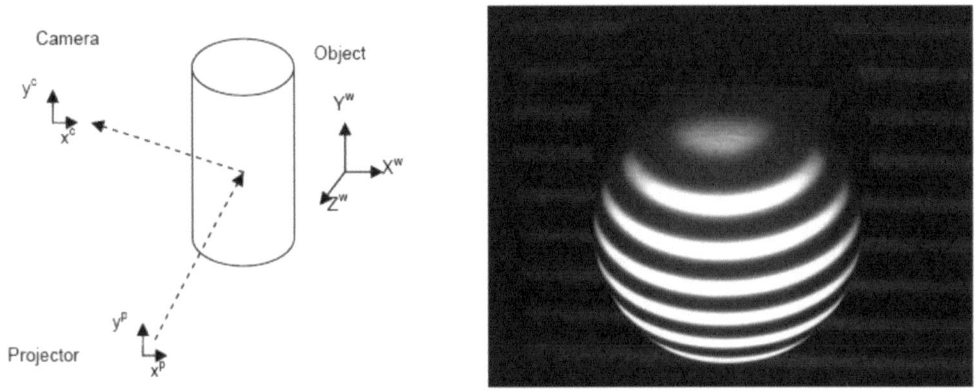

Fig. 1. (left) SLI geometry and (right) example stripe pattern on sphere.

Mathematically, the SLI measurement process is based on triangulation. Accurate results can be produced only when there is a well defined relationship between a single point on the projection plane and the corresponding point on the captured image, as shown in Fig. 1. It is to establish this relationship that projection patterns are utilized. A projection pattern (or more frequently a series of patterns) is designed such that each pixel (or row or column, depending on the specific implementation) of the projection image is uniquely characterized, either by some characteristic intensity value sequence or by some other identifiable property such as a local pattern of shapes or colors. When projected onto a subject, the captured image (or series of images) can be analyzed to locate these identifiable projection pattern points. Given a fixed placement of camera and projector, the location of any given pattern point on the subject creates a unique triangle with dimensions defined by the depth of the subject surface.

A well designed projection pattern can achieve significant accuracy and precision (Li et al., 2003). However, due to the difficulties involved in encoding each pixel uniquely, many of the most effective pattern types require more than one projection/capture instance in order to reconstruct the subject surface. These are known as time-multiplexed patterns. For example, the Phase Modulation Profilometry (PMP) (also known as sine wave shifting) technique utilizes a series of patterns in the form of sinusoidal grayscale gradient images, each shifted by a certain phase angle. Varying the intensity in this way will encode each row (or column) in the projector with a unique phase value. However, it has been shown that the accuracy of the phase value (and thus, the measurement of subject depth) is dependent on the number of shifts used. Therefore, a more accurate surface reconstruction requires more pattern projections and thus a longer scanning process.

2.1 Structured Light Illumination Motion Capture Methods

For many scanning applications it would be ideal to capture the required surface information in only a single projection/image instance. This is because during a multiple pattern scan, subject motion introduces error into the depth measurement. These techniques are therefore largely problematic for motion capture and human interaction. Fortunately, there are other options for single frame SLI capture, which offer not only reduced scan time, but also allow one to scan a moving subject. Most single pattern techniques fall into two categories; color-multiplexed types and neighborhood-search types.

Color-multiplexing simply combines individual patterns from some multi-pattern technique into a single pattern by coloring each differently. A three pattern PMP sequence, for example, can easily be combined into a single pattern by coloring each of the three patterns red, green, or blue. In this way, each pattern can be isolated independently of the others by considering only the R, G, or B channel of the captured image. Each channel image is effectively identical to a single frame of the corresponding multi-pattern PMP scan process. While the concept is simple, the number of patterns that can be combined in this way is usually relatively limited and analysis is plagued by non-idealities (Pan et al., 2006). In addition, color patterns introduce a strong dependence on subject coloration and luminance properties. If a subject is strongly colored blue, for example, there may be insufficient information in the R and G image channels to properly reconstruct the surface.

Neighborhood-search methods take a different approach entirely. These techniques utilize a pattern (usually binary in nature, that is, black and white colors only) in which subsections of the pattern can be uniquely identified in some way. Specific implementations may utilize patterns of noise or streaks (Maruyama & Abe, 1993) in which a point can be identified according to the known local statistical characteristics of the pattern, or deterministic sub-patterns defined by M-arrays or De Bruijn binary sequences (Morita et al., 1988) (Hall-Holt & Rusinkiewicz, 2001) wherein the identity of one point can be determined by the information contained in nearby points. Like color-multiplexed systems, the accuracy of neighborhood-search based techniques may be strongly dependent on subject surface characteristics. If pieces of the pattern can be obscured by subject features or distorted too much by local gradients, correct identification of the pattern points may be impossible. In addition, the primarily binary nature of the patterns can limit the resolution possible. Thus, only a small portion of surface points may be measured.

There are other methods of motion capture based on entirely different concepts. One method is to utilize high-speed hardware to simply run multi-pattern sequences faster (Zhang & Huang, 2006) reducing the effect that the subject's movement has on the depth measurement to a negligible amount. The composite pattern technique (Guan et al., 2003) combines component patterns of a time multiplexed method, such as PMP, into a single pattern by modulating each by a known frequency. This allows an effect similar to that of color-multiplexing, but avoids many of its drawbacks. Another new method, Lock and Hold (Hassebrook & Lau, 2006), utilizes a multi-pattern scan followed by a continuously projected tracking pattern (the Hold pattern) in order to scan moving subjects. The latter two options advantageously require no specialized hardware.

2.2 Composite Pattern

SLI systems frequently utilize patterns that vary only in a single direction (the "phase direction", a term taken from PMP and "y^p" in Fig. 1) and are constant in the other (the "orthogonal direction" or "x^p" in Fig. 1). In such a system, the camera is offset from the projector along the phase axis only. In this way, depth variation will cause variation in the pattern along the phase direction while leaving the pattern unaltered in the orthogonal direction. To visualize the effect, consider a square projected onto the surface of a sphere. If one views the sphere from an offset parallel to one set of sides of the square, these sides will still appear straight, while the other sides will appear curved. Composite Pattern multiplexing takes advantage of this fact by introducing sinusoidal variation along the orthogonal direction. When a surface illuminated with a composite pattern is viewed by the camera, the modulating signal will be unaltered by the surface features and can be used to isolate the component patterns in a way analogous to isolating each channel in an RGB color-multiplexed image.

Consider a four pattern PMP sequence. The intensity of each of the four patterns varies sinusoidally along the phase direction only. To combine the four into a single pattern, each is element-wise multiplied by a modulating image; patterns which vary sinusoidally in the orthogonal direction only, each at a unique (relatively high) frequency, as shown in Fig. 2. The modulated patterns are combined (and the resulting intensity scaled as necessary for the projection device) to create the composite pattern.

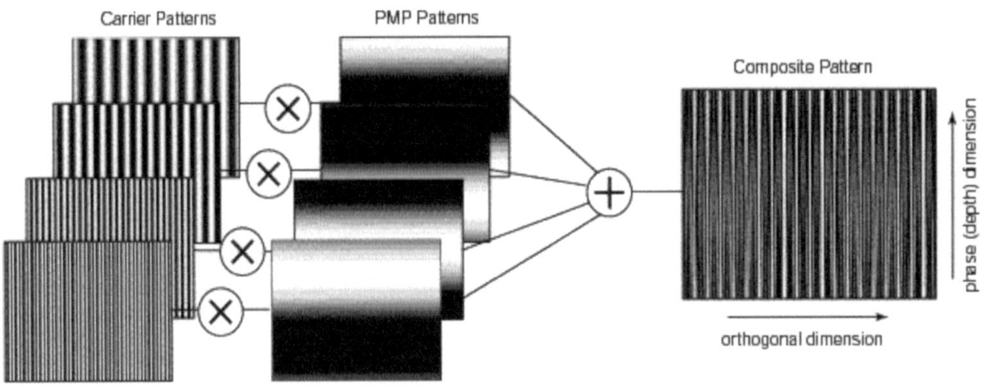

Fig. 2. Composite Pattern combining 4 PMP patterns into a single composite pattern.

When a composite pattern is used to illuminate a subject, the captured image must be processed in order to extract the original component PMP pattern images. These images can then be analyzed as though they were individual frames in a multi-pattern scan sequence. The process of isolating the component images is very similar to the process of isolating modulated communications channels. Considering the 2D Fourier transform of the image, component pattern information will appear as four signal envelopes shifted in the orthogonal direction by the modulating frequencies. Each pair of these envelopes (considering both positive and negative frequencies) is isolated using 2D band-pass filters. The inverse Fourier transform of these isolated bands are the equivalent component pattern images, and are then used to determine the surface depth according to standard PMP methodology. The method was combined with correlation filters to track hands (Guan et al., 2003) and used to control a virtual reality point of view as shown in Fig. 3. The left and right composite image of Fig. 3 have three component images; (upper left) the captured image, (upper right) the 3-D segmentation and hand tracking and (lower) the point of view of a virtual reality.

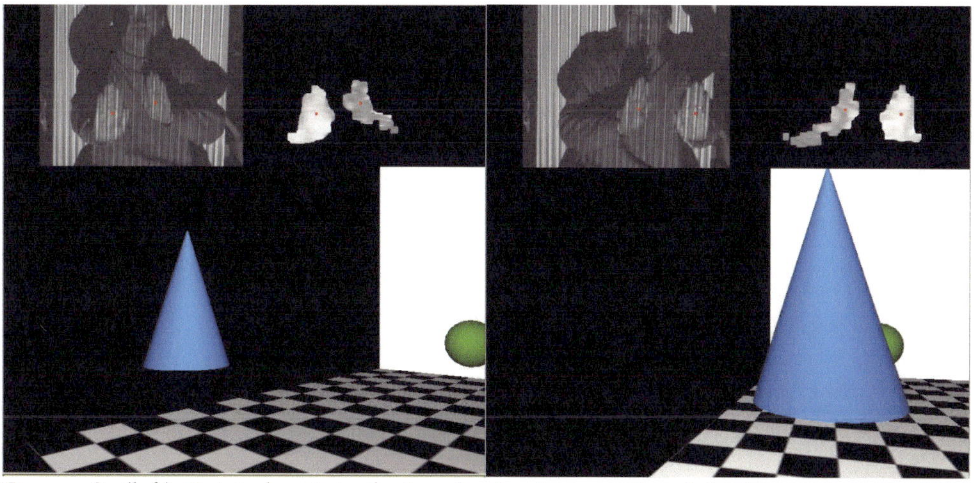

Figure. 3. (left) Rotated point of view by having one hand in front of another. (right) Translation of virtual reality to the left of the operator.

2.3 Lock and Hold Structure Light Illumination

Like the Composite Pattern technique, Lock and Hold motion capture was an idea inspired by communications theory. The idea is that, as in the operation of a phase-lock loop, if one can "lock on" to an unknown signal, then the changes in that signal can be easily tracked by compensating for the small incremental changes that occur through time. Lock and Hold motion capture uses an un-coded structured light pattern (usually a pattern of stripes with triangular cross sections) to capture the depth data of a moving surface. Changes in this "Hold pattern" are traced through the multiple frames of the capture video sequence in order to acquire a continually updated accurate depth map of the subject. Unlike similar systems that utilize un-coded SLI (Rodriguez et al., 2007) the system avoids difficulties involved with pattern ambiguity by the use of the "Lock sequence"; a preliminary 3D scan taken before the subject is allowed to move. Since an un-coded pattern has numerous identical elements, it can't generally be used to measure absolute depth in the same way as a coded pattern method (such as PMP or even Composite Pattern) since a projected pattern point may correspond to any number of pattern points on the captured image. By performing a preliminary 3D scan using PMP, the relationship between an identified point on the Hold pattern projection and Hold pattern capture can be unambiguously defined.
A simple explanation of the Lock and Hold process is as follows: to begin, a standard 3D scan of a subject is taken using a method such as PMP. Immediately following this, the Hold pattern projection begins and the subject is allowed to move, as shown in Fig. 4 (left and right). The Lock scan creates an unambiguous "phase map" which relates each point of the projection pattern to a single point that it illuminates on the subject image. If a Hold

pattern is immediately projected, the first frame of the Hold capture sequence is directly related to the phase map. In other words, each isolated feature of the Hold pattern maps to a single phase value from the PMP scan. In this way, the depth of each isolated Hold pattern feature (i.e., "snake") can be calculated using triangulation techniques.

Fig. 4. (left) Example of a Hold pattern projection and (right) resulting "snakes" representing depth of Hold image.

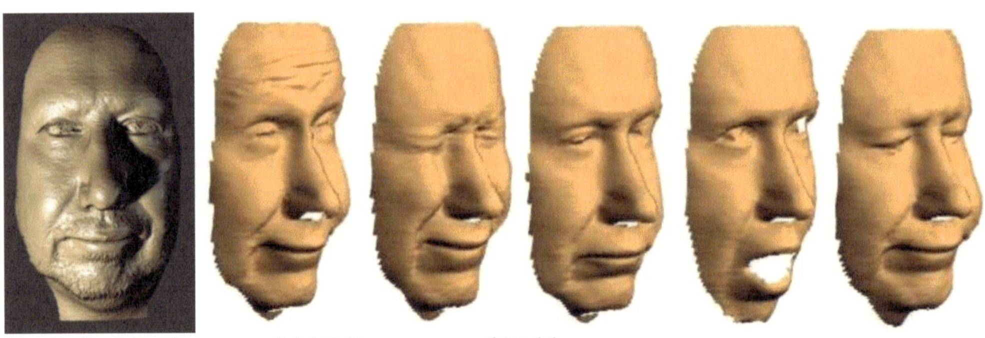

Fig. 5. (left) Lock scan and (right) sequence of Hold scans.

Once each feature in the first Hold frame is unambiguously identified, features in the next frame are isolated. Then, at each identified point in the first frame, a search is performed in a window around the corresponding position in the next frame. If a suitable feature is

found in that frame, it is assigned the appropriate identity. In this way features can be traced through the numerous frames of the Hold sequence, and a depth map for each frame can be calculated. A Lock scan and 5 samples of Hold scans are shown in Fig. 5.
Practical implementations of the process require additional steps, of course. Depending on the shape of the subject and the speed of its movements (relative to the capture rate of the camera), the initial tracking process may identify some features incorrectly. Thus, techniques for error prevention or correction are normally required for optimal results. However, for our purposes, a detailed description of this process is not necessary.

3. Augmented Reality 3D Computer Mouse Demonstration

In subsection 2.3 we demonstrate that surface details can be obtained by SLI. The Lock and Hold method was designed for special effects applications where a high resolution Lock scan is needed as well as a series of lower resolution Hold scans. The Lock scan takes about 1 to 3 seconds to capture and could be replaced by a method we call "leading edge lock" where the object enters the Field of View (FOV) and the leading edge is used to acquire a non-ambiguous measure of depth and thus, lock the snakes to an initial depth for tracking during the Hold process. However, for the convenience of demonstration we use our existing scanner to show feasibility for using a hand as a interface device to the computer. To do this, we must be able to track a hand feature such as a finger tip. We will use a simple correlation filter to conduct a five finger tip tracking operation and use the position and depth of the fingertips to convey control parameters to the computer. The value of this control is limited by the accuracy of the fingertip position measurement so we provide a final experiment to obtain the accuracy of the depth position of a finger.

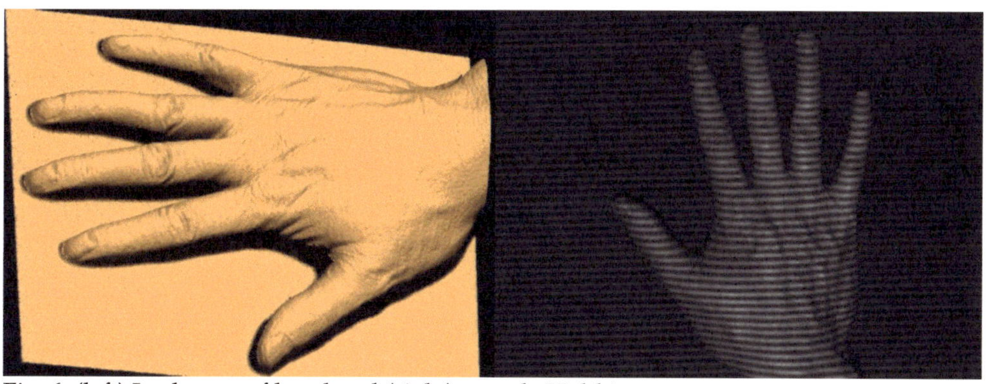

Fig. 6. (left) Lock scan of hand and (right) sample Hold image.

3.1 Fingertip Detection

The fingertip detection is accomplished globally by using a correlation filter designed to detect fingertips and suppress other regions of the hand. The Lock scan and a sample Hold scan are shown in Fig. 6 left and right, respectively. The captured image of the hand is down sampled to a course image for numerical efficiency has shown in Fig. 7 (left). That image is then correlated with a fingertip correlation filter leaving the detected fingertips as shown in Fig. 7 (middle). From those locations, the fingertip geometry is analyzed as a constellation of points to verify that they are actually fingertips.

Fig. 7. (left) Course image of hand, (middle) correlation response and (right) characterized fingertip constellation.

The fingertip correlation filter is designed to both detect the fingertips as a circular region and also suppress non-circular shapes. As shown in Fig. 8, the filter has a circular region of positive values surrounded by a ring of negative values.

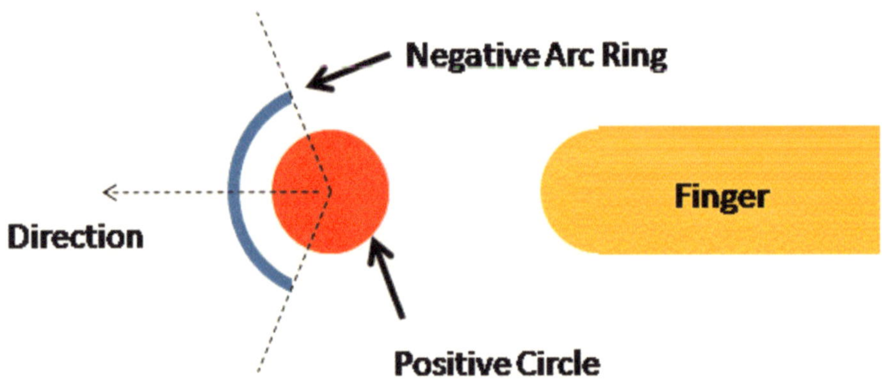

Fig. 8. The correlation fingertip filter.

The negative ring does not extend completely around the positive circle else it would partially suppress the tips. The positive and negative values are chosen such that when correlated with constant image intensity, such as the palm area, the resulting correlation is zero as shown in Fig. 7 (middle). Note that the filter only partially suppresses the fingers leaving the tips as the maximum correlation points. The number and positions of the points are checked to ensure their constellation is representative of a human hand configuration. Once the tip locations are established, the associated world coordinates, $\{X_w, Y_w, Z_w\}$, are used as the interface controls.

4. Results

We present two experiments and a discussion of numerical efficiency. The first experiment shows the tracking results for all 5 fingertips on a hand. The second experiment measures the depth accuracy of the fingertip position. The experiments were performed using an existing scanner system our group developed for a special effects application and then processing the data off line with a fingertip tracking algorithm used for biometric applications. So to evaluate the potential for a practical non-contact interface, we provide a discussion of numerical efficiency.

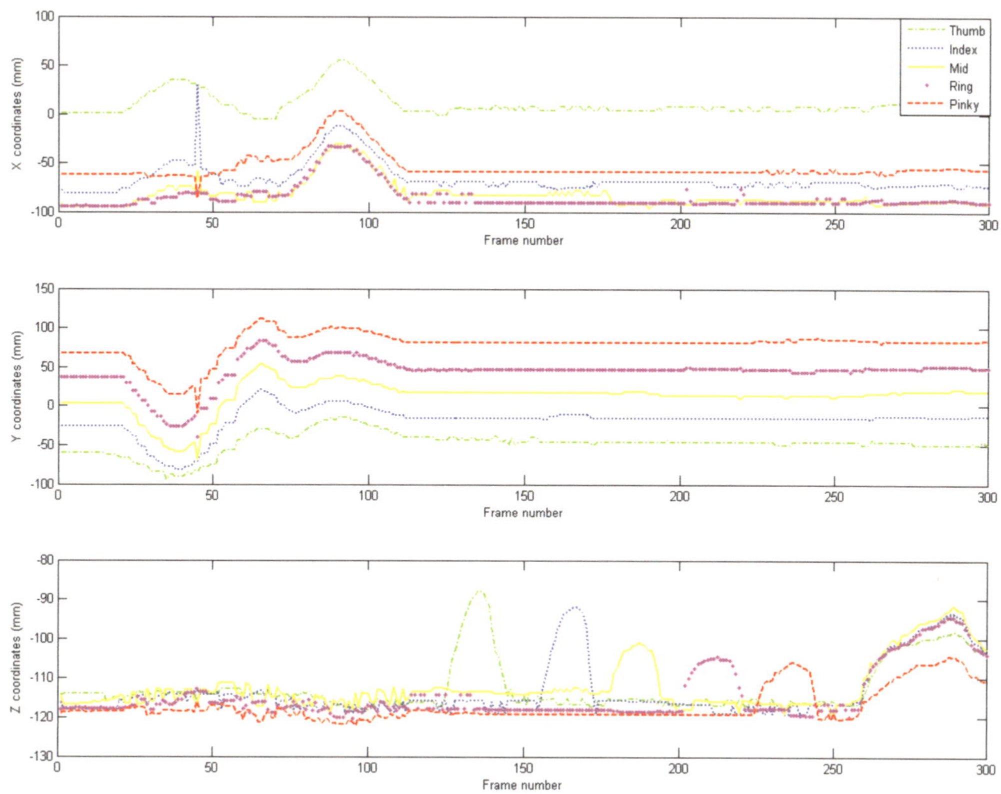

Fig. 9. XYZ tracking results of hand and finger movement.

4.1 Experiment 1: Five Fingertip Tracking

The fingertips were tracked for 300 frames at 30 frames per second (fps). The fingertip positions are shown in Fig. 9. The hand was moved in succession; left, right, back, and then forward to its starting position. Then, each finger, starting with the thumb, was raised up in sequence and finally all fingers were raised at the same time. The positive X axis in Fig. 9 is downward toward the wrist shown in Fig. 7. The positive Y axis is orientated toward the "pinky" finger side shown in Fig. 7. The positive Z axis direction is up off of the plane. A discontinuity occurred just before frame 50 and happened when three fingertips lost lock for one frame as shown in Fig. 9. The finger data is encoded by color such that the thumb (d1) is green, the "index" finger (d2) is blue, the "middle" finger (d3) is yellow, the "ring" finger (d4) is violet, and the "pinky" finger (d5) is red. The displacement of the thumb along the X axis, back towards the wrist, can be seen in Fig. 9 (top). The first hand movement is to the left as indicated by the Fig. 9 (middle) Y axis at about frame ~40. Note there is a rotation of the hand which also affects the X axis movement. The hand is then moved right to its maximum position at frame ~65. The hand is then moved back toward the wrist direction in positive X direction at frame ~90 and then returned to the original position at frame ~115. Next, starting at frame ~125, each finger is raised in the Z direction starting with the thumb (d1) followed by d2, d3, d4 and d5 ending at frame ~245. The last movement is the raising of all 5 fingers between frame ~260 through 300.

4.2 Experiment 2: Fingertip Position Tracking Accuracy

The final experiment yields the depth resolution of the system. In this experiment, a step ramp was placed underneath the middle finger (d3). Keeping the step ramp in place and the middle finger against the step ramp, the hand is pulled toward the wrist or positive X direction. The fingertip yielded a relatively constant Y value, and an X and Y position that linearly changed with hand position and ramp height, respectively. To estimate the depth, the X data was fit with a straight line. The straight line was then used as the horizontal value for the graph of Z in Fig. 10. A second line was fit to the Z coordinate and subtracted from the data in Fig. 10, leaving the noise. The slope of the line in Fig. 10 is $\Delta z/\Delta x = -0.1878$ and a standard deviation of 0.4971 mm.

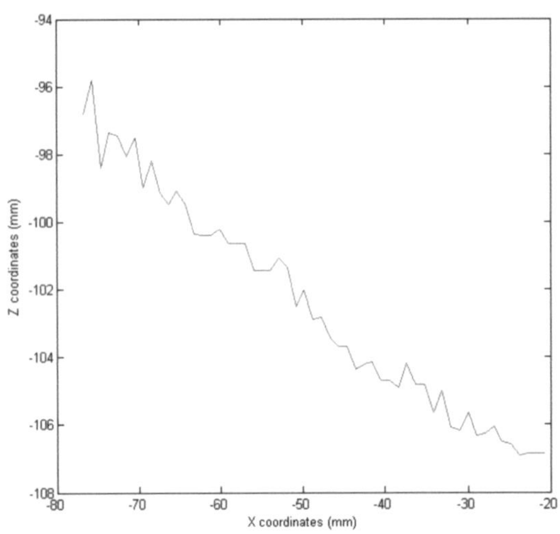

Fig. 10. Z coordinate of d3 fingertip as a function of X position on step ramp.

4.3 Discussion of Numerical Efficiency

For convenience, this research used offline processing of two different systems. That is the Lock and Hold scanner and the fingertip tracker. As such, the process would need to be combined and optimized for practical commercialization. For the acquisition component we introduced a new method called Lock and Hold SLI. In this application the Lock process is typically used to acquire a high resolution surface scan. In a non-contact human computer interface, this would not be necessary. Using only the stripe pattern shown in Fig. 6 (right) we could obtain lock by what we call leading edge lock where as the hand enters the camera FOV, the leading edge of stripes on the hand are identified and used to lock onto the hand surface. The absolute depth of the hand may be lost in this process but the relative depth of the hand and the fingertips is retained. Thus, only a single slide projection is necessary. In our experiments we capture 1.5 megapixels of data and then after initial preprocessing to 3D coordinates the result is downsampled by a factor of 150 to about 10,000 points. This takes about 1 second per frame using a dual core 2Ghz Intel Centrino processor. In a production system, this downsampling could be done upfront without preprocessing, with a lower resolution camera such as a 640 x 480 pixel camera. The processing is linearly proportional to the number of stripes and pixels used along the stripes. In theory we could have a 150x improvement but from experience we would expect at least a 15x improvement in speed primarily limited by the initial downsampling which involves an averaging process. The fingertip detection process runs at about 10 frames per second and uses a global correlation. Once the fingertips are located, the method could be adapted to local partition tracking (Su and Hassebrook, 2006) so if there are 5 partitions each of 1/25 the area of the entire scene, then the net speed up would be at least 5x and the partition filters could be optimized for each fingertip thereby achieving more robust and accurate tracking. So with a standard laptop Intel Centrino, we would expect to process at least 15 frames per second with just basic optimization. If a GPU or imbedded processor were used then the speed up would be considerably more and we would conjecture that the system could run at the frame rate of the camera.

5. Conclusion

Human to computer interfaces have been so far dominated by hand held and/or physical interfaces such as keyboards, mice, joysticks, touch screens, light pens, etc.. There has been considerable study in the use of non-contact interface technology that use image motion, stereo vision, and time of flight ranging devices. Using image processing of a single camera image, there is difficulty segmenting the feature of interest and poor depth accuracy. Stereo vision requires two cameras and is dependent on distinct features on the surface/object being measured, and time of flight systems are very expensive and lack close range accuracy.

We believe that Structured Light Illumination is a practical solution to the non-contact interface problem because of the simplicity of one camera and one projector, and its direct and accurate measurement of human hands and faces. Furthermore, with the advent of projected keyboards for augmented reality interfacing, a camera and projector are already present. In fact, the keyboard pattern could be used as the SLI pattern. In general, SLI, particularly the single pattern methods described in this research, are accurate, surface feature independent, and require only a simple slide projection in either visible or Near-Infra-Red light frequencies. The illumination source only requires efficient LED based illumination technology. As discussed in the results section, the accuracy of the depth measurement is within 1 mm so the demonstration is not just a non-contact "mouse" but a five finger analog controller. Full finger motion control could be used for a wide range of augmented reality interfacing that could be as simple as mouse and keyboard control or as sophisticated as a musical instrument interface or possibly even a sign language interface.

6. References

M. Betke J. Gips, and P. Fleming, "The Camera Mouse: Visual Tracking of Body Features to Provide Computer Access For People with Severe Disabilities." IEEE Transactions on Neural Systems and Rehabilitation Engineering, 10:1, pp. 1-10, (March 2002).

C. Guan, L.G. Hassebrook, D.L. Lau, "Composite structured light pattern for three-dimensional video," *Optics Express,* 11(5): pp. 406–17 (2003).

O. Hall-Holt and S. Rusinkiewicz, "Stripe Boundary Codes for Real-Time Structured-Light Range Scanning of Moving Objects," *Proc. Int'l Conf. Computer Vision,* pp. 359-366, (2001).

L.G. Hassebrook, D.L. Lau, "Structured Light Illumination Strategy INTRODUCTION OF LOCK AND HOLD STRUCTURED LIGHT ILLUMINATION," University of Kentucky EE Report #CSP 06-004, 2-20-06, Revised 5-26-06

Jielin Li, Laurence G. Hassebrook, and Chun Guan, "Optimized two-frequency phase-measuring profilometry light-sensor temporal-noise sensitivity," *J. Opt. Soc. Am. A,* 20(1), (2003).

M. Maruyama and S. Abe, "Range sensing by projecting multiple slits with random cuts," *IEEE Trans. Pattern. Anal. Mach. Intell.* 15, 647–651 (1993).

H. Morita, K. Yajima, S. Sakata, Reconstruction of surfaces of 3-d objects by *m*-array pattern projection method, in: IEEE International Conference on Computer Vision, pp. 468–473 (1988).

Jaihui Pan, Peisen S. Huang, and Fu-Pen Chiang, "Color-phase shifting technique for three-dimensional shape measurement," *Optical Engineering* - Vol. 45, Issue 1, 013602, (January 2006)

M.A. Rodrigues, A. Robinson, W. Brink, "Issues in Fast 3D Reconstruction from Video Sequences", Lecture Notes in Signal Science, Internet and Education, Proceedings of 7th WSEAS International Conference on MULTIMEDIA, INTERNET & VIDEO TECHNOLOGIES (MIV '07), Beijing, China, pp 213-218, September 15-17 (2007).

G. Schmaltz of Schmaltz Brothers Laboratories, "A method for presenting the profile curves of rough surfaces," Naturwiss 18, 315–316 (1932).

Wei Su and L. G. Hassebrook, "Pose and position tracking with Super Image Vector Inner Products" *Applied Optics,* Vol. 45, No. 31, pp. 8083-8091 (November 2006).

Song Zhang and Peisen S. Huang, "High-resolution Real-time 3-D Shape Measurement," *Opt. Eng.,* Vol. 45, No 12 (2006).

Head-mounted displays in ultrasound scanning

Juha Havukumpu*, Jari Takatalo*, Göte Nyman*, Jukka Häkkinen*,**
*University of Helsinki Department of Psychology,**Nokia Research Center*
Finland

1. Introduction

Ultrasound imaging, which is also called ultrasound scanning or sonography, is conducted by exposing part of the body to high-frequency sound waves to produce a visualization of the inside of the body. Ultrasound scanning is non-invasive, so it is usually painless. It is also widely available, easy-to-use and less expensive than other imaging methods. Because ultrasound imaging uses no ionizing radiation it is safer for the patients and medical staff.

Ultrasound is often used for the diagnosis and monitoring of pregnant women and the unborn infant (Dudley, 2004) . In Finland, an ultrasound scan is performed on mothers twice during pregnancy, the first in weeks 12+0 to 13+6 and the second after 19+0 to 20+0 weeks. The purpose of the screening is to check that the fetus is developing well and there are no abnormalities. As approximately 60 000 births occur per year, the total annual number of normal/routine fetus screenings is about 120 000. If mother has some illness, like diabetes, there is a reason to do more check-ups for the developing fetus.

The ultrasound scanning is based on a transducer that is located in a probe held by a sonographer and moved over the patient. The working position with the probe is often difficult, as it can cause a twisted position on users back, upper limbs and neck. For example, when investigating patient's heart, the patient is on the left side and the sonographer is doing sonography over the patient's body, which causes an abnormal working position (Morton & Delf 2007). The poor working position can cause tension to the neck, which could lead to uncomfortable feelings and headache.

Further problems can be created by the display of the sonographic machine, which is always placed on the top of the device. In most machines, the display is placed too high and when the gaze of the user changes between the patient and the display, the midwife must constantly look at either the display or the patient. This can place strain on the neck and other upper body muscles and can be uncomfortable during a long working day.

The situation can be especially problematic if the user has presbyopic vision and uses progressive lenses, because the user has to tilt his/her head to a very uncomfortable position, which can cause extra strain both to the neck and head (Figure 1.). An HMD could be used to reduce this strain, as the scanning result is constantly visible in the visual field of the midwife and the need to turn the head would be reduced.

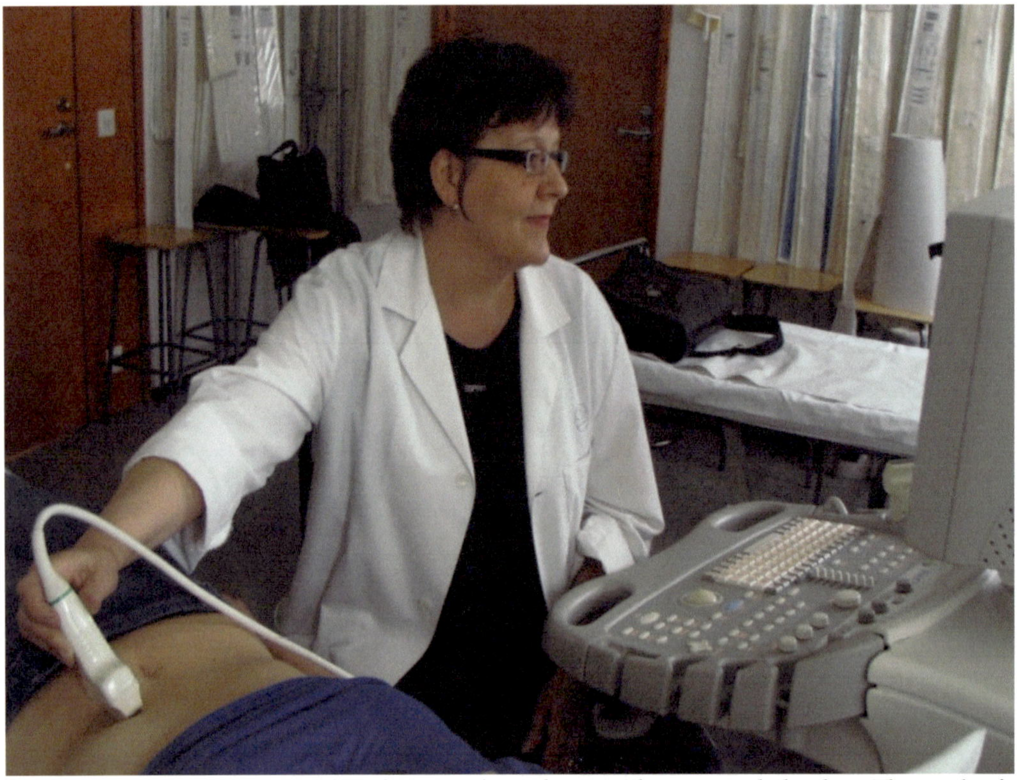

Fig. 1. Working position at the ultrasound machine with a normal display. The midwife must look at the display to see the results of scan, but has to turn her head toward the patient when repositioning the probe.

To avoid excessive work strain, special attention has been given to the work schedule of midwives. For example, at the Maternity Hospital of the Helsinki University Central Hospital there is a thirty-minute time for every ultrasound screening, so that gives to possibility to take a little break between the patients.. Furthermore, only two full working days with ultrasound screening tasks can be done sequentially. After that three resting days in other duties are required.

The most typical problems in ultra-sound scanning are musculoskeletal injuries and suffering of visual problems (Fernando, 1996). In a study focusing on the prevalence and causes musculoskeletal injuries among sonographers Morton & Delf 2007 report that experiences of pain and discomfort among sonographers is quite frequent, as 63.0% to 98.7% of the sonographers report some symptoms. Table 1 shows that shoulders, neck and upper back are quite often affected (Morton & Delf 2007). Visual discomfort among sonographers has been investigated less frequently, but some findings indicate that scanning work can cause eyestrain and a headache which can be related to eyes, neck or upper limbs (Fernando, 1996).

	Miles, 2005	Pike et al, 1997	Necas, 1996
Neck	66 %	73 %	76 %
Upper back	45 %	60 %	53 %
Middle back	29 %	40 %	---
Lover back	48 %	65 %	46 %
Shoulder	67 %	73 %	66 %
Upper arm	34 %	38 %	---
Forearm	29 %	35 %	33 %
Wrist	47 %	65 %	61 %
Hands/fingers	43 %	60 %	47 %
Elbow	32 %	---	33 %

Table 1. Findings of anatomical areas which are affected by pain and discomfort. (adapted after Morton & Delf 2007).

As there has been many suggestions of using a head-mounted display in medicine, and the results have been generally positive, we wanted to test the usability of a HMD in ultrasound scanning task (Howarth, 1994 ; Koesveld et al, 2003; Letterie, 2002 ; Ormerod et al. 2002; Ross & Naluai-Cecchini, 2002; Rosenthal et al, 2002; Reisman et al, 2002; Ryndin et al, 2005; Satava, 1994; Satava & Jones, 1998; Schuhaiber, 2004; Rosenthal et al, 2002; Reisman et al, 2002).

However, there are also a number of possible problems related to the using an HMD in an ultrasound scanning task. Firstly, earlier studies related to head-mounted displays have indicated subjective visual strain symptoms in users (Häkkinen et al., 2004; Hiatt et al, 2002: Mon-Williams et al. 1993; Howarth & Costello, 1997), although other studies have suggested that the symptoms are similar to those when using an ordinary display (Peli, 1998; Rushton et al., 1994; Sheedy & Bergström, 2002). Secondly, an HMD might occlude parts of the visual field and thus make the performance of the scanning task more difficult. We took these issues into account when creating the experimental setup.

2. Purpose of the study

In the present study the purpose was to investigate the issue of attention shifting in an ultrasound scan task, where a midwife has to alternately observe the patient and the display showing the scan results. We wanted to determine how midwives with previous experience of conventional ultrasound scanning would experience using an HMD in an ultrasound scan task. We also compared two different head-mounted display types in the scan task. The participants performed an abdominal ultrasound scan with a see-through Sony Glasstron in experiment 1 and with Micro-Optical SV-6 PC viewer in experiment 2.

The participant had to find, mark, identify and measure different abdominal organs. The organs were the uterus or prostate, depending on patients' sex, the both of the kidneys and the bladder. Each organ was measured linearly and crosswise and the volume of the bladder was also determined. Each of the identified organs was documented by printout. The task lasted 20 minutes. During the task the experimenter observed the user from behind. The experimental starting times were randomly distributed in the morning (9 am - 11 am) so that the existing eye strain would not affect the results. The participants did not know the ultrasound machine used in the experiment beforehand but they were able to familiarize themselves with the machine before the experiment.

2.1 Participants

Twenty-four registered midwives (mean age 43.1 years) with normal or corrected-to-normal vision participated in the two experiments: 13 in Experiment 1 (mean age 41.6 years) and 11 in Experiment 2 (mean age 44.8 years). The age of the youngest participant was 33 years and oldest 52 years. All participants were female and already had several years of experience of ultrasound methods in fetus scanning; 42.0% worked in a local hospital, 33.5% in Helsinki University Central Hospital, 17.0% in central hospitals, 4.0% in a healthcare centre and 4.0% of them were returning to working life, so they had no current working place.

2.2 Apparatus

We used two head-mounted displays: a see-through Sony Glasstron head-mounted virtual display in experiment 1 and a monocular Micro-Optical SV-6 PC viewer in experiment 2. The resolution of both displays was set to 640x480 pixels in both experimental conditions. The virtual image was at a distance of 1.4 meters with both displays. We placed a monocular display in front of the leading eye measured with the target aiming method (Figure 2.). We used a Vivid 3 ultra sound machine where we connected displays one at a time.

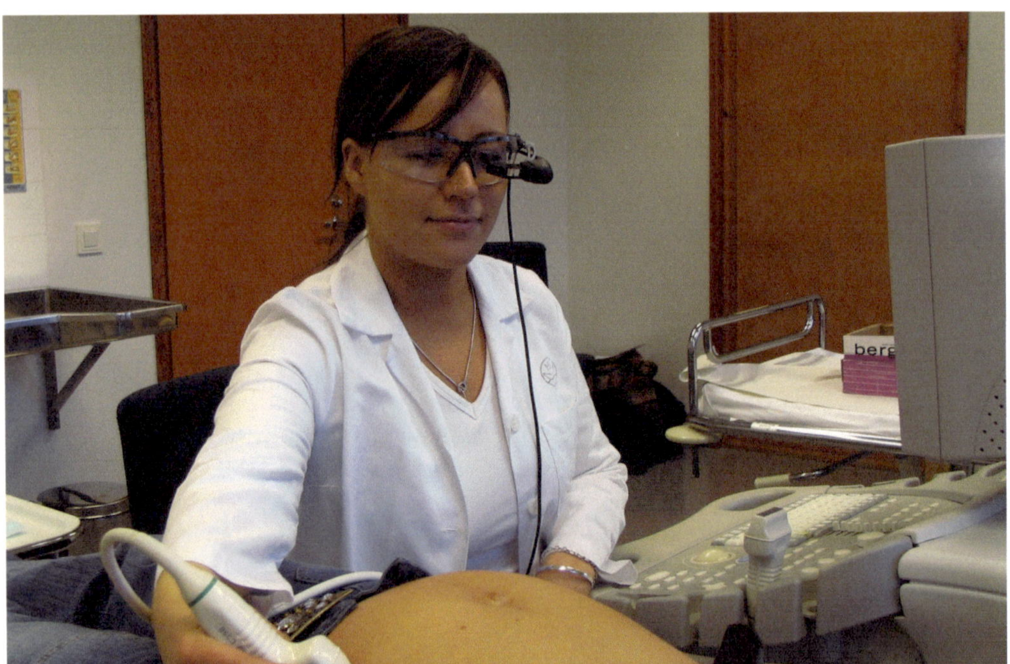

Fig. 2. Ultrasound scanning with the monocular display. The midwife can see the ultrasound scanning image in her left visual field and simultaneously follow the location of the probe with both eyes.

2.3 Procedure

In the main experiment the participant first completed a background questionnaire that contained general questions regarding the health of the participant. They described their head-mounted display and virtual reality experience, daily near-work time, computer-gaming frequency, motion-sickness frequency, headache frequency and handedness. We also asked when was the last time they had eaten and taken any medicines that made them more susceptible to nausea (sedatives or tranquilizers, decongestants, anti-histamines, asthma medicine or alcohol). Finally, the participants described their preconceptions and opinions about head-mounted displays. After completing the background questionnaire the participants began to do the task. After the task we gave the participants a questionnaire in which they described their opinions about the head-mounted display as well as the level of sickness symptoms they experienced after the use of the head-mounted display.

The participants performed an abdominal ultrasound scan with a see-through Sony Glasstron in experiment 1 and with Micro-Optical SV-6 PC viewer in experiment 2. The participant had to find, mark, identify and measure different abdominal organs. The organs were the uterus or prostate, depending on patients' sex, the both of the kidneys and the bladder. Each organ was measured linearly and crosswise and the volume of the bladder was also determined. Each of the identified organs was documented by printout. The task lasted 20 minutes. During the task the experimenter observed the user from behind. The experimental starting times were randomly distributed in the morning (9 am - 11 am) so that the existing eye strain would not affect the results. The participants did not know the ultrasound machine used in the experiment beforehand but they were able to familiarize themselves with the machine before the experiment.

3. Results

In the open questions the participants were asked about their positive and negative opinions about using the HMD. There were 18 positive and 22 negative responses in experiment 1 and 13 positive and 24 negative responses in experiment 2. The responses were diverse, but there were some issues that were brought up more frequently (Table 2). Only response categories with three or more answers are reported in the table, so the total number of answers in the table is less than in the complete experiment. 33.3 % of all the participants told in the post-experimental questionnaire that the ergonomics was better while using the HMD. In the answers the better ergonomics meant for example that using the HMD allowed the participants to move more and helped them to find out better working position. This matched their pre-task expectations, as the same number of participants expected better ergonomics before the task (positive pre-task answers in Table 2). The positive expectations meant that the participants expected to have a better working position and less strain in their neck and upper limbs with the HMD.

The image quality was also regarded as important, as 16.6% of the participants mentioned that the image quality was better with the HMD than with the ultrasound machine (positive post-task answers in Table 2). Interestingly, the participants expected this, as some had already mentioned this before the experiment (positive pre-task answers in Table 2). Focusing to the patient was also a significant issue, as 16.6% of all participants liked the opportunity to be able to focus to the patient. This was visible in the pre-task expectations, so it was an issue that the participating nurses did not regard as important when considering the use of a head-mounted dsplay.

The negative post-experimental findings were more divided (Table 2). Difficulties in wearing the display were most commonly mentioned negative post-task opinions (Table 2). Also, difficulties in communication with the patient and reduced visibility in the visual field due to the occluded areas were often mentioned. Interestingly, the sickness symptoms that were often mentioned in the pre-task questionnaire were not regarded as problematic in the post-task questionnaire.

If the two displays are compared, there are no clear differences in the post-task opinions (Tables 3 and 4).
However, certain display-specific issues were found to be disturbing. With the Glasstron the difficulty in wearing the display, the reduced visibility and difficulties in communicating with the patient were emphasized (Table 3). On the other hand, with the MD-6 the main problems were related to difficulties in keeping the display stationary in the correct position in front of the eye, the small size of the display and perceptual problems related to binocular vision experienced by the participants (Table 4). Positioning the display was especially difficult for the participants who used progressive or bifocal spectacles.

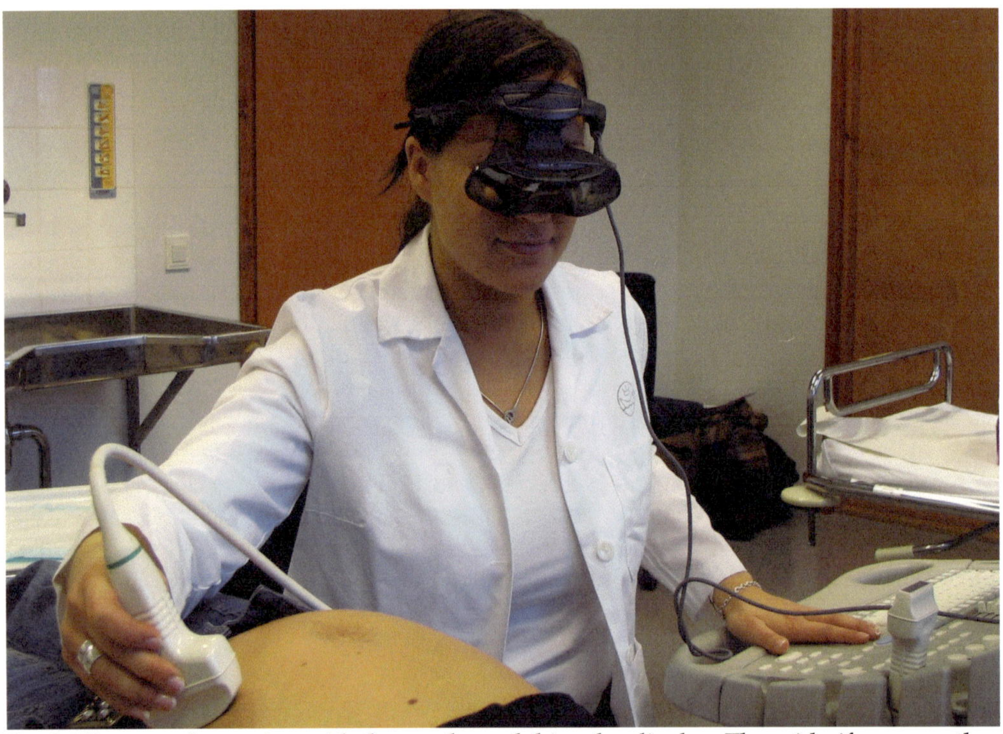

Fig. 3. Ultrasound scanning with the see through biocular display. The midwife can see the ultrasound scanning image in her visual field and simultaneously follow the location of the probe through the see-through display.

Positive pre-exp	Freq	Negative pre-exp	Freq
Ergonomics will be better	8	Adverse symptoms	8
Don`t know	6	Decreased contact patient	6
Better display quality	3	Lack of eye contact	6
Total	17		20
Positive post-exp	**Freq**	**Negative post-exp**	**Freq**
Ergonomics was good	8	Difficult to maintain contact to patient	4
Good image	4	Reduced visibility	4
Focus to the patient	4	Too much weight	4
Total	16		12

Table 4. The most frequent positive and negative post-task response categories in experiment 2 (MD-6).

Positive post-task	freq	Negative post-task	freq
Focus on patient	4	Difficult to wear the display	4
Ergonomics were good	4	Reduced visibility	3
Better consentration on examination	3	Difficult to communicate with the patient	3
Total	11	Total	11

Table 3. The most frequent positive and negative post-task response categories in experiment 1 (Glasstron).

Positive post-task	Freq	Negative post-task	Freq
Ergonomics were good	4	Difficult to keep the display in correct position	3
Good quality of image	3	Small working area through the display	3
Focus on patient	3	Problems with vision	3

Table 4. The most frequent positive and negative post-task response categories in experiment 2 (MD-6).

4. Conclusions

The use of head-mounted displays in medicine is in a preliminary stage and further research is needed to evaluate its long-term clinical impact on patients, nurses, doctors and hospital administrators. Other studies have shown that the use of a head-mounted display can be more precise than the use of a conventional desktop system. It also allows better accuracy and safety of clinical decisions based on images. However, psychological factors have a strong effect on the acceptance of the new technology. The widespread use and the universal transfer of such technology will remain limited until there is a better understanding of user experience issues related to this application.

Our results indicate that midwives regarded head-mounted displays as acceptable accessories to an ultrasound scanning task. Using the monocular head-mounted displays prompted slightly fewer negative comments than the use of a binocular see-through display. The reason for the differences might be related to the fact that the small monocular display disturbed the users less than the see-though display, which decreases the contrast of the visual scene and occludes peripheral vision.

The results showed both positive and negative ergonomics issues. The positive issues were related to the better working position made possible the head-mounted display. In other words, using a HMD requires less body rotation and less stretching out of the hands during scanning. This could ease adverse physical symptoms of sonographers in the long run. Furthermore, this might prevent the development of a musculoskeletal injury.

The negative ergonomics issues were complaints of difficulties in wearing the display and keeping the display stationary in front of the eye. In the long term, such issues might greatly decrease the satisfaction of users, so attention should be paid to the design of the displays so that wearing the display would be effortless and the display would remain stationary on the head in all work situations.

Generally our results suggest that the use of head-mounted displays is feasible during ultrasound scan. However, improvements in image quality as well as the design of the head-mounted display are necessary before the headset can be recommended for general use during ultrasound scanning. The test population in our experiment was fairly small, so it is difficult to generalize the results. A larger study will be needed to evaluate the possible trends in user performance over single sessions and over longer time periods. There may also be significant variability between users in accuracy and fatigue effects.

In the future, we are going to continue studies with the sonographers. Interesting questions are, for example, how a presbyopic person manage to use head-mounted display with the spectacles in the working situation. Also, we plan to investigate whether there are any differences with users who wear progressive lenses, normal single power lenses or contact lenses.

From ophthalmological point of view there are also several interesting research topics, like the possible relation of head-mounted display use and intraocular pressure (IOP) of the eye and the effect of HMD use to the dry-eye syndrome (Schaumberg et al, 2003).

5. References

Dudley, N.J. (2004). A systematic review of the ultrasound estimation of fetal weight. Ultrasound in Obstetrics and Gynecology. Volume 25, Issue 1 , Pages 80 - 89.

Fernando, R. (1996). Adverse Physical Symptoms in Radiographers Practising Ultrasound. *Radiography* 1996 2, 91-97

Hiatt K.L., Braithwaite, M.G., Crowley, J.S., Rash, C.E., van de Pol, C. Ranchino, J.,Statz, W.K., and Eke,A.J. (2002). "The effect of a monocular helmet-mounted display on aircrew health: A cohort study of Apache AH MK1 pilots, initial report," U.S. Army Aeromedical Research Laboratory, Fort Rucker, AL, USA *USAARL Report No. 2002-04*, 2002.

Howarth, P.A. (1994). Virtual Reality: an occupational health hazard of the future? *RCN Occupational Health Nurses Forum.* "Working for Health". April 1994

Howarth P.A. & Costello P.J. (1997). "The occurrence of virtual simulation sickness symptoms when a HMD was used as a personal viewing system," *Displays,* vol. 18, 107-116, 1997.

Häkkinen, J., Takatalo, J., Havukumpu, J., Komulainen, J., Särkelä, H. & Nyman, G. (2004). Simulator sickness symptoms caused by a visual search task in a monocular virtual display. *Proceedings of the 11th International Display Workshops (IDW '04)* December 8-10, 2004, Niigata Convention Center, Toki Messe, Niigata, Japan, 1511-1513.

Koesveld, J.J.M., Tetteroo, G.W.M. & Graaf, E.J.R. (2003). Use of head-mounted display in transanal endoscopic microsurgery. *Surgical Endoscopy* Volume 17, Number 6 / June, 2003.

Lee, P., Walt, J., Rosenblatt, L. Siegartel, L. & Stern, L. (2007). Association Between Intraocular Pressure Variation and Glaucoma Progression: Data from a United States Chart Review . *American Journal of Ophthalmology,* Volume 144, Issue 6, December 2007, 901-907.

Letterie, G.S. ; (2002). How virtual reality may enhance training in obstetrics and gynecology. *American Journal of Obstetric nd Gynecology,* 187 (2002) 37-40

Miles J. (2005). Work related upper limb disorders in sonographers. *Synergy;* 2005, 6-11.

Mon-Williams, M., Wann, J.P. & Rushton, S. (1993). "Binocular vision in a virtual world: visual deficits following the wearing of a head-mounted display," *Ophthalmic and Physiological Optics,* (1993) 387-391.

Morton, B., Delf, P. (2007). The prevalence and causes of MSI amongst sonographers, *Radiography* 2007. doi: 10.1016/j.radi 2007.02.004

Necas M. (1996). Musculoskeletal symptomology and repetitive strain injuries in diagnostic medical sonographers: a pilot study in Washington and Oregon. *J Diagn Med Sonogr* 1996,12:266-73.

Ormerod, D.F., Ross,B. & Naluai-Cecchini,A. (2002). "Use of a see-through head-worn display of patient monitoring data to enhance anesthesiologists' response to abnormal critical events," in *6th International Symposium on Wearable Computers (ISWC'02).* Seattle, Washington, USA, 2002, 131-132.

Peli, E. (1998). The visual effects of head-mounted display (HMD) are not distinguishable from those of desk-top computer display, *Vision Research* 38 (1998) 2053-2066.

Pike I, Russo A, Berkowitz J, Baker J & Lessoway VA. (1997). The prevalence of musculoskeletal disorders among diagnostic medical sonographers. *J Diagn Med Sonogr* 1997;13 219-27.

Reisman, M., Gray, W.A., Ormerod, D.F., Hyde, J.P. (2002) Use of a Head-Mounted Confluent Display of Fluoroscopic and Echocardiographic Images to Enhance Operator Feedback during Catheter-Deployed Closures of Cardiac Septal Defects. *Proceedings. of the 10th Annual Medicine Meets Virtual Reality Conference.* Newport Beach, USA 2002.

Rosenthal, M., State, A., Lee, J., Hirota, G., Ackerman, J., Keller, K., Etta, D. Pisano, E.D., Jiroutek, M., Muller, K., Fuchs, H._(2002). Augmented reality guidance for needle biopsies: An initial, randomized, controlled trial in phantoms. *Medical Image Analysis* (2002) 313-320.

Ross, B. (2002). Use of a See-Through Head-Worn Display of Patient Monitoring Data to Enhance Anaesthesiologists' Response to Abnormal Clinical Events. *Proceedings of the. Computer Society. Proceedings of the 6th International Symposium on Wearable Computers (ISWC.02)* (2002)

Rushton, S., Mon-Williams M., Wann, J.P. (1994). Binocular vision in a bi-ocular world. New-generation head-mounted displays avoid causing visual deficit. *Displays* issue 4 (1994) 255-260.

Ryndin, I., Lukasewycz, S., Hoffman, N., Nakib, N.A., Best, S. & Monga, M. (2005) Impact of Heads-Up Display Imaging on Endoscopic Task Performance. *Journal of Endourology*. October 1, 2005, 19(8): 964-967

Satava, R.M.(1994). Emerging medical applications of virtual reality: A surgeon's perspective. *Artificial Intelligence in Medicine* (1994) 281-288.

Satava R. M., Jones, S.B. (1998) Current and Future Applications of Virtual Reality for Medicine. *Proceedings of the IEEE 86* (1998) 484-489.

Schaumberg, D.A., Sullivan, D.A., Buring, J.E. & Dana, M.R. (2003). Prevalence of dry eye syndrome among US women. *American Journal of Ophthalmology* 136(2) 318-326.

Sheedy and N. Bergstrom, "Performance and comfort on near-eye computer displays," *Optometry and Vision Science*, vol. 79(2002) 306-312.

Shuhaiber J.H. (2004). Augmented Reality in Surgery, *Archives of Surgery* 139 (2004) 170-174.

18

Adaptive Real-Time Image Processing for Human-Computer Interaction

Bogdan Kwolek
Rzeszow University of Technology
Poland

1. Introduction

There is a need for computers to be capable to interact naturally with the user, in similar way as human-human interaction takes place. Adding perceptual abilities to computers would enable computers and humans to work jointly more in partner manner. A user-friendly computing system should be aware of the person's context so that it can respond appropriately to user's intentions and anticipate his or her needs. To achieve such functionality, the system needs to integrate a wide variety of visual functions, like localization, object tracking and recognition, action recognition, categorization, interactive object learning.

Human-computer interaction (HCI) is a research discipline that is concerned with the design, implementation and evaluation of interactive computing systems for human use. Most of the research in this area focuses on developing of user-friendly interfaces. Although existing interfaces are designed with human user in mind, many of them are far from being user-friendly end effective. So, if we put in a computer between two people communicating in a natural way, the effective bandwidth and naturalness of the communication will be reduced. Thus, a very important issue is how to accomplish synergism between man and the computer.

The idea of ambient intelligence is a promising area of human-computer interaction. An ambient intelligence environment is sensitive to the presence of people and responsive to their needs. It consists of devices that are integrated into environment and work in concert to support people in carrying out their everyday life activities. The unobtrusive layout should be adaptive, which means that it should change in response to user needs. Instead of single and predefined model, such a system acquires its knowledge via interaction with the user and the usage of multiple modules and pathways. To achieve goals of that kind the research interest has shifted from generic computer vision systems towards vision modules able to solve more specific tasks. However, multi-module vision systems running in real-world scenarios and integrating several different vision behaviors are only sparsely reported in the literature.

The objective of this work is to present the methods and techniques for construction of vision systems that can perform tasks oriented towards human-computer interaction. Particular emphasis is placed on algorithms using images acquired in realistic settings and through employing both static and dynamic information to allow knowledge acquisition and interpretation. It presents efficient and adaptive algorithms, which can operate over long period of time, in varying illumination conditions, with complex background. It is devoted to adaptive object tracking along with unsupervised learning algorithms. It presents adaptive observation models for probabilistic tracking. Particle filters built on such adaptive models are presented. A template based tracking, where the target is represented by a collection of rectangular regions is discussed. Every such a region votes in a common map reflecting the possible positions and the scales of the object. The mentioned above algorithms were tested using various test sequences. The attention is focused on human head/face, one of the most important features in tasks consisting in people tracking and action recognition. The efficiency of the algorithms is demonstrated in several real scenarios, among others in tasks consisting in person following via a real mobile agent, which is equipped with an on-board camera. The mentioned above algorithms constitute a vision system with adaptation and learning capabilities, which can operate on images with complicated background, taken in highly varying illumination conditions.

2. Current Research

Most of the research in human-computer interaction is connected with analysis of the dynamics of human face and body. HCI research devoted to human face is mainly concentrated on face detection, face recognition, tracking of location of the head/face, tracking of head pose, eye tracking, recognition of head gestures, recognition of facial expressions. Research work that is connected with the human body focuses on human detection, gesture as well as recognition of gestural commands, body motion analysis, human tracking, 3D body tracking. Although great progress has been achieved in human machine interaction, most researches still treat the above ingredients separately and the complete systems are reported only sparsely in the relevant literature. Little work has been done in order to endow computers with ability to see where humans are. Here, we evoke some recent surveys, then we present some methods that have been successfully applied in practice, and finally expand the discussion to areas not covered in previous surveys.

Extensive surveys have been published in several HCI fields such as face detection (Yang et al., 2002), face recognition (Zhao et al., 2003), facial expression analysis (Fasel and Luettin, 2003), gesture recognition (Pavlovic et al., 1997, Mitra and Acharya, 2007), human motion analysis (Gavrila, 1999, Aggarwal and Cai, 1999, Wang et al., 2003). A survey presenting the use of vision in HCI, particularly in the area of head tracking can be found in work (Porta, 2002, Kisacanin, 2005). The authors of work (Jaimes and Sebe, 2007) give an overview of multimodal human machine interfaces.

One of the methods that was applied in practice is eye tracking. The study of eye movements pre-dates the widespread use of personal computers. Eye tracking in the field of human-computer interaction has demonstrated modest growth both as a means of studying the suitability of computer interfaces and as a means of interfacing with the computer. An eye tracker is a device measuring both eye positions and eye movements. The commercially available eye tracking systems are mounted on the participant's head or remotely in front of the participant (Duchowski, 2002). Typically they acquire reflections of the infrared light from both the retina and cornea. The problem of constraining the relationship between the eye and the user is one of the obstacles for incorporation of eye tracking in broader scope of the practice use. Great progress has been made in reducing this barrier, but from the user perspective the existing solutions remain far from optimal (Jacob et al., 2003). Some recent advances in integrating computer interface and eye tracking make possible a mapping of fixation points to visual stimuli (Crowe et al., 2000, Reeder et al. 2001). The gaze tracker proposed in work (Ji and Zhu, 2004) can perform robust and accurate gaze estimation without calibration through the use of procedure identifying the mapping from the pupil parameters to the coordinates of the screen. The mapping function can generalize to other participants not attending in the training. A survey of work related to eye tracking can be found in (Duchowski, 2002).

The Smart Kiosk System (Rehg et al., 1997) uses vision techniques to detect potential users and decide whether the person is a good candidate for interaction. It utilizes face detection and tracking for gesture analysis when a person is at a close range. CAMSHIFT (Bradski, 1998) is a face tracker that has been developed to control games and 3D graphics through predefined head movements. Such a control is performed via specific actions. When people interact face-to-face they indicate of acknowledgment or disinterest with head gestures. In work (Morency et al., 2007) a vision-based head gesture recognition techniques and their usage for common user interface is studied. Another work (Kjeldsen, 2001) reports successful results of using face tracking for pointing, scrolling and selection tasks. An intelligent wheelchair, which is user-friendly to both the user and people around it by observing the faces of both user and others has been proposed in work (Kuno et al., 2001). The user can control it by turning his or her face in the direction where he or she would like to turn. Owing to observing the pedestrian's face it is able to change the collision avoidance method depending on whether or not he or she notices the wheelchair. In related work (Davis et al., 2001) a perceptual user interface for recognizing predefined head gesture acknowledgements is described. Salient facial features are identified and tracked in order to compute the global 2-D motion direction of the head. A Finite State Machine incorporating the natural timings of the computed head motions has been utilized for modeling and recognition of commands. An enhanced text editor using such a perceptual dialog interface has also been described.

Ambient intelligence, also known as Ubiquitous or Pervasive Computing, is a growing field of computer science that has potential for great impact in the future. The term ambient intelligence (AmI) is defined by the Advisory Group to the European Community's Information Society Technology Program as "the convergence of ubiquitous computing, ubiquitous communication, and interfaces adapting to the user". The aim of AmI is to expand the interaction between human beings and information media via the application of ubiquitous computing devices, which encompass interfaces creating together a *perceptive computer environment* rather than one that relies exclusively on active user input. These information media will be available through new types of interfaces and will allow drastically simplified and more intuitive use. The combination of simplified use and their ability to communicate will result in increased efficiency of the contact and interaction. One of the most significant challenges in AmI is to create high-quality, user-friendly, user-adaptive, seamless, and unobtrusive interfaces. In particular, they should allow to sense far more about a person in order to permit the computer to be more acquainted about the person needs and demands, the situation the person is in, the environment, than current interfaces can. Such devices will be able to either bear in mind past environments they operated in, or proactively set up services in new environments (Lyytinen and Yoo, 2002). Particularly, this includes voice and vision technology.

Human computer interaction is very important in multimedia systems (Emond, 2007) because the interaction is basic necessity of such systems. Understanding the meaning of the user message and also the context of the messages is also of great importance for development of practical multimedia interfaces (Zhou et al., 2005).
Common industrial robots usually perform repeating actions in an exactly predefined environment. In contrast to them service robots are designed for supporting jobs for people in their life environment. These intelligent machines should operate in dynamic and unstructured environment and provide services while interaction with people who are not especially skilled in a robot communication. In particular, service robots should participate in mutual interactions with people and work in partnership with humans. In work (Medioni, 2007) visual perception for personal service robot is discussed. A survey of the research related to human-robot interaction can be found in (Goodrich and Schultz, 2007, Fong et al., 2003). Such a challenging research is critical if we allow robots to become part of our daily life.. Several significant steps towards a natural communication have been done, including use of spoken commands and task specific gestural commands in order to convey complex intent. However, meaningful progress in the development is required before we can accomplish communication that feels effortless. Automating the use of human-machine interfaces is also a substantial challenge.

3. Particle Filtering for Visual Tracking

Assume that a dynamic system is described by the following state-space model

$$\begin{aligned} \mathbf{x}_t &= f(\mathbf{x}_{t-1}, \mathbf{u}_t), \; t = 1,2,..., \\ \mathbf{z}_t &= h(\mathbf{x}_t, \mathbf{v}_t), \; t = 0,1,..., \end{aligned} \tag{1}$$

where $\mathbf{x}_t \in R^n$ denotes the system state, $\mathbf{z}_t \in R^m$ is the measurement, $\mathbf{u}_t \in R^n$ stands for the system noise, $\mathbf{v}_t \in R^m$ express the measurement noise, and n and m are dimensions of $\mathbf{x}_t$ and $\mathbf{z}_t$, respectively. The sequences $\{\mathbf{u}_t\}$ and $\{\mathbf{v}_t\}$ are independent and identically distributed (i.i.d.), independent of each other, and independent of the initial state $\mathbf{x}_0$ with a distribution $\mathbf{p}_0$. For nonlinear models, multi-modal, non-Gaussian or any combination of these models the particle filter provides a Monte Carlo solution to the recursive filtering equation $p(\mathbf{x}_t \mid \mathbf{z}_{1:t}) \propto p(\mathbf{z}_t \mid \mathbf{x}_t) \int p(\mathbf{x}_t \mid \mathbf{x}_{t-1}) p(\mathbf{x}_{t-1} \mid \mathbf{z}_{1:t-1}) d\mathbf{x}_{t-1}$, where $\mathbf{z}_{1:t} = \{\mathbf{z}_1, ..., \mathbf{z}_t\}$ denotes all observations from time 1 to current time step t. It approximates $p(\mathbf{x}_t \mid \mathbf{z}_{1:t})$ by a probability mass function

$$\hat{p}(\mathbf{x}_t \mid \mathbf{z}_{1:t}) = \sum_{i=1}^{N} w_t^{(i)} \delta(\mathbf{x}_t - \mathbf{x}_t^{(i)}) \tag{2}$$

where δ is the Kronecker delta function, $\mathbf{x}_t^{(i)}$ are random points and $w_t^{(i)}$ are corresponding, non-negative weights representing a probability distribution, i.e.

$\sum_{i=1}^{N} w_t^{(i)} = 1$. If weights are i.i.d. drawn from an importance density $q(\mathbf{x}_t \mid \mathbf{z}_{1:t})$, their values should be set according to the following formula:

$$w_t^{(i)} \propto \frac{p(\mathbf{x}_t^{(i)} \mid \mathbf{z}_{1:t})}{q(\mathbf{x}_t \mid \mathbf{z}_{1:t})} \tag{3}$$

Through applying the Bayes rule we can obtain the following recursive equation for updating the weights

$$w_t^{(i)} \propto w_{t-1}^{(i)} \frac{p(\mathbf{z}_t \mid \mathbf{x}_t^{(i)}) p(\mathbf{x}_t^{(i)} \mid \mathbf{x}_{t-1}^{(i)})}{q(\mathbf{x}_t^{(i)} \mid \mathbf{x}_{t-1}^{(i)}, \mathbf{z}_t)} \tag{4}$$

where the sensor model $p(\mathbf{z}_t \mid \mathbf{x}_t^{(i)})$ describes how likely it is to obtain a particular sensor reading $\mathbf{z}_t$ given state $\mathbf{x}_t^{(i)}$, and $p(\mathbf{x}_t^{(i)} \mid \mathbf{x}_{t-1}^{(i)})$ denotes the probability density function describing the state evolution from $\mathbf{x}_{t-1}^{(i)}$ to $\mathbf{x}_t^{(i)}$. In order to avoid degeneracy of the particles, in each time step new particles are resampled i.i.d. from the approximated conditional density. The aim of the re-sampling (Gordon, 1993) is to eliminate particles with low importance weights and multiply particles with high importance weights. It selects with higher probability particles that have a high likelihood associated with them, while preserving the asymptotic approximation of the particle-based posterior representation. Without re-sampling the variance of the weight increases stochastically over time (Doucet et al., 2000). Given $w_{t-1}^{(i)} = 1/N$, the weighting function is simplified to the following form:

$$w_t^{(i)} \propto \frac{p(\mathbf{z}_t \mid \mathbf{x}_t^{(i)}) p(\mathbf{x}_t^{(i)} \mid \mathbf{x}_{t-1}^{(i)})}{q(\mathbf{x}_t^{(i)} \mid \mathbf{x}_{t-1}^{(i)}, \mathbf{z}_t)} \tag{5}$$

If a filtering algorithm takes the prior $p(\mathbf{x}_t \mid \mathbf{x}_{t-1})$ as the importance density, the importance function reduces to $q(\mathbf{x}_t^{(i)} \mid \mathbf{x}_{t-1}^{(i)}, \mathbf{z}_t) = p(\mathbf{x}_t^{(i)} \mid \mathbf{x}_{t-1}^{(i)})$, and in consequence the weighting equation takes the form $w_t^{(i)} \propto p(\mathbf{z}_t \mid \mathbf{x}_t^{(i)})$. This simplification leads to bootstrap filter (Gordon, 1993) and a variant of a well-known particle filter in computer vision, namely CONDENSATION (Isard and Blake, 1998).

The generic particle filter operates recursively through selecting particles, moving them forward according to a probabilistic motion model that is dispersed by an additive random noise component, then evaluating against the observation model, and finally resampling particles according to their weights in order to avoid degeneracy. The algorithm is as follows:

1. Initialization. Sample $\mathbf{x}_0^{(1)}, \ldots, \mathbf{x}_0^{(N)}$ i.i.d. from the initial density $\mathbf{p}_0$
2. Importance Sampling/Propagation. Sample $\mathbf{x}_t^{(i)}$ from $p(\mathbf{x}_t \mid \mathbf{x}_{t-1}^{(i)})$, $i = 1, \ldots, N$

3. Updating. Compute $\hat{p}(\mathbf{x}_t \mid \mathbf{z}_{1:t}) = \sum_{i=1}^{N} w_t^{(i)} \delta(\mathbf{x} - \mathbf{x}_t^{(i)})$ using normalized weighs:

$$w_t^{(i)} = p(\mathbf{z}_t \mid \mathbf{x}_t^{(i)}),$$

$$w_t^{(i)} = w_t^{(i)} / \sum_{j=1}^{N} w_t^{(j)}, \quad i = 1,\ldots,N$$

4. Resampling. Sample $\mathbf{x}_t^{(1)},\ldots,\mathbf{x}_t^{(N)}$ i.i.d. from $\hat{p}(\mathbf{x}_t \mid \mathbf{z}_{1:t})$
5. $t \leftarrow t+1$, go to step 2.

The particle filter converges to the optimal filter if the number of particles grows to infinity. The most significant property of the particle filter is its capability to deal with complex, non-Gaussian and multimodal posterior distributions. However, the number of particles that is required to adequately approximate the conditional density grows exponentially with the dimensionality of the state space. This can cause some practical difficulties in applications such as articulated body tracking (Schmidt et al., 2006). In such tasks we can observe weakness of the particle filter consisting in that the particles do not cluster around the true state of the object as the time increases, and instead they migrate toward local maximas in the posterior distribution. The track of the object can be lost if particles are too diffused. If the observation likelihood lies in the tail of the prior distribution, most of the particles will become meaningless weights. If the system model is inaccurate, the prediction done on the basis of the system model may be too distant from the expected state. In case the system noise is large and the number of particles is not sufficient, poor predictions can also be caused by the simulation in the particle filtering. To deal with the mentioned difficulties different enhancements to presented above algorithm have been proposed, among others algorithms combining extended Kalman filter/unscented Kalman filter with generic particle filter (Merve, 2001). Such particle filters incorporate the current observation to create the more appropriate importance density than the generic particle filter, which utilizes the prior as the importance density.

4. Head Tracking Using Color and Ellipse Fitting in a Particle Filter

Most existing vision-based tracking algorithms give correct estimates of the state in a short span of time and usually fail if there is a significant inter-frame change in object appearance or change of lighting conditions. These methods generally fail to precisely track regions that share similar statistics with background regions.

Service robots are designed for supporting jobs for people in their life environment. These intelligent machines should operate in dynamic and unstructured environment and provide services while interaction with people who are not especially skilled in a robot communication. A kind of human-machine interaction, which is very interesting and has some practical use is following a person by a mobile robot. This behavior can be useful in several applications including robot programming by demonstration and instruction, which in particular can contain tasks consisting in a guidance a robot to specific place, where the user can point to object of interest. A demonstration is particularly useful at programming of new tasks by non-expert users. It is far easier to point towards an object and demonstrate a track, which robot should follow, than to verbally describe its exact location and the path of movement (Waldherr at al., 2000). Therefore, robust person tracking is important prerequisite to achieve the mentioned above robot skills. However, vision modules of the mobile robot impose several requirements and limitations on the use of known vision

systems. First of all, the vision module needs to be small enough to be mounted on the robot and to derive enough small portion of energy from the battery, which would not cause a significant reduction of working time of the vehicle. Additionally the system must operate at an acceptable speed (Waldherr at al., 2000).
Here, we present fast and robust vision based low-level interface for person tracking (Kwolek, 2004). To improve the reliability of tracking using images acquired from an on-board camera we integrated in probabilistic manner the edge strength along the elliptical head boundary and color within the observation model of the particle filter. The adaptive observation model integrates two different visual cues. The incorporation of information about the distance between the camera and the face undergoing tracking results in robust tracking even in presence of skin colored regions in the background. Our interface has been used to conduct several experiments consisting in recognizing arm-postures while following a person via autonomous robot in natural laboratory environment (Kwolek, 2003a, Kwolek, 2003b).

4.1 State space and dynamics

The outline of the head is modeled in the 2D-image domain as a vertical ellipse that is allowed to translate and scale subject to a dynamical model. The object state is given by $\mathbf{x} = \{x, \dot{x}, y, \dot{y}, s_y, \dot{s}_y\}$, where $\{x, y\}$ denotes the location of the ellipse center in the image, $\dot{x}$ and $\dot{y}$ are the velocities of the center, s_y is the length of the minor axis of the ellipse and $\dot{s}_y$ is the rate at which s_y changes.
Our objective is to track a face in a sequence of images coming from an on-board camera. To achieve robustness to large variations in the object pose, illumination, motion, etc. we use the first-order auto-regressive dynamic model $\mathbf{x}_t = A\mathbf{x}_{t-1} + \mathbf{v}_t$, where A denotes a deterministic component describing a constant velocity movement and $\mathbf{v}_t$ is a multivariate Gaussian random variable. The diffusion component represents uncertainty in prediction.

4.2 Shape and color cues

As demonstrated in (Birchfield, 1998) the contour cues can be very useful to represent the appearance of the tracked objects with distinctive silhouette when a model of the shape can be learned off-line and then adapted over time. The shape of the head is one of the most easily recognizable human parts and can be reasonably well approximated by an ellipse. Therefore a parametric model of the ellipse with a fixed aspect ratio equal to 1.2 is utilized to calculate the likelihood. During tracking the oval shape of each head candidate is verified using the sum of intensity gradients along the head boundary. The elliptical upright outlines as well as masks containing interior pixels have been prepared off-line and stored for the use during tracking. The contour cues can, however, be sensitive to disturbances coming from cluttered background, even when detailed models have been used.
When the contour information is poor or is temporary unavailable color information can be very useful alternative to extract the tracked object. Color information can be particularly useful to support a detection of faces in image sequences because the color as a cue is computationally inexpensive (Swain and Ballard, 1991), robust towards changes in orientation and scaling of an object being in movement. The discriminative ability of color is especially worth to emphasize if a considered object is occluded or is in shadow, what can

be in general significant practical difficulty using edge-based methods. Robust tracking can be accomplished using only a simple color model constructed in the first frame and then accommodated over time. One of the problems of tracking on the basis of analysis of color distribution is that lighting conditions may have an influence on perceived color of the target. Even in the case of constant lighting conditions, the apparent color of the target may change over a frame sequence, since other objects can shadow the target.
Color localization cues can be obtained by comparing the reference color histogram of the object of interest with the current color histogram. Due to the statistical nature, a color histogram can only reflect the content of images in a limited way (Swain and Ballard, 1991). In particular, color histograms are invariant to translation and rotation of the object and they vary slowly with the change of angle of view and with the change in scale. Additionally, such a compact representation is tolerant to noise that can result from imperfect ellipse-approximation of a highly deformable structure and curved surface of face causing significant variations of the observed colors.
A color histogram including spatial information can be calculated using a 2-dimensional kernel centered on the target (Comaniciu et al., 2000). The kernel is used to provide the weight for color according to its distance from the region center. In order to assign smaller weights to the pixels that are further away from the region center a nonnegative and monotonic decreasing function $k:[0,\infty)\rightarrow R$ can be used (Comaniciu et al., 2000). The probability of particular histogram bin u at location $\mathbf{x}$ is calculated as

$$d_{\mathbf{x}}^{(u)} = C_r \sum_{l=1}^{L} k\left(\left\|\frac{\mathbf{x}-\mathbf{x}_l}{r}\right\|^2\right) \delta\left[h(\mathbf{x}_l)-u\right] \tag{6}$$

where $\mathbf{x}_i$ are pixel locations, L is the number of pixels in the considered region, constant r is the radius of the kernel, δ is the Kronecker delta function, and the function $h: R^2 \rightarrow \{1,...,K\}$ associates the bin number. The normalization factor C_r ensures that $\sum_{u=1}^{K} d_{\mathbf{x}}^{(u)} = 1$. This normalization factor can be precalculated (Comaniciu et al., 2000) for the utilized kernel and assumed values of r. The 2-dimensional kernels have been prepared off-line and then stored in lookup tables for the future use. The color representation of the target has been obtained by quantizing the ellipse's interior colors into K bins and extracting the weighted histogram. To make the histogram representation of the tracked head less sensitive to lighting conditions the HSV color space has been chosen and the V component has been represented by 4 bins while the H and S components obtained the 8-bins representation.
To compare the histogram Q representing the tracked face to the histogram I obtained from the particle position we utilized the metric $\sqrt{1-\rho(I,Q)}$, which is derived from Bhattacharyya coefficient $\rho(I,Q) = \sum_{u=1}^{K} \sqrt{I^{(u)} Q^{(u)}}$. The work (Comaniciu et al., 2000) demonstrated that the utilized metric is invariant to the scale of the target and therefore is superior to other measures such as histogram intersection (Swain and Ballard, 1991) or Kullback divergence.

Based on Bhattacharyya coefficient we defined the color observation model as $p(\mathbf{z}^C \mid \mathbf{x}) = (\sqrt{2\pi}\sigma)^{-1} e^{-\frac{1-\rho}{2\sigma^2}}$. Owing to such weighting we favor head candidates whose color distributions are similar to the distribution of the tracked head. The second ingredient of the observation model reflecting the edge strength along the elliptical head boundary has been weighted in a similar manner $p(\mathbf{z}^G \mid \mathbf{x}) = (\sqrt{2\pi}\sigma)^{-1} e^{-\frac{1-\phi_g}{2\sigma^2}}$, where ϕ_g denotes the normalized gradient along the ellipse's boundary.

4.3 Probabilistic integration of cues

The aim of probabilistic multi-cue integration is to enhance visual cues that are more reliable in the current context and to suppress less reliable cues. The correlation between location, edge and color of an object even if exist is rather weak. Assuming that the measurements are conditionally independent given the state we obtain the equation $p(\mathbf{z}_t \mid \mathbf{x}_t) = p(\mathbf{z}_t^G \mid \mathbf{x}_t) \cdot p(\mathbf{z}_t^C \mid \mathbf{x}_t)$, which allows us to accomplish the probabilistic integration of cues. To achieve this we calculate at each time t the L2 norm based distances $D_t^{(j)}$, between the individual cue's centroids and the centroid obtained by integrating the likelihood from utilized cues (Triesch et al., 2001). The reliability factors of the utilized cues $\alpha_t^{(j)}$ are then calculated on the basis of the following leaking integrator $\xi \dot{\alpha}_t^{(j)} = \eta_t^{(j)} - \alpha_t^{(j)}$, where ξ denotes a factor that determines the adaptation rate and $\eta_t^{(j)} = 0.5 \cdot (\tanh(-aD_t^{(j)}) + b)$. In the experiments we set $a = 0.3$ and $b = 3$. Using the reliability factors the observation likelihood has been determined as follows:

$$p(\mathbf{z}_t \mid \mathbf{x}_t) = \left[p(\mathbf{z}_t^G \mid \mathbf{x}_t)\right]^{\alpha_t^{(1)}} \cdot \left[p(\mathbf{z}_t^C \mid \mathbf{x}_t)\right]^{\alpha_t^{(2)}}, \quad 0 \le \alpha_t^{(j)} \le 1. \tag{7}$$

4.4 Adaptation of the color model

The largest variations in object appearance occur when the object is moving. Varying illumination conditions can influence the distribution of colors in an image sequence. If the illumination is static but non-uniform, movement of the object can cause the captured color to change alike. Therefore, tracker that uses a static color model is certain to fail in unconstrained imaging conditions. To deal with varying illumination conditions the histogram representing the tracked head has been updated over time. This makes possible to track not only a face profile which has been shot during initialization of the tracker but in addition different profiles of the face as well as the head can be tracked. Using only pixels from the ellipse's interior, a new color histogram is computed and combined with the previous model in the following manner $Q_t^{(u)} = (1-\gamma)Q_{t-1}^{(u)} + \gamma I_t^{(u)}$, where γ is an accommodation rate, I_t denotes the histogram of the interior of the ellipse representing the estimated state, Q_{t-1} is the histogram of the target from the previous frame, whereas $u = 1, \ldots, K$.

4.5 Depth cue

In experiments, in which a stereovision camera has been employed, the length of the minor axis of the considered ellipse has been determined on the basis of depth information. The system state presented in Subsection 4.1 contains four variables, namely location and speed. The length has been maintained by performing a local search to maximize the goodness of the observation match. Taking into account the length of the minor axis resulting from the depth information we considered smaller and larger projection scale of the ellipse about two pixels. Owing to verification of face distance to the camera and face region size heuristics it is possible to discard many false positives that are generated through the face detection module.

4.6 Face detection

The face detection algorithm can be utilized to form a proposal distribution for the particle filter in order to direct the particles towards most probable locations of the objects of interest. The employed face finder is based on object detection algorithm described in work (Viola et al., 2001). The aim of the detection algorithm is to find all faces and then to select the highest scoring candidate that is situated nearby a predicted location of the face. Next, taking the location and the size of the window containing the face we construct a Gaussian distribution $p(\mathbf{x}_t \mid \mathbf{x}_{t-1}, \mathbf{z}_t)$ in order to reflect the face position in the proposal distribution. The formula describing the proposal distribution has the following form:

$$q(\mathbf{x}_t \mid \mathbf{x}_{t-1}, \mathbf{z}_t) = \beta p(\mathbf{x}_t \mid \mathbf{x}_{t-1}, \mathbf{z}_t) + (1-\beta) p(\mathbf{x}_t \mid \mathbf{x}_{t-1}) \tag{8}$$

The parameter β is dynamically set to zero if no face has been found. In such a situation the particle filter takes the form of the CONDENSATION (Isard and Blake, 1998).

4.7 Head tracking for human-robot interaction

The experiments described in this Section were carried out with a mobile robot Pioneer 2DX (ActivMedia Robotics, 2001) equipped with commercial binocular Megapixel Stereo Head. The dense stereo maps are extracted in that system thanks to small area correspondences between image pairs (Konolige, 1997) and therefore poor results in regions of little texture are often provided. The depth map covering a face region is usually dense because a human face is rich in details and texture, see Fig. 1b. Owing to such a property the stereovision provides a separate source of information and considerably supports the process of approximating the tracked head with an ellipse of proper size.

A typical laptop computer equipped with 2.5 GHz Pentium IV is utilized to run the software operating at images of size 320x240. The position of the tracked face in the image plane as well as person's distance to the camera are written asynchronously in block of common memory, which can be easily accessed by Saphira client. Saphira is an integrated sensing and control system architecture based on a client server-model whereby the robot supplies a set of basic functions that can be used to interact with it (ActivMedia Robotics, 2001). During tracking, the control module keeps the user face within the camera field of view by coordinating the rotation of the robot with the location of the tracked face in the image plane. The aim of the robot orientation controller is to keep the position of the tracked face at specific position in the image. The linear velocity has been dependent on person's distance to the camera. In experiments consisting in person following a distance 1.3 m has been assumed as the reference value that the linear velocity controller should maintain. To eliminate needless robot rotations as well as forward and backward movements we have applied a simple logic providing necessary insensitivity zone. The PD controllers have been implemented in the Saphira-interpreted Colbert language (ActivMedia Robotics, 2001).

To test the prepared software we performed various experiments. After detection of possible faces, see Fig. 1. a,b, the system can identify known faces among the detected ones, using a technique known as eigenfaces (Turk and Pentland, 1991). In tracking scenarios consisting in realization of only a rotation of mobile robot, which can be seen as analogous to experiments with a pan-camera, the user moved about a room, walked back and forth as well as around the mobile robot. The aim of such scenarios was to evaluate the quality of ellipse scaling in response of varying distance between the camera and the user, see Fig. 1. e,h. Our experimental findings show that owing to stereovision the ellipse properly approximates the tracked head and in consequence, sudden changes of the minor axis length as well as ellipse's jumps are eliminated. The greatest variability is in horizontal motion, followed by vertical motion. Ellipse's size variability is more constrained and tends towards the size from the previous time step. By dealing with multiple cues the presented approach can track a head reliably in cases of temporal occlusions and varying illumination conditions, see also Fig. 1. c, even when person undergoing tracking moves in front of the wooden doors or desks, see also Fig. 1. c - h. Using this sequence we conducted tracking experiments assuming that no stereo information is available. Under such an assumption the system state presented in Subsection 4.1 has been employed. However, considerable ellipse changes as well as window jitter have been observed and in consequence the head has been tracked in only the part of the sequence.

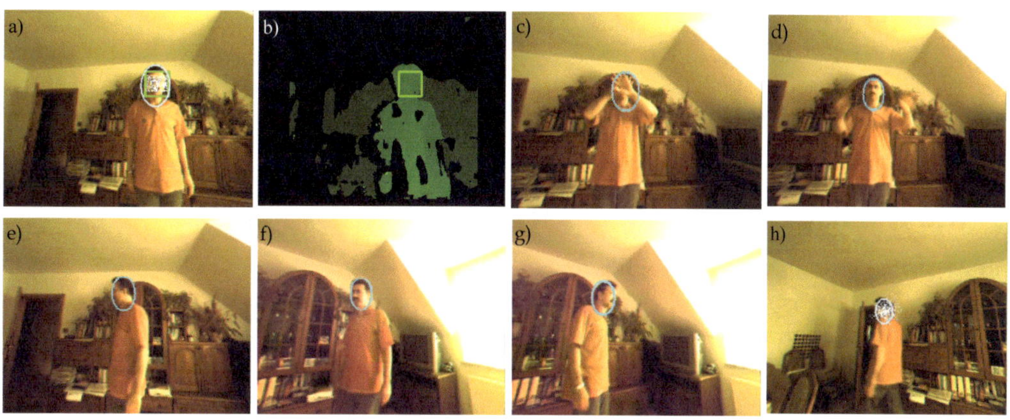

Fig. 1. Face detection in frame #9 (a), depth image (b), #44 (c), #45 (d), #69 (e), #169 (f), #182 (g), #379 (h)

Figure 2. demonstrates some tracking results that were obtained in experiments consisting in person following via the mobile robot. As we can see, the tracking techniques described above allow us to achieve the tracking of the person in real situations, under varying illumination.

The tracker runs with 400 particles at frame rates of 13-14 Hz. The face detector can localize human faces in about 0.1 s. The system processes about 6 frames per second when the information about detected faces is used to generate the proposal distribution for the particle filter. The recognition of single face takes about 0.01 s. These times allow the robot to follow the person moving with a walking speed.

Fig. 2. Person following with a mobile robot. In 1-st and 3-rd row some images from on-board camera are depicted, whereas in 2-nd and 4-th row the corresponding images from an external camera are presented

5. Face Tracking for Human-Computer-Interaction

5.1 Adaptive models for particle filtering

Low-order parametric models of the image motion of pixels laying within a template can be utilized to predict the movement in the image plane (Hager and Belhumeur, 1998). This means that by comparing the gray level values of the corresponding pixels within region undergoing tracking, it is possible to obtain the transformation (giving shear, dilation and rotation) and translation of the template in the current image (Horn, 1986). Therefore, such models allow us to establish temporal correspondences of the target region. They make region-based tracking an effective complement to tracking that is based on classifier distinguishing between foreground and background pixels. In a particle filter the usage of change in transformation and translation $\Delta\boldsymbol{\omega}_{t+1}$ arising from changes in image intensities within the template can lead to reduction of the extent of noise $\mathbf{v}_{t+1}$ in the motion model. It can take the form (Zhou and Chellappa, 2004): $\boldsymbol{\omega}_{t+1} = \hat{\boldsymbol{\omega}}_t + \Delta\boldsymbol{\omega}_{t+1} + \mathbf{v}_{t+1}$.

5.2 Head tracking for human-robot interaction

Let $I_{x,t}$ denote the brightness value at the location $\mathbf{x} = \{x_1, x_2\}$ in an image I that was acquired in time t. Let $\mathcal{R}$ be a set of J image locations $\{\mathbf{x}^{(j)} \mid j = 1,...,J\}$ defining a template. $Y_t(\mathcal{R}) = \{I_{x,t}^{(j)} \mid j = 1,2,...,J\}$ is a vector of the brightness values at locations $\mathbf{x}^{(j)}$ in the template. We assume that the transformations of the template can be modeled by a parametric motion model $g(\mathbf{x};\boldsymbol{\omega}_t)$, where $\mathbf{x}$ denotes an image location and $\boldsymbol{\omega}_t = \{\omega_t^{(1)}, \omega_t^{(2)},...,\omega_t^{(l)}\}$ denotes a set of l parameters. The image variations of planar objects that undergo orthographic projection can be described by a six-parameter affine motion models (Hager and Belhumeur, 1998):

$$g(\mathbf{x};\boldsymbol{\omega}) = \begin{bmatrix} a & d \\ c & e \end{bmatrix} \mathbf{x} + \begin{bmatrix} u_1 \\ u_2 \end{bmatrix} = A\mathbf{x} + \mathbf{u} \tag{9}$$

where $\boldsymbol{\omega} = (a, c, d, e, u_1, u_2)^T$. With these assumptions, the tracking of the object in time t can be achieved by computing $\boldsymbol{\omega}_{t+1}$ such that $Y_{t+1}(g(\mathcal{R};\boldsymbol{\omega}_{t+1})) = \hat{Y}_t(\mathcal{R})$, where the template $\hat{Y}_t(\mathcal{R})$ is in pose determined by the estimated state.

Given a set $S = \{\boldsymbol{\omega}_t^{(n)}, w_t^{(n)} \mid n = 1,...,N\}$ of weighted particles, which approximate the posterior distribution $p(\boldsymbol{\omega}_t \mid Y_{1:t})$, the maximum aposteriori estimate (MAP) of the state is calculated according to the following formula:

$$\hat{\boldsymbol{\omega}}_t = \arg\max_{\boldsymbol{\omega}_t} p(\boldsymbol{\omega}_t \mid Y_{1:t}) \approx \arg\max_{\boldsymbol{\omega}_t} w_t^{(n)} \tag{10}$$

The motion parameters in time $t+1$ take values according to the following formula:

$$\boldsymbol{\omega}_{t+1} = \hat{\boldsymbol{\omega}}_t + A_{t+1}[\hat{Y}_t(\mathcal{R}) - Y_{t+1}(g(\mathcal{R};\hat{\boldsymbol{\omega}}_t))]\,. \tag{11}$$

This equation can be expressed as follows: $\Delta\boldsymbol{\omega}_{t+1} = A_{t+1}\Delta\mathbf{y}_{t+1}$. Given N measurements we can estimate matrix A_{t+1} from matrices consisting of adjoined vectors $\Delta\boldsymbol{\omega}_{t+1}$ and $\Delta\mathbf{y}_{t+1}$ (Horn, 1986):

$$\Delta M_t = [\hat{\omega}_t^{(1)} - \omega_t^{(1)},...,\hat{\omega}_t^{(N)} - \omega_t^{(N)}] \tag{12}$$

$$\Delta Y_t = [\hat{Y}_t^{(1)} - Y_t^{(1)},...,\hat{Y}_t^{(N)} - Y_t^{(N)}]\,. \tag{13}$$

Using the least squares (LS) method we can find the solution for A_{t+1} (Horn, 1986):

$$A_{t+1} = (\Delta M_t \Delta Y_t^T)(\Delta Y_t \Delta Y_t^T)^{-1}\,. \tag{14}$$

Singular value decomposition of ΔY_t yields: $\Delta Y_t = UWV^T$. Taking q largest diagonal elements of W the solution for A_{t+1} is as follows: $A_{t+1} = \Delta M_t V_q W_q^{-1} U_q^T$. The value of q

depends on the number of diagonal elements of W that are below a predefined threshold value.
In the CONDENSATION algorithm we utilized the following motion model:

$$\boldsymbol{\omega}_{t+1} = \hat{\boldsymbol{\omega}}_t + \Delta\boldsymbol{\omega}_{t+1} + \mathbf{v}_{t+1}, \tag{15}$$

where $\mathbf{v}_{t+1}$ is zero mean Gaussian i.i.d. noise, independent of state and with covariance matrix Q which specifies the extent of noise.
When individual measurements carry more or less weight, the individual rows of $\Delta\boldsymbol{\omega} = A\Delta\mathbf{y}$ can be multiplied by a diagonal matrix with weighting factors. If the diagonal matrix is the identity matrix we obtain the original solution. In our approach such row weighting is used to emphasize or de-emphasize image patches according to number of background pixels they contain. The background pixels can be detected by a supplementing tracker, built on different cues, with different failure mode.

5.3 Appearance modeling using adaptive models

Our intensity-based appearance model consists of three components, namely, the *W*-component expressing the two-frame variations, the *S*-component characterizing the stable structure within all previous observations and *F*-component representing a fixed initial template. The model $A_t = \{W_t, S_t, F_t\}$ represents thus the appearances existing in all observations up to time $t-1$. It is a mixture of Gaussians (Jepson et al., 2001) with centers $\{\mu_{i,t} \mid i = w,s,f\}$, their corresponding variances $\{\sigma^2_{i,t} \mid i = w,s,f\}$ and mixing probabilities $\{m_{i,t} \mid i = w,s,f\}$.
The update of the current appearance model A_t to A_{t+1} is done using the Expectation Maximization (EM) algorithm. For a template $\hat{Y}(\mathcal{R},t)$ corresponding to the estimated state we evaluate the posterior contribution probabilities as follows:

$$o_{i,t}^{(j)} = \frac{m_{i,t}^{(j)}}{\sqrt{2\pi\sigma^2_{i,t}}} \exp\left[-\frac{\hat{I}_{x,t}^{(j)} - \mu_{i,t}^{(j)}}{2\sigma^2_{i,t}}\right] \tag{16}$$

where $i = w,s,f$ and $j = 1,2,...,J$. If the considered pixel belongs to background, the posterior contribution probabilities are calculated using $\hat{I}_{x,1}^{(j)}$:

$$o_{i,t}^{(j)} = \frac{m_{i,t}^{(j)}}{\sqrt{2\pi\sigma^2_{i,t}}} \exp\left[-\frac{\hat{I}_{x,1}^{(j)} - \mu_{i,t}^{(j)}}{2\sigma^2_{i,t}}\right] \tag{17}$$

This prevents the slowly varying component from updating by background pixels. The posterior contribution probabilities (with $\sum_i o_{i,t}^{(j)} = 1$) are utilized in updating the mixing probabilities in the following manner:

$$m_{i,t+1}^{(j)} = \gamma o_{i,t}^{(j)} + (1-\gamma) m_{i,t}^{(j)} \quad | i = w,s,f \,, \tag{18}$$

where γ is accommodation factor. Then, the first and the second-moment images are determined as follows:

$$\begin{aligned} M_{1,i+1}^{(j)} &= (1-\gamma) M_{1,t}^{(j)} + \gamma o_{s,t}^{(j)} \hat{I}_{x,t}^{(j)} \\ M_{2,i+1}^{(j)} &= (1-\gamma) M_{2,t}^{(j)} + \gamma o_{s,t}^{(j)} (\hat{I}_{x,t}^{(j)})^2 \,. \end{aligned} \tag{19}$$

In the last step the mixture centers and the variances are calculated as follows:

$$\begin{aligned} \mu_{s,t+1}^{(j)} &= \frac{M_{1,t+1}^{(j)}}{m_{s,t+1}^{(j)}}, \quad \sigma_{s,t+1}^{(j)} = \sqrt{\frac{M_{2,t+1}^{(j)}}{m_{s,t+1}^{(j)}} - (\mu_{s,t+1}^{(j)})^2} \\ \mu_{w,t+1}^{(j)} &= \hat{I}_{x,t}^{(j)}, \quad \sigma_{w,t+1}^{(j)} = \sigma_{w,1}^{(j)} \\ \mu_{f,t+1}^{(j)} &= \mu_{t,1}^{(j)}, \quad \sigma_{f,t+1}^{(j)} = \sigma_{f,1}^{(j)} \,. \end{aligned} \tag{20}$$

When the considered pixel belongs to background, the mixture center in the component expressing two-frame variations is updated according to:

$$\mu_{w,t+1}^{(j)} = \hat{I}_{x,l}^{(j)} , \tag{21}$$

where index l refers to last non-background pixel.
In order to initialize the model A_1 the initial moment images are set using the following formulas: $M_{1,1} = m_{s,1} I(\mathcal{R}, t_0)$ and $M_{2,1} = m_{s,1}(\sigma_{s,1}^2 + I(\mathcal{R}, t_0)^2)$. The observation likelihood is calculated according to the following equation:

$$p(Y_t \,|\, \boldsymbol{\omega}_t) = \prod_{j=1}^{J} \sum_{i=w,s,f} \frac{m_{i,t}^{(j)}}{\sqrt{2\pi\sigma_{i,t}^2}} \exp\left[-\frac{I_{x,t}^{(j)} - \mu_{i,t}^{(j)}}{2\sigma_{i,t}^2} \right] \tag{22}$$

In the particle filter we use a recursively updated mixture appearance model, which depicts stable structures in images seen so far, initial object appearance as well as two-frame variations. If a supplementing tracker with different failure mode is used, the update of slowly varying component is done using only pixels that are labeled as belonging to foreground. In pairwise comparison of object images we employ only non-background pixels and in case of background we use the last foreground pixels. Our probabilistic models differ from those proposed in (Zhou and Chellappa, 2004) in that we adapt models using information about background.

5.4 Face tracking using particle filter built on adaptive appearance models

Figure 3. shows tracking the face of a person on images acquired by a camera mounted on the computer monitor. The experiments have been done in a typical home environment. The camera was located in front of wooden doors or furniture. In such a scenario a typical color based tracker can have severe difficulties in following the face because the skin color form clusters, which overlap with colors of pixels belonging to wood. In the depicted images we can see that the jitter of the tracking window is relatively low. However, this gray-level image based tracker failed in frame #36.

Fig. 3. Face tracking using particle filter built on adaptive appearance models. Frames #1, #20, #25, #30, #35 (from left to right and from top to bottom)

Figure 4. depicts some tracking results which have been obtained in experiments with partial occlusions of the face undergoing tracking. In image #25 we can observe that despite of the considerable occlusion of the face, the template's location has not been shifted from desirable location. However, in images #45, #55 we can notice that in response to the occlusion of the face the template has been moved to left side. Therefore, the part of the template learned some background pixels. After the occluding book has been moved to the right a considerable jitter of the template has been observed in our experiment. Due to the mentioned above undesirable effects the tracking failed in some of our other experiments.

In Fig. 5. we present some tracking results that were obtained on another test sequence[1]. However, as we can see, the tracker failed in frame #33. In this experiment far larger tracking window has been utilized in order to cover the area of the face to be tracked.

6. Tracking using Multi-Part Object Representation

6.1 The algorithm

In work (Pérez et al., 2002) it has been demonstrated that multi-part object representation leads to better tracking. The authors proposed a method consisting in dividing the object to be

---

[1] Available on: http://research.microsoft.com/vision/cambridge/i2i

Fig. 4. Face undergoing tracking via particle filter built on adaptive appearance models. Frames #1, #15, #25, #45, #55 (from left to right and from top to bottom)

Fig. 5. Face tracking using particle filter built on adaptive appearance models. Frames #1, #32, #33 (from left to right and from top to bottom)

tracked into non-overlapping rectangular regions and then computing in each such a sub-region a color histogram. The observation model has been constructed under assumption that image data in different sub-regions are independent. The object likelihood was proportional to the exponential of negative sum of squared distances between histograms. In (Fieguth et al., 1997), rectangle sub-regions that are defined within the extent of the object to be tracked are employed to calculate the averaged color of pixels. The object tracking is achieved through an exhaustive search in a confidence region. An occlusion model has been developed to discriminate between good and spurious measurements.

Cognitive science states that complex entities are perceived as composition of simple elements. Objects are represented through such components and the relations between them (Ommer et al., 2006). One of the disadvantages of color histograms is the loss of spatial information. To incorporate such information in the object representation we divide the object template into adjoining cells, regularly spaced within the extent of the target to be tracked. We compute histograms within such regularly spaced cells using a fast method that has been proposed in (Porikli et al., 2005). Given the estimated position in the previous frame and the histograms within object at the estimated position we employ the chi-square test between such histograms and histograms extracted from cells within the template at candidate position.

The X^2 test is given by: $X^2 = \sum_i ((h_{e,i} - h_{c,i})^2 / (h_{e,i} + h_{c,i})^2)$, where $h_{e,i}$ and $h_{c,i}$ represent the number of entities in the i-th bin of the histograms, and a low value for X^2 indicates a good match. The distances are transformed into likelihoods through the usage of exponential function. We seek for the object in the new frame within a search window, which center is located at the previous object position. At each candidate position we compare the corresponding histograms and the result is utilized to vote for the considered position. Every cell votes in its own map. Then we combine the votes in a relevance map, which encodes hypothesis where the target is located in the image. In order to cope with partial occlusions we employ a simple heuristics aiming at detecting outliers. If the difference between corresponding histograms is below a certain level the score in the relevance map remains unchanged. The level for each cell is determined individually using the distances between histograms from the initial template and corresponding histograms from few first frames. Similar test is performed with respect to the actual medians.

6.2 Face tracking using multi-part representation

In Fig. 6 we can observe that this algorithm temporally failed in frame #35 and then recovered in later images. However, as we can see in frames #53 and #77 a considerable jitter accompanied the tracking of the face. The tracker is able to track the face under severe rotations, see frames #134 - #173. However, the tracking of the face ends with considerable jitter of the window, see frame #175.

Figure 7. shows some tracking results in case of partial occlusions of the face. In image #25 we can see that despite of the occlusion the window of the tracker has not been shifted from desirable location, see also Fig. 4. However, the occlusion of the face from the opposite side caused severe shifts of the tracked window, see also frame #48. In consequence, the tracker temporally failed in frame #55 and then recovered in the next frames.

In the tracking results presented in Fig. 8 we can see that the tracker can fail in some images. Its advantage is that it can deal with severe rotations of face undergoing tracking. However, in order to achieve such functionality, relatively large tracking windows should be employed in the course of the tracking. In the discussed experiments the template has been divided into four non-overlapping sub-regions. In order to take advantages of the tracker in the last sequence, the number of sub-regions should be something larger, say eight sub-regions.

7. Combined Face Tracker

Obtaining a collection consisting of both positive and negative examples for on-line learning is a complex task. In work (Zeki, 2001) the author argues that the human visual system consists of a number of interacting but still autonomously operating subsystems that process different object representations. Within such a mechanism, the subsystems can serve mutually in course of learning and bootstrapping of object representations. This inclined us to construct an object tracker consisting of two independent trackers with different failure modes, complementing each other and operating in co-training framework. The co-training approach has been employed in previous work (Levin et al., 2004), in which a tracker starts with a small training set and increases it by co-training of two classifiers, operating on different features.

In the combined algorithm we utilize the trackers presented in the last two Sections. Our

Fig. 6. Face tracking using multi-part object representation in case of occlusions. Frames #1, #15, #25, #45, #46, #48, #55, #65, #70 (from left to right and from top to bottom)

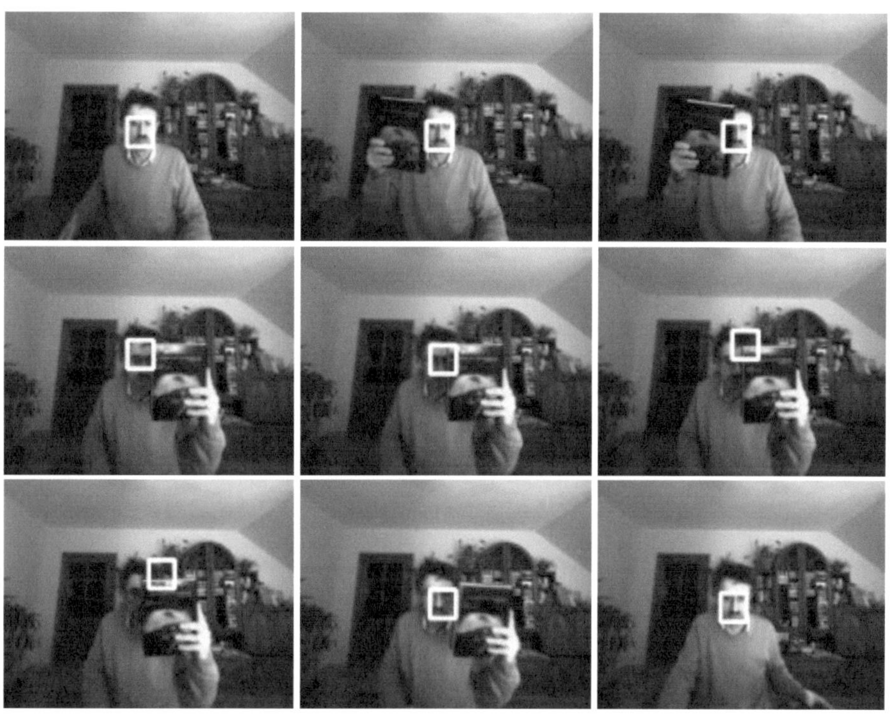

Fig. 7. Face tracking using multi-part object representation in case of occlusions.

Fig. 8. Face tracking using multi-part representation. Frames #1, #51, #86, #112, #126, #200

experiments demonstrated that even very simple combined algorithm based on the distance between the locations of windows, which have been determined via the employed trackers, leads to considerable improvement of tracking, see Fig. 9 and 10. As we already mentioned in the previous Section, in our combined tracker the adaptive appearance models are learned on-line using only foreground pixels, owing to the estimates determined by the complementary tracker. The information about distance between the locations of windows allows us to detect such pixels easily. What more, given such information we can accommodate the histograms of the object parts, which likely belong to the tracked object. In consequence, the drift of the part-based tracker is smaller. This in turn allows us to accommodate the histograms with rather lower risk that they will be updated via non-object pixels.
In the results depicted in Fig. 9 the size of the windows of both trackers has been estimated on the basis of depth map, which has been determined by the stereovision system. The depth map has also been utilized in labeling of the pixels for the adaptation. Assuming that the face is relatively flat we exclude pixels too distant from the distance of the template to the camera. Typically, in the combined face tracker the distance between the windows of the utilized trackers is small. In the part-based tracker we tried to determine the rotation of the template though searching for the best one using information on the similarities of the histograms. However, in the course of the tracking the orientation of the template estimated in such a way considerably fluctuates about the true template orientation. Therefore, better results were achieved using the orientation estimated by adaptive appearance model based tracker. This in turn allowed us to accommodate the histogram in experiments like these depicted in Fig. 11.

8. Conclusions

We have discussed adaptive algorithms for face tracking. Face tracking is one of the most important research directions in human machine interaction with many possible applications, for example see work (Tu et al., 2007). The algorithms were validated in various test sequences and demonstrated their great potential to be used in applications employing human face to complement the opportunities offered by the computer mouse.

Fig. 9. Face tracking via combined algorithm. Frames #1, #20, #25, #30, #35, #40 #59, #85, #104

Fig. 10. Tracking of the face undergoing occlusion using combined algorithm. Frames #1, #15, #25, #45, #55

The distance map provided by stereovision system offers great possibilities to construct robust algorithms for human-machine interaction. The proposed algorithms for adaptation and unsupervised learning were tested in real home/laboratory scenarios, and acknowledged great ability to deal with varying illumination conditions as well as complex background.

Fig. 11. Face tracking using combined algorithm. Frames #1, #51, #86, #112, #126, #135

9. References

Aggarwal, J. K.; Cai, Q. (1999). Human motion analysis: A review, *Computer Vision and Image Understanding*, vol. 73, no. 3, pp. 428-440

Birchfield, S. (1998). Elliptical head tracking using intensity gradients and color histograms, *IEEE Conf. on Computer Vision and Pattern Recognition*, pp. 232-237

Bradski, G. (1998). Computer vision face tracking for use in a perceptual user interface, *Intel Technoloy Journal*, vol. 2, no. 2, pp. 12-21

Comaniciu, D.; Ramesh, V.; Meer P. (2000). Real-time tracking of non-rigid objects using Mean Shift, *Proc. Int. Conf. on Computer Vision and Pattern Recognition*, pp. 142-149

Crowe, E. C.; Narayann, N. H. (2000). Comparing interfaces based on what users watch and do, *Proc. Eye Tracking Research and Applications Symposium*, ACM, pp. 29-36

Davis, J.; Vaks, S. A. (2001). Perceptual user interface for recognizing head gesture acknowledgements, *ACM Workshop on Perceptual User Interfaces*, pp. 1-7

Doucet, A.; Godsill, A.; Andrieu, Ch. (2000). On sequential Monte Carlo sampling methods for bayesian filtering, *Statistics and Computing*, vol. 10, pp. 197-208

Duchowski, A. T. (2002). A breadth-first survey of eye tracking applications, *Behavior Research Methods, Instruments, & Computers*, vol. 34, no. 4, pp. 455-470

Emond, B. (2007). Multimedia and human-in-the-loop: interaction as content enrichment, *Proc. of the ACM Int. Workshop on Human-Centered Multimedia*, pp. 77-84

Fasel, B.; Luettin, J. (2003). Automatic facial expression analysis: A survey, *Pattern Recognition*, vol. 36, pp. 259-275

Fieguth, P.; Terzopoulos, D. (1997). Color-based tracking of heads and other mobile objects at video frame rates. *Proc. IEEE Conf. on Comp. Vision and Patt. Rec.*, pp. 21-27

Fong, T.; Nourbakhsh, I.; Dautenhahn, K. (2003). A survey of socially interactive robots, *Robotics and Autonomous Systems*, vol. 42, pp. 143-166

Gavrila, D. (1999). The visual analysis for human movement: A survey, *Computer Vision and Image Understanding*, vol. 13, no. 1, pp. 82-98

Goodrich, M. A.; Schultz, A. C. (2007). Human-robot interaction: A survey, *Foundations and Trends in Human-Computer Interaction*, vol. 1, no. 3, pp. 203-275

Gordon, N.; Salmond, D.; Smith, A. (1993). Novel approach to nonlinear/non-Gaussian Bayesian state estimation, *IEEE Trans. Radar, Signal Processing*, vol. 140, pp. 107-113

Hager, G. D.; Belhumeur, P. N. (1998). Efficient region tracking with parametric models of geometry and illumination, *IEEE Trans. on PAMI*, vol. 20, pp. 1025-1039

Horn, B. K. P. (1986). Robot vision, The MIT Press

Isard, M.; Blake A. (1998). CONDENSATION - conditional density propagation for visual tracking, *Int. Journal of Computer Vision*, vol. 29, pp. 5-28

Jacob, R. J. K.; Karn, K. S. (2003). Eye tracking in human-computer interaction and usability research: Ready to deliver the promises. In: R. Radach, J. Hyona, and H. Deubel (eds.), The mind's eye: cognitive and applied aspects of eye movement research, Boston: North-Holland/Elsevier, pp. 573-605

Jaimes, A.; Sebe, N. (2007). Multimodal human computer interaction: A survey, *Computer Vision and Image Understanding*, no. 1-2, pp. 116-134

Jepson, A. D.; Fleet, D. J.; El-Maraghi, T. (2001). Robust on-line appearance models for visual tracking, *Int. Conf. on Comp. Vision and Pattern Rec.*, pp. 415-422

Ji, Q.; Zhu, Z. (2004). Eye and gaze tracking for interactive graphic display, *Machine Vision and Applications*, vol. 15, no. 3, pp. 139-148

Kisacanin, B.; Pavlovic, V.; Huang, T. S. (eds.) (2005). Real-time vision for human-computer interaction, Springer-Verlag, New York

Kjeldsen, R. (2001). Head gestures for computer control, *IEEE ICCV Workshop on Recognition, Analysis, and Tracking of Faces and Gestures in Real-Time Systems*, pp. 61-67

Konolige, K. (1997). Small Vision System: Hardware and implementation, *Proc. of Int. Symp. on Robotics Research*, Hayama, pp. 111-116

Kuno, Y.; Murakami, Y.; Shimada, N. (2001). User and social Interfaces by observing human faces for intelligent wheelchairs, *ACM Workshop on Perceptive User Interfaces*, pp. 1-4

Kwolek, B. (2003a). Person following and mobile robot via arm-posture driving using color and stereovision, In *Proc. of the 7th IFAC Symposium on Robot Control SYROCO, Elsevier IFAC Publications*, (J. Sasiadek, I. Duleba, eds), Elsevier, pp. 177–182

Kwolek, B. (2003b). Visual system for tracking and interpreting selected human actions, *Journal of WSCG*, vol. 11, no. 2, pp. 274-281

Kwolek, B. (2004). Stereovision-based head tracking using color and ellipse fitting in a particle filter, *European Conf. on Comp. Vision, LNCS*, vol. 3691, Springer, 2004, 192–204

Levin, A.; Viola, P.; Freund, Y. (2004). Unsupervised improvement of visual detectors using co-training, *Proc. Int. Conf. on Comp. Vision*, 626-633, vol. 1

Lyytinen, K.; Yoo, Y. J. (2002). Issues and challenges in ubiquitous computing, *Communications of the ACM*, vol. 45, no. 12, pp. 62-70

Medioni, G.; Francois, A. R. J.; Siddiqui, M.; Kim, K.; Yoon, H. (2007). Robust real-time vision for a personal service robot, *Computer Vision and Image Understanding*, Special issue on vision for HCI, vol. 108, pp. 196-203

Merve, R.; Freitas, N.; Doucet, A.; Wan, E. (2000). The unscented particle filter, *Advances in Neural Information Processing Systems*, vol. 13, pp. 584-590

Mitra, S.; Acharya, T. (2007). Gesture recognition: A survey, *IEEE Trans. on Systems, Man, and Cybernetics, Part C: Applications and Reviews*, vol. 37, no. 3, pp. 311-324

Morency, L. P.; Sidner C. L.; Lee, Ch.; Darrell, T. (2007). Head gestures for perceptual interfaces: The role of context in improving recognition, *Artificial Intelligence*, vol. 171, no. 8-9, pp. 568-585

Ommer, B.; Buhmann, J. M. (2006). Learning compositional categorization models, *European Conf. on Computer Vision*, pp. III:316-329

Pérez, P.; Hue, C.; Vermaak, J.; Gangnet, M. (2002). Color-based probabilistic tracking, *European Conf. on Computer Vision*, LNCS, vol. 2350, pp. 661-675

Porikli, F. (2005). Integral histogram: A fast way to extract histogram in cartesian spaces, *IEEE Computer Society Conf. on Pattern Rec. and Computer Vision*, pp. 829-836

Porta, M. (2002). Vision-based interfaces: methods and applications, *Int. J. Human-Computer Studies*, vol. 57, no. 1, 27-73

Pavlovic, V.; Sharma, R.; Huang, T. (1997). Visual interpretation of hand gestures for human-computer interaction: A review, *IEEE Trans. on PAMI*, vol. 19, pp. 677-695

Rehg, J. M.; Loughlin, M.; Waters, K. (1997). Vision for smart kiosk, *Proc. IEEE Comp. Society Conf. on Computer Vision and Pattern Recognition*, pp. 690-696

Reeder, R. W.; Pirolli, P.; Card, S. K. (2001). WebEyeMapper and WebLogger: Tools for analyzing eye tracking data collected in web-use studies, *Int. Conf. on Human Factors in Computing Systems*, ACM Press, pp. 19-20

Schmidt, J.; Fritsch, J.; Kwolek, B. (2006). Kernel particle filter for real-time 3D body tracking in monocular color images, *IEEE Int. Conf. on Face and Gesture Rec.*, Southampton, UK, IEEE Comp. Society Press, pp. 567-572

Swain, M. J.; Ballard, D. H. (1991). Color indexing, *Int. J. of Computer Vision*, vol. 7, pp. 11-32

Triesch, J.; von der Malsburg, Ch. (2001). Democratic integration: Self-organized integration of adaptive cues, *Neural Computation*, vol. 13, pp. 2049-2074

Tu, J.; Tao, H.; Huang, H. (2007). Face as a mouse through visual face tracking, *Computer Vision and Image Understanding*, Special issue on vision for HCI, vol. 108, pp. 35-40

Turk, M. A.; Pentland, A. P. (1991). Face recognition using eigenfaces, *Proc. of IEEE Conf. on Comp. Vision and Patt. Rec.*, pp. 586-591

Viola, P.; Jones, M. (2001). Rapid object detection using a boosted cascade of simple features, *The IEEE Conf. on Comp. Vision and Patt. Rec.*, pp. 511–518

Wang, L.; Hu, W. M.; Tan, T. N. (2003). Recent developments in human motion analysis, *Pattern Recognition*, vol. 36, no. 3, pp. 585-601

Waldherr, S.; Romero S.; Thrun, S. (2000). A gesture-based interface for human-robot interaction, *Autonomous Robots*, vol. 9, pp. 151-173

Yang, M-H.; Kriegman, D.; Ahuja, N. (2002). Detecting faces in images: A survey, *IEEE Trans. on Pattern Analysis and Machine Intelligence*, vol. 24, no. 1, pp. 34-58

Zeki, S. (2001). Localization and globalization in conscious vision, *Annual Review Neuroscience*, 24, pp. 57-86

Zhao, W.; Chellappa, R.; Phillips, P.; Rosenfeld, A. (2003). Face recognition: A literature survey, *ACM Computing Surveys*, vol. 35, no. 4, pp. 399-458

Zhou, S. K.; Chellappa, R.; Moghaddam, B. (2004). Appearance tracking using adaptive models in a particle filter, *Proc. Asian Conf. on Comp. Vision*

Zhou, M. X.; Wen Z.; Aggarwal, V. (2005). A graph-matching approach to dynamic media allocation in intelligent multimedia interfaces, *Proc. of ACM Conf. on Intelligent User Interfaces*, pp. 114-121

ActivMedia Robotics (2001). Pioneer 2 mobile robots

19

A Tool for Getting Cultural Differences in HCI

Rüdiger Heimgärtner
IUIC (Intercultural User Interface Consulting)
Germany

1. Introduction

The "Intercultural Interaction Analysis" tool (IIA tool) was developed to obtain data regarding cultural differences in HCI. The main objective of the IIA tool is to observe and analyze the interaction behavior of users from different cultures with a computer system to determine different interaction patterns according to their cultural background. Culture influences the interaction of the user with the computer because of the movement of the user in a cultural surrounding (Röse, 2002). To locate and find out the kind of different interaction behavior of the users from different cultural groups (at national level (country) between Chinese and German user first because of the high cultural distance) the interaction behavior of the users with the computer will be observed and detected. The objective is to be able to draw inferences *regarding differences of the cultural imprint* of users *by analyzing the interaction behavior* of those users with a computer system to get knowledge that is relevant for intercultural user interface design and a necessary precondition for cultural adaptive systems (Heimgärtner, 2006). E.g. the right number and arrangement of information units is very important for an application whose display is very small and at the same time the mental workload of the user has to be as low as possible (e.g. driver navigation systems).

2. Designing a Tool for the Analysis of Cultural Differences in HCI (IIA Tool)

Research of literature showed that there are no adequate methods for determining cross-cultural differences in interaction aspects of human machine interaction (HMI) and none for driver navigation systems. For doing this task on PC's, there are some tools like:

- UserZoom (Recording, analyzing and visualization of online studies)
- ObSys (Recording and visualization of windows messages) (cf. Gellner & Forbrig, 2003)
- INTERACT (Coding and visualization of user behavior) (cf. Mangold, 2005)
- REVISER (Automatic Criteria Oriented Usability Evaluation of Interactive Systems, cf. Hamacher, 2006)
- Noldus, SnagIt, Morae, A-Prompt, Leo, etc.

All the existing tools provide some functionality for (remote) usability tests and interaction behavior measurement. Nevertheless, I had to develop my own tool for this purpose, because this task presupposes intercultural usability metrics, i.e. a Cross-Cultural Usability Metric Trace Model (CCUMTM) or even better a Cultural HMI Metric Model (CHMIMM), which none of the existing tools offer explicitly for this purpose (because the parameters and

CCUMTM did not exist). This needs knowledge about variables depending on culture, which could not have been implemented in the existing tools. On the one hand, they are not known up to now. On the other hand, the architecture of the existing tools cannot be changed such that the potential cultural parameters can be determined by tests with the tools.

My theoretical reflections and deductions from literature led to a hypothetical model of intercultural variables (IV model) for the HMI design. It must be distinguished between variables, that can be determined at runtime, and variables, whose values must be determined in design phase to provide them for the runtime system. A benchmark test of systems from different countries with similar functions can help to determine differences in HMI. Furthermore, the interaction of cultural different users doing the same task should be observed (using the same test conditions i.e. the same hard and software, environment conditions, language, experience of using the system as well as the same test tasks). Helpful are also data of diagnose, debugging and HMI event triggering during usage of the system summarized in the Usability Metric Trace Model (UMTM). These data can be logged during usability tests according to certain user tasks. The evaluation of the collected data using statistical methods should show, which of the potential variables depend on culture (potential cultural interaction indicators (PCII's)). Having this knowledge, the UMTM can be optimized and verified empirically by further experiments within usability tests to get the cross-cultural UMTM (CCUMTM). This requires several development loops within integrative design.

To motivate the user to interact with the computer and to verify the postulated hypotheses, adequate task scenarios have been developed and implemented into the IIA tool. Even if the architecture of this new tool follows in some respect the already existing tools, it has been developed from the scratch because the existing tools did not measure intercultural interaction behavior according to driver navigation use cases which was a main requirement getting budget for developing the IIA tool. The resulting tool provides data collection, analysis, and evaluation for intercultural interaction analysis in HCI:

- recording, analysis and visualization of user interaction behavior and preferences
- localized tool for intercultural usability testing using use cases that are comprehensive in different cultures
- integration of usability evaluation techniques and all interaction levels according to the acting level model (cf. Herczeg, 2005).
- qualitative judgments by quantitative results (optimization of test validity and test reliability).

The preparation of the collected data takes place mostly automatically by the IIA data collection tool, which saves much time, costs, and effort. The collected data is partly quantitative (related to all test persons, e.g. like the mean of a Likert scale) and partly qualitative (related to one single test person, e.g. answering open questions) (cf. De la Cruz et al., 2005). Moreover, the collected data sets have standard format so that anyone can perform own statistical analyses. This also means that the results of studies using the IIA tool are verifiable because they can be reproduced using the IIA tool. The data will be stored in databases in formats (CSV, MDB) that are immediately usable by the IIA analysis tool, and, which also conducts possible subsequent converting and data preparation. Hence, statistic programs like SPSS, AMOS, and neural network can be deployed to do descriptive or explanatory statistics, correlations, and explorative or confirmatory factor analysis, to

explore cultural differences in the user interaction as well as to find a cultural interaction model using structural equal models. The data evaluation module enables classification with neural networks to cross-validate the results from data analysis. In future, it will be extended such, that it is possible to evaluate the analysis on the fly during data collection. The quantitative studies should reveal trends for the investigated cultures regarding the interaction behavior with the computer. Data mining methods and statistics e.g. cluster analysis for classification or linear regression for correlations can be exploited to find correlations between recorded cross-cultural user interaction values and values of the cultural variables (cf. Kamentz & Mandl, 2003).
Delphi was used to create a software tool, which can be installed online using the Internet as well as offline via CD. To avoid downloading and interaction delays, the IIA tool has been implemented also in one single executable program file on a server to be downloaded onto the local hard disk of the users worldwide because the tool has to measure the interaction behavior of the user during the online tests correctly and comparably. A huge amount of valid data can be collected rapidly and easily worldwide online via internet or intranet. Besides, the Delphi IDE allows transforming new HMI concepts and test cases very quickly into good-looking prototypes that can be tested very soon in the development process. E.g., some hypotheses could have been confirmed quantitatively addressing many test users online using the IIA tool within *one* month (implementing the use cases as well as doing data collection and data analysis). Hence, using the IIA tool means rapid use case design, i.e. real-time prototyping of user interfaces for different cultures.

3. Implementation of Test Tasks and the UMTM

The IIA tool has been developed to be able to determine the intercultural differences in the basic principles of HMI as well as in the use cases related to special products (e.g. driver navigation systems). Hence, the results can be general guidelines for every intercultural HMI development as well as context specific recommendations for the design of special products. The intercultural interaction analysis tool provides an implementation of the UMTM and therefore the ability to determine the peculiarities and values of the specified intercultural variables. Thereby, the IIA tool serves to analyze cultural differences in HMI. The following information scientific parameters (information related dimensions) can be determined quantitatively:

- Information density (spatial distance between informational units)
- Information speed (time distance between informational units to be presented)
- Information frequency (number of presented informational units per time unit)
- Interaction frequency (number of initialized interaction steps per time unit)
- Interaction speed (time distance between interaction steps)

Not all PCII's from IV model and UMTM could have been implemented into the IIA data collection module because of time and budget restrictions. Only the most promising PCII's requiring the least integrating effort to the test system have been implemented. Nevertheless, more than one hundred potentially culturally sensitive variables in HMI have been implemented into the IIA tool, and applied by measuring the interaction behavior of the test persons with a personal computer system in relation to the culture (as presented in table 1).

Measured variables in the single test tasks	URD (user requirement design) test task	PositionXBegin(URD), PositionYBegin(URD), PositionXEnd(URD), PositionXBack(URD), PositionYBack(URD), PositionXNext(URD), PositionYNext(URD), PositionXEnd(URD), PositionYEnd(URD), PositionXReady(URD), PositionYReady(URD), PositionXDisplay(URD), PositionYDisplay(URD), PositionXListbox(URD), PositionYListbox(URD), PositionXStatus(URD), PositionYStatus(URD)
	MD (map display) test task	NumberOfTextures(MD), NumberOfPOI(MD), NumberOfStreetNames(MD), NumberOfStreets(MD), NumberOfManoever(MD), NumberOfRestaurants(MD)
	MG (maneuver guidance) test task	MessageDistance(MG), DisplayDuration(MG), CarSpeed(MG)
	IO (information order) test task	InformationorderNumber(IO), InformationorderOrder(IO), FactorOfUnorder(IO), PixelOfUnorder(IO), PixelOverlapping(IO), CoverageFactor(IO), PixelSize(IO), DistanceImageMargin(IO), PixelDistance(IO)
	INE (interaction exactness) test task	InteractionexactnessSpeed(INE), InteractionexactnessExactness(INE)
	INS (interaction speed) test task	InteractionspeedExactness(INS), InteractionspeedSpeed(INS)
	QUES (questionnaire) test task	ChangeValueEndQues(QUES)
	IH (information hierarchy) test task	InformationhierarchyNumber(IH)
	UV (uncertainty avoidance) test task	UncertaintyAvoidanceValue(UV)
Measured variables at each test task	TestTaskDuration, TotalDialogTime, NumberOfErrorClicks, NumberOfMouseClicks, EnteredChars(where possible)	
Measured variables over the whole test session	TestDuration, TotalDialogTime, MaximalOpenTasks, NumberOfScrolls, AllMouseClicks, NumberOfErrorClicks, NumberOfMouseClicks, MouseLeftUps, MouseLeftDowns, ClickDistance, ClickDuration, NumberOfMouseMoves, MouseMoveDistance, NumberOfAgentMoves, NumberOfAgentHides, NumberOfShowMessages, NumberOfNOs, NumberOfYESs, NumberOfAcknowledgedMessages, NumberOfRefusedMessages, Lex (syntactical entries), Sem (semantical entries), (Interaction-)Breaks0ms, Breaks1ms, Breaks10ms, Breaks100ms, Breaks1s, Breaks10s, Breaks100s, Breaks1000s, Breaks10000s	
Measured variables before the test session	OpenTasksBeforeTest	

Table 1. Implemented variables from the UMTM in the IIA tool (the test tasks will be explained below in detail)

As mentioned above, the IIA tool allows the measurement of numerical values like information speed, information density, and interaction speed in relation to the user. These are hypothetically correlated to cultural variables concerning the surface like number or position of pictures in the layout or affecting interaction like frequency of voice guidance. Every one of the test tasks serves to investigate other cultural aspects of HCI. The test setting within the IIA tool contains two scenarios:

- an abstract scenario with tasks for general usage of widgets and
- a concrete scenario with tasks for using a driver navigation system.

In the first scenario, the user uses certain widgets. Those tasks can only be done by persons that have seen and used a PC before. The second scenario takes into account concrete use cases from driver navigation systems. The requirements of those tests are that the user has some knowledge and interaction experience about driver navigation systems as well as about PCs. The results of the abstract test cases are expected to be valid for HMI design in general because the context of usage is eliminated by abstract test settings, which are independent from actual use cases. The simulation of special use cases within the IIA tool can show usability problems and differences in user interaction behavior (similar to "paper mock-ups"). The test tasks are localized at technical and linguistically level, but are semantically identical for all users, so that participants of many different cultures can do the IIA test. Hence, the study can be extended from Chinese and German to other cultures in different countries by using the same (localized) test tool. Both abstract and special test cases have been implemented in this way as test scenarios into the IIA data collection tool in order to obtain results for the intercultural HMI design (cf. Heimgärtner, 2005). To transfer the results of general test cases in the abstract test settings to driver navigation systems, special use cases had been implemented as test scenarios in the test tool. E.g., the hypothesis "there is a high correlation of high information density to relationship-oriented cultures such as China" should be confirmable by adjusting more points of interest (POI) by Chinese users compared to German users. So, the use case "map display" was simulated by the *map display test task* to measure the number of pieces of information on the map display regarding information density (e.g. restaurants, streets, POI, etc.) (cf. figure 1).

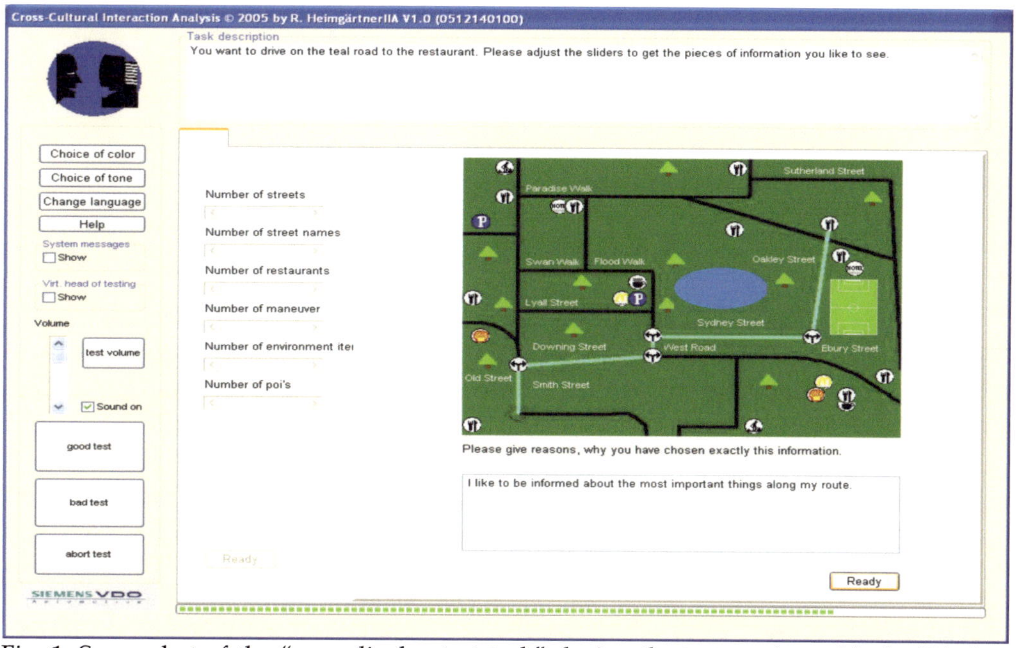

Fig. 1. Screenshot of the "map display test task" during the test session with the IIA data collection module. The user can define the amount of information in the map display by adjusting the scroll bars. The test tool records the values of the slide bars set up by the user.

Based on this principle, the test tool can also be used to investigate the values of other cultural variables like widget positions, menu structure, layout structure, interaction speed, speed of information input, dialog structure, etc. The test with the IIA tool was designed to help to reveal the empirical truth to such questions. Some of these aspects and use cases will be explained in more detail in this section to get an impression of the possible relationship between the usage of the system by the user and their cultural background. Along the implemented use case "map display" in the map display test task shown in figure 1, another important use case of driver navigation systems "maneuver guidance" has implemented as *maneuver guidance test task* into the IIA data collection module. The test user has to adjust the number and the time distance of the maneuver advice messages on the screen concerning frequency and speed of information (cf. figure 2).

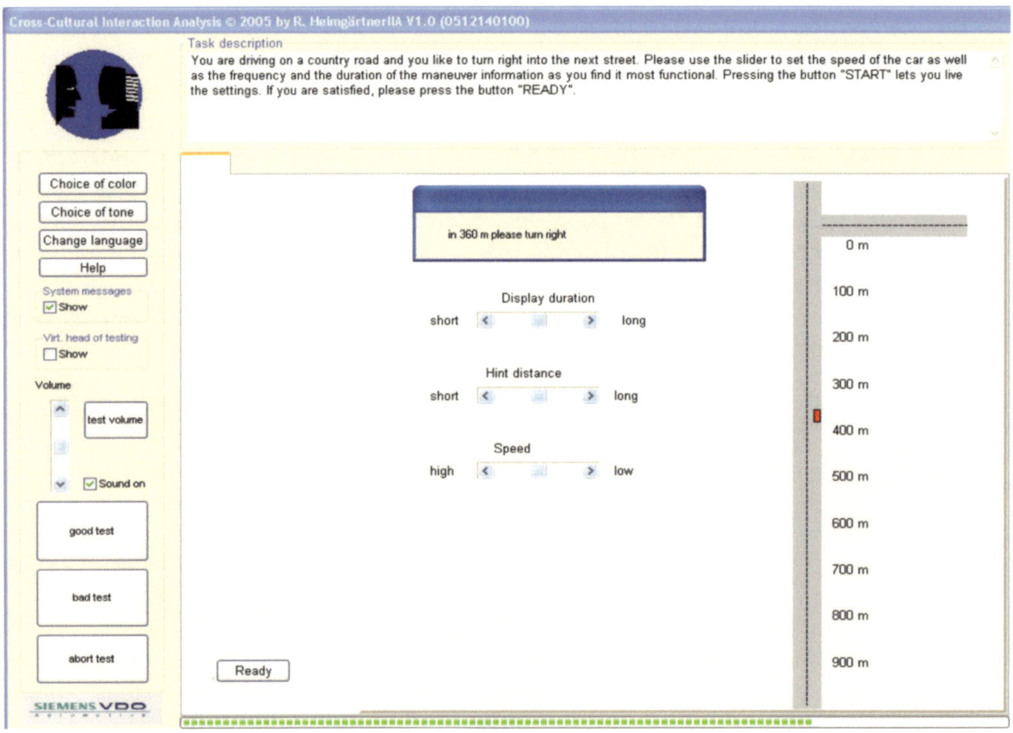

Fig. 2. Maneuver Guidance Test Task. The test person can use the sliders to select the car speed (indicated by the red rectangle), the duration of displaying the maneuver advice as well as the time distance of the given hints.

Another variable is e.g. measuring the acceptance of the "life-like" character "Merlin".[1] According to Prendinger & Ishizuka 2004, such avatars can reduce stress during interaction with the user. Hence, the agent "Merlin" was implemented in the IIA tool to offer his help every 30 seconds (cf. figure 3). On the one hand, according to cultural dimensions (cf. Marcus & Baumgartner, 2005), which describe the behavior of human beings of different

[1] The virtual assistant „Merlin" is part of the interactive help system of Microsoft Office^{TM}.

cultures, like high uncertainty avoidance or high task orientation, it was expected that German users switch off the avatar very soon (compared to Chinese users), because they do fear uncertain situations (cf. Hofstede et al., 2005). Furthermore, they do not like to be distracted from achieving the current task (cf. Halpin et al., 1957). On the other hand, if applying the cultural dimension of face saving, it should be the other way around. If Chinese users make use of help very often, they would lose their face (cf. Victor, 1997; Honold, 2000).

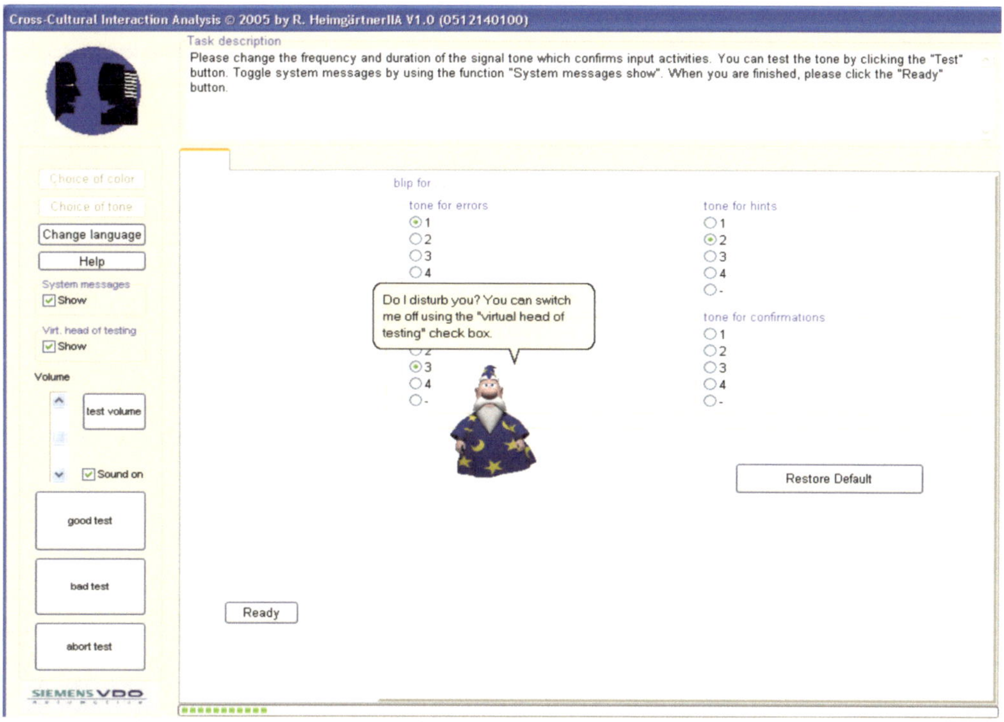

Fig. 3. Disturbing the work of the user by the virtual agent "Merlin"

The *interaction speed test task* is very abstract and is not related to DNS. Figure 4 shows the graphical user interface (GUI) for this test task. The user has to click away 16 randomly arranged dots at the screen to be able to measure interaction speed and sequentiality (clicking order). Similar to this test task is the *interaction exactness test task*, which measures the same parameters, but displays the points sequentially (to measure the clicking exactness, i.e. a deviation factor from the middle of the dots). Thereby, the following PCII's can be measured:

- Average time from clicking off one dot to another.
- Sequence of clicking off the dots.
- Exactness of clicking the dot in the middle.
- Number of interaction breaks during doing the task.
- Time period between information presentation and next user interaction with the system (user response time).
- Test task duration.

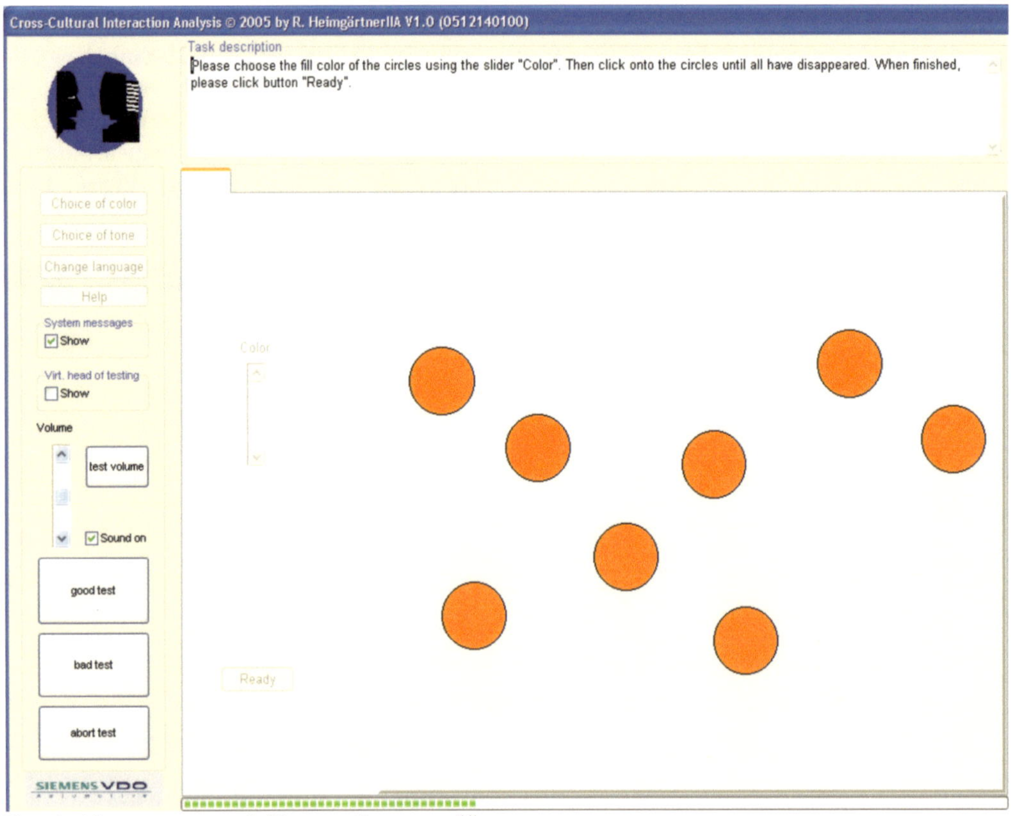

Fig. 4. Abstract test task "interaction speed"

In an additional test task, the user has the possibility to specify his requirements for widget position directly visually by designing the layout of the GUI e.g. by changing the widget position within the *user requirement design (URD) test task*. Figure 5 shows the main part of the GUI of the URD test task. Here, the following PCII's can be determined:

- Position of widgets.
- Duration of drag and drop process.
- Moving speed.
- Sequence of handling the widget.
- Number of function initiations (e.g. during testing the widget functions after finishing their arrangement).
- Sequence of function initiations (e.g. during testing the widget functions after finishing their arrangement).

During the whole test session, the IIA tool records the interaction between user and system, e.g. mouse moves, clicks, interaction breaks, or the values and changing's of the slide bars set up by the users in order to analyze the interactional patterns of the users of different culture. Thereby, all levels of the interaction model (physical, lexical, syntactical, semantic, pragmatic, and intentional) necessary for dialog design can be analyzed (cf. Herczeg, 2005). Figure 6 shows a part of a course of interaction of a user with the system during the test session represented by some parameters like mouse moves or mouse clicks as well as keyboard presses (at y-axis) displayed over time (at x-axis).

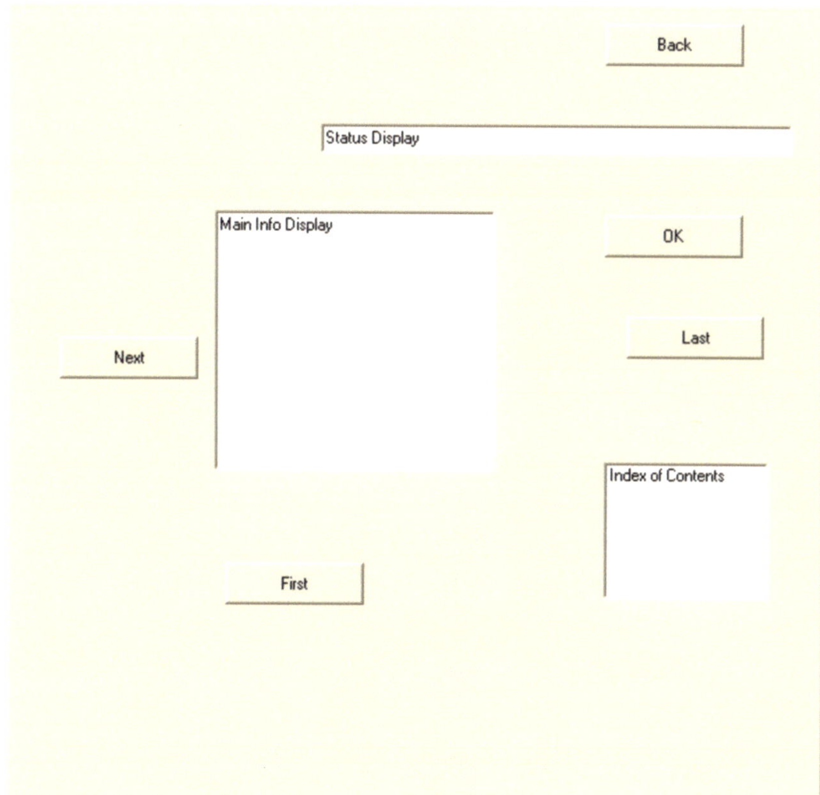

Fig. 5. Main part of the GUI of the URD Test Task

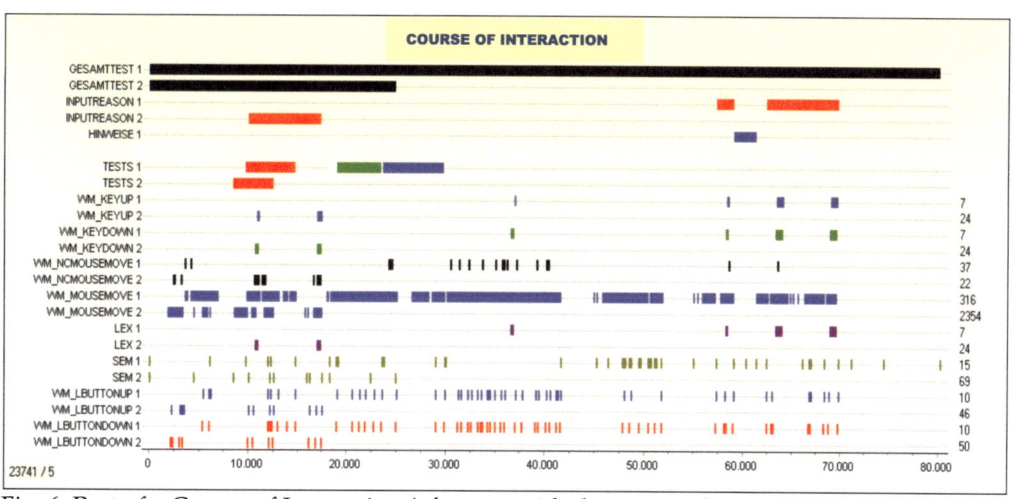

Fig. 6. Part of a Course of Interaction (of a user with the system during a test session)

4. IIA Tool Setup, Test Setting and Usage

To motivate the user to interact with the computer and to test the hypotheses, test tasks have been developed and implemented into the IIA tool as described in the last section, which the user has to work on. Figure 7 shows the IIA test procedure containing the sequence of tasks presented to the test participant (the brackets embraces the file names of the source code of the modules written in Delphi7).

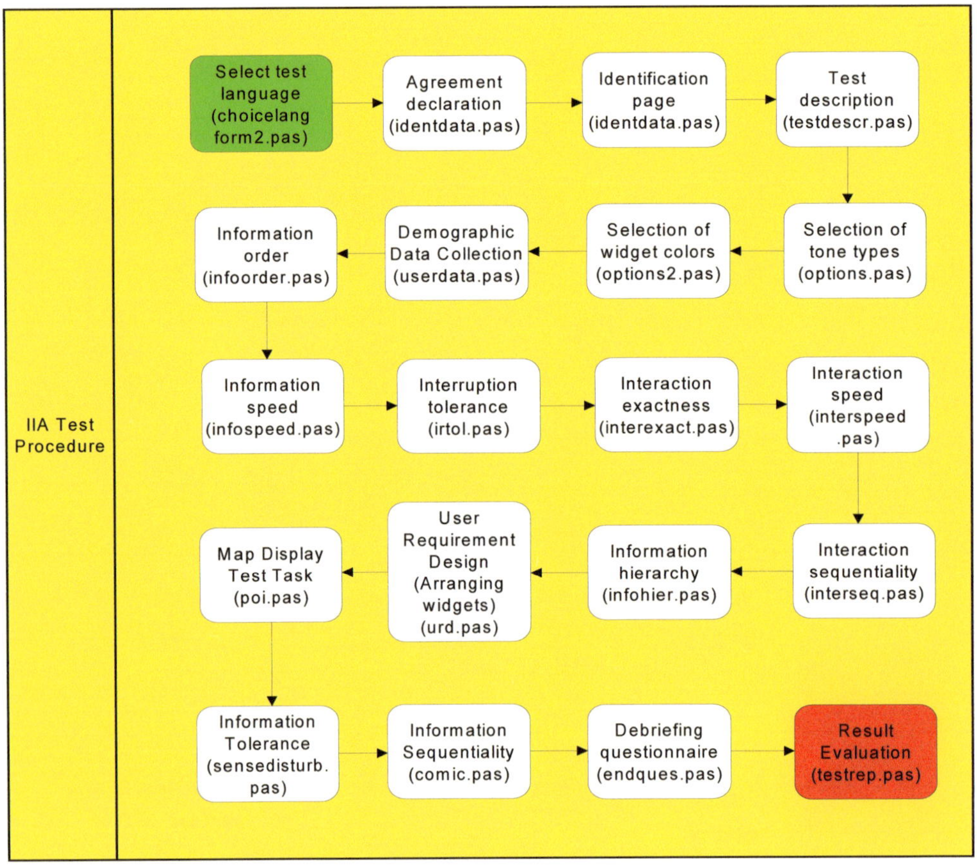

Fig. 7. Test procedure of the IIA test

A user test session with the IIA data collection module comprises five parts: collection of demographic data, test tasks, (cultural) value survey module (VSM94) questionnaire from Hofstede 1994, evaluation of results by the user, and debriefing questionnaire. The method to ask many users online by letting them do special test use cases and to collect the qualitative data (user preferences) emerged by this process quantitatively, has been used for Chinese (C), English (E) and German (G) speaking employees of SiemensVDO (SV) (now Continental) worldwide by an automated online data collection using the IIA data collection module to get cultural differences in HMI. After the start of the IIA data collection module, firstly, the user has to select his preferred test language (figure 8).

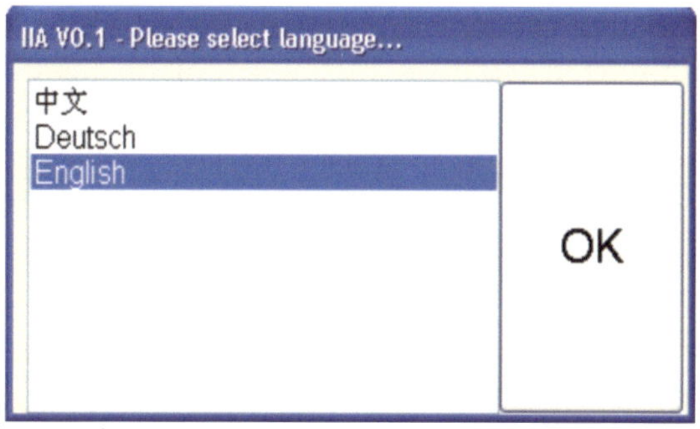

Fig. 8. The user can choose the language in which the test takes place (Chinese, German, or English)

Afterwards, greetings and a legend will be presented followed by a declaration of consent by the user that the collected data from the user may be used within the research project (figure 9). If the user disagrees, no personal data may be collected: the data collection will be anonymous.

Fig. 9. Test introduction and agreement to use personal data

The demographic "questionnaire" delivers the usual knowledge of demographic research especially about the cultural background of the user (like mother tongue, languages, nationality, residence in foreign countries, highest education, job description, age and PC experience) (figure 10).

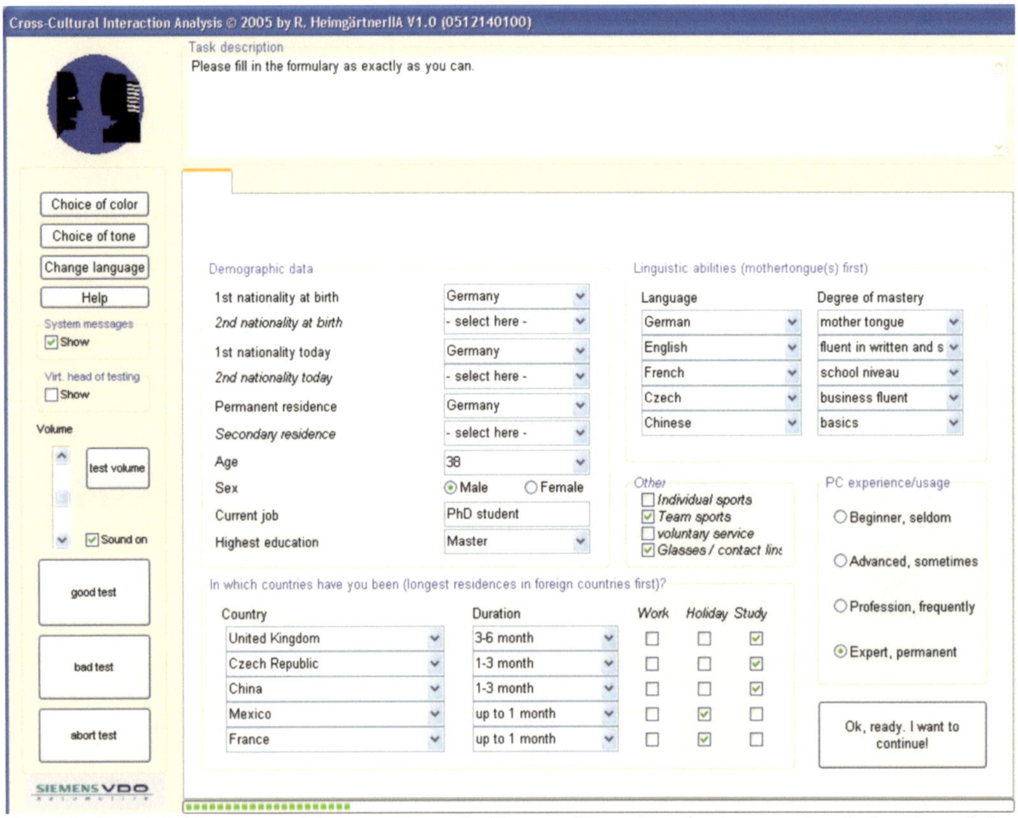

Fig. 10. Special "demographic questionnaire" recording also the interaction behavior of the user with the system

However, in this case, the demographic "questionnaire" is already a special test task, recording also many parameters regarding the interaction behavior of the user with the system.

- Sequence of asking the questions.
- Number of dialog steps to finish the test task.
- Number of interactions during doing the test task e.g. number of using optional functions and help initiations, color settings, mouse moves or clicks and drop downs.
- Length of interaction breaks during doing the test task.
- Number of premature trials to go on to the next test task because the user meant he has finished the current task already. It is assumed that (C)>(G), because C has lower uncertainty avoidance than (G).

- Number of help usage. The user can press a help button to get a hint about to do the test task. It is assumed in literature (cf. Honold, 2000), that Chinese user do not use this button as often as German users because of fearing to lose their face.
- Number of initiating optional functions supposed to be high for (G) because of the wish to work very accurately.
- Straightness of mouse moving direction is assumed to be linear for (G) because of high task-orientedness.
- Speed of mouse movement: probably higher for (C) than for (G) because of low uncertainty avoidance and high communication speed.
- Jerkiness of mouse movements concerning affectivity and emotionality: (C) higher than (G) because of their relationship-orientedness.
- Number of language switching probably higher for (C) because of cultural interest and openness as well as multilingualism by relationship-orientedness and collectivistic attitude.
- Number of dialog steps assumed to be lower for (G) than for (C) because of task-orientedness.
- Test duration can be both: (G) > (C) by doing tasks very exactly because of task-orientedness but also the other way around: (C) > (G) by discussing the tasks with other people because of relationship-orientedness.
- For all number of key presses like usage of return-key-presses and usage of keyboard (number and kind of key presses), (C) > (G) is expected because of high interaction speed coming from low uncertainty avoidance as well as high communication speed and density by relationship-orientedness.
- Number of sounds, words, sentences, and utterances higher for (C) e.g. because of higher affectivity and relationship-orientedness.
- Duration of selection (e.g. combo box) is expected higher for (G) than for (C) because of degree of reflection (R) and interaction exactness (hit exactness at motoric selection).
- Time between "Mouse-Move-Over-Widget and Click onto Widget": (G) > (C) because high degree of reflection and low interaction speed.
- Length of stay with mouse at widgets: (G) > (C) because of higher degree of reflection (R) as well as low interaction speed.
- Double click speed: higher for (C) than for (G) because of interaction speed, uncertainty avoidance (UV) and affectivity.
- Entering speed (e.g. on the keyboard): (C) > (G) because of interaction speed, (UV) and affectivity.
- Times between "selecting" and "using" (G)>(C) because of interaction speed, (UV) and (R).
- Sequence of user actions (e.g. „Selecting"): (G) > (C) because of action chain theory, i.e. high information sequentiality because of orientation to plan - avoiding coincidences - and doing things sequentially according to mono-chrone understanding of time as well as high uncertainty avoidance exposing a linear cognitive style.
- Number of backspace usage (number of wrong entering) and error clicks (= senseless or useless mouse clicks): (C) > (G) because of low (UV) and high interaction speed paired with high impatience or desire to get fast feedback (all initiations are expected to get immediate reactions).

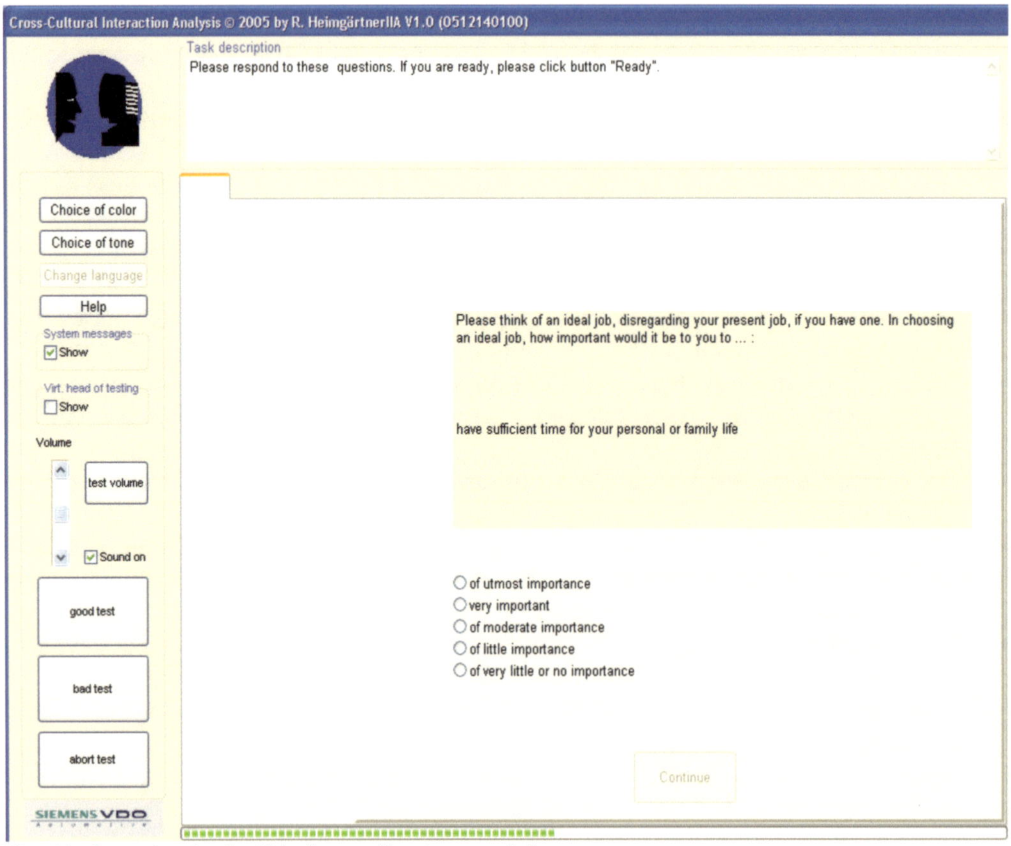

Fig. 11. Question in the IIA data collection module

Parameter	Example
ID	47
Number	42
Group	2
Category	DNS
Position	4
Source	Brown
Headline	Driver navigation system
Question	How polite should be a DNS?
Scale	Interval
Scale size	0,100
Attributes	polite honestly, polite-euphemistic
Layout	Vertical
Result	54
Reason necessary	False
Reason box headline	Please give a reason
Reason	no idea
Show values	False
Priority	4
Without question	False

Table 2. Flexible controlling of the questionnaires in the IIA data collection module by using simple excel sheets

Furthermore, to analyze the cultural characteristics of the users, the value survey module (VSM94) has to be filled in by the user (cf. Hofstede, 2002). The VSM94 contains 26 questions to determine the values of the cultural dimensions using the indices of Hofstede that characterize the cultural behavior of the users (cf. Hofstede, 1991). The questions are implemented within the IIA data collection tool (cf. figure 11) as flexible questioning module which can be controlled by a simple excel sheet (cf. table 2): not only the contents but also the kind of questions can be defined (nominal, ordinal, interval, with/without qualitative reason/text box, with/without numerical display, checkboxes or radio buttons).
After this, the results of the VSM94 and those of the test tasks are presented to the user who has to estimate whether or not the cultural and informational values found correlate or match to him (cf. figure 12).

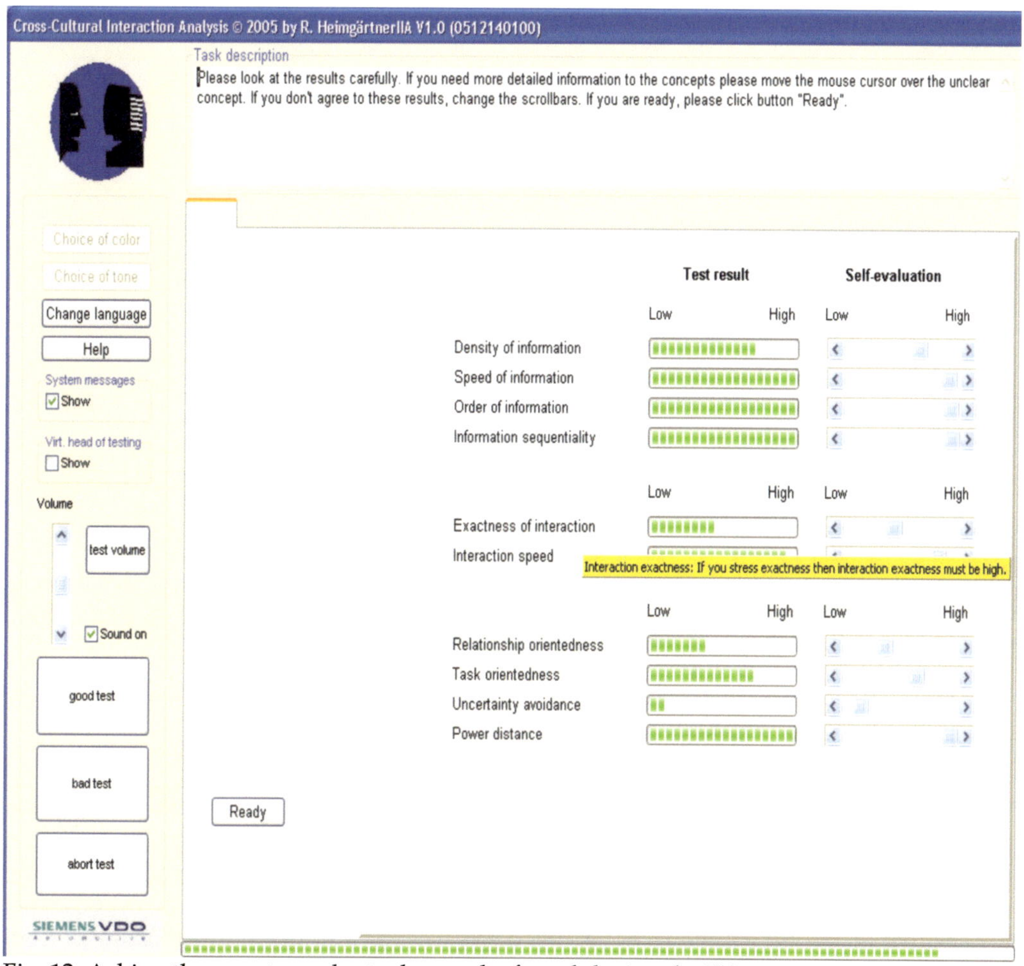

Fig. 12. Asking the user to evaluate the results found during the IIA test

The debriefing part reveals the purpose of the test to the user in greater detail. It collects data regarding the usability of the test system, the perceived difficulty of the test in general, if the user has recognized the implemented hypotheses in the test tasks during the test session, as well as e.g. asking the physical conditions of the test environment (cf. figure 13).

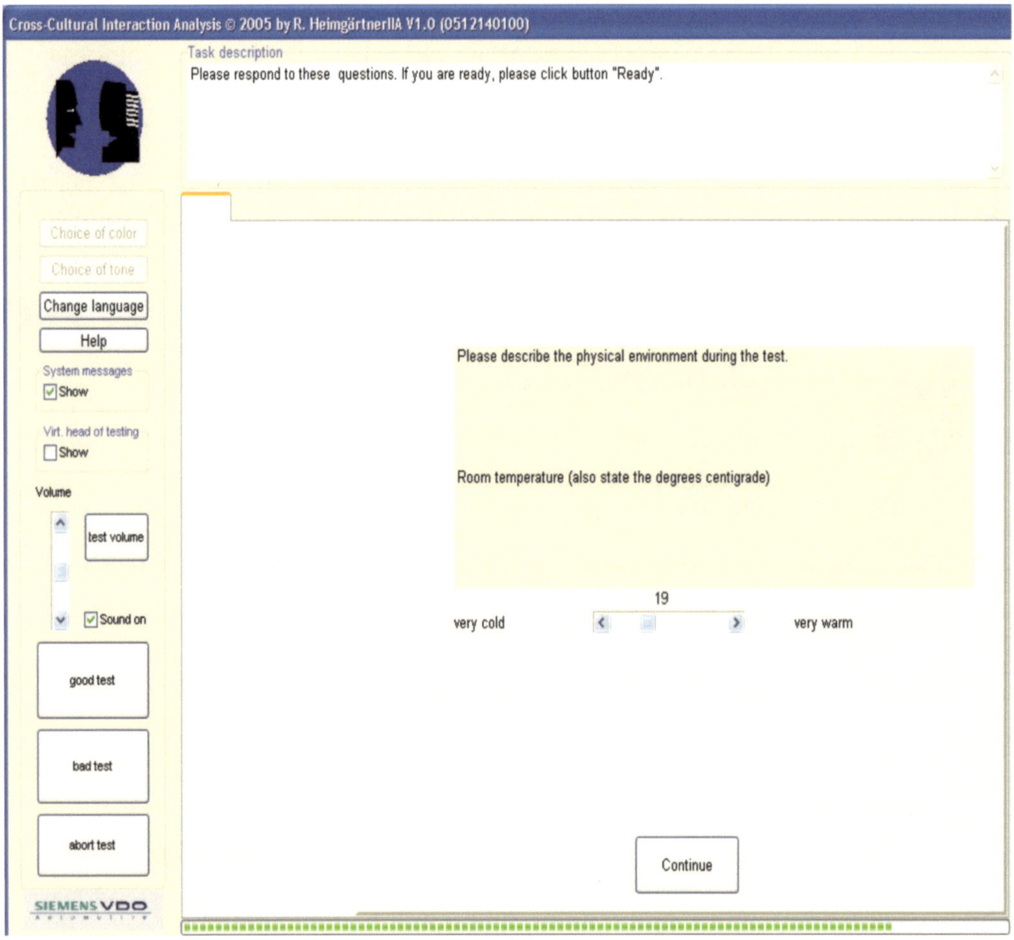

Fig. 13. Asking the user about the conditions of the test environment

5. Data Collection and Data Analysis with the IIA Tool

Two online studies timely separated by one year (in 2006 and 2007) served to verify the functionality and reliability of the IIA tool and to get the preferences of users according to their cultural background (especially regarding their interaction behavior). Randomly selected employees from SiemensVDO (now Continental) all over the world were invited per email to do the test session using the IIA data collection module by downloading it from the corporate intranet. The test participant (Siemens VDO employee) downloaded the IIA data collection module via the corporate intranet locally on his computer, started the tool and did all test tasks. Before closing the tool, the collected data has been transferred automatically onto a non public and secure network drive on a SV server by the IIA tool (figure 14). Using the IIA data analysis module, the data could have been analyzed there.

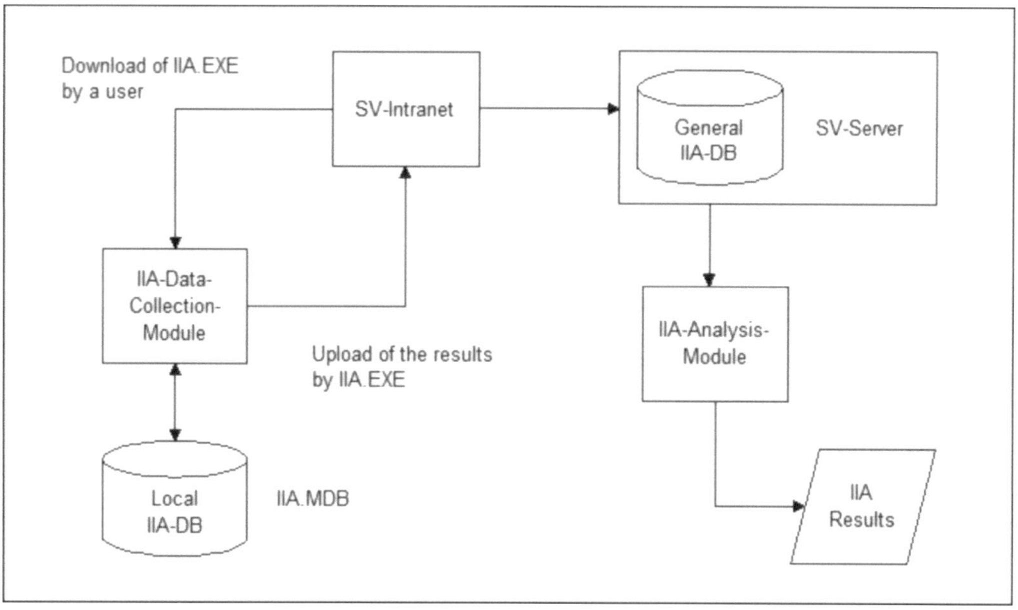

Fig. 14. Course of data collection flow

Table 3 characterizes the two online studies regarding sample size, tests downloaded, tests aborted, valid test data sets, and return rate.

Study	Sample size	Survey period	Number of downloaded tests	Tests Aborted [%]	Number of valid test data sets	Return Rate [%]
1	600	12/14/05 - 01/14/06	166	41,5	102	16,6
2	14500	11/14/06 - 01/19/07	2803	66,8	916	6,3

Table 3. Characterization of the two online studies conducted with the IIA tool

The tests have been aborted due to the following reasons: download time too long[2], no time to do the test now, test is not interesting or appealing. This type of qualitative data helped to optimize the testing equipment and to steer the direction of data analysis by asking the user for the reasons of his behavior during the test (e.g. by open questions using text boxes). Only complete and valid data sets have been analyzed using the IIA data analysis module and the statistic program SPSS (cf. Bortz & Döring, 2005). The discrimination rate of classifying the

[2] Notably in China because of slow network connections.

users to their selected test language by the variables concerning the cultural background of the user's mother tongue, nationality, country of birth and primary residence was 83.3% for the first and 81.9% for the second study.[3] Therefore, the differences in HCI in these studies have been analyzed in relation to three groups of test persons according to the selected test languages (Chinese (C), German (G), and English (E)) in order to reduce data analyzing costs. In the following, I concentrate on the more representative second main study, because it has been used nine times more valid test data sets (916:102). Furthermore, the second study almost mirrors the results of the first study. Nevertheless, I will contrast and discuss the differing results in some detail to be able to deduce the reliability of the IIA tool. Out of the 14500 test persons invited in the larger second main study, 2803 downloaded and started the test. The return rate of 19.3% is sufficient for reasonable statistical analysis. 66.8% of the tests have been aborted. The remaining 33.1% of the tests have been completed and only the data of these tests has been analyzed using the IIA data analysis module and the statistics program SPSS. The total remaining amount of valid data sets is 916.

To analyze the collected data, structural equation models have been used. Structural equation models belong to the statistical methods of *conformational* factor analysis.[4] In contrast, *explorative* factor analysis can be used to determine the correctness of the conducted classification of the parameters into factors (e.g. informational dimensions). Factor analysis serves to structure and to select the deduction of the cultural interaction indicators (CII's) of the information dimensions for HMI design. The objective of factor analysis is the grouping and reduction of the information quantity (judgments, questions, variables) simultaneously ensuring and protecting of information content. The main tasks of factor analysis are:

- Grouping variables to „factors" according to their correlation strength.
- Identifying variables resp. factors that correlate highly with information related dimensions or predict them greatly.
- Filtering of variables having low explanation value in regard to the factor or the informational dimension they represent.
- Resuming variables to indicators on the basis of factor and item analysis as well as reflections regarding content.
- Deducting indicators representing (parts of) the information related dimensions.

The methods used for these purposes are explorative factor analysis, regression analysis and item analysis (all feasible in SPSS). The analysis of the empirically collected data comparing the average values using the IIA analysis module, neural networks, and AMOS[5] revealed that some of the parameters do really depend on culture.

6. Results: Cultural Interaction Indicators (CII's) and Patterns (CIP's)

In the two online studies, some values of the implemented variables in the IIA tool showed

---

[3] The discrimination rate has been calculated using discriminance analysis (cross validated and grouped, Wilk's Lamda in study 1: $\lambda_{1\text{-}2}$=.072**, λ_2=.568**, Wilk's Lamda in study 2: $\lambda_{1\text{-}2}$=.192**, λ_2=.513**). The level of significance is referenced with asterisks in this chapter (* $p<.05$, ** $p<.01$).

[4] Cf. Backhaus et al., 2003.

[5] AMOS is short for **A**nalysis of **MO**ment **S**tructures. It is a statistical tool for data analysis providing structural equation modeling (SEM). For further details, please refer to Arbuckle, 2005.

significant differences, which represent differences in user interaction according to the different cultural background of the users. Therefore, these variables can be called *cultural interaction indicators*. Table 4 presents the cultural interaction indicators that can be derived from the quantitative results of the two online studies.[6]

Cultural interaction indicator	**First study**	**Second study**
MG.CarSpeed	F(2,102)=8,857**	χ^2 (2,916)=29,090**
MG.MessageDistance	F(2,102)=7,645**	F(2,916)=16,241**
MD.NumberOfPOI	F(2,102)=3,143*	χ^2 (2,916)=32,170**
MaximalOpenTasks	χ^2 (2,102)=12,543**	F(2,916)=15,140**
MaximalOpenTasksRatio (C,G,E)	2.5 : 1.4 : 1	1.7 : 1.03 : 1
MG.InfoPresentationDuration	χ^2 (2,102)=17,354**	χ^2 (2,916)=82,944**
NumberOfChars	χ^2 (2,102)=16,452**	χ^2 (2,916)=67,637**

Table 4. Cultural Interaction Indicators found in both studies

The significant cultural interaction indicators are the following: *MG.CarSpeed* (χ^2 (2, 916) = 29.090**) means the driving speed of the simulated car in the maneuver guidance test task ((C) less than (G) and (E)). *MG.MessageDistance* (F (2, 916) = 16.241**) denotes the temporal distance of showing the maneuver advice messages in the maneuver guidance test task. (C) desired about 30% more pre-advices ("in x m turn right") than (G) or (E) before turning right. This can be an indication for higher information speed and higher information density in China compared to Germany, for example. *MD.NumberOfPOI* (χ^2 (2, 916) = 32.17**) counts the number of points of interest (POI) set by the user in the map display test task. Information density increases with the number of POI and is two times higher for (C) than for (G) or (E). *MaxOpenTasks* (F (2, 916) = 15.140**) represents the maximum number of open tasks in the working environment (i.e. running applications and icons in the Windows ™ task bar) during the test session with the IIA data collection module. (C) tend to work on more tasks simultaneously than (G) or (E) (ratio (C,G,E) = 1.7:1.03:1) which can be possibly explained by the way of work planning (polychrome vs. monochrome timing, cf. Hall 1976) or the kind of thinking (mono-causal (sequential) vs. multi-causal (parallel) logic, Röse et al., 2001). *MG.InfoPresentationDuration* represents the time the maneuver advice message is visible on the screen. (C) and (G) wanted the advices to be about 40% longer than (E) do. *NumberOfChars* (χ^2 (2) = 67.637**) contains the number of characters entered by the user during the maneuver guidance and map display test tasks in answering open questions ((C) < (E) and (G)). This is explained by the fact that the Chinese language needs considerably less characters to represent words than English or German.

There are also possible cultural interaction indicators that are only significant in the second study which is more representative than the first because of n=916 in comparison to n=102 (cf. table 5).

[6] The variables in the valid test data sets are not distributed comparably in the first and the second online study. Therefore, partly the same variables have been analyzed either by ANOVA or by Kruskal-Wallis-test (indicated with F or χ^2).

Variables with borderline values	First study	Second study
OpenTaskBeforeTest	F (2, 102) = 3.129*	χ^2 (2,916)=5,965
OpenTaskBeforeTestRatio (C,G,E)	1.6 : 1.2 : 1	1.05 : 1.04 : 1
IE.InteractionExactness	F(2,102)=2,345 (p=.101)	χ^2 (2,916)=24,106**
IS.InteractionSpeedValue	F(2,102)=1,801 (p=.170)	F(2,916)=16,246**
MG.NumberOfManeuver	χ^2 (2,102)=4,785 (p=.091)	χ^2 (2,916)=54,051**
UV.UncertaintyAvoidanceValue	χ^2 (2,102)=5,297 (p=.071)	χ^2 (2,916)=26,239**
IS.InteractionExactnessValue	F(2,102)=2,698 (p=.073)	χ^2 (2,916)=40,862**

Table 5. Cultural interaction indicators with borderline values in the studies

OpenTaskBeforeTest represents the number of open tasks in the working environment (i.e. running applications and icons in the Windows ™ task bar) before the test session with the IIA data collection tool began. (C) tend to work on more tasks simultaneously than (G) or (E) which can be possibly explained by the way of work planning (polychrome vs. monochrome timing, Hall 1976) or the kind of thinking (mono-causal (sequential) vs. multi-causal (parallel) logic, Röse et al., 2001). *IE.InteractionExactness* (χ^2 (2, 916) = 24.106**) measures the exactness clicking onto dots in the abstract test task of "clicking dots away". (G) clicked the dots away almost twice as exact as (E) and (C). *IS.InteractionSpeedValue* (F (2, 916) = 16.246**) measures the duration of the abstract test task of "clicking dots away". (C) clicked the dots away almost twice as fast as (E) and (G).

The number of mouse clicks differs in both studies but in different significance peculiarities: E.g., *UV.MouseClicks* counts the mouse clicks in the test task "uncertainty avoidance". (C) are doing more than (G) and (E) which indicate the desire of (C) to get immediate system reaction according to their input requests (e.g. mouse clicks) is very high. This is also supported by *AllMouseClicks* (χ^2 (2, 916) = 15.235**) which counts all mouse clicks done by a user in the test and the nearly twofold amount of *ErrorClicks* by (C) in contrast to (G) and (E). *ErrorClicks* (χ^2 (2, 916) = 9.771**) counts the mouse clicks, which do not have any function for a test task (and hence, which can be a cue for impatience).

The peculations of the cultural interaction indicators regarding the different cultures are similar comparing them between first (n=102) and second (n=916) data collection. This indicates the correctness of the data collection. The analysis of the log files of the second data collection using 1632 valid data sets revealed the results shown in table 6.

Cultural interaction indicators (CII's) derived from log files of the second data collection						
df = 2	**Oneway ANOVA**			**Kruskal-Wallis**		**Interpretation**
Name of CII	**F**	**P**	**h**	**χ^2**	**p**	**CII is significant**
Test Duration	11,53	0,000	0,404	54,508	0,000	yes, quantitatively
MouseMoves_norm	26,20	0,000	0,225	57,900	0,000	yes, quantitatively
KeyDowns_norm	27,31	0,000	0,318	59,451	0,000	yes, quantitatively
LeftButtonDowns_norm	28,84	0,000	0,266	59,471	0,000	yes, quantitatively

Table 6. Cultural interaction indicators derived from log files of the second data collection

It is remarkable that all three CII's (MouseMoves_norm, KeyDowns_norm, and LButtonDowns_norm) concerning the kind of interaction behavior of the users are peculiarized very similar according to the nationality of the test participants indicating the same interaction behavior of the users of the same nationality which indicates the correctness of the test equipment and the study results.

The cultural interaction indicators can be visualized applying the IIA data analysis tool to plot "cultural HCI fingerprints" (in the style of Smith & Chang, 2003) which represent the cultural differences in HCI in respect to several variables for HCI design that depend on the cultural background of the potential target group of users (cf. figure 15). This visual representation of the CII's should ease information reception and improve comparative understanding of the cultural differences in HCI.

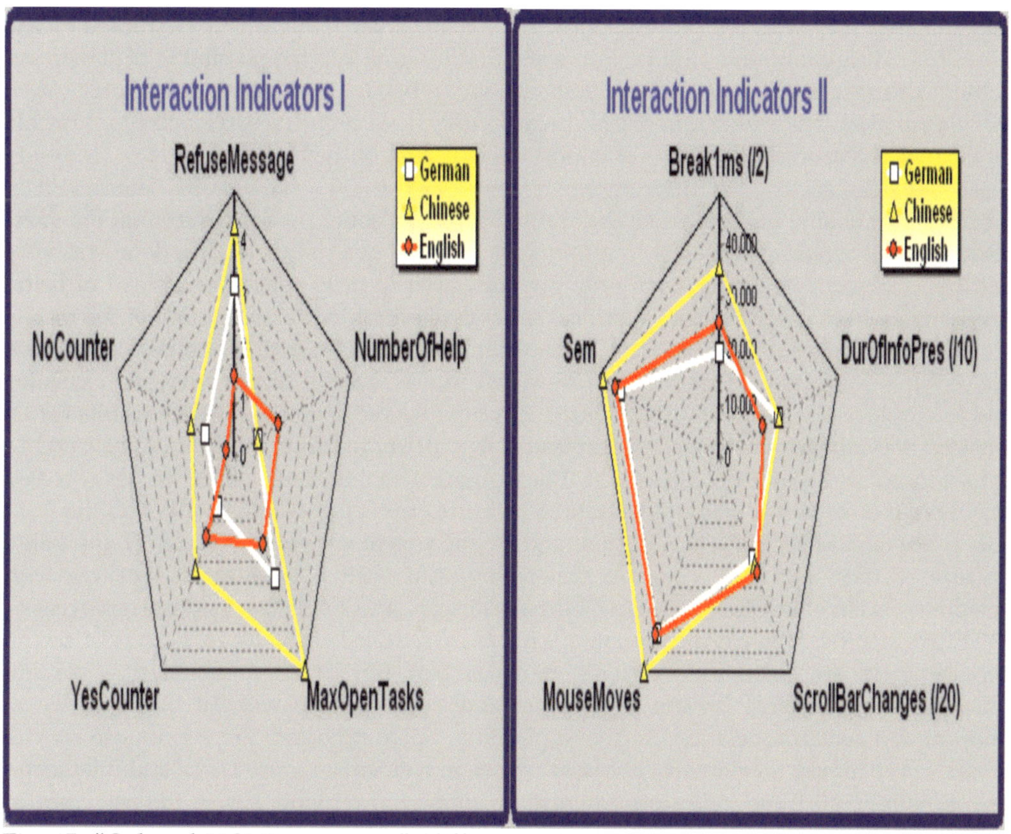

Fig. 15. "Cultural HCI Fingerprints" (different values of the cultural interaction indicators according to test languages) plot by the IIA data analysis tool

7. Discussion: Reliability of Results, IIA Tool and Design Recommendations

The two main online studies in this work revealed many aspects, which supported each other: a high discrimination rate of over 80% and the high accordance between the cultural interaction indicators found by one-way ANOVA and Kruskal-Wallis-Test respectively and the discriminance analysis on the other hand supports the high reliability and criteria validity of the statistical results received in this study using the IIA tool. Moreover, the tests with the IIA data evaluation tool using neuronal networks confirmed also the high classification rates of the several combinations of cultural interaction indicators of over 80%. This overall outcome proofs the high reliability and justifies the usage of the IIA tool in future. Furthermore, the reliability of the results and the IIA tool is also supported by the fact, that the results of other qualitative studies confirmed the results of the quantitative studies done with the IIA tool: the studies with the IIA tool comparing Chinese and German users revealed different interaction patterns according to the cultural background of the users regarding e.g. design (ample vs. simple), information density (high vs. low), menu structure (high breath vs. high depth), personalization (high vs. low), language (symbols vs. characters) and interaction devices (no help vs. help) that have been confirmed by qualitative studies e.g. by Vöhringer-Kuhnt 2006, Kralisch 2006 or Kamentz 2006. Results regarding e.g. the status bar position of the URD test task are qualitatively confirmed by e.g. Röse 2001. The quantitative studies gave some first insights into the possibility of classifying cultural different users on behalf of their interaction behavior concerning the *direct hidden cultural variables*. The results are *reliable* because they have been traceable and reproducible by the two online studies, finally yet importantly because of the high sample size. However, detailed values and higher discrimination power of the CII's have to be determined in future. Additionally, qualitative studies brought to light some results concerning the *direct visible cultural variables*. However, the sample size of the qualitative studies done was very small and hence, these results can only give direction to new guidelines instead of being precise guidelines for the future. A critical general objection to the application of the results yielded by the two studies using the IIA tool could concern the fact, that the collected data are selective samples because they are restricted to use cases of driver navigation systems and to employees of SiemensVDO. Hence, it is not allowed to generalize the results for all Chinese and all German users. Nevertheless, it is permitted and necessarily indicated to extract thumb rules for intercultural HMI design, because the results of the studies revealed that there is a metrics, which is adequate to measure cross-cultural HCI. Although the VSM values are similar to Chinese, German, and English speaking employees of SV (probably because of their common company philosophy) and their experience in working with computers is alike, the HCI between Chinese, German, and English speaking employees of SV differs significantly. Hence, *some results can be expected to be valid for HCI design in general* because there are culturally sensitive variables that can be used to measure cultural differences in HCI only by counting certain interaction events without the necessity of knowing the semantic relations to the application. Such indicators are e.g. mouse moves, breaks in the mouse movements, speed of mouse movements, mouse clicks and interaction breaks. Surely, all those indicators can also be connected semantically to the use cases or applications. However, simply counting such events related to the session duration from users of one culture and comparing them to users of another culture is obviously sufficient to indicate differences in interaction behavior of culturally different users. The possible implication that this is grounded in subconscious cultural differences imprinted by primary culture and learning the mother tongue which leads to different HCI independently of the conscious cultural propositional attitudes, has to be verified in future studies. Additionally, studies that are more detailed must show whether changing the metrics of potential cultural indicators (or using them in other situations, use cases, or circumstances) will improve their discriminating effect and yield appropriate values accordingly as well as the general usability of general cultural interaction indicators. The following criteria, which represent the *real* UMTM, have been identified as hypothetically depending on culture by literature research and reflection (according to the IV model) as well as actually depending on culture by empirical research (using the IIA tool):

- Information frequency (number of words per minute, number of dialogs per minute)
- Information density (number of images per page, number of words per dialog, number of words per information unit, image-text ratio or distribution, distance of pieces of information to each other)
- Information arrangement (widget positions, image-text arrangement)
- Information order (regularity and orderedness of informational units)
- Information sequentiality (sequential presentation of information units)
- Interaction speed (mouse clicks per minute, overall mouse clicks, length of mouse track per second)
- Interaction device (mouse, keyboard, menu control button, touch screen)

However, these confirmations of the postulated hypotheses do not finally proof cultural differences in the information related dimensions. One important reason for this is that the used metrics of the test setting must be optimized regarding the use cases and their logical relevance. Furthermore, the reliability of the metrics and the used indicators has to be determined more exactly and optimized. This requires applying test theory in much more detail.

8. Conclusion and Outlook

The IIA tool serves to record the user's interaction with the computer to be able to identify cultural variables like color, positioning, information density, interaction speed, interaction patterns and their values, which enable the deduction of design rules of thumb for cross-cultural HCI design. It is effective, efficient and reasonable to use the IIA tool within the process of cross-cultural HCI design because it can be used locally and worldwide and provides quantitative comparable and reliable results whose validity and method to get them is quantitatively and qualitatively confirmed by several studies. The results of two longitudinal studies proofed the reliability of the IIA tool and indicated that it should be possible to optimize the model of cultural dependent variables for the HMI design using structure equal models. Using the IIA tool means rapid use case design, i.e. real-time prototyping of user interfaces for different cultures as well as collecting huge amounts of valid data rapidly and easily worldwide online via internet or intranet.

The IIA tool will be continually optimized based on user feedback to extend the analysis and evaluation of cultural differences in HCI by exploring cultural interaction patterns and by improving the discrimination capability of cultural interaction indicators. Questionnaires in conjunction with recording biofeedback signals (heart rate and skin response) should give controlled insights into the user preferences. Another objective is to develop enhanced techniques using statistical methods (factors analysis, structure equation models, cluster analysis etc.), data mining and semantic processing to extract the cultural variables and its values as well as the guidelines for cross-cultural HMI design in a more automatically way. Moreover, it is intended to extend the method to implement new use cases e.g. by employing authoring tools or using HMI description languages.

9. References

Arbuckle, J. L. (2005). Amos 6.0 User's Guide. Amos Development Corporation. Spring House. USA

Backhaus, K., Erichson, B., Plinke, W., Weiber, R. (2003). Multivariate Analysemethoden. Eine anwendungsorientierte Einführung. Springer. Berlin, Heidelberg, New York. 10. Aufl.

Bortz, J. & Döring, N. (2005). Forschungsmethoden und Evaluation für Human- und Sozialwissenschaftler. 3. Aufl. Springer. Heidelberg

De la Cruz, T., Mandl, T., Womser-Hacker, C. (2005). Cultural Dependency of Quality Perception and Web Page Evaluation Guidelines: Results from a Survey. In Day, D., del Galdo, E., Evers, V. (eds.): Designing for Global Markets 7: Proceedings of the Seventh International Workshop on Internationalization of Products and Systems IWIPS 2005, The Netherlands, Grafisch Centrum, Amsterdam, 15–27

Dix, A., Finlay, J., Abowd, G., Beale, R. (1993). Human-Computer Interaction. Prentice Hall, London

Gellner, M. & Forbrig, F. (2003). ObSys - a Tool for Visualizing Usability Evaluation Patterns with Mousemaps. HCI International, Greece

Hall, E.T. (1959). The Silent Language. Doubleday, New York

Hall, E.T. (1976). Beyond Culture. Anchor Press, Garden City, N.Y.

Halpin, A.W. & Winer, B.J. (1957). A factorial study of the leader behavior descriptions. Bureau of Business Research, Ohio State University. Columbus, Ohio

Hamacher, N. (2006). Automatic Criteria Oriented Usability Evaluation of Interactive Systems. Dissertation. München: Dr. Hut-Verlag

Heimgärtner, R. (2005). Research in Progress: Towards Cross-Cultural Adaptive Human-Machine-Interaction in Automotive Navigation Systems. In: Day, D., del Galdo, E.M. (eds.): Proceedings of the Seventh International Workshop on Internationalization of Products and Systems. IWIPS 2005, The Netherlands, Grafisch Centrum, Amsterdam, 7–111

Heimgärtner, R. (2006). Measuring Cultural Differences in Human Computer Interaction as Preparatory Work for Cross-Cultural Adaptability in Navigation Systems. In: Useware 2006, VDI-Bericht Nr. 1946, VDI-Verlag, Düsseldorf, 301–314

Heimgärtner, R. (2007). Cultural Differences in Human Computer Interaction: Results from Two Online Surveys. In: Osswald, A., Stempfhuber, M., Wolff, C. (eds.). Open Innovation. Proc. 10. International Symposium for Information Science. Constance: UVK. 145-157

Herczeg, M. (2005). Software-Ergonomie. Grundlagen der Mensch-Computer-Kommunikation, 2. Auflage, München: Oldenbourg.

Hofstede, G. (1991). Cultures and Organisations: Software of the Mind. McGraw-Hill, London

Hofstede, G. (1994). Value Survey Module 1994 Manual, Institute for Research on Intercultural Cooperation, Maastricht

Hofstede, G. (2002). The Pitfalls of Cross-National Survey Research: A reply to the Article by Spector et al. on the Psychometric Properties of the Hofstede Values Survey

Module 1994. Applied Psychology: An International Review, Vol. 51, Nr. 1 (2002) 170–173
Hofstede, G. & Hofstede, J. G. (2005). Cultures and Organizations: Software of the Mind. 2nd Edition. USA, New York: McGraw-Hill
Honold, P. (2000). Interkulturelles Usability Engineering. Eine Untersuchung zu kulturellen Einflüssen auf die Gestaltung und Nutzung technischer Produkte. Reihe 10: Informatik/Kommunikation. Düsseldorf: VDI Verlag GmbH
Kamentz, E. (2006). Adaptivität von hypermedialen Lernsystemen : Ein Vorgehensmodell für die Konzeption einer Benutzermodellierungskomponente unter Berücksichtigung kulturbedingter Benutzereigenschaften, Dissertation
Kamentz, E. & Mandl, T. (2003). Culture and E-Learning: Automatic Detection of a Users' Culture from Survey Data. In Evers, Vanessa and Röse, Kerstin and Honold, Pia and Coronado, Jose and Day, Donald, Eds. Proceedings Fifth International Workshop on Internationalization of Products and Systems (IWIPS 2003) Designing for Global Markets 5: Proceedings of the Fifth International Workshop on Internationalization of Products and Systems (IWIPS 2003), pp. 227-239, Berlin, Germany
Kralisch, A. (2006). The impact of culture and language on the use of the internet - empirical analyses of behaviour and attitudes, dissertation
Lewandowitz, L., Rößger, P., Vöhringer-Kuhnt, T. (2006). Asiatische vs. europäische HMI Lösungen von Fahrerinformationssystemen. In: USEWARE 2006 (VDI-Bericht 1946).VDI/VDE-Gesellschaft Mess- und Automatisierungstechnik. Düsseldorf: VDI-Verlag. 301-314
Mangold, P. (2005). Proceeding studies on behavior - not only a challenge for professional tools. Usability Symposium 2005: 127-140
Marcus, A. & Baumgartner, V-J. (2005). A Practical Set of Culture Dimensions for Global User-Interface Development. In: Masoodian, M., Jones, S., Rogers, B. (eds.): Proceedings of Computer Human Interaction: 6th Asia Pacific Conference. APCHI 2004, New Zealand, Rotorua, 29 June - 2 July 2004, Volume 3101 / 2004. Springer, Berlin (2005) 252–261
Prendinger, H. & Ishizuka, M. (Eds.) (2004). Life-Like Characters. Springer
Röse, K. (2002). Methodik zur Gestaltung interkultureller Mensch-Maschine-Systeme in der Produktionstechnik. Fortschritt-Berichte pak. Band 5. Mensch-Maschine-Interaktion, Verlag Universität Kaiserslautern, Kaiserslautern
Röse K, Liu, L., Zühlke, D. (2001). Design Issues in Mainland China: Demands for a Localized Human-Machine-Interaction Design. In: Johannsen, G. (ed.): 8th IFAC/IFIPS/IFORS/IEA Symposium on Analysis, Design, and Evaluation of Human-Machine Systems. Preprints, Kassel (2001) 17–22
Shneiderman, B. (2002). User Interface Design. MIT Press
Smith, A. & Chang, Y. (2003). Quantifying Hofstede and Developing Cultural Fingerprints for Website Acceptability. In: Evers, V., Röse, K., Honold, P., Coronado, J., Day, D. (eds.): Proceedings of the Fifth International Workshop on Internationalization of Products and Systems. IWIPS 2003, Germany, Berlin, 17–19 July 2003. University of Kaiserslautern, Kaiserslautern, 89–102
Victor, D. (1997). International Business Communication. New York, Prentice Hall

Vöhringer-Kuhnt, T. (2006). Asiatische vs. europäische HMI Lösungen von Fahrerinformationssystemen. In: Useware 2006, VDI-Bericht Nr. 1946, VDI-Verlag, Düsseldorf (2006) 279–287

20

Detecting and exploiting user familiarity in natural language human-computer dialogue

Ludovic Le Bigot,* Philippe Bretier** & Patrice Terrier***
* *University of Poitiers & CNRS (CeRCA, UMR 6234)*
** *Orange Labs Research & Development*
*** *University of Toulouse II & CNRS (CLLE-LTC, UMR, 5263)*
France

1. Human-computer dialogue and usability

1.1 What is human-computer dialogue?

The fields of application for human-computer dialogue are both many and various. Users may dialogue with customer services over the phone or via a personal digital assistant in order to carry out banking transactions, find their way around a city, or book train or plane tickets (Wilkie et al., 2005).

The modality of interaction between user and system can also be either partially or totally speech-based. System messages or prompts can be delivered to the user via either a screen (text, graphics) or an auditory modality (pre-recorded or computer-generated voice). User data entry is possible through speech or via either a phone or a computer keyboard, and in the case of advanced systems, users can submit their requests in natural language (see Gorin et al., 1997, Le Bigot et al., 2007).

Furthermore, current systems propose a wide range of interaction styles. The dialogue can be guided by the system (system-initiated), the user (user-initiated) or both (mixed-initiated) (see Lai et al., 2008, for details). In system-initiated dialogue, which is the most common, the interaction is led by the system and may appear mechanistic. In the following examples, the system either questions the user or offers him or her a choice. For example, the system may say, "*To buy the share, press 1, and to sell the share, press 2*". The user then presses 1 or 2 on his or her phone keypad. For a speech system with explicit keywords, the "*Press 1*" or "*Press 2*" is replaced by a verb or a common noun: "*To buy the share, say Buy, and to sell the share, say Sell*". The user says the keyword aloud and continues the interaction. For a speech-based system with implicit keywords, the choices are suggested. The system may ask the user, "*Do you want to buy or sell the share?*". The user must then say the "*buy*" or "*sell*" verb aloud to continue the interaction (a system with natural language capability would be able to recognise a response such as, "*I want to buy the share*").

User-initiated systems are few and far between. However, they offer users greater freedom and flexibility. Once they have asked the user what he or she wants ("*What do you want?*"), the interaction continues in an open mode. Some systems offer a functionality which combines several different interaction modes. For example, the interaction may begin on a

user-initiated basis, but if several dialogue errors occur, the system may shift to a system-initiated mode.
Note that the degree of initiative displayed by the system to the user may not reflect the full extent of its understanding capabilities. In the case of the speech-based system-initiated example mentioned earlier, the system may accept greater flexibility from the user than it appears to. In addition to the keywords mentioned by the system, all the following user inputs may also be accepted as requests to buy a share: "*I want to buy a share*", "*Buy a share*", or "*The first choice*". This chapter, however, focuses on the degree of initiative displayed by the system to the user.

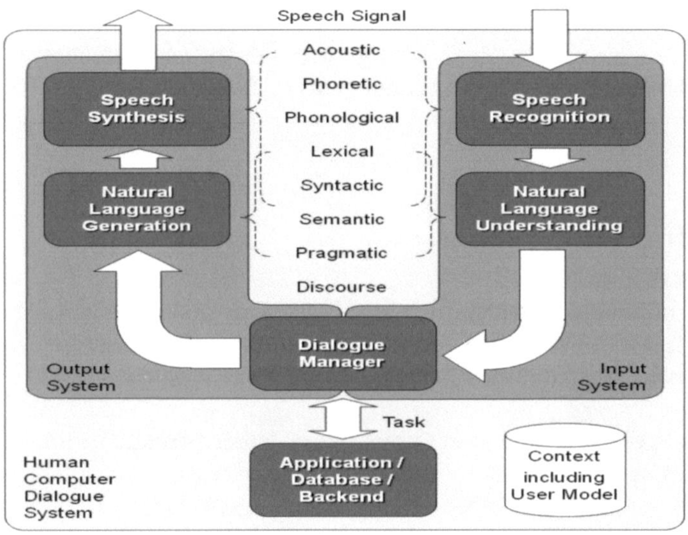

Fig. 1. General architecture of a human-computer dialogue system

As shown in Fig. 1, the architecture of a (speech) human-computer dialogue system is basically composed of a chain of five modules: *speech recognition, natural language understanding, dialogue manager, natural language generation* and *speech synthesis*. An additional module, linked to the dialogue manager, encapsulates the functional part of the system, which may take the form of a *computer application*, a *database* or some more complex *backend system*.
The module chain can be split in two subchains: the *input* and *output systems*. These two systems pass through different levels of analysis. The input system leads from the speech signal to the discourse level, passing through the acoustic, phonetic, phonological, lexical, syntactic, semantic and pragmatic levels. *Speech Recognition* is the first module in the subchain. Its role is to transcribe the user's speech signal into text, drawing on models at each level, from acoustic to syntactic. *Natural Language Understanding* is the second module. This processes text from the lexical and syntactic levels, converting it into dialogue action at the discourse level. The *Dialogue Manager* deals with user dialogue actions and reacts to them by implementing system dialogue actions. The output system moves in the opposite direction. Starting from the system's communicative actions at the discourse level, the *Natural Language Generation* module transcribes these into text at the syntactic and lexical

levels. After that, the *Speech Synthesis* module produces the speech signal, drawing on models at each level, from phonological to acoustic. During a dialogue between a user and the human-computer dialogue system, the processing follows the arrows displayed in the Fig. 1, in a pattern of user speech input processing followed by system speech output processing. This is the pattern that defines a *dialogue turn*, or *speaking turn*, for each dialogue partner (see Pietquin, 2004, for a detailed description of the general architecture of the human-computer dialogue system).
In the course of the speaking turns, all the modules retain a certain amount of data. These data are stored and made available to all the modules in a shared *context knowledge base*. This knowledge base contains the dialogue history at each level of analysis (e.g., speech duration and level, word occurrences and phonetics, utterances, dialogue actions, dialogue and task progress), together with knowledge about the user (e.g., age, gender, familiarity, average word count, average response time, language) and the environment (e.g., noise level) collected during the dialogue. This knowledge is used by the modules when they process each dialogue turn. The part of the knowledge base relating to the user is called the *user model* (see Part 2). The output and input systems must be designed homogeneously, primarily in accordance with the style of interaction. In the case of system-initiated interaction, the system asks the user to select an item (e.g., a keyword) from a list (see above example). The input system then has to process the user's speech input on the basis of the previous system's output. For obvious reasons, the system's understanding capabilities have to be at least on a par with the openness it displays to the user. Whatever the qualities of dialogue system's various components, its design must obey certain rules if it is to be easily understood by its users.

1.2 Usability of human-computer dialogue systems

Most of the recommendations for designing and assessing usable systems are also applicable to advanced human-computer dialogue systems (totally or partially speech-based). Usability is the key to designing a Web interface or software that is easy to use. The ISO standard 9241-11: 1998 defines usability as "*the extent to which a product can be used by specified users to achieve specified goals with effectiveness, efficiency and satisfaction in a specified context of use*". This notion is intended to help designers produce user-friendly systems. Many guidelines or heuristics have been put forward to ensure the usability of interactive systems. Nielsen (1994), for instance, recommended ten main heuristics for designing/evaluating a system. These heuristics range from giving the user clues about the system to providing assistance and documentation. Some of these heuristics are easy to apply to dialogue systems, and one example of Nielsen's heuristics (for complete list, see http://www.useit.com/papers/heuristic/heuristic_list.html) applied to spoken dialogue systems is set out in the following paragraph.
Nielsen's usability principle: *Flexibility and efficiency of use – Accelerators - unseen by the novice user - may often speed up the interaction for the expert user such that the system can cater for both inexperienced and experienced users. Allow users to tailor frequent actions.* For example, this opportunity may be offered in the message introducing a keyword-based interactive voice response system, by informing the user that a service can be directly accessed by activating a keyword: "*If you know* [...] *say the keyword corresponding to your request* [...]".
This example of the rule that has to be obeyed raise the question of whether the user should be taken into account as early as the design phase in order to enhance the usability of a

human-computer dialogue system; given that one of the keys to ensuring that human-computer dialogue systems are tailored to their users is to model the latter's behaviour or environment in order to create the optimum conditions for interaction.

2. Why model users in human-computer dialogue?

2.1 Static and dynamic user models

Due to significant variations in human-computer dialogue system performances according to the type of user and the type of dialogue, as is the case with more general interactive systems such as human-computer interaction, user modelling has become a critical aspect of designing systems and services (Litman & Pan, 2002). Like the knowledge pertaining to users that is contained in the context knowledge bases of human-computer dialogue systems, user models are constructed from both a priori and dynamically acquired knowledge about users. A priori knowledge is generally built into the system by domain experts (Fisher, 2001; Kobsa, 1990).

Most of the knowledge that forms the basis for user models is acquired during dialogues. Some of it is explicitly acquired in specific subdialogues (*"If you are an expert, say ..."*), while some is implicitly inferred from system observations (Shifroni & Shanon, 1992). Some knowledge is acquired once and for all, thus constituting the static part of the user model. Most of it, however, is dynamic: human-computer dialogue system observations (duration and modalities) and inferences (words, information, concepts and actions) at each level of analysis (see Fig. 1), as well as statistics (counts, averages and percentages) are continuously updated by the human-computer dialogue system during processing.

Categories of knowledge in the user model. The knowledge contained in user models can be divided into (at least) three categories: environmental, individual and use (e.g. Brusilovsky, 2001). Knowledge about the environment may concern the user's terminal (phone or personal digital assistant), the modality (speech or keyboard), the locality (GPS coordinates) and any other environmental characteristics (noise level). Knowledge about the user as an individual may be relatively static, such as his or her age and gender, occupational status (student, worker, unemployed, etc.), stereotype profile (disabled, elderly, expert, novice, etc., see Fink & Kobsa, 2000), preferences and interests (Elzer et al., 1994). Individual knowledge tends to be more dynamic and is continuously maintained by the human-computer dialogue systems during the dialogues. Users' mental states (knowledge and goals) represent one of the most precise, comprehensive and dynamic types of user model for the representation of individual knowledge (e.g., Bretier et al., 2004). Knowledge about use concerns users' behaviour. This can also be modelled at each level of analysis handled by a human-computer dialogue system (acoustic, phonetic, phonological, lexical, syntactic, semantic, pragmatic, discourse and task). For example, the plan libraries used in plan recognition constitute a type of use model that encapsulates a user's possible behaviour at the action level. Another example is human-computer dialogue system experiences, collected dialogue after dialogue. Statistical use models can be calculated on the basis of these corpora of experiences (Zukerman & Albrecht, 2001).

Exploiting user models. In general, user modelling is used for adapting human-computer dialogue systems. The purpose of this adaptation may be to enable a human-computer dialogue system to take a specific user's profile, preferences and goals into account (Fisher, 2001). The exploitation of user models consists mainly in taking individual knowledge into account when designing a human-computer dialogue system, particularly with regard to dialogue management. User modelling is extensively used to predict a user's behaviour. This prediction may concern problematic situations, such as those caused by speech recognition errors. Human-computer dialogue systems are then designed to avoid this situation (Litman & Pan, 2002). Prediction can be used by human-computer dialogue systems to anticipate a user's behaviour and minimise his or her contribution. Predicting that the user will ask for a specific item of information, a human-computer dialogue system may adapt its behaviour by proactively providing this information before the user asks for it (for a French-language example, see Baudoin, 2008). Prediction may also be used in a generative way in a user simulator. User simulators are used to automatically generate dialogue corpora for human-computer dialogue systems. These corpora allow systems to learn a number of dialogue strategies to complement their dialogue management design (Pietquin, 2004). Whichever approach is chosen, the literature on human behaviour provides a number of criteria which have to be taken into account when modelling users. The following section describes several studies of the effect of representing one's partner (system or human) on the content and dynamics of an interaction.

2.2 Impact of users' representations of a system on their utterances

When two human partners communicate via a computer system just as they would do if they were conversing face to face, they tend to share the same language. This phenomenon indicates that they have a mutual belief that they are referring to the same purpose (Brennan & Clark, 1996). Thus, the use of personal pronouns and reuse of the material contained in their partner's utterances reflect an active grounding in computer-mediated communication (McCarthy & Monk, 1994). In human-computer dialogue, the same sort of adaptation occurs between user and system (from the user's point of view): users naturally adjust their speech form to that of the system (e.g., Leiser, 1989; Walker et al., 2004). The fact that people adapt the form of their speech to that of their partner, even if the latter happens to be an artificial system, suggests that genuine dialogue processes can also take place during human-computer interaction. Some research has also indicated that people tend to anthropomorphize systems (Reeves & Nass, 1996). Arguably, the perceived capabilities of a system could also influence the way in which the user decides to interact with it. People may therefore interact differently with a dialogue system once they have adapted themselves to its capabilities/limitations.

How do a user's initial knowledge and/or beliefs impact on the way he or she uses the system for dialogue? During human-human dialogue, initial knowledge or beliefs about the interlocutor have a considerable impact on the way an individual constructs his or her messages, even if there is feedback from the interlocutor (Isaacs & Clark, 1989; Fussel & Krauss, 1991). For example, Isaacs and Clark (1989) demonstrated that speakers who were familiar with New York swiftly adapted their references according to which city landmarks were familiar or unfamiliar to their interlocutor. The influence of the interlocutor model, which can be defined as "*...the representation of the interlocutor's technical and linguistic skills, which is partly constructed during the dialogue process*" (Amalberti et al., 1993, p.551), extends beyond human-human dialogue, as individuals may profoundly modify the way they formulate their message according to the type of interlocutor that is being modelled (system or human operator).

Amalberti et al. (1993) found that the number of relevant items of information contained in an initial speaking turn was lower in a group interacting with an (simulated) artificial system than in a group interacting with a human operator. Users' knowledge (erroneous, in this case) of the system's understanding and problem-solving capabilities led them to provide fewer items of useful information in their initial request when they interacted with the system rather than with a human operator. Once several searches had been undertaken using the system, however, the number of items tended to increase. Richards and Underwood (1984) had previously drawn attention to this rise in the number of relevant terms for searches per utterance in the course of an interaction, associated with increasingly concise utterances (suppression of nonessential terms, such as articles, or politeness formulae). In short, it would seem that (1) the number of relevant items of information per utterance in a natural-language information search increases in the course of the interaction, especially following the initial speaking turn, and (2) the length of the utterances appears to remain relatively stable and may even increase during the interaction, at least in a spoken dialogue and especially following the initial speaking turn.

3. Detecting user familiarity – an empirical study

3.1 General methodology

Natural language dialogue systems have mainly been designed for use by people without any specific expertise who wish to consult or search for information. Task-oriented dialogue systems may be process-based (e.g., paying the bills of a service provider) or information-based (e.g., finding a restaurant, planning a trip.). The aim of the experiments described earlier (data taken partly from Bretier et al., 2004, and Le Bigot et al., 2006) was to determine whether the use of a real information-based, task-oriented human-computer dialogue system (a guide for performing a restaurant search) would confirm the findings reported in the literature. The hypothesis was that, whatever the interaction modality, (1) the number of relevant items of information in the initial speaking turn of a natural-language information search would increase in the course of the interaction, and (2) the length of the utterances in the initial speaking turn would remain relatively stable during the interaction.

The human-computer dialogue system took the form of a restaurant search service - a prototype designed to help members of the general public search for restaurants in Paris. The system cooperates with customers and offers solutions matching their query as closely as possible. The application allows users to base their search on three criteria: restaurant location, price and food type. Users can express their request in natural language. This allows them to supply all the items of information needed for their request: (1) in a single utterance, (2) one at a time, (3) in mixed mode. For example, a user looking for a restaurant serving Mexican dishes in the fifteenth district of Paris with no particular price limit can either provide these two search criteria within a single utterance (*"I am looking for a Mexican restaurant in the fifteenth district"*) or else begin with an utterance stating the speciality (*"I am looking for a Mexican restaurant"*, wait for the system to respond, then complete his or her request in a second utterance (*"in the fifteenth* [district]"). A typical search can be broken down into two phases (e.g., finding a restaurant, planning a trip). (1) In the criteria initialisation phase, users express a more or less specific request and the system helps them by asking them to specify their criteria. If they wish, users may supply several criteria within a single "speaking turn" (see Fig. 2: U_2, U_4). (2) In the refining phase, after the users

have entered their criteria, they browse through the solutions proposed by the system (see Fig. 2: U_6). They may also request more detailed information about the solutions. Users can switch from one phase to the other at any time. This system (as Fig. 1) was accessible over the telephone (spoken), using corpus-based speech synthesis and continuous speech recognition based on statistical models (Hidden Markov Model). This application was also accessible via a Web interface (the speech recognition module and speech synthesis were replaced by written interface: keyboard and screen).
The system's user model allowed it to represent the dynamic aspect (over time) of the user, together with his or her request and the words that were used. However, it did not have sufficient information about the user's "*profile*" for it to adapt the way the system reacted.
Both experiments were conducted using the same technology, but with two different interaction modalities (totally speech-based or totally text-based). One experiment featured a speech interface (phone, microphone), while the other featured a Web interface (screen, keypad). There were twenty-four participants per experiment (min. age = 18, max. age = 51). Participants were assigned information search tasks (scenarios), either in the form of a list of criteria or in the form of an utterance. Twelve scenarios based on either two or three criteria (location, food type and price) were created for making queries (e.g., location: Louvre; food type: Chinese; price: twenty euros). The number of possible replies for each scenario varied from one to six. The order of criteria, number of solutions and order of scenarios were counterbalanced. Prior to the experiment, the application was briefly presented to the participants. They were told that they could dialogue in natural language with the application, and were instructed to use the service to find restaurants *as quickly and accurately as possible.*

S1: Welcome to [...]. What do you want?
U2: I'm looking for a Chinese restaurant for less than 10 euros.
S3: You are looking for a Chinese restaurant for less than 10 euros. I have found more than 10. You can either be more specific - for example, what is the location? - or consult the solutions [...].
U4: uh, the Sorbonne.
S5: You are looking for a Chinese restaurant near the Sorbonne for less than 10 euros. I have found 3. You can either be more specific [...], or consult the solutions [...]
U6: I'd like to consult the solutions.
S7: The first restaurant is [...]

Fig. 2. Example of a dialogue with the restaurant search guide (S = system, U = user).

The exchanges between the user and the system were transcribed word for word. The number of relevant items of information contained in the user's first speaking turn was recorded. An item of information was considered to be relevant for the search if it corresponded to one of the search criteria (food type, location, price). The number of words uttered during the first speaking turn was also recorded for each participant.

3.2 Results

In order to simplify the presentation of the results, the mean number of items of information and the mean word count were calculated for 2 successive scenarios (i.e., 6 blocks: block 1 = scenarios 1 and 2, block 2 = scenarios 3 and 4, block 3 = scenarios 5 and 6, block 4 = scenarios

7 and 8, block 5 = scenarios 9 and 10, block 6 = scenarios 11 and 12). The data were subjected to an analysis of variance, with the position of the scenario block as a within-participants factor. The results of the experiment featuring spoken interaction are reported in Fig. 3. The results of the experiment featuring written interaction are reported in Fig. 4.

Concerning the spoken interaction, the analysis revealed a main effect of the position of the block, $F(5, 115) = 6.695$, $MSE = .240$, $p < .001$, *partial* $eta^2 = .225$. The trend analysis highlighted a significant linear trend in the number of items of information provided in the first speaking turn as the participants went through the various scenarios, $F(1, 23) = 14.58$, $MSE = .472$, $p < .001$, *partial* $eta^2 = .388$. Although the number of items in the first speaking turn gradually increased as the different scenarios were performed, the analysis failed to reveal any effect of the scenario blocks on the word count for the user's initial speaking turn, $F(5, 115) < 1$.

Concerning the written interaction, the analysis revealed a main effect of the position of the block, $F(5, 115) = 5.936$, $MSE = .196$, $p < .001$, *partial* $eta^2 = .205$. The trend analysis highlighted a significant linear trend and a more marginally significant quadratic trend in the number of items in the first speaking turn in the course of the scenarios, $F(1, 23) = 18.41$, $MSE = .242$, $p < .001$, *partial* $eta^2 = .445$ and $F(1, 23) = 4.22$, $MSE = .156$, $p = .051$, *partial* $eta^2 = .155$ respectively. There was a gradual increase in the number of items provided in the initial speaking turn, although this figure stabilized in the final scenarios. The analysis failed to reveal any effect of the scenario blocks on the word count in the user's first speaking turn, $F(5, 115) < 1$.

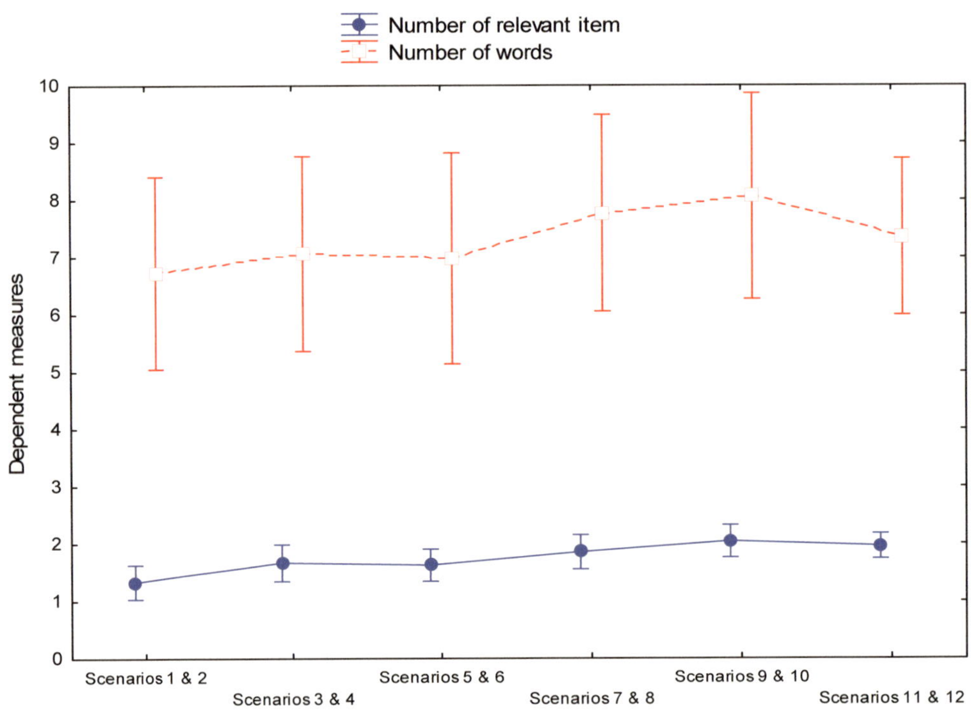

Fig. 3. Mean number of information items and mean word count for the user's initial speaking turn (spoken interaction).

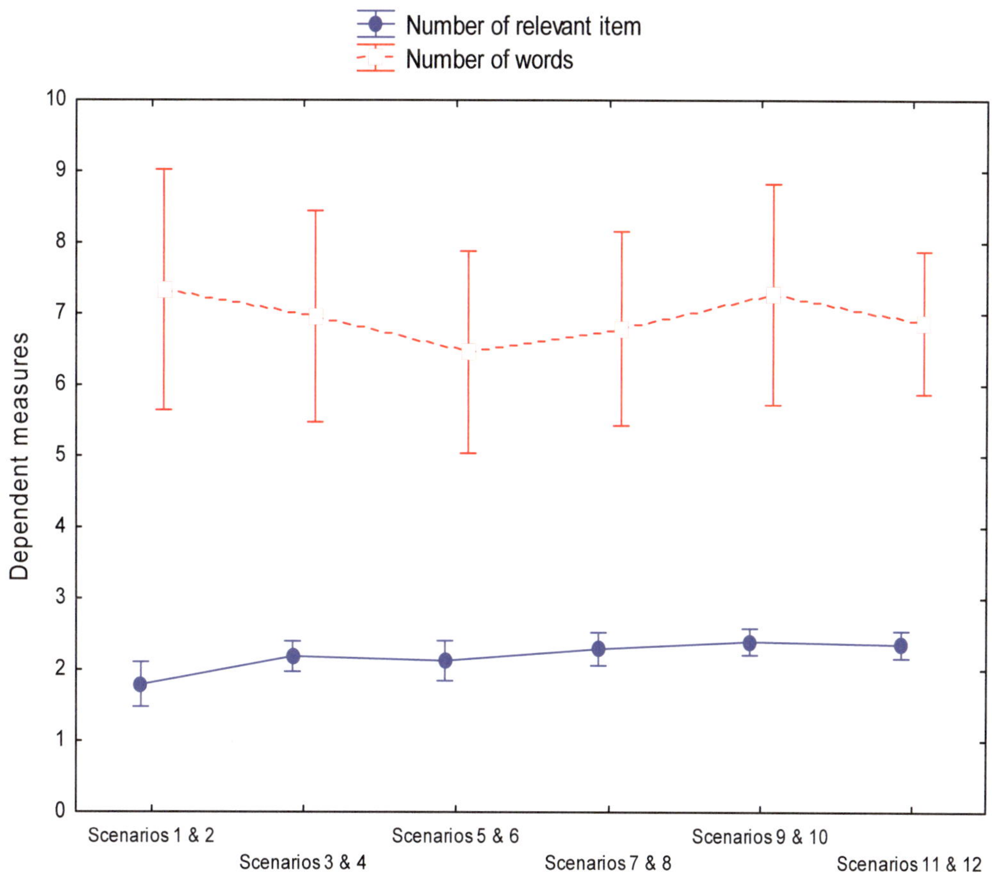

Fig. 4. Mean number of information items and mean word count for the user's initial speaking turn (written interaction)

4. Exploiting user familiarity to improve human-computer dialogue

4.1 User model and usability

These two experiments confirmed the findings in the literature concerning human-dialogue in a real system: the more a user interacts with a system, the more items of information he or she provides in the initial speaking turn, even though the word count remains relatively stable. These results appear whichever interaction modality is used, although user behaviour appears to stabilise more rapidly in the written modality than in the oral one.

The users had hardly, if ever, interacted with a dialogue system before, and in most cases, their representations of the system's understanding capabilities were most probably incomplete, if not erroneous. As they performed the blocks of scenarios, the users gradually increased the amount of information they provided. So, this finding, which can be interpreted in the light of psychological theories, could allow us to enhance the system's user model. The existing user model makes its possible to represent the dynamic aspect (over time) of the user's requests, but does not have sufficient information about the user's *"profile"* to adapt the system's reactions accordingly. Just as the data that were collected in our study made it possible to identify clues to the user's degree of familiarity with the system so, too, should modelling. It should be entirely possible to detect the user's degree of familiarity with the system by calculating an index based on the number of items of information and the number of words used to convey these items in the first speaking turn. This index could then be exploited to enrich the application's user model in order to enhance usability. If the system detected that the user had little or no knowledge about the system, it could provide assistance or information about its capabilities (following Nielsen's usability principles: *Visibility of system status* and *Help and documentation*). Given that we are dealing with the capability of understanding natural language, this assistance could take the form of an example which the user could then use as a template for interacting with the system.

It is important to try and match the interlocutor model with the system's actual capabilities in order to promote human-machine cooperation. The system's construction of a user model can be seen as a strategy to reduce the need for the user to construct a (truthful) model of the system.

Hence, current information systems place a great many demands on their users because the latter must know what sort of information is relevant for their goals and what information is irrelevant, what proportion of the relevant information is contained in the dialogue system and how to find the relevant information within that system (Kobsa, 1990). Clearly, the last two points mean that the user must possess a "model" of a dialogue system. However, it should not be up to the user to build a model of the dialogue system. Rather, the system should build a model of the user. In the course of the interaction, the system should generate assumptions about aspects of the user that may be relevant in the task domain in question.

Lastly, natural language-based systems are often designed for use by the general public. Consequently, a great many default assumptions may be generated about the user's goals (e.g., all users of a hotel reservation system can be assumed to be searching for accommodation) and the user's knowledge and beliefs about a particular domain (i.e., a system with a user modelling component may assume that all its users possess basic knowledge in a given domain). Importantly, assumptions based on the user's inputs into the system are seen as the most direct and most reliable ones. Detecting and exploiting the user's familiarity is a possible alternative to relying on the user's inputs to make information systems more cooperative. The literature provides other examples (see Kobsa, 1990) of how a system's ability to make assumptions about a user's beliefs, goals and plans can enhance its cooperativeness - an ability that is especially important if the system is intended to be accessible to the general public.

4.2 Conclusion

In this chapter, we sought to underline the fact that user modelling must rely on the identification of relevant indicators for performing a given activity. The aim is primarily to improve the degree to which systems can adapt to human characteristics. As we have already discussed, user models accumulate knowledge about users gleaned from observations by the systems. These systems then apply design patterns (recommendations and heuristics) that are known to optimise usability according to the nature of their user model.

It is worth noting that when the system's observations are erroneous, the application of recommendations and heuristics may have a negative impact on usability. This is the principal motivation for regarding uncertainty as the standard situation.

In user modelling, statistical and probabilistic models both use observed sample results to make statements about unknown, dependent parameters. These parameters represent aspects of users' behaviour, such as their goals, preferences, and forthcoming actions or locations. Design patterns should be implemented by system designers as possible but not systematic behaviours. Implementing approaches that draw on the science of stochastic processes (e.g., dynamic Bayesian networks, see Zukerman & Albrecht, 2007), a user model may be able to cope with behavioural uncertainty stemming from human error or individually preferred interaction paths. For example, some user modelling work has been done using Bayesian networks and the resulting models applied to system behaviour design (e.g., Zukerman & Albrecht, 2001; Lemon & Pietquin, 2007; Williams & Young, 2007).

Improvements in the user model should logically lead to an improvement in the usability of the system, by adapting its behaviour to that of the user. For example, with respect to the heuristics discussed at the beginning of this chapter, one can imagine systems storing the user model they have constructed during an interaction and retrieving it at the beginning of the next session. This would certainly be relevant if the system was intended to be used frequently by the same user and for similar purposes, and could serve as the basis for personalization. Today, user profile modelling is clearly perceived as a prerequisite for Web service personalization, as illustrated by technologies such as profiling (painting a portrait of users based on fill-in forms), click-stream analysis and web usage mining, or collecting data about a user's movements in a Website (Manber et al., 2000; Pierrakos et al., 2003).
Going back to the specific issue addressed in this chapter, we have emphasised that users provide information about themselves via the pattern of their (first) request: they implicitly provide information about their familiarity with the natural language interaction task being performed with the system. Familiarity could arguably be assessed on a basis other than the index we have proposed for the first request (number of relevant items of information/number of words), including other linguistic parameters, or the speed of message production. Indeed, other criteria are clearly needed and may well be found in the course of future research. Furthermore, these criteria could be tested with respect to their external validity, by changing the environmental parameters (e.g., is the result independent of the message production modality?) or the user's parameters (e.g., is the same result observed in different age groups?). Lastly, once the user model has been enriched with this information, the latter must be exploited: providing assistance to someone who has no accurate knowledge of the system's capabilities by providing an example he or she could use as a template, or correcting a misconception; reducing the amount of guidance and offering greater flexibility when the system detects a degree of experience on the part of the user.

To conclude, the design of human-computer dialogue is very much an interdisciplinary enterprise. On the one hand, computer sciences (e.g., speech processing, artificial intelligence) are applied to phonetics, linguistics and discourse. On the other hand, these "technological" fields are cross-fertilised by the human sciences. Studies in psychology and ergonomics help system designers to take users' needs and behaviours fully into account. We believe that this is particularly true in the case of user modelling for dialogue systems. Other specialised applications that have recently been proposed (Griffith et al., 2007; Slaney et al., 2003), including user group modelling and cooperation or multitasking user modelling, will also strengthen the case for the application of cognitive research.

5. References

Amalberti, R., Carbonnel, N. & Falzon, P. (1993). User representations of computer systems in human-computer speech interaction. *International Journal of Man-Machine Studies*, Vol. 38, 547-566.

Baudoin, F. (2008). Personnalisation des systèmes de dialogue en langage naturel : une méthode d'anticipation rationnelle d'actions communicatives [Trans. Personalization of natural-language dialogue systems: a rational method for anticipating communicative actions]. *Unpublished doctoral thesis*, Paris 6: Paris (France).

Brennan, S.E. & Clark, H.H. (1996). Conceptual pacts and lexical choice in conversation. *Journal of Experimental Psychology: Learning, Memory, and Cognition*, Vol. 22, 1482-1493.

Bretier, P., Le Bigot, L., Panaget, F. & Sadek, D. (2004). De la représentation de l'interlocuteur vers un modèle utilisateur formel pour le dialogue personne-machine [Trans. From the interlocutor's representation to a formal user model for human-computer dialogue], *Proceedings of the 16th international conference of the Association Francophone d'Interaction Homme-Machine IHM 2004*, pp. 21-28. Namur (Belgium), August-September, 2004, ACM Press.

Brusilovsky, P. (2001). Adaptive Hypermedia. *User Modeling and User-Adapted Interaction*, Vol. 11, No. 1-2, 87-110.

Gorin, A.L., Riccardi, G. & Wright, J.H. (1997). How may I help you? *Speech Communication*, Vol. 23, No. 1-2, 113-127.

ISO 9241-11. (1998). Ergonomic requirements for office work with visual display terminals (VDTs) - Part 11: Guidance on usability.

Elzer, S., Chu-Carroll, J. & Carberry, S. (1994). Recognizing and utilizing user preferences in collaborative consultation dialogues. *Proceedings of the Fourth International Conference on User Modeling*, pp. 19–24, Hyannis (MA), August 1994, Springer, Vienna, New York.

Fink, J. & Kobsa, A. (2000). Adaptable and adaptive information provision for all users, including disabled and elderly people. *User Modeling and User-Adapted Interaction*, Vol. 4, 163–188.

Fischer, G. (2001). User modeling in human-computer interaction. *User Modeling and User-Adapted Interaction*, Vol. 11, No. 1-2, 65–86.

Isaacs, E. & Clark, H.H. (1987). References in conversation between experts and novices. *Journal of Experimental Psychology: General*, Vol. 2, No. 6, 26-37.

Kosba, A. (1990). User modelling in dialog systems: potentials and hazards. *AI & Society*, Vol. 4, No. 3, 214 -240.

Lai, J., Karat, C.-M. & Yankelovich, N. (2008). Conversational speech interfaces and technologies. In *The Human-Computer Interaction Handbook: Fundamentals, Evolving*

Technologies and Emerging Applications, 2nd edition, A. Sears & J.A. Jacko (Eds), (pp.381-391), Lawrence Erlbaum Associates, ISBN: 978-0805844689, New York.

Le Bigot, L. , Jamet, E., Rouet, J.-F., & Amiel, V. (2006). Mode and modal transfer effects on performance and discourse organization with an information retrieval dialogue system in natural language. *Computers in Human Behavior,* Vol. 22, 467-500.

Le Bigot, L., Terrier, P., Amiel, V., Poulain, G., Jamet, E. & Rouet, J.-F. (2007). Effect of modality on collaboration with a dialogue system. *International Journal of Human-Computer Studies,* Vol. 65, 983-991.

Lemon, O. & Pietquin, O. (2007). Machine learning for spoken dialogue systems. In *Proceedings of Interspeech, 2007,* Antwerp (Belgium), pp. 2685-2688, August 2007.

Leiser, R.G. (1989). Exploiting convergence to improve natural language understanding. *Interacting with Computers,* Vol. 1, No. 3, 284-298.

Litman, D.J. & Pan, S. (2002). Designing and evaluating an adaptive spoken dialogue system. *User Modeling and User-Adapted Interaction,* Vol. 12, No. 2-3, 111-137.

Manber, U., Patel, A. & Robinson, J. (2000). Experience with personalization on Yahoo! Communications of the ACM, Vol. 43, No. 8, 31-34.

McCarthy, J.C. & Monk, A.F. (1994). Channels, conversation, cooperation and relevance: all you wanted to know about communication but were afraid to ask. *Collaborative Computing,* Vol. 1, 35-60.

Nielsen, J. (1994). Heuristic evaluation. In *Usability Inspection Methods,* J. Nielsen & R.L. Mack, R.L. (Eds), (pp. 25-64), ISBN: 0-471-01877-5, John Wiley & Sons: New York.

Pietquin, O. (2004). *A Framework for Unsupervised Learning of Dialogue Strategies,* Presses Universitaires de Louvain, ISBN: 2-930344-63-6, Louvain.

Pierrakos, D., Paliouras, G., Papatheodorou, C. & Spyropoulos, C.D. (2003). Web usage mining as a tool for personaization: a survey. User Modeling and user-Adapted Interaction, Vol. 13, No. 4, 311-372.

Reeves, B. & Nass, C. (1996). *The Media Equation: How People Treat Computers, Television, and New Media like Real People and Places.* Cambridge University Press and CSLI, ISBN: 1575860538, New York.

Richards, M.A. & Underwood, K.M. (1984). How should people and computers speak to each other? In *Proceedings of Human-Computer Interaction (INTERACT'84),* pp. 33-36, London, September 1984, Elsevier Science Publishers.

Shifroni, E. & Shanon, B. (1992). Interactive user modeling: an integrative explicit-implicit approach. *User Modeling and User-Adapted Interaction,* Vol. 2, No. 4, 287–330.

Wilkie, J., Jack, M.A. & Littlewood, P.J. (2005). System-initiated digressive proposals in automated human-computer telephone dialogues: the use of contrasting politeness strategies. *International Journal of Human-Computer Studies,* Vol. 62, 41-71.

Walker, M.A., Whittaker, S.J., Stent, A., Maloor, P., Moore, J.D., Johnston, M. & Vasireddy, G. (2004). Generation and evaluation of user-tailored responses in multimodal dialogue. *Cognitive Science,* Vol. 28, No. 5, 811-840.

Williams, J.D. & Young, S.J. (2007). Partially observable Markov decision processes for spoken dialogue systems. *Computer Speech and Langage,* Vol. 21, No. 2, 393-422.

Zukerman, I. & Albrecht, D. (2001). Predictive statistical models for user modeling. In *Proceedings of the Eight International Conference on User Modeling,* pp. 5–18, Sonthofen (Germany), July 2001, Springer, Vienna, New York.

Zukerman, I. & Albrecht, D. (2007). Introduction to the special issue on statistical and probabilistic methods for user modeling. *User Modeling and User-Adapted Interaction,* Vol. 17, No. 1-2, 1-4.